C0-ARI-375

If You Think This Is
Just Another Book About Rock, Think Again....

"The music of a well-ordered age is calm and cheerful, and so is its government. The music of a restive age is excited and fierce, and its government is perverted. The music of a decaying state is sentimental and sad and its government is imperiled."

—Lu Be We, ancient Chinese philosopher

"Break out the hash pipe and heat up the gumbo—Dr. John is back again with music from that steamy, swampy place in your mind that only Dr. John can reach. If you get stoned to watch TV commercials while eating Colonel Sanders fried chicken and drinking warm Ripple—then you are weird enough for Dr. John. And he is, sure as sin and rain, weird enough for you."

—David Gancher, reviewing
Remedies, by Dr. John,
The Night Tripper

THE ROLLING STONE RECORD REVIEW
is an original
Pocket Book edition.

Are there paperbound books you want
but cannot find in your retail stores?

You can get any title in print in **POCKET BOOK** editions. Simply send retail price, local sales tax, if any, plus 25¢ to cover mailing and handling costs to:

MAIL SERVICE DEPARTMENT
POCKET BOOKS • A Division of Simon & Schuster, Inc.
1 West 39th Street • New York, New York 10018

Please send check or money order. We cannot be responsible for cash. *Catalogue sent free on request.*

Titles in this series are also available at discounts in quantity lots for industrial or sales-promotional use. For details write our Special Projects Agency: The Benjamin Company, Inc., 485 Madison Avenue, New York, N.Y. 10022.

The Rolling Stone
Record Review

by the editors of
Rolling Stone

PUBLISHED BY POCKET BOOKS NEW YORK

THE ROLLING STONE RECORD REVIEW

POCKET BOOK edition published August, 1971

The reviews and letters in this book, some of which have been slightly abridged, originally appeared in *Rolling Stone* Magazine during the years 1967-1970.

This original POCKET BOOK edition is printed from brand-new plates made from newly set, clear, easy-to-read type. POCKET BOOK editions are published by POCKET BOOKS, a division of Simon & Schuster, Inc., 630 Fifth Avenue, New York, N.Y. 10020. Trademarks registered in the United States and other countries. L

Standard Book Number: 671-78531-1.
Copyright, ©, 1967, 1968, 1969, 1970, 1971, by Straight Arrow Publishers, Inc. All rights reserved. Published by POCKET BOOKS, New York, and on the same day in Canada by Simon & Schuster of Canada, Ltd., Richmond Hill, Ontario.

Printed in the U.S.A.

Table of Contents

Introduction

Out of the first three years of *Rolling Stone,* we have distilled a collection of critical writing about music which could be said to trace the rise of the rock and roll singer from juvenile delinquent to *auteur*.

That's no mean task. Not in these heavy times. Heh, heh.

By the time this book hits the stands (if not the best-seller lists, and in *this* business you don't even have a "bubbling under the Hot 100" chart) it may have already begun to take on some of the finer aspects, if not yellowed appeal, of an Oldies But Goodies collection. Such is the perishability of modern art.

Unlike literature, where a huge body of example and theory have set forth the modes of criticism, popular music criticism has had few guidelines. Jazz men developed some, but rock and roll critics, finally descending upon us *circa* 1967, were mere babes in the woods.

Let that be our excuse, both in editing and in writing, for the many omissions and errors in judgment that become evident in the clear light of a new decade. In trying to define the styles and principles of rock criticism and to determine what was relevant—while editing a new-born and not extravagantly financed publication—some things inevitably are missing.

From the sometimes erratic, nearly always amusing review pages we've attempted to add a little structure by dividing things up into sometimes fairly arbitrary categories. For instance, there are chapters on the music of

London and Los Angeles and San Francisco, but none on New York. Why? Not that New York didn't remain the capital of the music business, but we have here a period in which the making of the music itself left Tin Pan Alley for the streets.

The music covered here is basically from the end of 1967 through the end of 1970, years of a great popular explosion of rock (as it then became known). This fits well the delineation of the 1963–1967 Beatle years as a distinct period in the rock of the Fabulous Sixties. And as 1970 closes, we sense the coming to an end of yet another great era in rock.

Some of the chapters (particularly the selections on the fathers of rock and roll and on soul music) are incomplete and sketchy. But for further reference, some excellent published work is already available in these areas. For the early history of rock and roll, get Charlie Gillette's *Sounds of the City,* and in the soul music area, three books are recommended: *Urban Blues,* by Charles Keil; *The Sound of Soul,* by Phyl Garland; *Blues People,* by Le Roi Jones.

Although we frequently reviewed and recommended great classics and contemporary jazz and blues, we have decided not to include that here, as a vast body of literature already exists in these areas which we could barely improve on.

We have tried to make room for some of the levity which arose out of the record reviewing trade and, as an opening shot, even attempted to give the "big picture"— an overview. An occasional moment of lightheadedness is one of the hazards of the trade. Hopefully you'll also find the places where we tried to take record reviewing beyond known bounds.

The *Rolling Stone* records section was edited at various times by myself, Greil Marcus, Ed Ward and Jon Landau, all of whom also aided in the preparation of this book and without whom . . . Love also goes to Langdon Winner for his great help and to June Auerbach who did, in her phrase, "the chick work," which makes the world go round.

JANN WENNER

The Rock and Roll

Record Reviewer:

An

Historical Overview

Noah was lucky. He had an ark, two of everything, Mount Ararat, and plenty of advance warning. After a mere forty days of bobbing around in The Flood trying to avoid the wreckage of a condemned civilization, he washed ashore to begin a life of pastoral simplicity.

The flood in which we are currently engulfed is of a different sort. In its own way it is much more treacherous and persistent. The deluge of American mass technological culture moves inexorably forward, capturing everything that walks in whirlpools of automobiles, tract houses, Doggie Diners, television sets, radios, drugs, computers, extra-drys, frozen foods, and throw-away boxes, bottles, cans and books. Evidently, there is no longer a beneficent deity watching from on high to offer the modern Noah a piece of dry land. It's a wonder that any of us have survived at all.

Fortunately, the world is not totally without salvation. There is still hope. For in an age of apathy and escapism there remain a few diligent souls who struggle bravely against the flood of mediocrity for the benefit of mankind. The best known of these self-appointed cultural life rafts are the famous Raiders led by Mr. Ralph Nader. A measure of their selfless dedication, the Raiders are pledged to leave no Volkswagen undemolished, no turkey unthawed in their quest to protect the consumer from the evils of the marketplace.

A less well-known but equally important kind of culture hero in this vein is the rock and roll record reviewer. Working behind the scenes with a minimum of fanfare or national recognition, the reviewer stands between the listeners and the incredible mass of phonograph records cast forth by the music industry every month. Compared to the burdens and responsibilities of the reviewer, the work of Nader's Raiders is mere child's play. For, unlike a Plymouth or Chevrolet with defective brakes, a bad rock and roll record cannot be sent back to the factory for relining. Once you've bought the thing, you're stuck with it.

The difficulties here are compounded by the fact that those who read the reviews often pay no attention to them. In some cases they deliberately go out of their way to purchase a record that an established reviewer has labeled "worthless" or "unadulterated garbage." Such treachery by the audience, however, only increases the reviewer's dedication to his cause. It is an uphill fight, but an honorable one, nonetheless.

In his novel, *The Glass Bead Game,* Hermann Hesse offers some interesting comments on the relationship of music and society, comments which may prove useful to those who read this or similar books on rock and roll. Quoting from an ancient Chinese text, Lu Bu We's *Spring and Autumn,* Hesse observes:*

When the world is at peace, when all things are tranquil and all men obey their superiors in all their courses, then music can be perfected. When desires and passions do not turn into wrongful paths, music can be perfected. Perfect music has its cause. It arises from equilibrium. Equilibrium arises from righteousness, and righ-teousness arises from the meaning of the cosmos. Therefore one can speak about music only with a man who has perceived the meaning of the cosmos.

* * *

Decaying states and men ripe for doom do not, of course, lack music either, but their music is not serene. Therefore, the more tempestuous the music, the

---

* Hermann Hesse, *The Glass Bead Game* (Magister Ludi), translated from the German *Das Glasperlenspiel,* by Richard and Clara Winston, New York, Holt, Rinehart and Winston, 1969, pp. 29-30.

more doleful are the people, the more imperiled the country, the more the sovereign declines. In this way the essence of music is lost.

* * *

The cause of the degeneration of the Chu state was its invention of magic music. Such music is indeed tempestuous enough, but in truth it has departed from the essence of music. Because it has departed from the essence of real music, this music is not serene. If music is not serene, the people grumble and life is deranged. All this arises from mistaking the nature of music and seeking only tempestuous tonal effects.

Therefore the music of a well-ordered age is calm and cheerful, and so is its government. The music of a restive age is excited and fierce, and its government is perverted. The music of a decaying state is sentimental and sad, and its government is imperiled.

It is not entirely clear which, if any, of the ages described by Lu Bu We we now inhabit—one of order and harmony, one of ferocity and political perversion, or one of decay, sadness and resignation. It is also far from certain whether the music we hear is one of the causes of the peculiar phenomena of our time or merely a reflection of something deeper. If Hesse's sage is correct, however, one conclusion is now beyond doubt: we must never assume that the nature of our music and the order of things in the world are independent of each other. If one listens carefully and then ponders what he has heard, at least some of the mysteries disappear.

The historical record indicates that the music review had its birth in the mid-thirteenth century. A man named Albert De Groot had spent thirty years of his life developing a machine which could produce distinct vocal sounds. One day Thomas Aquinas, the famous medieval philosopher, chanced to hear the mechanism performing one of its peculiar songs. Horrified that such a thing could exist at all, Aquinas grabbed a large stick. Whack! Whack!

In a few swift blows he totally destroyed the singing machine and its music.

Twentieth-century reviewers, of course, have difficulty living up to Aquinas' splendid example. No longer is it possible to deliver such a definitive comment with so few words. But the essence of the review itself remains unchanged. The reviewer listens carefully to the music in question, ponders its aesthetic qualities and offers his humble judgment. And just as Aquinas had to face the wrath of Albert De Groot, so must a *Rolling Stone* reviewer face the reactions of a highly partisan readership.

Consider, for instance, the plight of John Mendelsohn in the following:

~~~~~~~~~~~~~~~~~~~~~~~

LED ZEPPELIN
Led Zeppelin
(Atlantic SD 8216)

The popular formula in England in this, the aftermath era of such successful British bluesmen as Cream and John Mayall, seems to be: add, to an excellent guitarist who, since leaving the Yardbirds and/or Mayall, has become a minor musical deity, a competent rhythm section and pretty soul-belter who can do a good spade imitation. The latest of the British blues groups so conceived offers little that its twin, the Jeff Beck Group, didn't say as well or better three months ago, and the excesses of the Beck group's *Truth* album (most notably its self-indulgence and restrictedness), are fully in evidence on Led Zeppelin's debut album.

Jimmy Page, around whom the Zeppelin revolves, is, admittedly, an extraordinarily proficient blues guitarist and explorer of his instrument's electronic capabilities. Unfortunately, he is also a very limited producer and a writer of weak, unimaginative songs, and the Zeppelin album suffers from his having both produced it and written most of it (alone or in combination with his accomplices in the group).

The album opens with lots of guitar-rhythm section exchanges (in the fashion of Beck's "Shapes of Things" on "Good Times Bad Times," which might have been ideal for a Yardbirds' B-side). Here, as almost everywhere else on the album, it is Page's guitar that provides most of the excitement. "Babe I'm Gonna Leave You" alternates between prissy Robert Plant's howled vocals fronting an acoustic guitar and driving choruses of the band running down a four-chord progression while John Bonham smashes his cymbals on every beat. The song is very dull in places (especially on the vocal passages), very redundant, and certainly not worth the six-and-a-half minutes the Zeppelin gives it.

Two much-overdone Willie Dixon blues standards fail to be revivified by being turned into showcases for Page and Plant. "You Shook Me" is the more interesting of the two—at the end of each line Plant's echo-chambered voice drops into a small explosion of fuzz-tone guitar, with which it matches shrieks at the end.

The album's most representative cut is "How Many More Times." Here a jazzy introduction gives way to a driving (albeit monotonous) guitar-dominated background for Plant's strained and unconvincing shouting (he may be as foppish as Rod Stewart, but he's nowhere near so exciting, especially in the higher registers). A fine Page solo then leads the band into what sounds like a backwards version of the Page-composed "Beck's Bolero," hence to a little snatch of Albert King's "The Hunter," and finally to an avalanche of drums and shouting.

In their willingness to waste their considerable talent on unworthy material the Zeppelin has produced an album which is sadly reminiscent of *Truth*. Like the Beck group they are also perfectly willing to make themselves a two- (or, more accurately, one-and-a-half) man show. It would seem that, if they're to help fill the void created by the demise of Cream, they will have to find a producer (and editor) and some material worthy of their collective attention.

—JOHN MENDELSOHN
3-15-69

SIRS:

Mendelsohn's review of Led Zeppelin was a 100% lie. Pure bullshit. Never has there been such a great band since Winwood's departure from Traffic.

ERIC CHARLES
BROOKLYN, N.Y.

SIRS:

If I used your record reviews as a guide to my personal record purchases, I would have the worst pile of garbage in the history of record collecting.

A few issues back, your unbelievably fucked review of Led Zeppelin. This, plus past reviews of Creedence Clearwater, Cream, etc.

I don't know where the musical taste of San Francisco is at, but if your magazine is an indicator—perhaps you all ought to come east on your vacation this summer.

CHARLES LAQUIDARA
WBCN-FM
BOSTON, MASSACHUSETTS

LED ZEPPELIN II
Led Zeppelin
(Atlantic SD 8236)

Hey, man, I take it all back! This is one fucking *heavyweight* of an album! OK—I'll concede that until you've listened to the album eight hundred times, as I have, it seems as if it's just one especially heavy song extended over the space of two whole sides. But, hey! you've got to admit that the Zeppelin has their distinctive and enchanting formula down stonecold, man. Like you get the impression they could do it in their sleep.

And who can deny that Jimmy Page is the absolute number-one *heaviest* white blues guitarist between 5'4" and 5'8" in the world?? Shit, man, on this album he further demonstrates that he could absolutely fucking *shut down* any whitebluesman alive, and with one fucking hand tied behind his back too.

"Whole Lotta Love," which opens the album, has to be the heaviest thing I've run across (or, more accurately, that's run across me) since "Parchmant Farm" on *Vincebus Eruptum*. Like I listened to the break (Jimmy wrenching some simply indescribable sounds out of his axe while your stereo goes apeshit) on some heavy Vietnamese weed and very nearly had my mind blown.

Hey, I know what you're thinking. "That's not very objective." But dig: I also listened to it on mescaline, some old Romilar, novocain, and ground up *Fusion*, and it was just as mind-boggling as before. I must admit I haven't listened to it straight yet—I don't think a group this heavy is best enjoyed that way.

Anyhow . . . Robert Plant, who is rumored to sing some notes on this record that only dogs can hear, demonstrates his heaviness on "The Lemon Song." When he yells "Shake me 'til the juice runs down my leg," you can't help but flash on the fact that the *lemon* is a cleverly-disguised phallic metaphor. Cunning Rob, sticking all this eroticism in between the lines just like his blues-beltin' ancestors! And *then* (then) there's "Moby Dick," which will be for John Bonham what "Toad" has been for Baker. John demonstrates on this track that had he half a mind he could shut down Baker *even without sticks*, as most of his intriguing solo is done with bare hands.

The album ends with a far-out blues number called "Bring It On Home," during which Rob contributes some very convincing moaning and harp-playing, and sings "Wadge da train roll down da track." Who said that white men couldn't sing blues? I mean, like, *who?*

—JOHN MENDELSOHN
12-13-69

SIRS:

I have yet to read one of your review sections that didn't motivate me to pull my hair out of my goddam skull. Now your Romilar freak-turned rock critic John Mendelsohn has made the mistake of writing his *Led Zeppelin II* review while trying to reach the "cough control center."

Granted, Led Zeppelin is a fine rock band, superior in the British tradition, but to run down a rap that Jimmy Page is "the best white bluesman alive" is a little too far out. I hate to be the one to break the news, but there's a cat named Eric Clapton who is certainly the best white guitarist in the world.

JAMIE MARTIN
PITTSBURGH

SIRS:

The gullible innocence of reader Jamie Martin was touching in its instant acceptance of John Mendelsohn's satirical review of *Led Zeppelin II*. That's what is so reassuring about the Masked Marauder generation: the sophisticated naivete of all the well-informed literates who can read without thinking.

The perceptive Pittsburgher views the distinction of Jimmy Page being the heaviest white blues guitarist between 5'4" and 5'8" (name them, Jamie), his ability to sound as if playing with one hand behind his back (quite melodious, wouldn't you say?), and the criterion for enduring this excessive album (being dulled unconscious on novocain), as being somehow complimentary. In fact, J. Martin's letter seems such a satiric exercise in lack of insight that one just might credit the clever Mr. Mendelsohn with having written it himself.

JOHN'S GROUPIE
LOS ANGELES

SIRS:

Coming soon to your local drivein—destined to be a horror classic—*John Mendelsohn Meets Led Zeppelin III*. Don't miss it.

THE CRETIN
LOS ANGELES

And finally, one must consider the other side of the travail of being a record reviewer. Charles Perry, writing under the pseudonym Eleanor Roosevelt, did just that in the following review that mysteriously appeared in one section.

PRESENTING
BURTON GREENE
Burton Greene

(I forgot the number—but the record stores are in the business, just ask them for Burton Greene.)

I took this record home, but I didn't put it on just right away. For one thing, I was too stoned to function pretty soon and frankly, I just forgot.

Next morning, I put it on. I played it as background music, letting it insinuate itself quietly, naturally, into my morning routine. Usually, I shave, glance through the *Chronicle,* take a crap, and think about things I should get around to doing.

There's a certain, very special kind of delight that comes from listening to a record you know you are never again going to hear. It's like meeting a drunken stranger on a train you took in error, or a long awkward conversation with a Baptist minister you come across by chance in the middle of Syria (both these things have happened to me). *Einmal, nur einmal*—"just once, once only," as Rilke said—a subtle, ephemeral pleasure that derives its charm more from the idea that in the future, you will not *be* experiencing this experience, than from the experience itself *qua* experience.

I never felt that I knew Burton Greene before hearing this record: now that I have, I find my mind filled with thoughts and feelings, all different, all the same. The important thing is to get them down on paper, and I'm sure I'll be able to.

This is a record you can't *listen* to too much. I found —whether shaving, crapping, scanning the *Chron*—that once in a while my mind would wander from its appointed task and mosey out, as it were, to the frontiers of the senses where it would contact the music: then, almost as quickly as it began, it would retreat foaming with thoughts and feelings. The image that came to my mind on reflection was of a snail nearsightedly (as if a snail could be nearsighted with those long eyestalks!) wallowing into a patch of salt. It must really be a strange trip for the snail, quite *unlike* anything else in his realm of experience, and certainly something to give him pause for reflection.

In the end, all music though is unanalyzable, inevaluable. Burton Greene is an experience; this album is an experience. An experience like all experiences—$3.98.

TRULY,
ELEANOR ROOSEVELT
9-20-69

The End of the Beatles

Sergeant Pepper's Lonely Hearts Club Band was the summit of the Beatles' career as a group. That album overshadows every other long playing record of the decade as a complete and perfect work. It took the long playing record to the point of its furthest development as an artistic medium.

It seemed that the Beatles couldn't do any more as a band. They certainly couldn't perform *Sergeant Pepper* with its use of countless tape recording tricks, brass and string sections and complement of musical sounds and instruments which could only be reproduced with a company of perhaps 250 musicians, singers and engineers in one place.

The Beatles' work from that point on can be seen as the work of individuals rather than as the work of a group. The Lennon-McCartney song-writing team came to an end. According to John, the breakup of the Beatles as a group was obvious from the "white album," the two-record set titled *The Beatles*. What took place was that each member of the group came to recording sessions for new albums with his own songs, which he then produced and arranged with the others performing basically as session men. So it all came out as Beatle music. Much in the same way as before.

But the magic, to some, was gone. In the following reviews one sees little of the unqualified enthusiasm that accompanied the Beatles in their career through *Sergeant Pepper*. But of course, that was also before there were such things as rock critics. Despite the several reservations

13

expressed, they are all excellent albums and all unqualified musts in any rock library.

At times it seemed heretical to criticize the Beatles' work, but as the group fell apart, the unity of their concept began to fragment at the edges. But both this loosening and other criticisms expressed in the following reviews simply pale in the face of the overwhelming talent seen on these records: talent for singing, songwriting, arranging, playing, producing and every other phase of the recording art.

~~~~~~~~~~~~~~~~~~~~~~~~

MAGICAL MYSTERY TOUR
The Beatles
(Capitol 2835)

"There are only about 100 people in the world who understand our music."

—JOHN LENNON, 1967

THE BEATLES
The Beatles
(Apple SWBO 101)

The power of rock and roll is a constantly amazing process. Although it is Bob Dylan who is the single most important figure in rock and roll; and although it is the Rolling Stones who are the embodiment of a rock and roll band; it is nonetheless The Beatles who are the perfect product and result of everything that rock and roll means and encompasses.

Never has this been so plainly evident as on their new two-album set, *The Beatles* (Apple SWBO 101).

Sgt. Pepper's applied the concept of the symphony to rock and roll, adding an incredible (and soon overused) dimension to rock and roll. Nothing could have been more ambitious than the current release: *The Beatles* is the history and synthesis of Western music. And that, of course is what rock and roll is, and that is what the Beatles are.

Rock and roll, the first successful art form of the McLuhan age, is a series of increasing hybrids of musical styles, starting from its basic hybrid of country and western music and black American music (blues, if you will). That merger represents the distantly effected marriage of the music of England and Africa, a yin and yang that could be infinitely extended.

Not only the origin of rock and roll, but also the short history of it can be seen as a series of hybridizations, the constantly changing styles and fads, as rock assimilates every conceivable musical style (folk, blues, soul, Indian, classical, psychedelic, ballad, country) not only a recent process, but one that goes back to the Drifters, Elvis Presley, Little Richard, Buddy Holly, and so on. Rock and roll's longevity is its ability to assimilate the energy and style of all these musical traditions. Rock and roll at once exists and doesn't exist; that is why the term "rock and roll" is the best term we have, as it means nothing and thus everything— and that is quite possibly the musical and mystical secret of the most overwhelming popular music the world has known.

By attempting such a grandiose project with such deliberation and honesty, they have left themselves extremely vulnerable. There is not the dissemblance of being "our boys" from *Hard Day's Night*, nor the disguise of Sgt. Pepper's Band; it is on every level an explanation and an understanding of who and what the Beatles are.

As usual, the personal honesty is met with an attack. (The secret is that innocence is invulnerable, and those who rush too quickly for the kill, are just themselves dead.) On the level of musical ignorance, I read the very first review of this record that appeared; it was in the New York Times. In about 250 words the "critic" dismissed

the album as being neither as good as the Big Brother *Cheap Thrills* LP nor as the forthcoming Blood, Sweat and Tears album. You come up with only one of two answers about that reviewer: he is either deaf or he is evil.

Those who attacked the Beatles for their single "Revolution," should be set down with a good pair of earphones for a listen to Side Four, where the theme of the single is carried out in two different versions, the latter with the most impact. And if the message isn't clear enough, "Revolution No. 9" is followed by "Goodnight."

To say the Beatles are guilty of some kind of revolutionary heresy is absurd; they are being absolutely true to their identity as it has evolved through the last six years. These songs do not deny their own "political" impact or desires, they just indicate the channelling for them.

Rock and roll has indeed become a style and a vehicle for changing the system. But one of the parts of the system to be changed is "politics" and this includes "New Left" politics. There is no verbal recognition required for the beautifully organized music concrete version of "Revolution." A good set of earphones should deliver the message to those we have so far been unable to reach. Maybe this album would be a good gift for them, "with love from me to you."

As to the Beatles, it is hard to see what they are going to do next. Like the success of their earlier albums and the success of all others in this field, whether original artists or good imitative ones, the success of it is based on their ability to bring these other traditions to rock and roll (and not vice versa, like the inevitable excesses of "folk-rock," "raga-rock" and "acid-rock") and especially in the case of Dylan, the Stones, the Beatles and to a lesser extent all the other good groups in rock and roll, the ability to maintain their own identity both as rock and roll and as the Beatles, or as Bob Dylan, or as the Rolling Stones, and so on.

Thus, the Beatles can safely afford to be eclectic, deliberately borrowing and accepting any outside influence or idea or emotion, because their own musical ability and personal/spiritual/artistic identity is so strong that they make it uniquely theirs, and uniquely the Beatles. They are so good that they not only expand the idiom, but they are also able to penetrate it and take it further.

"Back in the USSR," this album's first track, is, of course, a perfect example of all this: it is not just an imitation (only in parts) of the Beach Boys, but an imitation of the Beach Boys imitating Chuck Berry. This is hardly an original concept or thing to do: just in the past few months we have been deluged with talk of "going back to rock and roll," so much that the idea is now a tiresome one, because it is, like all other superficial changes in rock and roll styles, one that soon becomes faddish, over-used and tired-out.

It is all open to the Beatles. It would be too simple to say that "Back in the USSR" is a parody, because it operates on more levels than that: it is fine contemporary rock and roll and a fine performance thereof; it is also a superb commentary on the United States S. R., hitting every insight—"honey, disconnect the phone." As well as a parody, it's also a Beatles song.

The song is undoubtedly the result of Paul McCartney's three trips to the United States in 1968 before the album was made. It is the perfect introductory song for this set. What follows is a trip through the music of the US (SR).

"Looking through a Glass Onion" is, of course, the Beatles on the subject of the Beatles. Whatever they may feel about people who write about their songs and read things into them, it has undoubtedly affected them, eating away at their foundations and always forcing that introspection and that second thought. And so here is a song for all those trying to figure it out—don't worry, John's telling you right here, while he is rolling another joint.

Part of the phenomenal talent of the Beatles is their ability to compose music that by itself carries the same message and mood as the lyrics. The lyrics and the music not only say the same thing, but are also perfectly complementary. This comes also with the realization that rock and roll is *music,* not literature, and that the music is the most important aspect of it.

"Obladi Oblada," where they take one of the familiar calypso melodies and beats, is a perfect example. And it's not just a calypso, but a rock and roll calypso with electric bass and drums. Fun music for a fun song about fun. Who needs answers? Not Molly or Desmond Jones, they're married with a diamond ring and kids and a little "Obladi Oblada." All you need is Obladi Oblada.

"Bungalow Bill," the mode of the Saturday afternoon kiddie shows, is a tribute to a cat the Beatles met in Marrakesh, an American tiger hunter ("the All American bullet headed saxon mother's son"), who was there accompanied by his mother. He was going out hunting, and this song couldn't put the American in better context, with his cartoon serial morality of killing.

"While My Guitar Gently Weeps" is one of George Harrison's very best songs. There are a number of interesting things about it: the similarity in mood to "Bluejay Way" recalls California, the simple Baja California beat, the dreamy words of the Los Angeles haze, the organic pace lapping around every room as if in invisible waves.

Harrison's usual style, in lyrics, has been a slightly self-righteous and preaching approach, which we have here again. One cannot imagine it being a song about a particular person or incident, rather a general set of incidents, a message, like a sermon, impersonally directed to everyone.

And this song speaks at still another level, the very direct one of the title: it is a guitarist's song about his guitar, how and why and what it is that he plays. The music mimics the linear, continuous line of the lead guitarist. It is interesting to note that the song opens with a piano imitating the sound of an electric guitar playing the heavily Spanish lead line well before the guitar picks up the lead. I am willing to bet something substantial that the lead guitarist on this cut is Eric Clapton, yet another involution of the circular logic on which this song is so superbly constructed as a musical piece.

The title, "Happiness Is a Warm Gun," comes from an advertisement John read in an American rifle magazine. That makes this track the first cousin of "Revolution." The three parts of it; the break into the wonderful 1954 C-Am-F-G style of rock and roll, with appropriate

"Bang Bang, shoot, shoot." What can you say about this song except what is obvious?

Part of the success of the Beatles is their ability to make everything they do understandable and acceptable to all listeners. One needn't have an expert acquaintance to dig what they are doing and what they are saying. The other half of letting rock and roll music be receptive of every other form and style of music, is that rock and roll must be perfectly open and accessible to every listener, fulfilling the requirement of what it is—a popular art.

Paul demonstrates throughout the album his incredible talent as one of the most prolific and professional songwriters in the world today. It's embarrassing how good he is, and embarrassing how he can pull off the perfect melody and arrangement in any genre you would care to think of.

Just name it and Paul will do it, like say, for instance, a love song about a dog in the Gilbert and Sullivan style, with a little ragtime, a little baroque thrown in. "Martha, My Dear," about Paul's English sheepdog of the same name, with hairy puns ("when you find yourself in the thick of it") and all. And of course, it works on the level of the send-up and also as an inherently good song, standing fully on its own merits.

"Blackbird" is one of those beautiful Paul McCartney songs

in which the yin-yang of love is so perfectly fitted: the joy and sorrow, always that ironic taste of sadness and melancholy in the lyric and in the minor notes and chords of the melody (remember—"Yesterday," "Eleanor Rigby," "Good Day Sunshine," prominently among many). The irony makes it so much more powerful.

Not only irony: these songs and "Blackbird" share other qualities—the simplicity and sparseness of instrumentation (even with strings) make them penetrate swiftly and universally. This one is done solely with an acoustic guitar. And of course there is the lyric: "Take these sunken eyes and learn to see; All your life you were only waiting for this moment to be free."

"Rocky Raccoon" is another one of those McCartney offhand tour-de-forces. Perhaps the Mound City Blues Blowers, circa 1937? Paul is so incredibly versatile not only as a writer, but also as a singer and a musician. Dig the vocal scatting, the saloon-hall piano; then the perfect phrasing, enunciation, the slurring (as in the phrase "I'm gonna get that boy . . ."). The song is so funny and yet dig the lyrics: "To shoot off the legs of his rival." Not just to kill, mind you, but to maim. And so why does this song come off so funny? Death is funny.

If Paul can do songwriting as

easily as some people do crossword puzzles (and that is not to say that he is flippant or careless, because Paul has allowed himself to display his absolute professional ability with song to a point that it can only be seen as a form of personal honesty), John's songs are agonizing personal statements. They are painful to hear.

"Julia" is a song to his mother, whom John saw killed in a car accident when he was 14 years old. It is the most emotionally revealing piece on the album. The whole world has been witness to the personal lives of the Beatles, and it seems that a record album is the most appropriate place for such a message, sung to, sung for, his mother. And as always, John is protected by his innocence.

"I'm So Tired" begins in the manner of the late night jazz singer ("I wonder should I get up and fix myself a drink") if not, again, one of the many early styles of rock and roll with those elegantly placed electric guitar chops. And again, it uses this only as a base, a take off point to go on into completely modern, extremely powerful choruses: "You know, I'd give you everything I've got for a little peace of mind," where everything—arrangement, vocal, instruments, melody—perfectly evokes the agony of the plea.

David Dalton says of this song: "It reminds me of how many changes John has gone through since he was the plump cheeky leader of the Fab Four. Jesus Christ, Sgt. Pepper leading the Children's Crusade through Disneyland: a voyage to India as victims of their own propaganda; Apple, a citadel of Mammon . . . Even two years ago, the image of Lennon as a martyr would have seemed ludicrous, but as his trial approaches, a gaunt spiritual John hardly recognizable as his former self emerges. This metamorphosis has taken place only at the cost of an incredible amount of energy, and the weariness of this song seems to fall like the weight of gravity."

Other songs on side two include one by George and one by Ringo. George's "Piggies" is an amazing choice to follow "Blackbird," with such an opposite mood and message; "Blackbird" so encouraging, "Piggies" so smug (though accurate: "what they need's a damn good whacking"). Ha! By comparison, both "Piggies" and Ringo's polka, "Don't Pass Me By" (trust Ringo to find the C&W music of any culture) are weak material against some of the superb numbers, although on their own, they're totally groovy.

But it brings forward two interesting points: neither Paul's near-genius ability with notes nor John's rock and rolling edge of honesty are *sine qua non* for the Beatles. The taste and sense of rightness in their music, to choose the perfect musical setting, the absolutely right instrument, are just as important.

The second is that there is almost no attempt in this new set to be anything but what the Beatles actually are: John, Paul, George and Ringo. Four different people, each with songs and styles and abilities. They are no longer Sgt. Pepper's Lonely Hearts Club Band, and it is possible that they are no longer the Beatles.

When they get together, it's "Why Don't We Do It In the Road," which—whatever else it may sound like—tain't nothin' but a Beatles field holler.

This is one of many observations to be made about this album. It is at once both their simplest (plain white cover) and yet most complex effort to date.

Someone will do the work, and maybe come up with a list of old and new rock and roll songs and styles which each of these tracks is supposed to be based on. "Birthday" might be Hendrix or Cream, maybe even Larry Williams. The point is that it is, like "Helter Skelter" and "Everybody's Got Something to Hide" as well, all of these, the very best traditional and contemporary elements in rock and roll brightly are suffused into the Beatles. The "hard rock" aspect of the Beatles is one often overlooked and neglected, often times pur-

posely in the attempt to get them to be something they are not. They are a rock and roll band, after all, and they can do that thing. The straight rock is some of their most exciting and mature material. (They don't, however, cut the best of the Stones or of the Who.)

If "Birthday" is based on, say, the guitar licks of Jimi Hendrix or Clapton, it takes what is best from it and uses it in its own fashion, perfectly within context and joined with something new in rock and roll *sound recording,* which in this case is the wavering piano sound, obtained by using the leakage from the original piano track onto an empty track as the final take for the mix.

In "Everybody's Got Something to Hide Except Me and My Monkey," all the old elements of the Beatles are brought back, right up to date, including use of all the old fashions and conventions in such a refreshingly new manner.

Take the structure of the song, for example: it is based on the old I-IV-V twelvebar progression in approach, but in actuality they never do the old thing. From IV they go to VII. When they get back to V after that, they take the most unusual way—in sound and melody—to get back to I. They also use those old Beatle harmonic tones. (By way of comparison, set this song against what Steppenwolf is now popular at doing with this same material.)

"Helter Skelter" is again both traditional and contemporary—and excellent. The guitar lines behind the title words, the rhythm guitar track layering the whole song with that precisely used fuzz-tone, and Paul's gorgeous vocal. Lord, what a singer! Man, you can't sit still. No wonder you have blisters on your fingers.

As completely wide-open-eyed artists, sensitive like all others in McLuhanville, they are of course caught up and reflective in their music of what's happening around them, especially the recent scenes they have been through.

Many of these songs—if not the vast majority of them—were written while the Beatles were with the Maharishi. "Everybody's Got Something to Hide" is certainly reflective of it in its lyric. "Sexy Sadie" is the Maharishi. The harmonies and other vocal lines are exquisite, especially the "s's." The lyrics and the vocal delivery are so sincere and yet so sarcastic. John is still John.

"You may be a lover, but you ain't no dancer." What a choice for the next track.

Another very deliberate parody is "Yer Blues," a song that does away with most all of this "blues revival" nonsense out of Great Britain these days. With the exceptions of Eric Clapton, the Jeff Beck Group, and may-be one or two as-yet unfamous individuals, the Beatles are simply better at it. And that makes it so ludicrous.

The organ riff at the end of the last chorus so perfectly tells the whole story; it is based on the very boring and repetitious style of these new blues musicians who will pound the shit out of some mediocre change or short riff as if it is *the* riff which has got them to such incredible heights of feeling and style.

The Beatles of course, make it interesting, because it is so stylistically in context with the piece in which it is set. Same with the opening lyric "Yes I'm lonely wanna die." The line "black cloud crossed my mind" is in phrasing and content a parody of the "black cat crossed my path," and yet a good line by itself and as part of this song.

Forgetting the parody for a moment, it's a very good modern rock and roll blues. Dig the lines "My mother was of the sky/My father was of the earth/But I am of the universe/And you know what it's worth."

Getting back to the message (even in the title), here's Mr. Dalton again, on the English blues scene:

"The trendy transvestites of the English blues scene: Pretentious and ludicrously out of context; drawing room blues singers have created a cult of the blues bordering on intellectual snobbery and purism. It is hard to imagine anything more incongruous: the English blues fans fanatically denouncing a group for adding horns, fights breaking out in the audience at the Hampton Blues Festival. Mr. Jones [whom the Beatles refer to in this song] is said to be Dylan's grisly portrait of the folk purist, with his intellectual hang-ups, who could not accept the brash commercial forces of rock and roll. The blues purist who looks down on Soul Music as a debased commercial form is just Mr. Jones in a sheepskin jacket."

If you take any one of these songs and really get down with it, to where every piece of excellence and craftsmanship is explained and understood fully (and it's always just as good, and often even better, when you do), whatever you say about that one song is as true for the rest.

"Revolution No. 1" is a better piece, in texture and substance, than the single, although the latter was better *as* a single. "No. 1" carries the message more easily and more successfully. The horns at the end are a gas, and even, I think, a little "Daytripper" by George on the left earphone.

"Cry Baby Cry," hits me at first as a throwaway, but the further acquaintance says this: another top-notch Beatles song. Every time they are exploring

and opening new possibilities and combinations. Every time they make them work.

So many factors enter into the success of the Beatles in what they do. Some of them have been touched on. In addition to everything else, they are excellent musicians (Ringo's drumming on this LP is his best, and among the very best to be heard on any rock and roll record; George's leads are continually well-placed, well-written and well-played). We see them all in their varied strengths on this record.

"Honey Pie" is another one of those perfect Paul McCartney evocations of a whole musical era, understanding the essence so finely, that it could be as good as the original. Lovin' the rhymes: crazy-lazy, tragic-magic, frantic-Atlantic. He not only is able to re-create such moods and eras with his melody, his words, his arrangements, instrumentation, but also with his voice. He is equally expert in all these areas.

"Honey Pie" is also a more sophisticated version of "When I'm 64," just as "Savoy Truffle" is a more sophisticated look at "Lucy In the Sky With Diamonds," and "Back in the USSR," a more sophisticated "Sgt. Pepper." It is unlikely that "With A Little Help From My Friends" will ever be topped as a song for Ringo. The question is whether they are *better* songs.

If these are weaker songs,

they are the only flaws of this album set. It is a relatively minor point, and considered at a longer view, an almost irrelevant one. No creative persons in history were able to match their own brilliance with absolute consistency.

—JANN WENNER
12-21-68

ABBEY ROAD
The Beatles
(Apple SO 383)

Simply, side two does more for me than the whole of *Sgt. Pepper,* and I'll trade you *The Beatles* and *Magical Mystery Tour* and a Keith Moon drumstick for side one.

So much for the prelims. "Come Together" is John Lennon very nearly at the peak of his form; twisted, freely-associative, punful lyrically, pinched and somehow a little smug vocally. Breathtakingly recorded (as is the whole album), with a perfect little high-hat-tom-tom run by Ringo providing a clever semi-colon to those eerie *shoo*-ta's.

George's vocal, containing less adenoids and more grainy Paul tunefulness than ever before, is one of many highlights on his "Something," some of the others being more excellent drum work, a dead catchy guitar line, perfectly subdued strings, and an unusually nice melody. Both his and Joe Cock-

er's version will suffice nicely until Ray Charles gets around to it.

Paul McCartney and Ray Davies are the only two writers in rock and roll who could have written "Maxwell's Silver Hammer," a jaunty vaudevillian/music-hallish celebration wherein Paul, in a rare naughty mood, celebrates the joys of being able to bash in the heads of anyone threatening to bring you down. Paul puts it across perfectly with the coyest imaginable choir-boy innocence.

Someday, just for fun, Capitol/Apple's going to have to compile a *Paul McCartney Sings Rock And Roll* album, with "Long Tall Sally," "I'm Down," "Helter Skelter," and, most definitely, "Oh! Darling," in which, fronting a great "ouch!"-yelling guitar and wonderful background harmonies, he delivers an induplicably strong, throat-ripping vocal of sufficient power to knock out even those skeptics who would otherwise have complained about yet another Beatle tribute to the golden groovies' era.

That the Beatles can unify seemingly countless musical fragments and lyrical doodlings into a uniformly wonderful suite, as they've done on side two, seems potent testimony that no, they've far from lost it, and no, they haven't stopped trying.

No, on the contrary, they've achieved here the closest thing yet to Beatles free-form, fusing more diverse intriguing musical and lyrical ideas into a piece that amounts to far more than the sum of those ideas.

I'd hesitate to say anything's impossible for the Beatles after listening to *Abbey Road*. To my mind they're equalable, but still unsurpassed.

—JOHN MENDELSOHN
11-15-69

ABBEY ROAD
The Beatles
(Apple SO 383)

Eeeeeeeeeeeeek, it's the Beatles. Look. Look. They're crossing Abbey Road in London—John all leonine and scrunched up and dressed in white with tennis shoes, and Ringo in a tux, and Paul out of step with the others (what do you suppose *that* means?), and George looking very intense and with much better posture than the others. Up the block a ways a police van is watching, but it's cool because they're crossing in the pedestrian crossing area and I'm sure that thing Paul is carrying is a Players—they're playing it very safe. A nice yellowish colored picture on one of these nice new instant fall-apart covers. Sixteen new Beatles songs for just under seven bucks.

What's it like? Well, I don't much like it, but then I have a thing about the Beatles. Since

Revolver I've been buying their albums, playing them a couple of times, and then forgetting about them. The last album was, admittedly, exciting in places, but I still don't play it much because there's still too much stuff on it that should have been edited. Singles are a different matter, since for some reason they are more exciting, but the albums just don't seem very vital. They are masterpieces of the engineer's art, containing a melodic gift that is rare these days, and, occasionally, lyrics that are truly excellent. In fact, about as close to perfect as one can come in this field. And as Crosby, Stills & Nash have shown, perfection can be carried to the point of sterility, yet the Stones are close to perfect and are anything but sterile.

Part of the reason can be found, I think, in a comparison of the production techniques used by the Beatles and Stones. The Beatles create a sound that could not possibly exist outside of a studio. Electronically altered voices go *la la la* in chorus, huge orchestras lay down lush textures, and the actual instruments played by the Beatles themselves are all but swallowed up in the process. Indeed, *Abbey Road* is the address of a studio in London. On the album, tape splices go whizzing by, and the ear strains to dissect layers of over-dubbing. For the first time they play with their new Moog, which disembodies and artificializes their sound. Too often the result is complicated instead of complex.

In direct contrast with this we have the Stones. They all play real instruments and exactly at that. Additional instrumentation seems to be used only when there is no alternative and then it is kept to the minimum and mixed in unobtrusively. They, too, spend a lot of time remixing and overdubbing, but the end result is always credible—one can imagine little Stones performing in the speakers. The tape splices are there, but it is hard to tell just where, and the one time they really overextended themselves on record, *Their Satanic Majesties Request,* is looked upon as pretty much of a failure for just that reason. After that, they got a producer to help keep them in check and went back to making good music. I wonder what the Beatles would sound like if Jimmy Miller produced them?

Of course, the Beatles are still the Beatles, but it does tread a rather tenuous line between boredom, Beatledom, and bubblegum. "Come Together," the first track, is a superb bit of Lennonian babbling about such things as toejam football and mojo filter which contains such memorable lines as "got to be good looking 'cause he's so hard to see," and "hold you in his armchair, you can feel his dis-

ease." It's all very catchy, very funny, and quite mad, all of which is just fine with me.

Unfortunately, it is followed by "Something," by George Harrison, which Time magazine says is the best song on the album, and it's sure easy to see why. It's got a nice, easy-listening melody, vapid lyrics and a gigantic string section oozing like saccharine mashed potatoes all over the place. The vocal is comparable to Glen Campbell in the fervor of its delivery. It's so vile that I'm sure it will be covered by eight or ten artists in the next month and will rate with "Yesterday," and "Michelle" as one of the fab four's top money makers.

Things get a little better (it couldn't get worse) with the next cut, "Maxwell's Silver Hammer," about a guy named Maxwell Edison, a student majoring in medicine, who goes around killing people. It's all done as a nice bouncy catchy little song, quite hummable and singable, sort of like something left over from *Sgt. Pepper* and featuring some pale imitation Buddy Holly vocal hiccups. It's cute and pretty well done, but not particularly memorable.

Side two is a disaster, although it begins well enough with George's "Here Comes the Sun," a pleasant number with lots of Top 40 appeal, even if the lyrics are nothing special. The arpeggios at the end, along with those at the end of the last song on the first side, are motifs that keep cropping up throughout the rest of the album. At first I thought that this might indicate some unifying and thematic thread running throughout all the little songs at the end, but that doesn't seem to be the case.

The slump begins with "Because," which is a rather nothing song, featuring lots of little Ellington saxophone-voiced Pauls singing harmonies that are not unlike the Hi-Los. The backing, lyrics, everything but the vocal, sounds like the Bee Gee's, but it's not—it's the Beatles. "You Never Give Me Your Money" is a song with so many sections that it never gets anywhere, but the biggest bomb on the album is "Sun King," which overflows with sixth and ninth chords and finally degenerates into a Muzak-sounding thing with Italian lyrics. It is probably the worst thing the Beatles have done since they changed drummers. This leads into the "Suite" which finishes up the side. There are six little songs, each slightly under two minutes long, all of which are so heavily overproduced that they are hard to listen to and only two of which have decent melodies—"Golden Slumbers" which features a large string section, but doesn't suffer for it, and "Carry That Weight" which is quite infectious. The side closes with the obligatory funny trick (it's not over when you think it is), and there you are.

Now, much has been made of the "get back" phenomenon, with so many artists eschewing the complicated and returning to roots of one kind or another. It is ironic that the Beatles should have put out a single with that advice, as well as an admonition not to let them down, followed that advice quite well with the follow-up record, and then released an album like this. We're told that their next one will be all Beatles playing instruments with no overdubbing or any of the other things that mar *Abbey Road* so badly. It is tempting to think that the Beatles are saying with this album that the only alternative to "getting back" for them is producing more garbage on this order, and that they have priced it so outrageously so that fewer people would buy it. But if that's so, then why bother to release it at all? They must realize that any album they choose to release is going to get a gold record just because so many people love, respect, and trust the Beatles. They've been shucking us a lot recently, and it's a shame because they don't have to. Surely they must have enough talent and intelligence to do better than this. Or do they? Tune in next time and find out.

—ED WARD

11-15-69

LET IT BE
The Beatles
(Apple AR 3400)

To those who found their work since the white album as emotionally vapid as it was technically breathtaking, the news that the Beatles were about to bestow on us an album full of gems they'd never gotten around to polishing beyond recognition was most encouraging. Who among us, after all, wouldn't have preferred a good old slipshod "Save The Last Dance For Me" to the self-conscious and lifeless "Oh! Darlin'" they'd been dealing in?

Well, it was too good to be true—somebody apparently just couldn't Let It Be, with the result that they put the load on their new friend P. Spector, who in turn whipped out his orchestra and choir and proceeded to turn several of the rough gems on the best Beatles album in ages into costume jewelry.

Granted that he would have preferred to have been in on the project from its inception rather than having it all handed to him eight months after its announced release date (in which case we would never have been led to expect spontaneity and his reputation would still be intact), one can't help but wonder why he involved himself at all, and wonder also, how he came to the conclusion that lavish decoration of several of the tracks would enhance the straightforwardness of the album.

To Phil Spector, stinging slaps on both wrists.

He's rendered "The Long and Winding Road," for instance, virtually unlistenable with hideously cloying strings and a ridiculous choir that serve only to accentuate the listlessness of Paul's vocal and the song's potential for further mutilation at the hands of the countless schlock-mongers who will undoubtedly trip all over one another in their haste to cover it. A slightly lesser chapter in the ongoing story of McCartney as facile romanticist, it might have eventually begun to grow on one as unassumingly charming, had not Spector felt compelled to transform an apparently early take into an extravaganza of oppressive mush. Sure, he was just trying to help it along, but Spectorized it evokes nothing so much as dewy-eyed little Mark Lester warbling his waif's heart out amidst the assembled *Oliver* orchestra and choir.

"I Me Mine," the waltz sections of which remind one very definitely of something from one of *The Al Jolson Story*'s more maudlin moments, almost benefits from such treatment—it would have been fully as hilarious as "Good Night," after all, had Spector obscured its raunchy guitar with the gooey strings he's so generously lavished on the rest of it. As he's left it, though, it, like "Winding Road," is funny enough to find cloying but not funny enough to enjoy laughing at.

Elsewhere, Spector compounds his mush fixation with an inability to choose the right take (it is said that nothing on the "official album" comes from the actual film sessions, mind you). Inexplicably dissatisfied with the single version of "Let It Be," for instance, he hunted up a take in which some jagged guitar and absurdly inappropriate percussion almost capsize the whole affair, decided that it might be real Class to orchestrally embellish the vocal, and thus dubbed in—yes!—brass. Here the effect isn't even humorous—Spector was apparently too intent on remembering how the horns went on "Hey Jude" to listen closely enough to this one to realize that they're about as appropriate here as piccolos would have been on "Helter Skelter."

Happily though, he didn't impose himself too offensively on anything else, and much of what remains is splendid indeed:

Like John's "All Across The Universe," which, like "Julia," is dreamy, childlike, and dramatic all at once and contains both an unusually inventive melody and tender devotional vocal.

Like the two rough-honed rockers, the crudely revival-ish "I've Got A Feeling" and "One After 909," both of which are as much fun to listen to as they apparently were to make. "C'mon, baby, don't be cold as ice" may be at once the most ridiculous and magnificent line Lennon-McCartney ever wrote.

Like John's crossword-puzzlish "Dig a Pony," which features an urgent old rocker's vocal and, being very much in the same vein as such earlier Lennonisms as "Happiness Is a Warm Gun," nearly makes up for the absence of "Don't Let Me Down" and "The Last Dance." And especially like everyone's two favorites, "Two of Us," which is at once infectiously rhythmic and irresistibly lilting in the grand tradition of "I'll Follow the Sun," and the magnificent chunky, thumping, and subtly skiffly "Get Back," which here lacks an ending but still contains delightful camping by John and Billy Preston.

All of these are, of course, available on the bootleg versions of the album, a further advantage of which is their pure unSpectoredness and the presence of various goodies that didn't quite make it to the official release.

Musically, boys, you passed the audition. In terms of having the judgment to avoid either over-producing yourselves or casting the fate of your get-back statement to the most notorious of all over-producers, you didn't. Which somehow doesn't seem to matter much any more anyway.

—JOHN MENDELSOHN
6-11-70

The Fathers

of

Rock and Roll:

Wop-bop-

aloo-bop-

awop-bam-boom

Thus spoke Little Richard in 1956. Rock and roll was in full swing. Late in the sixties, when they began to teach rock and roll in the colleges, there was a rich and glorious history to look back on. There were giants in those days.

"Elvis, kids," J. R. Young says in his review in this section, "is gonna blow your mind." And indeed he does, 'cause Elvis was King. And his records sound as modern, clean and contemporary today as they did then.

Jerry Lee Lewis was there, Bo Diddley, the Everly Brothers, Fats Domino, Buddy Holly, Richie Valens and Chuck Berry Himself. Among many.

These are the fathers of rock and roll: many of them, although not even Chuck Berry is reviewed at length in this selection. Most of the great records are in the "shopping guide" to Oldies at the end of this chapter. Once you have sought these out and loved them, the rest comes naturally.

Rock and Roll Will Never Die.

WORLDWIDE 50 GOLD AWARD HITS, VOL. 1
Elvis Presley
(RCA LPM 6401)

I really loved Elvis back in '56. Loved his face, loved the way he moved, loved the way he sang, and devoured every little word he said that I could find. So did a lot of other kids, lots of them. And the best part was that we never cared why.

Sure, Pat Boone was "too much," sure, with his clean white bucks and diploma from Columbia (he refused to do "Ain't That A Shame" for a while because it was "bad grammar" and wasn't "good for the kids") and his lovely wife and daughters (in his first movies he wouldn't kiss the leading lady or anybody, insisting that he would "never kiss anyone but his wife"), and Harry Belafonte, natch, because the calypso was the rage ("Mama Look At Bubu" and all the others, cha cha), but Elvis was it, really *it*.

He had acne and everything, man, dirty jeans and sideburns. Sideburns!!! And only hoods had sideburns. Hoods that loved their mothers and could kiss them in public. Elvis was a hood at heart. Everybody knew it. And he changed the world.

My dad played checkers with him back in '56, on a train trip that my folks took. My dad beat him somewhere between L.A. and Memphis, because that's where Elvis got off. My folks continued on to Florida. Can you dig what it meant to a skinny kid four foot eight and in the seventh grade collecting Elvis Presley cards. *My dad played checkers with Elvis.*

I carried the autographed picture (To Jeff, from Elvis) that my dad brought home for the next eight years, and would probably be carrying it today if my wallet hadn't been stolen when I was cleaning swimming pools. It was the only important thing I carried in it, a strange link to a well-spent youth.

I have a cousin who was born in '56 and she says she hates Presley's ass because he's dumb. She doesn't see the same thing

in those drooping Gladys Presley eyes he's worn all these years, because what I see is still magic. Elvis' new music isn't magic by any means, but Elvis himself, well, there's no escaping that aura built into him.

Modern Elvis is nothing more than a terrible facade that time has built over him, a tasteless wrapping of Koolwhip and "mod neckerchiefs." No wonder she hates him. She can't see him, can't quite look in those eyes and see the hood still residing, still resplendent in his baggy beige wool pants, and pink and grey and black shirt (when Elvis was hot on buying Cadillacs, his favorite was the pink one. He had three, a marvelous fact back then).

But it really isn't too hard to grasp. Think about hearing "Bossa Nova Baby" or "If I Can Dream" (and hearing them a lot) *before* ever hearing "Blue Suede Shoes" or "I Want You, I Need You, I Love You." That thought appalls me, literally, the fact that something so insipid as "Bossa Nova Baby" could taint "Blue Suede Shoes." Horrifying. Perhaps that's why the Biggest and Most Expensive package to ever hit the rock and roll racks will rectify the misinformation inherent in "(You're The) Devil In Disguise."

Worldwide 50 Gold Award Hits, Vol. 1. ELVIS ELVIS ELVIS. It's really an astounding package playing out the whole disintegration of taste and style on four albums, spanning the last 15 years, "Heartbreak Hotel" (January '56) to "Kentucky Rain" (January '70). It's enough to make a grown man cry.

If the album, however, has any value in its totality, it's that maybe some kids will buy it for "In the Ghetto," "Suspicious Minds," and other of that ilk, and discover the real Elvis of the early years, that hood from Memphis. And if there are any of you others out there who pooh-pooh Elvis, but haven't listened to the first stuff lately, I'd recommend that you go through that bottom drawer and get out those old 45s, put them on your Panasonic, and turn it up, way up. It'll really knock you out 'cause it's like the best Rock and Roll ever made. It isn't even nostalgic. It just rocks your ass off.

And if you're lucky enough to have the very first album, *Elvis Presley* (LPM/LSP 1254, and on RCA of course), then you're in for Super Treat, 'cause the Kid was really together with their sound. That's the good, hopefully, that will come out of this ten-dollar-plus package, that the real Elvis may be heard for the first time by so many kids.

If it were up to me, however, I'd recommend that the Big One *(50 Hits)* be skipped, and in its stead everybody buy *Elvis' Golden Records* (LPM/LSP 2075), and, if you still don't have it, the first album, *Elvis Presley*. It would be cheaper to do this, and infinitely more rewarding. *50 Gold Award Hits* is too concerned with presenting the Elvis continuum, a chronological rendering of his career, the good and the bad. The other albums are just his music, the best of his career, the Important Years, and they're good. Mean stuff. So put your collar up, cats, and all you kittens stand in line 'cause Elvis, kids, is gonna blow your mind.

—J. R. YOUNG
10-29-70

FROM ELVIS IN MEMPHIS
Elvis Presley
(RCA LST 4155)

Elvis and Memphis have changed, along with everything else. Country music has been polysyllabized, and rhythm and blues, which was once just that, has long since dropped the blues from its make-up. When Elvis was in high school he could have heard Muddy's "Long Distance Call" or "Honey Bee" as popular new releases, and Sonny Boy Williamson's "Don't Start Me to Talkin'" came out at just about the same time as Elvis' own first song. Sam Phillips, Elvis' reluctant discoverer, had in the course of a few years recorded Howlin' Wolf, Bobby Bland, Little Junior Parker, Johnny Ace and B. B.

King, all for the first time. Some records had been leased; others had appeared on his own Sun label. There was a relaxed interplay—musical and probably social—between white and black that was the product as much of naivete as of conscious commercial exploitation.

When Elvis first recorded fifteen years ago there was no name for the kind of music he was playing. It was just the sort of thing you heard at roadhouses and country fairs all through Mississippi, Arkansas, and Tennessee. Country singers like Sonny Burgess were known for raucous blues like "Red Headed Woman," and Harmonica Frank, the Great Medical Managerist recorded by Phillips, was popular with his blues and novelty numbers. All of this was at Elvis' fingertips, and he could sing Arthur Crudup's "That's All Right" as naturally as "Isle of Broken Dreams" or "My Happiness" (the song he recorded originally on a Sun demo for his mother's birthday).

Elvis' first commercial release, Crudup's blues backed by a Bill Monroe bluegrass tune, changed everything. For one thing, it changed Sun Records. From a white-owned blues label which might have given the Chess brothers (to whom much of Phillips' material was leased) stiff competition Sun became first the harbinger and then the king of the new rockabilly

sound. It's generally been assumed that the phenomenal commercial success of this music reflected a correspondent deterioration in quality, but I think that in reality no such decline took place. In just three years Phillips put together a list that could rival that of any other recording company in any other field. There was room for the talents of artists as diverse as Jerry Lee Lewis, Carl Perkins, Roy Orbison, Charlie Rich, Billy Riley, Warren Smith, Johnny Cash, and Elvis himself, and really the only conclusion to which we are led is that Phillips was a man of exceptional, wide-ranging taste who possessed extraordinary producing ability.

Dewey Phillips, a popular Memphis DJ with a big rhythm and blues following, broke Elvis' song on the radio, and according to legend the station was flooded with calls demanding the song be played over and over again. Elvis himself hid out in a movie theatre, and at last appeared on Dewey Phillips' radio show to quiet the public uproar, and, at Phillips' prodding, to give assurance (in order to authenticate his color) that it was indeed all-white Humes High School that he had attended. We listen to these accounts not with disbelief but with a kind of incomprehension, unable to imagine so electrifying a triumph, unable to recapture so revolutionary a moment. In those days Sonny Boy Williamson was on the radio broadcasting from West Helena, Arkansas with his King Biscuit Boys, Elmore James and B. B. King, among others. Rufus "Bear Cat" Thomas, the novelty blues singer, was a regular DJ on WDIA—as he remains today—and it was just a couple of years before that Howlin' Wolf left his job at WKWM and went north to Chicago after five years of spinning records and selling fertilizer. It seems in retrospect like such a fabulous time—yet many of these same singers are still around, and Elvis is still on top.

The new album is great. I think flatly and unequivocally that it is the equal of anything he has ever done. If it were made only of its weakest elements it would still be a good record and one that would fulfill in many ways all the expectations we might have had of Elvis.

"In the Ghetto," a hit big enough to substantiate Elvis' continued popularity, is for all its lush orchestration convincingly sung and phrased with sensitivity. It substantiates as well the whole liberal complex we grafted onto Elvis in adopting him for our hero, and despite a message fuzzy enough to allow the song considerable C&W popularity it gives us a statement as explicit as any we are ever likely to get. "Only the Strong Survive," while a little

stiff and tightly sung, is a creditable soul offering, and even "Any Day Now" is palatable enough in this vein. Finally "Gentle On My Mind" offers us Elvis in the new mod buckskin image of country music, as he triumphs forcefully over the banality of the lyrics with a willingness to use dramatics, even at the risk of seeming melodramatic, and all this on a song that has previously been the bland property of singers like Glen Campbell and Bobby Goldsboro.

Most striking are the powerful evocations of an earlier style with "Power of My Love," a tough blues with a popular bridge, and "After Loving You," a stammered blues very much like "One Night." Both have basic rock and roll accompaniment, both are marked by the boastful sexual swagger of earlier days, and "After Loving You" is highlighted by what sounds like Elvis' own lowdown guitar (with the same runs that brought cries of "Play it dirty, play it dirty" on the TV special). "True Love Travels on a Gravel Road" gives us a well-written love ballad, eerily updated with scarcely a hint of the anachronistic style of "Love Me," "Love Me Tender," and "Loving You." It's put across in Elvis' best genteel manner, offering a glimpse of real sophistication while at the same time "It Keeps Right On A-Hurtin'" and "Movin' On" are masterful reminders of El's earlier country and western roots. "It Keeps Right On A-Hurtin' " showcases fine Jerry Lee Lewis-styled country piano, and "Movin' On," Hank Snow's driving classic, complete with whining steel guitar, is nicely understated by Elvis' normally extravagant voice. Both cuts are marked by the same sensible arrangements which distinguish the greater part of the album, and both are vivid, highly successful performances.

All of this is merely confirmation of what we already knew about Elvis, though. What is new, and what is obvious from the first notes of the record, is the evident passion which Elvis has invested in this music and at the same time the risk he has taken in doing so. From the hoarse shout that opens the album to the hit song that closes it, it seems clear—as indeed it was clear on the TV special—that Elvis is trying, and trying very hard, to please us. He needs to have our attention, and it comes as something of a shock to discover that a hero whom we had set up to feel only existential scorn, a hero who was characterized by a frozen sneer and a look of sullen discontent should need us in the end. It is his *involvement* after all which comes as the surprise.

And thus it's "Long Black Limousine" and "I'll Hold You in My Heart" which mark the high point of the album and indeed may mark the high point of Elvis' career to date. "Long Black Limousine" is the almost quintessential C&W ballad, the melody of which bears traces of such mournful standards as "Old Shep" and "Green Green Grass of Home." It tells the classic story of the country girl who goes to the city in search of riches, only to be corrupted by city ways:

> *When you left you know
> you told me that some-
> day you'd be returning
> In a fancy car for all the
> town to see
> Well now, everyone is
> watching you, you've
> finally had your dream
> And you're riding in a long
> black limousine*

Ordinarily a song like this will be treated as a kind of grim cautionary tale, delivered in a flat unadorned voice with simple sentimental country backing. Here the accompaniment is ornamented with bells, horns, and female choir, but it is Elvis' voice upon which the words depend for their dramatic effect. In a departure quite uncharacteristic of most country music, there is a fierce, almost shocked indignation in the voice, and the passionate intensity of Elvis' voice transforms a fairly ordinary song into a vehicle for savage social protest.

"I'll Hold You In My Heart ('Til I Can Hold You In My Arms)," an Eddy Arnold composition, is a simpler kind of song with words almost altogether, the arrangement is just country-gospel piano, strong supporting guitar, piano and rhythm, and the message consists only of one or two verses repeated hypnotically over and over. The effect is all-enveloping, though, and nothing could better exemplify the absorbing character of Elvis' unique and moving style. At the same time nothing could more effectively defy description, for there is nothing to the song except a haunting, painful emotionalism. It goes on and on, long past the point where you'd have thought it might logically have stopped, as Elvis himself is seemingly caught up in the mesmerizing effect of words and rhythm until he is lost in the song, using the dynamics of his voice to marvelous effect, calling up an aching vulnerability which he has never before exposed. He doesn't let go of the song until he has wrung every last ounce of feeling from it, and listening to this performance is an absorbing, emotionally riveting experience. Elvis has never sung better.

And yet it's still not the same. There is that unavoidable tightness in his voice. For a moment we lose sight of it in "I'll Hold You In My Heart," but it's a function of knowledge as much as anything else. You can't recapture the innocent ease of those first sides, you can't bring back the easy innocence of new adulthood, whether for listener or for singer. What is so striking about the sides cut for Sun Records, even today, fifteen years after their first release, is the freshness of style, the cleanness and enthusiasm. There is a total lack of pretentiousness in Scotty Moore's crisp lead guitar and in the easy swing of the combo. The sound is without affectation or clutter, and the songs—about equally divided between blues and country and mostly available on two RCA albums, *A Date With Elvis* (LSP 2011) and *For LP Fans Only* (LSP 1990)—are all of them timeless. Most of all the voice, free of the mannerisms with which it has inevitably become infected, is joyously full of confidence and youthful vitality.

The first arrangement of "That's All Right," it is said, was worked out during a coffee-break between takes of a ballad called "Without You." Really, all the early songs sound like some kind of inspired accident. It's as if some musicians got together and fooled around to make music for themselves, and the result somehow found its way onto record. There's the unexpected falsetto and chuckle with which Little Junior Parker's "Mystery Train" trails off, the bubbly beginning to "Baby

Let's Play House," and the too perfect, beautiful slow take of Kokomo Arnold's "Milkcow Blues" when Elvis says, "Hold it, fellas. That don't move me. Let's get real gone for a change."

Well, he got gone. Sun sold his contract to RCA for $35,000 plus $6000 in back pay they owed to Elvis, Elvis and Colonel Parker got rich, and Sam Phillips lived to regret his one real lapse of judgment. "I knew he'd be big," Phillips is reported to have said, "but I never knew he'd be that big." Elvis, too, must have been a little bewildered, but he never let it show, for he withdrew from the world to make movies. He made more money, and the Colonel's formulaic approach to show business continued to pay off, and Elvis didn't go back to record in his home town of Memphis until 1969.

His homecoming can now be accounted a triumph. But then his whole career can be counted a triumph. There's no point in wasting any sympathy on Elvis or on anyone else. Because if he lost what he had he certainly got what he wanted, and that's all you can really hope for, isn't it? When he first came to our attention it would have been difficult to imagine the seriousness with which rock and roll would one day be greeted. We took Little Richard's outlandish screams for a welcome relief, and the nonsense lyrics

of Chuck Berry and Carl Perkins seemed to express an implicit view of the world that each of us secretly shared. Now the secret is out, and everyone is covering up.

—PETER GURALNICK
8-23-69

FATS IS BACK
Fats Domino
(Reprise RS 6304)

Just out of the back of the left speaker comes this scratchy, but very hip piano, then at the right speaker it's an old Fats Domino hit ("You made!! me cry!! when you said!! goodbye!!") and back and forth between the speakers run the opening riffs of songs—not just "Blueberry Hill"—nearly forgotten.

A voice announces that "Fats is Back," and he is up full with a song called "My Old Friends." From the very beginning, put perfectly in the mood, the album is just fantastic: the production is modern, the mixing superb, and Fats is Fats, better than ever, a remembered, beautifully deep and mellow voice and he's there.

The segue into the next second track, a perfect set of drum triplets, illustrates how precisely, how masterfully and how tastefully the past and present have been combined into this amazing album. The segues are not all; the horn arrangements are contemporary, sometimes a little thick, but good; and the King Curtis solos are superb (King Curtis, after all, being a man who was very much there in the beginning and is still a superb session man, as he is here, as well as a soloist in his own right).

The dominant instrument is the piano, and Fats is a fine piano player. ("Gonna rock it, gonna roll it, till the broad daylight.") The musicians on the session—and this includes the Blossoms who did the vocal back-ups, including a total job of "Lovely Rita"—have done their parts perfectly.

One would really expect that something like this—a new recording by an old artist, long past his time, with a new record company, and during the "rock and roll revival," yet—would inevitably be totally without taste, dull, a tepid rehash at best and a waste of money and time.

But one can be wrong. *Fats Is Back* is unequivocally a fine record in all respects. The closing track on side one is "Lady Madonna," surely as good a cover of a Beatles' song as ever has been done. It's a very logical song to use, "something very simple and catchy," as Fats is quoted as saying in the liner notes. Fats on the grand piano and in his vocal, which is quite excellent, brings a new depth to the song. (The only disturbing thing in this number is the

choral and muted horn parts behind Fats on the verses. Otherwise, it is a rendition which must be heard to be believed.)

"Honest Papas Love Their Mamas Better," like nearly everything on this album, has a great rocking shuffle, with a very strong and understated horn section. Listening to collections of oldies and other golden greats can only go so far, usually because the production of the record or whatever engineering techniques then available were invariably very thin and just don't hold up on a second or even first listen ten years later. This difficulty simply does not obtain here and the record is not a collection of oldies but a tastefully programmed set.

"One For the Highway (Two For the Road)" recalls the great instrumental figures and techniques of early rock and roll, strong, immediate, swinging music. And, at the same time, it is terribly modern, not just because of the mixing, but because those involved with this recording understood that the values of good 1956 rock and roll are the exact same values of good 1968 rock and roll.

If "One For the Highway" does not illustrate this, then take Fats' version of "Lovely Rita, Meter Maid," a totally surprising song to include in this production. But the thing that must be realized, and that is realized here, is that it is not surprising at all: the same things that made rock and roll great then still make great rock and roll today.

"Lovely Rita" begins with a full soprano chorus, picks up Fats' perfectly suited vocal, a chorded piano melodically equal to the Paul McCartney bass line and a set of maracas doing the double-time. Fats does this song like it should be done—*that* is the very simple proof of the viability of it all. And it's just too fucking much when Fats cries out "Nobody but you, Rita."

Everyone involved with this album, not least of all Antoine "Fats" Domino, has done an excellent job. But Richard Perry, the producer, who one assumes to be responsible for the segues, the repertoire, the perfect final fade, the selection of arrangers and so many other aspects, deserves especial credit, for Perry, second only to the man himself, has brought Fats back.

—JANN WENNER
9-14-68

LITTLE RICHARD'S GROOVIEST 17 ORIGINAL HITS
(Specialty SPS 2113)

Wop-bop-aloo-bop-awop-bam-boom . . .

Thus spoke Little Richard in 1956, on his first Specialty single, "Tutti-Frutti." Richard Penniman's first record was a hard-driving semi-novelty number, characteristic of a good deal of what followed. Unlike Chuck Berry, whose material used to emphasize a narrative, Little Richard combined scatting, nonsense, and a vague story line with a super-presence and a masterful, authoritative delivery. Like Jimi Hendrix today, nothing mattered as long as Richard was doing it.

While Little Richard was unquestionably one of the great figures of early rock and roll he has only recently enjoyed the renewal of interest that people like Chuck Berry have experienced. He was not one of the English scene's lost idols, judging from the fact that groups like the early Stones and Yardbirds, and others specializing in early American rock ignored him. In the mid-Fifties he did exert great influence on people like Elvis Presley who recorded many of his songs. And on the contemporary scene there are two musicans who have been influenced by him tremendously: Paul McCartney and Otis Redding.

The Beatles were one of the few groups from England to record Little Richard songs. Paul McCartney is a brilliant mimic of Richard's hoarse, gospel vocal style. In the early days the Beatles used to say that the hardest kind of song for them to write was hard rock, which is why most of the hard rock on their early albums was written by someone else. They finally solved the problem with "I'm Down," the flip side of "Help." That McCartney song was almost identical in structure to Richard's "Long Tall Sally," a song McCartney performed on the second Beatles album. Also the version the Beatles recorded of "Kansas City," on *Beatles VI,* is an exact copy of Richard's version which can be heard on *The Fabulous Little Richard,* an old Specialty album.

Otis Redding's ties to Little Richard's music were more direct. Redding spent his early years in Macon, Georgia, Little Richard's hometown. Redding grew up with Richard as his boyhood idol. On his first album, *Pain In My Heart,* Redding recorded "Lucille," a famous Little Richard song. He also did one of his own compositions, "Hey Hey Baby," in a style so close to Richard's that the casual listener wouldn't be able to tell who was singing, except for the backing of Booker T. and MGs.

Hearing how influenced Redding was by Richard at this early stage in his career, one can discover innumerable touches of Richard's influence in later Redding recordings. However, at that stage in his career, Redding was no longer relying on Richard's techniques and his use of Richard's nu-

ances was not obviously derivative.

Perhaps as a result of the general interest in older rock stars which has been kicked up over the summer, there is now a renewed interest in Little Richard's music. His label, Specialty, has gone back into business. They were a very important company in the Fifties, having been responsible for records by Larry Williams, Lloyd Price, and Sam Cooke, all of whom eventually found their way on to bigger labels. They are now trying to cash in on the interest in Richard by releasing a collection of his old records called *Little Richard's Grooviest 17 Original Hits,* electronically reprocessed for stereo. The stereo doesn't help the original sound one bit, but beyond that it is a magnificent collection of the music of a man whose contribution to rock and roll was second to none. It points up all the strengths and weaknesses of an era in American popular music. And as entertainment it is unlikely that a dozen albums will be released this year of greater interest.

Little Richard's music was rhythm centered. Unlike Chuck Berry, the central rhythm instrument was the piano, which Richard played himself. The era of guitar dominance had not yet emerged in Richard's day and piano oriented rock was at least as common as guitar music. For examples one need look no further than Jerry Lee Lewis and Fats Domino. (And Berry himself relied on his pianist Johnny Johnson almost as much as he relied on his guitar.) Little Richard was not a great pianist. Like Berry on guitar, he had a few licks he would use to identify himself with, but unlike Berry, who was a marvelous and fluid soloist the rest of Richard's bag was simple boogie woogie piano figures. Little Richard's most characteristic instrumental chorus is heard on two cuts of the new album, "True Fine Mama" and "Good Golly, Miss Molly." The only difference between the two is that on the former he plays the chorus an octave higher than on the latter.

Richard rounded out the rhythm section with electric bass, guitar and drums. The bass mainly played two types of shuffle figures. Most often he would do a straight boogie woogie figure, for example, on "Tutti-Frutti." Occasionally he would go to a more stylized shuffle, as on "All Around the World." That latter figure was turned into a talking instrumental by Jimmy McCracklin called "The Walk," and eventually became a standard rock figure.

Little Richard's guitarist played chords and simple rhythm figures. Only on the last records Little Richard recorded for Specialty (on *The Fabulous Little Richard*) did the guitar ever take the lead. Occasionally the guitar would be used for the intro as on "Kansas City" (on the aforementioned album) and "Hey Hey Hey Hey," on the new *Original Hits* album. The figure is the same in both cases.

The thing that dates any Little Richard record is the drumming. In line with the custom of the time, the drums were under-recorded, the snare sounded ludicrously bassy, and the instrumentalist did next to nothing. On some of Richard's later records it got worse, because the guy gave up on keeping the beat.

Finally there was a simple horn section made of a few saxes. On some of the cuts I can make out only a lead sax. The lead sax would take a solo. It was as Motown horn solo is today. Part of the routine. While the tone of these solos is always clean and occasionally fits the song, by and large their only purpose was to fill out the song. Like most pop instrumental solos their main purpose was to vary the lead sound for fear that the vocal wasn't interesting enough to sustain interest for the entire length of the record. It could have been worse.

Ultimately a Little Richard record was exactly what Little Richard put into it. He had the voice, he dominated the record, he was what moved you or failed to move you. His vocal style was, above all, crude. He paid little or no attention to the subtleties and niceties of pop singing, a fact which in itself isn't particularly praiseworthy.

However, like Hendrix on guitar, Richard had the talent to make his deliberate violations of decent formal technique a meaningful way of singing. His basic approach was to take everything from the top and work it up from there. Sometimes the results would be fairly comical, as when he runs out of breath at the end of "Jenny, Jenny." More often it served as an excellent means of knocking the listener out. The simple concentration of energy is so great that one is forced to respond.

Little Richard's background was gospel, not blues. He was a predecessor of contemporary soul music. It is not widely understood that modern soul is an offshoot more of gospel than blues. Every important practitioner of soul got his start in the church. Soul derives its hyperactive and intensely involving qualities from this gospel source. The blues represent a separate and distinct counter tendency in black American music. The blues have always reflected a more cerebral, reflective, contemplative side of life. It is for that reason that few if any black vocalists are both good soul and blues singers.

Richard was no exception and the only use he ever made of

blues was in borrowing some of its forms. The singing style, the frenetic quality to all of his work, is directly related to gospel music and has no parallel among blues singers. In the Fifties, as now, there is a broader general attraction to this hot medium of communication than there is to the usually cooler approach of the straight blues singers, which helps to explain why Richard sold so many records while equally talented blues singers sold so few.

Of the songs on *Little Richard's Grooviest 17 Original Hits* almost all illustrate some particular facet of Richard's style. Perhaps the best known songs included on the set are two of his earliest, "Long Tall Sally" and "Tutti-Frutti." The songs are very similar. They both have verses sung over no accompaniment (except a chord on the first beat of each measure), blues choruses, a sax solo, and concluding choruses. "She's Got It" and "Ready Teddy" are in the same vein.

This was a very common song from in the mid-Fifties and people like Fats Domino ("Ain't That A Shame") and Jerry Lee Lewis ("High School Confidential") made use of the broken time type of verse. It is a highly efficient way of putting some tension into a performance right from the beginning. The trick in using such a technique is to, on the one hand, excite the listener's interest by use of the unorthodox device, but at the same time hold his interest for the duration of the piece. To me, "Ready Teddy" is the best instance of Richard's use of the form. It works best because it extends the unaccompanied verses to a greater length than on the other songs. This creates the more tension and sustains a greater degree of interest. But any one of these times should be enough to get you out of your chair through sheer excitement.

Richard recorded numerous songs with straight shuffle blues forms. The two best illustrations of this approach are "Ooh, My Soul" and "True Fine Mama." "Ooh, My Soul" is the fast version. It begins with Richard simply saying "Ooh, My Soul" and crashing into the song ("Honey, honey, honey, honey, honey/Get up all of that money"). At the end of each chorus he stops everything and repeats "Ooh, My Soul." It is amazing to listen to for the sheer power of Richard's performance. "True Fine Mama" is really straight, done at an even-paced, moderate tempo. No novelty lyrics, just straight blues words with a gospel background. It is one of the songs with the greatest lasting appeal. I still dig it, eleven years after the first time I heard it.

The pace of a Little Richard album is always absurdly fast. He recorded very few slow numbers in the Specialty days.

There are only three on this album, the best of which, by far, is "Send Me Some Lovin.'" That cut features the pounding piano style so common in the Fifties, a very intense and moving delivery, and a fine song based on "Down In the Valley." However, the very best ballad Richard ever recorded was omitted from the new set and is available only on his very first Specialty album, Here's Little Richard, or on the flip side of the single version of "Keep A-Knockin," another song unaccountably left off the new set. That ballad was "I Can't Believe You Wanna Leave," a classic rock and roll song but done in a style of incredible intensity. There isn't a modern rock singer on the scene who could get that much power, control, and energy into a two-and-a-half-minute, three-chord ballad.

I have two favorites on Little Richard's Grooviest 17 Original Hits. They are the two cuts which best illustrate Little Richard's achievements as a rock and roll artist. "Hey, Hey, Hey" was originally the flip side of "Good Golly, Miss Molly." It is a song which was obviously put together in twenty minutes and recorded in less. It is a blues done, us usual, at an unbelievable speed. It simply says, "Goin' back to Birmingham/Way down in Alabam' ". There is a long sax solo (two choruses) and then a series of verses which Richard used at the end of his version of "Kansas City." As the verses build up there are some subtle changes in the horn and bass figures and then Richard winds it up by singing "I'm hollerin' and screaming/Baby please come home" (which, by the way, is inconsistent with the opening verse which announces that Richard is going back to Alabama, not that he wants his woman to come home to him). The performance is perfect. It contains all the elements of a great Little Richard performance, plus one of his band's best performances, plus the spontaneity that comes with just throwing together an arrangement.

The other song that knocks me out is "All Around the World." That song has the "walk" beat, mentioned earlier. It is similar in form to the Cadillacs' classic recording, "Speedo." However, what really knocks me out are the words.

All the flat top cats
With their rock and roll queens
Just a-rockin and rollin
In their red & blue jeans
Rock and roll is all they play
All round the world

That says it, doesn't it?
—JON LANDAU
11-9-68

ROCKIN' RHYTHM AND BLUES
Jerry Lee Lewis
(Sun 107)

SHE EVEN WOKE ME UP TO SAY GOODBYE
Jerry Lee Lewis
(Smash SRS 67128)

I saw Jerry Lee Lewis *live* for the first time in 1965. Eight of us made what was a kind of personal pilgrimage to Canobie Lake Park in Salem, New Hampshire to see him perform. What impressed us most about him then, even more than the energy and inventiveness of his performance, was the fierceness of his dedication to the music itself. "I love this music," he announced from the stage. "I'm never going to stop playing it. I'll go on playing just as long as there are people to listen."

At the time it seemed like something of an empty promise. For while he performed with all the fire and exuberance of his early sides—entertaining effortlessly with a wiggle of the finger and a quizzical grin, kicking back the piano stool and shaking his blond hair forward for the inevitable "Whole Lotta Shakin'"—for all the enthusiasm of the crowd and his equally enthusiastic response, it seemed impossible to disguise the fact that after ten years on the road Jerry Lee Lewis was stuck on the sock-hop circuit of garrulous disc jockeys and grinding one night stands.

Well, times have changed, and Jerry Lee Lewis is back on top. But it's as a country singer that he's made his comeback, and at a time when he might be turning a good profit from the so-called rock and roll revival, too. He still features the old songs in his act, but the new ones have titles like "What Made Milwaukee Famous (Has Made a Loser Out of Me)" and "Sing Me a Song I Can Cry To," and a country fiddle has replaced the rockabilly guitar. We might well feel a nostalgic twinge if it were not for the fact that country music is so obviously the underpinning for the whole Sun rockabilly sound and the equally obvious fact that Jerry Lee Lewis loves the music, has always loved the music, that he is performing today.

"I've always sung country music," he insists today. "I've been country all my life, only thing is I'm a little bit more serious about it now," he told a Memphis reporter. "I'm just a hillbilly singer and I play hillbilly speeded up." If you take a closer listen to his early sides you realize that it's true. He might have once billed himself as the man who did a little bit of everything ("You're looking at the cat here," he said on his first *live* album for Smash, "I might do a blues tune one minute, and then I might turn around and do a good country tune . . ."), but underlying everything that he did was a feeling for country music and a big helping of country soul.

What is most striking about him, though, and what distinguishes him from nearly any other performer that you will ever see, is his engagement with his material. In person this has expressed itself in his consummate sense of showmanship. On record it has been made apparent in the unabashed exuberance of his early sides and the evident sincerity of his latest ones.

This quality comes through, both in his new Sun release, *Rockin' Rhythm and Blues,* which includes previously unissued material, and in his new country album for Smash, *She Even Woke Me Up to Say Goodbye.* The Sun album is made up mostly of blues and vintage rock and roll. In addition to newly recorded titles like "Johnny B. Goode" and "Good Rockin' Tonight" it includes alternate takes of "Hello Josephine" and "Sweet Little Sixteen" which are sufficiently different from the original issues as to seem like new songs. "See See Rider," from the same session as "Hang Up My Rock and Roll Shoes," demonstrates once again the use to which a great singer can put even a presumed handicap, as Jerry Lee not only triumphs over but actually capitalizes on a raspy throat. "Little Queenie" comes close to rivaling Chuck Berry with that quality of slit-eyed, almost indifferent amusement which Jerry Lee has always used to such effect. But it's on "Big Leg Woman," a composite blues very much like "Hello Hello Baby" from his second Sun album, that Jerry Lee Lewis really goes to town. Here his pumping piano literally lives up to its name, and Jerry Lee delivers the lyrics

> Let me tell you, tell you,
>   tell you something
> What I'm talking about
> I'll bet my bottom dollar
>   there ain't a cherry in
>   this house
> Oh big leg mama ease your
>   dresses down
> 'Cause when I start drilling
>   on you, baby
> You gonna lose your
>   nightgown

with his customary verve and patented chuckle ("Oh, you want the one where he laughs," said the girl in the record store in Soho when we bought "Mean Woman Blues"). At the end he makes what should have been the definitive pronouncement on the song's fate, when he shouts, "It's a hit!"

It wasn't a hit, because it was never released. And it was never released, probably because Jerry Lee got too much into the spirit of the song.

And Jerry Lee Lewis has always been the most adventurous of rock performers. More than Little Richard, more than Chuck Berry or Elvis even, he will respond to the demands of the moment to create a vocal or instrumental improvisation or simply an instant of pure theater which could never be fully anticipated or exactly recreated. His "Walkin' the Floor Over You," for example, was a good enough song on the album (*She Still Comes Around*), but by the time I saw him do it on *Hee-Haw* it had evolved into one of his most satisfying performances. "High School Confidential" varies from show to show, and even "Whole Lotta Shakin' " is never the same.

His country albums have up till now been characterized by a slightly greater restraint than is evident on his Sun sides or in live performance. I don't know whether it's because he's less familiar with the material or simply to establish his credentials as a country singer, but generally he has seemed less free with his interpolations, and the result, while always good, has been markedly more sober. The new album, though, signals a confident return to his old manner, as he runs through a tasteful selection of new tunes and country standards. The highlight of the album is, of course, "She Even Woke Me Up to Say Goodbye," a beautiful country-styled blues and one of the finest songs Jerry Lee has ever recorded.

He unveils a yodel on Jimmie Rodgers' "Waiting for a Train," and just in case you missed it brings it out again for "Wine Me Up." "When the Grass Grows Over Me" features a fresh baritone for effect, the chorus is generally used much more imaginatively than on his other Smash recordings, and his sidemen are unexceptionable. What's best about the album, though, is that he really feels at home and lets you know it. "Down in Louisiana we call that boogie woogie," he shouts over a rolling piano figure on "Workin' Man Blues." And on "Since I Met You Baby," an imaginative departure from the Ivory Joe Hunter standard, he seems to give himself over to the music entirely as he says, half-amused, half meaning it, "Oh, play the fiddle, Mr. Kenneth Lovelace. I want to hear those blues, son. I likes it, I likes it, I likes it."

Anyone who has not seen Jerry Lee Lewis perform in person is missing a unique experience. He builds his act around a fairly stable number of devices, but he can vary them endlessly and if his piano is not as technically innovative as it has sometimes been claimed to be, it is always engaging and always energetic. His vocals, too, may occasionally err on the side of enthusiasm; his voice has coarsened a little over the years, and he will sometimes reach for an effect that isn't there or simply try to overpower a song. But the impression that you'll walk away with is one of electric excitement, puckish good humor, and an almost staggering inventiveness. For Jerry Lee Lewis is a born entertainer, something no one who knows anything about him would ever deny, least of all himself.

He doesn't undervalue himself. I've seen him shush a blonde ("Honey, will you kindly quit your yakking? There's lots of our loud numbers, you can do all the talking you want. But this here's a real sad song, and you ought to listen"). And stop a couple from dancing with the admonition, "I'm the show."

He is, and he has every right to be. He's a uniquely gifted performer, and just as much as any blues or emotive soul singer he sings what's inside of him. Recently he was asked, what about the rock and roll revival? He shook his head and said he'd stick to country. Couldn't he be lured back to singing rock? No, he said, the country fans had stuck with him, and he guessed he'd stick with them now. "I'm singing real country music," he said, "the way I remember it. I think it is the best thing for me, the best thing for country music, the best thing for everyone concerned . . . I sing the way I sing because I feel that way."

—PETER GURALNICK
4-2-70

**ORIGINAL GOLDEN GREATS,
  VOL. 1
Jerry Lee Lewis
(Sun 102)**

**ORIGINAL GOLDEN GREATS,
  VOL. 2
Jerry Lee Lewis
(Sun 103)**

Nowadays, Jerry Lee Lewis is a respected country and western star, instant success following each release. Actually, he's always been country. But he hasn't always been such a well-respected man.

These two albums of re-releases return us to the Fifties, when Jerry Lee was the Mick Jagger of his day. If his (for then) outlandishly long blond hair, wild clothing, and frenzied act didn't aggravate the public sufficiently, he made up for it in other ways. He married three times before his twenty-third birthday; the last marriage, to his thirteen-year-old cousin, came before his second divorce was final and he found himself tossed out of England as a result. Headlining several of the late Alan Freed's cross-country rock circuses, he was crucified by the press. And when Dick Clark brought rock to prime time TV, Lewis was the opening night star. Singing "Great Balls of Fire" and "Breathless," the Pete Townshend of the piano discarded the stool, pounded the keys with his el-

bows, and transformed himself into a golden mass of perspiration. Jerry Lee was then at his peak, but the public wasn't ready for him, and he soon faded. His style, both on stage and off, was part of his downfall.

It's "Jerry Lee Lewis and his Pumping Piano," as the labels of his old Sun 45s once boasted; a distinctive vocal style, a country sound, a crazed piano, a guitar break, an occasional sax. His biggest hits are here: "Whole Lotta Shakin' Going On," "Great Balls of Fire," "Breathless," and the equally good but lesser known "High School Confidential." They remain among the best examples of pure rock. The other numbers are straight C&W or rhythm and blues, all reflecting the musical flavor of the Fifties. We have a "Teen-Age Letter," a "Break-Up," and "Save the Last Dance for Me."

Many of the lyrics and arrangements are, of course, antiquated. People simply don't sing about "boppin' at the high school hop" or dancin' shoes anymore. And background "doo-wahs" are scarce today. Yet the result overshadows these distractions.

Lewis' voice, that slow southern drawl filled with power, urgency, sureness, and sexuality, is the same sort of voice that most of the early English groups tried to recreate, and it is still the voice of today. The white use of black pronunciation ("Great Balls of Fire," "Little Queenie") which Lewis carried on in true country tradition is now more common than ever. His fascination with boogie ("Lewis Boogie," "What'd I Say") reflects a knowledge of a form that many people today feel they have just uncovered.

"Whole Lotta Shakin' Going On" and "Great Balls of Fire" speak for themselves as Lewis' own contribution to the permanent history of rock, and "High School Confidential" is beautiful. Here he is, ordering his woman to open her door and get her dancing shoes before the juke box blows a fuse. The music stops, he sings; it stops, he sings. The song is so fast it stuns, the voice so urgent it spells emergency. So what if they're going to a high school hop? It could be anywhere, and it could be *any* fuse getting ready to blow. He also does Chuck Berry's "Little Queenie" and Barrett Strong's "Money," long before the English "discovered" them for white audiences. Jerry Lee knew back when.

Again, while millions are only now finding country music, Lewis always knew it. The C&W numbers also show shapes of things to come, as well as what had been. "Move on Down the Line" reminds me of the putdown songs of the Stones. "Fools Like Me" and "I'll Make It All Up to You" are country,

but like much country, they are also the blues. And everyone tries his hand at the blues today. Especially with Hank Williams' "You Win Again" do we see why Lewis is a top country figure today. The music is not as smooth as country's Top Forty, nor is the singing. But the beginnings are there, the feeling if you want to get corny.

For me, however, "Breathless" remains his masterpiece. The piano *is* pumping, the voice is raw Louisiana, and only the tired adjective "frantic" can describe the song's total effect. The gasp for air each time he confesses he's breathless, the substitution of squeals and groans for words, the half-talk, half-sing style; everything is perfect. There is a bit of "Breathless" in most good rock today. Only the "good-*ness* gra-*ci*-ous" of "Great Balls of Fire" matches the creativity of this song.

Lewis is not a great singer, a great musician, nor does he write much. He is a great interpreter. He takes the words and the music that others have put on paper and makes them his. Not many of today's groups have this ability. The best write their own material. The others don't last very long. It is this ability that makes "Breathless," "Great Balls of Fire," and "Whole Lotta Shakin'" great.

Like a few of the other rock stars of his time, like Presley, the Everlys, and Roy Orbison, he unwittingly foresaw the future. The forecasting is one of the remarkable aspects of these albums. His rock numbers still stand up. His country flavor is again the big thing. The blues, the boogie, the monologue; it's all here. Those who saw him in the earlier days will recall one of rock's wildest, yet best performers. A wild white singer, Mick Jagger with a piano. Those who never saw him can visualize it all by listening to these numbers, songs running from self-pity to gloating overbearance to simple statements of fact. And Jerry Lee was a revolutionary before it became fashionable. He just did what he thought was right.

A few of the songs on the albums are truly great. Most of them are good. There are a few duds, which is remarkable considering that Sun probably scrounged through their files to find enough material for the set.

Lewis is now enjoying a revival among rock listeners as well as among country fans, but he's only doing what he's always done; a bit more subdued, but basically the same thing. Hearing these albums won't conjure up visions of him singing "What Made Milwaukee Famous Has Made a Loser Out of Me." But it's so very easy to close your eyes and be back in the balcony of the Brooklyn Fox seeing Alan Freed intro-

duce the one and only Jerry Lee Lewis.

—BOB KIRSCH
10-18-69

BOPPIN' THE BLUES
Carl Perkins and NRBQ
(Columbia CS 9981)

WHOLE LOTTA SHAKIN'
Carl Perkins
(Columbia CL 1234)

KING OF ROCK
Carl Perkins
(English: CBS 63309)

COUNTRY BOY'S DREAM
Carl Perkins
(Dollie LDP 4001; in England,
London [E] HAP 8366)

RESTLESS
Carl Perkins
(Columbia 4-44723)

NRBQ was on the same bill with Ricky Nelson recently, and the difference between them pointed up a lot of the difficulties with the so-called rock and roll revival. Nelson, himself a second generation product of rock and roll, did a tight, well-rehearsed set. He presented his songs without apology or pretense, the music was fresh and to the point, and his group played crisp punched-out arrangements.

But what won over an audience that had come as much to scoff as out of curiosity was his thorough-going sense of professionalism.

NRBQ, on the other hand, acted like clowns. They pranced around the stage, indulged in pointless time-wasting, their songs were drawn-out, their music undisciplined, and generally they seemed anxious to give the impression that it could just as well have been anyone who was up on stage, that their presence was no more than an accident of circumstance. They treated the music as a kind of a goof.

A great deal of this contrast comes through on the new Carl Perkins-NRBQ album. Carl Perkins plays, as always, with taste and with economy. His voice is grainy, his guitar says only what needs to be said, and his sound is never cluttered. NRBQ, backing him up or on their own, don't seem able to settle on a style. It isn't so much that they don't know what to play as that they don't know what to leave out.

As so often happens, NRBQ seem to feel compelled to prove themselves, and what was undoubtedly intended as a sincere tribute turns instead into a kind of cutting session. On four of the six cuts that they share with Perkins, Steve Ferguson, NRBQ's guitarist, takes the lead. And on "Sorry Charlie," probably the session's most successful collaboration, the song is allowed to go on several choruses too long, due largely to the organist's self-indulgence.

There are, of course, compensations. It's good to hear Carl Perkins romping through some of his old numbers again. And he does turn in a couple of good new songs as well as a disarming guitar solo to end the record better than it started off. But probably the best thing about the album is its cover. With its disc-centered design, star-shaped snapshot cut-outs, Loonytunes lettering and cartoon technicolor it captures more of the deliberate raunchiness of the era than any of NRBQ's music and immediately brings to mind the classic artwork of Carl Perkins' LP for Sun, *Dance Album*.

The real problem with groups like NRBQ is that their music has no clear need to exist. Unlike Carl Perkins, or unlike Creedence Clearwater, say, they have never been forced to define themselves within a commercial structure. Instead they have taken rock and roll as a kind of disembodied phenomenon, a mystique rather than a music with roots and a legitimate background of its own. So that when they do songs like "Rip It Up" and "Jenny Jenny Jenny" or Carl's own beautiful ballad, "Sure to Fall," it comes out halfway between self-conscious put-on and honest tribute. And while their music may be eclectic in the extreme, it never has the urgency, it never has the necessity of the real thing.

Carl Perkins, by contrast, has always been the most guileless of musicians. He plays music that is simple and straightforward and limited by commercial considerations (of length, of subject, of form). But it has been his particular genius to transform these considerations into art, and as a result, he along with Chuck Berry has given us some of the watchwords of our times.

And yet, for an artist of his stature, Carl Perkins has had a curiously undignified career. He went from Sun to Columbia off the enormous success of "Blue Suede Shoes," "Boppin' the Blues," and a whole string of hits. But while he enjoyed fair-sized sales at first, he never equalled the kind of popularity he had known with Sun. Nor did he ever again achieve the artistic heights.

Probably they misgauged his talents (Columbia promoted him for a while as their answer to Elvis Presley, which clearly he was not). But the main reason for his popular decline was Columbia's total misreading of the new market and their obvious contempt for the music itself.

The first album that Columbia released, *Whole Lotta Shakin'*, is pretty good evidence of this insensitivity. Taking its title from the Jerry Lee Lewis song, it consists almost exclusively of covers of Elvis Presley and Little Richard material. It features as well the most pedestrian sort of arrangements, and in a confused attempt to obscure Carl Perkins' country

sound adds a honking sax on top of a tinkling honky-tonk piano. The mixture never jells, Carl's guitar suffers in the confusion, and the overall effect—with its noisy texture, frenetic pace, and cluttered arrangements—is a middle-aged adman's fantasy of rock and roll.

At times Carl does manage to triumph over the material. His "Where the Rio de Rosa Flows" is full of bouncy good-natured enthusiasm. "Hey, Good Lookin'" sounds a little like a hopped-up Hank Williams; and "Shake Rattle and Roll," too, conveys some of the desperate drive that underlay the good-humored surface of his early music. ("I actually wasn't describing a pair of shoes. I was a country boy proud of a pair of blue suedes and didn't want them stepped on.") But the album as a whole is only for those interested in collecting rock and roll memorabilia, or in getting an idea of just where Columbia thought rock and roll was really at back in 1958.

The singles are generally much more successful. For one thing, they include a fair number of originals. For another, they were aimed at a real market. Produced, like the album, by Frank Jones and Don Law, at that time heads of Columbia's C&W division, they were increasingly slanted towards the country market. And while they suffer from some of the same defects of production as the album, they are on the whole a much more honest kind of music and in their own way come close to rivaling the great early sides for Sun.

They have been collected for the most part in a 16-track English album called *Carl Perkins: King of Rock*, which is about equally divided between irrepressible rockabilly and slow heartfelt ballads. It continues to catalogue Carl Perkins' fascination with clothes ("Pink Pedal Pushers," "Pointed Toe Shoes," "Levi Jacket"), an obsession that must go down with Chuck Berry's infatuation with cars and Johnny Cash's thing about trains as touching reminders of the simplicities of an earlier age. It includes as well the demonic "Sister Twister" with its leering echoes of Jerry Lee Lewis' "I've Been Twistin'" ("Sister twister, they say you really go/I think the boys are all scared/To get you on the floor") and a song as expressive as any for every child of the Fifties, "Pop Let Me Have the Car."

"Pink Pedal Pushers," it says in the liner notes, made #1, but if any of the others did it has escaped notice and Columbia dropped Carl Perkins' contract about seven years ago. He made sporadic recordings after that, cutting singles for Decca and Brunswick among others. But it wasn't until 1967 when he cut some singles and an album for Bill Denny's Dollie label that he had anything like a regular contract. In 1969 Denny worked out a leasing arrangement under which Denny produces and Columbia once more packages Carl Perkins.

The Dollie album, *Country Boy's Dream*, is made up exclusively of country numbers and represents in a way a turning point in Carl Perkins' career. For while he has always sung in a country style and obviously must be considered a country artist at least in part, the Dollie album amounts to the first open acknowledgment of that fact.

For rock and roll, it must finally be admitted, was a music for the middle class. A compromise between blues and country mixed in about equal parts, it was in a sense the truest kind of folk music and created a market of previously unimagined proportions. But what we lost sight of at the time, and something that the instant glamor of rock and roll itself tended to obscure, was that each of these artists had a past. Fats Domino, for example, was already an established rhythm and blues star when he got swept up in the tidal wave of rock. Singers like Little Richard were no overnight sensations; Richard had himself been recording as far back as 1950. And Big Joe Turner was no youngster when "Shake Rattle and Roll" established him as a teenage idol.

The white artists were, of course, much younger, but all sprang from equally legitimate backgrounds. Carl Perkins, Gene Vincent, Elvis Presley, Jerry Lee Lewis all had their roots in country music, and it's only appropriate that they should now at last be going home.

None of the songs on the Dollie album is particularly outstanding in itself, but the overall mood is relaxed and mellow and it gives Carl the opportunity for some clean country picking on acoustic as well as amplified guitar. "Country Boy's Dream" and "Home (That's Where the Heart Is)," a Perkins composition, both embody affecting and heartfelt sentiments, and on a number of songs Carl really does sound like an antic Hank Williams, whose death he memorializes in "The Star of the Show." But I think the highlight of the album is "Shine Shine Shine," a buoyant composition which comes closest to his old style and closest to "Restless," the song that launched his new career with Columbia, a fair-sized hit recently on the country charts.

"Restless," in its single version at least, embodies for me nearly all of Carl Perkins' best qualities. It has all the infectious enthusiasm of his early sides together with that wry sense of absurdity (I walked up to the window/I said, "Give me a ticket please/She said, "Where

to, mister?"/I said, "That's all right with me") which he shares with Chuck Berry. The guitar, too, echoes Chuck Berry in a bright attractive way, and his voice plays engagingly with the lyrics and makes good use of a falsetto break. But what distinguishes a Carl Perkins performance more than anything else is the odd contrast between mood and manner, the way in which a flat vocal tone is set against his almost frenzied involvement with the music. "Come on, Stella, let's ride this gray dog," he calls out encouragingly, as the song gathers momentum and the guitar picks up an already exuberant pace. His voice begins to sing along behind the verse, drawing it out and manicly echoing itself, and at the fade-out you hear Carl still shouting, "Give me two tickets, I want to keep riding, honey, let's go," desperately pleading for time.

For some reason Columbia released a different take on the album *Carl Perkins' Greatest Hits*. But pick up the single if you can. And pick up the album with NRBQ. It might have been better if they had shown themselves a little less presumptuous. But Carl Perkins is always engaging. And hopefully with the push that Columbia is now giving him and his new assured place with the Johnny Cash show we'll have even better records in future. But Carl

Perkins doesn't really need anyone else's words of introduction. He has always been an eloquent man, and in "Lake County Cotton Country" he speaks for himself best of all:

> I nearly about remember
> the day I was born
> Mama, papa said it was
> early one morn
> Pop liked his boy; I'd soon
> be a man
> He started me out in that
> cotton land.
> He put a nine-foot tarbot-
> tom on my back
> He said, take your hand,
> boy, and fill that sack.
> I worked my fingers down
> to the bone
> Folks, that ain't funny
> But it's about the only way
> I had to make a living
> In the Lake County cotton
> country . . .
> I finally saved enough nick-
> els, got myself a guitar
> I had visions of the Opry,
> I'd soon be a star
> Picked cotton by day and
> guitar at night
> I got my lessons on the
> floor by a coal oil light
> I wore hand-me-down
> britches every day to
> school
> That's enough to disillusion
> any ordinary fool
> Kept on picking my old
> guitar
> It meant that much to me
> Lord, I kept on picking my
> old guitar

> In the Lake County cotton
> country . . .

There's not much anyone could add to that.

—PETER GURALNICK
3-19-69

THE EVERLY BROTHERS' ORIGINAL GREATEST HITS
The Everly Brothers
(Barnaby BGP 350)

No matter what else happens, my summer's made. The Beatles may be dead as a group, but two of their mentors, two of the great rock and roll originals, the brown-eyed, everlovin' Everly Brothers, are back—and back strong. Forget that Don and Phil are holding down the Opry stage for Johnny Cash and ABC. What counts, what you've absolutely *got to* take notice of, is *The Everly Brothers' Original Greatest Hits*—two whole records of the merely beautiful rockabilly stuff that inspired Beatles, Hollies, Byrds, Burritos and, hell, you and me to get up each day and face the dreary Fifties with a smile.

We've all carried the Everlys' twangy, piercingly precise harmonies and simple pickin'-and-strummin' riffs around in our heads for about 13 years now. But anybody who didn't hang on to the old Cadence 45s and out-of-print LPs was stuck with his memories: "Bye Bye Love," "Wake Up, Little Susie," "Bird Dog," "Problems," plus the slow-dance, pump-and-dip, hug-her-close flip sides like "All I Have to Do Is Dream" and "Maybe Tomorrow."

For a half dozen years now, I've been wondering when some producer-genius would get smart and re-release the original Everly material—and now everybody's favorite, Andy Williams, has gone and done it. (Evidently, he owns much of Archie Bleyer's Cadence catalog—the label Andy himself started on.) About time too—the grooves of my battered 45s are about gone.

Well, what of it? What's all the folderol about? What's Barnaby offering for our edification and pleasure? Patience, friends. Twenty, count 'em, 20 splendid tunes gleaned from the Everlys' three or four Cadence albums— a little country, a bit of rhythm 'n blues, a batch of rockabilly, all adding up to a whole lot of good ol' rock 'n roll. Most of the familiar numbers are here, the "situation" rockers like "Wake Up," "Bird Dog," and "Problems," and some of the slow stuff too; but fully half of the numbers are much less familiar—Everly covers of Ray Charles and Little Richard, like "Leave My Woman Alone" and "Keep A-Knockin'," and several numbers which must be from that early sampler of country roots, *Songs Our Daddy Taught Us* ("Rockin' Alone," "Long Time Gone," and a couple others).

Amazing how much superb music Don and Phil could get from drums and acoustic guitars, from an upbeat shuffle coupled with their clear, free-wheeling wailing. There's no cut here that doesn't have something going for it. Some representative favorites: " 'Til I Kissed You" because the kettle drums or whatever and breathless vocals are so compelling; "Love of My Life" because it's just so *purty* and because I used to watch Dick Clark's cool cats cha-cha-cha to it; "Like Strangers" because it's one of the Everlys' all-time best attempts at that pure Kentucky harmony and high mountain sound; "Be-Bop-a-Lula" because—forgive me, Gene—the Everlys do it more musically and maybe more excitingly too; "Poor Jenny" because it takes "Wake Up, Little Susie" and goes it bigger, better and faster; "Lightning Express" because it's not, instead being an unexpected, five-minute folk tune; and, best of all, because it started the whole Everly Brothers thing on its way, "Bye Bye Love."

But I've a few bones to pick as well. Maybe it's just my faulty memory, but has the impact of the Everlys' "Let It Be Me" always been dissipated by a string orchestra? If it has, at least that's the only cut so burdened among these 20. Considerably more damaging is the inexplicable omission of several significant hits. Where's "Claudette," one of the brothers' fastest and flashiest? Why leave off the bee-yoo-ti-ful flip sides of "Bird Dog" and "Bye Bye Love" —that is, those two exquisite samples of Everly harmony, "Devoted to You" and "I Wonder If I Care as Much?" Also, what's happened to "Take a Message to Mary," another of their memorable country-folk numbers?

A final note: the two records come packed in a jacket that offers a snazzy "Rock 'n Roll Quiz" as well. Samples: "What was the name of Ahab's camel?" and "What movie starred Jayne Mansfield and had its title sung by Little Richard?" The answers to the 50-odd questions total up to 100. I scored just 83, but the Everlys' *Original Greatest Hits* rates a big, fat 95. Now, Andy, how's about those missing sides?

—ED LEIMBACHER
9-17-70

Buddy Holly and Ritchie Valens

Clear Lake, Iowa, Feb. 3 (UPI)

Three of the nation's top rock-'n-roll singing stars— Ritchie Valens, J. P. (The Big Bopper) Richardson, and Buddy Holly—died today with their pilot in the crash of a chartered plane.

The singers, members of a rock-'n-roll troupe touring Midwest cities, died because they wanted to make a fast hop between dates so they could get their shirts laundered.

The tragedy that ended the careers of the three rising stars symbolized, in a way that was powerfully real, the decline of the strange new music that was carrying us into adolescence and adulthood. In rock and roll one has to be a fan as well as a listener, and the energy of the music depends on stars as much as it does on expertise and creativity. Send Jimi Hendrix to prison for a few years, bust John Lennon and Mick Jagger just one more time, and it won't matter much how good the next album by the Byrds sounds. Rock and roll is not composed in conservatories or judged in museums—this is one world where infinity does not go up on trial. 19 and 59—the stars were gone.

The sound Buddy Holly had brought together was left to the second stringers, members of the bands who previously had been happy to back him up or copy his material. Then Bobby Vee appropriated the Crickets for an LP, and hired a young piano player, Bob Dylan, for his road band. That was where the momentum was. Rock and roll, as Dylan himself put it, became "a piece of cream."

Today, we can discover that the heritage of that flimsy, beautiful era comes to more than just the million-sellers everyone remembers. The spirit of the old music, brash, innocent, is a spirit our best craftsmen have never lost, and the memories are more than music —they jump out of an awareness of crucial, sometimes tragic events that exaggerate every note of "La Bamba" and "Peggy Sue" until there's just a lot more there to hear.

Following an appearance before 1000 fans at Clear Lake last night, they chartered a plane at the Mason City Airport, two miles east of here, and took off at 1:50 AM for Fargo, North Dakota. Their Bonanza four-seat single engine plane crashed minutes later.

If Buddy Holly were alive today I've no doubt that he, like Johnny Cash, would be recording with Bob Dylan. (The band, for their part, tried to get Gene Vincent to visit the sessions for their latest album, only to discover him living in a hospital in Los Angeles, crippled by an accident.) When young Bob Dylan brought an electric rock and roll band on stage at a junior high school music pageant back in Hibbing, Minnesota, to a reception similar to the one he received when he

did the same thing at Newport years later, Buddy Holly tunes were most likely part of the program. Traces of Holly's vocal style, his phrasing rather than his insane changes from deep bass to something resembling soprano, pop up all through Dylan's career: on an obscure 1962 Columbia single, "Mixed-Up Confusion," on "Absolutely Sweet Marie," on "I Shall Be Free No. 10," anywhere you look. Dylan and Holly share a clipped, staccato delivery that communicates a sly sense of cool, almost teenage masculinity.

This spirit is captured at its best on one of Holly's finest albums, *The Great Buddy Holly* (Vocalion VL 3811), recently released as a budget item ($1.98). The LP contains ten cuts recorded in Nashville before Holly made it as a star (these are the songs discussed by Barret Hansen in "Tex-Mex," the article in *Rolling Stone* [12-7-68], but they *are* available). The accompanying musicians, lacking the flash and the excitement of Holly's later band, do all the right things and put the burden on Holly. He carries it with ease, on an early version of "That'll Be the Day," on love songs, on schoolboy rockers. It's with the last two songs, "Don't Come Back Knockin' " and "Midnight Shift," that Holly gets into rock and roll like a young Carl Perkins singing about women who cheat on him, not people who step on his shoes. This isn't the blues—there is no self-pity, not even a tear. Buddy has the last laugh. "Annie's been working on the midnight shift"—he's glad to let you know, and he's not referring to overtime pay at the all-night drugstore. The phrasing is simply what we know as pure Dylan—

If she tells you she wants
to use the caahhhh!
Never explains what she
want it faaahhh!

—what Phil Spector meant when he heard the Four Tops doing "Reach Out" and said, "Yeah, that's a black man singing Dylan." In an odd way, it was the Four Tops doing Buddy Holly. If things had been different, Holly and Dylan might be surprising us all with a snappy duet on "I Don't Believe You."

The plane skidded across
the snow for 558 feet. Hol-
ly, 21, was found twenty
feet from the wreckage.

Following his death, Coral Records released half a dozen albums of Holly's hits and memorabilia. While *The Buddy Holly Story* (biggest hits, Coral CRL 757279) ought to be part of everyone's collection, there is much more. Holly's obscure recordings, made on home tape-recorders, in high

school with his pal Bob Montgomery, demos and rehearsal acetates, have been re-recorded with studio musicians, often the Fireballs, supplementing the original vocal tracks.

The feeling one gets from listening to these cuts, an uneven collection of various Number One records ("Smokey Joe's Cafe," "Shake Rattle and Roll," "Blue Monday," "Love Is Strange," "Rip It Up," and so on), is that of visiting a funeral parlor to watch an embalmer touch up the face of a body mangled in an accident. The guy does a great job but you still don't recognize the face. For the most part, these records are interesting historically, not musically—they show where Holly came from, sounding like an anemic Carl Perkins on "Blue Suede Shoes," until he finally emerges as an original, able to master any sort of material in a way that is unique and compelling. His vocal on "Love Is Strange" steals the song from Micky and Sylvia. Holly had it all down.

Sometimes, these ancient cuts provide a real sense of what rock and roll might have become had Holly lived. The same shock of recognition that knocked out the audiences at the Fillmore West when the band from Big Pink lit into Little Richard takes place, with the same song, when the ghost of Buddy Holly is joined by the Fireballs for "Slippin' and Slidin'" (from

Giant, the "new" Holly release, Coral CRL 757504). An agile, humorous vocal is carried by a band that knows all the tricks. They break it open with the Everly Brothers' own seductive intro, constantly switching, musically, from song to song while Holly ties it together. The guitarist actually sounds like Robbie Robertson, throwing in bright little patterns around the constant whoosh of the cymbals. The excitement and confusion that comes from a precise marriage of the two songs is irresistible—it's certainly one of the best things Buddy Holly never did. He was only twenty-one, so Coral Records just brought him out of the grave.

Valens, a 17-year-old recording sensation hailed as "the next Elvis Presley," was thrown forty feet. Valens, from Pacoima, California, was rapidly becoming one of the hottest singing talents in the country. His first record, of a song he had written called "Come On, Let's Go," was released last summer and made him famous.

Richard Valenzuela, a Southern California boy. Ruben of Ruben and the Jets was patterned after Ritchie, and much of the material on the *Cruising* album is a fair representation of Valens' music. Today, it might all seem rather laughable, but for Ritchie and his fans, as Zappa would be the first to admit, it was no joke, it was just the way it was. "We made this album because we really like this kind of music: just a bunch of old men with rock & roll clothes on sitting around the studio, mumbling about the good old days."

Valens was a hero to the Mexican-American community in Los Angeles, and they cheered him on with the same kind of support they gave when one of their boys faced a black welterweight in the annual Golden Gloves Tournament. It meant a lot to break into a field that had always been in the hands of larger, more established minorities—blacks, Italians, Okies—Ritchie was the first Chicano singer, a hero, just a kid, but a hero.

Valens sang fragile melodies with the enthusiasm and commitment of Little Richard, and the tension that resulted from a fusion of these two elements in a single song captivated his audience and made him a star. Imagine Little Richard singing "Whispering Bells" or perhaps something like Mary Hopkin's "Goodbye" the way he sang "Lucille" and you have Ritchie Valens. He could turn it around: "Donna" is as touching a ballad as "I Threw It All Away."

Valens took an old Mexican festival song, "La Bamba," gave it a rock and roll beat, and scored with one of the most exciting records of the era. The split second flashes of the intro, the guitar break that happens before Ritchie has finished with the words—they were all in so much of a hurry the notes pile up on top of each other until the song itself explodes. And Valens traveled twenty feet farther than either Buddy Holly or the Big Bopper. What is left?

The only LP by Ritchie Valens that is still in print is a weird budget album (88c) on Guest Star Records (GS-1469), available in supermarkets and drugstores, "a product of the Synthetic Plastics Co." "Fine records need not be expensive" is their slogan. Again, more graverobbers. The company has taken Ritchie's audition tapes (vocal and fine acoustic guitar playing), studio jams that were recorded for vocals that were never sung, and some unreleased masters, added the hit version of "Donna," and come up with "an album." Surprisingly, it works as a record: starting with the early tapes, a kid trying to get his first contract, the sense of melody is there and there is no doubt about the talent. As with the Holly albums, we go through a period of uncertainty, the tracks randomly titled ("Rock Little Donna" is really about a girl named Susie), Ritchie finding himself, beginning to work with a band. Then the triumph, his perfect "Donna," a few pleasant songs,

two jams, and it's over. This is Juke Box Heaven, courtesy of Guest Star Records. This is what is left. When Valens died "La Bamba" was right up there in the Top Ten; a week later it was slipping down off the charts, and Bobby Vinton was there, holding Ritchie's coat.

> *The wreckage and the bodies were not discovered until long after dawn. The other members of the troupe, including singer Frankie Sardo, the "Crickets," and "Dion and the Belmonts," made the trip by bus. Although grief-stricken, their performance tonight in Moorhead, Minn., took place as scheduled.*
>
> —GREIL MARCUS
> 6-28-69

GENE VINCENT'S GREATEST
Gene Vincent
(Capitol DKAO-380)

I'M BACK AND I'M PROUD
Gene Vincent
(Dandelion/Elektra D9-102)

BEST OF GENE VINCENT
Gene Vincent
(EMI/Capitol ST 20957)

THE BEST OF GENE VINCENT, VOL. 2
Gene Vincent
(EMI/Capitol ST 21144)

Gene Vincent was the most

tortured of the Fifties rock stars. I only saw him in concert once and that was weird. He was in pain throughout and sang kneeling, his bad leg stretched out straight behind him. In the faster numbers he gyrated on his knee, swinging his straight leg right round over the microphone, wriggling across the stage, sweat pouring over his leather suit.

He was fat, ugly, and greasier than Joe Cocker. There were no girls in the audience, but for the assembled rockers he was the ultimate in rock and roll—offering nothing but music and sacrificing everything to that music, their music. I've never seen another rock star so worshipped and held in such awe by an audience.

The white, drawn, agonized Gene Vincent had entered into myth (he hurt his leg in the crash that killed Eddie Cochran)—but the pain was real enough. It interfered with his career and with his music. He was always disappearing and coming back, changing groups, managers and record companies.

For the last two years he has been the great missing figure of the rock and roll revival. His music suffered even more—we forgot about it. Everyone remembered Gene Vincent, but the only song of his they remembered was "Be-Bop-A-Lula." We forgot that the reason he was a great rock star was be-cause he made great records. Now to celebrate (cash in on) his return, Capitol has at last issued a "Greatest Hits" album and we can remember and rejoice.

Gene Vincent's music was tough and very edgy, and his best records were extraordinarily tense. The excitement of "Be-Bop-A-Lula" comes less from the beat than from the feeling of suppressed energy and the feeling that Vincent and the Bluecaps are holding themselves back.

Gene Vincent had one of the most remarkable voices of the Fifties, with great range and perfect control (most noticeable in slow numbers like "Important Words"), but it always had a neurotic feel, slightly anxious. He used his voice as an instrument (listen to the famous hesitation style in "Woman Love" or his very effective vocal support for the lead guitar in "Race with the Devil") and the sound of the voice was always more important than the words in giving his songs atmosphere.

The tension was a result of the conflict between Vincent's originality and the demands of the rock and roll single. The Bluecaps added to this tension. Both Cliff Gallup and Johnny Meeks, who succeeded Gallup as lead guitarist in 1957, had an extraordinary ability to play all the instrumental-break cliches while still sounding original. On "Bluejean Bop," for example,

Gallup sounds as though at any moment he might break out and destroy the record altogether. He never quite does and the results were some of the greatest rock singles.

Long before we worried about the significance of record production Gene Vincent and the Bluecaps were *issuing* total creations, not just good songs but good *records* with everything going in to make a complete three-minute experience. The best examples on this album are "Lotta Lovin' " and "Yes I Love You Baby" where the interplay of voices and instruments is perfect, the total effect being built up from the conflict between all the elements rather than from the superimposition of layers of sound behind the lead vocal. These tracks quite transcended the normal rock and roll singles of 1957-58— listen to the wonderful biting guitar which fights the chorus line in "Yes I Love You Baby."

This is a great album; however, the cover, art, packaging, and historical data (there is none) leaves much to be desired. Originally Capitol planned a Gene Vincent special—color pictures, comprehensive liner notes, and biographical information—but they killed that project at the last minute and instead included Gene's album in their banal *Greatest* series. Their choice of Gene's "greatest hits" is not as strong as it might be, but Capitol in En-

gland has had a two volume *Best of Gene Vincent* out for some time (available from EMI Records, the many American stores that carry imports of any mail order English dealer) and it contains some classics that no greatest hits set should be without. Most remarkable is "Git It." Also not to be missed are rockers like "Say Mama" and "Right Here on Earth," which faultlessly sum up rock and roll, songs like "Wild Cat" and "Wear My Ring" (not the Elvis number) which are beautiful displays of Vincent's unique voice, and his strange version of "Frankie and Johnnie" (much more interesting than the straight version of "Over the Rainbow" which is on the American album).

Gene Vincent was one of the masters of the rock and roll single, but the days of the rock single are all but over and on his new album *I'm Back and I'm Proud,* we have something else: a fine country singer singing his favorite songs. The tension has gone, he is at ease with his voice and behind him the sounds can be built up lovingly, with no need to fight him or the conventions of rock. The new version of "Lotta Lovin'" is a bouncy country song, discarding the backing voices; and it's good, but it doesn't stop me dead. Four other tracks are straight country and western— "Black Letter," "Rainbow at Midnight," "Circle Never

Broken," "I Heard That Lonesome Whistle"—nice enough but not startling. Four are rockers: "Rockin' Robin," "Be-Bop-A-Lula '69," "Sexy Ways," "Ruby Baby"—in which Gene demonstrates his vocal control with such relaxation that the excitement has to come from the instrumental build-up.

The most interesting tracks are "In the Pines" and "White Lightning." The latter is reminiscent of the Band, in its integrated but easy improvised sound and its Southern, rural theme. "In the Pines" is a disturbing song, and the melancholy of the words is brought out by the contrast between Vincent's talking voice and the increasingly frantic bass and piano line. Finally there is a pretty (icky?) version of "Scarlet Ribbons" in which Gene is joined by his wife Jackie.

What is there to say? Vincent's performance is impeccable, the musicians (including old Bluecap Johnny Meeks) are very fine and the production is good enough. It is a relaxed, enjoyable record and for true Gene Vincent fans it is worth getting just to hear Gene's exuberant spoken introduction, "I'm back and I'm proud . . ." It's great that he is and that he's content at last. But for true rock and roll fans the money's better invested in getting hold of his old hits with the Bluecaps. Nobody makes records like that anymore, not even Gene Vincent.

—SIMON FRITH
3-7-70

THE CRUISIN' SERIES
(Increase INCM 2001-2007)

Put simply, the *Cruisin'* Series is a good example of a nice idea that worked. Set up and produced by Ron Jacobs (whose excellent 48-hour *History of Rock and Roll* can still be heard on well-meaning FM stations), the seven-album set was designed to provide a re-creation of Top 40 pop radio in the magic years from 1956 to 1962. To accomplish this, Jacobs found seven of the more popular disc jockeys from that period, gave them a whole slew of oldies from the golden grooveyard, and then simply let them loose to do a typical show, complete with actual commercials, station breaks, "back to school" contests and other fascinating sidelights of teen history.

However, good ideas sometimes get lost in the translation, and so actually having something like this come off could be quite another matter. Most of us are living in 1970 now, not the late Fifties, and it's a hard-edged fact that what might have come naturally then has a great potential to sound contrived and self-conscious today.

We've already seen it happen in a great number of rock 'n' roll revival shows, where the familiar old brands of nostalgia are dredged up in ever-growing amounts (sort of making you wonder what appeal there could have been even in those early times), and it doesn't necessarily have to stop there.

But Jacobs and his crew have avoided all the pitfalls. They've seen that all the standard pieces have meshed exactly together, forgetting none of the little parts that were fully as important as any of the larger ones. Each "show" comes rolling out of your record player just as free and easy as you could want it, a blast from the past, exactly like it might if you had a time tunnel station on your radio.

More, if the chosen jockeys are all properly in there, each one is so different, so involved in his own little world, that it makes each separate album stand on its own, complete almost in itself. I couldn't begin to recommend one over another —obviously, regional preferences are going to play a large part in anyone's individual decision—though Hunter Hancock makes me wish I had grown up in Los Angeles, while Joe "Rockin' Bird" Niagra makes me happy I spent some summers around Philadelphia. I miss not seeing New York's legendary Jocko, who used to make the Rocketship Show soar late at night over WADO radio, but then I guess you can't have everything.

Still, if the work of the disc jockeys starts this series of albums going, the choice of songs manages to take it on over and home. From each year, whether it be 1956 (with the Cadillacs' "Speedo" and the Cadets' "Stranded In The Jungle"), or 1960 ("Fannie Mae" and "Alley Oop"), or even 1962 (with Joey Dee's killer "Peppermint Twist"), the selection is nearly impeccably good. They're all your super-hit favorites, of course, nothing obscure since this is *top* radio, and having them come at you like they would in the year of their release only serves to make them sound even better.

A word about the album covers. In the context of the series, they are great: finely-detailed pop art depictions of America, year by year, from its Peg and Eddies to its Edsels to its hanging dice in the window, full of life and twice as bright. A Hatlo tip of the hat should go to Jere Briane and Paul Gruwell (who thought it up) and Mike Royer (who drew it). You can easily tell that they've gone through the whole scene, have ridden in the wing-backed Chevvies and hung out at the Dairy Queens, and have picked up on the very things that made those times special, that gave them a peculiar touch of greatness.

In fact, that's the kind of

thing you could say about the entire series. *Cruisin'* has a lot of love surrounding it, and it adds a special dimension to the records which you might not find anywhere but your store of golden memories. Sure, it's nostalgia, and sure, the very fact of it having to be a "re-creation" means that an era has died, but the people who have put together *Cruisin'* have gone beyond the obvious and into the ozone. And when it gets out there, past the usual sort of boundaries, you know that you're into it where it counts.

—LENNY KAYE
11-12-70

OLDIES

In recent months various companies have issued a host of rock and roll and rhythm and blues albums, often spotlighting music that has not been available to the general public for a decade or more. The audience that in the past has had to be satisfied with Original Sound *Oldies But Goodies* and Roulette *Golden Goodies* LPs is now in a much better position to gather a collection of some of the best music the Fifties and early Sixties had to offer, and it's along those lines that we have prepared something of a consumer guide to these re-issues and to other old albums of special interest. This "guide" is not really intended for the serious collector, haunting the fabled oldies shops in New York, Los Angeles, Memphis and Chicago, but for the listener intent upon putting together a solid, if not complete, collection of the best of rock and roll.

Many of the important companies have sold out or folded, and while their vaults have in most cases been transferred to current labels, several problems have come up that are hurting re-issues in general. Most of the re-issues are put on the market in reprocessed stereo, since many stores will no longer stock mono; in virtually all cases this weakens the sound and in some cases it virtually destroys it. In addition, the packaging of the new re-issues is almost uniformly shoddy and uninteresting, often inaccurate, and usually lacking in recording data, historical photos, and intelligent commentary. Truly careful repacking is rare; only the Imperial *Rhythm and Blues, End of An Era* set has been done as well as one could hope, and even that omitted pictures.

This guide covers the major recent re-issues by label, as well as some excellent LPs available in most record stores. This is by no means a comprehensive digest, nor a complete analysis of all the LPs. Hopefully, it's a competent shopping list.

BUDDAH RECORDS

Buddah Records recently purchased the old Vee Jay catalogue and from it has prepared a whole series of blues, R&B and rock and roll LPs designed to cash in on current trends and contemporary hype. The cover art is without exception miserable, and the liner notes vary from inaccurate (Sun Records locating in Muscle Shoals, Alabama?) to informative. Formal recording data is absent on all but the blues LPs. The most noteworthy:

The Rock and Roll Stars, Various Artists (BDS 7503)

Biggest hits by R. Valens, J. Clanton, B. Day, H. Dorman, M. Williams, F. Ford, etc. Poor liner notes, poorly programmed, and lots of fine songs, most of which are still available as singles. Consult your local oldies shop first.

Great Groups, Various Artists (BDS 7509)

A well-organized and extremely mellow, soothing, listenable album, containing some of the sweetest R&B ever recorded, including such masterpieces as "Down the Aisle of Love" by the Quintones, "Golden Tear Drops" by the Fla-mingos, and "Story Untold" by the Nutmegs. Buy it.

Little Richard (BDS 7501)

Re-recordings of the original greats cut for Specialty, and not up to those by any means. Avoid this album and buy *Little Richard's Grooviest 17 Original Hits* (Specialty S2113). The Specialty album is one of the all-time dynamite rock and roll albums and it is easily available. *Greatest Hits,* a live album, is also excellent (Okeh 1412).

First Generation Soul, Various Artists (BDS 7504)

Pointless liner notes, and some excellent material ("Duke of Earl," "You Can Make It If You Try," "Goodnight My Love") randomly organized.

SUN RECORDS

Sam Phillips' fabled Sun Records has been quiescent for many years; the old "chicken shack with the Cadillacs out front" issued no new recordings and kept only a few Johnny Cash LPs in print. Recently Shelby Singleton bought all of Sam Phillips' stock and began a massive re-issue.

Sun, along with Atlantic and

Chess was among the labels most important to the founding of rock and roll. Scotty Moore on guitar (he can be heard backing Tracy Nelson on her *Country* album, Mercury SR 61230, on a song he first recorded for Elvis' initial smash, "That's Alright Mama"), Bill Black on drums and Phillips' own production created a striking, immediate sound, never overwhelming like that of Little Richard but always seductive and irresistible; and though many have tried to recapture it (most notably Carl Perkins, after he moved to Columbia) none but Creedence Clearwater Revival have been able to do so. If you dig Creedence you'll definitely want most of these LPs.

All albums are unobtrusively reprocessed, though the cover photos have no historical value and the general packaging of the records is extremely poor; cheap fall-apart covers and lousy graphics. No recording information is included and there are no liner notes. Nevertheless, the historical and musical value of the albums makes most of them essential.

Original Golden Hits, Vols. I & II, Johnny Cash (Sun 100 & 101).

It should be mentioned that all of the material included here was available on Cash's original LPs—if you have those, most of

which have been currently in print, you don't need these. Those who have only, say, *Folsom Prison* will find these albums a fine introduction to the original, pre-Columbia recordings of "I Walk the Line," "Folsom Prison Blues," etc. There's also that pop classic, "Ballad of a Teenage Queen." These are necessary albums.

Get Rhythm and *Showtime,* Johnny Cash (Sun 105 & 106)

Get Rhythm is a good LP for someone who wants *still more* early Cash, but it is definitely secondary to the *Original Hits*. The material doesn't measure up to that of those two LPs. *Showtime* is the worst of the lot; dubbed in applause mars each cut in an attempt to simulate a "live" album à la the million-selling *Folsom Prison* and *San Quentin* LPs. All cuts appear on the other reissues. Avoid this unless you're a student of bad special effects.

Songs of the Trains & Rivers, Johnny Cash (Sun 104)

Many repeated cuts from the *Original Hits* albums, but a fine, listenable record all the same. Is it a "concept" album?

Lonely Weekends, Charlie Rich (Sun 110)

Rich, from Arkansas, was one of the many Southerners, black and white, who made the trek to Memphis, and his early material as represented here makes a superb album, a brilliant and valuable LP for anyone interested in the rock and roll that came out of the South or for any fans of Bob Dylan or Elvis Presley. Rich's deep, mellow voice, with a phrasing and style that on these recordings especially is close to that of Presley, transforms each cut into a lasting work. Particularly fine are "C. C. Rider," "Lonely Weekends," and "Who Will the Next Fool Be." Rich's piano is outstanding. (Those who dig this will want Rich's most recent LP, *Set Me Free*, Epic BN 26376. This can be ordered. Also often to be found in drugstores and oldies shops is *The Many New Sides of Charlie Rich*, Smash SRS 27070, issued in 1965, which includes the hit "Mohair Sam," and the brilliant "Down and Out.")

Original Golden Hits and *Blue Suede Shoes*, Carl Perkins (Sun 111 & 112)

What a joy to have Perkins' first records available again! His first sides, cut in the early and middle Fifties, projected an honesty and warmth unmatched on any other Sun releases, and his enthusiasm goes without saying. Perkins fans who have blanched at his two recent Columbia LPs (the re-recorded *Greatest Hits*, monstrously overproduced, and the somewhat better *On Top*, featuring excellent material and a new song co-authored with Dylan) will flip over these albums. The two taken together include all the sides included on Carl's orginal Sun LP, *Dance Album*, but if you're only going to buy one, *Original Hits* is what you have to get. Included are: "Blue Suede Shoes," "Boppin' the Blues," "Matchbox," "Everybody's Trying To Be My Baby," (the Beatles must have played the grooves off their copy) and what is perhaps Perkins' masterpiece, his cover of the Platters' "Only You," featuring stunning slow guitar work. *Blue Suede Shoes* is also excellent, while containing more novelty material ("Movie Magg").

The Original Sound, Roy Orbison (Sun 113)

Orbison's high, clear tenor drives through eleven brilliant cuts, all previously rare or completely unavailable. The guitar work is astounding, the material straight young love/young sex, and the delivery dynamite. Included here is Orbison's first hit, "Ooby Dooby" (which translates simultaneously as a new dance and a sexual score). The flip, "Go, Go, Go," is not included, which hopefully means another LP is forthcoming. This is an album of the purest rock and roll that may well be the gutsiest of all the Sun reissues (most of Orbison's later Top 40 hits are available on *The Very Best of Roy Orbison*, Monument SLP 18045; avoid the material recorded for MGM).

~~~~~~~~~~~~~~~~~~~~~~~~

SPECIALTY RECORDS

Specialty Records, based in Los Angeles, was perhaps the most important West Coast label in the early days of rock and roll and R&B, its historical position threatened only by cross-town rival Dootone Records, which was founded a good deal later. Best known for the early Little Richard recordings, Specialty too has begun a series of re-issues that so far are of varying quality musically, but anything but shoddy in terms of presentation. Their reprocessing is adequate. The two mentioned below will be

of the greatest interest to those looking for rock and roll:

Doo Wop, Various Artists (Specialty SPS 2114)

An oldies comedy album for true Ruben and the Jets fans only. Packaged with nostalgic humor and good visuals, the music is occasionally excellent ("Bad Boy" by Larry Williams, "Dream Girl" by Jesse and Marvin, "Wheel of Fortune" by the Four Flames) and mostly for laughs. Not a bad present for anyone over twenty-five.

This Is How It All Began, Various Artists (Specialty SPS 2117)

This LP, with fourteen first-rate cuts—emphasis on big city blues and R&B—features complete recording data and stiff, pseudo-scholarly liner notes, as well as photos of historical value. More for the blues collector than the rock and roll fan. Highlights include Percy Mayfield's "Please Send Me Someone To Love," Frankie Sims' "Married Woman," and Mercy Dee's "One Room Country Shack."

~~~~~~~~~~~~~~~~~~~~~~~~

KING RECORDS

King Records (along with Federal) headquartered in Cincinnati, and recorded many early sides by James Brown, Little Willie John, and Billy Ward, among others. Some LPs are supposedly still available from King Records, 1540 Brewster Ave., Cincinnati, Ohio. *Mr. Little Willie John* (King 1012), Billy Ward's best album (King 952), a Hank Ballard LP with the "Annie Trilogy" (King 541), and James Brown's *Unbeatable 16,* which includes the best of his early hits and is absolutely essential to any representative collection (King 919). Also:

> *Anthology of Rhythm 'n' Blues, Vol. 1,* Various Artists (Columbia CS 9802)

This Columbia album is made up of sides originally issued on the King and Federal labels; no photos but adequate liner notes. The material is excellent: seventeen cuts by Hank Ballard, Little Willie John, James Brown and others; but what we need are full albums by these men, not random collections.

~~~~~~~~~~~~~~~~~~~~~~~~

ALREADY IN STOCK

Many beautiful early albums are still in print and easily available at most record stores. A few of the best:

The Coasters (Atco 33-101)

This is a fantastic album with a great cover and good liner notes; it includes "Searchin'," "Down in Mexico," and the unbelievable play-within-a-song, "Riot In Cell Block Number Nine."

The Coasters' Greatest Hits (Atco 33-111)

Just what it says it is: essential.

Coast Along With the Coasters (Atco 33-135)

Later hits from the Sixties: "Little Egypt," "Run Red Run," "What About Us," and more. A marvelous record.

Chuck Berry's Golden Decade (Chess LP 1514D)

This two-record set is *the* Chuck Berry album, though all of his Chess LPs have a lot to offer. All are in print, reprocessed only, and the reprocessing is irritating. It's worth it to hunt around for mono copies, which are common. *The Golden Decade* album also includes excellent photos and liner notes. As a document and as pure fun, it should probably come before any of the other albums listed here (avoid the Mercury releases unless you simply can't stop).

The Best of Sam Cooke, Vols. I & II (RCA LSP 2625 & 3373)

Again, reprocessed, and fairly badly. No real liner notes, no recording data. Still, the music is so good you should buy them anyway without hestitation. Cooke was the true founder of modern soul music, and the first LP has most of his biggest hits. Records of greater beauty have rarely, if ever, been made. *Vol. II* includes a great deal of weak material, but it too is a must if only for "Another Saturday Night," "Little Red Rooster," "Shake," and Cooke's masterpiece, "A Change Is Gonna Come." Otis Redding fans avoid these albums at their own peril.

All of Elvis' LPs are still in print; but the early albums, the best, for the most part, come in truly abominable reprocessed stereo, so bad as to make the albums virtually unlistenable. You should hunt for mono copies, which are not hard to find, or buy those listed below and listen to one channel only.

Elvis Presley (RCA LSP 1254e)

Great photos and good music on Elvis' first LP for RCA. Mostly cover versions of then-recent hits, it stands up well.

Elvis (RCA LSP 1382e)

A good album, with "Old Shep," among others.

The liner notes are almost worth the album price: they are outstanding in their honesty and interest.

Elvis' Golden Hits (RCA LSP 1707e)

All the early RCA hits, an absolute necessity for any rock and roll collection. Liner notes give fascinating details about each recording session. Look for the mono copy before you buy; but buy it.

For LP Fans Only and *A Date With Elvis* (RCA 1990e & LSP 2011e)

Two albums that include Elvis' first recordings for Sun, some of the best sides he ever put down, including "That's Alright Mama," the great "Milkcow's Calf Boogie," and "Mystery Train." Excellent albums with a sound only Creedence Clearwater has captured.

Elvis Is Back (LSP 2231/true stereo)

Elvis' first out-of-the-army LP, cut with an extremely strong blues band. Definitely one of his best albums, virtually on a par with his recent *From Elvis In Memphis*. Includes the great "Reconsider Baby" and lots of army-life photos to boot.

New Orleans, Home of the Blues, Vol. 2 (Minit Records LP-0004)

This unusual record, recently re-issued by Liberty in tolerably reprocessed form, contains a number of delightful examples of the kind of black rock and roll that was coming out of the South as late as the early Sixties. There are six cuts by Irma Thomas; but most interesting are one hit and one non-hit each by Ernie K-Doe, Benny Spellman, and the Showmen. The Showmen were responsible for one of the best songs ever about rock and roll, the perfect "It Will Stand," included here. Imagine what kind of spirit—coldly commercial or actually religious—it must have taken to set down these lines: "It swept this whole wide land/Sinking deep in the heart of man." Then K-Doe's "Mother-In-Law," which had the same sort of surrealistic humor as Tommy Tucker's "High-Heeled Sneakers": "Satan should be her name/Seems they're 'bout the same . . . Sent from down below/Mother-in-law." Finally there's Spellman's "Fortune Teller," later recorded by the Stones.

—GREIL MARCUS AND
GARY VON TERSCH
2-21-70

ACAPPELLA
The Persuasions
(Reprise 6394)

There are very few acappella albums worth buying, even at the bargain prices for which they usually sell. The records listed here are of varying quality, but should be considered the core collection for anyone interested in the form. The first three are essential; the others present facets of acappella of interest to the serious collector. Any albums not on this list are considered as being for masochists only.

THE BEST OF ACAPPELLA, VOLUME 1 (Relic 101)
THE BEST OF ACAPPELLA, VOLUME 2 (Relic 102)
I DIG ACAPPELLA, VOLUME 1 (Cat-Time LP 201)
ACAPPELLA SOUL, The Royal Counts (Catamount 901)
ACAPPELLA BLUE-EYED SOUL, The Cordials (Catamount 902)
ACAPPELLA: THE SOUND OF THE CITY (Times Square 201)

Applause, and then: three beautiful interlocking bits of harmony, just hanging there in the air, rising together, falling together, rising again . . . And over it:

"Thank you. Singing first tenor . . . Calvin Washington!" [applause]

"Singing second tenor . . . I call him Big Joe, but his name is . . . Jesse Russel!" [applause]

"Singing baritone . . . Tizzy Bizzo!" [applause]

"This is my main man . . . my guy . . . singing bass is my boy . . . Jimmy Hayes!" [applause]

Then a velvety smooth bass voice:

"Thank you. Thank you very much." A voice from the audience shouts out "Whaddabout da leeduh?" and the bass voice replies "The leader? . . . This is my *man* . . . my *Main Man* . . . this is . . . Jerry Lawson!"

There is wild applause in the State Theatre in Jersey City from over 1500 people in the audience as the Persuasions, from all the way over in Bedford-Stuyvesant, launch into the last number of the evening, their version of the Temptations' "Don't Look Back." The audience is young, but you won't find much long hair in it, except, of course, on the girls. There's a lot of white-on-white, pointy Italian shoes, and see-through black stretch sox. They have gathered for the latest in a series of all-acappella shows, paying homage to the great group harmony sounds of the Fifties which they all love.

They've heard it all before, of course, because they've cut class to get into that stairwell down by 205 where the echo is just *perfect*. Or one night coming home late from a date and passing in front of Rosie's and seeing the guys out front drinking wine, trying to work some life into a mangled version of "When I Fall In Love."

And tonight they've come to see it all again . . . the parade of kids just like themselves up there on the stage singing their re-interpretations of the immortal old classics: "Gloria," "Stormy Weather," "When I Fall In Love," "Over The Rainbow." All acappella, of course.

> For those of you who are not hep, 'Acappella' means '*without music*.'
> —from the liner notes of *The Best of Acappella, Vol. I*

Without *music*? Well, not really. Without instrumental accompaniment, actually, although sometimes you wonder if the definition isn't being taken literally. At its best, acappella can be a thrilling experience, with the voices skillfully locking into tight, difficult harmonies that send involuntary shivers up and down your spine. At its worst it's—well, better that the kids go back to work at the car wash. It owes a lot to gospel, and there's little doubt that most of the makers of those "great group sounds" today's acappellists admire so much originated their harmonies without the aid of instrumental accompaniment.

It all started at about the same time as the British Invasion, with lower-middle-class kids who resented the new sound and loved their "oldies" —the Orioles, the Zodiacs, the Spaniels. Not only was the new sound alien, but if you wanted to perform it, you had to shell out all kinds of money for equipment, not to mention the time it took you to learn your instrument. With acappella, you'd been using your instrument from the moment the doctor whacked your fanny, and you'd been developing your skill on it ever since.

Acappella seems to have been centered around the New York-Philadelphia area, if one goes by the groups that got recorded, although every large city in the country had (and has) informal acappella groups who have never been recorded or recognized. The reason that New York and New Jersey cared enough about the form to record it and put it on stage is that the area had a long tradition of group singing and a long tradition of these singing groups getting recorded by tiny labels who would tape a dozen similar songs in the hopes of getting one into the Top Ten. This practice resulted in scores of obscure records that lay on shelves gathering dust, until, in the late Fifties, the scene began to wane and the resulting scarcity forced record collectors to rely on the services of several specialty shops that sprang up to meet the demand.

The most famous of these was Times Square Records, located in a subway arcade at Sixth Avenue and 42nd Street. It was begun by Irving "Slim" Rose, a veritable legend among oldies collectors. "He was a funny man," remembers Harold Ginsburg, who took the store over after Slim left in late 1966. "He was the start of everything because he knew about the really rare oldies . . . He used to be able to find them cheap." Slim had come from California with his wife and had opened a novelty shop in the arcade. One day, he introduced a few records into his stock, and shortly thereafter Allen Fredericks, who had a late-night rock and roll show on WADO, played a few and plugged the store. The next morning when Slim came to open up there was a line that stretched through the arcade and on up the subway steps.

Noticing the demand, Slim began releasing reissues of some of the rarer stuff. In the course of acquiring rights to some of this material, he bought out entire labels with all their material, released and unreleased, including such labels as Herald, Standard, and Klick. While going through this material, he found the first of what were later to be known as acappella releases—practice tapes by such groups as the Nutmegs ("Story Untold") and the Five Satins. He put them out, and the rest is history. "Immediately, there was a big demand," Harold remembers. "I guess people who heard this music really saw themselves."

Another important store in the acappella rush was the Relic Rack, located on Main Street in scenic Hackensack, New Jersey. Like Slim, Eddie Gries of the Relic Rack had started his own reissue label to give more widespread circulation to the rarer oldies, but, unlike Times Square, they began to search out and record talent in the area, which was not a particularly difficult task. All they had to do was walk outside, pick five likely-looking individuals, sit them down in front of a microphone and say "Sing!" The air would fill with the strains of "Stormy Weather," almost like the Spaniels' version, but not quite.

Acappella drifted along for a while, racking up some small sales and becoming a minor fad among oldies collectors. It took the Zircons, a group from the Bronx, doing a rendition of the Skyliners' hit, "Lonely Way," to take it out of its limited circle and into a restricted, but decidedly mass, circulation. "Lonely Way" was played on AM radio, on the Danny Stiles *Kit Kat Klub* show out of Newark, and it sold 3000 copies—not as many as "Sugar, Sugar," perhaps, but still a pretty good figure for something that almost nobody had known about the week before. It really is a remarkable record—you might listen to it several times before you notice the lack of accompaniment, and the singers are *tight*.

"Lonely Way" firmly established acappella as a genre of rock and roll unto itself. With its success, a horde of record-store-based labels entered the market, each with one or two good groups and a host of hangers-on. Predictably, Times Square and Relic led the field with the best groups and production. Relic, in fact, was the first to release an all-acappella album, called, with much justification, *The Best of Acappella*. Along with *Best, Volume 2*, it remains one of the few good albums devoted to acappella, featuring the cream of the groups: The Chessmen, the Camelots, the Nutmegs, the Velvet Angels, and the Delstars' immortal "Zoop Bop," which has been described by one listener as "a bunch of cough-syrup freaks in an echo chamber."

The most interesting, as well as one of the most professional, of the above groups is the Velvet Angels, whose records bear the cryptic notation "This Acappella Recording Was Made In A Jersey City Hotel Room." In reality, the Velvet Angels were a rather more famous group called Nolan Strong and the Diablos, whose incredibly lovely version of "The Wind" had been a moderate hit in 1952. As the story goes, they were all sitting around feeling pretty good and someone turned on a tape recorder and thus were born a half-dozen acappella classics.

The Camelots were from the heart of Brooklyn's Coney Island. In a sense, they single-handedly brought acappella to Philadelphia when Jerry Blavat ("The Greator With The Heator") broke their record of "Don't Leave Me Baby" on his oldies show. Blavat had, and still has, a large following in the area, so it wasn't much later that the Zircons could be heard doing "Lonely Way" on WIBG, Philadelphia's biggest rock station at the time. The Camelots followed this success up with "Chain of Broken Hearts," and from there tried for the really big dough by recording with instrumental backing. "Pocahontas" is a nice song (especially the line "The chipmunk and the squirrel are in a lasting dream"), but it wasn't much of a hit. Undaunted they turned up a few months later as the Harps on the Laurie label. Of all the acappella groups, they were the tightest and most professional, and must have had quite a stage act, if we can go by their promo picture.

When mentioning the Zircons, make sure you know what you're talking about, since there were two groups by that name, with nothing in common except the lead singer, Mario Ibanez. The first group was the one that recorded "Lonely Way" and disbanded shortly thereafter, since several of their members were drafted. The second Zircons were originally known as the Prophets, a group formed by Coolsound Records to do an original called "Silver Bells." After becoming the Zircons, they went to the Old Timer label, cutting a masterful fast version of "Stormy Weather" and less noteworthy readings of "Unchained Melody" and "Remember Then." They eventually declined into obscurity, and a recent phone call to one Mario Ibanez in the Bronx brought forth a "Whaat?" when asked about the Zircons.

The Citadels were the first acappella group to feature a girl. She was Jane Eckerson, sixteen years old at the time, and blessed with a crystal-clear voice. The Citadels' music has a definite Everly Brothers tinge to it; the harmony is free of "blue notes" and vibrato, sort of like southern Sacred Harp singing. The Young Ones were four Puerto Rican kids from Brooklyn who recorded the best acappella version of "Gloria" and later went on to record "with music." The Chessmen were from Manhattan and appeared on the stage of the Apollo Theatre in Harlem several times, as well as in Hackensack and Lodi, N.J. They did a lot of rather narcissistic stuff, but they were good, and each member of the group was a capable performer. They were also one of the few groups to record a solo album.

Unfortunately, the above-named groups, plus a couple of others that we'll get to in a minute, are about all there is to acappella. Almost immediately with the arrival of the Golden Age of Acappella came the beginning of the decline. Dozens of groups sprang out of nowhere, glutting the market with gimmicky variations of overdone standards and ridiculous originals. "These are acappella firsts!" announced the cover of *Best Of, Volume 4*. "Barbershop Harmony! Girl Groups! An Acappella Recording in a Foreign Language! Little Joe and the Majestics, featuring Little Joe Rivera, 12 Years Old!" The Girl Group! was Ginger Scaglione and the Adorables, a bunch of dolls who looked like Jerry Lee Lewis with Wild Thing hair-dos. It takes them only eight bars of a song to slide exactly a half-tone flat.

Since the base of support for acappella was concentrated among such a small number of people to start with, it quickly collapsed under the added weight of so much schlock. The good was dragged down with the bad; while such groups as the Semesters and the Durhams slipped back into well-deserved oblivion, they also pulled with them such fine acts as the Camelots and the Young Ones. By the end of 1965 acappella was dead, once again filed in those piles of ten-for-a-buck singles from which it began its rise to fame.

Indeed, the only bright spot in this entire period was the beginning of a series of acappella stage shows, featuring such groups as the Five Sharks and the Meadowbrooks. They took place primarily in northern New Jersey in such towns as Hackensack and Jersey City. The first show, at the Fox Theatre in Hackensack, a decaying old movie palace, took place auspiciously enough on the night of the Great New York Blackout. This didn't stop close to fifteen hundred stone acappella freaks from jamming the place to see their favorite performers (or those that turned up, anyway). Also on the bill, for reasons unknown, was a pseudo-English group called the Whatnots, whose very appearance elicited a stream of boos and catcalls from the audience that didn't let up until they slunk off stage. One thing these people *hated* was the English sound. "Unfortunately," say the liner notes on *Best Of, Volume 2,* "New York is starving for group sounds due to the mass brainwashing of the public with imported English garbage," and in an oldies fan magazine of the period, an insult tossed at the editor (all in fun, of course) was that he was a "Beatles lover."

The man behind most of the acappella shows was one Stan R. Krause of Catamount Records. Krause had begun his acappella career working with the Relic Rack, finally leaving when he found his ambitions in the direction of record production being stifled there. He began his own label with a group from Newark called the Savoys. Throughout its history, Catamount never produced an overload of masterpieces; instead, its main virtue was that it was unerringly consistent. When it came time to produce an album, Krause put together *I Dig Acappella, Volume 1,* with such artists from his stable as the Five Fashions and the Versailles. The original cover was graced by a scantily clad and slightly chubby young lovely holding a shovel (she digs . . .), who had to be pulled off the covers of subsequent editions due to numerous complaints.

In retrospect, Krause seems to have been the only acappella promoter to have been moti-

vated by a genuine love for the music. "I believed in it," he says today. "If I hadn't cared, I wouldn't have put five years of solid work into it . . ." Even in the early days, he was thinking of ways to showcase the music. To promote his groups, he would take them down to the boardwalk at Seaside Heights, New Jersey, where they would draw crowds of up to four hundred people. And Krause's acts always showed up on time for stage shows, always well-rehearsed and tight.

Even in acappella's dog days, Krause kept pushing. "It was really weird," he remembers. "When things began to go bad everyone started to dump their stuff on the market, selling them to wholesale warehouses and the like."

Krause, in reaction, pulled his stuff off the market and in time was the only one still producing new material. His first venture was a group from Dickinson High in New Jersey called the Royal Counts. They cut an album for him called *Acappella Soul,* featuring material originally done by the Temptations, the Four Tops and others, and to date, the album has sold an amazing 15,000 copies. Its success convinced Krause that there yet remained a mass market for acappella.

Almost immediately, he began making the rounds of major labels, looking for someone who would support him in a mass venture. "I was trying to prove it to everyone in the world . . . I heard something that couldn't be found anywhere else, and it meant something to me." Among the labels Krause saw was Epic, who told him flatly that he was two years ahead of his time, after which he was thanked politely.

In the meantime he continued headlined until they were re-producing acappella shows, moving from Hackensack to the State Theatre in Jersey City. For a while, the Royal Counts (along with the Chessmen) placed by some kids from New Rochelle High School who called themselves the Cordials. "Every summer," Krause wrote on the back of their album, *Blue Eyed Soul,* "they are in demand at the many shore clubs in Westchester County. They have appeared at the famous Glen Island Casino, and at many proms all over Westchester and Long Island." One member of the group was described thusly: "He collects old records and is interested in cars. He is now stationed in the Naval Reserve in Boston." Ah, yes . . .

The Cordials reigned supreme for a time, but were finally shut down by what must be the finest group that Krause has yet discovered: the Persuasions. He found them backing a nondescript white girl singer in a New York supper club, doing a mixed bag of pop numbers and show tunes. Krause had good taste; the Persuasions had been in show business a collective twelve years—one, in fact, had been a member of the Dixie Hummingbirds, while another had recorded as a solo artist for Sue Records. He took them into the studio and cut about a dozen numbers (including the first acappella "My Yiddishe Mama"), using stereo for the first time in acappella recording history. He also recorded them live on the stage of the State Theatre.

With this latest triumph in hand, Krause went knocking on doors again, but this time, he got an answer, although he had to go to California to get it. His tapes eventually came to the attention of the noted social historian Frank Zappa, who bought the rights to them for his Straight label. Zappa had been aware of the use of acappella singing in working out group harmony; in an interview he did with Richard Barry of the Pharoahs (the group that did the original "Louie, Louie") he was told that they get together, turn off the lights, and work out their vocal arrangements. He was unaware, however, of the Times-Square-Relic-Rack-type acappella scene when he played Krause's tape for the first time, but he thought that the Persuasions were extremely good and admired the way that Jerry Lawson, their lead singer, sang and phrased. And so, half a decade after it surfaced, acappella was on its way towards national distribution.

"Something is stirring on this," Krause explains it. "The market is so mixed—everybody is looking for something. That's why you have the 'Rock and Roll Revival.'"

The album, titled *Acappella* (Reprise 6394), marks either a glorious end or a new beginning for acappella. The live side, with its free interplay between audience and performers, captures perfectly the ambience of a live acappella show. The other side, with such numbers as "Up on the Roof" and "Since I Fell For You," is incredibly clean and mellow, a fine testimonial to the beauty of acappella at its best. It closes with a group original called "It's All Right," a soft recitation by Jerry Lawson done over a mellow four-part harmony background: "It's all right," they croon, and when they're finished, you know that it really is.

The Persuasions, more than any other acappella group, show a marked reliance on gospel harmonies and techniques. In their hands, "Old Man River" becomes the spiritual it was meant to be, while a simple teenage dance song, "The Bounce," carries the feeling of a revival hymn. Moreover, the Persuasions sing with an assurance, a precision, that most haphazard street acappella groups were unable to master. If any group is to carry acappella to a mass audience, it will be the Persuasions.

Happily, it looks like they're about to do just that. Aside from the release of their album, a score of personal appearances are being set up coast-to-coast to bring acappella, with its superb visual aspects, to a generation that might never have known it existed. Zappa is thinking of presenting them in a package with his own quartet, an all-instrumental act which would act as the drawing card as well as a contrast to the all-vocal Persuasions.

With luck, today's audience will react to it in a big way. "There's no truer sound for living and having fun than the old street-corner singing," insists Krause. "The human voice is the greatest instrument of all."

One of the things that marked the acappella craze, along with the oldies craze, were "charts" which listed the Top 150 or so group singles by sales, popularity, or availability in the stock of a given oldies shop. The authors of this article, in keeping with the tradition, have listed, after many hours of arduous research, what they feel to be the ten best acappella singles of all time. Most of these are available on the albums listed in the discography.

1) "Lonely Way"—
   The Zircons
      (Mellomood)

2) "Don't Leave Me Baby"—
The Camelots (Aanko)

3) "Sweeter Than"—
The Young Ones
(Times Square)

4) "Lola/Johnny Johnny"
—The Velvet Angels
(Relic)

5) "The Storm"—
The Vitones
(Times Square)

6) "Silver Bells"—
The Zircons
(Coolsound)

7) "Zoop Bop"—
The Delstars
(Mellomood)

8) "Comes Love"—
The Five Fashions
(Cat-Time)

9) "Sunday Kind of Love"—
The Five Shadows
(Mellomood)

10) "New Love Tomorrow"—
The Citadels (Relic)

—LENNY KAYE AND
ED WARD
4-16-70

THE CHANTELS
The Chantels
(End LP-301)

The balloting is in on the Best Female Vocalist in Rock and Roll History. The results: second place—Aretha, third place —Tina Turner, fourth place— Janis Joplin. First place, the winner—ARLENE SMITH!

What? You say you've never heard of Arlene Smith? How could an unknown place first ahead of Aretha and the others?

Let me assure you that this review is entirely serious. It is not a put on, not an artsy reviewer's way of saying that esoteric "oldies" are always the best. For although the "poll" was taken among a small handful of rock fans, we were able to agree after listening to *The Chantels* that their lead vocalist, Arlene Smith, could out-sing any of her competitors before or since.

The Chantels were a quintet of young, pretty black chicks popular in the late Fifties. They were the earliest pioneers of the gospel-rock big sound later developed by Phil Spector. You have probably heard their two biggest hits, "Maybe" (redone by Janis on her new album) and "I Love You So," classics in anybody's book. They were the marvelous prototype for a host of female rock groups— the Crystals, the Ronettes, the Supremes, Martha and the Vandellas—and they were better than all of them put together. When they stopped singing in the early Sixties, it was a sad moment in American music.

The thing that always surprises me about a Chantels song is that the Cleveland Symphony and the Duke Ellington Orchestra are not backing them up. It only sounds like they are. For the Chantels never used heavy instrumentation in their work. On most records it's just piano, bass, snare drum and organ, and playing damn quietly at that. The remarkable power and fullness of the sound comes solely from the voices of the Chantels, in particular the astounding voice of Arlene Smith.

What's so great about her voice? Well, to be frank, it starts where all other voices in rock stop. Arlene sounds like twenty Arethas (and I dig Aretha), eighty Dionne Warwicks, and three hundred of anybody else you can name. When she reaches for a high note she just keeps going. There is never a hint of strain. Nothing drops out. Her tone expands in breadth to match the requirements of high pitch. Most singers have to rely on well-produced crescendos by the horns and strings to cover up the fact that the voice can't cut it up there. Listen to Diana Ross, for example. This simply doesn't happen with Arlene. Like a three thousand dollar stereo system playing Beethoven's Ninth, the high, lows and mid range extend into infinity. Arlene Smith's is not only the best voice I've ever heard, it is also the best instrument of any kind I've ever encountered. It sounds like mythical bells preserved by the gods which the world's best pipe organs try to emulate but never quite reach.

What's most amazing about it is that Arlene's incredible range and tone quality are not purchased at the cost of phrasing. With the possible exception of Billie Holiday, I've never heard a woman make every word count the way she does. There's an edge on her voice that's at once very sexy and very, very deep. Listen to the trill in the phrase "I want you to *know*" in the song "I Love You So." You'd have to ransack the archives of all contemporary music to find another line that would even come close to its impact.

On the album *The Chantels* we find some of Arlene's best work preserved. In addition to the songs already named, it contains "The Plea," "Every Night," "Whoever You Are" and several others. My favorite of them all is "If You Try," a song I'd never heard until someone pushed the album into my hands a couple of weeks ago. It combines the conviction and warmth of "Maybe" with the sheer force of "I Love You So." The sound is so big that I'm afraid I'll have to ask the city council for a zoning change in order to keep it in my house. Most unbelieveable of all, however, is the fact that Arlene was only fifteen years old when she made these cuts. Amazing.

Until we can hear some new recordings from Arlene, we'll just have to thrive on the cuts from volumes #3 and #10 of

Golden Goodies albums (Roulette 24217 and 25218). Hopefully, *The Chantels* will also be released again by whoever owns the rights to it.

From the best information I've been able to gather, Arlene Smith now lives in the Bronx and has stopped singing professionally. It's entirely possible that the only people who hear that wonderful voice nowadays are her children as she rocks them to sleep at night.

—LANGDON WINNER
11-1-69

The Rolling

Stones

Their own introduction is their best: "Ladies and Gentlemen, the greatest rock and roll band in the world . . ." Here are five reviews that explain why, beginning with Jon Landau's account of how the group took a wrong turn on one album, followed by his review of an album that went right back to the core of their identity. Then a single review by Greil Marcus and his review of the Stones' *fin de decade* masterpiece, *Let It Bleed*. The section closes with Lester Bangs' account of their 1969 American tour live shot at Madison Square Garden, *Get Yer Ya-Ya's Out!*

Don't miss their earlier works, classics all—*The Rolling Stones, 12 x 5, December's Children, Out of Our Heads, Flowers* and *Between the Buttons*.

THEIR SATANIC MAJESTIES REQUEST
The Rolling Stones
(London NPS-2)

The Rolling Stones have been the best of all possible worlds: they have the lack of pretension and sentimentality associated with the blues, the rawness and toughness of hard rock, and the depth which always makes you feel that they are in the midst of saying something. They have never impressed me as being kitsch.

Their Satanic Majesties Request, despite moments of unquestionable brilliance, puts the status of the Rolling Stones in jeopardy. With it, the Stones abandon their capacity to lead in order to impress the impressionable. They have been far too influenced by their musical inferiors and the result is an insecure album in which they try too hard to prove that they too can say something new.

The album is marred by poor production. In the past there has been a great gulf between production styles of the Beatles and the Stones. The Beatles' production is often so "perfect" that it sounds computerized. *Sgt. Pepper* really does sound like it took four months to make. The Stones have never gotten hung up on that kind of thing. There is far greater informality to their sound and they probably have recorded more mistakes than any other group in pop music: vocals out of key, out of tune twelve strings (*December's Children* is loaded with them), forgetting lyrics, you name it.

In the past such mistakes all made sense because it was part of the Stones' basic statement, their basic arrogant pose. With the shift in pose to something quite different, something nearly "arty," the weak guitars and confused balance merely become annoying. Instead of tightening up the rudiments of their production, the Stones confuse the issue with their introduction into the instrumental tracks of countless studio gimmicks.

These production gimmicks create the aura of newness which surrounds this album. It gives the listener the feeling that he is hearing something that the Stones haven't done before. However, shorn of all extraneous artifacts, the songs that comprise this album are nothing new. We get simple folk chorus type stuff, ("Sing This Song All Together"); English folk melodies *à la* "Lady Jane," as in "In

Another Land"; occasional attempts at the old audacity and guttiness ("And I awoke/Is this some kind of joke?"), all of this in combination with the ever-present intent of proving that they are poets, like John Lennon or Donovan, and all that.

What is missing from all this, and what is so obviously and desperately needed to turn the whole thing into good Stones, is the instrumental and vocal style that has made the Stones so potent in the past, right down until *Between the Buttons*. But, those styles have been replaced by the kind of amorphous and aimless instrumental styles characteristic of American freakouts (at least if they had borrowed from the Who . . .). Thus we get oscillators and vacuum cleaners, pathetic doodling on the guitar, fuzz-tones without end, and we get the mandatory eight minute freakout. Groovy.

The Stones were always exemplary of one of the best of all rock qualities: tightness. They have always been economical, the opposite of ornamental. Having a very clear idea of what they wanted to say they could go into a studio and make it all up on a three minute cut.

One song which best illustrates the virtues of this approach is "Connection," from *Buttons*. It contains all of the Stones' virtues, but particularly the tightness. It is stark: just staring at you absolutely naked, no embellishment, no pretense, no apology. That is what the Stones have done, to varying degrees of effectiveness, on all of their former recordings. They were the exemplars of telling it like it is.

But, like everyone else, the Stones' heads do not stand still. They are a little less certain now. They are unhappy with their old style but they lack the artistic certainty to create a wholly new one. The result is that *Satanic Majesties* is necessarily a transitional album and, as such, it contains few of the old virtues. The new ideas are presented in such an undeveloped state that they do not achieve a valid identity of their own.

The basic motive of this album is a kind of meandering undercurrent of production effects and electronic gimmicks, meandering instrumental breaks which do not follow the songs they are a part of, and an attempt at either creating, or possibly satirizing, *Sgt. Pepper* type unity. In substance, the songs and much of the instrumental style used in the body of the songs offer very little which is new, and much which is inferior to what they have done previously.

"Sing This All Together" has a pleasant enough melody combined with its idiotically pretentious chorus. The horn riff they use at the end of each verse is a variation of the horn riff on Otis Redding's "Love Have Mercy" (*Dictionary of Soul*, Volt 415).

What bothers me about the cut musically is the archetypical (for this album) instrumental break which, in a word, is the superficial masquerading as depth. The quick guitar runs in the middle are brilliant. Unfortunately, no meaningful musical context has been created for them. They lie suspended over some musically irrelevant piano doodling and an absence of directed rhythm. For those who want to tell us that this cut contains anything startlingly new, I would point out that the break ends with the oldest rock cliche in the book, a single chord repeated first in half notes, and then accelerated into quarter notes, as in "Hang On Sloopy." And for those who wish to argue that the Stones make brilliant use of the rock cliche, they clearly don't as the absence of a related context virtually precludes it.

"Citadel" further illustrates the point that the Stones are not creating a genuinely new sound on this album, as melodically, vocally, and in intent, there is nothing new about this cut. What is new is the unnecessarily distorted guitars and the noisy instrumental track, as a whole. The old Stones would have done this cut very much the same way, except that the sound would have been tighter and more to the point.

To this end, Charlie Watts deserves great recognition. Of all the Stones, he seems to be least impressed with himself and he consequently turns in what is clearly the most consistent and best instrumental performance on the record.

In fact, Charlie hasn't changed very much since *Heads,* nor has there been much reason for him to do anything more than refine his style. Unfortunately, the two best examples of Watts in full bloom are not included in this album, "Dandelion" and "We Love You". The former was recorded well over a year ago and the latter was of more recent vintage. Even if you didn't dig the songs (I think each is significantly better than anything on this album, "We Love You" being the most advanced, sophisticated, and musically coherent thing the Stones have recently done), dig the power, brazenness, and guts of Charlie's elemental style. In any event, "Citadel" is certainly one of the more passable cuts on this album, due largely to Watts' drumming.

Bill Wyman's debut as a vocalist and a songwriter is fairly inconspicuous. The song, "In Another Land," is typically Stones, with the chorus resting comfortably in the *Aftermath* mold. Bill's solo voice, deliberately obscured by the trem-

olo effect, is of no consequence in any event. The nicest thing about the cut is the transition from the verse to the chorus. Watts continues to drive things and the acoustic guitars create solidarity and tightness. The lyrics to the chorus are among the few that recall the toughness of the past.

"2000 Man" is one of the strong points of the album. The rhythm change is quite nice, Watts' drumming is very strong, the acoustic guitars are more effective than usual, and the contrast between Jagger's weak voice on the verses and his gutsier style on the chorus is quite effective. However, the mix could have been better, particularly with reference to the bass, and the long organ chord that ends the song is stupid.

"Sing This All Together," round two, is the most annoying cut on the album by virtue of the fact that it includes some absolute strokes of genius which are lost by the totally inadequate arrangement and lack of musical direction. Particularly brilliant is Keith's guitar sound. The high of the track comes after two minutes of random doodling, when Richard gets into a lovely riff and is slowly joined by the horns. For about thirty seconds, it sounds like they are going to pull the whole thing together. They don't. The whole thing dies. There are a couple of other similarly isolated spots that occur during the cut, before Jagger gives the whole thing his kiss of death by singing the lyrics in a voice even more pretentious than the words call for, with the aid of an unbearably vulgar use of echo to make his voice and the words sound "deep." It is embarrassing.

The best cut on the album is easily "She's A Rainbow." Happily, Jagger abandons his wispy, small voice pose. He allows no doubt about what he wants to get across and his voice carries a positiveness and forcefulness lacking on most of the other cuts on the album. Even so, it is a remarkably asexual love song for the Stones and as such does not approach the power of the earlier Stones' singing on the same subject.

The performance is startlingly strong, with those rhythm guitars right up front and some very nice piano and strings, which I presume, they have nothing to do with. The dissonant instrumental break that comes before the last verse is excellent in this case because it gives the chorus added force when the band comes back in. It is short, succinct, and economical, the very qualities which are missing from so much of the rest of the album.

"Lantern" is another comparatively successful effort in which some excellent instrumental efforts help transcend a rather boring time and a poor lead vocal. Particularly of note are Wyman's guitar runs on the bass and his syncopated playing over extended chords at the end of each chorus. Watts' performance is again exemplary, particularly during the verses where he leads off each line with those tight little rolls.

Richard's guitar playing on "Lantern" is his best on the album. Richard has always been my own favorite lead guitarist in rock and he is certainly the best hard rock lead around. But after the first three Stones' albums I never felt he got into the groove again. On *Buttons* he showed he was moving in some new directions, and on this cut he turns in a beautiful performance, crowding into a few small runs a great deal of musical force.

The duration of the record motion is downward. "Gomper" is a total loss, the instrumental break having nothing whatever to recommend it. The vocal is unbearable. One thing Jagger is not very good at is trying to sound innocent. The cut simply does not cohere and was produced horribly.

By the time we get around to "2000 Light Years From Home" it is possible that even enthusiasts of the sound effects and production gimmicks, and that is what I think they are, will begin to tire of them. The song itself is fine—the drumming holds a comparatively good instrumental track in place—but the continuity is murdered by oscillators and what have you. Jagger just cannot sing consistently well in this kind of restrained voice and his attempts at whispering the line, "It's so very lonely, you're two thousand miles from home," are again embarrassing. He isn't much as a poser in the image of "teller of truths."

In a review of *Between the Buttons* I wrote, "The Stones make you feel their presence in a way that is so immediate, so essential, so relevant, that one can't turn his mind away from what they're doing." At the time I believed that the Stones were best of all our white groups, even superior in several respects to the Beatles. And I still think that.

The current album is an obvious detour in which the Stones manifest an understandable insecurity. With everyone getting into seemingly new things and other pop groups cutting huge prestige albums it is reasonable for the Stones to have felt the need to try to say something different, if for no other reason than to please their friends and the cultists.

Unfortunately they have been caught up in the familiar dilemma of mistaking the new for the advanced. In the process they have sacrificed most of the virtues which made their music so powerful in the first place: the tightness, the franticness,

the directness, and the primitiveness.

It is largely a question of intent. The old Stones had the unstated motto of "We play rock." And there was always an overriding aura of competence which they tried to generate. They knew they did their thing better than anyone else around, and, in fact, they did. The new Stones have been too infused with the pretentions of their musical inferiors. Hence they have adopted as their motto "We make art." Unfortunately, in rock there seems to be an inverse ratio between the amount of striving there is to make art and the quality of the art that results. For there was far more art in the Rolling Stones who were just trying to make rock than there is in the Rolling Stones who are trying to create art. It is an identity crisis of the first order and it is one that will have to be resolved more satisfactorily than it has been on *Their Satanic Majesties Request* if their music is to continue to grow.

—JON LANDAU
2-10-68

BEGGAR'S BANQUET
The Rolling Stones
(London PL 53)

On the surface rock and roll changes at an amazing pace. The influence of a figure like the Maharishi can appear and disappear in a matter of months. Talk about old fashioned rock and roll finds itself dead before it begins. Yet some things do remain, while others maintain enough of their former selves so that the logic of their growth at least makes itself obvious.

The Rolling Stones are constantly changing but beneath the changes they remain the most formal of rock bands. Their successive releases have been continuous extensions of their approach, not radical redefinitions, as has so often been the case with the Beatles. The Stones are constantly being reborn, but somehow the baby always looks like its parents.

In many ways 1968 was another one of those blues revival years. The Stones were into that when it was still verboten to show up at Newport with an electric guitar. It wasn't until five years after they recorded "King Bee" that Slim Harpo finally made it into a white rock club. Happily, even back then, the Stones never got bogged down in the puritanism that mars so many of the English blues bands. They were from the beginning a *rock and roll* blues band. They may have mimicked Harpo note for note, Keith Richard may have played a straight Chuck Berry bag for three-quarters of their first album, but it always wound up sounding like rock and roll: loud, metallic, and trebly. The Stones were the first band to say, "Up against the wall, motherfucker" and they said it with class.

Since that beginning the Stones have tried their hands at a lot of things: arrogance, satire, social commentary, "psychedelia," lewdness, love songs, you name it. Each phase seemed to flow naturally from the one that preceded it and none of their phases ever really changed their identity as a band. In every album but one it seemed to me that they managed to feel the pulse of what was happening now and what was about to happen. For example, "Satisfaction," that classic of the rock and roll age, both expressed the feelings of a moment and foreshadowed what was about to unfold: the elevation of rock and roll to the primary cultural means of communication among the young. There we were in the early summer of 1965 with folk music dead and nothing really exciting going on. And then there were the Stones sneering at the emptiness of what so many people saw all around them, not telling you to do anything about it, but letting you know that they feel it too. The music, with its incessant, repetitious, pounding guitar and drums, and that tension-filled voice, was so permeated with violence that just listening to it was cathartic.

And the Stones live. If the violence of their music was cathartic, how to describe their concerts? I saw them several times during their early American tours, most memorably in Lynn, Massachussetts, in the spring of 1966. The Stones had their usual major dates lined up on their itinerary and the Lynn gig was not one of them. Lynn is a suburb of Boston and they must have decided to do a quickie number for less than their usual fee in order to fill in an open night. The concert was held in an open air football field that held 10,000 people. It rained that evening, a steady drizzle, and when they finally came on there was a lot of tension and movement.

Everyone wanted to get the show done so that they could put the money into the bank. There was no possibility of a makeup date. Jagger emerged in a tee shirt and spread his hands out like Jesus. He thanked everyone for being there and the band went into "19th Nervous Breakdown." The instruments were out of tune, as well as nearly inaudible. Watts had trouble keeping the beat. Everything was a mess except for Jagger who miraculously managed to deliver. He filled the song with drive and energy and it was enthralling to hear him ringing out through the drizzle over practically no instrumental support. The band went on its disjointed way for the entire set unable to worry about the sound while the rain

was pouring down on them, and Jagger continued to go his.

The crowd that night was filled with high school kids and they were very restless. A group of them had massed in front of the stage and the local DJ who had presided over the show decided to come on stage and tell the kids that the concert wouldn't go on until they all pulled back. The Stones ignored him and went on with "The Last Time."

As the set drew to a close they went into "Satisfaction." I had seen them do it under ideal circumstances a year earlier and it had been superb. They had gone through the song then with full energy and intensity and then quieted things down a little. Jagger had taken off his jacket and put it near the drums. Then he had picked up a tambourine and walked around the different sides of the stage, talking to the chickies. Towards the end, the band had picked up to full volume, Jagger had thrown the tambourine into the audience, draped his jacket over his shoulder, and done a Frank Sinatra exit. As soon as he had vanished, the band followed him. It had been an altogether beautiful and tragic spectacle.

Jagger attempted the same bit that night and got as far as picking up the tambourine. The audience broke the police line and completely surrounded the stage. Brian Jones signalled to Jagger, who was in a trance, that they had better split. The cops did their best to clear a path but by this time there were literally hundreds of kids milling around what was supposed to have been the Stones' exiting area. When the Stones got into their limousines the cops started exploding tear gas. Idiots that they are, they neglected to put on masks to protect themselves from the gas and were soon incapacitated by their own tear gas canisters. A great deal of commotion ensued but presumably the group made it out of there safely.

Violence. The Rolling Stones are violence. Their music penetrates the raw nerve endings of their listeners and finds its way into the groove marked "release of frustration." Their violence has always been a surrogate for the larger violence their audience is so obviously capable of.

On *Beggar's Banquet* the Stones try to come to terms with violence more explicitly than before and in so doing are forced to take up the subject of politics. The result is the most sophisticated and meaningful statement we can expect to hear concerning the two themes—violence and politics—that will probably dominate the rock of 1969.

Politics has not been fashionable since Dylan left it among musicians. There have always been the few hold-outs left over from the folk music period, but despite the mass media's continually mistaken references to rock and roll as "protest music," rock musicians have done remarkably little protesting. Protest is a hallmark of the liberal. It is an appeal to the conscience of the majority to remedy some injustice being done to the minority. It presupposes a belief that meaningful change can be worked out within the system. Rock and roll musicians, for the most part, don't buy that. They don't take things like government seriously unless they are forced to. They find the whole political process something worthy of contempt.

Protest singers in the past were most often ideologues who set pallid verse to semi-musical melodies. The idea that it is the music that should convey the brunt of their meaning never occurred to them. There were words and there were notes but there wasn't any music.

The people who are turning to political themes in their music now are different. They don't do it as a luxury, or for moral reasons. They are doing it because it is part of their lives and they have to express themselves in terms of how what is happening in the streets is affecting their lives.

Beggar's Banquet is not a polemic or manifesto. It doesn't advocate anything. It is a reflection of what goes on at the Stones' house, with a few pictures of the house itself thrown in for good measure. Part of what that house looks like has to do with what it's surrounded by and the most startling songs on the album are the ones that deal with the Stones' environment: "Salt of the Earth," "Street Fighting Man," and "Sympathy for the Devil." Each is characterized lyrically by a schizoid ambiguity. The Stones are cognizant of the explosions of youthful energy that are going on all around them. They recognize the violence inherent in these struggles. They see them as movements for fundamental change and are deeply sympathetic. Yet they are too cynical to really go along themselves. After all, they are rock and roll musicians, not politicians, and London is such a "sleepy town."

They make it perfectly clear that they are sickened by contemporary society. But it is not their role to tell people what to do. Instead, they use their musical abilities like a seismograph to record the intensity of feelings, the violence, that is so prevalent now. From the beginning they themselves have been exponents of emotional violence and it's hard to imagine any group more suited to voicing the feelings of discontent we all share in these most violent of times. Wherever they wind up themselves, they are writing songs of revolution because they are giving power-

ful expression to the feelings that are causing it.

Musically the Stones express themselves through three basic elements: rhythm, tension, and energy. "Street Fighting Man" is prototypical of the approach. Drummer Charlie Watts lays down an elementary drum pattern, the same one he has been using since "Route 66." He strikes the high-hat with a near compulsive regularity and hits the snare drum with such a wallop it's hard to believe the sound is coming out of only one drum. The rhythm guitar is laid over the drum and is characterized by a violent attack which emphasizes the "*on*" beat. The bass pattern is simple and restrained. Like the guitar it serves to magnify the impact of the beat. The collective effect of the instrumental track is of fantastic thrust forward.

The beat is constantly being pushed, the guitars constantly re-emphasizing the basic movement of the song, the bass providing the perfect floor to the arrangement. And then the voice: Jagger is the source of the tension. At his best (definitely on this track) he sounds like he's fighting for control, fighting to be heard over the din of the instruments. For all its simplicity it is an amazingly complex style of arranging and a perfect vehicle for expressing the lyrics.

The words are beautiful. Notice how Jagger emphasizes

them: *"Ev-*ry *where* I *hear* the *sound* of *charg-*ing, *march-*ing *peo-*ple." The Stones obviously revel in the images of charging people: they've sure seen enough of them at their concerts. But they are too mature and too realistic to fall into the trap of slogans and easy answers. All they can really do is sing in a rock and roll band.

"Salt of the Earth" continues in the same vein and serves as Jagger's tribute to the "other half." Lyrically, the song's point of view is again ambiguous. Jagger obviously wants to empathize with the "common foot soldier," the working man, the man who is forced to throw his life away on "back-breaking work" without ever achieving satisfaction. On the other hand, when he looks into their "faceless crowds," they look "strange." He has gotten to a point where he can't really come to terms with their way of thinking. Nonetheless, the tribute goes on and begins to sound a bit like a drinking song. At one point I expect them to all be standing around the bar toasting the veterans of the Spanish Civil War. The double time at the end pushes the song past that stage and helps it regain its movement and vitality. It is typical of Jagger's honesty that he was unafraid to use a soldier as symbol of "Salt of the Earth." They are as much victims as anyone else.

"Sympathy for the Devil"

rounds out the group of ambiguous, socially aware songs. To me, it is the most distinguished song and performance of the year. Lyrically, it is a striking picture of a world gone mad. Cops are criminals. Saints are sinners. God is the devil. Whoever is on top makes whoever is beneath him the enemy; actually, it is always the men on top who are the enemy. Those who claim righteousness for themselves are only interested in perpetuating their own power. Those they vilify are really the righteous ones, until they achieve power for themselves. Then they imitate their predecessors and the process repeats itself through history. The narrator, Lucifer, was there when "Jesus Christ had his moment of doubt, of pain." He was there when "the blitzkreig raged and the bodies stank." And he lays "traps for troubadours who get killed before they reach Bombay." And who is telling us all this? A man of wealth and taste. Sounds like what a lot of people would like to become.

The music is brilliant. The cut opens with just the percussion—a sort of syncopated Bo Diddley, precisely the kind of thing Watts excels at. Then they add Nicky Hopkins' rhythm piano, perfectly understated. Wyman's simple bass line matches Watts' syncopation perfectly. Throughout the cut he adds color to the basic rhythm pattern by throwing in some very pretty, loopy bass lines. After two verses of Jagger's singing, the background voices add that ultra simple "oo-oo" accompaniment which continues to grow for the duration of the cut. By the time they reach the end, they sound like a plane taking off, accelerating at an inexorable pace until it finally reaches its normal flight speed, at which point it levels itself off.

Jagger sings with tension and control, constantly pushing himself as far as he can go, but never crossing over that line between power and excess. The guitar solo by Richard is among the finest rock solos I have heard recently. He only uses about five of the simplest rock lines around but he plays them with such finesse they seem to be oozing out of the guitar. His style is pure eroticism and he seems to linger over each note, making sure it comes out exactly like it's supposed to.

Watts, with Jagger, provides the energy. He keeps his little riff going like a computer. Towards the end he expands his part by a bit: he starts throwing out cymbal smashes on the first beat of each measure. It provides just that extra bit of rhythm and drive.

The rest of the album is made up of largely conventional Stones styled songs. There are some mediocre ones among them, but then that's

part of the Stones. Consistency is not their bag. Among the really fine cuts are "Doctor, Doctor," "No Expectations," "Factory Girl" and "Stray Cat Blues." "No Expectations" is noteworthy for its sentimental melancholy. It has a lovely country feel to it, without actually being an attempt at country music. "Factory Girl" is more of the Stones' interest in the working class (remember "Backstreet Girl") and has a New Lost City Ramblers type accompaniment, complete with old-timey styled fiddle.

"Stray Cat Blues" is easily the best of the lot and is pure Stones. It deals with their favorite subject: naughty boys and girls. The lyrics are about a groupie and Jagger comes up with some very tough lines: "I've heard you're fifteen years old/But I don't want your ID" and signs off with "I'll bet your mother don't know you can bite like that."

Musically, it is one of the songs that make use of the rhythm, tension, energy pattern mentioned earlier. The verse is in the form of one of those great *Between the Buttons* cuts, "All Sold Out." That is followed by a simple chorus. Later, a second chorus is added on top of that ("Oh yeah, you're a stray, stray cat . . ."). Each element of the structure adds to the tension of the body of the arrangement. But at the end of each chorus the energy level drops back down to that of the more restrained verse part of the song. It provides the listener with a perfect release. Instrumentally, Keith Richard's performance is again brilliant.

Beggar's Banquet is a complete album. While it does not attempt *Sgt. Pepper* type unity it manages to touch all the bases. It derives its central motive and mood from the theme of "revolution" but isn't limited to that. Over at the Stones' house there's plenty of room for groupies, doctors, jigsaw puzzles, factory girls, and broken hearts as well. Yet even these subjects are colored by the impact of "Sympathy for the Devil" and "Street Fighting Man." *Beggar's Banquet* ought to convince us all that the Stones are right. By putting all these different themes on the same album the Stones are trying to tell us that they all belong together. They do.

—JON LANDAU
1-4-69

"HONKY TONK WOMEN"
"YOU CAN'T ALWAYS GET
WHAT YOU WANT"
The Rolling Stones
(London 45-910)

"Honky Tonk Women" would have made a great twenty minute cut on the Stones' new album; as it is this disc is most likely the strongest three min-

utes of rock and roll released in 1969. It deserves twenty minutes because the Stones give us just the most tantalizing taste of everything they do well, of everything they do the best. In spite of Mick's screaming, joyful singing, this time the star of the show is Keith Richard. He combines the cleanest, toughest guitar lines in rock with Charlie Watts' jingling cowbell and steady drum shots for an introduction very similar to and equally as dramatic as that of Marvin Gaye's "I Heard It Through the Grapevine." Keith moves off after that, really fronting Mick himself, stretching sex with a smile out of every note, running up to the choruses with the same kind of perfect excitement Mike Bloomfield displayed on "Like a Rolling Stone." On the last two choruses Richard sings beautifully behind Mick, bending the words in counterpoint to Mick's straight shouts: "It's a haaaaawwww-aw-aw-aw-aw-kytonky woman! Bam! Gimme, Gimme, Gimme, Gimme . . ." It would have been a gas to hear Keith sing a chorus all by himself.

Mick sounds as if he had more fun recording this number than since I don't know when, kicking off the marvelous sax, bass, and guitar break with a sizzling "All *reeeet!*," ending it all with his out-of-breath shout "now *woooh!*" Hero producer Jimmy Miller has it just right for Bill Wyman, bringing the bass up for the choruses to fill in all the gaps. And the lyrics fit Ethan Russel's sneaky color photo on the single's cover: "I laid a/dee-vor-say/in New York City/Bomp ba-da . . ." A Stones classic.

The flip side is simply the other side of the Rolling Stones: from the cheap pubs of "Spider and the Fly" and the barrooms of Memphis Mick treads his way up the ladder of the upper class, back to the girls of "The 19th Nervous Breakdown" and "Play With Fire" in their mansions in St. Johns Wood, Hampstead, and Chelsea. Slow notes on the guitar and the moaning of a french horn lead into a melancholy story in which no sympathy is wasted on anyone: "You can't always get what you want . . . Oh, no, you can't always get what you want . . . you can't always get what you want . . . But if you try sometimes, you might find . . . that you get what you need." The arrangement of this masterful tale of decadence is very reminiscent of Traffic, the chorus seemingly a marriage of "Feelin' Alright?" and the best riffs from "Smiling Phases." Al Kooper sits in on piano and organ, and comes up with his best music since Blonde on Blonde. For a man who's been put down a great deal lately —if for good reason—Kooper shows that when discipline is imposed the fruits of his imagination are as good as they come.

We really couldn't ask for more—the life and times of the Rolling Stones on one little record, and a cover picture that says it just as well as the music. Buy it, lay it on your stereo and hang it on your wall. It'll look good there.

—GREIL MARCUS
8-23-69

LET IT BLEED
The Rolling Stones
(London NPS-4)

Let It Bleed is the last album by the Stones we'll see before the Sixties, already gone really, become the Seventies; it has the crummiest cover art since Flowers, with a credit sheet that looks like it was designed by the United States Government Printing Office (all courtesy of the inflated Robert Brownjohn), and the best production since, well, "Honky Tonk Women." The music has tones that are at once dark and perfectly clear, while the words are slurred and often buried for a stronger musical effect. The Stones as a band and Jagger and Mary Clayton and Keith Richard and Nanette Newman and Doris Troy and Madelaine Bell and the London Bach Choir as singers carry the songs past "lyrics" into pure emotion. There's a glimpse of a story— not much more. And like Beg-

gar's Banquet, Let It Bleed has the feel of *Highway 61 Revisited*.

On songs like "Live With Me," "Midnight Rambler," and "Let It Bleed," the Stones prance through all their familiar roles, with their Rolling Stones masks on, full of lurking evil, garish sexuality, and the hilarious and exciting posturing of rock and roll Don Juans. On "Monkey Man" they grandly submit to the image they've carried for almost the whole decade, and then crack up digging it: "All my friends are junkies! (That's not *really* true . . .)." And there are other songs, hidden between the flashier cuts, waiting for the listener to catch up with them: the brilliant revival of Robert Johnson's exquisite "Love In Vain," and Keith Richard's haunting ride through the diamond mines, "You Got the Silver."

And yet it's the first and last of *Let It Bleed* that seem to matter most. The frightening desperation of "Gimme Shelter" and the confused frustration of "You Can't Always Get What You Want" give the lie to the bravado of "Midnight Rambler" or "Live With Me." Not that those songs don't work—they do, of course, as crunching, soaring dreams of conquest and pop supremacy. They're great numbers. But "Gimme Shelter" and "You Can't Always Get What You Want" both reach

for reality and end up confronting it, almost mastering what's real, or what reality will feel like as the years fade in. It's a long way from "Get Off My Cloud" to "Gimme Shelter," a long way from "I Can't Get No Satisfaction" to "You Can't Always Get What You Want."

That's not to say the Stones can't move fast and play all their roles at once—they can, right on stage—but the force of the new vulnerability blurs the old stance of arrogance and contempt. The music of these two songs is just that much stronger than anything else on the album—they can't be ignored. Once the Stones were known, someone said, as the group that would always take a good old-fashioned piss against a good old-fashioned gas station attendant. And now Mick sings it this way too: "I went down to the demonstration/To get my fair share of abuse . . ."

"Gimme Shelter" is a song about fear; it probably serves better than anything written this year as a passageway straight into the next few years. It's a full-faced meeting with all the terror the mind can summon, moving fast and never breaking so that men and women have to beat that terror at the game's own pace. When Mary Clayton sings alone, so loudly and with so much force you think her lungs are bursting, Richard frames her with jolting riffs that blaze past her and take it back to Mick. Their answer and their way out matches the power of the threat: "It's just a shot away, it's just a shot away . . . it's just a kiss away, it's just a kiss away." The truly fearful omen of the music is that you know just a kiss won't be enough. This song, caught up in its own momentum, says you need the other too.

You remember the Stones' girls, the common, flirty (or was it "dirty"?) machine operator of "The Spider and the Fly," or for that matter the poor girl back home who said "when you've done your show go to bed"? They're all still here on Let It Bleed, with their masks on so you can use them —all the cooks and maids, upstairs and downstairs, in "Live With Me," or the presumably well-mangled victims of The Midnight Rambler. But the real women of this album seem to be women who can shout like Mary Clayton—gutty, strong, and tougher than any of the delightful leering figures that are jumping out of the old Stones' orgy. She can stand up to Mick and match him, and in fact, she steals the song. That's what makes "Gimme Shelter" such an overwhelming recording—it hits from both sides, with no laughs, no innuendoes, and nothing held

back. The Stones have never done anything better.

That's not a pace to maintain, obviously.

Meanwhile, as the Rolling Stones close out the Sixties and move into the Seventies with Let It Bleed, a new book's been published, photographs by David Bailey (once the Stones' photographer) of the celebrities who meant something in London these last ten years. It's called Goodbye Baby & Amen —to translate the subtitle, "A Wild Dance for the Sixties." It attempts to capture, in pictures and print, the liberation London found when the Empire was jettisoned, when Christine Keeler cut the boards out from under the platform of the British Establishment, when John Lennon, Mick Jagger and Peter Townshend drove out the old with the noise of the new music, when movie stars and directors and models took art out of the museums and took their clothes off at the same time. The book reaches for that sense of freedom already past, urging images of one long party lasting through the years, some still looking for it.

This era and the collapse of its bright and flimsy liberation are what the Stones leave behind with the last song of Let It Bleed. The dreams of having it all are gone, and the album ends with a song about compromises with what you want— learning to take what you can get, because the rules have changed with the death of the Sixties. Back a few years, all of London's new lower-class middle-class aristocracy were out for just what they wanted and they damned well got it. But no one can live off a memory; that vanished sense of mastery fell in, when was it, '65, '66? If "Gimme Shelter" is the Stones' song of terror, "You Can't Always Get What You Want" looks for satisfaction in resignation. And *that* sort of goal isn't what made "Satisfaction" the unanimous nation-wide poll-winning choice for the greatest rock and roll song of all time. But then the radio stations don't hold those polls anymore. You have to reach for this song yourself.

This is one of the most outrageous productions ever staged by a rock and roll band, and every note of it works to perfection: the slow, virginal choral introduction; the intensely moving, really despairing sounds of Kooper's horn and Keith's slow strum; and then the first verse and first chorus by Mick, singing almost unaccompanied. From there it dissolves and builds again with surges of organ, lovely piano ripples, long lead electric runs by Richard, drumming that carries the song over every crescendo—music that begins in a mood of complete tragedy and fatigue and ends with optimism and complete exuberance. The song, in a way, is as much a movie as *Blow-Up*—beginning and ending with a party in a Chelsea mansion, the singer meeting a strung-out, vicious girl he apparently knew from some years before, when things were different all around. It moves from there into street-fighting and frustration, and then to the strangest scene of all, a young man trying to strike up some sort of friendship with an old man who's past it. The results are much grimmer than anything out of "Midnight Rambler."

> *I went down to the Chelsea*
> *   drugstore*
> *To get your prescription*
> *   filled*
> *I was standing in line with*
> *   Mr. Jitters*
> *And man, did he look*
> *   pretty ill*
> *We decided that we would*
> *   have a soda*
> *My favorite flavor's cherry*
> *   red*
> *I sang my song to Mr.*
> *   Jitters*
> *And he said one word to*
> *   me*
> *And that was death . . .*

From there, of course, it's back to the party.

So in *Let It Bleed* we can find every role the Stones have ever played for us—swaggering studs, evil demons, harem keepers and fast life riders—what the Stones meant in the Sixties, what they know very well they've meant to us. But at the beginning and the end you'll find an opening into the Seventies—harder to take, and stronger wine. They have women with them this time, and these two magnificent songs no longer reach for mastery over other people, but for an uncertain mastery over the more desperate situations the coming years are about to enforce.

—GREIL MARCUS
12-27-69

GET YER YA-YA'S OUT!
The Rolling Stones
(London NPS-5)

The Rolling Stones barnstormed their way across America last fall for a tour which left most audiences satisfied and well-nigh spent. But they got reviews mixed and ultimately perplexed because few of us were sure what to expect or, once the hysteria of the actual performance had drained away, how to react. In 1965, caught up in a hurricane of bopper shrieks, we accepted the whole thing as sort of a supernatural visitation, a cataclysmic experience of Wagnerian power that transcended music. In 1969 they were expected to prove themselves as a stage act, but the force of their personalities and the tides of hype and our expectations cancelled all our

cynical reservations the moment Mick strode out and drawled hello to each home town. There they were in the flesh, the *Rolling Stones,* ultimate personification of all our notions and fantasies and hopes for rock and roll, and we were enthralled, but the nagging question that remained was whether the show we had seen was really that brilliant, or if we had not been to some degree set up, pavlov'd by years of absence and rock scribes and 45 minute delays into a kind of injection delirium in which a show which was perfectly ordinary in terms of what the Stones might have been capable of would seem like some ultimate rock apocalypse. Sure, the Stones put on what was almost undoubtedly the best show of the year, but did that say more about their own involvement or about the almost uniform lameness of the competition? Some folks never did decide.

All of which is why *Get Yer Ya-Ya's Out!* is such an unfettered delight. This album, at last, proves the fears of those who cared to fear groundless. More than just the soundtrack for a Rolling Stones concert, it's a truly inspired session, as intimate an experience as sitting in while the Stones jam for sheer joy in the basement. It proves once and for all that this band does not merely play the audience, it plays *music* whose essential crudeness is so highly refined that it becomes a kind of absolute distillation of raunch, that element which seems to be seeping out of Seventies rock at a disturbing rate. Where most live efforts seem almost embarrassing in their posturings and excesses, and even *The Who Live At Leeds* held tinges of the Art Statement, *Ya-Ya's* at its best just rocks and socks you right out of your chair. You can not only love it for what it is, you can like it for what it isn't.

The set opens with a brief collage of MC introductions from all their tour stops, and then rolls right into a solid, methodical "Jumpin' Jack Flash." Neither it nor the next three songs on side one quite match the energy level reached in "Midnight Rambler" and sustained through all of side two, but subsequent playings reveal the live "Jack Flash" to have a certain fierce precision which the studio single lacked and which makes the latter sound almost plodding by comparison. Here the bottom is full and brooding and the group as a whole has a bite as sharp as a pair of wire cutters.

Next comes Mick, teasing the little chickies: "Uh oh, I think I bust a button on mah trousahs . . . you do' want mah trousahs to fall down, now do ya?" I had a friend once who

nearly provoked me to fisticuffs when he remarked that Mick's appeal was "perverted." Now, the thing that strikes me here is how essentially positive and even *wholesome,* in terms of what's in the wind in 1970, Mick's onstage stud-strut is.

"Carol" is fine but definitely weaker than the version of *Liver,* and for me "Stray Cat" and "Love in Vain" provide the low points of the album, the former by a certain clutter and the latter by not being that inspiring a vehicle in the first place.

But all traces of disinterest or disappointment disappear with the first swaggering chords of "Midnight Rambler." Mick can hardly wait to get started, flinging out rippling harp riffs and muttering lyrics before the others even begin, and certainly this great song made to be done live, has never been rendered with more purging viciousness. Every riff in it is so pristinely simple, yet so directly and deliberately placed that its locomotive rushes and icy invective take on more power the closer you come to learning them by heart. *Let It Bleed*'s version seemed sinuous, somehow cool and detached in its violence, like one of Norman Mailer's Fifties hipsters. Here the song's celebratory rage comes bursting with a juggernaut wallop, Mick wrenching inchoate nonverbal vocalisms from his throat in the stop-time middle section, the audience roaring back (one crazed cat hollering "God damn!" in between), and the final frosting some wiry, lunging new riffs from Keith that build magnificently to the crashing climax.

The second side opens with another great audience riff—an insistent chick yells " 'Paint It Black,' you devils!" and the Stones answer with an airborne "Sympathy For the Devil" that beats the rather cut-and-dried rendition on *Beggar's Banquet* all hollow, and spotlights a ringing Richard solo that's undoubtedly one of his best on record.

From there on out the energy level of the proceedings seems to soar straight up. "Live With Me" is just great ribald jive, but "Little Queenie" as done here is alltime classic Stones. Just strutting along, leering and shuffling, the song has all the loose, lipsmacking glee its lyrics ever implied. This kind of gutty, almost offhand, seemingly effortless funk is where the Stones have traditionally left all competitors in the dust, and here they outdo themselves. I even think that this is one of those rare instances (most of the others are on their first album) where they cut Chuck Berry with one of his own songs.

"Honky Tonk Women" is just a joy, but "Street Fightin' Man" takes the show out on a level of stratospheric intensity that simply rises above the rest of the album and sums it all up.

Keith's work here is a special delight, great surging riffs reminiscent of some of the best lines on the first Moby Grape album, or the golden lead in Stevie Wonder's "I Was Made to Love Her." I don't think there's a song on *Ya-Ya's* where the Stones, didn't cut their original studio jobs. and this one leaps perhaps farthest ahead of all.

The Seventies may not have started with bright prospects for the future of rock, and so many hacks are reciting the litany of doom that it's beginning to annoy like an inane survey hit. The form may be in trouble, and we listeners may ourselves be in trouble, so jaded it gets harder each month to even hear what we're listening to. But the Rolling Stones are most assuredly not in trouble, and are looking like an even greater force in the years ahead than they have been. It's still too soon to tell, but I'm beginning to think *Ya-Ya's* just might be the best album they ever made. I have no doubt that it's the best rock concert ever put on record. The Stones, alone among their generation of groups, are not about to fall by the wayside. And as long as they continue to thrive this way, the era of true rock and roll music will remain alive and kicking with them.

—LESTER BANGS

11-12-70

The

British

Invasions

When the history of rock in the sixties is written, two great British Invasions will be seen: the first was led by the Beatles, the Rolling Stones, the Animals and many others like them at the time. These great names, of course, have left huge bodies of work. The second wave really began with Cream at the time when the physical locus of rock consciousness shifted from London (where Cream lived) to San Francisco (where they made their initial breakthrough).

In the wake of Cream came a host of hard rock trios and quartets, usually heavily blues-based and of less and less musical worth, culminating in Led Zeppelin (cf: The Record Reviewer, An Historical Overview).

Many of the first wave survived—either in original or permutated form—and became a part of the second wave.

In this collection, The Kinks and The Who are examples. Traffic, Cream and the Small Faces are permutations of groups that existed during the first wave. Their particular origins are discussed within the reviews of these groups, which are from their post-1967 period.

The Kinks' reviews in this collection merit some particular attention. They have devoted and loving critics. Paul Williams, editor and founder of *Crawdaddy,* contributed his as a guest review to one issue. *Tommy,* perhaps the most popular and long-lasting accomplishment of the post-*Pepper* period in Great Britain, was never reviewed as an album in the pages of *Rolling Stone.* Having published the interview (see *The Rolling Stone Interviews,* Straight Arrow Books) in which Pete Townshend originally formulated the rock-opera and his later analysis of the completed work, it seemed somehow extraneous. What was there to say except that it would have been better if it were condensed into a single album. Ah, ambition . . .

Again, it must be kept in mind that this selection is neither a comprehensive nor a complete one. The Animals, Manfred Mann and a number of other groups are not represented here. And pre-1968 albums are for the most part missing, including the great early work of The Who and a number of others. And in the selection of the blues-based groups, one will right away notice that, regretfully, there are no reviews of John Mayall, the father figure of the English blues scene, from whose group came Eric Clapton, Mick Taylor and a dozen others.

~~~~~~~~~~~~~~~~~~~~~

FRESH CREAM
Cream
(Atco SD-33-206)

ARE YOU EXPERIENCED?
The Jimi Hendrix Experience
(Reprise 6261)

It is only natural that as part of the overall experimentation going on in pop, attempts at using new combinations of instruments would be tried. The earlier pop groups of the new wave, starting with the Beatles, the Animals, the Stones, and the Beach Boys, were all four-instrument groups, and tended to influence others in that direction. But from the beginning some American groups have attempted to enlarge this concept.

The result has been a certain denseness in the music of these expanded ensembles, with the West Coast in particular developing an ornamental sound, emphasizing lots of embellishment, and lots of interaction among soloists.

Oddly, in England the trend has been in the other direction. The Who, the current Yardbirds, the Cream, and Jimi Hendrix are all three-instrument groups. They represent attempts to tighten the music, to eliminate the superfluous, and to get closer to the mythical nitty-gritty. In some cases they are going so far as to eliminate the distinction between background and foreground sounds.

In considering the work of two major new trios, the Cream and Jimi Hendrix, it must be remembered that there is no point in eliminating the rhythm instrument if it is a group's intention to play the kind of rock in which it is important to have one. Any rock form in which there is a solo-accompaniment idea, such as the blues, or hard rock, will require more than a bass and drums for rhythm. It is therefore self-defeating to start a three-man group to play those types of music. Hendrix has been more successful in realizing this and in using the three-instrument idea more meaningfully.

Eric Clapton, of the Cream, is still very tied to the blues and doesn't seem to know which way to go. On the *Fresh Cream* album he fools around with attempts to make the straight three-man thing work but dubs a fourth instrument on several tracks. The results are pretty confusing.

First of all, in terms of his own performance, when he does a straight blues he sounds bored. He has done it all before and it isn't likely that he will soon surpass his blues playing on cuts like "Have You Heard" from the Bluesbreakers album. Hence, on a cut like the totally charming "Sleepy Time Time" he doesn't really get into it. Most of the instrumental excitement of the cut is instead created by Jack Bruce's full and imaginative bass playing. Bruce's bass is recorded very loud to compensate for the lack of rhythm, yet the total sound remains

thin and, on this cut, the fourth instrument is very much needed.

On another blues cut, Muddy Waters' "Rolling and Tumbling," they try it without a bass. Guitar, harp, by Jack Bruce, and vocal all play identical lines in an attempt to create a harsh, unified, violent effect. It is a good attempt at a three-instrument thing, but unfortunately, Bruce's poor harp solo destroys the concept and prevents the cut from fulfilling itself. (It is absolutely beyond me how three such technically gifted musicians were unable to spot this fact in listening to the playbacks.)

On "Four Until Late" the group turns in a tight but conventional performance which is quite effective, without relying on dubbing a second guitar. And on "Cat's Squirrel" they get into a real three-instrument thing and it works wonderfully, giving us a real taste of Clapton's marvelous chord style.

The real standout on the album is "I'm So Glad," primarily because it is one of Eric's few really creative moments on this record, and because the vocal arrangement is so fine. His solo is beautifully constructed and shows off his capacity to improvise harmonically off the melody line to excellent advantage. Few rock guitarists have this capacity and none more so than Clapton. However, on the solo he felt the need to dub a second guitar which again illustrates the limits of three instruments for this kind of material.

As good as Ginger Baker is on the drums, he can be faulted for failing to move out in the manner of Keith Moon, or Mitch Mitchell, when the group's instrumental sound takes off.

When the Cream does make good music, as on their last single, "Strange Brew," it isn't because they are doing anything really new, but because they are doing the old thing, the blues, extremely well. And to work in this idiom they know they need the extra guitar and dub it in to give the arrangement more substance.

Ultimately the Cream will have to decide if this is what they want to continue to do or not. If they do, they may eventually find it aesthetically advantageous to add another instrument. If not, then perhaps they will evolve their own version of a three-instrument group, in which case, with their vast individual talents, they will really come up with something.

On the British *Are You Experienced?* album there is a straight blues called "Red House." Prior to his guitar solo on that cut, Jimi Hendrix announces, "I've still got my guitar." It's a good thing, because Jimi is neither a great songwriter nor an extraordinary vocalist.

He is, however, a great gui-

tarist and a brilliant arranger. On "Red House," the only straight blues he has recorded (he wrote it himself, but it sounds like B. B. King), he establishes himself as an absolute master of that musical form. The blues and hard rock used to be Jimi's *forte* when he toured the country in bands fronted by Little Richard and Joey Dee, the latter being the place where Felix Cavaliere and Eddie Brigati got their starts, but he is no longer interested in those seemingly limited musical forms. In a way it's a shame because for me this simple little blues is the most exciting cut he's yet recorded. Even Jimi seems to realize this when he says to the engineer, at the end of the cut, with the smug confidence that has become his trademark, "How about that one?"

On the American album we find a totally unified presentation of a sound altogether different from that of "Red House." Unlike Clapton, Jimi really does think in terms of three instruments, and despite some small amount of dubbing, he has given us the first really new sound in this idiom since the Who's first album with its "Out in the Streets," and "My Generation."

Jimi relies exclusively on his drummer, Mitch Mitchell, for his whole rhythm concept. Mitchell has clearly been influenced by the best of all British drummers, the Who's Keith Moon, and goes after that heavy metallic tone that Moon introduced two years ago. He is an extremely busy drummer who has better technique than most and a very clear concept of what he is trying to do.

Noel Redding is likewise a fine bass player and rhythm guitarist, but unlike Jack Bruce, he doesn't feel the need to compensate for the lack of another rhythm instrument and therefore tends to limit the range of his playing a great deal more.

And then there is Jimi himself who feeds and fuzzes just about everything, knows every gimmick in the book, and has a fantastic touch. On some of the cuts he goes to a bassier guitar sound than is usual for this kind of playing ("The Wind Cries Mary") and on some cuts he concentrates on just a few lengthily sustained notes ("Fire"), but on most of the others he just pulls out the stops and what results is indescribable.

"Purple Haze" is the perfect beginning for this album because the intro is a perfect expression of Jimi's charismatic style. In words it seems to be saying, "Now, dig this." There is no real sense of foreground-background once Jimi starts to sing on the cut, as is often the case. Only on "Hey Joe" and "The Wind Cries Mary" does Jimi play in a more conventional style and on these cuts

he gives us a brief taste of his melodic sense—on the solos—which in both cases is perfect. On the latter he uses the eclectic perfectly, placing a country and western based guitar solo right where it belongs.

Everything else is insane and simply a matter of either you dig it or you don't. Basically I don't for several reasons. Despite Jimi's musical brilliance and the group's total precision, the poor quality of the songs, and the inanity of the lyrics, too often get in the way. Jimi is very much into state-of-mind type lyrics, but even so, lines like "Manic depression is a frustrating mess," just don't make it. It is one thing for Jimi to talk arrogantly, and without any pretense at artistry; it's another to write lyrics in that fashion. In this context "I Don't Live Today" can be seen as both the best and worst cut on the album. The best because it is performed with such exquisite precision and control, and the worst because what Jimi is trying to get across is such a drag: "There's no life nowhere."

On the *Are You Experienced?* album Jimi has made a tremendous technical advance in the use of three instruments. The superfluous has been eliminated, the tightness of the arrangements is total, the ornament and the background-foreground concept have been limited, if not eliminated, and the level of individual virtuosity is extraordinarily high. But in Jimi's case, the sum total of all this is pure violence. Above all this record is unrelentingly violent, and, lyrically, inartistically violent at that.

Dig it if you can, but as for me, I'd rather hear Jimi play the blues.

—JON LANDAU
11-9-67

AXIS: BOLD AS LOVE
Jimi Hendrix
(Reprise 0281)

Jimi Hendrix sounds like a junk heap (Ben Calder crushed monolithic mobiles bulldozed), very heavy and metallic loud. Rock's first burlesque dancer, superman in drag, his music is schizophrenic. *Axis: Bold as Love* is the refinement of white noise into psychedelia, and (like Cream) it is not a timid happening; in the vortex of this apocalyptic transcendence stands Hendrix, beating off on his guitar and defiantly proclaiming "if the mountains fell in the sea, let it be, it ain't me." Such cocky pop philosophy shall not go unrewarded.

"EXP" is Hendrix's white tornado advertisement aperitif (come-on), "my God Martha, it's a white tornado": "There ain't no life nowhere." The science fiction continues (Mose Allison) in "Up from the Skies," while "Spanish Castle Magic"

transforms the Clovers; in fact, much of *Axis* demonstrates that Hendrix stands in relation to rhythm and blues of the fifties as the Who stand in relation to mainstream rock of the fifties—two useful transplants, indeed. "Ain't No Telling" is all Mitch Mitchell, who is by now definitely one of rock's most frantic drummers (from Moon to Baker). "If 6 Was 9" cracks foundations with banalized hippie lore ("wave my freak flag high"), while "She's So Fine" positively destroys walls. If "One Rainy Wish" repairs everything (like "May This Be Love"), pomp and circumstance ushers out "Bold as Love"—we all know that she by now *has* to be experienced.

Jimi Hendrix may be the Charlie Mingus of Rock, especially considering his fondness for reciting what might loosely be called poetry. But his songs too often are basically a bore, and the Experience also shares with Cream the problem of vocal ability. Fortunately both groups' instrumental excellence saves the day, and Hendrix on *Axis* demonstrates conclusively that he is one of rock's greatest guitar players in his mastery and exploration of every conceivable gimmick. Uneven in quality as it is, *Axis* nevertheless is the finest Voodoo album that any rock group has produced to date.

—JIM MILLER
4-6-68

ELECTRIC LADYLAND
The Jimi Hendrix Experience
(Reprise 6307)

Being a bit fed up with music as "reactive noise" ("God man, the world's a drag, let's play loud and drown it out"), I was sort of set *not* to dig this LP, but I had to. Hendrix is a good musician and his science fiction concepts surmount noise. There isn't really a concept (no Sgt. Pepper trips here)—instead there's a unity, an energy flow. The LP opens with an electronic track using tape loops and phasing (think of "Itchy Coo Park" by the Small Faces for an example of phasing) called "And the Gods Made Love." Hendrix said in an interview, "We knew this was the track that most people will jump on to criticize, so I put it first to get it over with."

The "I" in that sentence is true—Hendrix produced and directed these sides himself. Following is "Electric Ladyland," a fairytale trip that serves as introduction to the rest on the LP; "I want to show you the angels spread their wings." Next is "Crosstown Traffic," a stomp under with a heavy beat. "90 miles an hour is the speed I drive, girl," sings Hendrix as he compares the woman with a traffic jam—"It's so hard to get through you."

Then a live cut, which sounds as though it was recorded late at night in a small club, at one of the jamming sessions Hendrix is known for. It features Stevie Winwood on organ and Jack Casady on bass, and is called "Voodoo Chile." It begins with a very John Lee Hooker-like guitar intro, and keeps a blues feeling all the way through, although Hendrix's lyrics ("My arrows are made of desire/ From as far away as Jupiter's sulphur mines") are a far cry from "Rolling Stone" (the Muddy Waters song that's an ancestor to this track, as well as a lot of other things). After some feedback screech, a listener says "Turn that damn guitar *down!*" and the track ends with Hendrix and a chick discovering that the bar in the club is closed. "The bar is closed?" she says unbelievingly.

But yes it is. Side B opens with a song by bassist Noel Redding, "Little Miss Strange," probably the most commercial of the numbers included. Basically hard rock, the best thing about it is some nice unison guitar lines, probably an overdub, unless Hendrix has grown another couple of arms. "Long Hot Summer Night" is next, a song set in the "Visions Of Johanna" scene, although Hendrix has a way out—"my baby's coming to *rescue* me—." An Earl King number, "Come On," follows. Mostly rock/soul, the guitar break in the middle is one of the nicest things Hendrix has done.

"Gypsy Eyes" begins with a drum thumping, a simple bass line and a compelling guitar line, it's a light groovy time that really sticks to your synapses. (If it was possible to hum or whistle Hendrix, this would be the tune you'd most likely do.)

The side ends with "Burning of the Midnight Lamp," which was Hendrix's last single in England, released a year ago this summer. It's a freaky ballad, with particularly nothing lyrics and on the whole a drag . . . it goes nowhere. Side C is the sea or water side. It opens with "Rainy Day, Dream Away," using a small group that includes Buddy Miles from the Flag on drums. In it Hendrix does a lot to restore the grooviness of rainy days, previously much maligned in many songs.

This fades to "1983: A Merman I Should Be" (a merman is a mermaid's mate, of course). Hendrix's vision of the future shows a world torn by war, on the verge of destruction as he and his lady go for a walk by the sea, and dream of living in the water. With tape loops, melancholy guitar and the flute of Chris Wood (also from Traffic) Hendrix structures a beautiful undersea mood—only to destroy it with some heavy handed guitar. My first reaction was, why did he have to do that? Then I thought that he created a beautiful thing, but lost faith it it, and so destroyed

it before anybody else could—in several ways, a bummer.

Another electronic track, "Moon Turn the Tides Gently Gently Away," heals some of the rent in your head, and the side ends peacefully. Side D opens with a continuation of "Still Raining, Still Dreaming," only heavier and funkier—maybe just a bit too much so (iron raindrops hurt, man). "House Burning Down" could be taken as Hendrix's first socially conscious statement, but it ends in typical Hendrix fashion; "an eerie man from space . . . come down and take the dead away."

Then comes the new single, Dylan's "All Along the Watchtower"—in many ways one of the most interesting cuts here. On Hendrix's original numbers, it's sometimes hard to see the structure at first; the rhythm starts and stops, the changes are a bit hard to follow sometimes. But here, if you listen to the rhythm guitar track, and keep the original song in your mind, you can see the way Hendrix overlays his beautifully freaky sound on the already established framework of the song. He is true to its mood and really illustrates the line "the wind began to howl." Last is "Voodoo Child (Slight Return)," done this time with his usual backup men in a studio cut, heavier and more driving.

In other words, an extended look into Hendrix's head, and mostly it seems to have some pretty good things in it (who among us is totally free of mental garbage?). A few random thoughts to sum up; Hendrix is the Robert Johnson of the Sixties, and really the first cat to ever totally play *electric* guitar. Remember, he used the wah-wah pedal before "Brave Ulysses," and he's still the boss. And it's nice to see that he is confident enough so he can play some blues again—I'd like to hear more.

Hendrix, psychedelic super-spade??? Or just a damn good musician/producer? Depends on whether you want to believe the image or your ears. (And if you wanna flow, dig this on earphones, and watch the guitar swoop back and forth through your head.) Hendrix is amazing, and I hope he gets to the moon first. If he keeps up the way he's going here, he will.

　　　　　　　—TONY GLOVER
　　　　　　　11-9-68

BAND OF GYPSYS
Jimi Hendrix
(Capitol STAO-472)

This is the album that Hendrix "owed" Capitol for releasing him over to Reprise Records and significantly, it isn't a studio effort, as his Reprise albums have been. Which is not to imply that it is any better than those Experience albums. The context of the album is vital—*Band of Gypsys* was one of Hendrix' 1969 amalgamations consisting of Buddy Miles on drums and Billy Cox on bass, among others. They hadn't been together very long when this session was recorded live at the Fillmore East, New Year's Eve 1969/70, and the music shows it.

Both sides are basically extended jams with lots of powerful, together guitar by Hendrix, able bass by Cox, at times overbearing drums by Miles and rather lame, buried vocals by both Hendrix and Miles. The group sound is surprisingly similar to Hendrix' old "Foxy Lady" and "Purple Haze" days, with the significant difference that here Hendrix really gets into his guitar playing. No more the flashy, crotch-oriented gimmickry and extended wah-wahs—here he just stands still and shows us how adept he is with the ax. The support from Cox is always inventive, but Miles' drumming is definitely disturbing and exceedingly pedestrian at times. Hendrix overcomes on pure tension alone, as both "Message To Love" and "Who Knows" aptly demonstrate.

The problem is the vocals—all the tunes are new ones and with Hendrix' weird poetic sensibility (akin to LeRoi Jones in effect at times: catch the poem on the inside cover), it would have been a large improvement had we been presented with a little less drumming and a lot more vocal. The excitement and hypnotic compression so apparent in the music would have been pressed home even more forcefully behind Hendrix' drawling, heavily inflected voice, because Hendrix is not just a run-of-the-mill R & B singer—his voice is just as much an instrument as his guitar. But, it's all just potential this time out, with the one exception of the twelve-minute "Machine Gun," dedicated to "all the soldiers that are fighting in Chicago, Milwaukee and New York and . . . oh, yes . . . all the soldiers fighting in Viet Nam." Here the Hendrix vocal is in the forefront and perfectly matched to his most desperate, driving guitar solo ever. You can hear the sirens wailing and the entire mood, even down to Miles' drumming, is one of confrontation and freneticism mixed in equal parts.

This album is Hendrix the musician. With just bass and drum support he is able to transfuse and transfix on the strength of his guitar-work alone.

—GARY VON TERSCH
5-28-70

THE YARDBIRDS FEATURING PERFORMANCES BY BECK, CLAPTON & PAGE
(Epic EG 30135)

This two-volume set of Yardbirds material, culled from their previous albums, is purportedly "the Yardbirds at their best and most complete." Not so. While it is an interesting and somewhat elucidating selection of tunes, the neglect of some of the Yardbirds' most revolutionary and trend-setting songs is evident. I have in mind such gems as their first single smash "For Your Love" and the song that launched the whole onslaught of what was soon termed "psychedelic music," "Still I'm Sad." Other necessities for an album of this ilk would be "I'm A Man," "Heartful of Soul" and the drone-spun "Evil Hearted You." Instead of such trivialities as "Got To Hurry" and "A Certain Girl," this album would have been more representative had more of the above-mentioned songs, which are really indicative of the contributions the Yardbirds made to what was then still called rock and roll, been included.*

What contributions, you ask? The Yardbirds were one of the best R & B bands, outside of the Stones, in the early Sixties (fortunately "The Train Kept A Rollin'" and "Drinkin' Muddy Water" are included), were the first band to include extended, improvised solos in their material, were one of the first to explore the then "new" fuzz-tone guitar technique (the reason "Still I'm Sad" is sorely lack-

---

* The album issued prior to the above does contain those songs not included here. (Ed.)

ing), experimented with the sitar and the whole Eastern music aura before the Beatles ("Hot House of Omargarashid" gives some indications of this, but there were better tracks on their *Over Under Sideways Down* album) and, though not documented on disc, were the first band to employ feed-back in a constructive fashion, yea even before Hendrix. Some cuts on this album do offer indications of these achievements—the discursive "White Summer," "Turn Into Earth," the Bo Diddley rave-up "Here 'Tis" and the call-and-response fashioned "I Ain't Done Wrong" being the most outstanding.

A word of caution: Don't purchase this album for the Eric Clapton cuts—there are only two, "I Wish You Would" and "I Ain't Got You," on which he takes nice but limited solos. While interesting, they are hardly worth the lavish heraldization of his name all over the album covers. But, if you want a glimpse at the achievements the Yardbirds accomplished in the mid-Sixties, the album is sufficient, but it would have been a must-get set had a little more judiciousness been used in the tune choosing.

—GARY VON TERSCH
8-27-70

DISRAELI GEARS
Cream
(Atco SD 33-232)

Within the grooves of this record are miles of listening pleasure. Eric Clapton, Jack Bruce and Ginger Baker are simply superb musicians with the gift of unending virtuosity. The title of the album, as Eric explains it, is a pun. The group was driving along one day trying to think of names for the record, coming up with things like "Elephant Gerald" (Ella Fitzgerald) and hit upon "Disraeli Gears," a word play on English racing bicycles which have derailer gears.

Unfortunately the album does not totally hang together, marred by some poor material. They usually compensate for what they lack as composers and songwriters by thorough brilliance of performance. But in some tracks ("We're Going Wrong," "Dance the Night Away" and "Blue Condition," among them), the material is too pale to support the heavy instrumental work which makes Cream such an overwhelming trio.

"Strange Brew" stands out as the most complex song and rather an unusual one in that Eric uses reverb—to stunningly mean and sensual effect—and it is really very far away from the usual blues stylings for which he has been noted. In some places in the song, it sounds like the guitar has been triple-tracked.

"Sunshine of Your Love" (an incredibly strong number) and "Tales of Brave Ulysses" are typical Cream pieces. They are structured on a simple, repeating run of heavily syncopated descending (or ascending) chords. In these songs, and on "Outside Woman Blues," where the chord structure is classic, the beauty of Cream becomes readily evident: Clapton's lines, Baker's dynamics, and, to a slightly lesser extent, Bruce's runs are so simply put together that the listener has no choice but to stand in awe of their precision, grace and exquisite sense of time.

"Swlabr" (pronounced "slobber") and "Take It Back" are also two excellent cuts (these written by Jack Bruce and Peter Brown). Cream's new album is more difficult to get into, and thus more rewarding, than the first one. *Fresh Cream* was recorded over a year and a half ago, at a time when the group was less than two months old. This new LP reflects a more original direction, greater musical sophistication (the guitar is double-tracked throughout) and the polish of a year together.

Despite their recorded shortcomings, Cream happens to be one of the great modern rock and roll groups. If you aren't already hip to it, pick up on *Fresh Cream* (Atco 33-206) and John Mayall's *Bluesbreakers* (London PS 492), a highly polished album which features Eric in a strict blues context.

On top of the music in the new LP, there is the cover done in exploding day-glo style. The photo-montage on the back is reflective of the fact that Eric Clapton happens to be a Nikon-freak.

—JANN WENNER
1-20-68

WHEELS OF FIRE
Cream
(Atco SD 2-700)

Cream is good at a number of things; unfortunately songwriting and recording are not among them. However, they are fantastic performers and excellent musicians. Their latest recording, *Wheels of Fire,* a two-record set inside a silver jacket, proves all this.

One record is subtitled "In the Studio." The set begins with a Jack Bruce original, "White Room," which is practically an exact duplication of "Tales of Brave Ulysses" from their *Disraeli Gears* album, including the exact same lines for guitar, bass and drums. The lyrics are not much to speak of and it's very difficult to imagine why they would want to do this again, unless of course, they had forgotten that they had done it before. The Sonny Bono-ish production job adds little.

"Sittin' On Top of the World," a Howlin' Wolf song, is a fine slow blues, done much closer to the original than the familiar speeded-up version by the Grateful Dead. The song is a good vehicle for Clapton, but that's about it. Wolf's ballad-style singing and melody is far superior to Bruce's. (Those interested in comparisons might want to pick up Wolf's *Real Folk Blues* LP on the Chess label, and compare the two, and then compare that comparison to what the Electric Flag did with Wolf's "Killing Floor," also on the same record. The Flag wins.)

"Passing the Time," a soft sad-circus tune with various instrumental paraphernalia thrown in, is a stone bore. The transition from verse to chorus is absolutely absurd. Ginger Baker stands out on glockenspiel. Of all of Jack Bruce's compositions in this release, only one of them is good, "As You Said." The structure is thoughtful and pleasant. Clapton is totally absent from this cut; Ginger Baker uses only his high hat and Bruce plays acoustic guitar and cello. The way they play back and forth and with each other, each on the melody together, is musicianship worthy of their reputation.

"Pressed Rat and Warthog," a Ginger Baker poem recited to a good background of drum rolls and Clapton's chording, is a track open to individual taste. It's nice, but not what you want to get the album for. The trumpet solos spoil whatever mood was trying to be evoked by their superfluousness and obviousness.

It is unfortunate that the group chose to do "Born Under a Bad Sign," that fine blues that Booker T. Jones wrote for Albert King. King's guitar solo can hardly be improved, although Clapton does do it with his own style. The real mistake is that Jack Bruce doesn't have a good voice for blues, but he chooses to try it out on one that is currently popular in an exceptionally fine original version. His throaty breathing is just plain *wrong*. Ginger Baker also ought to learn that knocking on a cowbell and woodblock does not make a song funky.

There is really only one good side to come out of the studio, and that is "Politician," a track which really gets to the heart of Cream's very real problem. Because only rarely do they have a good original song to work with, their standard procedure is to put a strong rhythm and chord structure behind it and sort of recite the lyrics, spoken almost rather than sung because there is no melody. The trouble with this studio LP is that confronted with this problem—and their predilection to use miserable originals rather than revive a good blues—they have choosen to add layers of superfluous instrumental work. This is particularly ironic in that Cream is the group that initiated the concept of a trio with only the three essential instruments really commanding a piece.

What makes "Politician" the most successful is that, although it is not a song of much merit, they don't muddy it with a lot of meaningless studio garbage, but use the studio to overdub two more guitar parts. In "Those Were the Days," half of it is studio garbage and the other half is the driving drum-bass-guitar combination.

Disraeli Gears had this same problem of paucity of material. In that previous release they had three good originals, used a few good blues, and for the rest of it wailed with only three instruments, so that despite the lack of good original material, it was still fine listening. It took only four days to do *Disraeli Gears* "from stem to stern," as their producer, Felix Pappalardi, has put it, and several weeks for the studio work in their new release. *Disraeli Gears* was far better.

Fortunately, however, the other record in this set is "Live At The Fillmore" where it was recorded several months ago. For one thing, it at least proves

that you can do an excellent live recording of a rock and roll group (something, amazingly enough, none of the San Francisco groups have yet done, despite the popular belief that their sound is designed for live performances).

By and large, the live performance is excellent. Jack Bruce is not very good with a harmonica and it amazes me why he plays it at all. His solo on "Traintime" is loudly amateurish. If they had dumped this cut and put in three of the studio sides ("Sittin' On Top of the World," "As You Said," and "Politician"), we would have one really fine record instead of a set that is 1¾ good and 2¼ mediocre.

"Toad" is a fine number; the live performance is much better than the previously recorded studio version. Here Clapton really displays his superlative chording and rhythm abilities. Ginger Baker's long drum solo is pretty good, on the whole. His tendency to be sloppy is not evident, and he gets moving quickly and sustains the tension well (though he nearly loses it once when he seems to have momentarily choked and come out of it with a few repetitive minutes).

The really fine side of this whole business is the one with "Crossroads" and "Spoonful." This is where Cream really shines because it is where they are at: live, without superfluity of any kind, and into the blues. Clapton is a much better blues singer than Bruce, and his vocal on "Crossroads" is a relief. The tune is Clapton's showpiece, and he does it just like he's supposed to. It's far and away the best cut on the album.

"Spoonful" only really gets going about a third of the way into it. The only criticism I have about this cut is that Jack Bruce's bass-playing is much too busy when he should be the bottom of the sound. On the other hand, he and Clapton really move. The way they do it as a trio is excellent: Clapton and Bruce get going into their "rolling and tumbling" groove, making it madly through the record while Ginger Baker is playing vertically, walking along at just as mad a clip. This is the kind of thing that people who have seen Cream perform walk away raving about and it's good to at last have it on a record.

Anyway, the whole bundle comes in a double-fold packet with this exploding, psychedelicized imitation Saul Steinberg (of the *New Yorker*) cartoon mural on the cover and a totally tasteless Ken Kesey-ism on the inside.

The album will be a monster.

—JANN WENNER
7-20-68

GOODBYE
Cream
(Atco SD 7001)

"What a Bringdown." The last title of (probably) the final Cream album serves as a capsule summation of *Goodbye* and, indeed, the whole Cream mess. Certainly Jack, Eric, and Ginger deserved a better fate.

Goodbye is not a very worthwhile album. Critics will probably tear it apart, while even bonafide Cream Freaks will have to be a little disappointed. It's like the once-famous tycoon who dies an anonymous pauper; it's just a bad way to go out.

The studio version of "I'm So Glad" from *Fresh Cream* is far superior to the live one. What melody the song had is lost as Jack and Eric get involved in a shouting match. "Politician" wasn't an overly brilliant song in the first place, and the live recording doesn't improve upon the original version. "Sittin' On Top of the World" is the best of the live cuts; it is dominated by Jack with a convincing vocal and a creaky bass. Eric comes in with a flash of guitar at the end; it all fits together tightly.

As for the studio cuts, they are plagued with the same fault which hindered *Wheels of Fire*. Cream was best at playing blues; however, none of the stuff they wrote was blues. Hence, whether or not they work depends largely upon the taste of the individual. If you're a fan of pure, simple blues you won't like these; however, if you can appreciate a few studio effects, they'll be quite listenable.

A double-tracked vocal helps Eric on "Badge," while a guy named L'Angelo Misterioso adds rhythm guitar. Felix Pappalardi plays piano and mellotron on "Doin' That Scrapyard Thing." And Jack Bruce abandons his bass guitar for piano and organ on "Bringdown."

There's a little nostalgia here; buy the record, listen to it, and hang the poster on your wall. And shed a quiet tear—not for Eric Clapton, Jack Bruce, or Ginger Baker, but for Cream. Goodbye.

　　　　　　　—RAY REZOR
　　　　　　　4-5-69

TRUTH
The Jeff Beck Group
(Epic BN 26413)

The album that catapulted John Mayall & Eric Clapton to fame, *The Bluesbreakers with Eric Clapton,* was a special one. It hipped the U.S. to two good blues interpreters, held a fresh approach to the blues, and was performed by good musicians all around. Two months ago everyone was saying "Jeff Beck's in town and you must see his group . . . blah, blah, blah."

It was an unnerving experience to hear the Beck group. I had to leave after three numbers. The band was blowing changes, the bass player was losing time, Beck was uncomfortably and bitingly over-volumed, the singer was doing deep knee-bends holding the mike stand like a dumbbell (original, but so what). It didn't make a hell of a lot of sense to me.

When his album came out, I expected to hear England's revenge for Blue Cheer or Jimi Hendrix and his Electric Period. Not a chance. This album is quite another story. It's called *Truth*.

I wonder what is the truth: the record or what I saw that night? This remains to be seen. However, this album is a classic, much the way the Clapton-Mayall album is. *Truth* is probably the current equivalent of that album.

The album opens with a considerably reworked version of "Shapes of Things" and it is more successful than the original *except* for Beck's solo. I believe the solo on the Yardbirds record (by Beck) to be one of the classic guitar soli on a pop record. I was hoping he would top it. The singing (Rod Stewart) is just great and many will now realize just how impotent a singer Keith Relf really was.

After a "Strange Brew"-ish opening, "Let Me Love You"

gets into a Mayall-Clapton "Little Girl" structure with an honest and relaxed feel. Beck sounds really comfortable here. The bass line (Ron Wood) is as correct and tasteful as could be for this particular groove. The ending is beautiful.

Tim Rose's "Morning Dew" comes in for a good turn next. Most covers of this song have been quite good and it's probably a credit to Tim's original, which gave everyone a lot to work with. It sounds like they phased Beck's "wah . . . wah" without moving the frequency to give it a close-up sound (like the vocal on "Punk's Dilemma" by Paul Simon). Bonnie Dobson would be proud of the occasionally faded-in bagpipes on this cut. The piano playing by Nicky Hopkins is quite good.

On "You Shook Me," no credit is given the organist or the pianist, but the organ is up front and slows the groove down a great deal. Beck plays his our-de-force (sic) on this cut. The close of the first side and a highlight of the album is "Old Man River." A very orchestral beginning featuring tympani gives way to a Percy Sledgeish track and vocal. The tympani are a bit overbearing after a certain point, and you wish "you know who" hadn't gotten hung up with them at the session. The singing is gorgeous and actually in order not to repeat myself, the singing is first-rate throughout the album. It was not half as groovy in person however, which might tell the story of the Jeff Beck Group's "fame" in the coming months.

An acoustical "Greensleeves" opens side two. It's not very impressive. B. B. King's bastardized "Rock Me Baby" called "Rock My Plimsoul" uses a quarter note triplet turnaround which is very effective and the track bounces around like a pinball machine. Beck sounds a lot like Hendrix on this. "Beck's Bolero" is on here. It's a B-side from one of his old singles and it's a chapter in a book that includes "Jeff's Boogie" and his other instrumentals. Beck is actually a lot better than Clapton at playing four guitar overdubs and fusing them. Hendrix is better than both of them; he does it all at once.

"Blues Deluxe" is a seven-minute jam. Supposedly "live" (it sounds quite studioish) it slugs along and sounds like any other blues by a competent group. Nothing special. "I Ain't Superstitious" starts off like a Yardbirds record but gets into Beck's new groove. He does dog's barking with his wow-wow pedal, changes tempos and just generally eases around Stewart's lucid singing.

As a group they swing like mad on this record. It remains to be seen what will happen to them in person. I hope the public is honest enough to make them work out.

—AL KOOPER
9-28-68

BECK-OLA
The Jeff Beck Group
(Epic BN 26478)

This is a brilliant album, dense in texture, full of physical and nervous energy, equally appealing to mind and body. There is a guiding intelligence which enables these five excellent, assertive musicians to work with and not against each other. The group benefits from the addition of Nicky Hopkins, the perfectionist rock pianist (although his playing is sometimes over-shadowed by the electrical *sturm und drang* around him, something of an occupational hazard for pianists). Ron Wood's very prominent bass provides the rhythmic background of the album, and Tony Newman's drumming is solid and wonderfully varied, especially on "Spanish Boots" and "Plynth." Rod Stewart's voice is a little high and raspy, but this is a matter of personal taste; the singing itself is emotive, displaying a good grasp of blues-rock singing technique. The rasp, in fact, is somehow appropriate; it's really the vocal equivalent of electric distortion.

Beck himself, of course, is the star. His playing doesn't quite have the excellence and logic of Clapton, but his ideas are unsurpassed. Outside of Jorma of the Airplane, Beck plays the most unpredictable guitar lines in rock, yet manages to combine them with a heavy blues feeling. He is capable of enormous speed and precision, yet his technique is almost always in service to a fertile, bizarre imagination. Listen to the eastern, Arab quality of his playing on the Yardbirds' "Heart Full of Soul" and "Over Under Sideways Down." Beck miraculously manages to adapt this quality to a straight blues —the most obvious case being "Let Me Love You" on *Truth*— a very unlikely fusion.

Much is made of Beck's egotism (in concert he will interrupt a song to play, by himself, Earl Scrugg's "Beverly Hillbillies Breakdown"), but really, he has the resources to support it.

Truth, the other Beck album, contained individually outstanding cuts, particularly some ingenious reworking of traditional blues, but the entire album was not so much good or bad as patchy. "Greensleeves" and "Old Man River" came across as fillers, and another cut was an old B-side. *Beck-Ola* has greater aesthetic unity, but the problem of working up material still remains. The new album has only seven cuts (five of which are original) and a playing time of under thirty minutes.

Beck-Ola includes two oldies, "All Shook Up" and "Jailhouse Rock." While Beck throws in a little new-fangled feedback on the latter, the original echo, sounding very campy by now, is preserved for Stewart's voice. This cut contains the strongest vocal performance of the album (Stewart's best singing altogether is on a very soulful number called "Drinking Again," which for some reason is not on the album). The Beck Group's "Jailhouse Rock" boils with all the virulence the Fifties could muster. There's a change of pace with "Girl From Mill Valley"—a lovely, wistful gospel tune written by Hopkins, which towards the end teeters unfortunately on the edge of Mancini-land. The addition of a vocal part would have made it even better.

The last cut, "Rice Pudding," is teeming with ideas. There's lots of rhythmic interest and a driving, syncopated riff which is returned to regularly as if for recharging when the semi-improvisations start to wear thin. There is the same kind of mood control, even metabolic control, which the Stones displayed on cuts like "The Last Time." In the middle of the finale, the tape is cut, leaving the listener hanging unmercifully in the group's thrall until the release of the next album.

—BEN GERSON
8-9-69

FLEETWOOD MAC
Fleetwood Mac
(Epic BN 26402)

The Blues has always been popular in England. Performers like Screamin' Jay Hawkins, Howlin' Wolf and even Freddie King and Bo Diddley were stars in England before making it big in their own country. When John Mayall formed the Bluesbreakers it was out of respect and admiration to those performers; and he's stayed with the blues, cultivating a number of fine young blues musicians including guitarists Eric Clapton and Peter Green. After Clapton left Mayall, moving on to form Cream, Peter Green replaced him. Now Green has formed his own group, Fleetwood Mac (along with another former Bluesbreaker, bassist John McVie).

Whereas Clapton expanded onto new horizons with Cream, Green has chosen to remain dedicated to the blues, and on this, their first recorded effort, Fleetwood Mac have established themselves as another tight English blues band—joining Mayall's Bluesbreakers, Ten Years After and Savoy Brown as chief practitioners of blues in England.

Green, like Mayall, has studied the records and performances of Howlin' Wolf, Memphis Slim, Junior Wells and Elmore James carefully.

The piano riffs on "Hellbound on My Trail" are lifted directly from Slim's classic "If You See Kay," but it's done well, if perhaps a little too self-consciously. Fleetwood Mac (the name is a combination of the names of members of the group) know what they're doing, they dig the music they're playing and that's great—but the drawback here is that they don't put enough of themselves into it instead of what they've heard from the original artists.

Green is a more than competent guitar player, and the Mac's treatment of "Shake Your Moneymaker" is just as powerful as the first Butterfield version (on the *Paul Butterfield Blues Band* album). The harp work is proficient in most places but rather weak on "Got to Move," the old Sonny Boy Williamson song. Green's composition "Long Grey Mare" is one of the best cuts on the album, anchored by McVie's strong bass line. The record has a strange, prematurely vintage (if there can be such a thing) sound to it, like an old classic recording made in the late Forties or early Fifties.

Like most modern white bluesmen, Fleetwood Mac try very hard to live the kind of music they play—not picking cotton in the Delta, but maintaining the hard-life blues tradition, gigging at small clubs in Northern England and in scruffy halls in the East End. Their music retains an unaffected rough quality. They play well, and if it sounds a little scratchy at times it's because that's the way they happen to feel at that particular moment. The licks they've copied from other performers are natural enough—it's more of a tribute than an imitation.

The English continue to prove how well into the blues they really are, and know how to lay it down and shove it back across the Atlantic. Fleetwood Mac are representative of how far the blues has penetrated—far enough for a group of London East-Enders to have cut a record potent enough to make the South Side of Chicago take notice.

—BARRY GIFFORD
8-10-68

HEAVEN IS IN YOUR MIND
Traffic
(United Artists UAS 6651)

Stevie Winwood, all of 18 years old, has probably the best blues voice of his generation. If this wasn't already apparent on the two Spencer Davis Group albums released in this country and the other records so far unreleased, and from the monstrous smash song "I'm A Man," then with the R&B tracks Stevie sings on the American release of Traffic's first album, it should be even more so. His voice has matured, acquired new depth and new reaches, a more individual feeling and a greater range in both style and tones.

The albums that feature Stevie Winwood are all pretty much great albums, and *Heaven Is In Your Mind* (or *Dear Mr. Fantasy,* to which the title was changed after the first pressing of the album) is no exception.

Traffic is the group that Winwood formed after he and his brother Muff split the Spencer Davis Group a year ago. Winwood got three other musicians (Dave Mason, guitar and sitar; Jim Capaldi, drums; and Chris Wood, flute and bass) to join him. Together they set out for the country, where they lived for three months in an isolated cottage in Berkshire. (Hence the song "Berkshire Poppies," with all its pleasant references to country life, disgust at the sadness of the city, and "Rainy Day Woman" type refrains . . . leading one to draw hasty, and probably not incorrect, assumptions about what went on in the cottage in the field of Berkshire poppies.)

Just as the group was releasing its first record, and fame appeared imminent, Dave Mason left the group. Not because of any conflicts, just that he didn't want to be famous. He still expects to record and write for Traffic. The American release of the album leaves off two of Dave Mason's songs, but it does pick up all the sides of the two American single releases not on the English LP and the great R&B-styled cut "Smiling Phases," which is one of the best pieces on the album.

"Hole In My Shoe" and "Paper Sun" are the singles which never went anywhere. They are excellent examples of what Traffic, with Mason, is capable of without Winwood's vocals or R&B strength. Both use a sitar, and on "Paper Sun," the sitar lines are phrased much like Jimi Hendrix's guitar. "Hole In My Shoe," has got an almost insane beat and melody, but still they both work very well as songs. They're not as good as the Winwood-styled stuff, but they stand on their own because they are much different. "Dealer" is another one of these, with a gypsy guitar woven around a variety of flute solos. These songs are "comprehensibly far-out."

But the strongest points of this album are where the elements of Traffic's "comprehensibly far-out" and Winwood's great R&B style are combined. "Heaven Is In Your Mind" is one of those, but it doesn't really make it in the way that "Dear Mr. Fantasy," the opus of the album, does. "Heaven" is too scattered in instrumentation and arrangement to be a real grabber. "Mr. Fantasy" has excellent lyrics ("Do anything to take us out of this gloom, sing a song, play guitar, make it snappy;"), the Hendrix riffs again, and attractive guitar solo, soul chorus and accurate crescendos in pace and volume from the bass and the guitar. Winwood does the vocal and gives us some real "British soul."

"Giving to You" is an interesting cut. The members of the group are excellent musicians, and so anything they do is bound to be interesting. Also interesting are the one-eighth level faded segues between tracks and the close to "Mr. Fantasy."

The most successful—or attractive—tracks include "Colored Rain" with excellent lyrics ("Yesterday I was a young boy, searching for my way, not knowing what I wanted, living from day to day;") and an incredibly up-tempo bridge. The drumming here is very well-rounded and precise with little repetition. Also on "No Face, No Name, No Number," Winwood's vocal is exquisite, full of the most restrained passion, the best phrasing and indescribable whispered overtones. "No Name" is also strengthened by classical piano chording and violins.

"Smiling Phases" is the most out and out R&B song on the album, and it is also the strongest song. The reasons have all been given above. Winwood is simply incredible. He has a top group of musicians with him

and they have made an album which, although it needs one unity that time will provide, is one of the best from any contemporary group.

—JANN WENNER
4-27-68

TRAFFIC
Traffic
(United Artists UAS 6776)

Traffic is a group that excels at everything except getting it together. This has been evident not only from the drawn out personnel and touring problems they have had, but also from their records—excruciatingly good in terms of *real* music— but frustratingly plagued with a severe case of what could only be called "loose-endism."

It is difficult to say that there is anything wrong with them or their two records, including their newest, other than that. Every criterion you could think up, they meet—material, performance, creativity, vocals, production, mixing, etc., etc.— yet . . . Living in a cottage in Berkshire may be fun, but it hasn't done what 710 Ashbury did for the Grateful Dead nor what Big Pink did for the Band.

Their new record is a large improvement on their previous LP, the United States version of which you could fairly say was butchered by whoever handles those things at United Artists. (Having decided that they hold one of the potentially hottest acts in the new rock and roll scene, United Artists has put more of a push behind the new LP, and allowed for a nice eight-page insert in the package, but when it gets back down to it, here's what producer Jimmy Miller says in his liner notes to the LP: "And the UA man still thinks that some underground DJ should write the liner notes. It's all a shame!")

To the music: it's superb. Dave Mason is a top-notch rock and roll composer and the Steve Winwood/Jim Capaldi team is equally good. Winwood and Capaldi have a perfect understanding of each other's groove, coming up with material on a level with the Young Rascals' best work. On top of this, they have stunning command of their instruments and voices and the capability of bringing it off in new and fresh ways.

"You Can All Join In" is one of those opening, get-in-the-groove, numbers. It's a fun, very bouncy, and yet a hard Dave Mason number—good tune, good lyrics. Steve's guitar playing is not worth noting for a technical exercise, but he has a superb gift of phrasing and understanding of notes. Mason brings a gift for a very hip naivete to his lyric and his melody. Doing the child-like approach in a very heavy musical setting is what gives this such power as a piece of material.

"Pearly Queen," is a Steve Winwood showcase—he does practically everything except the drums, including bass, lead guitar, organ and vocals. "I bought a sequined suit from a pearly queen." Such English country mysterioso! Tremendously effective mixing in the two bridges, where the quick movement from channel to channel imitates the rhythms of the guitar, all of it ending up in the phantom middle speaker.

Their ability as musicians with any material is phenomenal. One mustn't overlook Chris Wood who is always drifting around somewhere in the middle or on the side with the best sax and flute to be heard in a contemporary rock and roll setting. In fact, Chris Wood is the only musician in the contemporary scene who has added a not-often-used instrument to the group effort in any consistently strong way.

The problem is that although they can each write material in the style of the others, they never form together a single performing and composing unit. Mason does his songs; Winwood does Winwood songs. The performance is Traffic; never the material.

What makes this especially sad is that we may never really hear or see what this combination is capable of. They'll break up first. What makes it so potentially good is that Mason is a gifted writer and Winwood demonstrates time and time again his agility and ability with material that is not R&B in its inception or orientation. He is fully capable of bringing all the technique, style and energy he has learned from soul music to original material in another vein.

"Dear Mr. Fantasy" was an example of that; all the songs on this new LP ("40,000 Headmen" and "Pearly Queen") point in that direction. His piano and bass figures on "Vagabond Virgin" are excellent; the way Wood's doodling on the flute and Mason's Spanish rock rhythm fit right in the new combination at work. Capaldi keeps time like Al Jackson.

After Traffic, in their full four man version, returned from their recent one-weekend tour of the States, Dave Mason left and the remaining three went right into the studios. Maybe this will be the answer.

Steve's vocal talent is, as always, overwhelming. He has matured, and his approach is no longer that of the 17-year-old Ray Charles, but his own powerfully realized original style, shifting easily and dramatically from the singsongy slow material to the grooving uptempo passages, such as those on "40,000 Headmen." His vocal transmits the power because he never really cuts loose when he gets into the fast stuff, always holding that edge of re-

straint on it so that the listener must propel himself forward.

I would like to hear Steve doing the vocal instead of Dave on Dave's song "Crying to Be Heard." It would have given it that last little push so that we would have a great *whole* Traffic piece. The refrains must have been unconsciously written for Steve: " 'Cause there's somebody crying to be heard, and there's also someone who hears every word." This would have been that new combination that would fulfill the promise of Traffic.

It would be pretty obvious and a bit too clever to say that Traffic is the R&B equivalent of the country & western oriented band from Big Pink, but check out the closing song, "Means to an End," and see if this isn't true.

—JANN WENNER
1-4-69

BLIND FAITH
Blind Faith
(Atco SD 33-304B, identical to Atco SD 33-304A)

The year 1969 has not been a very good one for rock and roll. Outside of *Tommy* and the Band's decision to go on tour, we haven't had much to get excited about. But the other arts have suffered as well. Like Jim Morrison in Miami and John and Yoko on their album cover, the "best" of the novel —(*Portnoy's Complaint*), film— *I Am Curious (Yellow)* and theatre—numerous examples, have practically had to jerk off to their audiences in order to draw attention to otherwise-undistinguished products.

Art theories have hypothesized that artists are usually most inspired in times of crisis, that the forces of history push them to greater personal achievements. Perhaps the reason this does not hold true today is that while crisis is one thing, times are getting out of hand. With scientists calmly packing away quart bottles of nerve gas that can kill fifty people with one drop, military helicopters staging air attacks on their own populations, and atrocities bizarre beyond the imagination, the artist, too, must eventually feel the strain. Art suffers at the hands of Reality.

Blind Faith can be viewed as an attempt to jar rock out of these doldrums. The group is based on the idea that if you take three of the best soloists around and form them into a single smooth-functioning unit, the result will be one incredible rock band. Ego conflicts must be kept at a minimum; solos are taken not because someone feels like flashing for a while, but because the song calls for a solo at that point.

The formula works nearly perfectly on this album—when it is followed. The music is phenomenal in places, weak in others. Unfortunately, the weakest song on the album is fifteen minutes long and takes up almost a whole side.

By far the best song is "Presence of the Lord," an Eric Clapton hymn which explains in part how Blind Faith ever came to be. The majesty of the organ even makes it sound like a church song, until Clapton wah-wahs off on a quick solo that's so good it makes me want to apologize for every snide thing I've ever said or thought about him. The first time I heard this song, it brought me out of my listening chair, mouth wide open in awe. It still does. Never has a guitarist said so much so beautifully in such a short time. The solo is so inspirational it can't help but make the lyrics that much more believable.

In fact, it's so good it tends to overshadow two other very fine cuts on the album. "Had to Cry Today" goes through several interesting changes, Clapton always bringing it back to the main theme. The choice of Rick Grech, heretofore almost unknown, as bassist is fully justified by his work on this song. "Can't Find My Way Home," a pleading Stevie Winwood tune, features Ginger Baker's highly innovative percussion and the delightful line, "Well I'm wasted and I can't find my way home."

"Do What You Like" is a fine

five-minute rock song which is destroyed when it is dragged out ten extra minutes by solos for the sake of solos. Baker's lyrics state the Blind Faith formula ("Do right use your head/ Everybody must be fed/Get together break your bread/Yes together that's what I said."), but the music then proceeds to obliterate it. Winwood's solo is the only one worthy of remaining in the song; he is the most consistent musician on the album. Clapton's is perfectly competent, but nothing new or exceptional. Baker confuses quantity with quality; his solo starts out nicely enough, but quickly falls apart despite his insistence on continuing. Poor Ginger is bound and determined to *someday* match the original version of "Toad"; he is, at this rate, destined to retire a very frustrated drummer. The bass solo is sheer self-indulgence.

I don't know what the explanation for this cut is, but I could venture a calculated guess. Atlantic President Ahmet Ertegun was recently quoted as saying, "If we'd known they were going to do this well (on the American tour), we wouldn't have rushed the album." I wouldn't be surprised if this song falls into the throwaway solo rut because Blind Faith didn't have enough new material to fill an album in time to meet Atlantic's deadline, and resolved the problem by extend-

ing a song they already did have. If so, add avaricious businessmen to the list of handicaps the artist must face.

This album is better than any of Cream's and about as good as any of Traffic's. On the basis of the potential shown in the best cuts, and writing off "Do What You Like" as a fluke mistake that won't be repeated, I'm already anxious for the next Blind Faith album. If they ever get it together all at once, rock and roll will never be the same.

—JOHN MORTHLAND
9-6-69

**JOHN BARLEYCORN
  MUST DIE**
Traffic
(United Artists 5504)

ALONE TOGETHER
Dave Mason
(Blue Thumb S 19)

We have before us two inexorably linked albums: *John Barleycorn Must Die* by Traffic, a trio now, continuing their group saga, and *Alone Together* with Dave Mason, formerly one-quarter of Traffic, off on his own trip. They're both good albums, careful, well-played, occasionally brilliant, well-conceived, but neither of them breaks its vinyl bonds and soars.

Take Traffic. "Glad," the instrumental cut which opens the album, has some glorious piano work by Steve Winwood and some inventive, imaginative sax playing by Chris Wood. It's all so perfect, so exquisite and so dull. "Freedom Rider" is much more like it. Wood's flute and Winwood's piano are both extraordinary, and Jim Capaldi's drumming is fine, very sympathetic, but . . . if this train is moving, why isn't the scenery changing?

The best cut on the album is probably the title tune, a traditional English ballad arranged by Winwood for acoustic guitar and flute. Wood's flute is again exceptional, delicate and ornate, and Steve sings the song just right, with an admirable sense of restraint and simplicity. Simple, but it works.

Winwood's two virtuoso cuts, "Stranger To Himself" and "Every Mother's Son," are equally satisfying. Jim Capaldi's lyrics are almost perfect, and Winwood's singing is just stunning, lean and clear. And he is a *good* virtuoso—the guitar on "Stranger" and the organ on "Every Mother's Son" are both powerful and moving. But that kind of control-board masturbation can take the music only so far. Steve Winwood may be the best at it that there is, but it still isn't a very rewarding art form.

Perhaps part of the problem is my high expectations of any Traffic album. This is a good album of rock and roll music,

featuring the best rock and roll woodwind player anywhere and one of the best singers, and maybe the trio is still just getting together again, feeling each other out. *Traffic,* after all, was a light-year jump from *Mr. Fantasy;* maybe the next album will soar again.

In terms of expectations, *Alone Together* is much better. Mason's talent as a song writer remains undiminished, and his easy, fluid voice, long in Winwood's giant shadow, is used to maximum effect.

This is, of course, the marbled LP, a brilliant burst of color spinning on the turntable, the grooves barely discernible so the needle seems to be floating across the record. Maybe the next step could be a little cartoon around the edge of the record, like those flip-the-pages funnies, or a slow inward spiral so you could be literally hypnotized by the record.

The music is vintage Mason, veering here and there towards commercialism but never quite getting there, slick but not offensive. Falling in line with the rest of Great Britain, Mason chose old Delaney and Bonnie sidemen for the session, including Leon Russell, Jim Keltner, Carl Radle and Rita Coolidge, plus old Mother Don Preston. Russell, as always, is much in evidence, and his piano (if it is him—the album doesn't say and we have only internal evidence), particularly on "Sad and Deep As You," is masterful.

The high point of the album is clearly "Look at You Look at Me," a song Mason wrote with Trafficker Jim Capaldi, whose tight, urgent drumming on the cut moves the song along with discretion and skill. Mason's singing is simply superb. The other exceptional cuts are "Shouldn't Have Took More Than You Gave" (Mason is not, between you and me, a great song titlist), which features the best wah-wah guitar since Clapton's initial exposition on "Tales of Brave Ulysses"; and "World in Changes," with Mason's deceptively simple lyrics pulled along by some brilliant organ work.

High commercial potential on the album is represented by "Only You Know and I Know," which has a ricky-ticky rhythm reminiscent of "You Can All Join In." It's really a trivial song (like others on the album, particularly "Waitin' On You" and "Just A Song"), but it will sound great on a tinny AM radio at 60 miles an hour.

But the Mason album, too, is more potential than realization. It too is, in a very real sense, flawless, but, as Paul McCartney is beginning to learn, great music is much better than flawless music.

—JON CARROLL
9-3-70

ARTHUR
The Kinks
(Reprise 6366)

Remember the English Invasion in 1964—Capitol had the Beatles, Epic had the Dave Clark 5, Kapp had the Searchers, London the Rolling Stones, Ascot had Manfred Mann, and Reprise' acquisition was the Kinks. Four guys: Ray Davies —leader, songwriter, vocalist, rhythm guitarist and keyboards; Dave Davies, lead guitarist, second vocalist, and Ray's younger brother; Mick Avory—drummer; and Peter Quaife on bass, now replaced by John Dalton.

The Kinks' image is so strange, a group making it on the fact that they've never made it. The ultimate recording group—that's all they do, they just make records, you never see them but once a year they put out an album—a gift from themselves to their audience. The Kinks' last two albums, *Something Else* and *Village Green Preservation Society* sold a combined total, in America, of 25,000 copies—that ain't very many. I don't know whether people actually don't like their stuff or if they've just never heard it—whatever the reason, somebody's missing something, because the Kinks, since 1964, have been making some of the finest rock music this side of the Stones and the Beatles.

Things like "You Really Got

Me"—really tough, grinding hardrock; and "All Day and All of the Night"—strange, stumbling, go-stop-go tempo; and "So Tired of Waiting For You" —repetition working, monotony makes it: "So tired, tired of waiting, tired of waiting, tired of waiting for you-ooh-oo . . ." Those were three hits in a row they had back in '64 and '65, but from then on it was pretty sporadic: hit and miss, one would make it: "Set Me Free"—while the next record might not even get played: "See My Friends"— the first sitar record in pop music, as Dave had once before been first with the fuzz-tone on "All Day and All of the Night," before Keith Richard and "Satisfaction." These cats are not lightweights, they are heavy musical dudes—some of their things just happen to be light-hearted, like "A Well Respected Man," the first of Ray's little social stories. Or "Dedicated Follower of Fashion"—God, remember Carnaby Street?; and then "Sunny Afternoon"—the all-time good-time music song, the Seurat landscape set to a Pabst Blue Ribbon commercial, *Jules and Jim,* 1910.

The Kinks have always done it, one little gem after another, six years of treats: "David Watts," "Waterloo Sunset," the *Face to Face* album, with Ray's coverwork; it's all there, folks, in the world of Ray Davies, the magical kingdom of the Kinks—the Disneyland of rock in its most beautiful form.

Arthur, the Kinks' new movie: such an incredible album, the band in their finest form, turning it in from start to finish, the first time their songs are longer than three minutes, the first time they get into playing for a while and really let it out—their longest album.

Arthur—The Decline and Fall of the British Empire: Ray's England with a brass section.

"Victoria"—the old queen, covered in pomp and circumstance, kicks it off in real shitkicker style—what an opener— a declaration of love for one's mother country. "Victoria" is a statement of fact in the nineteenth century, the Kinks' hymn to tradition—and with such fucking exuberance, man! Dave is yelling his head off, and Mick Avory's drumming is so fine, he's always there, to the Kinks as Charlie Watts is to the Stones. Being English with a vengeance.

"Yes Sir, No Sir"—Ray's voice marches to the cadence of Mick's drums, with Dave tossing in these little licks, refuting the orders. The first of *Arthur*'s two soldier songs—the Army, the need for this incredible order, the reason for constant authority—the generals are insane.

"Some Mother's Son"—you just cry; it's the whole story, from childhood to the battlefield to a grave, for no fucking reason at all; the waste, the absurd waste of a life—Ray's voice puts it across so movingly. The home fires are still burning, mom knows but she can't quite understand . . . "some mother's memory remains."

"Drivin' "—forget the hassles, for three minutes and fifteen seconds tragedy doesn't exist anymore—who's to say what's real. The Kinks take us on a picnic with them, skipping over the hills to John Dalton's bass patterns, listening to the birds, watching the dogs run, falling out on the grass and just dreaming away, mmm . . .

"Brainwashed"—the eight-to-five syndrome, Dylan's "Only a Pawn in Their Game": stay in your place, man, stay in your place. Ray tells it in his pissed-off manner, and Dave's guitar is just like "All Day and All of the Night."

"Australia"—The English-man's promised land, the Kinks acting as travel agents, saying hello to the Beach Boys along the way. The group takes the song sauntering up into the break and then wraps the in-strumental around your head like the Stones did in "Sym-pathy for the Devil," heavy and very different for the Kinks, al-most seven minutes, complete with sax and a wobble board.

"Shangri-la"—Paradise on earth. Starts off slowly, Ray speaking to an old man who's worked his ass off all his life, showing him all the little things he's earned, and then laying into the whole scheme of the man's life, coming back at the end to reassure the poor old guy: it's alright pops, it's OK—you *did* do your best.

"Mr. Churchill Says"—Ray reads Winston Churchill's speech and makes it work! The British people prepare to get together and repel the Nazi hordes, and the Blitz of Britain is on! "The War That Had To Be Fought" —the air raid sounds, it's real now, it's in the streets: "Did you hear that plane flying over-head, there's a house on fire and there's someone lying dead."

"She Bought a Hat Like Princess Marina"—Dreams are nice: the scrubwoman cinderel-la-izes into Mr. and Mrs. An-thony Eden; they go to the Derby at Ascot and after stop-ping off at the local pub and meeting up with the Stones in "Something Happened To Me Yesterday" they're finally es-corted home again, with all the boys in the band just cooking their asses off—listen for Dave's happy yelling.

"Young and Innocent Days" —Such a soft, beautiful hazy hymn to childhood and every-thing that went with it. Dig this: "I look back at the way I used to look at life/Soft, white dreams with sugar coated outside . . ." Someone like Bob

Lind would have said, "Eating from the cake of life . . ."

"Nothing To Say"—Continued from the above; You Can't Go Home Again, Part Two. Such a great statement to rap to your parents . . . after all that time together you've just got nothing to say to each other . . . and finally—

"Arthur"—the poor dumb well-meaning guy, all he wants is just a bit of peace and quiet and a few little comforts; I mean, everybody's entitled to that.

—MIKE DALY
11-1-69

THE KINKS ARE THE VILLAGE GREEN PRESERVATION SOCIETY
The Kinks
(Warner-Reprise RS 6327)

I certainly love the Kinks; it's been fifteen months since I've had a new Kinks album in my house, and though I've been listening to them I've missed that pleasure. Bob played *The Village Green Preservation Society* for me when he bought a British copy, about a month ago, and I've played it twice since it arrived here this afternoon, and already the songs are slipping into my mind, each new hearing is a combined joy of renewal and discovery. Such a joy, to make new friends! And each and every song Ray Davies has written is a different friend to me.

Ray makes statements, he says the sort of stuff that makes you delighted just to know that someone would say stuff like that. "As long as I gaze on Waterloo Sunset I won't feel afraid." "I'll remember everything you said to me." "There's too much on my mind, and I can't sleep at night thinking about it." "There's a crack up in the ceiling." "I'm not content to be with you in the daytime." "The world keeps going 'round." "I'm on an island." "You just can't stop it, the world keeps going 'round."

Oh, wonderful Kinks. They remind me of Erik Satie. "We are the Village Green Preservation Society." The vocal is under-recorded, so you turn up the volume. The bass and drums sound so easy and sure. Everyone's determined; no one's in a hurry. "What more can we do?" Such very fine vocals. The tune, the rhythm, are more of a delight with each verse. Dave Davies' lead lines are never wasted. It would be unbearable that the song's over, but here's another. "Walter, isn't it a shame our little world has changed?" Now why is it Ray's songs always sound like something else, a different something else with each song and sometimes with each hearing? Sure, he's the world's master plagiarist, but it's more than that. It's more a feeling that it's all part of the same thing, it's all music and isn't it nice to run across this melody again? And it is, it's never a repetition, it's always some sort of opening. Ray Davies makes you realize how much there is all around us, waiting to be explored and explored again. Boredom? Every place you've been is a new frontier, now that you're someone different.

It doesn't matter what I say, I'm just happy to be writing about my boys. Ray, Dave, Pete and Mick: I've bought their every album as it's been released, and that's four years now and ten albums, every one satisfactory and worth far more than double your money back. "I'm the last of the steam-powered trains." The song is completely itself, but you can't overlook even on the first hearing the fact that it's Howling Wolf's "Smokestack Lightning." And that makes me smile, good old Kinks, finally recording "Smokestack Lightning," and a good job of it too. A little fancy kineticism in the break, harmonica and bass and lead buildup, just so you know all the old tricks are as relevant to their music as any new tricks they might enjoy could be. They even throw on a " 'Til the End of the Day" ending, and that's not the second time they've done that. Might be the fifth.

Each Kinks song a friend. I really mean that. I can lie in my bed thinking about "Love Me Till the Sun Shines," and I wonder when I'll hear it again, happy at the thought of its existence. Hearing "Big Sky" on this new album, I know we'll get along just fine. "I think of the big sky and nothing matters much to me." This is true, an experience I've shared. "Big sky's too big to sympathize; big sky's too occupied, though he would like to try." What a fine modification of Stephen Crane. And who but Ray Davies would share my interest in the theme of "The Open Boat"?

You can dance to the Kinks. Move your arms up and down as you walk across the room to get a glass of water. Bob your head. Get up and rhumba. I don't know what a rhumba is, but it sounds right, and you know that's all that matters.

Ten albums. Have you ever listened to *The Live Kinks?* It's almost musique concrete. Never has an audience been so unselfconsciously part of the experience. Maybe because nothing could come off of a Kinks record that wasn't part of their unique world-system, or maybe there's some sort of real bond between Kinks-lovers the world over. I mean it's not just some rock group. It's more like a taste for fine wines from a certain valley, a devotion to a particular breed of cocker spaniel. How many people are there who would feel good to know that "Waterloo Sunset" 's Terry and Julie are Terrence Stamp and Julie Christie—that is, they inspired the names, by appearing together in *Far from the Madding Crowd?* How many would understand not feeling afraid, as long as you gaze on that sunset? We're a select few, no doubt, so we may as well love each other and stick together.

This Kinks-love is, I think, something that can be consciously related to the sense of nostalgia, which in turn is something that has less to do with time and things past, and more to do with texture. Texture is sensuous; if style is how you do it, texture is the way you make it feel. Ray Davies' voice, with Dave Davies' guitar just behind it, not only feels a certain way regardless of what it's doing, it also establishes for you a certain relationship to things, which is maybe one reason why *deja vu* is such a large part of the Kinks listening experience. It's not that you heard this before, necessarily, but that you felt this way about something before, the common denominator is that the relationship between A and B is the same as the relationship, with which you're more familiar, between D and F. Looking at a little Maurice Sendak kid looking at a Wild Thing, you identify, not because you felt just that way when you last saw a Wild Thing, but because you know

that exact feeling, you felt just that way when you last saw . . . Whatever it was, Maurice Sendak (or Ray Davies) couldn't possibly know about it. But you two, artist and audience, still share something, a great deal in fact. The texture of that moment. Doesn't it feel good?

Nostalgia is the recapturing of a certain feeling you once had before. How else classify a feeling, save through personal past experience? Ray Davies' songs have a second-order relationship with the way people feel, not necessarily joy but the reaction to joy, if you follow me. Ray's vignettes are wry, ironic—and one suspects it's not just that he's capable of a certain detachment, but also that he can't escape that detachment, it's the way he's always known things are. "People take pictures of each other, just to prove that they really existed." Can you reach through that to a certain sincere sadness? and further through to that most tenuous necessity, affirmation? It is, after all, kind of nice that we're really here.

And when texture is beautiful, as it always is with Maurice Sendak, as it is in the gatefold photo of the Kinks on this new album, as of course it is in all (even despairing) Kinks-music, it's an affirmation in itself, just for things to feel this fine is enough for now. "Sunny Afternoon" is the song

Ray wrote after or maybe during his famous breakdown. It may be one of the songs of the century. Doing nothing, feeling like nothing or worse, you still feel like this song ("The taxman's taken all my dough/And left me in my stately home/Lazing on a sunny afternoon/And I can't sail my yacht/He's taken everything I've got/All I've got this sunny afternoon") and it's one of the highest feelings man has yet recorded in art. Maybe just because it's so real. Or maybe something more than that. ("Help me, help me, help me/Sail away/Give me, two good reasons/Why I ought to stay/Cause I love to live so pleasantly/Live this life of luxury/Lazing on a sunny afternoon.") It's so far down, and raises me so far up. ("In the summer time . . .") Surely, this is greatness.

I'm frustrated now. I was okay, trying to make you feel how good the Kinks make me feel, but I can't pass on greatness. I can't sit here and come up with phrases to argue genius, I can only shout, as modestly as possible, about how deeply I'm affected. I'm thinking, only genius could hit me so directly, destroy me and rebuild so completely, but that's ontology, proving has nothing to do with making you believe. I've never had much luck turning people onto the Kinks. I can only hope you're onto them already.

If you are, brother, I love you. We've got to stick together.
—PAUL WILLIAMS*
6-14-69

THE WHO SELL OUT
The Who
(Decca DL 4950)

This album is fantastic, it has an exquisite sense of humor (songs of the humbly homespun) and consummate musicianship. The cover, of course, is amazingly funny: deodorant, pimple cream, baked beans and the Charles Atlas course, each shot perfectly suited to the character of the person in the group. It's almost too English.

The first thing you are going to see are the commercial plugs and Radio London spots. They take various forms; the cover is the first. The others include segues between the songs which are either real singing house ads from Radio London, or the Who's versions of commercials for other products. Some of the songs themselves incorporate stories of products, for instance Peter Townshend's bitterly funny "Odorono." It is the tale of a young chick singer who has a successful performance, meets the handsome man backstage where the following ensues: "But his expression changed,/

---

* Paul Williams is the former editor of *Crawdaddy!* This is a guest review.

She had seen,/As he went to kiss her face./It ended there, he claimed a late appointment,/She quickly turned to hide her disappointment./She ripped her glittering gown,/couldn't face another show, no,/Her deodorant had let her down/She should have used Odorono."

What makes the song so good—and the whole album so fantastic—is not the surface concept of incorporating commercials but the absolute musical mystery which is used to bring them off. The girl who should have used Odorono is obviously meant to be a laugh, but it is bittersweet laughter. The Who have caught the embarrassing reality of it, and reality is the essence of humor (as is more readily apparent with the Beatles in most everything they do).

The opening song of the album, "Armenia City in the Sky," is one of the best tracks on the album, and one which well illustrates why the Who are among the very best of the contemporary groups. First of all, they have such a firm grasp of the basics of rock and roll that they, like the Beatles, do not stumble when they move on to newer and more creative endeavors in rock and roll; they've learned their stuff and are thus practiced enough to come up with a wholly original instrumental sound.

Within that framework, the Who set various electronic miniatures, including passages of guitar feedback and distortions, variations on a theremin and a tonal puddle from an organ. These are not extended breaks completely outside the structure of the song (which is the mark of a group trying to be experimental with too little real substance), but tight and intelligently thought out placements. And, there are the lyrics: "If you ever want to disappear, just take off and think of this: Armenia City in the Sky."

"Marianne With the Shakey Hands," has a Spanish beat and guitar strum. The barely-beneath-the-surface humor of the lyric and whole Who attitude is reflected stroke for stroke in the music.

"Tattoo" is one of those gems of guitar playing from Peter Townshend, one which shows flawless mastery of rock and roll chording. "Our Love Was Is" has some fine choral work of "la, la, la" simplicity and graceful harmony and mixing, which is another part of the Who's sound. "I Can See For Miles" is a fine demonstration of Keith Moon's insanely strong drumming, perhaps at his recorded wildest, slamming and scattering rim shots all over the place and hitting the bass drum on every beat. It's a curious ecstasy. Townshend's one note fuzz line in one of the inside instrumental bridges is a fine use of this rock and roll cliche.

"Silas Stingy"—the money,

money man, there goes mingy stingy—recalls the mini-opera of their last album. Entwistle blows five seconds of fine french horn. It is a longish story with an organ added which becomes light in its heaviness and heavy in its lightness. "Sunrise" is a strange piece for the Who; the voices call to mind Simon and Garfunkel as well as the instrumental work—a double tracked acoustical guitar.

"I Can't Reach You—Spotted Henry," which opens side two, makes use of a piano. One supposes that some member of the group also plays it, as they are themselves responsible for all the other sounds on the record. Like all the others, the track is characterized by alternatingly soft and hard chord patterns set in interplay with Moon's drums and over John Entwistle's loping bass patterns. The "Spotted Henry" part of the song is the amusing pimple commercial ("This adolescent little fella was nicknamed by his friends 'Old Yellah.'") The underside of the Who is incredibly hard.

—JANN WENNER
2-10-68

THE WHO ON TOUR/ MAGIC BUS
The Who
(Decca DL 75064)

This is not so much a review as a complaint.

Decca is well known as one of the more myopic record companies—"If you liked the Who, you are sure to enjoy Len Barry," read their notes to *My Generation*—and Decca has also gained special fame for the inattention they have lavished on the Who, such as their forgetting to send review copies of some of the group's singles to *Billboard* and *Cashbox*.

But the Who, thank God, made it on their own, and Decca, afraid of losing any of the golden eggs, has released this album in hope of keeping Pete Townshend and Co. in the public eye while the Who work on their *Blind Deaf and Dumb Boy* opera.

Thus we're presented with this random collection of tracks, some superb ("Magic Bus," "Pictures of Lily" and "Disguises"), some good (like "Bucket-T"), some bad (John Entwistle's cuts on this LP just don't touch "Whiskey Man" or "Boris"), and as a real drag, even three repeats from earlier albums.

Why Decca didn't choose to release the live material recorded at Winterland and Fillmore East I don't know (just think—"Summertime Blues," "A Quick One," "Shakin' All Over"), but there is no excuse for the jumble of *The Who On Tour/Magic Bus*. There are over a dozen fantastic cuts by the Who that have never been released on American LP's, most of them singles that received little airplay or were never released at all in this country.

We could have had a classic record, *The History of the Who,* starting with their stone-tough "I Can't Explain," along with their strange version of "I'm A Man," from their first English LP. Then "Substitute," maybe the best song the Who have ever done: "I was born with a plastic spoon in my mouth/The north side of my town faced east/And the east was facing south"—a song powered by really startling harmony and the kind of humor only Pete Townshend can project.

Then "I'm A Boy," an absurd story about our very own rock and roll parents, even crazier than those Leiber and Stoller summoned up for Coasters' "Yakety Yak." Keith Moon fans could have screamed to his falsetto "Barbara Ann"—"Yes," he said at the Fillmore once, "my walls are covered with pictures of the Beach Boys, my heroes . . ."

And then the Who coming through when so many others turned their backs:

The WHO consider Mick Jagger and Keith Richard scapegoats for the drug problem and as a protest against the savage sentences imposed on them at Chichester yesterday, the WHO are issuing today the first of a series of Jagger-Richard songs to keep their work before the public until they are again free to record themselves.

—with their pounding, angry, smashing versions of "The Last Time" and "Under My Thumb," featuring some of the most exciting guitar work Townshend has ever put on record. They meant it, and it shows. Close the LP with "Magic Bus" and "Pictures of Lily," a wonderful song about puberty and sex-without-girls (real-life girls, that is), and you have, and we should have, *The Who's Greatest Non-Hits,* every cut a delight, each one better than before, no matter in what order they might be arranged. Each one uniquely the Who, with gutty harmony and blazing drums and crashing guitars, telling outrageously funny stories, getting made for all of us.

The Who *are* the spirit of rock and roll—and because of that even Decca's clap-trap collection is worth buying, for "Magic Bus" and "Pictures of Lily" and "Disguises." But maybe we all ought to be writing angry letters—the Who deserve better, and so do we.

—GREIL MARCUS
11-9-68

HOLLYWOOD DREAM
Thunderclap Newman
(Track SD 8264)

How anyone will manage to remain a nasty narrow-minded jade in the presence of this unremittingly delightful album defies the imagination.

There's simply no exaggerating the pimply splendor of Speedy Keen's lead voice, a reedy, breathless, disarmingly earnest affair that resides in the No-Voice's-Land between little-boy soprano and grown-up falsetto. There's simply no describing the charm of Andy Newman's keyboard-tickling, which takes the form of a dazzling assortment of boogie-cum-piano-bar chops laid down with unerring clumsiness only in the least likely places (and there without accompaniment, as there's apparently no keeping up with it). Nor could one exude excessively in behalf of wee Jimmy McCulloch's precisely lyrical lead guitar.

Put alternatively, nothing in Thunderclap's music has anything much to do with anything else in Thunderclap's music, the result being that Thunderclap's is at once unexaggerably bizarre and a mightily refreshing rock and roll sound. That sound couldn't in a month of Halloweens be better suited to Speedy's imbecilically catchy little songs, which abound with surreal, nostalgic, surreally nostalgic, and other wonderful lyric sentiments.

Try on for size "Wild Country," in which he glorifies the great outdoors because, simply, it's such a nice place to ball in. Try on both the modest and colossal (the latter featuring all manner of domestic and exotic percussion) takes of "Hollywood," an eminently hummable little ditty in which Speedy laments the passing of bigger-than-life film-stars who used to make him sick, and a very *McCartney*-ish instrumental exploration of this theme, "Hollywood Dream." And the delightfully-dated "Accidents," which here bends the mind with its late 1966 psychedelic ambiguity for nearly ten minutes and contains dazzling piano and kazoo freak-outs by Andy. And, of course, "Something In The Air," which you'll find as emphatic a knock-out on 600th hearing at it was on first. "Pass out the arms and ammo . . .": have you ever encountered a TV revolutionary line that can match that for sheer charm?

To top it all off, they're the oddest-looking bunch you've ever laid eyes upon. Newman, with slicked-back, receding hair, a corncob pipe, and the face of a 40-year-old mailman (in actual fact he's a 27-year-old *former* mailman who used to attend art college with Pete Townshend) is so straight he's surreal, while Speedy's your workaday big-nosed English longhair. And McCulloch is the archetypal moddie, a tiny teen with an adorable toothy smile who a casual groupie of my acquaintance has informed me will find long lines of takers should he ever venture onto the stage of the Whisky A-Go-Go.

—JOHN MENDELSOHN
10-15-70

SHAZAM
The Move
(A&M 4259)

The Move were born in Birmingham, where they began with Tamla-Motown-brand R&B replete with synchronized Miracles-cum-Shadows dance-steps. Roy Wood, their songwriter, lead-guitarist, and mastermind, had been to art school, was naturally musical, and a little reclusive. Carl Wayne, the lead-singer, was glib, worked hard at being suave, and was recruited from a position as an insurance clerk. Trevor Burton, bass-guitarist, wore a perpetual rocker's sneer, drank and doped too much. Guitarist Chris Kefford (whose adoring fans were soon to christen him Ace) came from a family with an illustrious history of psychological irregularities. And Bev Bevan, who played drums, spoke in a sonorous basso, and was quite handsome, had, according to legend, played football with some success and phoned his mother daily.

Eventually they were discovered by Tony Secunda, a London pop entrepreneur with a reputation for shrewd stroke-pulling and bandwagon-jumping, who outfitted them in gangster pin-stripes, encouraged their natural nastiness, and booked them into the famous Marquee, in London, where they proceeded to impress the pop public.

When the style changed and standing in a straight line looking infinitely bored and nasty lost its appeal, the Move took to attacking TV sets, old automobiles, and likenesses of various political baddies with axes at the ends of performances while strippers stripped and strobes flashed. The idea was Secunda's (although Wayne today maintains that it may have been the brainstorm of a mysterious little Russian chap who had read Artaud).

Granted that the whole trip was blatantly second-hand Whoish, it did make the Move famous, didn't it? Why, even we in America heard about it (the Association, on one memorable occasion, are reported to have cancelled out of a gig in preference to sharing a stage with the Move for fear of being assaulted with axes). The Move, mind you, had themselves never been terribly enthusiastic about it, and forever banned such carryings-on from their act as soon as they'd evoked sufficient press hysteria. Wayne explains in retrospect. "It was very dangerous—when we used to stick axes through televisions someone could have lost an eye or something, which would have cost us a fortune."

With the summer of 1967 came *Sgt. Pepper,* San Francisco, and the short-lived age of peaceloveandflowers. Secunda had his boys change from Al Capone suits into kaftans and beads and pose for publicity photos in bucolic meadows. Quite by chance, they had months before recorded a slightly trippy little fantasy number called "Flowers in the Rain," which Secunda, having noted the appeal of such themes, had them release as a single. He decided to publicize it by way of a postcard depicting Prime Minister Wilson in bed with a personal secretary with whom he'd been rumored injudiciously involved, above the caption, "Disgusting, despised, and despicable though Harold may be, beautiful is the only word to describe 'Flowers in the Rain' by the Move." The group balked, but Secunda, fortified by the reassurances of unnamed attorneys, was not to be dissuaded.

"The next thing we knew," reminisces Wayne, "Mr. Wilson, bless his heart, was slapping a writ down on us." The Move, whose prosecutor was made a Lord immediately following the case, wound up handing over all their royalties from the record (which, unsurprisingly, was a smash) to charities of Mr. Wilson's designation.

Thus comfily ensconced Britain's pop reigning Bad Boys circa early 1968, the Move settled down to producing a slow stream of exceptional singles (among them "I Can Hear the Grass Grow," "Blackberry Way," and last summer's "Curly"), storming incessantly up and down Britain, and not getting around to recording a follow-up to their first album, most of which was cut way back in the late summer and fall of 1967.

Wood kept letting his hair grow. Wayne worked at his moustache and sunned himself a lot. Burton, wishing to play more blues than the Move's dedicatedly commercial repertoire allowed, took his nasty leer elsewhere. Kefford, the ultimate singing skull, became impossible to work with and was invited to take *his* eaten-away flesh elsewhere. Rick Price, from another Birmingham group called Sight and Sound, replaced them both. Eventually the Move ceased to be controversial.

Last October they toured America for the first time, if you'd call playing three cities and driving across the country in a crowded rent-a-van a tour. Aside from assorted groupies and some hostile cowboys in

Arizona, no one much noticed them, this despite the fact that, with Cocker & Co., they were the most exciting British act to debut here in 1969.

Upon their return to England Carl Wayne began explaining to the English pop press how the polarity between Wood's and his own personality somehow served to make the group cohesive. No sooner had his remarks been transcribed and set in print than he announced that he was leaving the group to embark on a solo career that would ultimately make the world forget Engelbert Humperdinck.

Then Price announced that he was about to leave the Move to start his own group, which would hopefully—get this—sound like the 5th Dimension vocally and Blood, Sweat & Tears instrumentally. Wood announced that he, Bevan, and Idle Race leader Jeff Lynne were shortly to join a string quintet in forming something to be called the Electric Light Orchestra.

By the time of the subsequent issue of *Disc* everyone had changed his mind again.

Which, finally brings us to the Move's new album, *Shazam,* an honest, happy child of that heavily electronic brand of rock and roll which was born of the Who and later massively popularized by Cream and their imitators.

Those tens of thousands of tours they've endured have paid off handsomely for the Move: their music, both in performance and on this album, is both powerful and intricately structured and flowing. *Shazam* is a brutally energetic rock and roll album.

It opens with "Hello Susie," which, in a substantially different form, was a large hit by a popular British teenybopper act called Amen Corner a while back. The Move introduced it during their American visit with some sarcastic remarks about how they'd restored it to its original state, and surely their own version will make even the hardiest teeny wilt with horror. Devastatingly brutal and containing some absolutely lewd guitar, it's sung with unutterable viciousness by Wayne, who, delivering some of the nastiest growling ever captured on vinyl, sounds like he'd just as soon bite off Susie's head as look at her.

"Beautiful Daughter," a tuneful little pop ditty embellished by a string section that sounds like it just arrived from a McCartney session, is a definite throwback to the first Move album (*The Move* Regal Zonophone SLRZ 1002), where, between the occasional syrupy Paulie imitations are to be found: an hilarious Bev-sung duplicate of the Coasters' comic adaptation of "Zing Went the Strings of My Heart"; the magnificent Duane-Eddy-reverb-guitar-decorated "Fire Brigade"; a great copy of Eddie Cochran's "Weekend" sung by nasty little Trevor with enormous greasy zeal; the charming Gilbert & Sullivan-cum-electricity-cum-acid "Flowers in the Rain"; and five or so lovely helpings of the early Move's catchily simple, vocal-dominated and mildly strident, and distinctively British rock and roll.

In "Cherry Blossom Clinic Revisited," an adaptation of a charming song about confinement in a mental hospital from that first album, the Move show us all their new tricks. Poundingly rocking and energetic, its orgasmic choruses are yanked in by siren-screech guitar-slides from Wood, after the last of which there appears a short acoustic bridge that introduces an amazing series of composed movements that alternately feature a baroque Spanish guitar line in front of Price's stalkingly sinister bass, explosive drumming, and finally a choral repetition in falsetto of the baroque guitar line. The walls of the Whisky very nearly crumbled when the Move performed this one there last October.

"Don't Make My Baby Blue" is a Mann-Weill semi-schlocker which the Move have converted into a stunning display of all the techniques that characterize the most compelling, "heavy" rock and roll. Wood here employs a monstrously ferocious

Jimmy-Pagish guitar tone that he makes work perfectly in the context of the song. He slices the song in half in the middle with a screechingly dissonant wah-wah explosion that will floor you, and then at the end hands it over to Bev, whose drum explosion signals the torrent of sirenish harmonies that end the song.

"The Last Thing On My Mind" clinches it: what the Move here do with Tom Paxton compares quite favorably with anything the Byrds ever did with Dylan. And perhaps not coincidentally, the Move use all the Byrds' tricks, right down to the dense-sounding twelve-string guitar and massive high choruses that will remind you of jets taking off.

Do what you can to prevent this from being the last Move album. Petition Regal Zonophone in England or A&M (who's still sitting stupidly on the first album, afraid to release it). Or write your congressman. The Move must be kept going to give us more albums like this one.

—JOHN MENDELSOHN
5-14-70

SHINE ON BRIGHTLY
Procol Harum
(A&M SP 4151)

Procol Harum is a hard group to review, if only because they have chosen stylistically to place themselves in competition with middle-late *(Blonde on Blonde)* Dylan and the Band *(Music from Big Pink)*; thus Keith Reid can write uncannily like a certain period Dylan (see "Rambling On" on *Shine On Brightly*), and B. J. Wilson often sounds like Levon Helm taught him how to play drums. It has been remarked how much the Band album showed the influence of the first Procol Harum album; it might also be remarked how much the second Procol Harum album shows the influence of the Band album. Perhaps this juxtaposition is unfair—it must be admitted Procol Harum suffers in these comparisons—but Gary Brooker, in spite of his unique style, just cannot match Richard Manuel's vocals, and Robin Trower can't begin to touch Robbie Robertson's guitar playing.

In spite of these limitations Procol Harum is nevertheless quite capable of powerful music when not being wantonly eclectic (note the absurd quote from Rodrigo's *Concierto de Aranjuez* in the middle section of "Skip Softly"). The dilemma of the group is illustrated quite bluntly by "In Held Twas in I," a seventeen minute sonic blitz that ranges from an anecdote concerning a koan the Dalai Lama presumably once delivered, to an electric mass of sorts. Sandwiched in the midst of all this often patent

nonsense is a very moving song, decidedly (and effectively) schizoid, about the "autumn of my madness." "Shine On Brightly" is also a beautifully constructed little song, an effective wedding of lyrics and music.

"Quite Rightly So" and "Rambling On" are nice tracks, while "Magdalene" is certainly pleasant enough. Having said this however, it must be noted that *Shine On Brightly* is not the album one might have hoped for. The Procol Harum's first release was generally more satisfying, especially since this new album displays little in the way of startling growth—the group has apparently chosen to refine their old approach and the musical result, while usually listenable, is not consistently interesting. One question that the album does raise is whether the Procol Harum have the imaginative and musical potential to creatively evolve, and on this score *Shine On Brightly* must remain an ambiguous statement.

—JIM MILLER
12-7-68

A SALTY DOG
Procol Harum
(A&M SR 417)

A Salty Dog is a confusing album. At its best it represents the group's greatest success to date with the brand of rock for which the group is known, at its worst it is both surprisingly mediocre and trivial. The most tenable explanation for this unevenness of quality is that Procol Harum, now produced from within by organist Matthew Fisher and boasting three songwriters where it once boasted one (or one and a half if you wish to consider Fisher's infrequent early contributions), is growing, but not without suffering growing pains.

Three cuts fit comfortably into the familiar Procol mold. "All This And More" is quite reminiscent of "Homburg," although not nearly so good. "The Milk Of Human Kindness" features a sort of torchy (i.e. late Thirties musical-style) guitar line and some nice Procol Harum country funk on the choruses. The best of the three, however, is "The Devil Came From Kansas," which nearly overflows with latent energy. B. J. Wilson here alternates march and bolero rhythms behind gigantic piano chords and a powerful vocal by Brooker.

Each of Fisher's entries is lovelier than the one before. "Boredom"'s gentle calypso feeling is created by some very pretty marimba work (by Fisher) and various exotic percussion instruments. On "The Wreck of the Hesperus" he sounds a little like Paul McCartney. The song's essential prettiness will no doubt be lost on those who, because of its Wagnerian-sounding arrangement and theme (lots of talk of Valkyries here), will dismiss it as pretentious. "Pilgrim's Progress" is even prettier, with a melody gorgeous enough to have been written by a Bee Gee (not meant sarcastically). Keith Reid's introspective, confessional lyrics are backed by a "Whiter Shade of Pale"-sounding organ.

And now to the really magnificent parts. "Too Much Between Us" is the kind of song you can float away on—its background and vocal of marimba and acoustic guitar in a perfectly understated waltz-time are beautifully ethereal. This is probably the best non-mold song Procol have yet produced.

"A Salty Dog" opens with eerie strings and seagulls (and threatens for a moment to become just a bit too luxurious). On the part where the words are: "How many moons and many Junes have passed since we made love?" (my favorite line on the album) the drums come in hard, the strings swell mightily, and Brooker's voice soars excitingly (leaving you so knocked out that you won't even notice the rather gauche strings that start the cycle up again until your third or fourth listening).

This could have been an astonishing album. But where Procol Harum is staying where they've been (especially Trower's recorded guitar work and

Wilson's drumming) they're becoming a bit too predictable, and they're a little awkward in their pursuit of the new directions suggested by Trower and Fisher. Also, Reid's lyrics, which might have served as the glue that unified the diverse sides of the album, are becoming too diffuse, too self-conscious to function in that way. And one can't help but wish that Brooker and Fisher will resist their urge to fool around with string arrangements until such time as they can make them something more than superfluous.

Get it anyway. Its several incredible moments will make it well worth your while.

—JOHN MENDELSOHN
5-31-68

HOME
Procol Harum
(A&M SP 4261)

Procol Harum has undergone some changes since its "Whiter Shade," "Repent Walpurgis" and "Salty Dog" days. Gone is Matthew Fisher, whose Brahms-ed and Bach-ed organ playing was the back-bone of the Procol Harum sound from the outset. Throughout Harum's first three albums Fisher's role lessened more each time—on the last effort he even competed with strings and horns. Chris Copping has replaced him (Copping also replaces former

bass guitarist Dave Knights), but the most important switch in Harum's sound is due to the fact that guitarist Robin Trower has stepped up and is truly playing a lead guitar. On their earlier albums Trower played nothing but endless drone and repetitive filler riffs—here he unleashes an atmospheric, Hendrix-style wailing, screeching assault that successfully replaces the vanished organist. Efforts such as the extended miniepic "Whaling Stories" and "Whiskey Train" are good examples of the transfusion of textures that Trower has brought to Harum's sound. On "Whiskey" he even gets into the blues idiom with no harmful side effects.

Gary Brooker hasn't lost any of his vocal charisma as he alternately sings and talks the lyrics in his emotional, mystical and ofttimes buried fashion. Next to Trower it is Brooker's piano playing that is the crux of the Harum sound and it hasn't changed much—it's just as pounding, arpeggio-ridden and disturbingly melodic as ever. Offset against Trower's guitar the piano is magnified that much more and balances out the dimensionality of that Harum sound.

And let's not forget Keith Reid, whose lyrics are just as fine as ever. True, his themes are still the graveyard, religion-ridden and netherworldly, but his depth and convoluted intensity at times are overwhelming. Highlights here include the violent "Still There'll Be More," the muted Eleanor Rigbyish "Nothing That I Didn't Know" or down to the expansive, image-taut "Whaling Stories" that culminates wondrously in the last four lines, as the song shalimars onto a whole different level of meaning. Reid is the master of the compact line in pop music and we have multifarious examples of it here—from "Watch the book, the page is turning" to "Sack the town, and rob the tower/and steal the alphabet" his sense of reality conflicts not a notch with the classical/rock evocations of the instrumentation.

But Reid still insists on rhyme and in some cases it is his downfall—"Your Own Choice" is too simplistic and unnatural. Maybe some free verse experimentation would be rewarding. And haven't we had enough of these pseudocerebral/Katzenjammer covers for this season?

—GARY VON TERSCH
9-3-70

THE ROD STEWART ALBUM
Rod Stewart
(Mercury SR 61237)

Rod Stewart, lead singer with the off-again on-again Jeff Beck group, has come up with a superb album of his own. Imagination pervades the music, in the choice of material, in the frequent use of beautiful bottleneck guitar work to draw out the subtler aspects of many cuts (Ron Wood is responsible here), and in the range Stewart himself displays on virtually every vocal.

British albums are often over-done, with good ideas transformed into gimmicks; on this record the music sustains itself through innumerable listenings. A bass solo is not an indulgence here but a perfect lead-in to striking piano; the bottleneck is so sparing that you simply hunger for more of that brilliant sound. What is more amazing is that the musicians make their statements with the same sort of friendly sympathy that recently has been displayed only by the Stones and by the three geniuses of Traffic. Their soul is in their timing.

Stewart opens by taking the big risk, with "Street Fighting Man." And, like Johnny Winter's "Highway 61 Revisited," Rod's performance shows no self-consciousness, no worry about the "right way" to do it. He starts in the middle, brakes with a crash, and then a familiar "We Love You" riff on the piano carries the song back to the Stones' beginning, Rod's ending. It's just a fine piece of music, not a cover.

"Man of Constant Sorrow" is next; Stewart's own guitar is up front, while Wood's bottleneck creeps in from the other channel, adding depth to a vocal that is just about the definition of English soul. The richness of this album begins to suggest itself here—this is not just another solid Joe Cocker LP, but something more. You don't hear Ray Charles or anyone else looking over Stewart's shoulder, but an echo of lessons well learned.

"Handbags & Gladrags" clinches it. It will remind most of the Stones' "No Expectations"; the same soft despairing heart-breaking Floyd Cramer-style piano played by Mike D'Abo, and again, the sort of restraint and timing that make the listener wish the song would never end. It's a very sophisticated composition, a brief story that's full of emotion but which never slides into dull sentiment. Like the rest of the songs Stewart is singing here, it's not going to get old.

Stewart's LP is perhaps the only album released this year that reflects something of the feeling of *Beggar's Banquet*, aside from *Let It Bleed*. And, unlike so many of the records of 1969, issued with a flood of hype and forgotten after a dozen playings, this one is for keeps. Many LPs are a lot flashier than this one, but damn few are any better.

—GREIL MARCUS
2-7-70

GASOLINE ALLEY
Rod Stewart
(Mercury 61264)

The music of Rod Stewart helps us to remember many of the small but extremely important experiences of life which our civilization inclines us to forget. Compassion. Care for small things. The textures of sorrow. Remembrance of times past. Reverence for age. Stewart has a rare sensitivity for the delicate moments in a person's existence when a crucial but often neglected truth flashes before his eyes and then vanishes. The amazing character of Stewart's work is largely due to the fact that he can recall these fragile moments of insight to our minds without destroying their essence.

As I listened to *Gasoline Alley* the first time, I found myself saying again and again, "He *can't* understand *that.*" But he does. The tone of his voice and the authenticity of his phrasing let you know that he's doing much more than just singing the required lyrics. "The one who shared just about all he had/In a one sided love affair," he moans in "Lady Day." As he goes on he admits "I get scared when I remember too much" and at the end of the song recognizes that the girl to whom his confession is dedicated is not even listening. I suspect that experiences like this are virtually universal. Ever pour your heart out to someone and then find that he (or she) just couldn't care less? These are the moments Stewart is interested in and he never fails to capture their distinctive colors. It's almost frightening.

"Country Comforts," for example, conveys perfectly the situations, personalities and feelings of rural life. I've been listening to country-rock albums of the recent vintage for some time now, but Stewart's version of this song is the only recording I can remember that awakens in me a genuine nostalgia for the rural life of my own childhood. Old Man Grayson, that stubborn old coot, refuses to use those new-fangled machines in his mill. "It just ain't natch'rl." "He's a horse drawn man until his dying day." And Grandma's really looking fine—well, fine for 84. She asks you if you could come by and fix the barn. You say "yes," but quietly hope that in her senility she'll forget your promise. "Poor old girl, she needs a man down on the farm."

At his best Stewart comes very close to Thoreau's meaning in the early pages of *Walden:* "The mass of men lead lives of quiet desperation."

The two Rod Stewart albums are together the most important listening experience I've had since the Band's first album. His music speaks with a gentleness and depth which seem to heal the wounds and ease the pain. The question of which of the two albums is the better does not interest me in the least. The music and spiritual content of them both is so totally extraordinary that I cannot really separate the two in my mind. *Gasoline Alley* is for me merely the second volume in what I hope will be a continually expanding "Collected Works" of a supremely fine artist.

—LANGDON WINNER
9-3-70

THE AUTUMN STONE
The Small Faces
(Immediate IML 01/2)

Behind the kings of rock and roll stand the workers who make up the boredom and blarney, the fervor and humbug of pop. They are usually dwarfed by it all, and looking back it is surprising how much enjoyable music they have given us. The Small Faces are part of this crowd—they broke up in 1969 after three years of English hits and the most indifferent sort of success in America—and *Autumn Stone* is a final English "Best of" two for the price of one double album, easily available here in the many shops that carry imports. It is very enjoyable indeed.

The Small Faces started as a controllable Who, a hasty group of four mods emerging from the mod movement of 1965. They looked set for a brief, derivative career under an exploitative manager in the time-honored British pop tradition—but they were *real* mods. They had their own ideas and the songwriting and instrumental abilities to pursue them. They remained derivative, they jumped on every bandwagon, they never did anything startlingly original, but the style of their imitations wasn't show-biz-there's - money - to - be - made - in-this, but London-mod-hey-man-that's-cool. They had a naive eagerness to try everything without understanding anything, and the results had their own appeal.

Their drug song, "Itchycoo Park," is ridiculously coy, but it does capture the joy of getting high. Their folk-rock song, "Just Passing," has wretched words but it is nicely innocent; and even their most arty song, "The Autumn Stone," is saved by its corniness. Whatever they tried to do, in the end their real strength came through. Their songs are all high-powered dance tunes straight from the mod discotheques.

This is a very English record. The Small Faces didn't look very far for their influences. Steve Marriot, their lead singer, has a very powerful voice (one of the great sights of English rock and roll used to be tiny, neat Steve Marriot opening his mouth slightly and

screaming like a dervish) but he had no idea what to do with it and so turned to Steve Winwood for inspiration. It's obvious as well that the band never gave up trying to catch the Who. In the end, one can pick out all the elements of the British pop scene 1965-1968, from Herman's Hermits to Geno Washington.

The Small Faces never really made it. They lacked an evil genius like Andrew Loog Oldham to discipline and mold their obvious talent for his own ends (the beautiful, soaring chorus of "Afterglow of Your Love" makes one wish a Phil Spector had got hold of Marriot's voice and given it *real* power). By themselves the only place the Small Faces could decide to go was after everyone else and they never caught up. But their pursuit was always innocent and enthusiastic, very happy and defiantly infectious—the essence of good rock and roll.

—SIMON FRITH
3-7-70

FIRST STEP
The Small Faces
(Warner Brothers 1851)

The Small Faces are now into a more sophisticated and mature commerciality. The addition of Rod Stewart as vocalist and Ron Wood on lead guitar has altered the substance of their music noticeably. The three remaining Faces—Ian McLagen, organ; Ronnie Lane, bass; Kenny Jones, drums—all are very good instrumentalists and coupled with Stewart and Wood they make a fine rock band. The basic weakness with the album is that although the music is original, it is also highly derivative. The final effect leaves one considerably less excited than the lineup promises.

They are slick, playing tight changes and neat licks all the way through the record. McLagen's organ work is competent, more so than many better-known rock organists, and Ron Wood's guitar playing is economical and fluid. Though he played with Jeff Beck on bass, Wood has done sessions with Donovan (among others) as a guitarist and has recorded with a group called Santa Barbara Machine Head. He is far more proficient than he is thrilling; nowhere on the album does he play with any abandon.

Rod Stewart, on the other hand, sings his butt off. His raspy, sore throat voice lends itself well to the Faces' music. But Stewart's value lies in his unpredictability. His phrasing and delivery are filled with the unexpected.

The songs on the album are varied and come from all kinds of places. They do Dylan's "Wicked Messenger" with a bland but precise arrangement.

Lane wrote and sang a funky traditional-type folk song ("Stone") featuring Stewart on banjo, Wood on harp and himself playing guitar. "Around the Plynth" is a fine bottleneck workout for Ron Wood. Unfortunately, stereo "effects" on this number almost ruin it. "Pineapple and the Monkey," a Ron Wood instrumental composition, would sound exactly like Booker T. if it weren't for the tone of the guitar.

The Small Faces play with more control than soul. They know exactly what they are doing and they do it well, as good musicians should, but the precision and purity of their sound seems a little sterile, and they lack the drive and power to make their music work without subtleties.

—JOEL SELVIN
5-28-70

DAYS OF FUTURE PASSED
The Moody Blues
(Deram DES 18012)

IN SEARCH OF THE
   LOST CHORD
The Moody Blues
(Deram DES 18017)

One of the several English groups that has survived more or less intact since the days of the Beatles is the Moody Blues, who take their place next to the Rolling Stones, Hollies, Kinks, Zombies, and Who in this regard. To be sure, this is a mixed bag of company, but it is certainly surprising to what extent the old English groups still share certain qualities that mark them off from their American counterparts.

The Moody Blues are part of the English rock group family that includes as nearest relatives the Hollies, the Beatles, and the Who. All these groups give prominence to their vocal work, and all still adhere to the basic English rock instrumentation (guitars, bass, drums, occasional organ or piano) with occasional orchestral augmentation. Their historical lineage may be traced back to the American rock and roll (not blues) of the late Fifties. Granted these not insignificant similarities, the English groups have each by and large developed their own stylistic character.

The Moody Blues, on the evidence of their most recent recordings, have matured considerably since "Go Now," but their music is constantly marred by one of the most startlingly saccharine conceptions of "beauty" and "mysticism" that any rock group has ever affected. To be specific: *Days of Future Passed* claims to "have extended the range of pop music," finding "the point where it becomes one with the world of the classics." This is pure nonsense.

There are some quite fine rock tracks on *Days of Future Passed* ("Tuesday Afternoon" especially), but all of these songs have next to nothing to do with "the classics." In any case "the classics" for the Moody Blues apparently are Rimsky-Korsakov, Brahms, David Rose, and Elmer Bernstein; the London Festival Orchestra is generally used between tracks to play Hollyridge Strings changes on the rock compositions in the album. The whole execution of the album is so perverse that the only real surprise is the discovery that between the movie soundtrack slush there is some quite palatable rock which makes no compromises, even in the direction of orchestral accompaniment—as a matter of fact there is almost none on the rock tracks. Then why the Festival Orchestra? Why the hideous spoken introduction and conclusion? If this crap is supposed to be breathtakingly beautiful or the aesthetic raison d'etre of the album, God deliver us back into the hands of prosaic rock, like "Peak Hour," or "Forever Afternoon," or "Nights in White Satin." Or even the triteness of "Twilight Time."

This must remain the real curiosity of *Days of Future Passed*: what is obviously a fine, tight English rock group has chosen to strangle itself in contextual goo. Ironically almost every one of the rock tracks has something to recommend it—but what might have been a quite capable, even exciting, album is willfully turned into something musically akin to Milo's chocolate cotton. Which is too bad.

If *Days of Future Passed* is the Moody Blues being self-consciously "beautiful," *In Search of the Lost Chord* is the Moody Blues being self-consciously "mystical." Too bad again. But let us be charitable: we will say nothing further of the seven minute closer on the album, "Om." Nor the opening "Departure." The rest of the album is very well produced and generally tasteful; John Lodge's "Ride My See-Saw" and Ray Thomas' "Dr. Livingstone, I Presume" are both well done, solid rock tracks. On the other hand we have "House of Four Doors," an overblown piece of literal psychedelia with four (count 'em: four) squeaky door sound effects sandwiched in between some rock mood music.

The dilemma of this whole album is illustrated by "Legend of a Mind," featuring a nifty lyric about "Timothy Leary's dead." If you don't listen to the words it sounds like a better than average rock song with interesting flute work by Ray Thomas and appropriately swooping cellos—but then there

are those insane lyrics that keep bombarding you with Timothy Leary's name. Mike Pinder's "The Best Way to Travel" sounds indebted to the Pink Floyd, while the inevitable sitar pops up painlessly on Justin Hayward's "Visions of Paradise." Whoever does the vocal on "The Actor" and "The Word" (they run together) does one hell of a job; beautiful, unabashedly emotional singing.

So what are we finally to make of the Moody Blues? The conceptions of both of their recent albums have been disastrous, but in both cases some interesting, listenable music was surfaced. Their writing is not consistently imaginative, but it is not especially derivative either; the singing is consistently good and the arrangements are effectively executed with little reliance on studio musicians. Hopefully next time around the Moody Blues will leave their London Festival Orchestra and Yantra at home and get together a straight-ahead, no bullshit album of rock; judging from even these albums they should be quite capable of doing this and, furthermore, doing it well.

—JIM MILLER
12-7-68

Soul

Here is the voice of the black man, the wellspring of the greatest popular music in the history of man. Like jazz before it, rock and roll comes directly from the music and experience of the Negro in America. Originally recorded as "race" music during its days as blues, it was later called "rhythm and blues" when it began to cross over and attract a substantial white audience in the postwar era—in *all* its variety, rock does not exist without it.

In the sixties, it became known as "soul music." Except for a few words about R&B in the fifties, this chapter is a quick look at a few major events in soul music in the late sixties. The selection is incomplete at best, but gives us nonetheless a look at several of the most important figures and sounds that were heard.

ROOTS

HISTORY OF RHYTHM & BLUES
Various Artists
(Atlantic SD 8161-4)

Volume 1—*The Roots* 1947-52; Volume 2—*The Golden Years* 1953-55; Volume 3—*Rock & Roll* 1956-57; Volume 4—*The Big Beat* 1958-60.

The term "rhythm & blues" first came into general usage as a postwar euphemism for what had been known as "race records." The Negro audience that bought these records had, through defense plant prosperity and the broadened outlook occasioned by migration from Down Home to the industrial centers of the North, become sensitive to the patronizing overtones of the earlier designation. But the music it demanded was if anything "blacker" and in terms of the European (for which read "white") tradition, more vulgar and less schooled, than the classic, country and early urban blues (Bessie Smith, Robert Johnson and Leroy Carr are, respectively, examples of these styles) that appeared on the old Okeh, Bluebird and Vocalion labels during the Twenties and Thirties.

Unlike Okeh and the others, subsidiaries of recording industry giants, the companies that produced rhythm & blues were —and for the most part still are—small and independently, sometimes Negro, owned— Chess-Checker, Atlantic, King, Savoy, etc. Atlantic, one of the pioneers in the field, has gone into its vaults to compile this 57-cut history.

The collection's title would be more appropriate if it read "History of R&B on Atlantic Records." The notes maintain the pretense that this is a complete and accurate representation of the style and period; if they had dropped the hoke and included at least the names of other important vocal groups, singers and instrumentalists the series would be not only more honest but less flawed a "document" than it now is.

I suppose it is too much to ask, given the competitive, produce-it-at-minimum-cost and therefore shortsighted nature of the record business, for a truly inclusive anthology of this or any other Twentieth Century (i.e. post-Edison) music, with sides by artists still under contract to—or whose output is

still the property of—disparate labels: wouldn't it be a gas, though? ("You'd think he'd be satisfied with Joe Turner, Ray Charles, the Coasters, Drifters, Ravens, Orioles, Ruth Brown, Clyde McPhatter and Carla Thomas.")

It's not that I doubt these are a good selection of Atlantic and Atco releases. Especially in its last two volumes, covering the late Fifties when those labels dominated the scene, the *History* resurrects some memorable and important sides. But there's a lot more to the music than the novelty numbers, popular songs with a Negro accent and occasional heavily-arranged blues that we find here. *18 King Size Rhythm and Blues Hits* (Columbia CS 9367), compiled from King Records releases, gives a much broader musical spectrum in one-third the number of tracks. Though some of the songs are less than exciting, inclusion of material like "Sixty Minute Man" by Billy Ward & The Dominoes brings this album closer to the down the line R&B feel.

Many late Forties records, for example, were so explicitly sexual in their lyrics and overall sound that it would be pussyfooting to call them suggestive. Yet the closest things to "Baby Let Me Bang Your Box," Dinah Washington's "Long John" or "I've Got a Big 12-Inch . . . Record of the Blues" that appear in the Atlantic collection are "Young Blood" by the Coasters and "Smokey Joe's Cafe" by the Robins, both of them Leiber-Stoller tunes that come absolutely clean in the clinches.

Or, with so many fine saxophone solos sandwiched in on these numbers (King Curtis on "Yakety Yak," Gene Barge on Chuck Willis' "C. C. Rider," and assorted unidentified heroes on the Ruth Brown and Joe Turner cuts), why are the only two instrumentals by Frank Cully and Tommy Ridgeley? It is as if the classic R&B tenor player—Big Jay McNeeley, whose acrobatics are described below, and the others, similar in sound but less visually dramatic: Louis Jordan, Joe Houston, Lockjaw Davis, Vido Musso—lying on the floor, kicking his legs in the air as he strips off his jacket and shirt and all the while blowing repeated notes and honking phrases until he, his horn and his audience reach a collective climax that even by today's Jimi Hendrix standards could hardly be called ersatz, it is as if those men, who headlined the R&B shows they appeared in, those masters of showmanship who could make the same "battle of the bands" seem like a be-all-or-end-all showdown in town after grimy town, had never existed.

There is likewise no mention of Earl Bostic, the late alto saxophonist and bandleader. His band, in which John Coltrane played during some lean years, was constantly on tour of nightclubs, dance halls, etc. of the Great American ghetto —primarily in the Northeast and the South—during the period these records span. His LPs were steady sellers, his singles were on jukeboxes everywhere and he attracted a sizable white following, but . . .

The most glaring omission involves straight blues. True enough that Joe Turner is a Kansas City blues shouter who first came to prominence in the company of boogie-woogie (heavily rhythmic "eight to the bar" blues) pianist Pete Johnson and that Ray Charles is a phenomenally talented stylist and innovator whose wedding of the blues to the inflections and choral techniques of gospel singing was the genesis of the Stax and Motown approaches to "soul music."

But to speak of rhythm and blues without taking note of B. B. King, not to mention Bobby Bland, Wyonie Harris, Jimmy Reed, the early, electrified Lightnin' Hopkins, etc., is left-handed to say the least. The Atlantic catalog itself could have provided some exemplary material by T-Bone Walker and Champion Jack Dupree; even the Ray Charles items included are not his bluesiest. And where is Jimmy Witherspoon, also from Kansas City but better-voiced and more sophisticated than Turner, who, though lately associated with jazz, was an R&B presence to be reckoned with around 1950? What about the "Queen of the Blues," Dinah Washington?

One thing the *History* does document very clearly is the extent to which rhythm and blues performers found themselves "fattening frogs for snakes." By this I mean the situation where a white group covered a release and found acceptance—and the lion's share of the money—in the popular music market. LaVern Baker's "Tweedle Dee" and Joe Turner's "Shake, Rattle & Roll" were well-known victims of this process, but did you ever think about what the Weavers did to Leadbelly's "Goodnight Irene," which appears on Volume 1? This routine has pretty much petered out—and has even been reversed in such instances as Otis Redding's version of "Satisfaction"—but it was a harsh fact of life ten or fifteen years ago.

One additional note. These records were remastered, largely from old 78s and 45s, and supposedly "enhanced for stereo." After listening to them on three different sound systems, my conclusion is that enhancement is where you find it: a lot of the cuts sound about like they would if you found the original 78 in the bargain bin of a local record store.

There are any number of outstanding songs on these records. Besides those already mentioned, "Drinking Wine Spo-Dee-O-Dee" by Sticks McGhee, Ruth Brown's "Mama, He Treats Your Daughter Mean," Charles' "Greenbacks" and Ben E. King's "Spanish Harlem" are almost Chekhovian slices of life . . . with music. The best thing to do is check the songs on each record. There are bound to be some you thought you'd never hear again —and others you hoped you never would. Volumes 1 and 3 are closest to being essential.

—JERROLD GREENBERG
4-6-68

RHYTHM & BLUES, THE END OF AN ERA, VOL. I
Various Artists
(Imperial LP 94003)

> *Keep your feet on the floor,*
> *Because blues and rhythm is stealin' the show . . .*
> *Get way back and clap your hands,*
> *Do the camel walk until you meet your man . . .*
> The Jewels, 1955

At first glance it's hard to believe that this album even exists. There have been so many cop-outs lately—major labels content with merely oldies albums of the sure-thing solid-hit variety, filled with material usually easily available on 45's and other LP's. And the approach of such records is generally very catch-as-catch-can, with very little scholarly interest devoted to continuity, a sense of era, or a sense of mood. And yet here it is—an album of mainly *un-issued* sides by *early* R&B vocal groups, pre-Coasters, pre-Moonglows, pre-Drifters, superb, unique combos from a ghostly era all their own, groups about which most of today's listeners know little or nothing.

End of an Era is presented in a well-documented fashion, with extensive, informative liner notes and a compendium of the titles of the remaining un-issued sides by the groups in question, with matrix number, group personnel, dates, hometowns. All of the sides have been culled from the defunct West Coast Aladdin label and from the catalogues and vaults of Imperial. These cuts offer listeners an excellent chance to hear what went down in those halcyon days of rock and roll and R&B from 1952 to 1956. And these aren't the sure-thing hits of the era—these are flip sides and nitty gritty rarities for collectors and aficionados of those zoot-suited, white-bucked, sequined, duck-walking times. One might venture the statement that this is the first oldies album with that vital element that so much of the music really has—atmosphere.

Back then all the R&B 45's actually did have "two sides" —the ballad side and the jump or novelty side—and the groups all had elaborate vocal and visual mannerisms (authentic remnants of this ancient showmanship can be seen in the ageless explosions of James Brown and His Famous Flames, and to some extent, in the Ike and Tina Turner Review).

Driving, intertwined saxophone solos dominated the jump/novelty sides, while a simplistic and enchanting one finger piano wandered through the ballad sides. Acappella and spiritual echoes vibrated in the tempos and in the choruses that backed the lead vocalist, who somehow always seemed to be singing like he really meant it —sometimes even the old Ink Spots technique of the emotion-charged spoken interlude was employed for greater effect. Listen to the Shaweez' 1952 version of "No One to Love Me"— *it* features, in *addition* to the interlude, a weeping vocal which was an oft-used piece of gimmickry back then—remember Billy Ward and the Dominoes doing "The Bells"? To get some idea of what a single from this era sounded like listen to both cuts by the Jewels included here—"Keep Your Feet on the Floor" is a jump blues *in toto,* while "Please Return" is a classical ballad.

The most memorable of the jump blues cuts on the album

is "I Want Your Love" by the Mellow Drops, which sounds like it could be the flip-side of the new Rolling Stones single, "Honky Tonk Women"—it's gritty, low-down, out-and-out rock and roll street music: "C'mon baby rock and roll/I want you body and soul/Meet me in the alley Sally/Sally don't make me wait!!" A soft step to the ballads, with "Teardrop Eyes" by the Dukes, presenting their Harptones/Moonglows sound, and of course the brilliant "Red Sails in the Sunset" by the Five Keys, who have had a long string of hits over the years, lasting well into the Sixties. "Red Sails" is the earliest cut on the album (1952), and its success led to new versions of many old standards. I can still hear Little Richard's remake of "By The Light of the Silvery Moon" and Gene Vincent singing "That Old Gang of Mine." And as a topper, anything by the Spiders, who I don't think ever made a less-than-great record, must be well-received. "You Played the Part," included here, is a gem—previously un-issued.

This album delineates a distinctive sound that is pre-Motown, pre-Spector, pre-Stax, and the beauty of it is that the music never seems contrived or stylized or over-arranged; it just appeared and spread, as this disc demonstrates, from the West Coast to New Orleans (the Spiders were discovered at

the Pelican Club there) to New York City. Henry Vestine and Bob Hite of Canned Heat deserve congratulations for getting this project started, and Volume II is eagerly awaited. Now how about an album of all those *further* un-issued items by which we're tempted in the liner notes? We can only wait so long.

—GARY VON TERSCH
9-20-69

RHYTHM 'N BLUES, VOL. 2
Various Artists
(Imperial LM-94005)

That doo-wopping, hucklebucking golden group era of the early Fifties lives again with the music on this album. Although this disc lacks the extensive liner notes and label photos that enhanced Volume One in this important series, it is every bit as good tune-wise. Nine groups from the Aladdin and Imperial archives are represented by fourteen selections that range from the up-tempo "Miss Lucy" by the Pelicans to the lush, emotional vibrations of "Love Me" by the Avalons.

All the stops in between are hit also. One of the few chick groups of the era, prophetically named the Crystals, are represented by both sides of their only Aladdin release, circa 1957. Their sound is a cross between the Teen Queens ("Eddie My Love") and the Six

Teens ("A Casual Look"). In fact, the Crystals' rendition of "I Do Believe" sounds very similar to the melody used by the Six Teens in "Only Jim." Novelty or flip-side tunes are not in abundance, but the two Pelicans/Kidds cuts (both previously un-issued) "Miss Lucy" and "Down In Mexico" are as fine as anything later written by the Leiber/Stoller team. The fascinating thing about these two cuts, besides the marvelous jive-oriented lyrics, is the fact that the former is sax dominated, while the latter features a percussive guitar interlude—nuances such as this often led to a group's rise or fall back in those stylized, gimmick-oriented years. Also notable is the Shaweez' rendition of the Guitar Slim/Ray Charles tune "Feelin' Sad" that demonstrates very aptly the reason for the word "blues" in the label "rhythm and blues." Very few groups ever tackled the postwar blues songs, although versions of classics like "Old Man River" and "Red Sails in the Sunset" were common. Perhaps if this had been issued . . . ?

Just as we were given a taste of the Five Keys on Volume One of this series, here we are tempted with the Robins' first release, circa 1949, entitled "Around About Midnight." This group, which had huge success in the mid-Fifties, survived the R & B jungles for more than a

decade, and were the first to record the novelty efforts of the renowned Leiber/Stoller team. In 1957 half of the group left to form the fabled Coasters for Atlantic, while an augmented Robins continued to record on Whippet. The rest of this story strays over into rock and roll history, as the Coasters took the genius of Leiber/Stoller with them from "Idol With the Golden Head" on down, while the Robins soon drifted into obscurity. Little of this can be heard in the bluesy "Midnight" but the rarity of the disc is undeniable in the early development of groupdom.

Which is really the purpose of this album. Fully eleven of the cuts heard here were never released until now. Further, groups like the Fideltones, the Avalons and the Shades never had a single release during the era, though it is hard to see why. The five selections from these groups were all culled from demo tapes in the Aladdin/Imperial files and are fully as fine as any released ballads by any of the known groups of the era. But, better late than never, which also sums up this album, which offers a page in the history of what was going on before the onslaught of Mister Presley and company.

—GARY VON TERSCH
9-17-70

THE GOSPEL SOUND OF SAM COOKE WITH THE SOUL STIRRERS, VOL. 1
(Specialty SPS 2116)

This is a first-rate introduction to the gospel environment that has nurtured so many latter-day R&B and soul singers. The mid-1969 success of "Oh Happy Day," the pop success of the Staple Singers, and the lasting memory of Sam Cooke (not to mention the presence of Johnny Taylor, who now records for Stax) all contribute to the commercial and musical timeliness of this LP.

The group itself was founded in 1934 by bass man Jesse J. Farley during his high school days in Trinity, Texas, where all the original Stirrers sang in the school glee club. They performed locally in churches as well as in concert, and in September, 1944, the group, by then based in Chicago, signed with Aladdin Records in LA and recorded many popular spirituals, gaining a large following.

In January of 1949 the Stirrers went to Specialty Records, then a fledgling LA label. Sam Cooke stepped in as lead singer, replacing R. H. Harris. The group, at this point fully fifteen years old, gained a second life, and their popularity soared. Still operating out of Chicago, they played Madison Square Garden and Carnegie Hall with the likes of Mahalia Jackson. Cooke toured with them until 1956, when he entered the pop world; Johnny Taylor then took over as lead singer.

The selections here all feature Cooke, with close support from the "second decade" Soul Stirrers, foremost among them being S. Roy Crain with his wavering falsetto. All of the later Cooke mannerisms can be heard on this record; the emphasis was on close, often insistent harmony accompanied by an infectiously rhythmic chorus. Cooke's rise to fame in 1958 with "You Send Me" seems only natural when one listens to his perfect phrasing, his mellow and sensitive evolutions of lines, and his half-humming, half-singing vocal style as it's presented here. Like many other artists before him, Cooke paid his dues, but few have left such a marvelous documentation of their early days. "Just Another Day" or the overbearing "Old Man River," included here, would have made excellent flip-sides for his early Specialty/RCA hits, and it really is a shame that Cooke never returned to gospel before his death.

The liner notes to this album write off the present day Soul Stirrers, though they had a successful LP in 1966; though Cooke's ghost hangs over their present sound, Little Willie Rogers still makes it work. The bum-tripping liner notes seem the sly result of label rivalry, and not much more.

—GARY VON TERSCH
4-30-69

AGAIN . . . JOHNNY SINGS
Johnny Ace
(Duke LP-71)

On Christmas Eve, 1954, at the age of twenty-five, Johnny Ace killed himself playing Russian Roulette. He'd been a star since 1952, and it was during these two years that so-called "pop" music and R & B began to merge; the result was rock and roll. This LP gives us not only an excellent portrait of the late Johnny Ace, but a perfect example of rock in its earliest stages.

In the early Fifties, national hits went to "pop" stars such as Rosemary Clooney, Eddie Fisher, and Perry Como. It was these artists, often doing covers of R & B material, who held the Cashbox charts. At the same time, Johnny Ace, Sonny Till, and the Clovers (recording on small, regional labels), reigned as kings of R & B. It was people like Alan Freed who first forced black music on the nation, only to discover that after the initial push, kids *wanted* to hear more. With Johnny Ace, Duke records made good use of its chance.

Both Ace and this album are somewhat enigmatic. Though he won virtually every blues award available, his voice was much smoother and his delivery more sedate than that which we commonly associate with "soul" music. The same characteristics fit the bands that backed him. Everything is controlled. Yet he was not alone; The Platters and the Clovers possessed similar qualities. It's almost a compromise music, not black enough, yet not white enough. The answer may be that these artists were in a transitional stage, for it was the "smooth" blacks who first appeared on the white charts.

Most of the songs on Ace's album are the sort we used to hear on the "Dreamy Side" of the Oldies But Goodies series. The music varies little—soft drums, jazzy guitar, mournful sax, occasional big band sound and a domineering piano. The songs will seem hopelessly trite to those hearing them for the first time. Yet Ace molded them into things of his own. He combined control and emotion, a rare talent indeed.

The LP opens with "Pledging My Love," released after his death and his biggest hit. Employing his mellowest voice, enunciating perfectly (another quality not associated with R&B), he sings in exact harmony with a soft piano and vibes. A softer sax drifts in as he begs his woman to come to him, pledging his love. The next cut is "Don't You Know," a blasting blues that reminds one of "Kansas City." We have a boogie woogie piano and big breaks that let the horns blow. Ace changes his voice from mellow to deep and bellowing, slurring the words this time. Again, all is controlled. He's yelling "DON'T YOU KNOW" without really yelling. A good, loud song.

These cuts set the standard for the album. All the following songs are love ballads or blatant blues. But Ace is always the blues. He's *always* the underdog, *always* begging, never dominating.

Of the other big hits included two stand out: "My Song," and "Saving My Love For You." The first is a typical but fine sample of early rock. The music bounces from cocktail lounge to solid rock and back. The second number is simply a great song. The vibes, the piano, the soft voice all fall together. The horn is just right, and the words just mushy enough to mean something.

The other cuts on the LP were not hits: "So Lonely" is a slow piano blues with a sad guitar and nervous vibes. Ace's voice slurs. It's the only song with the standard AAB blues verse arrangement, almost like sophisticated Chicago blues and strictly black. "How Can You Be So Mean" combines a big band backup with the blues. Johnny deepens his voice,

slurs the lyrics, and repeats the title. There's a rock guitar and a Sam "The Man" Taylor sax. Between breaks Ace tosses in phrases and seems to abandon his control.

It's ridiculous to ask whether Johnny Ace was a great influence or was greatly influenced. The answer is both. One thing for sure; he was a master of early rock. His voice, his backup (which is good; Johnny Otis much of the time), and his subject matter are all fairly typical. Yet he was not. A certain degree of masochism runs throughout the LP, it did in most vintage rock (the Platters' "The Great Pretender," or Guitar Slim's "The Things That I Used To Do," for example). Ace is always on the bottom, ready for more.

Johnny seemed caught in transition, as were those who immediately followed. Clyde McPhatter and Sam Cooke sang in the same manner, and Fats Domino was the most prominent to use similar backup. They, however, lived to move into the white market.

We are left with Ace in transition, which is where he stopped. His kind of music is rarely heard these days. Our rock revival (Lewis, Haley, etc.) is actually a reactivation of rock's second wave. Johnny was with the first.

Everything here is typical: everything but Johnny Ace. And the album is a masterpiece for what it is; a first step in the evolution of rock.

—BOB KIRSCH
3-19-69

THE BEST OF
SOLOMON BURKE
Solomon Burke
(Atlantic 8109)

KING SOLOMON
Solomon Burke
(Atlantic 8158)

The business of soul is salvation, and no one is better at it than Solomon Burke. Today the music is sometimes less important than the image, as James Brown gets more and more caught up in his messianic quest and the familiar churchy sound is abandoned for more self-conscious statements of roots. When soul music consisted only of that earnest preaching style, though, it was Solomon Burke, the Bishop, who was crowned King of Rock 'n' Soul, and indeed, the title was well earned.

His reign didn't last very long. It was just about five years ago that I saw him headlining a show that featured Otis Redding and also included Joe Tex, Rufus Thomas, and a torrid Sugar Pie De Santo slipping off her "Slip-in Mules." As the headliner, Burke of course came on last, with all the attendant panoply of startime. He wore a gold lame suit with a gold cummerbund stretched tight across his substantial middle. As he ran through his old hits —standards like "Cry To Me," "If You Need Me," "Down in the Valley"—he captivated an audience of brothers and sisters that is not always easy to please, and when he launched into his then-current hit "Goodbye Baby," there were shouts of recognition. He stood on the edge of the stage, jacket thrown off, tie loosened and sweat pouring down his face, moaning out his song to the familiar gospel changes. Suddenly some kids rushed the stage, pushing each other forward and clambering towards him. Instead of retreating, in a spontaneous gesture of magnanimity Solomon handed them the mike and allowed them to finish out his song. He stood there in the wings, eyes closed and swaying, while the kids sang and danced until the sound was finally cut off.

"There's a song that I sing and I believe if everybody was to sing this song it would save the whole world," he preaches with fervor in a song the Stones were later to popularize for another audience, "Everybody Needs Somebody To Love." Every song he does seems to have this underlying conviction that somehow or other by his investment of emotion he might indeed change the world's course. For some singers soul was a mixture of church and blues, but for Solomon Burke, the boy preacher from Philadelphia, it's all church, and even his celebrated adaptation of country music (with "He'll Have to Go," "Just Out of Reach" and a host of Jim Reeves songs) failed to change the character of his message. When he sings even a trivial pop song like "Get Out of My Life, Woman," he injects the evangelical note with his verse, "Get out and vote now, baby, I might run for president. You won't have a chicken in every pot, but I'll give out stamps to pay your rent"; and on "I Wish I Knew (How It Would Feel to Be Free)," a song with an admittedly explicit message, he declares, "Most of all I wish I had the answer and the secret to peace, I'd give this secret to every leader of the world . . ."

Probably his best selection on record is *The Best of Solomon Burke,* which includes all of his most familiar hits and one of his greatest compositions, "The Price." Almost equally good, however, is his next to best album for Atlantic, *King Solomon.* It offers a free selection of the throbbing soul ballads he does so well, including his best big hit, and one of his very best songs in the preaching vein, "Take Me," as well as a driving version of the Staple Singers' "It's Been a Change." Throughout the album his rich, resonant voice is shown off to great advantage, at times reminiscent of Sam Cooke in its smooth, almost syrupy quality, occasionally suggestive of Elvis Presley (another singer who passed from country to soul, going the other way), in the sudden swoops from high to low, in the lush vocal orchestration he will allow himself. What sets Solomon Burke off from every other singer, though, is the suppressed energy which lurks just beneath the surface of all his best songs. There's always the impression of barely controlled power which, if unleashed, could overwhelm the listener.

He was in town again a couple of years ago for New Year's Eve. He had been a long time without a hit, and the turnout at Louie's Showcase Lounge in Roxbury, Massachusetts, was sparse. He put on his show as usual, though, working hard, and playing guitar himself, with feeling. At the end of the night he delivered a New Year's Eve sermon that was to be the basis for his great message in "Take Me." "But I believe there's different strokes for different folks. And if you give your woman what she wants, when she wants it, how she wants it, where she wants it, every time she even thinks she wants it, you won't ever have to worry about anything." That audience was moved, too. They turned out in much greater numbers for Otis Redding a couple of months later; when Joe Tex came to town Louie's was packed and everyone knew the words to "Skinny Legs and All"; but no audience was as moved as the audience that saw Solomon Burke.

Now Solomon's finally got his hit with "Proud Mary." It's not so unlikely a choice, because Solomon Burke has always been the most eclectic of soul singers—doing everything from Dylan and Woody Guthrie to "By the Time I Get to Phoenix"—but it's sad, in a way, because it does probably mark the end of an era. Otis is gone; it doesn't look as if Aretha will ever again match the heights of her lovely "Do Right, Woman" or her ballsy "Dr. Feelgood"; James Brown is sticking to his capitalism and his rhythms; and Solomon Burke has finally made the Top 40.

—PETER GURALNICK
8-19-68

〰〰〰〰〰〰〰〰〰〰〰〰

MOTOWN

〰〰〰〰〰〰〰〰〰〰〰〰

I WAS MADE TO LOVE HER
Stevie Wonder
(Tamla 279)

Three of the biggest exponents of the Motown sound in recent months have been Stevie Wonder, the Temptations, and the Four Tops, and all three have recently released new albums.

Stevie Wonder's latest, *I Was Made To Love Her* (Tamla 279), is typical of a lot of Motown albums in at least two respects. First, the cover is terrible. Cheesey looking. And secondly, the range of material is very limited, making it difficult to listen to the album as a whole.

Stevie's recent style is essentially a variation on the kind of thing he did on "Uptight," a fine record. On that cut he added to the standard components of a Motown single a very personal lyric, and then sang the whole thing in a driving style from beginning to end. Stevie doesn't go in for dynamics, rhythm changes, or crescendoes, but prefers to sing frenetically for the duration of a piece.

The "Uptight" style continues to be the basis for all of Stevie's recordings, and the title song of his new album, *I Was Made to Love Her,* is a beautiful example of what Stevie can do using this approach. By far the best cut on the album, it contains a personal, down home lyric, some of Stevie's wild harmonica, and the basic overdrive that characterizes all of his records. In the middle there is a very kinetic spot in which Stevie sings perfectly over just the rhythm. And the sidemen, particularly the drums and bass, get into some very groovy riffs.

Everything after the title song is a comedown. Stevie's style is too limited to sustain an entire album and when he tries to vary it, as on Ray Charles' "A Fool for You," the results are more than unsatisfactory. In fact, the album has all the worst characteristics of the Motown sound with only a very few of the saving graces. The whole thing has a blatantly manufactured quality to it typical of Motown's capacity to crank out albums without giving any thought to experimentation or expanding the range of its artists' capacities. The result is an album of second-rate single material.

Unfortunately the Temptations' latest, *With A Lot O' Soul* (Gordy 922), is a similarly manufactured job in which the distinctive qualities of this fine group are largely lost. They are the bluesiest of all Motown groups and on some of their earlier releases they frequently reminded one of the R&B groups of the late fifties, especially via their use of a deep bass voice.

On the new album their distinctive style is obscured, the artifacts of Motown production predominate, and the resulting album hardly does them justice. Songs like "Two Sides to Love" and "Don't Send Me Away" don't even qualify for flip side material and the performances are totally uninspired. Predictably, the only cuts worth talking about are the ones released as singles.

"All I Need" is first-rate Motown. The song is the typical Motown circle of repetition, but with two very nice breaks. The back-up vocal fits perfectly. The rhythm guitar gets into some very nice chord things. And David Ruffin's lead drives the whole thing home. "You're My Everything" on the other hand is a little disappointing. Eddie Kendicks took the lead on this one, and his high soulful voice gives some welcome variety to the group's overall sound (he also sang lead on "Get Ready"), but the cut is wildly over produced, with the strings coming on much too strong. The Righteous Brothers type break in the middle doesn't quite come off either. On the whole, though, it is an entertaining cut.

The masterpiece of the album is "(I Know) I'm Losing You." Here the basically bluesy sound of the Temptations is permitted to come through and the background is a little less regimented. The song itself is out of sight, with fantastic lyrics, ("It's in the air, it's everywhere . . .") and a tough chord progression. The only thing that slows the song down is a very poor instrumental break after the second chorus. Still it is a very moving cut with a lot of momentum. This is Motown at its best.

On the latest Four Tops album, *Reach Out* (Motown 660), Motown makes an effort to get away from the problem with the Wonder and Temptations albums, mediocre material, but the Tops fare no better. Whenever a group gets to be as big as the Tops, Motown, as I noted earlier, likes to show how versatile they are. So, in the middle of some of their greatest singles ever, like "Reach Out," and "Bernadette," we get the Motown version of "Last Train to Clarksville" and "Cherish." It wouldn't be so bad if at least they tried a different approach in arranging the material. But they are totally incapable of turning out anything but the Motown sound, and the result is that if you didn't know that "Cherish" was written by the Association, you would think it came from Detroit.

Only when you get to Motown's collections of singles albums do you get an inkling of just how good Motown can really be and fortunately the most recent such album is *The Four Tops Greatest Hits* (MS 662). I personally think it to be one of the greatest rock albums ever produced. The problem with Motown albums that I've already discussed is that Motown doesn't really try. They know that on the strength of a beautiful single like "I'm Losing You" they can sell a whole album. But instead of seeing the album as a vehicle in which the artist can explore musical ideas in depth, free of the limitations of having to make it on commercial radio, they see the record as a way to make a quick killing and generally hand you the artist's latest single, combined with a lot of stale material that simply wasn't good enough to be released as single material. The resulting albums are bound to be disappointments. However, when they release an album which is a collection of single hits, then we are at least getting the invariably high quality of Motown singles, and some of these albums are nothing short of fantastic.

Such is the case with the *Four Tops Greatest Hits*. The Tops have emerged at this point as the finest Motown has to offer. The songs they record, primarily Holland-Dozier-Holland tunes, are the finest being written in Motown land these days. The arrangements they use are the most advanced and sophisticated found on any Motown records. And riding over the whole thing are the Tops themselves. The background voices sing the best parts of any Motown group, (check "Bernadette" or "Reach Out") and of course, lead singer Levi Stubbs just drives a song until there is nothing left. The Hits album is uninterrupted fulfillment of everything good at Motown. The bass is consistently incredible, the arrangements fit the songs to a T, the drumming is steady enough to be coming out of a computer, and, of course, there are the songs and the vocals, turning the whole thing into art.

If "soul music," in the sense that the term is used by the music industry, refers to music aimed specifically at the Negro market then Motown is black music but it is not soul music. Its appeal is aimed as much at the white audience as it is at the black one.

This isn't to say that Motown artists are not popular among black record buyers. It does mean that Motown is happiest when it can broaden the base of its popularity to include the white audience. And it is willing to move away from a straight soul sound to accomplish this.

It has long been the goal of Motown to put its big artists into the rich white night club circuit. To this end it has groups like the Supremes, the Four Tops, and the Temptations incorporate pop tunes and standards into their live acts. For the same reason, the Tops have recorded an album of show tunes, and the Supremes an album of Rodgers and Hart songs.

In a similar vein, Motown has hit upon a general musical formula which has yielded great success with both Negro and white record buyers. The elements of this formula have become so standardized that anyone with even the slightest familiarity with Top 40 radio can identify a Motown tune immediately. The four beat, stomp drumming, the high-pitched vocal backgrounds, the rigid big band arrangements, and those repetitive melodies. All these things are the key to the public's identification with Motown's music.

Motown is above all a commercial enterprise. But in recent months the thing that has impressed me most about their records has been the capacity of the individual artist to get past the limitations Motown imposes on them. This is especially true of Marvin Gaye, Stevie Wonder, the Temptations, the Miracles, and the Tops. Motown believes in routinizing its music, in formalizing it. But the really great Motown artists use the Motown formula to go beyond it. They can take all the good things about Motown, and there are plenty, and use it all to say something more than Motown ever intended. Therein lies the beauty of the best things in Motown, and therein lies the beauty of *The Four Tops Greatest Hits*.

—JON LANDAU
12-14-68

DIANA ROSS PRESENTS THE JACKSON FIVE
The Jackson Five
(Motown MS 700)

The Jackson Five stand in the tradition of super young rock singers that goes back to Frankie Lymon and the Teenagers and, more recently, Little Stevie Wonder. Ever since the day that Frankie Lymon lied about his age to producer George Goldner and earned the right to sing lead on "Why Do Fools Fall in Love," there has been a prominent place in rock and roll for the very young, exceptional voice.

The Jackson Five range in age from 10 to 16. Michael Jackson, the magnificent lead singer, is a scant ten years old. Supplied with some good arrangements and instrumental backing from the Motown assembly line, the boys from Gary, Indiana, perform with an exuberance and flair which many of the older groups on the same label rarely achieve these days.

The hit single, "I Want You Back," sets the tone for the whole album. Here is the most energetic piece of soul music since Aretha's "Respect." A very urgent and rapid bass line supports the moaning and crooning of young Michael. The other Jacksons shout their support and give every evidence that they too can sing. A surprising sidelight of the number comes when Michael defies twenty years of jazz-blues-rock propriety and puts the EEEE back in "baby." Doesn't he know that it's pronounced "Bay bay"? His "Ooo Ooo Bay Bee" is brash to the point of subversion.

The rest of the album combines some authentically good songs with the inevitable Motown blueprint specials. "Zip A Dee Doo Dah," the same version recorded by Bob B. Soxx and the Blue Jeans in the early Sixties, comes off very well. "Stand," done first by Sly and the Family Stone, captures the rhythmic complexity and poignant message of the original. Unlike the Temptations, who are falling all over themselves trying to copy Sly Stone with bombs like "Psychedelic Shack," the Jackson Five seems capable of incorporating Stone's new directions into their sound. The disappointments come with the hack Motown standards like "Standing In the Shadow of Love" and the ridiculous "My Cherie Amour." In songs like these the whole burden rests on the glossy facade constructed by the Motown arrangers. It's a nice trick, but the question remains, why not use the same ingenuity to come up with songs of real substance?

Given any kind of decent material at all, the Jackson Five should be able to give us many years of good, tight music.

Who's this "Diana Ross" anyway?

—LANGDON WINNER
3-7-70

ABC
The Jackson Five
(Motown MS 709)

This is the Jackson Five's first fully realized album. Their own previous album consisted mainly of earlier Motown songs done over with arrangements which were generally good, but which failed to express the spirit of the Jackson Five any more than they expressed the spirit of the original versions. *ABC*, however, is an album wholly in the spirit of those great Jackson Five singles, two of which, the title cut and the incredible "The Love You Save," are included. Catchy melodies, explosive rhythm backgrounds and energetic vocals are the rule here, especially on the first side, which is as strong as anyone could want.

The second side does get into some slow stuff; "La La" and "I Found That Girl" aren't really the type of material this group should be doing, though the arrangement of the latter (unlike that of "La La," where the Delfonics' understated force is replaced by Michael Jackson's wonderful screeching) has some interest insofar as it shows Motown looking back over its shoulder at the Delfonics and

at Gamble-Huff cuteness in general. But it took just the right exercise of imagination to borrow Funkadelic's "I Bet You," the most substantial song this minor Detroit group has done and one that would be a credit to any Motown group, and the result is a superlative arrangement.

The basic limitation of the album has to do, of course, with the fact that its material is necessarily the kind that can be handled by young voices. The only really heavy cut is "Don't Know Why I Love You," and this is the one for which a more mature vocalist would be most desirable. But aside from that, I like the album. A good Jackson Five song is one that is not only fast, with heavily accented rhythms, but also loose and playful, with built-in irregularities and breathing spaces that Michael and the others can fill with their delightful vocal improvisations. I'm happy to report that almost all the songs on *ABC* fit this description.

—ARNOLD BRODSKY
9-3-70

"THE TEARS OF A CLOWN"
Smokey Robinson and
the Miracles
(Tamla T-54199)

Motown does some questionable things. It refuses to print liner notes that say anything insightful about company acts or music. It keeps deserving performers on the shelf for months at a time. And it buries records that anyone with ears can tell are definite hits.

"Road Runner" was kept hidden on the *Shotgun* album for over a year before release. Marvin Gaye's "I Heard It Through the Grapevine" was in the can for two years before it was put on record. And "The Tears of a Clown," the last cut on the 1967 album *Make It Happen,* is only now released as a single.

On first listen it's a certain smash, as England confirmed when it shot the song to Number One this summer. Soul stations played the cut three years ago, and Miracles cognoscenti cherished it as they would a hit single. Now they will gladly share it with the plebes.

A circus atmosphere is established by the opening phrase that works as effectively as (but ever-more-subtly-than) the intro to James Darren's "Goodbye Cruel World." This phrase reoccurs throughout, giving the song an air of levity that belies the misery-and-woe lyrics.

And what lyrics! Smokey Robinson may or may not be America's greatest living poet, but he is certainly its most erudite writer of soul songs. Not only would no other composer mention Pagliacci in his verses, few would understand the allusion.

It's worth noting that "Tears of a Clown" is structured precisely, more so than some of the recent stiffs that were freer in form. In this sense it is vintage Miracles and should enjoy the success of another 1967 release, "I Second That Emotion."

The big question—why now and not then—remains unanswered. Perhaps Motown wanted to play down the uptempo side of Smokey's talents when his ballads were doing great business. If so, now may be the time for the fast singles. And if three years isn't too long to wait for "Tears of a Clown," can we still hope for the release of the four-year-old "More More More Of Your Love"?

—PAUL GAMBACCINI
11-12-70

PUZZLE PEOPLE
The Temptations
(Gordy 949)

CLOUD NINE
The Temptations
(Gordy 939)

Black music in America has always had an implicit relationship to the lives of black people, in the sense of its being true "folk" music, but until recently Motown's albums were often Tom travesties, weighted down with wretched cutesy renditions of lame Broadway show songs, and largely given the kind of production that sounded as if several quarts of linseed oil had been poured into the mixing machine.

But at Motown, as so many other places these days, the times seem to be changing at last, and their lineup of fall releases may be (with the sole exception of the Supremes, who've foresworn roots for Ed Sullivan anyway) the solidest they've ever had. Among all these great, grooving albums, each fully as gutsy in its own individualistic Motown way as Stax/Volt's best, *Puzzle People* is the absolute standout. Not only is it one of the most creative, diversified and fully-realized soul albums yet released, it's just plain brilliant as a rock album—stomping, shaking, thrilling, chilling music.

A preview was offered last year in *Cloud Nine,* which featured the title hit (one solid shot of relentless, corrosive fire and the Tempts' best single since "My Girl") as well as "Runaway Child Running Wild," their great careening nine-minute ride through the jungles of the cities. Also innovative as one of soul music's first forays into extended performance this blistering, beautifully sustained workout never seemed to get old through endless replayings. I thought *Cloud Nine* was a great album when it came out, but *Puzzle People* is a seven-league advance. The Tempts have a postive, effortlessly energetic unity to their music which in-

sures that everything they attempt will prove successful. All the many components of their music are essential to the subtle building and dissolving of awesome, enveloping waves of sound. Unlike many hip white groups, the Tempts and most soul folk always know exactly what they want to achieve and what the end product will sound like. In the past this has often made for dull, contrived music, but when all is handled right, the result, as on "Cloud Nine," is ecstatic and unforgettable.

Puzzle People extends and diversifies the Tempts' driving new sound. "I Can't Get Next to You" is one of their best songs ever, a rumbling *tour-de-force* utilizing the harmonized voices like rhythm instruments. The Isley Brothers' "It's Your Thing" is probably the standout, arching well-handled fuzz and Temptation choruses through a breath-taking exercise in dynamics. And there is also a great eight minutes called "Slave," follow-up to "Run Away Child," giving the same somewhat euphemistic and sentimentalized but nevertheless moving treatment to an earlier aspect of black sociology.

These albums suggest that there is a new spirit at work in the Motown enclave today, something more in tune with the spirit of the times and the tastes of the audience. Now that Motown artists have *really* begun to get it on, there should be no stopping them from challenging Stax/Volt in a very positive way, and the result can only be steadily rising standards for all concerned.

—LESTER BANGS
2-7-70

PSYCHEDELIC SHACK
The Temptations
(Gordy GS-947)

Listeners already familiar with *Cloud Nine* and *Puzzle People* will need no general introduction to the dominant style of *Psychedelic Shack*, a a bit too familiar by now. Nonetheless, those who have been turned off by the routineness of the title song shouldn't keep away from the album on that account, for the recent Tempts have been a rarity among Motown groups—a group whose obscure album cuts have been more adventurous and more arresting than their hit singles. This album deserves a favorable notice if only for its magnificent eight-minute version of Gladys Knight's "Friendship Train," which milks the gospel potential of the song and is tightly held together by some brilliant guitar work by one of those ever-anonymous great Motown musicians. Not all the extended cuts that have been coming out lately on soul albums really justify their length; this one does.

On first playing, *Psychedelic Shack* is a lot less fun than *Puzzle People*. Certainly its individual cuts lack the same kind of definition and are less memorable as *songs*—they all seem to blend in with each other, submerged in the heavy rhythms of the title cut—and there is nothing comparable to the variety achieved on the previous album by such diversely exciting things as "Message from a Black Man," "It's Your Thing," and "You Don't Love Me No More." But the new album improves with each playing and its apparent limitations have come to sound like something else again. *Puzzle People* was a more song-oriented album, with each three minutes promising a totally different experience from the three minutes before—an album equally suited to playing in full or jumping around selecting favorite bands. *Psychedelic Shack*, on the other hand, gains decidedly from being played through from beginning to end, its individual songs seemingly growing out of each other with a cumulative effect.

Another advance can be seen in the predominantly middle-range length (four minutes) of the tracks—long enough to accommodate the kinds of internal flexibility and playfulness which previously stood out as a special feature of those eight-minute exercises, "Runaway Child" and "Slave." Thus the album has its own kind of diversity, one that shows up more within the cuts than between them, and a more subtle unity replacing the sharp contrasts between eight-minute extravaganzas and tightly structured three-minute spinoffs. A related subtlety characterizes the use of psychedelic instrumental effects, which on *Puzzle People* seemed at times a little too flamboyantly applied—a matter of techniques just being discovered and not yet completely assimilated. Here they are kept more under control, and support the vocals better. It is a pleasure to listen to the highly complex opening of "You Make Your Own Heaven and Hell," the complete adequacy of the seemingly insubstantial "Hum Along and Dance," and the beautifully integrated arrangement of "Take a Stroll Through Your Mind," which quietly outclasses more pretentious "jazz-rock" groups.

This album also continues the Tempts' movement into "message" lyrics, with more songs cast in a poetic-philosophical vein than on any previous album. A problem here (analogous to the overly mechanical rhythms commonly occurring when commercial soul groups "go psychedelic") is that the message tends to be too explicit, too expository. In "War," a very effective song where the vocal bursts out like gunfire from a military march back-

ground, the rhetorical question "War, what is it good for?" is met with a resounding "Absolutely nothing!" It might be better if the answer were left blowin' in the wind.

—ARNOLD BRODSKY
9-3-70

MY WHOLE WORLD ENDED
David Ruffin
(Motown MS 685)

FEELIN' GOOD
David Ruffin
(Motown MS 696)

When David Ruffin was fired as the lead singer of the Temptations, Motown intimated that Ruffin's ego was leaping ahead of the rest of the group and, rather than allow it to become "David Ruffin and the Temptations," they let him go. Ruffin's story was different and probably more to the point. He said he had been fired because of his insistence on knowing how much the group was actually making from appearances and records beyond their limited weekly salary. Because he didn't know his place in the Motown establishment, he was severed from the Tempts but not released from a just-renewed contract. About half a year after his dismissal, Ruffin was appearing as a solo at the Apollo, still bitter but far from ready to perform on his own. Not long after that, some sort of "understanding" must have been reached with Motown, who announced Ruffin was working on a solo album.

Intrigues aside, David Ruffin has now put out two fine solo albums for Motown: *My Whole World Ended,* titled after his first and most successful single (with a typically literal cover: David looking downcast, head in hand, a world globe slightly out of focus over his shoulder) and *Feelin' Good.* Both have the feel of middle-period Temptations, when the group moved away from the Smokey Robinson masterpieces ("My Girl," "Since I Lost My Baby") to harder stuff (beginning with "Ain't Too Proud to Beg"), and Ruffin's leads began to take on more grittiness. Since his departure, the Temptations, through their producer Norman Whitfield, have fallen under the influence of Sly Stone, and Ruffin carries on much of their old sounds alone.

Ruffin has one of the few remaining unbleached voices at Motown and one of the most exciting anywhere. He sings with a kind of harshness, a husky tension that adds warmth and a genuinely felt quality to his material. His special flourish—a rising falsetto cry that isn't quite a scream—is used beautifully as punctuation, as transition or to carry the last word of a line up and out. Sometimes it's piercingly sweet,

sometimes more strained and anguished, but always effective.

If the anonymous choruses (both male and female) used here are nothing when compared with the rich backing work of the Tempts, their smooth sweetness provides an even better foil for Ruffin. But on two cuts—"World of Darkness" (from the first album) and "I'm So Glad I Fell For You" (his last single, on the second album)—the chorus is whipped into a righteous gospel spirit and they drive Ruffin to even greater heights. Both are fine examples of gospel-influenced rhythm and blues and are two of the best songs here. "I'm So Glad" is rather sparse instrumentally (a heavy bass and shrill organ taking over from a piano intro), throwing David and a large women's chorus up front. The song builds relentlessly to a repeated gospel close full of such rejoicing that it sounds more like true religion than true love. The interaction with the choruses of men and women, the women in the forefront, in "World of Darkness" is even more striking. The song rises and falls on waves of rushing voices. Ruffin's always on top. At a few points, the chorus breaks into separate voices counterpointed against each other and Ruffin's lead, full of gospel clapping and church shouting.

Like much of the best Temptations' material, the songs on Ruffin's two albums are usually concerned with lost love: the I'm-just-no-good-without-you school. It is at its highest point in a run of four beautiful songs that open up the first album —the title song, "My Whole World Ended (The Moment You Left Me)," "Pieces of a Man," "Somebody Stole My Dream," and "I've Lost Everything I've Ever Loved"—whose lyrics (composed by various Motown teams whose common member is a man named Bristol who is probably the uncredited producer of the album) are perfect examples of this exalted R&B genre. For instance, the movingly specific (and carefully pronounced) lines from "Somebody Stole My Dream": "Every morning at 7:45/You'd call to say that you loved me/The moment you opened up your eyes./I still wait for your call baby . . ." Or the rather exquisite lines from "Pieces of a Man," whose lyrics are equally well-chosen: "With an invisible knife you cut me clean in two." "I've Lost Everything I've Ever Loved" tends to fall into the maudlin (enumerating his dog "Jeff" in there with his parents, "granny" and his girlfriend), as does the unfortunate "Flower Child" on the other side, but Ruffin manages to make both songs surprisingly touching.

If there is no song that stands out lyrically quite as much as

these four songs, the material on the second album is on the whole more solid. "Loving You (Is Hurting Me)" is probably the best of this group, backed up by a bouncy string arrangement and giving Ruffin a chance for some of his soaring wails. "The Letter," a Smokey Robinson song included here, is marred by some rather frivolous chorus work, but again David rescues the number with admirable style.

The second album contains a greater amount of borrowed material (only "Message from Maria" on the first album is from another identifiable source), all in respectable but hardly remarkable versions. "Feeling Alright" is also subverted by a too-smooth chorus. "What You Gave Me" ("is more than enough to last") was made by Marvin Gaye and Tammi Terrell and although Ruffin's is superior (especially nice is the chorus crooning the word "reality" for emphasis throughout), the song is not really worth two interpretations. "I Could Never Be President" was more convincing in Johnnie Taylor's original, but is here preceded by a short music-box intro of "The Battle Hymn of the Republic," a real Motown touch.

Even though Motown seems to be trying to ignore him, treating him like a wayward child to Berry Gordy's Organization Man, David Ruffin has produced two of their best, most substantial albums of the past year. He deserves a lot more attention than he's been getting.

—VINCE ALETTI
8-6-70

M.P.G.
Marvin Gaye
(Tamla 292)

Marvin Gaye has been around for a long time—ever since the beginning of Motown. He's already earned the distinction of *two* albums of his own greatest hits, but it's only since the beginning of this year that he's achieved truly mass popularity. His version of "I Heard It Through the Grapevine" became the all-time best-selling single for Motown, and Marvin's follow-up, "Too Busy Thinking About My Baby," was another national number one. For some reason, Marvin has been able to escape the plague that has fallen on all of the other Motown groups—the need to include overdone sentimental songs like "The Impossible Dream" or "The Look of Love" on his albums. All of the cuts on *M.P.G.* are fully representative of Marvin Gaye at his best—a display of his voice against strong arrangements of top material.

The album leads off with "Too Busy Thinking About My Baby," and it sounds even better in stereo than it did coming out of a car radio. The female voices backing Gaye on this song are a richly balanced setting for his own smoothly syncopated singing. Over the years Marvin Gaye has teamed with Kim Weston and Tammi Terrell for special LPs. He sounds best when he has the counterpoint of a female voice or voices singing with him.

I'm sure Marvin's success with "Grapevine" encouraged him to do versions of other songs first recorded by Gladys Knight. Marvin's "The End of Our Road" is outstanding and very much his own interpretation. He uses his unique falsetto to great effect and the song is very moving.

Smokey Robinson is responsible for a couple of the cuts on side two, "It's a Bitter Pill to Swallow" and "More Than a Heart Can Stand." Both tracks are irresistible. They also show off Marvin's special way of presenting a lyric, as he manages to keep a song driving forward with an incredible momentum while always holding the intricacies of rhythm under control.

"I Got to Get to California" is my particular favorite; Marvin again strides through the song, building the intensity as his voice goes through an exquisite range of changes. There's also a tribute to the Drifters with Gaye's version of "This Magic Moment," but Ben E. King wins hands down on this one. Marvin Gaye does not thrive on songs that require a more melodic and less staccato style of singing.

M.P.G. treats the listener to the same infectious music and subtly varied singing that made Gaye's last two singles so popular. Since the days of "Hitch-Hike" and "Pride and Joy," Marvin has mellowed and expanded his emotional range to include a versatile series of voices. He can bite into the words of a song, suddenly sing against the rhythm of the arrangement, and then slide into a smooth and flexible falsetto for an emphatic "oooh" or "oh yeah" or drive up to a note with an amazing burst of power.

Marvin Gaye does not aim for spectacular effects—he screams and shouts with restraint, if that's not a contradiction. His control of the rhythm and momentum of a song is unique to him, and his specialty is still the delivery of a staccato vocal with a syncopated assurance and conviction. Judging from the way he projects the songs on this album, Marvin still "just wants to testify."

—JACK EGAN
8-23-69

SILK 'N' SOUL
Gladys Knight and the Pips
(Soul SS 703)

FEELIN' BLUESY
Gladys Knight and the Pips
(Soul SS 707)

NITTY GRITTY
Gladys Knight and the Pips
(Soul SS 713)

Every Motown group must have at least one super-stone masterpiece, a production so powerful it moves you far past the boundaries that keep you from bestowing the *obsessions* on most soul music that you get almost daily in hard rock. Martha and the Vandellas capsulized the summer of '64 in one smoky vision in "Dancin' in the Streets," and I still get chills every time I hear Stevie Wonder's "I Was Made to Love Her." When I first heard Gladys Knight and the Pips' "I Heard It Through the Grapevine" on the radio, I stopped stockstill and just listened, openmouthed, to the most searing single I'd heard in months. Gladys and the Pips don't occupy the top stratum of the Motown pantheon, but they have sustained themselves beautifully while continuing to release some of the most powerful soul blasts around: last year's "The End of Our Road" was a searing rage-filled exorcism in the great

"Grapevine" tradition. After listening to their last three LP's, their strategy becomes obvious: divide the material about equally between violent outer-edge wailers, standardized Motown soul grooves that sometimes harken far back as the Fifties, and the tamest, lushest of "sweet-soul" stylings.

At first you feel the urge to skip the lush ballads and make a beeline for the grinding bedrock. When I first got these albums, I played *Feelin' Bluesy* constantly, dipped into *Nitty Gritty* on occasion, and filed *Silk 'n' Soul* impatiently away after one half-completed playing. After a while, though, I found myself beginning to dig their soft sides almost as much as the churning blues, and before I knew it I was playing *Silk 'n' Soul* repeatedly and listening to it in amazement at the sincere bluesy melancholy Gladys imparted to such slices of pure schmaltz as "Theme From Valley of the Dolls" and "The Look of Love." Maybe it's true when they say that a true artist can make *any* kind of shit, no matter how intractable, into something beautiful. The reason it's so convincing here is that the treatment Gladys gives those lame Broadway/Hollywood shots seems like a radically toned-down expression of that same fierce urgency with which she ignites songs like "Grapevine." The tenderness so often has just the tangy edge of ever-so-subtle bitterness, with none of the oozing, gushing histrionics all those white chicks give these songs on the *Merv Griffin Show*.

Nitty Gritty is a beautifully balanced album, with a refreshing variety to the songs and arrangements. Aside from a "Cloud Nine" almost identical to the Tempts' version, there's not a dull or banal moment on the album, and one song, "The Stranger," is extraordinarily good, with an unusual melody and arrangement as haunting as some of Martha and the Vandellas' old masterpieces like "Dancin' in the Streets," impressing its subtle twists of tone and feeling in your consciousness until it's the first thing you play on getting home from a day of it running mesmeric circles in your head. Shirley Ellis' old "Nitty Gritty" also gets a gutty, propulsive workout.

But *Feelin' Bluesy* has still gotta be my favorite, because this is where Gladys and the Pips excel: on the one hand, throat-wrenchingly soulful ballads that pass the usual Motown pyrotechnics to touch the heart; on the other, showcase pieces like "The End of Our Road"—burning, incredibly intense blues shouts slashing through charging, grinding rhythms as razor-edged chorus exclamations explode from the Pips with sizzling ferocity.

Many more albums like

these, and Motown just might reclaim its lost throne as supreme force in the soul music industry. In any case, the rewards for our ears are all right here, right now.

—LESTER BANGS
12-27-69

GREATEST HITS
Gladys Knight and the Pips
(Soul SS-723)

This is another supplement to what might be called the Motown Songbook, each volume issued in wrap-up format as "greatest hits" by Mary Wells, The Temptations, The Marvelettes, whoever, and each one becoming an instant classic soul album. Of course, the early collections were the best—and the two-record set of The Miracles' *Greatest Hits from the Beginning* remains one of the most important albums released—but Gladys Knight and the Pips have no trouble living up to the original standards and their own compendium is typically fine.

It opens with remakes of the group's three pre-Motown hits—a risky business at best but here brought off rather well (under the supervision, one assumes, of their current producer, Norman Whitfield). The variation on "Every Beat of My Heart" is minor enough, consisting mainly of a string background and some harps (Oh, Motown!) where in

the original, the chorus carried the full weight. "Letter Full of Tears," written by Don Covay, is at first startling and unsatisfactory but given some time, it settles in as one of the best cuts on the album. The Pips are brought out front to comment and echo Gladys' beautifully lush lead, singing, "Wait a minute, wait a minute, y'all." Although strings come rushing in a little too often, they're played off to good effect against some gently biting guitar. The only disappointment is "Giving Up." Stripped of its original heavy horn punctuation and incredibly robust chorus work, the song limps along to some low-key organ movement (plus inevitable violins, etc.). Yet much of the emotional power is retained by Gladys' steady, measured phrasing and her convincing cry, "Oh Lord, he's all I got!"

The rest is more familiar, often excessively so. As with most Motown Songbook material, nearly every song included here has been done before or was followed-up by another Motown group. "I Heard It Through the Grapevine"—creatively remade for Marvin Gaye but copied with all the excitement of a duplicating machine by more people than anyone but the songwriters would care to remember—is still a standout in the original, bursting with Gladys' rich, gutsy voice, vibrant male back-up voices and more rocking soul than one thought Motown capable of at the time.

With the exception of "Didn't You Know (You'd Have to Cry Sometime)," by the Ashforn-Simpson team, and a truly inspired remake of "The Nitty Gritty," all of the new material was written by producer Whitfield in collaboration with one or two others, usually Barrett Strong. Since Whitfield and Strong are responsible for all the new Temptations' work, there is a great deal of practically incestuous cross-over between the two groups. "Everybody Needs Love" and "I Wish It Would Rain" are both Temptations originals copied here as mere repetitions. The Tempts turn about and borrow "Friendship Train" and "You Need Love Like I Do (Don't You)" for their *Psychedelic Shack* LP, again leaving the arrangements essentially intact. "You Need Love" is a spectacular, driving song in both versions (the Tempts, with Eddie Kendricks in the lead, have the edge on this one)—the kind of relentless dance number that put Motown where it is today, and one of the best. "It Should Have Been Me" is another neglected Motown masterpiece, with a story straight out of the love comics but a production made in heaven.

Gladys Knight and the Pips are the best thing to happen to Motown in years (Oh, yes, and there's that *other* group . . .). Look no further for proof.

—VINCE ALETTI
10-29-70

GREATEST HITS
Jr. Walker & the All Stars
(Soul SS 718)

WHAT DOES IT TAKE TO WIN
YOUR LOVE
Jr. Walker & the All Stars
(Soul SS 721)

What a Greatest Hits album may lack in freshness and the excitement of surprise, it makes up for in known excellence as well as in meaning acquired through the years of familiarity. This applies with particular force to the Motown output. Amid myriad albums of dubious value on that label, every Motown Greatest Hits album is outstanding, and the new Jr. Walker collection is one of the best.

Rhythmically as tight as anything Motown puts out, Walker's band sounds like nothing else in creation. Its trademarks are, of course, Walker's sax solos alternating with his pleasantly gritty vocals (his instrumental style is smoother and more graceful than his vocal style, but both are exquisite). There is always a great deal else going on underneath, though, to the point that what really makes Walker's arrangements so distinctive and powerful is the heavy use to which he puts the supporting instruments—bass, piano, guitar—not just in sustaining the rhythm but in working out interesting countermelodies of their own. These instrumental lines mean everything to "Home Cookin'" and "Pucker Up Buttercup," and together with a low-register wind instrument (a baritone sax?) they make "Road Runner" probably Walker's finest achievement.

This album spans a longer time period than almost any comparable collection, stretching from the early-Sixties "Shotgun" to last summer's "What Does It Take," the latter a last-minute substitution (the back cover still lists "Hip City—Pt. One" in its place). But the material is consistent in style and quality. Side One in particular is a run of classics all the way—simply incomparable. And while the major songs on Side Two are less striking, that side also includes some more diverse material. "Hip City—Pt. Two" seems aimless, but the slow and silky "Cleo's Mood" is a fine change of pace, and "Money" is done up as a raucous live clap-and-shouter like "Quarter to Three" or the Stones' "It's All Right."

Remakes, Walker's stock in trade, are becoming an obtrusive problem in rock in general and especially in soul. How discouraging it is to see the various Motown groups fill their albums with each other's songs without sensing a need for any genuine creative reinterpretation. In the case of Jr. Walker, those distinctive instrumental components which make his arrangements sound so unique also guarantee his remakes a validity like that of Wilson Pickett's or Aretha Franklin's. They may not always supplant the originals, but they always have some life and interest of their own. His *Greatest Hits* include the two important remakes—"How Sweet It Is," which now stands as the definitive version of that song even over Marvin Gaye's original, and "Come See About Me," which seems to me demonstrably inferior to what must be one of the Supremes' two or three best things. The Walker version is not as subtly and smoothly integrated as the original; the contrapuntal vocal line stands out as an independent assertion instead of blending with the lead. But it is still good enough, and different enough, to be worthwhile on its own account.

The *What Does It Take* album is built around the title song, one of the biggest-selling and also one of the best singles of 1969. Walker puts over its catchy melody in a leisurely and measured way, keeping strict boundaries between the gently repetitious sax sections and the double- and single-tracked vocal mixes—the whole arrangement tied together by a superbly simple bass line that carries great weight. For me, at least, this release came across as that memorable surprise—an indefinably apt combination of elements—that makes one throw away any preconceived criteria for good songs and acknowledge a concrete success.

The rest of the album, which includes the more recent singles "These Eyes" and "Gotta Hold On To This Feeling," carries on in a singular style, but nowhere else is the classic simplicity and clarity of the title song recaptured. The recent Walker material probably represents a departure from the characteristic sound of the *Greatest Hits* greater than any internal variation within the *Greatest Hits* itself. Too much clutter is slipping in, caused by ingredients like strings and soft choral backgrounds that seem to be working away from Walker's strengths, which are in the direction of stark sound contrasts. Nonetheless, Walker holds everything together quite satisfactorily.

Though Walker's "These Eyes" makes the original Guess Who version seem flaccid, it is so stuffed with competing brilliancies as to obscure the *song,* and to recapture it. I find myself going back to the Guess Who. In stereo Walker's choral voices and bass line do tricks that don't show up on radio; still I think there's something to be said for the Guess Who's simpler yet more authoritative bass line, with its more compelling interactions with the lead vocal. And if Walker at least earns a draw with "These Eyes," with "Proud Mary" the excellence of the original drives him to unprofitable extremes of shrill embellishment.

The album has its share of fillers, but also such good things as the distinctively funky "Hot Cha" (this doesn't sound new, though) and the four-minute sax blast "Ame Cherie" bolstering the strong singles. Too many things are repeated from other albums, and there are the usual signs of opportunistic commercial album-making. (Why waste a band on "How Sweet It Is" *three years* after its release as a single, especially with the *Greatest Hits* just released!) But while not a classic album like the *Greatest Hits,* this one stands up well enough.

—ARNOLD BRODSKY

4-2-70

SOUL SINGLES

"PSYCHEDELIC SHACK"
The Temptations
(Gordy 7096)

"POINT IT OUT"
The Miracles
(Tamla 54198)

**"GOTTA HOLD ON TO
    THIS FEELING"**
Junior Walker
(Soul 35070)

"ABC"
The Jackson Five
(Motown 1163)

"I SHOULD BE PROUD"
Martha and the Vandellas
(Gordy 7098)

"THE BELLS"
The Originals
(Soul 35069)

"IT TAKES TIME"
Edwin Starr
(Gordy 7097)

**"NEVER HAD A DREAM
    COME TRUE"**
Stevie Wonder
(Tamla 54191)

**"GIVE ME JUST A LITTLE
    MORE TIME"**
Chairmen of the Board
(Invictus 19074)

**"DANGER, HEARTBREAK
    AHEAD"**
Kim Weston
(People 1001)

"DIG THE WAY I FEEL"
Mary Wells
(Jubilee 5684)

Since New Year's there has
been a great deal of activity out
of Detroit's soul center, much

of it good, not enough of it
accessible to white AM listeners. The Temptations' "Psychedelic Shack" has been the most
successful Motown single since
"I Want You Back," though not
the best. It continues in the
now familiar *Puzzle People*
vein, but after some of the
genuinely exciting songs on that
album it seems disappointingly
slick, its music and lyrics both
representing too facile an approach to the integration of
soul and acid rock styles that
the Tempts have been attempting. Still, it has one line—"music so high you can't get over
it, so low you can't get under
it"—that would serve as a good
short review of *Puzzle People*.
Incidentally, for those who
want "Message from a Black
Man" (a much better Temptations song) as a single, it has
been put out by the Whatnauts
in a version that stays close to
the original.

Anything by the Miracles is
important by virtue of their distinguished history, and "Point
It Out," only a minor hit on the
soul stations, does contain some
promise of renewal. The decline of power and richness in
Smokey Robinson's voice seems
irrevocable, but there have been
some masterpieces in his later
vocal style, like "The Love I
Saw in You Was Just a Mi-
rage." "Point It Out" has some
of the tension of "Mirage,"
though it is not consistently

maintained. This is one that grows with every hearing.

So is Jr. Walker's "Gotta Hold On to This Feeling." It starts out beautifully, though the soft chorus doesn't add much and the vocal is awkward. But if you want to "learn the meaning of soul," as the Temptations put it, listen closely *between* some of those sung lines.

That key second release has always been crucial to the durability of rock and roll groups. Therefore it is heartening that in "ABC" the Jackson Five have come up with a strong follow-up that doesn't lean on their first hit but establishes its own groove, utilizing all the voices in quick succession. The group is boisterous as before, but more rhythmic than melodic here.

An antiwar song from Martha and the Vandellas? Really? Up to now Motown's war songs have been of the bland seeing-Johnny-off variety, but now Johnny comes home in a coffin and the lyrics go, "He wasn't fighting for me; he was a victim of the evil of society." The orchestration is a little schmaltzed-up, a la recent Supremes, but the song is rescued by its driving rhythms and by a truly dynamic vocal done by one of the best and most underrated lady soul singers. The "I should be proud" refrain is strong indeed. This song is brand new, and could be a big hit if enough people demand that it be given air play.

As always, some of the best Motown singles out now are by lesser-known artists who stick closer to the straight R&B approach from which some of the label's big names have "graduated." With "The Bells" the Originals continue their mellow but expressive reformulation of the Fifties ballad style which was so successful in "Baby I'm for Real." And Edwin Starr, best known for "Agent Double-O-Soul" and last year's great "25 Miles," now has "It Takes Time," which builds upon recent Temptations rhythms but with funkier vocal support.

But the cup of excellence among the current Motown crop goes to Stevie Wonder, who specializes in sentimental novelty songs which are very good when they work, very bad when they don't. "Never Had a Dream Come True" works. The best is reminiscent of "A Place in the Sun," one of Stevie's best early songs, but there is less of a dominant regularity here, and the added looseness enables his vocal straining to fit in better here than on the more stiffly structured "Yester You, Yester Me, Yesterday." What finally makes the song distinctive is the harmonized humming section, which is given an appropriate and repeated emphasis.

To go from Motown to imitation Motown (though in this

case it's really self-imitation),
Holland-Dozier-Holland's new
independent enterprise has
scored its first big hit with the
Chairmen of the Board's "Give
Me Just a Little More Time," a
standard 1965 Four Tops arrangement featuring a lead singer who sounds as close to Levi
Stubbs as possible, with some
Billy Stewart tweeting and
chirping added. Routine, but
there hasn't been anything like
it for a few years.

Marvin Gaye's two old flames
are alive, if not so well, on
other labels. One of them,
Kim Weston, has just brought
back the Marvelettes' "Danger,
Heartbreak Ahead." The new
version is good, but then so
was the original, so what's the
point? Kim is best known for
"Take Me in Your Arms," but
the one to look for in the oldies
shops is the earlier "Feel Alright Tonight," which Smokey
wrote. Anything Smokey wrote
for any vocalist in the early
Sixties is worth having. Though
the tunes he gave to others tend
to be more mechanical than the
ones he sang himself, all make
good economical use of bluesy
chord patterns. Marvin Gaye's
original duet partner, Mary
Wells, whose voice served as
the vehicle for some of those
great early Smokey songs, recently had a big soul radio hit,
"Dig the Way I Feel." Though
lively and accomplished, it
didn't move me much in weeks
of exposure. But Mary has a

secure place in the history of
rock and roll, if only for "Bye
Bye Baby," that non-stop scream
which she wrote herself and
which, along with "Way Over
There," started it all going in
Detroit a decade ago.

—ARNOLD BRODSKY
4-16-70

~~~~~~~~~~~~~~~~~~~~~~~

SOUL MEN:
STAX' GOLDEN YEARS

~~~~~~~~~~~~~~~~~~~~~~~

SOUL MEN

There are in effect two different types of soul artists: country and urban. The same distinction exists among the older
blues artists, and between folk
songs of rural and urban origin. In soul, James Brown and
Wilson Pickett, regardless of
what part of the country they
may have originally come from,
represent the urban style, while
Otis Redding, Carla Thomas,
and Sam and Dave represent
the more rural style.

The basic characteristics of
the urban sound are its professionalism and its polish. A
Wilson Pickett record utilizes
modern recording techniques,
including a lot of overdubbing
when necessary plus things like

female trios backing up the lead vocal. The rural type of soul artist goes in for a more low-down, less slick, more spontaneous sound. Otis Redding usually records his whole tracks at once, no dubs, and seldom goes through more than a few takes. Sometimes he even finishes the writing of a tune while he is recording it.

This type of soul artist has a rougher and more gravelly type of voice (compare Otis to Wilson) and his arrangements are apt to be extremely straight forward (as on Otis' "Hawg For You," *Dictionary of Soul*, Volt 415). Basically, it is a difference in feel and the more you listen to soul in general, the more obvious these basic distinctions become.

The only reason why I go through the trouble of making these distinctions is to point out that the emergence of Sam and Dave at the top of the pop charts with their new single of "Soul Man" is of particular importance. It is one thing for the urban stars like Brown and Pickett to make it with the general pop audience. Their music, due to its polish and professionalism, is something that young record buyers should have no trouble relating to.

When "Soul Man" becomes a national number one record, it indicates that a much more earthy, low-down kind of soul is beginning to get to white America.

The music of Sam and Dave is, after all, a very simple, though not simplistic, type of music. It is spontaneous and primitive and is much less removed from country blues and folk styles than the music of a Wilson Pickett whose new single, "Stagolee," while a folk song originally, exhibits all the characteristics of urban soul. A good place to acquaint ourselves with the subtleties of the rural style of soul is on the album that "Soul Man" spawned, namely *Soul Men*, Stax 725.

Sam Moore and David Prater have been together since 1961 (Otis Redding, in a wonderful Hit Parader interview with Jim Delephant, says that they have been together for closer to a decade) and it is safe to assume that a good deal of that time has been a struggle for them. The first taste of acceptance they received was with their beautiful and classic recording of "Hold On, I'm Comin'", which was a hit some years back. The single resulted in their first fine album of the same title (Stax 708).

In *Soul Men*, Sam and Dave reveal a heightened sense of sophistication over the earlier album, and the recording itself is considerably improved, but basically the boys are in the same bag as before. In music like soul, the artist doesn't seek to grow by expanding, but by penetrating. Sam and Dave's idea of musical growth is not the assimilation of new eclectic influences, but the refinement of the essence of the basic ideas and forms which dominate their own style of music. This refinement and penetration is what Sam and Dave have largely achieved on their newest record.

To get into an album of this type may not be easy for one unfamiliar with Stax-Volt style soul. The first time I listened to *Dictionary of Soul* I was impressed with some of the individual cuts but I found a lot of the material to be boring. But I eventually went through a thing where each cut on the album was my favorite until I wound up just digging the whole thing from beginning to end, every last second of it. (I still think it is *the* classic soul album.) Something similar, although not to the same extent, occurs with this record. The first time through a lot of it seems old hat and unimpressive. But listen to it all the way through three or four times and some of the seemingly dull cuts begin to get to you.

When you do get into this record, the first thing that has to impress you is the instrumental back-up. It is by Booker T. and the M.G.s and the horns of the Mar-Keys, both wonderful recording artists in their own right. In addition, the production by Isaac Hayes and David Porter is excellent. My criterion for calling it excellent has nothing to do with the pol-

ish or smoothness of the recording, because neither are particularly pronounced.

What I like about the production is that one can distinguish everything that is happening. For example, drummer Al Jackson, easily the best drummer in all of soul, does some beautiful things with his bass drum and using normal production techniques you would not be able to clearly distinguish what he is doing. The same holds true for Steve Cropper's guitar which, if it were recorded at Motown, would probably have been lost in the shuffle. The virtue of the Hayes-Porter style of production is in its honest reproduction of what actually takes place in the studio, without relying on gimmicky techniques or excessive echo.

Getting into the record itself, "May I Baby," written by Hayes-Porter, is the flip side of "Soul Man" and illustrates what I was talking about a moment ago. The first few times you listen to it, it sounds kind of trite. But then Cropper's up front rhythm guitar reaches you, being tied so nicely into what the drums and horns are doing. And then the clarity of both vocals, especially when they ring out over the horn riffs, has to reach you. This is a typical example of Sam and Dave's ballad style and it is a fine cut.

"Let It Be Me" is quite similar to "May I Baby" and is a frequently recorded ballad by soul artists. The Everly Brothers had the first recording of it six or seven years ago. Here Booker's lovely melodic chord style on the organ fills in the sound very nicely and the horn riffs on the chorus are particularly effective. But despite the fine vocal, the song has become a bit cliched and the impact is not particularly strong.

Not so of "Broke Down Piece of Man" and "Hold It Baby," two uptempo tunes on the first side. The former is quite interesting as a song. The verse part of the chord progression is typical soul I-IV-V, in this case E-A-B7, which resolves into a flatted III-VII-IV, or G-D-A pattern. (All chords are major.) The use of the major flatted III is typical of a lot of Stax-Volt soul, (the root progression of "Hold On, I'm Comin'" is I-flatted III-IV-I, or C-E flat-F-C, which is the most common use made of it) and the movement from G to D-A is very effective, for all you music majors. Also, the words are filled with the kind of graphic phrases typical of the best soul songs. Just dig the title, "Broke Down Piece of Man."

On "Hold It Baby" we get into a slightly different type of thing. First there is the stomp drumming, which entails the drummer hitting the snare on every beat. But it is not the usual stomp in that Jackson does all kinds of fancy things with the bass drum instead of relying on the usual "four" (stomp) there as well. Also, listen to the way Jackson does his eight on the hi-hat. He gets the perfect sound out of them. After that, notice how the arrangement is handled when they get to the four "Hold It Baby" lines. The first is done over just the bass, slight organ, and drums. Next time the piano comes in, then the guitar, and the last time the whole band resolves it into a one line riff and then, back into the song.

The whole thing shows perfect understanding of rock dynamics and tension. It would take the average rock band four or five minutes to try and get across what these people do in fifteen seconds, and even then they wouldn't do it right. This is tight. The band doesn't dawdle around, they don't use any tricks. Tight.

Finally, notice that the instrumental break does not follow the same chord progression as the melody, which is a frequently used Stax-Volt arranging device. (On this particular break they utilize those flatted III and VI chords just as in "Broke Down Piece of Man.") In all, a fine song, fine arrangement, and fine vocals.

Side two has most of the cuts which best illustrate the rural roots of Sam and Dave. "Just Keep Holding On" has a chorus which sounds like it could be a folk tune. Like many of their ballads the melody is very long winded, ultimately resolving into an eloquently simple chorus. The first verse and chorus are followed by a good bit of Sam's talking style which is quite good. He recites it all over a beautifully building instrumental track which takes us back into the one line chorus, "Just Keep Holding On."

The reason why someone as knowledgeable about the pop scene as Hit Parader editor Jim Delephant says Stax-Volt has the best rhythm sound on records is plainly in evidence on "The Good Runs the Bad Way." First, dig our main man, Steve Cropper. His rhythm is so right and so simple that it makes you wonder why he hasn't received the recognition that infinitely inferior guitarists have. Also, Duck Dunn shows what it means to play the bass, as opposed to playing a four string guitar. Perfect timing and perfect understanding of the uses of his instrument. And Sam and Dave riding over all of it showing us how blues harmony is supposed to be done.

"Rich Kind of Poverty" is so low down, particularly in the verse part, that it is the perfect follow up to "The Good Runs the Bad Away." The traded leads on this cut allow us to see just how well Sam and Dave complement each other.

As good as most of the rest of this album is, there isn't anything on it which can compare with "Soul Man," which is definitely in the "Try a Little Tenderness," "Respect" category. From the first four bars of Cropper's guitar over just the drums you know they have it, and then there's that vocal: "Comin' to you on a dusty road/Good lovin', I got a truck load." Listen to everything: Dig the way Duck's bass interacts with the band. And then notice how Cropper's rhythm guitar, playing that silly little riff (Ami7-G), which is very similar to what Keith Richard does on the live "Under My Thumb," ties the whole thing together. And then there is Al's drums, (I don't think he plays an actual roll on the whole cut) with a beat that cuts through everything with its deep, dry, unechoed sound. And, of course, there are the two of them blurting out: "I was brought up on a side street/Learned how to love before I could eat," and then "I'm a soul man, and that ain't all."

Sam and Dave's virtue is that they are alive. More alive than a lot of people who blather about "reality" and "love" from behind their lack of musical sensitivity and competence. The feeling that music can create in a listener doesn't come from our opinion or image of the artist who makes the music, if our response is at all genuine. It doesn't come from the artist telling us what he is trying to do, or acting it out. It is there in the way he says the words more than in what the words say. And if Jim Morrison screams at us to "Break on through to the other side," well, Sam and Dave don't have to tell us about it because their music is *on* the other side.

—JON LANDAU
1-20-68

SOUL ROLL

Almost a year after his death, Atco records continues to release new Otis Redding records. The latest is *Otis Redding in Person at the Whiskey a Go Go* and was recorded in April, 1966.

The repertoire of the new album consists primarily of Redding standards, many of them recorded by Redding several different times, with a previously unrecorded Redding song—"I'm Depending On You"—and a James Brown number thrown in for good measure. The familiarity of the material in no way mars the effectiveness of the recording, because in several instances Redding turns in the best performances ever of songs long identified with him.

Volt records released a live album of Redding two summers ago called *Otis Redding Live in Europe*. The record was universally recognized as a spectacular performance. However, this new set surpasses it in certain respects. The recording here is of almost studio quality, thanks to engineer Wally Heider. Redding is in somewhat better voice than on the earlier record. The mix is superior and the sound tighter and more controlled than on the earlier album.

Redding recorded this album with his touring musicians. They are the same band he used to produce Arthur Conley's "Sweet Soul Music" and they are superb. While there are a few technical errors in their playing, they are no more than we find Booker T. and company making on *Live In Europe*. And for the bulk of the record they establish complete rapport with Redding. On several cuts—notably "Satisfaction" and "I Can't Turn You Loose"—they simply cut both the studio and live performance of the Stax-Volt band.

In Person at the Whiskey A Go Go is animated by Redding's professionalism as are few other Redding albums. As his manager Phil Walden describes it, Redding decided to do some extra preparation for the taping the day before it was to take place. He finished his regular set at the Hollywood Club late in the morning and then told the band that he wanted them to stick around for a while just to go over some of the rougher numbers.

Redding wound up keeping them there from 2:30 AM until 10:00 AM at which time he gave them some time off.

Around noon they were told to reassemble and Redding kept them there until evening show time, going over every last detail and nuance of each musician's part.

And, adds Walden, when Redding practiced, it wasn't like he sat around on his butt and watched musicians struggle over their arrangements. He would be up on the stage going over things personally, cajoling that extra bit of togetherness out of each of them. And the fruits of his labors are in evidence from the beginning to end on this album.

The set opens with one of Redding's lesser songs, "I Can't Turn You Loose." Redding invests that ordinary piece of material with a performance of such power that he transforms it into one of the outstanding numbers in the Redding catalogue. Over an incessantly repeated guitar-bass figure and an elementary horn part he sings the words with methedrine-like energy.

As he does throughout this album, drummer Elbert Woodson pushes the beat like there was no tomorrow. When Otis wants to emphasize the lines "Hip shaking woman I told you/I'm in love with only you," Woodson momentarily switches over from his closed high hat cymbal to one of his big ones, giving Redding just that bit of instrumental emphasis the line required. It is that kind of sympathetic support from all of the musicians that makes their collective performances so satisfying.

The Chambers Brothers have a cheap, bastardized version of "Turn You Loose" on their latest album (and now released as a single). It is a crime that their version is the one receiving mass media exposure and that boppers are buying their single without even knowing about Redding's version.

On "Just One More Day" Redding again transforms one of his lesser songs into a major performance. The ballad opens with a beautiful, folky-sounding horn introduction. Redding's vocal is simple and eloquent. The entire five minute cut is marked by a sort of "I've Been Loving You Too Long" buildup and crescendo. Redding adds a long coda to the body of the song which includes a call and response between him and the band. In the middle of the coda, the band, except for the rhythm section, cuts out, suddenly creating a tense and dramatic mood. When they re-enter, they provide a perfect dramatic conclusion to the flawless recording.

From "Just One More Day" Redding charges into the lightning fast "Mr. Pitiful." The song is not one of my favorites but this is Redding's best recording of it. As "Mr. Pitiful" is drawing to a close the band suddenly breaks into "Satisfaction." The first lines are played just by the rhythm section, as Redding calls out, "Here's one you can't sit still over." And then they hit you with what is by far the best recording on the album and the best recording Redding ever did of this song.

Some people have never warmed to soul singers doing the Rolling Stones' opus. After all, the lyrics to the Stones' song have little to do with the experience of an Otis Redding or an Aretha Franklin. Overlooked in such a view is the fact that "Satisfaction" was an Otis Redding song. At the time Jagger and Richard wrote this song they were enormously influenced by Redding and had recorded several of his songs. "Satisfaction" in its rhythm, drive, and deliberateness, is perfect Redding material.

It was Steve Cropper and Booker T. who sensed this and asked Redding to try recording it. Incredibly, he had never heard the song. Nor was he overwhelmed by it the first time he heard it. Presumably, he had trouble making it through the lyrics. When he eventually did record it, he kept the basic rhythm motif and the intensity of the arrangement, but completely re-wrote the lyrics and tacked on a riff from Ray Charles' "I've Got a Woman," composing new lyrics on the spot. The result was one of the great virtuoso performances in recent pop music history.

The version included on the *A Go Go* album is almost twice as long as any of the versions included on other Redding albums. Redding structures the song so that each time it seems like he has no place to go with it he manages to increase the tension a bit more, until towards the end he goes into a speeded up double time which is sensational. It is the highest form of energy music I know of. One has to be awed not only by Redding's precision and artistry, but by his physical endurance as well. Like the man says.

> *Early in the monin'*
> *You've got to get you some*
> *And late in the evening oh man,*
> *You've got to get you some.*

All of the above mentioned cuts are on the first side of the album and unfortunately, the second side is not quite up to it. However, side two does have Redding's recording of James Brown's "Papa's Got a Brand New Bag." That cut, which has now been issued as a single, illustrates something which I have believed for some time: James Brown, despite his background, couldn't shine Otis Redding's shoes.

Otis Redding in Person at the Whiskey A Go Go is a significant addition to the available recordings of Otis Redding and a powerful testament to his ability as a stage performer. It's music to "get down with it" by.

When Otis Redding toured Europe with the Stax-Volt Revue in the summer of 1967, he used to close the show by following Sam and Dave. Legend has it that Redding would look on from back stage, sweating and mumbling to himself that he would never be able to follow *that*. And indeed, there was more than a little justification for his fear.

Redding contributes "Try a Little Tenderness" as the closing cut on the *Stax-Volt Revue Live in Paris* album. At the very end of the record, you can hear Sam Moore grabbing the mike and picking up where Otis left off and he sounds awfully good. Then again, Aretha Franklin tried to follow them at last summer's *Soul Together* concert and couldn't quite cut it either.

As live performers, there is little doubt that Sam and Dave are the finest soul performers working today. Many people involved with soul music professionally believe Sam Moore, the high voice of the duo, is the finest male singer of black music around.

Phil Walden, Otis' manager, handled the two of them for years. Recently they came to an unpleasant parting of the ways. Yet after hearing their latest single, "Everybody Got to Believe in Somebody," he felt he had to send them a telegram telling them again how good they are, an action that reflects both on Walden's generosity and Sam and Dave's brilliance.

While best known for their concert work, Sam and Dave have recorded some of the great standards of contemporary soul music. "Hold On, I'm Comin' " was their first giant record and represents one of the highpoints of the history of Stax-Volt. Al Jackson's drumming on that record, as well as Cropper's off-beat chording, is a triumph of the Stax style of simple, pounding rhythmic, yet always musical performance.

"When Something Is Wrong With My Baby" was a great piece of material, a beautiful soul ballad, but did not receive the performance it deserved until it was recorded live at the Stax-Volt revue in 1967.

"Soul Man," their single of a year ago, and their only gold record, was a gem on the order of "Hold On, I'm Comin'." The arrangement had all the elements of an outstanding Stax record: a archetypal horn figure, a memorable chord riff by Cropper, Jackson's incessantly rhythmic drumming (particularly his bass drum work) and vocal work, particularly by Sam, that cannot be topped.

Despite these highpoints, the group's recordings have been generally spotty. A single released earlier this year—"Can't You Find Another Way of Doing It"—was so atrocious hardly anyone would play it. Such records are the product of careless and hurried recording sessions, made necessary by the duo's constant touring. They are degrading to stars of Sam and Dave's stature.

Fortunately, their new album, *I Thank You,* shows evidence of great care. "I Thank You" is their well known follow up to "Soul Man" and is more of a rock and roll song that the duo usually record. "Wrap It Up" was the flip side and is almost as good. Particularly noteworthy is the driving horn line used on the chorus. "You Don't Know What You Mean To Me" features Sam's rock bottom preaching and a delightful, simple, hummable chorus.

The only lapse in the preparation of the album is in evidence on this cut—as is often the case, Atlantic has either remixed or used the wrong master, pointlessly altering the sound of the original 45. Anyway, the song is done better live.

Otis Redding's "These Arms of Mine" is given a lovely, unself-conscious reading and side two features five new Stax-Volt songs of unusually high quality. The core of this album is three songs done with strings and the closing cut, "That Lucky Old Sun." "Everybody Got To Believe in Somebody" is one of the string cuts and was released as a single. It is not doing well, primarily because soul stations do not like to program songs which use

string orchestration. It is a beautiful song, in perfect harmony with the Stax-Volt style. None of Sam and Dave's basic drive is sacrificed, but the accompaniment is given an added, and in my opinion, welcome dimension. Sam's lead is exceptional.

"Talk to the Man" is a similarly well done number, with a particularly exciting chorus. But it is on the ballad, "If I Didn't Have a Girl Like You" that the new approach produces a really magnificent cut. The song itself is a ballad in the "When Something Is Wrong with My Baby" mold.

Sam takes the lead for most of the song and his soaring voice is dramatically pitted against the dense, full instrumental track. The crescendo at the end—slow, heavy, inexorable—is a perfect fruition of everything Sam and Dave have sought to do. If the magnitude of their accomplishment on this cut does not hit you at first listening, listen a bit more. It is not the kind of thing that will necessarily strike you first time around.

For that kind of cut may I suggest "That Lucky Old Sun." For the body of the song Sam, who takes most of the lead, sings it straight. But at the end of the bridge there is a sudden and startling rhythm change and the two together unleash a powerful, driving conclusion to the song. Jackson's drumming is particularly exciting and after hearing the cut innumerable times I begin to think that this is supposed to be Sam and Dave's answer to "Try a Little Tenderness." If so, it's a mighty good answer.

—JON LANDAU
12-21-68

DOCK OF THE BAY
Otis Redding
(Volt S-419)

When Stevie Winwood first heard the single after which this album is named, he said "Is it a Dylan song? Eric Burdon? Sounds like Otis." Stevie's credentials are excellent, and his answer is very revealing. "Dock of the Bay" does sound very much like something that Dylan could have written. Both he and Otis were headed in the same direction.

As it is, it is.Otis' last single (Stax-Volt thinks they have enough *good* unreleased tapes to make another album) and the only indication left of where Otis was going to take us. It is possible to think that the tremendous emotional impact of this song—and that would be the indication of its soul—is in part due to his death, but the song itself, a distillation of all that's best in soul ballads, stands as one of Otis' very best recordings. "Dock of the Bay" indicated a real change in Otis' ballad style; he refined down to

two beautiful lines the techniques of tension against melancholy that he used in "Fa Fa Fa Fa Fa" and "Try a Little Tenderness."

The cuts on this "memorial album" were selected by Jon Landau, who went through all of Otis' recordings and picked his best performances with the exception of most of the best-known material. People who don't buy R&B singles should be especially grateful as should those who are not disc jockeys and did not obtain the Stax "Stay in School" album, a release which featured all the Stax-Volt performers in an anti-drop out propaganda piece. "Huckle-Buck" from that album is a performance that swings like mad. Where the horns aren't carrying it, the bass is. Just great.

"I'm Coming Home," a nearly faultless display of Otis' voice, because of the arrangement, particularly the horns which provide the primary texture, is relatively uninteresting and should probably not have been included in this set. "Ole Man Trouble" is too loose on this recording. While it is a fine song and a moving one with which to close this album, it can be found in a much better version on *Otis Blue*.

Dock of the Bay is one of the finest collections of Otis' recordings: the others are *History of Otis Redding* which contains all of his big hits; and *Dictionary of Soul* ("Complete and Unbelievable").

Dock of the Bay is one of the essential LP's for Redding fans. It is an excellent collection, obviously put together with both love and respect for what Otis Redding did and who he was. In many ways, *this* is the history of Otis Redding. "Tramp," his duet with Carla Thomas, really brings it home. Carla says "You know what Otis? You're country; you straight from the Georgia woods." And Otis says "That's *good.*" It sure is.

—JANN WENNER
4-27-68

〜〜〜〜〜〜〜〜〜〜〜〜〜〜〜〜

ARETHA: A SOUL QUEEN'S COMEBACK

〜〜〜〜〜〜〜〜〜〜〜〜〜〜〜〜

I NEVER LOVED A MAN
Aretha Franklin
(Atlantic SD 8176)

ARETHA ARRIVES
Aretha Franklin
(Atlantic SD 8150)

The record business is a well known drag. Even if it isn't a drag for everybody, up until recently it has certainly been a drag for Aretha Franklin. Six years ago she made the mistake of signing a long term contract with a label that didn't know what to do with her—Columbia —and for five years she struggled with material like "Rock-A-Bye Your Baby" and "Try A Little Tenderness." She did the best she could with it, and some of her recordings were extremely good, but it obviously wasn't her scene.

It was only when the Columbia contract expired that Aretha's luck began to change. In 1966 she had the good fortune to encounter an aspect of the music scene which is definitely not a drag, namely Jerry Wexler, the Vice-President of a non-drag label, Atlantic Records.

Wexler has been largely responsible for the soul revival, and while he is certainly not averse to commercial success, he seems to have a high regard for the integrity of his artists. Under his leadership Atlantic and its subsidiaries have been coming up with thoroughly inspired and revitalized soul music, in the form of Joe Tex, Otis Redding and Wilson Pickett, i.e., the whole Stax-Volt thing. It was under Wexler that the old Ray Charles records were done which set a standard for modern blues artists. The importance of Wexler in allowing Charles artistic freedom can be seen when we compare the Atlantic Ray Charles to the ABC Ray Charles. ABC simply did not know what to do with the genius and as a result he never produced a satisfying album during his entire tenure on that label.

When Aretha finally got away from Columbia Jerry moved in and set her up with Atlantic's regular soul sidemen and songwriters, and in a very short time she emerged as a super-star. Now she books for incredible sums of money and her recent records sell in incredible numbers.

The new Aretha is obviously her own girl with an easily identifiable sound. While Wexler himself produces her, it is obvious that, as with Charles, his commercial and artistic sense tells him that Aretha will do better left alone. Let her do her things, after all, she's the one with the talent. That's the way to treat an artist. Motown wouldn't have been good for Aretha because just like Columbia they would have tried to stick her with a sound that wasn't her own, and for Aretha it never would have worked.

Musically, Aretha is obviously into gospel. She is the daughter of a well known gospel singer and she has listened to Alex Bradford and Marion Williams, although Aretha's style is more lowdown than either of theirs. She has also listened to B. B. King and other urban, gospel-oriented, blues vocalists. But above all, standing behind her like a shadow is Ray Charles.

Aretha's own synthesis of all these basically frenetic styles first appeared on *I Never Loved A Man the Way That I Love You.* On it, Aretha got into some very fine things. She did a very nice job with the rhythm on "Respect" and she laid down a very fine vocal on King Curtis' old instrumental, "Soul Serenade." Also, "Don't Let Me Lose This Dream" showed her off as a fine songwriter, and again her very subtle rhythmic sense predominates. The verses are almost Latin. The main hang-up with the album as a whole was the lack of versatility on the part of the sidemen. The drums weren't hard enough, the guitar was weak, and the production lacked polish.

On her latest album, *Aretha Arrives,* these problems are completely removed. Most of the people who do Wilson Pickett's sessions were brought in for the new job, and particularly crucial here was the use of drummer Roger Hawkins. He turns the whole thing into rock and roll which was what the first album lacked. On four of the slow cuts Wexler tries out some strings and I think they work quite well.

Aretha's performance on *Aretha Arrives* is not faultless. On the contrary, she herself has two distinct hang-ups, both of which were present on the first album, and both of which really begin to grate on the new one. The first of these has to do with her choice of material. All these slow ballads begin to drag after a while, especially because there is so little attempt at doing anything distinctive with some of them. On the first album this problem was particularly evident on Aretha's thin attempt at recreating Ray Charles' gorgeous "Drown in My Own Tears." On the new album there is too much of stuff like "Never Let Me Go," which fits into this category of uninspired slow stuff.

A cut like "Prove It," or "Change's Gonna Come," on the first album, are both very inspired ballad performances, and show fully Aretha's capacity in this direction. Nonetheless, dull stuff takes up too much space on *Aretha Arrives* and helps to destroy the continuity of the album as a whole.

Aretha's other problem takes the form of a gimmick. It seems whenever she gets into a weak spot in one of the arrangements she runs for the gospel shouts. She overuses two or three phrases to the point of distraction from whatever else is going on during the cut. To someone who doesn't listen to a lot of soul music this reliance on shouts and screams can be very exciting, but to people more accustomed to the idiom, it is likely to wear very thin. The only soul star who knows how to handle the technique consistently is Ray Charles. Even James Brown can get to be a drag when he overdoes that

kind of thing, which lately he hasn't.

So much for the hang-ups. The rest of what is happening here is first rate all the way. On side one Aretha turns in a knockout "Satisfaction," (dig the drums) and a solid remake of Charles' "You Are My Sunshine." She is a hundred per cent successful with her vaguely comical "96 Tears," and "Prove It" is the best ballad on the album, making the most successful use of strings on any of the bands. Side two has most of the real winners though.

Leading off is a version of "That's Life" which convinces you that not only Aretha, but the song as well, is great. "Going Down Slow" is the best blues on the album and is very tough, especially the ending, and the riff that the band backs her with. "Ain't Nobody," written by sister Carolyn, is a gospel thing that shows how well Aretha works with those minor gospel chord progressions. The gospel shouting in the background is breath-taking. And finally there is the opus, by far the best cut on the record, "Baby, I Love You." This cut smoulders eroticism, has beautiful piano, fine rhythm guitar, great lyrics, great vocal back-up by Aretha and her sisters, double tracked, and a perfect lowdown dirty lead vocal. I think I got it all.

Basically, *Aretha Arrives* is a high impact album in which

neither the sophistication nor the subtlety of the musicians involved gets in the way of the basic primitivism of Aretha's music. The best cuts on the record hit with tremendous immediacy and force, and do so in a totally artistic way. The only defects are the occasional reliance on unnecessary gimmicks, and the weakness of some of the material.

It will be interesting to see where Aretha goes from here. The only single that she has released since this album is quite distinct from anything else she has done for Atlantic. "A Natural Woman" was written for Aretha by the team of Goffin and King who do so much writing for big white groups like the Righteous Brothers, the old Animals, and the Monkees. They are songwriters who can write a song to fit anyone's style, and "A Natural Woman," while it is an extremely commercial record, is also a significant improvement over some of the material Aretha's been recording. The production is more within the mainstream of big pop production and makes far better use of strings and horns than was done on either of the two albums.

It is a good sign for the future of Aretha's career because, even while taking her away from some of the more lowdown stuff she has already done, it gives her a chance to work with the really big sound her

voice is capable of without sacrificing her identity. It shows that she can go beyond what she has already done. And when one has done as much as Aretha already has, that is no mean accomplishment.

—JON LANDAU
11-23-67

ARETHA NOW
Aretha Franklin
(Atlantic SD 8186)

The new Aretha Franklin album, shows America's most important and popular singer walking a very thin line between progress and regression. The best things, although few in number, are among her best ever; the lesser items show that both she and the entire Atlantic staff are having trouble trying to keep the ball rolling. And even the good stuff doesn't sustain itself over repeated listenings.

For some of Aretha's fans, her first album was her best and each successive one has decreased in interest. Up until this album, I thought that the reverse has been the case. *I Never Loved A Man* was her least refined and, to me, was fairly dull and repetitious. *Aretha Arrives* was a solid improvement, and *Lady Soul* was her very best— in fact, it may well prove to be the best album of the year. On that record Aretha is heard in command of absolutely everything: "Natural Woman" to "Sweet, Sweet Baby"; "Groovin'" to her triumphal "Ain't No Way." She proved herself capable of encompassing a variety of moods, tempos, lyrics, and styles and yet she remained on top of them all. There was no slackness and no throw-away cut. Her every nuance was perfectly controlled and executed.

On *Aretha Now* Miss Franklin aims for a second edition of *Lady Soul*. According to Jerry Wexler, it was an easier album to record. It took only five days of studio time. The musicians were as enthusiastic as ever, and presumably, thoroughly cooperative. These sessions were done in precisely the same manner as the earlier ones. The lead vocal and rhythm were laid down together, in the first stage. Then the vocal backgrounds of the Sweet Inspirations were added on the second track. Finally, the horn section added its parts on the last track. This is how Aretha has done her sessions right from the beginning with Atlantic when she cut "I Never Loved A Man" and "Do Right Woman—Do Right Man" in Muscle Shoals, over a year and a half ago.

But the fact that these sessions did go so well may not have been a good sign. Three albums of the same bag were enough. On *Lady Soul* Aretha refined the style just about as far as it can be refined. *Aretha Now* over-saturates us with a statement that cannot stand too much more repetition. Only on some of the ballad material does it push in any new direction. The 2/4 uptempo (like "I Take What I Want") is boring. On much of the album, the musicians sound like they have done it all before. Their enthusiasm just doesn't come across like it did when they socked it to us on "Sweet, Sweet Baby." They haven't grown. Drummer Roger Hawkins, for whom my admiration is well known, is stagnating.

Wexler tried to anticipate some of the problems by cutting down on the size of the rhythm section but that hasn't given the record the tightness he was hoping for. The bass and drum combination isn't as strong with Tommy Cogbill (bassist on all previous sessions) now playing lead guitar and Jerry Jammot playing bass. Not only that, Cogbill, who is among the finest bassists in popular music, is a boring and inconsequential lead guitarist. While he does a fairly good job on some of the slow material ("I Can't See Myself Leaving You") he isn't nearly as good as Bobby Womack playing the same bag on Wilson Pickett's records (like "I'm In Love"). And on the fast cuts he clutters things up with a semi-country style of flat-picking ("Think") which is just nowhere.

There is no question that

most of this record would have been improved if it had been recorded in Memphis with an expanded version of the Stax-Volt band, which, along with the Motown studio band, remains the finest soul band in the world.

But enough of these generalities. The following is a detailed commentary of the album's ten cuts. There are also some suggestions on what new directions Aretha might seek to explore in the future.

"Think" ties "Chain of Fools" as Aretha's worst single. I was hoping it would bomb, as a deterrent to further such records being released as singles, but Atlantic is confident it will be her sixth million-seller. Which is a fantastic achievement for anybody. The song has virtually no melody. The lyrics are trite and banal. (Aretha and her husband composed the song.) The vocal is disturbed by Cogbill's super-busy lead. The piano is the best thing on the cut, and is quite nice. Vocally the only good segment is the "Freedom" chorus, primarily because it is sung over a I-III-IV-V progression, which manages to appear once and not be repeated for the rest of the song. The overall franticness of both song and vocal are grating to this listener and do not achieve the personal level of communication which soul is supposed to be all about.

"I Say A Little Prayer": One of the real successes of the al-

bum. Wexler heard Aretha fooling around with this one in the studio and it sounded so good he decided to record it on the spot. What Aretha has done with the arrangement is among the most creative things I have ever heard her do. After whipping through the song, she gets into a very kinetic buildup with the chorus doing a very nice job. After several repetitions of the basic melody-lyric line, the ensemble moves very nicely into the chorus again, with a beautiful crescendo. The whole structure of the thing reveals tremendous sensitivity on the part of all concerned. It is just that level of personal communication that is lacking on the opening cut which is utilized so well here. To improve a Bacharach-David-Warwick performance is really an event and it shows that we would all profit if Aretha were willing to spend a little more time with material like this and "Natural Woman."

"See Saw" is a Don Covay-Steve Cropper song which is given very mediocre treatment here. The vocal is quite good, but the omission of the original harmony from the chorus was foolish, because it is an integral part of the song's identity. Again the lead guitar is inadequate. It is more the feeble sound that Cogbill gets out of his amp that hurts than the ordinary licks he uses. Other than that, the song falls into Aretha's 2/4 drag trap. It just crawls along, despite her best efforts to give it a push with her voice. The drums don't punch and the bass lacks sock. Tunes like "Money Won't Change You" from *Lady Soul* said the same thing with infinitely more zest and flash.

"Night Time" is a Ray Charles staple and was recorded at Wexler's suggestion. Of course, Wexler recorded almost all of the Atlantic Ray Charles sides and if that was all he had ever done it would still have been enough to make him one of the major A&R men of the post-war period. Wexler minimizes any contribution he made by saying that when the Genius recorded the only thing anyone ever had to do was turn on the microphones.

Anyway, Wexler obviously loves to see Aretha do an occasional Ray Charles selection and this was intended as pure fun. For the most part it is. The band does some very swinging big band things and the piano is very solid. Still, the trouble with doing Ray Charles is that Aretha is not Ray Charles and she just can't cut it vocally. She's not in his class and that's all there is to it. She proved the same thing when she messed up "Drown In My Own Tears" on an earlier album. If after I'm through hearing it I can pull out a record made ten years ago and realize that it is better in every respect, right from the original's opening, wailing sax solo, then I seriously question

the wisdom of Aretha trying to do it at all.

"You Send Me": Well, if Aretha should stay out of the Ray Charles bag, she should do more in Sam Cooke's. She does wonders with Sam's biggest selling record, and this has to be the best cut on the album. It is simple, straightforward, uncluttered ballad singing at its best. The piano intro is superb, the harmony and horns perfect. I can't imagine the drums, the lyric improvisations, or the entire arrangement being any better. Sam Cooke would have smiled.

"You're A Sweet Sweet Man" is a Ronnie Shannon song. Ronnie Shannon is Aretha's own discovery and composed two of her best earlier hits: "I Never Loved A Man" and "Baby, I Love You." While his lyrics here are, as usual, exceptional, the melody lacks direction and the band goes around in circles. Hawkins' drum intro could have been better. The best thing about the cut is really the Inspirations singing "Sweets for my sweet, sugar for my honey," in the background.

"I Take What I Want" is Sam and Dave, and Aretha's version is no match for theirs. Wexler told me that he has tried to get Hayes and Porter (Sam and Dave's writing-production team) to write some new material for Aretha, but most of what they have come up with is of a decidedly inferior quality compared to what they do for their Stax artists. The vocal chorus is contrived on Aretha's version and wholly superfluous. During the break Aretha sings over just a bass. Sam and Dave do the same bit over the bass and Al Jackson's drums, and it really makes a difference. In fact, for a cut like this, there is no question that Jackson is the man they need.

"Hello Sunshine" was first recorded by Wilson Pickett on his *I'm in Love* album. The song is a major work and certainly bears re-recording by Aretha. The difference between Cogbill and Jammot as bassists is pointed up here because Cogbill's bass on the earlier version was vastly superior to what Jammot puts down here. Nonetheless, the horns and arrangement in general are overpowering, the vocal superb, and the cut emerges as one of the best Aretha has ever done. The last 45 seconds are particularly gorgeous. Aretha shows real creativity in the way she interacts with the Inspirations and the horns at the same time. Cogbill's chord style is also good and the way they have all altered the tail end of the melody is excellent.

"A Change" is an uptempo piece of very mediocre quality given a very ordinary reading by all concerned. The lead guitar gets in the way again but that's really the least of their problems. Wexler should have

shown more discrimination and refused to have let this cut pass.

"I Can't See Myself Leaving You" is another Ronnie Shannon tune, a very pleasing ballad. The vocal and guitar work together intimately to build the mood and the arrangement complements the development more than adequately. No big pretense, no frenzy, just a highly listenable cut.

Atlantic seems to be not unaware of the fact that all kinds of ugly things can happen if they let Aretha settle in a rut. Consequently they are thinking now of bringing out some different kinds of things in the future. They have already recorded a live album in Europe which should be a real brain buster. And they are considering doing a live gospel album as well, which should be even more exciting. What I would like to see is Atlantic bring out a greatest hit album this summer as kind of a landmark indicating that this phase of Aretha's career is behind her. Such an album would be an immediate million dollar album and could easily be filled with nothing but the best of what Aretha has already done. Then Atlantic ought to consider in just what ways they could help Aretha move beyond the plateau she has already reached. The following are some observations and comments intended to suggest some possible approaches open to them.

The first thing Aretha needs is a song writing team. Every major artist in every different field of pop music relies on one. If an artist doesn't write too much original material he simply must have somebody with whom he can work, capable of furnishing him an album's worth of material several times a year. The Beatles have themselves, as do most of the white groups, but the soul and pop stars need non-performers most of the time.

Otis was an exception but Sam and Dave rely on Hayes and Porter, Albert King on Booker T. and William Bell, and Dionne Warwick on Bacharach and David. And I needn't add anything about the Motown artists. The reason why Aretha needs to find such people is that it simply will not do for a star of her stature to continue devoting large percentages of her album cuts to dressed-up versions of old soul hits. Of course there are exceptions ("You Send Me") but as a general rule she just can't do her best when she is working with five year old Don Covay material and ten year old Ray Charles numbers.

One way or another, she's got to be able to present the public with something that is fresh and new. There are, I might add, several song writing teams around who might easily

fit into Aretha's needs, the most notable being Dan Penn and Spooner Oldham, who have been writing some of the best new soul songs around.

Secondly, Aretha needs a new band. I yield to no one in my appreciation of what the Muscle Shoals group has done for Aretha on her first three albums, but its time for a change. They have had their say, they've played their song, and they have now stopped growing. And when that happens new people have to be found.

Finally, Aretha's full range as a vocalist must be developed. And to do that, the range of her material has to be expanded. Her soft side, her ballad singing, which even now is one of the finest things about her, has to be given more opportunities to make its presence felt.

Atlantic may be a little reluctant because "Natural Woman," despite the fact that both the song and the arrangement were extraordinarily beautiful, was Aretha's poorest selling single, her only one, in fact, which failed to reach a million. But such reluctance must be overcome. Sooner or later people are going to get tired of the one dimension Aretha has settled into and she damned well better have some place to go because if she doesn't she isn't going to last.

This all may seem a little harsh and in a way it's very unfair. Unfair because Aretha didn't expect to become an over-night super-star, and now that she has it is only human that after three albums she is beginning to falter. But she is a super-star and she ought to be treated like one. I for one think she can cut it. Sure, she has limits. She also has talent. More of it than any female vocalist singing rock and roll right now. But because she has so much, it is that much more important that she continue to develop it, that she continue to grow into the beautiful musician she is destined to become.

—JON LANDAU
11-23-67

SOUL '69
Aretha Franklin
(Atlantic SD 8212)

It does no good to say Aretha Franklin can't sing as well as Ivy Anderson; Ivy Anderson is dead, and not a dozen of the dedicated music-lovers who read this journal remember the great Duke Ellington vocalist. We must make do with what we have, and the best female singer we have now is Aretha. There are cleverer singers, and there are one or two with more impressive technical abilities, but no one does so many things so well. At her best, Aretha is more exciting and more believable than any other lady now singing. She does not break our hearts, as did Ivy, or Billie

Holiday, but she moves us with her ballads and grooves us with her soul shouts. We could be worse off.

After a rather long apprenticeship, during which she sang gospel for her father, the celebrated Reverend C. L. Franklin, and pop for Columbia Records, Aretha joined the Atlantic Recording Company, whose vice-president and producer, Jerry Wexler, took her to a studio in Muscle Shoals, Alabama, to record with a group of musicians from Memphis. The rest, to mint a phrase, is history. A steady stream of million-selling records in an advanced rhythm-and-blues style have earned for "Lady Soul" tremendous public and critical approval, including the ultimate accolade of American pop civilization, the cover of *Time*. The effect of all this acclaim, however, has seemed unfortunate. While Aretha's first three Atlantic albums were mostly excellent, her fourth was not so good, and her fifth, a desultory "live" album, was miserable. Perhaps she had become bored, feeling that there were no more worlds to conquer.

Now, however, Wexler has once more expanded her horizons. Aretha's latest, though camouflaged with the title *Soul '69*, is an album of blues, or more specifically, jazz-blues. It is quite possibly the best record to appear in the last five years. Certainly it is excellent in ways in which pop music hasn't been since the Beatles spear-headed the renaissance of rock, a musical genre which, notwithstanding its recent eclecticism, is extremely limited, having neither the musical complexity nor the emotional variety of jazz.

Though some groups, like Blood, Sweat & Tears, are getting into jazz, none of them could have made an album like this one with musicianship of such subtlety, individuality and seemingly effortless power. Wexler gathered musicians from such revered sources as the Count Basie Orchestra and the Miles Davis Quintet, put them together for eight-hour recording sessions, and the result is that the band sounds as if it had been together for years. The horn arrangements, by Arif Mardin, are simply beautiful, alternately driving and mellow, with rich, warm harmonies. Aretha sings better than ever; she is freer, more relaxed, and each time she hits a note it makes a dramatic point.

Though this album is a departure from her usual style, Atlantic has eased the transition in several ways. Besides the protective coloring of the title, there are on some tracks the background singers familiar from her earlier records, and on two tracks—"Today I Sing the Blues" and "Tracks of My Tears"—the rhythm section is her usual funky crew from Memphis' American Studios. The choice of tunes, including "Gentle On My Mind" and "Elusive Butterfly," will also make *Soul '69* more palatable to Aretha's pop-oriented fans, some of whom will probably buy the album and enjoy it without even knowing that they're listening to heavy jazz.

This album could have a tremendous effect on contemporary popular music, but it probably won't. The devices on an album like the Beatles' *Sergeant Pepper* are easily imitated, but musicianship that has paid its dues for decades cannot be. The electric-haired heads of today's rock musicians will have turned white before they make an album like this one.

—STANLEY BOOTH
3-11-69

SPIRIT IN THE DARK
Aretha Franklin
(Atlantic SD 8265)

When I was an innocent 17-year-old freshman, a black grad student I met invited me to play guitar at this "discussion group" he "chaired" at a downtown Pittsburgh "hall." Well, that sounded good enough, so one evening I went to the address he gave me and found myself the only white person—youngest to boot—in the middle of a Pittsburgh-ghetto-preaching and shouting non-denominational-holy rollering one - preacher - 30 - parishioner store-front church.

My grad student friend was the one preacher.

He stepped up to the pulpit to face his flock, and immediately you could feel the religious energy in the room start to build. First he said isn't it nice the way all God's children can come together and raise their voices on high to the glory of God. A-men. Amen. That's right, and he said when we *all* get together, *all* God's children, and sing unto Him, I know His light shines upon us. That's *right*. Amen.

Next he's introducing brother Isaac Turner who's gonna play the organ for us while we sing His praises: Brother Isaac. And Brother Isaac sits down and *stomps* on that organ, and Reverend Thomas sings the first line of his song and the congregation sings its answer, and he shouts the next line and they shout back, and ten verses later, when he had done all the hymnal verses, when Brother Isaac was *wailing* that organ away, when you were jumpin' up and down just to keep from getting knocked over by the people rollin' on the floor, at that height of religious pandemonium, Reverend Thomas started testifying . . . singing his soul out to the Lord, confessing, shouting: testifying with

the heart's words his love supreme for the Almighty.

And that's just where Aretha Franklin starts to sing. Whether denying her man's two-timing or declaring her love for him, Aretha makes her song sound like a "testifying" of her feelings.

This is the spirit she lavished on "Chain of Fools," "Think," "See Saw" and the like, and which has been sorely missed since her *Soul '69* album. That record saw her strapped to a big band jazz format in a concerted but somehow unexciting effort; maybe it just never stood a chance following her hard stuff. The next album, *This Girl's in Love With You,* was back to soul grits, but smelled like something had gone amiss in the kitchen. It was concocted from cuts which had probably been lying around in the can, refried hits of white groups— "Let It Be," "Eleanor Rigby," "Son of a Preacher Man," "The Weight"—and one Aretha original, "Call Me." Spice with uninspired arrangements and vocals. Cook at below standard temperature (for Muscle Shoals). Serve tepid.

But, Aretha fans, relief has arrived. *Spirit in the Dark* has the soul (and spirit) of the Aretha Franklin we all know and love. The Queen has made a strong return to her gospel roots, and therein lies the success of this album. Cut after cut is underlined by her rolling, gospel piano on solid fills and funky solos. Aretha's piano work on "The Thrill is Gone" typifies her unique gospel way of interpreting blues material. She delivers her message tersely and, incredibly, maintains the musical tension and aura of desperation which haunt the tune.

I don't know what to say, what to single out, about the arrangements on this album. They possess a kind of soul freakishness in their constant flow of fresh ideas and subtle, stoney effects hidden under layers of innocent-sounding, hardass, rocking soul. The do-wah-bop-sha-bang girls (besides singing in shimmering harmony) pop up at weird moments to offer words of advice or warning when Aretha makes a particularly impassioned confession of love. Sort of a latter day Greek Chrous in their effect. Other remarkable feats of arrangement: steadily rising, ass-kicking climax on almost every tune, guided by the sure hand (foot?) of master musicians and producers. If the MGs were at their best under Otis Redding, these various bands sound best under Aretha. Yup, she pulled a good performance out of everyone on these sessions.

Aretha wrote five of the tunes on this album and all are strong compositions and excellent vehicles for her. The standouts, "Pullin" and "Spirit in the Dark" are masterpieces of composition and performance. Why "Don't Play That Song" was chosen over either of them for the single release is beyond me. Only two tunes here have been hits previously (both by B. B. King), "The Thrill is Gone," and "Why I Sing the Blues," and both, if you believe it's possible, are *more* chillingly done than the originals.

'Nuf said about *Spirit in the Dark*. If you're into Aretha's singing you already know the majesty and supreme power she's capable of. Its all here: sweet soul music done as only Aretha Franklin can do it.

Turns out Reverend Thomas played a pretty mean game of tennis too.

—BILL AMATNEEK
11-12-70

SOUL TODAY: THE PAST MAKES THE FUTURE

LIFE
Sly and the Family Stone
(Epic BN 26397)

The most adventurous soul music of 1968 is being put out by two groups who really aren't part of the mainstream R&B

scene at all. Both the Chambers Brothers and Sly and the Family Stone are primarily black, but both have white members. And both spend more time on the white rock circuit than in the black clubs and theaters.

The Family Stone emerges as the real revolutionary force on this, its third album. Sly's people have made a mighty progression since their first album just eight months ago. That album (*A Whole New Thing*) was a rather conventional program enlivened by two or three heavy flashes. *Life* is a flash from beginning to end. Easily the most radical soul album ever issued, it is an exhilarating success in a time of disappointments.

Soul music, like blues, was born in an environment of noisy clubs and parties. R&B records are made for instant pleasure, not concentrated listening, and they have always thrived on simplicity. A single sonic texture usually suffices for a song, sometimes for a whole album. But not with Sly and the Family Stone. Rarely does Sly let any element sink in before he socks you with a change. The group has several capable lead singers in various voice ranges from bass to soprano, and they are forever trading off; some of the vocal arrangements almost sound like Lambert, Hendricks & Ross revisited. Same deal with the instruments—guitar, organ, bass, drums, horns ap-

pear in new combinations and voicings about every other bar. Like the Mothers, this group revels in the element of surprise. The contrast with the predictable fare you get on R&B stations is incredible.

Take, for example, the first cut, "Dynamite!" Opening with an unaccompanied blues guitar lick, turned up all the way, it goes into a heavy riff. With fuzz guitar out front, it's more a San Francisco riff than a Motown one. Then comes the vocal. The melodic line and progressions are fairly standard soul, but the words move into a new realm. Even more radical is the way the vocal lead is split up between at least three different singers. Each new one is a flash, yet the continuity never gets lost. Next flash: the word "Dynamite" is repeated, three times, to the accompaniment of a building drum roll that amply suggests the impact of an explosion. Back to the top, and the verse is repeated in a slightly longer form, with heavier instrumentation. (Relatively standard soul procedure here.) The "Dynamite" climax is doubly strong. Then the opening blues guitar once again, but here it dissolves into some of the "bomp-bomp" vocalizing that has always been a Sly trademark, and we are suddenly in the presence of a very well-executed Beatle-style fade. Suddenly we think we hear one of the horns doing the familiar lick from "Dance to the Music." Only *after* that are our suspicions confirmed, as someone actually sings the title line of that memorable song. More quotes from "Dance" and the music dissolves into happy talk and laughter. The whole sequence, the whole track, is ecstatic listening in any situation.

So that's one cut, time 2:43. All the cuts on this album are single length (range 2:12 to 3:28), but each one goes through flashes equal to those on "Dynamite!" Some of the flashes are cute—as on "Chicken" where voices dissolve into clucking, and on "Harmony" where the voices go into a fancy jazz chord everytime the title comes up. (I'll let the rest of these be surprises—the good taste and naturalness holds throughout.) Other flashes are musically very strong, like the double-time jazz turn-around figure on "Into My Own Thing," and the Staple Singers counterpoint on "Chicken."

Still another flash technique is the use of quotes. "Dance to the Music," not itself on this album, becomes a sort of *leitmotif*, a wonderful device to tie the album together and emphasize the group's identity. It crops up in various guises on several different cuts. One whole cut, "Love City," is generated from the tune of "Dance"; note how the soprano sax line is a very interesting development from the one in "Dance." This may seem like self-plagiarism or lack of originality. I rather think it's intentional. In any case, it's highly effective, just one more of the innumerable subtle things Sly thinks up to keep you glued to your stereo. "Eleanor Rigby" also comes in for a couple of masterful quotes.

Sly's words are still another radical factor. R&B lyrics have generally had more sociological than intrinsic interest; Sly's have plenty of both. He often deals with standard subjects, but his pithy, cliche-free language is quite a departure from the norm. Then again, Sly gets into some message and story things that are much closer to new rock than to soul as in "Plastic Jim." "Jane Is A Groupee" is the most incisive song ever written about rock's camp-followers, not excluding Frank Zappa's several comments on this theme. "I'm an Animal" is perhaps the best of all—and I'd quote it, except that those words really have to be heard to be enjoyed. Some rather sensual sounds which I could only write as "ugh ugh" are an integral part of the message. The music, the words and the meaning are all one great experience.

In a very curious way, this album reminds one of the big swing bands of the 1930s in their prime. It's because everything depends on the arrangements, and the arrangements are constructed to spotlight many different solo elements, each very briefly, with the interest heightened by a constantly changing background. The frequent use of riffs is another thing Sly has in common with old Count Basie records. Early rock and roll, with its absolute simplicity to the point of intentional monotony, was a great rebellion against this very approach. Now here we are with Sly and the Family Stone. Such things make rock history interesting. Soul music up to this point has continued to pursue the simplicity approach, its year-to-year progress coming mainly out of the advancement of vocal techniques, electric bass and drum playing, and improved recording quality. Sly's vocalists and instrumentalists are all more than competent, but they are content to serve their purpose within the arrangements, which are *the thing* here.

Sly and the Family Stone are opening the door to a whole new era in soul music. With their emphasis on flash, on never-let-up entertainment of the senses rather than on the orderly telling of a story, they might well be the first McLuhanian soul group. But perhaps they haven't got the door all the way open yet; there are still a few bugs in the machine.

The biggest bug is a real paradox, not at all easy to describe but evident nonetheless. Despite the uniform quality of all the cuts, and despite all the variety of texture and all the flashes, *Life* is not the best album to hear all the way through at one sitting. This is partly because certain changes pop up in similar form in many cuts, the trade-off vocal parts especially. But a much more important reason is that there is very little variety in the tempos—fast straight time all the way. There is even less variety in the dynamics, which are of course loud all the way. "I'm An Animal" has a fleeting few bars that are gently scored, with some really sensual soft singing. They are incredibly beautiful in this context, and I'm sure Sly could do a lot more with dynamic variation if he cared to. A change into shuffle or ¾ time could also have been very effective.

This album contains, of course, the group's current single "Life." Despite a fine flash in which a 1900 brass band becomes a soul horn section, and some brilliant effects on organ, it's not quite the best cut. This itself signifies a welcome change from all those R&B albums that sink or swim with their hit singles.

The recording is superb technically. Incredibly enough, this group performs this material on stage in very much the form it appears here. But the record is really a greater experience, because the flashes of subtleties are much clearer and more dramatic in stereo. The only complaint one might have is that one can't hear the bottom very well. But I suspect it was intended that way; it's just one more element to set *Life* apart from ordinary soul albums. Also it helps the clarity. The drums, recorded up front and very percussive, preserve the motion unfailingly.

—BARRET HANSEN
8-24-68

STAND!
Sly and the Family Stone
(Epic BN 26456)

Like Frank Zappa's Mothers, Sly Stone's group is unique. And, in fact, a comparison of the two groups is not as far fetched as it first might seem. Both exude a superficial formlessness in their sounds. Both demand, on one level at least, to be taken seriously. But while the Mothers have taken pop music to previously unimaginable levels of complexity, Sly and the Family Stone has gone in the other direction—to basics.

At first, *Stand!* seemed like soul music distorted, or soul music lacking its usual polish, but a couple of listenings showed this to be a superficial impression. John Mayall once called soul music "all showmanship," which, while typically purist of him, is largely true. While the Stone Family puts on a show, it isn't showmanship.

First of all, there is no attempt at sophistication. While all the Family Stones are competent musicians, their overall sound comes across more like a noisy clamoring street gang who just happen to have some musical instruments in their possession, than a polished blend of musicians. And, vocally, they're much closer to the mid-Fifties black groups than present-day soul, even the Memphis variety.

But, if they're a noisy young street gang, they're a gang with a very evident sense of moral purpose (like the Mothers). Almost all their songs on *Stand!*, which includes their hit single, "Everyday People," are openly idealistic, telling of things as they *should* be, dealing with vast social problems in abstract terms, which is not usually within the scope of soul music. *Stand!* is not, however, simply a polemic. It's also extremely vital body busic. It really can't be listened to at a low volume and communicate. *Stand!* depends on sheer energy more than anything else.

The most powerful instrument in the sound is usually the bass, which is incessant and repetitive. And, in fact, the most bothersome thing about this album, at first, was its insistent, almost defiant, repetition. But, it was bothersome simply because I sat there trying to figure it out; once I stood up (like the title says) it was fine. It's not a contemplative piece.

There's one long instrumental cut included, called "Sex Machine," that's really different. Except for the number of instruments used, it's pretty close to Jimi Hendrix's stuff. They use a single heavy bass line and pile up a lot of slurpy, buzzy, electronic sounds including the strange sound of Sly scatting into a microphone that is hooked up to a wah-wah pedal, and for a unit that isn't primarily an instrumental group, they come out with one of the most listenable hard rock instrumentals I've heard in quite a while.

One of the other cuts that really stood out is pointedly titled, "Don't Call Me Nigger, Whitey." It's just that phrase and the converse, "Don't call me whitey, nigger," repeated endlessly in voices that sound like a black David Seville and the Chipmunks. It's done in a taunting, almost snotty tone of voice and irritated the hell out of me until I realized that it was intended to do just that. It works. You get the message.

And, that, perhaps, sums up *Stand!* It's effective. You can criticize each or any particular point regarding the music or the content of the message, but in toto, it works. *Stand!* is not an album for someone who

demands perfection or sophistication, although it's by no means crude—just basic. It's for anyone who can groove on a bunch of very raucous kids charging through a record, telling you exactly what they think whether you want to hear it that way or not. If you don't mind being pushed a little, then *Stand!* will move you.

—ALEC DUBRO
7-26-69

COLD SHOT
The Johnny Otis Show
(Kent 534)

This is a monster of a blues album, one of the very best and freshest in recent years. Otis, of course, is well known as the leader of a highly successful package revue that toured extensively during the Fifties and enjoyed great success with Negro audience. His recent disclosure that he is not black but white blew a lot of minds, for his command of modern Negro popular music has been more than sufficient for him to have gained unqualified acceptance in the black community.

Now he's back blowing minds again with his imaginative, exciting album. Despite the name of the group "The Johnny Otis Show," the basic instrumentation is that of a trio—Otis, thanks to multiple recording, doubling on piano and drums, both of which he plays authentically; his 16-year-old son Johnny "Shuggie" Otis Jr. on guitars and bass (and occasionally harmonica) and a young, very impressive singer Delmar "Mighty Mouth" Evans. Occasionally a number of local Los Angeles bluesmen augment this basic format, but the honors definitely go to the trio. The three men create a lot of honest, inventive music, reaffirming the communicative power and continuing relevance of the blues (if there were ever any question of this). And there's a great deal of humor in their approach too.

The music is very contemporary sounding, thanks largely to the work of young Shuggie Otis, who has the sound and tonal effects of recent rock guitar down cold. Despite his youth, he plays solid, interesting lines—not just strings of licks—that move surefootedly and, most often, with real power. He has something to say and says it directly. And his concern with tone production is obvious in everything he plays. To say he's promising is to be condescending of his already solid accomplishment; such a qualification is irrelevant anyway. He's got the idiom covered.

There are any number of excellent performances. "The Signifyin' Monkey" is a very musical and forceful treatment of an old Negro bawdy toast that boasts flawless backup work and a pair of strong solos by Shuggie Otis. It doesn't mince words either, being a totally unexpurgated version of the old toast. Its only flaw is a clumsy ending. Equally impressive is "Country Girl," again with solid, imaginative guitar work, and a great amount of humor in the vocal. The instrumental "Cold Shot" is a bitch, with fine solos by both Otises and by amplified-violinist Sugarcane Harris (one half of the old Don and Dewey recording team). The track's only drawback is that it doesn't go on long enough; I could listen to a whole LP of this kind of music. Harris' playing especially is very bluesy. "Sittin' Here All Alone" and "Bye Bye Baby" have some very effective T.-Boneish guitar work and fine Otis piano. And Evans' singing throughout the album is excellent, rhythmically relaxed and full of feeling. Just like a blues singer should be, in fact.

All in all, this is a very fine, successful album of contemporary blues. At its best (and there's a lot of this), it's tremendously exciting and will provide the blues listener plenty of food for thought. And enjoyment. Highly recommended.

—PETE WELDING
4-19-69

RIVER DEEP-MOUNTAIN HIGH
Ike and Tina Turner
(Spectacular Productions on
    A&M Records SP 417)

OUTTA SEASON
Ike and Tina Turner
(Blue Thumb Records BTS 5)

Ike and Tina Turner have been packing suitcases and riding buses for years, playing the Sportmen's Clubs and the Showcase Lounges, sometimes making it into the class rooms, occasionally breaking into the middle of the R&B charts, once or twice getting onto *Billboard*'s Hot 100, moving from label to label, options not picked up, not well-known enough to get to black high school kids the way the Impressions and the Temptations do. Ike and Tina have a rock and roll legend to their credit, though: Tina's magnificent performance of Phil Spector's "River Deep-Mountain High" is part of the story of a record that should have been an automatic Number One but never made the charts. Backed up by what sounds like ten thousand Ikettes, challenging and conquering the difficult changes of mood Phil created for the production, Tina outsang Bill Medley and the Crystals and Veronica and put herself on a level with Darlene Love. But it bombed. Phil took out ads reading "Benedict Arnold Was

Right!" when the record scored in England, and then he quit the music business and dissolved his record company.

But not even Phil Spector was able to get a first-rate album out of smoldering Tina and poker-faced Ike. While the Spector album, enjoyable and well-produced, is certainly their best, being mainly a reprise of their greatest hits ("Fool In Love" and "It's Gonna Work Out Fine"), R&B standards, and a few big-deal efforts by Phil, only three cuts create the excitement and intensity of the best R&B—the driving, gutty, sly "Make 'Em Wait" (a song about virginity from Tina Turner, if you can believe that), a job on "Everyday I Have To Cry" that brings back all the firecracker explosions of the Crystals, and, of course, "River Deep-Mountain High," which is simply in a class by itself. The power of its emotion might be compared to Dylan's "One Of Us Must Know," but the musical inventions of Spector and Tina's control over her almost anarchic vocal weapons make any comparison pointless. It stands alone.

The rest of the album is a disappointment. Spector's job on "Save the Last Dance for Me" seems to owe more to Elmer Bernstein and the Academy Awards than to Wagner or Verdi; the arrangement is mushy, something fit for the

Fifth Dimension. On "A Love Like Yours (Don't Come Knocking Every Day)" Phil does everything right, but the real problems begin to emerge. With some exceptions, Tina is not a very interesting or creative singer, and when they say "don't scream on this one" and then let her take it from there, she hasn't the ability to evoke much emotion—she seems to be straining or falling down flat, as if it all ought to be about three more rungs up the ladder but there's not a chance of getting there.

The numbers produced by Ike (the greatest hits and standards) illustrate this problem even more clearly. Tina is not in a class with Martha Reeves or Carla Thomas or Gladys Knight, and without the kind of direction Spector provides only when he is totally committed to a production (and he has made it clear his commitment comes on singles), Tina rarely demonstrates even the kind of vocal agility of which Dusty Springfield is capable. Tina Turner's performance of "River Deep-Mountain High" is strikingly better than anything the artists mentioned above ever have or ever will achieve, a masterpiece, but perhaps it was for once and then never again, like a cab driver spending one night with a fare that turned out to be Jeanne Moreau.

The Turners' new album on Blue Thumb is a package that looks great but fails to go anywhere. The cover art—Ike and Tina in whiteface, chomping on watermelon—is a brilliant come-on, with the magnetism Tina projects with her fabulous and dazzling sexiness breaking through even on a gag photo. The material, almost all blues, looks fine—"Honest I Do," "Dust My Broom," "Rock Me Baby," and many other classics. The possibilities for letting Tina loose seem terrific. Maybe so, but it doesn't happen.

All the cuts are done straight, without invention or excitement. The one saving grace is Ike's guitar playing, very tough, melodic, at times almost dazzling, great debt owed to B.B. King and all that, but in fact a good lesson for young musicians who can't make their instruments speak but who don't want to sound like Blue Cheer either. But that's it. The band sounds tired and bored, as if they've done it all a million times before and just couldn't be bothered.

Only on the opening track, "I've Been Loving You Too Long," does the band really seem to care—a very sparsely illustrated accompaniment following Tina's sustained and convincing vocal, a fine tribute to Otis Redding. The drummer sounds as if he is playing in church. From then on nothing happens in the rhythm section, and Tina is no more interesting than the bass guitar. Most of the cuts are too short for Tina or the band to get into, and they don't bother. The fade-outs are pointlessly timed and abrupt, jarring whatever feeling might have been about to develop.

"Reconsider Baby" is done with an easy, rolling beat that is totally inappropriate to the spirit of the song, which is more or less equivalent to Dylan's description of "Don't Think Twice": "It isn't a love song, it's a statement you can say to make yourself feel better." That's to say the song should have an edge on it, a hardness; here there is a smoothness to the music and to Tina's uninvolved vocal that makes the cut a throw-away instead of a triumph. It just passes by as the record winds its way to the end of the side, nothing there at all. The only cut that breaks up the monotony is Ike's instrumental, "Grumbling," which is the sort of thing that is put out on a B-side, to be revealed years later by John Lennon as something everyone should be ashamed of missing. But we will miss it—the album provides little reason to get to it.

—GREIL MARCUS
5-17-69

FIRST TAKE
Roberta Flack
(Atlantic SD 8230)

CHAPTER TWO
Roberta Flack
(Atlantic SD 1569)

With the appearance of her first album a little less than a year ago, Roberta Flack immediately established herself as worthy to enter the pantheon with the two other truly great black female singers of the Sixties, Aretha and Nina Simone. It is impossible to classify her. She is not a "soul" singer like Aretha, who emphasizes gospel rhythms and blues harmonies. She is not a shouter like Aretha, either. She is not a jazz musician, as Nina Simone essentially is, though, Roberta resembles Nina in her amazing ability to get further inside a song than one thought humanly possible and to bring responses from places inside you that you never knew existed. However, where Nina Simone overpowers one with her strength, bitterness and anger, Roberta Flack underplays everything with a quietness and gentleness. More than any singer I know, she can take a quiet, slow song (and most of hers are) and infuse it with a brooding intensity that is, at times, almost unbearable. With her, Leonard Cohen's "Hey, That's No Way To Say Goodbye" and

Ewan MacColl's "The First Time Ever I Saw Your Face" become the basis for meditation.

Her weakness is uptempo songs and the weakest song on this album is the first cut, "Compared to What." Her gentleness fails to convey the bitterness and sarcasm of the song. Les McCann's rendition is far superior and truer to the song. But that is the album's only failure. *First Take* is one of those rare albums that has the power to enlighten the emotional content of one's life. You feel the world differently after listening to it.

Her just released second album, *Chapter Two*, is successful, but not wholly. Again there is one uptempo cut, and, again, it is the first one, "Reverend Lee." Listening to it, one wishes for Aretha. Roberta Flack is simply not funky enough, which is not to say she isn't funky. She is, but her contribution has been to infuse the lyrical with funk, something one would have heretofore thought impossible. This album is also marred by two sentimental "message" songs—"The Impossible Dream" and "Business Goes On As Usual." The failing is not the messages, but that the songs are simply bad songs and Roberta's soft approach makes them too saccharine for consumption.

The rest of the album, however, is equal to her first one and she gives unequalled per-

formances to songs like, "Do What You Gotta Do," Buffy Ste. Marie's beautiful "Until It's Time To Go," Dylan's "Just Like a Woman" (which she personalizes, changing the "she" to "I"), and the Sweet Inspirations' big hit, "Let It Be Me."

Her singing is characterized by an adherence to the melody line, with occasional embellishments that have adumbrations of the Baptist church, but never to the point where the embellishments have taken over, as they do in Aretha's singing. Roberta emphasizes the melody of songs and de-emphasizes rhythm. Where Aretha adapts every song to her particular style, Roberta Flack tries to convey the essence of the song without remaking it. The meaning of the song is everything and everything is made to serve that one end. The result is a kind of purity that is rarely heard in this world.

Like Nina and Aretha, Roberta accompanies herself on piano, but it is difficult to know what her playing is like because of the string and brass orchestra backing her, sometimes for the better, more often for the worse. She takes a solo on only one cut in the two albums, "Hey, That's No Way To Say Goodbye," and it is merely a succession of chord changes which follow the melody closely, not improvisation. However, it is tasteful and exquisite.

The hallmark of Roberta

Flack is an ability to make sure that nothing stands between you and the experience of the song. She is merely the transmitter and puts herself at the service of the song so that you not only hear the music, but become a part of it. If you can stand the intensity and don't mind risking your life, listen.

—JULIUS LESTER
10-29-70

Singles

Rolling Stone came along at a time when the album began to dominate the single as *the* form of recorded art. That is not to slight the single, as it probably can be proven that most of the best songs were originally recorded to be singles (and released as such), or that entirely wasteful albums were really only worth (and constructed because of) one or two single tracks on them.

But it was the era when the sales of albums, first in terms of dollar sales and finally in terms of actual unit volume, overtook the sales of singles. This was accompanied by the rise of FM rock radio where albums and album cuts were nearly 90 percent of the floating, free-form playlists. Traditional AM rock radio ignored albums entirely until the interest and influence of FM was made undeniable as album artists such as Jimi Hendrix, Cream and a string of others made it to the top of the charts without any AM hits whatsoever. FM even broke single hits by continual airing of album tracks, "Get Together" by the Youngbloods being a major example.

In any case, *Rolling Stone*'s singles coverage was nearly non-existent until early 1970, even though many singles (some never to be seen on follow-up albums) were among the best music being issued during that time.

These, then, are a few of the singles we did write about. The selection is opened by a complete series of reviews by Ed Ward, who edited the record section in the summer and fall of 1970, and who initiated and continues to contribute to our new regular singles columns.

Back in the dear old deadly doldrum days of rock, when seemingly every overnight phenomenon bore the name Bobby, I used to sit with my RCA transistor radio on my desk and dream of having my own radio station. Surely, I thought, there were good records, being made out there *somewhere;* all that I'd have to do would be find them. And, to make things complete, I could call the station WARD.

When I got in college, I got my chance—a DJ spot on the college FM station. I'd already found out that WARD was already a station somewhere in Pennsylvania, I think, but that hardly mattered—there were hundreds of singles coming in every week. The trouble there was that even if I *did* find something, who listened to our punky programs that cared? But I retained my love of singles, and, a few weeks ago, feeling massively uninspired by the album fare I'd been hearing, I took home about 200 of them and began winnowing them down.

What follows here is the result of that winnowing. Some of the singles are listed by their A-side only, due to the fact that the record companies send out their promotional copies with the A-side on both sides, just in case some radio station P.D. (Program Director) wants to get adventurous and plug some side the company doesn't want him to plug. This is a shame, because some of the best songs listed below are B-sides.

And just in case you think what follows is some kind of chart, the records are listed alphabetically by artist.

"THIS WHOLE WORLD" b/w "SLIP ON THROUGH"
The Beach Boys
(Brother/Reprise 0929)

"Slip on Through," promoted as the A-side, is a clumsy pseudo-Rascals thing, hardly worthy of a listen, but "This Whole World" has got to be the best thing the Beach Boys have done since "Good Vibrations." Once again, Brian Wilson proves that Crosby & Co. still have plenty of lessons to learn about harmony and counterpoint, and the music echoes almost everything the group has done in the past. Lyrics are Wilson-cosmic, and who else but the Beach Boys could sing a backup vocal line like "Auuuum-dop-diddit?" My only complaint is that if it had a few seconds longer to resolve itself it would be perfect, instead of ending on a weak fade as it does.

"AVAILABLE SPACE" b/w "GOIN' TO BROWNSVILLE"
Ry Cooder
(Reprise 0910)

Ry Cooder is the finest slide guitarist and mandolinist in rock today, as his work with Taj Mahal and the Stones has amply demonstrated. "Available Space" is a funky, happy instrumental; short, to the point, it is a fine spacefiller in between records on an FM rock station. "Brownsville" is a traditional blues, played on mandolin, with a vocal. Both of these cuts are light and snappy and a great change of pace from the turgid heaviness so much in evidence on the airwaves.

"SOUL SHAKE"
Delaney & Bonnie and Friends
(Atco 45-6756)

This is the B-side of "Free the People," a fine cut reviewed in these pages a few issues back. Atco is now pushing this side, and, while "Free" is still a great song, this is a fifth-encore, all-stops-pulled-out rave-up performance. Any AM station that doesn't pick up on this is fucked. Of course, you can help by flooding the station with requests. If D&B don't get on the charts with this one, I'll be amazed.

"YOUR OWN BACKYARD"
Dion
(Warner Brothers 7401)

With anti-drug campaigns all the rage on the AM stations, it's strange that so few have picked up on this heartfelt autobiography. It's hackneyed to say that Dion tells it like it is, but that's just what he does. No preachifying, no grass-leads-to-mainlining bullshit, just a conversational ballad about getting fucked up on drugs and then getting straightened out. And not only that, but it's good music, too.

"WORLD IN HARMONY" b/w "THE GREEN MANALISHI"
Fleetwood Mac
(Reprise 0925)

Why Reprise is pushing a klunker like "Manalishi" is beyond me. It's another of those aimless heavy things that goes nowhere. "World," on the other hand, is a beautiful instrumental, featuring placid guitar work through several tempo changes, sounding very much like a world in harmony. This recording, incidentally, was made before guitarist Peter Green left. It is unlikely that it'll ever be on an album.

"ALL RIGHT NOW"
Free
(A&M 1206-S)

Yeah, I know it sounds like "Honky-Tonk Women" and its vocalist grunts like he's been listening to too many Motown records, but it's currently number one in England and there's a reason: it's good. Good beat, good chorus, good guitar, good melody. A sure FM winner, and a winner for any AM station who'll program something clocking in at 4:14.

"STEPPING STONE" b/w
"IZABELLA"
Hendrix Band of Gypsys
(Reprise 0905)

Now here's a hot little item that's only a few months old, released before the Capitol album and a dozen times as good. Hendrix and the guys rocket through "Stepping Stone" with its outrageous lyrics ("You're all woman—at least you taste like you are") and ever-increasing tempo, culminating in a frenzied guitar solo which ends with the engineer breaking in and saying "You made it!" Indeed. "Izabella" ain't much, though.

"MEXICO" b/w
"HAVE YOU SEEN THE
SAUCERS"
Jefferson Airplane
(RCA 74-0343)

Not for the chicken-hearted. The single comes packed in a sleeve which shows some very lovely looking marijuana flower tops, very red and potent-looking. The music is the same way. Opening with the "Volunteers" leitmotiv, "Mexico" is a rather-too-specific-for-airplay ditty about Nixon and Operation Intercept which closes with some not unrelated thoughts about Woodstock. "Saucers" is less leisurely paced, and reflects Paul Kantner's increasing fascination with science-fiction. But it, too, seems too radical for your average P.D., as it urges the child of the Woodstock Nation to "Open the door/That's what it's there for." If you're an Airplane fan, you better buy this, because the word is that there won't be an album for quite a while, and these two songs are masterpieces you can't afford to miss.

"THE WITCH'S PROMISE" b/w
"TEACHER"—"INSIDE"
b/w "A TIME FOR
EVERYTHING"
Jethro Tull
(Reprise 0899 and 0927)

I ain't much of a Jethro Tull

fan, but I know good music, I think. "Promise" and "Inside" beat out anything on *Benefit*, for my money, as does "Teacher." If you like Tull, you'll love these, and they're not gonna be on any albums for a while. Incidentally, one side of the bootleg *My God!* is nothing but forgotten Tull singles from England.

"STEALING IN THE NAME OF THE LORD"
Paul Kelly
(Happy Tiger HT 541)

This is the first single I've mentioned so far that is getting the kind of attention it deserves. It is the tightest, freshest soul record I've heard in months, tension-building and dramatic, but very sparingly produced. The lyrics deal, of course, with ghetto religious extortion.

"LOLA" b/w "MINDLESS CHILD OF MOTHERHOOD"
The Kinks
(Reprise 0930)

The first Kinks single in a long, long while. Unfortunately, it'll never be a hit because: 1) it's 4:06 long and 2) its subject matter is just a bit controversial. Musically, it's even stronger than anything on *Arthur*, almost sinking away at

one point but resurging stronger than ever—a credit to Ray Davies' genius. But it concerns itself with a young man's first sexual experience, and a most unusual one it is, at that; he can't understand why she "walks like a woman and talks like a man." "Boys will be girls and girls will be boys," he declares, later adding "I know what I am, and I'm glad I'm a man/And so's Lola." Take it as you will, it's a great song. The other side is by brother Dave, and it's a tight rocker with enigmatic, angry lyrics.

"LET THE MUSIC TAKE YOUR MIND"
Kool and the Gang
(De-Lite De 529)

This is a snappy instrumental workout, and it sounds like the Gang sure had fun making it. There must be a dozen members of the Gang, and although the song consists of a simple riff and the title chanted over and over, the background noises put it in a category with such classics as Gary Bonds' "Quarter to Three" and "Bang Bang" by Joe Cuba.

"BRONTOSAURUS"
The Move
(A&M 1197)

A&M isn't helping to promote

this any with their ad showing a couple of brontosauri fucking. If you got off on *Shazam,* you'll love this song, heavy as its namesake, describing a dance ("She could really do the Brontosaurus") that must be fun to do. Much too long for AM radio, this oughta be one of those "underground hits" you hear so much about.

"ACCIDENTS"
Thunderclap Newman
(Track 45-T-2718)

A followup to "Something in the Air," this record has all the makings of yet another one. Newman's trip is a strange one, and this engaging number is a catalogue of children hit by trains, run over, and such, all set to a wonderful tune. "Love is just a game/You fly your paper plane/There is no wind" say the words to the fadeout. Meditate on *that.*

"MULE SKINNER BLUES"
Dolly Parton
(RCA 47-9863)

A little change of pace here as Dolly revives the Jimmie Rodgers classic and adapts it to her inimitable country style If this doesn't bring a smile to your lips ("I'm a lady *mule-* shkinner") then nothing will.

"THE EAGLE AND ME"
Van Dyke Parks
(Warner Brothers 7409)

When Parks disappeared after the failure of his *Song Cycle,* he was reported to be working in some way for ecology. This Thirties show tune is right up that alley, performed in the same *Song Cycle* style, far too complex for AM and probably FM. The layers and layers of sound fit right in with the lyrics, each layer being indispensable to the finished product—a kind of musical ecology, if you will. I'd sure like to hear the B-side, which I'm told is just great.

"LET'S GET TOGETHER
AND LOVE"
The Rance Allen Singers
(Reflect RF-1)

I was alerted to this by one of our readers, who was good enough to send a copy. The Rance Allen Singers is a gospel trio from the midwest who play their own instruments and turn in an electrifying live performance. This side combines modern R&B with a crackerjack instrumental backing, and might go over big if it ever got exposed. Meanwhile, write Reflect Records in Monroe, Michigan, and find out when the album's due.

"BLUEGREENS"
William Truckaway and
the Stovalls
(Reprise 0935)

2:41 of sheer nonsense. My guess is Norman Greenbaum backed by Bernie Krause at the Mighty Moog, but I might be wrong. This is an instant hit, something to truck away the rest of the summer to, and I don't see how it can avoid getting played. It's especially nice in stereo, where it can be heard in all of its hand-clapping grandeur, with the Moog bass lines sliding across the picture. Demand it.

"SUGAR MOUNTAIN"
Neil Young
(Reprise 0911)

This is a rather obscure Neil Young cut, recorded live at Ann Arbor's Canterbury House. Five and a half minutes of Neil and his guitar weeping away acoustically. Part of his next album may be like this, and here's a chance for a preview. On the B-side is "Cinnamon Girl."

Now, most of the above records are in stereo, and most are of good fidelity. Not a one offends the taste as much as the Pipkins or some of the other goodies being pushed down our throats today and most of them are not getting played. If you feel you want to do something about it, call up your local station (whichever one seems to be most suited to the song in question—i.e., don't try to get the Airplane played on AM, it's a losing battle) and ask for the P.D. Ask him why the record isn't getting played, and listen courteously to his explanation. Thank him, hang up, and then have a couple of friends do the same.

Who knows? You might even get somewhere.

—ED WARD

9-3-70

"COME AND GET IT"
Badfinger
(Apple 1815)

P. McCartney (he of "Urban Spaceman." "Those Were the Days," and others fame) has scored once again from the producer's side of the street, the score this time being a somewhat wonderful McCartney-composed and -produced Badfinger single which comes to us from the *Magic Christian* soundtrack, which ought not to be confused with "Come and Get It" *by* the Magic Christians (Commonwealth C-3006).

"Come And Get It" on first listening seems a trifle more easily resisted than your usual McCartney song, because it's a trifle less tuneful than your usual McCartney song. Its catchiness is rather in its understated but insistent rhythmicness.

The most striking thing about the record is the excellent drum work (Paul certainly knows how to get the best out of his drummers, judging from this and recent Beatle recordings), which is beautifully recorded and perfectly mixed with the tambourine and bass. In the absence of an out-front lead instrument (the piano is just blocking chords), the drums in fact come out as the lead instrument. Considering how few are playing, the instrumental fullness on the record is amazing.

Don't miss the B-side, another excerpt from the *Christian* score called "Rock of All Ages" (an original), which, with its screechy voices and thundering eight-beats-per-bar bass, reminds one of "I Saw Her Standing There." A nice English counterpart to the most recent Creedence Clearwater single.

[A note of immense historical interest.] Before being convinced by their Beatle mentors to switch to Badfinger, the boys used to rush about billing themselves as the Iveys, under which name they did a splendid early-English-Sound slowie last year called "Maybe Tomorrow" (Apple 1803). Perhaps you had the inestimable good fortune of hearing it on AM radio. If not, find a copy and buy it. It's contrived datedness will refresh you.

—JOHN MENDELSOHN
3-7-70

"HE AIN'T HEAVY, HE'S MY BROTHER"
The Hollies
(Epic 5-10532)

Two men appear on the horizon just as the curtain lifts. A harmonica straight out of *Shane* or something like it moans melancholy, giving way to the rich twangy Orbison-cum-Everlys baritone of handsome Alan Clarke: *The road is long, with many a winding turn . . . The two men grow closer and we recognize them as David Niven and Sidney Poitier. Sidney, wounded and limping, is being sort of dragged along by Dave . . .* "But I'm strong enough to carry him/He ain't heavy, he's my brother." The title song from the film, uh . . .

Well, friends, there is no such film, but this amazing new Hollies single is perfect for it in spite of such obstacles, being all priceless melodrama.

Mind you, this single has no more to do with rock and roll than did Matt Monro's "Born Free," but remember, the Hollies are in for the charts. This is something like their twentieth successive hit in England. What, after all, could have greater chart appeal in these troubled times than a disarmingly overdone version of a tear-jerkingly inspirational universal-love-plea inspired (as rumor has it) by one of those Give Generously charity posters?

Sure it sounds better suited to Lulu than to the Hollies, the emotions so evocatively voiced are coming to us second-hand, having been written by Bobbys Scott and Russell (of, I believe, "A Taste Of Honey" fame), but never you mind—this record is fun, not to mention certain to appeal to the older, less rowdy, folks out there is Radioland.

—JOHN MENDELSOHN
2-7-70

"MY BABY LOVES LOVIN' "
White Plains
(Deram 85058)

"THAT SAME OLD FEELING"
Fortunes
(World Pacific 77937)

"UNITED WE STAND"
Brotherhood of Man

It started out as a little scratch with "Smile a Little Smile For Me," became a festering sore with "Baby Take Me In Your Arms," grew into general pustulation after "Love Grows (Where My Rosemary Goes)," and has now erupted in a flood of rancid ooze thanks to an influx of horrendo 45s. The phenomenon is the arrival on our shores of an increasing volume of English shlock that makes even Herman's Hermits seem heavy.

All of these records seem tailor-made for Bill Drake—undistinguished, forgettable but innocuous forays into a world where the only requirement seems to be to keep a song moving towards its inexorable end two minutes and some fifty-odd seconds after the needle touches the first grim groove.

They have some common characteristics. The writers and producers, all from the Tony Macaulay school, are more important than the performers, all second-string groups who in some cases don't exist outside of the studio and in others do little else more exciting than cut soft-drink commercials. Form is more important than substance. The lyrics always lack any semblance of depth and are harder to recall than the names of President Nixon's lesser cabinet members (quick, now, what are the first two lines of "Love Grows"? Even after you've heard the song 100 times on the car radio, you *still* can't remember). All of the musical lines to some degree feature a slur of several notes, space similar to the "peace" in "Silent Night's" "Sleep in heavenly peeeeeeace." A few basic phrases are repeated almost as often as "Na na na na na na na na hey hey goodbye."

Yet these records are played and these records sell, while the "River Deep Mountain Highs" of the world collect dust. The answer can only lie in the fact that they provide excellent background music for a housewife or bopper who doesn't want to have to pay attention to a lyric or melody but just wants to have the security of a sustained monotonous musical continuum as she does her hair. AM radio, which was always bad, is now going muzak. Choke.

If these British producers have their hands on the pulse of the musical silent majority, perhaps someone should slash the wrist. Or at least threaten to send Davy Jones back to England for good if they can't keep these mediocrities on their side of the Atlantic. What are they trying to do, make Chinese water torture obsolete?

—PAUL GAMBACCINI
6-25-70

**"FREEDOM BLUES" b/w
"DEW DROP INN"
Little Richard
(Reprise 0907)**

The self-proclaimed King of Rock and Roll is back, this time with a new recording contract from a company that apparently respects and knows how to use his talents.

Avoiding the error of trying to capitalize on the never-was "rock revival," this first Reprise release finds a Little Richard working out in an entirely new musical context, very much remindful of the Muscle Shoals back-up heard on many of Aretha Franklin's sides. The change is an abrupt one, but the results

are so effective that references to Little Richard's halcyon days of the mid-Fifties are gratuitous. From the "na-na-na" acappella opening, to the *de rigeur* sax break, down to, three minutes later, the tasty brass fade, Richard Penniman's "Freedom Blues" is confidently and securely based in the Seventies.

As easefully as ever, Little Richard still slides from his gravel-voice lower register upwards to his trade-marked falsetto, and as of yore, the elusive, but ever-present E. Blackwell is still credited as co-producer. But, at least on the "A" side, Little Richard is taking chances, by working within a new musical framework.

This unfamiliar instrumentation—acoustic guitar, heavily milked electric bass, and dampened Memphis-style horn section —compliments the game-as-ever vocalizing. I miss Little Richard's telegraph-key pianistics, though.

The flip, "Dew Drop Inn," however, affords Little Richard a chance to not only cart out the piano, but also to take us on a brief trip up to rock and roll heaven, subtly interweaving musical quotations from several of the big ones on Specialty.

The naive sentiment of the lyrics of "Freedom Blues" excepted, Little Richard has travelled through time better than almost any of his musical contemporaries. Reprise seems justified in billing its latest contracted artist as "the best rock and roll singer since Little Richard."

—BILL REED
6-25-70

"BAND OF GOLD"
Freda Payne
(Invictus 20201)

Thumpthumpthumpthumpthuumpthumpthump. A drummer practices his part in a Holland-Dozier-Holland song.

1-2-3-4. Thumpthumpthump thump. He's been doing it for years. He did it in "Reach Out I'll Be There." And now he's doing it for "Band of Gold."

Eddie, Lamont, and Brian still can't write for their Invictus label because of legal hassles with Motown, but that doesn't matter as long as they can produce. They could give "Okie From Muskogee" the Detroit sound if they were granted five minutes to figure out the basic harmonies. In this case they have taken a simple Dunbar lyric and carted out some of their old staples—the sometimes fluid, sometimes staccato strings, the subliminal supporting voices, the inconclusive fadeout. There is one variation on the theme, a concession to five years of musical development: the standard Motown sax bridge from the early days has been replaced by a strong guitar line.

Not enough change to keep us from viewing "Band of Gold" as a pleasant anachronism. It seems like part of our youth because it was; the similarity between this and Kim Weston's "Helpless" is uncanny, particularly when both vocalists return again and again to the major melodic line during the denouement.

Freda Payne is no Diana Ross and maybe even no Kim Weston, but she is gutsy on this one. She asks no sympathy, and she recites her lines like she's been left ten times before and no longer is surprised when dumped upon. The strange effect renders the lyrics about as meaningful as a recitation of the "K" section of the Detroit phone book, but in so doing makes Freda's voice the most important of HDH's instruments. She says most in her wavering, junglecatlike "Ohhhhhh," an exciting deviation from the Detroit formula.

"Band of Gold" is certainly not a classic, but it is, as somebody used to say, one of the all-time good records. It's a great deal of fun, and a reminder that Holland-Dozier-Holland will be making the same kind of records until the Apocalypse.

Somewhere a drummer rehearses for his next HDH session.

Thumpthumpthumpthump.

—PAUL GAMBACCINI
6-25-70

"GOVINDA"
Radha Krishna Temple of
London
(Apple 1821)

For my money, the Hare Krishna movement is peopled with the same kids you'd find in an urban Methodist church in the Midwest, and I generally cross to the other side of the street when an encounter with one of their clanging, cater-wauling street-kirtans seems imminent. However, the devotion to their cause is just as sincere as the Midwestern Methodists', and, as we all know, devotion to a faith has inspired some pretty good music over the years. "Govinda," unlikely as it may seem, is not only good music, but it has the earmarks of a Top 40 smash hit.

It starts out innocently enough, with an organ and some plunking Indian-style instrument laying down the basic changes, joined by the lead singer, who sings through the chorus once and is joined the next time through by the rest of the singers. The verse is next, overflowing with quarter-tones and other musical oddities, and then they swing (and they really do) into the "Govinda" chorus again and you're hooked. By the time the second (and last) verse is over and the mellotron comes in and the tempo starts accelerating and accelerating you notice your foot jumping and you start singing along. And by the time it's over, you're floored.

What makes "Govinda" so good again and again is the superb production that George Harrison (who else?) has given it. Some people say it sounds like an old Del Shannon hit, others say it's like Phil Spector or the Moody Blues or King Crimson or Mahler. Everybody (except, of course, AM program directors, who are turned off by the 4:45 playing time) thinks it sounds like a hit. And what with the dearth of good lyrics these days. "I worship Govinda the primeval Lord, who is adept in playing on his flute with blooming eyes like lotus petals" sung in ancient Sanskrit is certainly a change.

At any rate, until the deejays wake up, you should get this record and listen to it a lot. Who knows—you might even find yourself handing your local Hare Krishna monk a nickel in spite of yourself.

—ED WARD
5-28-70

"1862 B.P." b/w
"48 HOURS"
Rev. Ether, The Kingdom,
The Power & The Glory
(Etcetera 45-201)

Oh, boy. I don't know who in hell (you should pardon the expression) Rev. Ether is, but he wails like nobody I've ever heard, except maybe Little Richard. This is the best single I've heard in *months,* a bizarre story of the Civil War, concerning a naked soldier wandering through the state of Arkansas, the Emancipation Proclamation, and a lot of other things that you mostly can't make out because of the fucked-up quality of the recording—not that that's bad at all; it's sort of like the 1950s all over again. Were it not for the fact that this song is so *weird,* it would probably make number one in a flash, what with the great tag lines (*"You* get to hear the *story,"* followed by a great downward guitar sweep into silence, and the inimitable—literally—beginning which goes "South Carolina through Virginia Georgia Tennessee/Louisiana Alabama Texas Florida Mississippi") and a vocal that just won't stop. Hear it once and you'll just have to hear it again. It oughta be a hit, dammit, at least in South Carolina through Virginia Georgia Tennessee. The other side is fascinating, a tale of someone who works 48 hours a week at a job he hates, goes out and gets drunk at night and some more stuff that can't be deciphered because the lyrics are even more garbled than on "1862." Whoever these people are, they should lay an album on us soon, so watch out, and don't say I didn't warn ya. Oh, and if you want to bother your

local radio station, the Etcetera label is distributed by Atlantic.

"HOLY MAN" b/w "HALLELUJAH, BABY" Diane Kolby (Columbia 4-45169)

Diane Kolby is a stone country genius from Texas who makes up dozens of quasi-religious songs and sings them in a voice that is powerful, versatile, and soulful. Somebody at Columbia had the good fortune to hear her, and this single is the result. "Holy Man"'s lyrics are a shade eerie, and when you hear the beginning of the song, you might wonder where it could possibly go from there, but it builds at a just-right speed to an ending that features some truly hair-raising scat singing. This record should also be a hit, as it is in Texas, but I hope somebody up north has the sense to start playing it. The B-side features yet more of her earthy gospel shouting—Diane is, to judge from her pictures, a big girl, and she sounds it—but it's not as well-controlled as "Holy Man." She'll be making her public debut soon. Watch for her.

"HEART ASSOCIATION" The Emotions (Volt VOA-4045)

I had just about given up on

Stax/Volt when I heard this one. Ever since Otis Redding died, they seemed to be chasing after Motown's coattails, featuring the same kind of overlush arranging and insipid songwriting; a little more grit, maybe, but not much. Well, if this record is any sign, I owe them an apology. The Emotions are three very petite girls who don't look like they're out of their teens yet, and they sing in three very petite voices, breathy and sexy and very hard to capture on a record with any success. Well, Volt did it. They didn't glom it up with strings, they built in some nice crescendoes and decrescendos, and they came up with a very fine record. I've never heard of the Emotions, but if this is a sample of what they can do, let's have more. Oh, yes. As I thought, a glance at the Hot 100 and the Soul 50 shows this record is nowhere to be found . . .

"WITCHI TAI TO"
Topo D. Bill
(Charisma CB-116, British
Import)

This song is on its way to becoming a "standard" in the rock field, and no wonder, since it lends itself to myriad interpretations so readily. This particular one, produced by ex-Bonzo "Legs" Larry Smith, is a sheer knockout. You see, the chant "Witchi Tai To" has basically only one note, so it is possible to weave all kinds of intricate harmonies around it. A nice sax break early on, and a superlative trumpet line at the end that reminds me of the Royal Brass Music of King James I, are like a tasty frosting on this cake. God only knows who Topo D. Bill is, although it seems evident that he's using that name for a reason, but some enterprising record company in the States should pick this one up. It's a longshot, sure, but it could make it.

"CARRY ON (GLITTERING
DANCER)"
Ruthann Friedman
(Reprise 0941)

Ruthann Friedman delighted the audience at a Big Sur Folk Festival once with one of her songs, released an album that seemingly delighted nobody but the folks at Reprise, and then disappeared for a while. Where she's been, it seems, is collaborating with Van Dyke Parks on this single. It is his most approachable bit of production in a while, featuring his familiar Southern California brand of pointillistic pantonality, but helped along by some neat conga work and a darn good tune. FM stations should pick up on this, and if it's any indication of what Ruthann is into now, then, in the words of the song, "Carry on, follow through. . . ."

"TELL THE TRUTH" b/w "ROLL IT OVER"
Derek and the Dominos
(Atco 45-6780)

This is Eric Clapton's new group, as if you didn't know, and the record is good, as if you didn't expect that. It seems that Eric has found happiness for a while with this four-man outfit that sounds like nothing more or less than something left over from the British Invasion of Beatles/Animals/Herman's Hermits/Kinks/etc. fame. "Tell the Truth" rocks out nicely, and my only complaint is that the producer (some cat named Phil Spector) chose to do some sloppy phasing with the drums, but it's hard to even notice that when you're trying to keep up with the Dominos' break-neck pace. The other side is a slower number, which is to say that it's merely frantic, and it is a blues-based thing, very funky. Messrs. Clapton, Whitlock, Gordon, Radle, and Spector have acquitted themselves nicely. Congratulations, and keep up the good work.

Well, there it is, the all-star lineup. The first four records reviewed have already made it into my Golden Hall of Fame due to their outstanding excellence and extreme durability in the face of extensive play. If your excitement has been whetted by reading this, let me repeat that your local rock station will be glad to play these hot sides if you pester them politely enough,—just call and ask for the program director—and I'll be glad to answer any questions you juke box operators, P.D.s and so on might have.

Oh, yes. Reverend Ether, get in touch . . .

—ED WARD
10-15-70

"HAMBURGER MIDNIGHT" b/w "STRAWBERRY FLATS"
Little Feat
(Warner Brothers 7431)

This is the masterpiece. It is perhaps the best record I've heard in several months. As usual, Warner's has picked the wrong side as the A-side. "Hamburger Midnight" is indeed a fine song, reminiscent of Johnny Winter, crackling and sizzling through two minutes packed with incredible energy. Yet it pales against "Strawberry Flats,"* which must be one of the definitive statements of "where youth is at today." Dig these (partial) lyrics:

> Ripped off and run outa town
> Got my git-tar burned when I was clownin'

_____

* © Abraham Music

Haven't slept in a bed for
a week
And my shoes feel like a
part of my feet
(Chorus:) Let me come
down
Where I won't be a bother
to no-one
Let me around
Give me a hole to recline
in . . .
Knocked on my friend's
door in Moody, Texas
Asked if he had a place for
me
His hair was cut off 'n' he
was wearin' a suit
He said
"Not in my house! Not in
my house!"
It seemed like part of a
con-spir-a-cy.

The singer is "six hours out
on Strawberry Flats" and trying
to get past the schoolbus Texas
roadblock where they're "stop-
pin' everyone who looks too
weird." The music sounds like
the Band taken one step further,
and it is difficult to believe that
they generate so much excitement in two minutes and 21
seconds. This anthem of the
Age of Paranoia deserves to be
in your collection and on every
radio station in the country, although I realize as I write that
it is wishful thinking. The group
Little Feat seems to have ex-
Mother Roy Estrada, a guy
named George, and another guy
named Payne in it. Warner
Brothers says that they have an
album coming, but they're not
too sure when. Watch for it,
and if you don't believe me, in-
vest 77¢ or whatever in the
single.

"DOMINO"
Van Morrison
(Warner Brothers 7434)

Ordinarily, I wouldn't mention this, mainly because the album'll be out in short order,
but if the album is as good as
this, then watch out. Meanwhile,
all you P.D.s out there better
put it on your playlist, cuz it's
gonna be a hit, his biggest since
"Brown-Eyed Girl."

"HOUNDOG TURKEY" b/w
"SAW A MAN"
Jeffrey Cain
(Warner Brothers 7428)

Jeffrey Cain picked me up
one day as I was hitchhiking to
work, but that's not why I like
"Houndog Turkey." I like it because it's outrageous, because it
deals with the fact that you
should never trust your houndog
with your turkey, but you
should never trust your turkey
with your cornfield and so on.
It is simple enough that it has a
chance of being a hit, with one
of those great Marin County
throw-together backup bands
chortling away in the background. It was produced by
Rick Turner of the late great

Autosalvage (whose record is now out of print, incidentally) and is released on the Youngbloods' Raccoon label, which may indicate that we'll be hearing more from Jeffrey. "Saw a Man," incidentally, is a good B-side; you hardly even notice it's there.

"I WOULDN'T LIVE IN NEW YORK CITY (IF THEY GAVE ME THE WHOLE DANG TOWN)" b/w "NO MILK AND HONEY IN BALTIMORE"
Buck Owens and His Buckaroos
(Capitol 2947)

Recorded live in the streets of New York, this is a lovely song. Direct and honest, and setting the old tradition of let's-stick-in-as-many-place-names-as-possible-so-it'll-sell-all-over-on-its-ear, this song lays it on the line: "Talk about a bummer/It's the biggest one around." Surprised at Buck using language like that? Well, you haven't been following him very closely. "Baltimore" also has the feel of having been recorded on the spot, and its story line is credible and well-stated. This is one of the best country singles I've heard in a long time, and the *musique concrete* aspects of the streetnoise are not to be sneered at. I wonder if the New York FM stations (not to mention the San Francisco ones) will pick

up on this one? Oh, and those sirens at the end of "New York City" are the cops coming to bust Buck for singing in the streets . . . (Really!)

"FREE THE PEOPLE" b/w "THE RAINMAKER"
Barbara Keith
(A&M 1191)

You may remember Delaney and Bonnie's version of this song, and how good it was. Well, Barbara's the one who wrote the thing, and she does it up just as well as you might expect. It lacks the Salvation Army feel of the D&B rendition, substituting instead a deeply-felt intensity that shocks the listener into realizing that this is, after all, a religious song. "Rainmaker" fares nowheres near as well, but it isn't quite as good a song to start with. But I feel that Barbara Keith is a talent to be reckoned with, and we'll be hearing more from her.

WHISKEY TRAIN" b/w "ABOUT TO DIE"
Procol Harum
(A&M 1218)

Some albums that are coming out these days remind me of maple sap. It's sticky and watery and kind of tasteless, but it can be boiled down into a useable and supremely delicious commodity. Thus with *Home*, the latest from Procol Harum. A lot of people like it, and more power to them, but this single kind of sums it all up for me. If you don't have the bread to buy all the albums you want, an awful lot of them can be boiled down into a good single, and usually are. Ask your dealer.

"UP ON THE ROOF"
Laura Nyro
(Columbia 4-45230)

I hate Laura Nyro and her blackboard-and-fingernails voice and daintily soulful pretensions, but, dammit, when a good record comes along I've gotta acknowledge it. This is one, and I was shocked upon consulting the latest Billboard chart and seeing it nowhere upon it. Laura's reading of this old classic is unbeatable, and the production by Felix Cavaliere (Felix Cavaliere?) and Arif Mardin is flawless. If this is indicative of the kind of thing Miss Nyro will be handing us from now on, I hereby take back all the nasty things I've ever said about her.

—ED WARD
11-26-70

San

Francisco

~~~~~~

San Francisco. Where it all came down. Golden Gate Park—the Panhandle, especially, where there were free concerts. The Avalon. The Fillmore. Acid Tests. Hell's Angels' Dances. Tribal Stomps.

And it spread. To the East Bay, where Oakland and Berkeley nurtured some of the groups that were, to outsiders, the epitome of the "San Francisco sound." Northward to Marin County, where weary bands from the East mellowed out behind some fine wine and a sunset with Mount Tamalpais as a spectacular backdrop.

Yet another feature of the San Francisco Scene (you should pardon the expression) was the fledgeling rock paper *Rolling Stone.* Since it was founded toward the end of 1967, reviews of some of the most seminal San Francisco albums never appeared, i.e., the first two Jefferson Airplane albums *(Take Off* and *Surrealistic Pillow),* the first Country Joe and the Fish album *(Electric Music for the Mind and Body)* and the first albums by the Moby Grape and the Grateful Dead.

What is chronicled here, then, is San Francisco after the boom. Bands straining to maintain the impetus they had created themselves, sometimes succeeding, sometimes not. The second-, third-, and seventeenth-wave bands. The stalwarts, like the Airplane, Quicksilver and the good old Grateful Dead. The newcomers that weren't so new after all—Creedence Clearwater Revival.

San Francisco. What more could you say?

THE THREE ORIGINALS

AFTER BATHING AT BAXTERS'
Jefferson Airplane
(RCA LSO-1511)

It is entirely possible that after one eliminates certain products of the Stax-Volt house band and some combinations that Bob Dylan has brought together for his back-up group, Jefferson Airplane could be the best rock and roll band in America today.

The criteria, to list a few, are that a group be able to provide from within itself enough good original material to sustain a prolonged effort both in performances and on recordings; that a group prove its ability as a professional and capable unit in live performance (not necessarily be able to reproduce a recorded work, but to bring off to general satisfaction a live performance if the group is involved in live performance); and that a group contain members who are able to sing and play like professional musicians.

You have Grace Slick, surely one of the two or three best non-operatic female voices in the world; Jack Casady, perhaps the strongest bassist around outside of a blues band; Marty Balin and Paul Kantner whose words and melodies are among the best currently available, outside of the obvious exceptions; and Jorma Kaukonen and Spencer Dryden who, while not outstanding instrumental virtuousos, are certainly original and inventive within the context of rock and roll, a wide context indeed. Got it?

It isn't very surprising that the Airplane is so good and that they have come up with probably the best, considering all the criteria and the exceptions, rock and roll album so far produced by an American group.

Hey all you out there with personal favorites which blow your heads off, listen closely. Marty and Grace may not make love on stage, either with each other or their respective microphone stands, but "Ballad of You & Me & Pooneil" happens to be a fine song. The instrumental backing is traditional Airplane 2/4 rhythm, whiplash chording and all, brought up to date with a subtle variety of electronic and melodic refinements. The tune itself is a groove: a pretty melody with a rocking beat against a sort of atonal line.

The electronic segue is well-positioned and a nice dip into the modern classical music school. The most important use of electronics on this album, and by the Airplane in general, is not their long extended electronic jams which are oftentimes a bore, but where they use electronics—as in the superb tune "Young Girl Sunday Blues," an excellent product of the Balin-Kantner team—for enrichment of the instrumental and vocal melodies.

"Rejoyce" is not something that's particularly easy to hum along with, but it's a good display of Grace's amazing vocal control, her piano and Spencer's jazz ear. "Watch Her Ride" has a very south-of-Santa Barbara feeling; it wouldn't be a surprise to learn that it was composed in Los Angeles. "Spare Chaynge" proves both Jorma and Spencer to be gifted musicians fully capable of sustaining an instrumental, not highly complex, but highly *interesting*.

"Street Masse" and "How Suite It Is" are the best sections on each side, excellent in all respects. Jefferson Airplane is still the group that'll "get you there on time."

—JANN WENNER
1-20-68

CROWN OF CREATION
Jefferson Airplane
(RCA LSP-4058)

The Jefferson Airplane, for all their commercial success and artistic importance, have had a peculiarly checkered recording career; after hearing each album in toto one gets the impression that it somehow could have been better—even if what we are given is quite admirable in many aspects. Thus *The Jefferson Airplane Takes Off* has several rock masterpieces amid mediocrities and up against the liability of a recording that is in general poorly engineered. *After Bathing at Baxters'* can at times sound over-indulgent, particularly "Spare Chaynge," and coupled with some tight, innovative rock tracks are several highly stylized songs that fail to hold up to repeated listenings.

Style in fact is both the curse and the achievement of the Jefferson Airplane. Certainly there is a constancy to the Airplane's output (as there is to that of the Byrds) that immediately marks an Airplane Album or track by style alone. Yet the problem with style (which is not only essential but a prerequisite for any work of art) is the danger of degeneration into stylization which can become a crutch and a refuge from artistic development. The new Jefferson Airplane album, *Crown of Creation*, shows the group caught in the midst of a struggle between style and stylization, and the results are sometimes ambiguous.

Obviously one of the strong points of the Airplane, as well as the source of the group's problem, is the fact that the Jefferson Airplane has among its personnel a number of distinct and forcible stylists: Grace Slick, Jorma Kaukonen, and Marty Balin are only the most obvious figures in the group in this respect. Take the case of Grace Slick: here is an obviously talented vocalist who can transform a song into something unique—but at the same time, Grace is not beneath the distorted mannerism offered up in place of thoughtful style. Her "Greasy Heart" is, by and large, a satisfactory performance, but the phrasing is, to say the least, eccentric. At times peculiar words and phrases are accented in such a way as to jump out at the listener; in "he wants to sell his paintings but the market is slow," "slow" is dragged out and given such prominence to be jarring beyond ostensible purpose. On the other hand the phrase "woman with a greasy heart, automatic man" is rendered beautifully, a nice clip being applied to "automatic." The point is that Grace is not immune to the dangers of her own style which can, through exaggeration, verge on self-parody and mannerism.

Jorma Kaukonen also has developed a distinctive style; his guitar playing owes more to Kaukonen than anyone else, which is a rarity in these days of mini-Claptons, Bloomfields and B. B. Kings. However, in contrast to Grace, Kaukonen is less likely to fall into mannered playing, although often his style contributes to a stylized texture.

Which brings us to Marty Balin, whose "Share a Little Joke" is a prime example of uninteresting Airplane. "Share a Little Joke" sounds like bits of other Airplane songs strung together, yet it makes the mistake of not being particularly cohesive, a characteristic quality of the best Airplane songs. Now "Share a Little Joke" is *not* a terrible track—by this fourth album, the Airplane are to the point where there is little chance that they will commit a truly howling musical blunder. But taking their music as in process of development, a song like "Share a Little Joke" is highly disappointing.

Of course *Crown of Creation* has its share of excellent moments which reflect the kind of creative rock we have come to expect from the Airplane. For instance, the use of acoustic guitars (sometimes mixed with electric guitars) on several tracks is noteworthy, especially in the case of Balin and Kantner's "In Time." On "In Time" Kaukonen, Jack Casady, and Kantner spin a gentle yet complex web that surrounds Kantner's vocal; here also Grace does a beautiful job of vocal embellishment, an object lesson to all practitioners of the art. "Ice Cream Phoenix" is an odd but effective song that sounds refreshingly dissimilar to anything the Airplane have recorded before; it includes a marvelous passage with Kaukonen and Grace phrasing together the line "the wall of your memory will echo your sorrow. . . ." Unfortunately the record's ambitious closing song, "The House at Pooneil Corners," does not fare so well; it can best be described as a noble failure. To carry off an explicitly apocalyptic song is a difficult task, even for someone like Jimi Hendrix, but the Airplane nevertheless at times achieve striking success. The song builds nicely in its churning way, and when Grace sings of "jelly & juices & bubbles—bubbles on the floor" the effect is pretty chilling. Yet for some strange reason the track is allowed to drag on for too long with little essential musical development: the chaos and drive is solidly present from the beginning, and after almost six minutes the effect begins to wear off.

Most of the rest of *Crown of Creation* is capably executed, particularly Kaukonen's solo on the otherwise undistinguished "Star Track." Kaukonen here, as elsewhere on the album, uses the wah-wah pedal, making clear that the new sound is a perfectly natural outgrowth of his earlier playing. Apart from "Greasy Heart," Grace's only other song is "Lather," which rather unsubtly uses sound effects; apparently the Airplane saw nothing ludicrous in underlining the phrase "his mother sent newspaper clippings to him" with the sound of scissors clipping paper.

Of special interest is "Triad," a David Crosby composition. One of the great losses to the rock world was Crosby's departure from the Byrds where his writing (not to mention his singing) was always a bright spot. "Triad," with its acoustic guitar arrangement, texturally is reminiscent of the Joni Mitchell set Crosby produced; like so many Crosby songs, this one is rather sad, and (as usual with his work) "Triad" makes a haunting impression. Its inclusion in *Crown of Creation* is a big plus for the album, doing credit to both Crosby and the Airplane.

Caught between style and stylization the Jefferson Airplane seem momentarily trapped artistically in a position where they may engulf themselves through their own exemplary aesthetic efforts. *Crown of Creation* (like the other Airplane albums) has its high points, but it certainly also has its disappointing low points. Nevertheless the Airplane has steadily (if slowly) evolved, and it is refreshing to have a group refrain from rushing into *Sgt. Pepper* changes and instrumental augmentations. If the Airplane can avoid the pitfalls of mannered stylization there is every possibility that they will remain among the best solid rock units in the country—and perhaps then we may get, one day, the completely satisfactory album the Airplane should be capable of recording.

—JIM MILLER
10-26-68

VOLUNTEERS
Jefferson Airplane
(RCA LSP-4238)

I guess it's all in what you look for in a rock and roll record.

Now, I happen to think that the Jefferson Airplane, on the basis of what they have done on *Bathing at Baxters'* and now *Volunteers,* are musical pioneers. But tell this to some people and they tell you that the Airplane is dull, leaden. They don't *swing,* for chrissakes. And on *Volunteers,* man, the politics . . .

But there is most assuredly something there with the Airplane, something that may raise the musical sophistication and complexity of rock and roll to new heights. The only trouble is that in the process, the Airplane is turning off a part of their audience, those who might be called successors to the it's-got-a-nice-beat-and-you-can-dance-to-it people. This same thing has happened to jazz a dozen times, and although I hate to start drawing parallels between rock and jazz, still I think it's fair to say that pretty soon we'll be seeing the emer-gence of a whole new brand of "serious rock," which will prob-ably get even less airplay than "progressive rock" does today, appeal to a smaller audience, and generate a good deal of very heated debate.

Now, I am neither a musi-cian nor a musicologist, so I would be hard pressed to tell you exactly what it is that the Airplane is doing that inspires me to all of these rash feats of prophecy, but if you com-pare the fine collective impro-visation "Spare Chaynge" on the *Baxters'* album to the general musical level of your average "super-session," or compare the well thought-out guitar work of Jorma Kaukonen to your aver-age wind-up guitarist, maybe you'll see what I mean. Or may-be you won't. Like I say, it's all in what you're looking for. For instance, one thing I really appreciate is the way the Air-plane plays around with the rhythmic and harmonic struc-tures they set up in a song; in "Spare Chaynge" they are mere-ly hinted at, while in "Hey Fredrick" they are emphasized while the musicians play around with the value of the metrical unit. *I* find that kind of thing exciting, at least when the musi-cians are good enough to know what they're doing and to do it well; you may be indifferent or bored by it all, or you may feel that to have to put as much effort as it takes to figure all

that out into a piece of rock
and roll is ridiculous.

So, with the prejudices up
front, let's take a look at *Volunteers.*

Probably the best cut on the
album is their version of
"Wooden Ships," which has
been given new life by Paul
Kantner. Kantner seems to be
a true innovator; in almost all
of his songs the vocal harmonies
come to the fore, rich and
weirdly un-harmonic, consisting
as they do of lots of unresolved
seconds and other strange inter-
vals. "Wooden Ships" emerges
as a new and better "Won't
You Try Saturday Afternoon"
with the same apocalyptic bass
(Casady was credited with playing "Yggdrasill bass" on *Crown
of Creation,* Yggdrasill being
the Norse sacred tree of life)
and a fine searing lead guitar.
The song comes off as more of
a scream of desperation than
does the Crosby-Stills-Nash version, with the "wooden ships
on the water" part supported by
some mellow harmony that re-
inforces the lyrics nicely. It is
an epic performance, and one
of the best the Airplane has
ever done.

The other major song on the
album is Grace's "Hey Fredrick," which contains some really inspired instrumental work
by Jorma and Nicky Hopkins,
who seems to turn nearly everything he touches into gold.
Jorma's duet with himself is
remarkable in that neither of

the parts is anything special by
itself, but they are different
enough so that the combination
of the two parts results in a
separate, third musical entity.

"We Can Be Together" and
"Volunteers" are more or less
the same song (and I have a
feeling that the chord progressions used show up in somewhat different forms in several
of the other songs—"Good
Shepherd" and "The Farm," for
instance). Kantner's harmonies
are here in all their glory, and
the tune(s) is (are) undeniably
catchy. Some people are disturbed by the words. Well,
they're certainly no more or
less stupid than the average
rock lyrics, and right about now
lyrics about revolution are becoming about as trite as most
of those about love have always
been. Is "We Can Be Together"
a political statement? Listen to
how the "revolutionaries" sing
the line "And we are very
proud of ourselves" before
launching into the self-indulgent
"Up against the wall" part. If
there's a political statement
here, maybe it's between the
lines. And don't forget, the kid
who buys the album to hear
them say "motherfucker" will
listen to the rest of it and
maybe get musically, if not
politically, radicalized.

The rest of the album, with
the possible exception of Spencer's "A Song for All Seasons,"
which I think is a cute slap at

the music business, but little more, is excellent. "The Farm" and "Turn My Life Down" have supporting vocals by the Ace of Cups, who wind up, due to the exigencies of 16-track recording, sounding like a chorus of angels squished way down in there somewhere. Marty's voice has never sounded better than on the latter cut, and the pyramiding of the voices on "The Farm" is delightful. "Good Shepherd" is a beautifully relaxed reworking of the old gospel tune, "Eskimo Blue Day" sounds like a combination of "Crown of Creation" and "Bear Melt," with the best features of each, and "Meadowlands" is just fine.

The Jefferson Airplane will never replace the Rolling Stones or the Grateful Dead, and the Rolling Stones and the Grateful Dead will never replace the Airplane. More power to all of them.

—ED WARD
2-21-70

HOT TUNA
Hot Tuna
(RCA LSP-4353)

What a mystery this record is. I'd been hearing rumors for a long while that said that the Airplane was in a kind of semi-retirement, and that Jack and Jorma were playing around with various sit-in drummers, including, I think, Mitch Mitchell. All of which sounded like a gas. I still think that "Spare Chaynge" on *Baxters'* is the greatest instrumental achievement of rock to date, and that's kind of what I expected from this splinter group, which, I later learned, was calling itself Hot Tuna. Then came the news that they would be releasing an album. My mouth watered with anticipation.

And here it is, I guess. Acoustic guitar, electric bass, vocals, and, here and there, a little harp. Recorded live at the New Orleans House in Berkeley. Playing what appears to be, on first examination, Dave Van Ronk's Greatest Hits.

But appearances deceive, and I should kick myself for trying to second-guess two of the finest musicians in the country today. Hot Tuna is a couple of guys from a rock band who got bored sitting around waiting for the rest to get over their throat-node operations and various forms of tripping around, so they started jamming the old favorites back and forth and came out with an album. A convenient fiction which we will let stand while we talk about the music on RCA LSP-4353.

To begin with, I have sat in on jam sessions, lazed around Washington Square Park when the folk boom was at its height, attended concerts and hootenannies, and consorted with all manner of speed demons and would-be guitar virtuosi, and have not, until this point, heard anyone play guitar as rapidly as Jorma Kaukonen. Ever. There are times when he sounds like Bert Jansch *and* John Renbourn, with a third person playing rhythm. And it's all tasteful and blessedly free of wretched excess. Casady's bass is very subtle and unfortunately not crisply enough recorded to make the kind of impact that it should, but any close listening will reveal that he is in just as fine shape here as he ever was.

The songs, though, are just jumping-off places for instrumental excursions, usually carried off with lightning inventiveness, as if the players' heads were so jam-packed with ideas that they could hardly wait to dispose of one so that they could get the next one in. The mysterious Will Scarlett provides harp textures that are very reminiscent of the extreme sensitivity of Mel Lyman, and, while he never really lets go and blows his brains out, it is hard to imagine any more fitting addition to Jorma and Jack's dynamism.

Still, the album is not the titanic masterpiece that an Airplane fan might expect. Its uncomplicatedness fits in well with the atmosphere of the place where it was recorded; one can hear glasses being dropped and the engineers discussing equipment problems. It is a relaxing album, one to sip wine and sit

on the back porch by, but it isn't gonna do your head in like you might expect. And as far as talking about any individual cut, well, you've heard them all before, with the exception of the lovely "New Song" and the instrumental "Mann's Fate," which stand out mainly because they are nothing like the ragtime-blues that make up the bulk of the album. Relaxing music, all of it, regardless of how fast or slow it is. Which is probably why that guy dropped his glass.

But still, this Hot Tuna bears very little resemblance to the electric Hot Tuna that so many San Franciscans have seen playing at the clubs and ballrooms. That band is loud, includes a drummer (Joey Covington, the new Airplane drummer, started out with them), and is supposedly into a whole nother trip. It's just too bad that we never got to hear any of what they could do. Oh, well, until the next Airplane album, "Spare Chaynge," anyone?

—ED WARD
7-9-70

ANTHEM OF THE SUN
The Grateful Dead
(Warner Brothers WS 1749)

On the Grateful Dead's *Anthem of the Sun* the studio with its production work dissolves into live performance, the carefully crafted is thrown together with the casually tossed off, and the results are spliced together. The end product is one of the finest albums to come out of San Francisco, a personal statement of the rock aesthetic on a level with the Jefferson Airplane's *After Bathing at Baxters'*. To be sure, the album has its weak points, but as a total work it is remarkably successful, especially when compared to the first Dead album.

The first side of *Anthem of the Sun* is a masterpiece of rock, "That's It for the Other One" and "New Potatoes Caboose" being particularly noteworthy. The main theme of "Other One" is an eminently memorable quasi-country melody that starts right off with the tasteful guitar of Garcia that dominates the record; a second movement starts the confusion between live and studio (nice stereo production work here), fading into a restatement of the main theme; then there is some beautiful musique concrete leading into "Caboose." Already there is evident carefully arranged vocal work, a departure from the Dead's previous release. The end of "Caboose" is a driving solo by Garcia that builds into structured frenzy thanks to Lesh's bass, the drums of Hart and Kreutzmann, and especially Garcia's masterful playing. Garcia is that rarity among rock guitarists, a thoughtful phraser

who logically constructs his solos in a manner not unlike a capable jazz musician. Together Lesh, Weir and Garcia (along with McKernan's fat globs of organ) produce a complex, tight sound that stands with the best hard rock around.

Kazoos open "Alligator," which is that kind of song, hardly dead serious. But it includes another fine Garcia solo; Lesh shows here as elsewhere that he is a fine bass player, while Hart and Kreutzmann work together to form one of the most powerful (and inventive) percussion units in rock. With "Caution (Do Not Stop on Tracks)" we are confronted with the album's most curious track, which ranges from a white-imitation blues riff vamp-until-ready to 60-cycle hum and microphone feedback. The vocal sounds like Danny Kalb (poor in other words), but this in fact is the main consistent problem with the album: the vocals. Often the voices are muddy and on blues none of the Dead sound particularly persuasive; but this is a minor quibble when so much else is right on this album. The mixture of electronic and serious music achieved by Edgar Varese on "Deserts" stands as one of the most impressive achievements in this area; on their own terms the Dead have achieved a comparable blend of electronic and electric music.

For this reason alone *Anthem of the Sun* is an extraordinary event. It's been over a year since the first Dead album. It was worth waiting.

—JIM MILLER
9-28-68

LIVE DEAD
The Grateful Dead
(Warners 1830)

Live Dead explains why the Dead are one of the best performing bands in America, why their music touches on ground that most other groups don't even know exists.

A list of song titles would mean very little in terms of what actually goes on inside the album. Like the early Cream, the Dead in concert tend to use their regular material as a jumping-off point, as little frameworks that exist only for what can be built on top of them. In "Dark Star," for example, they give a token reading of the song itself, waiting patiently until the vocal drops and Garcia's guitar comes out front to begin the action. About ten minutes later, if you can manage to look up by then, you might realize that what is happening bears as little resemblance to "Dark Star" as all that rollin' and tumblin' stuff did to "Spoonful." But of course, by that time, it just doesn't matter, and when the Dead slowly bring the song back around to "Dark Star," each change made with care and a strange kind of tact, you can only marvel at the distance you've traveled in such a short period of time.

Live Dead also exhibits the group's quite considerable ability in tying together differing song-threads, letting them pass naturally into one another, almost as if they had been especially designed for such a move. A jamming band (and the Dead are that, if nothing else) has to rely on its sense of Flow, on its talent in taking that small series of steps which will ultimately bring it to some entirely different place from where it started. On side two, they begin with "St. Stephen," working at that until they magically appear in "The Eleven," and then, just before the final tape cut-off, you can hear them changing again with "Turn On Your Lovelight." It's beautifully conceived and done, each piece clicking together perfectly.

One of the finer things about the record is that the cuts seem to have been chosen with a great deal of care. Even on the best of nights, the group as a whole has a tendency to be spotty, with the many good moments intermingled with the bad. This is not necessarily a minus factor; when you work on such tenuous ground as the Dead, where each note means holding a balance between seven very different people and a less concrete mass out front, it's only logical to expect a large number of misses. If you've ever seen them live, you know that there are times when they simply can't do it, when the thread that has been so carefully nursed is suddenly snapped apart, when they amble around, trying to find the key that will unlock the door again.

Live Dead contains none of this searching. It's all there, up moment after moment, everything snugly tucked in place. "Turn On Your Lovelight," the usual Pigpen show-stopper, is right to the point here, all the different sections coming together in a nice ripe whole, moving quickly with nary a jerk or piece left hanging. Even a long eight-minute section of feedback on side four is handled well, each individual howl pinpointed with unerring accuracy. And as in concert, a piece from the Incredible String Band's "A Very Cellular Song" is a perfect way to close out the show.

I'm not going to end this by using some overworn phrase about how this is possibly the best live album ever a must for your record collection something no fan should be without etc. etc. But if you'd like to visit a place where rock is likely to be in about five years, you might think of giving *Live Dead* a listen or two.

—LENNY KAYE
2-7-70

WORKINGMAN'S DEAD
The Grateful Dead
(Warner Brothers WS 1869)

It's so nice to receive a present from good friends.

Workingman's Dead is an excellent album. It's a warming album. And most importantly, the Dead have finally produced a complete studio album. The songs stand up quite nicely right on their own merits, which are considerable.

"Uncle John's Band," which opens the album, is, without question, the best recorded track done by this band. Staunch Dead freaks probably will hate this song. It's done acoustically for a starter. No Garcia leads. No smasho drumming. In fact, it's got a mariachi/calypso type feeling. Finely, warmly-lush tuned guitar work starts it off, with a statement of the beat and feeling. When Garcia comes in with the vocal, joined by a lot of tracks of everyone else's voices, possibly including his, it's really very pretty. The lyrics blend in nicely with the music. "All I want to know/ How does the song go?" "Come hear Uncle John's band/playing to the tide/Come with me, or come alone/He's come to take his children home." Near the end of the song there is an *a cappella* section done by everyone, sounds like about 62 tracks, maybe 63. Just listen to it, and try *not* to smile.

The years of playing together have shown handsome dividends. "Dire Wolf" points this out. It's a country song, Garcia's steel guitar work is just right, and everyone sings along to the "Don't murder me" chorus.

The country feeling of this album just adds to the warmth of it. "Cumberland Blues" starts off as a straight electric cut, telling the story of trying to make ends meet in bad times. Slowly, imperceptibly at first, a banjo enters the song. By the end, I was back at the old Gold Rush along with everyone else. The banjo brought me there.

Even the cuts that are not directly influenced by country stylings have a country feel to them. I suspect that this is due to the band's vocals. Living out on their ranch seems to have mellowed them all, or at least given a country tinge to their voices. "Casey Jones" is not the theme song you might remember from television. "Driving that train/High on cocaine/Casey Jones you better watch your speed." Listen closely, especially to the cymbal work. Then listen to Phil Lesh's bass mixing with Weir's guitar. Now listen to the cymbal again. Yep. They did it. I don't know who's train is better, Casey's or the Dead's. Living sound effects. Just fine.

—ANDY ZWERLING
7-23-70

QUICKSILVER MESSENGER SERVICE
Quicksilver Messenger Service
(Capitol ST 2903)

Quicksilver's initial and long-awaited excursion into the primordial clear light of San Francisco isn't quite what was expected, due to the production staff headed by the Electric Flag's Nick Gravenites and Harvey Brooks. The Quicksilver Messenger Service don't sound quite the same since they've heard the Flag and Mike Bloomfield, late arrivals on the San Francisco scene. As a result, most of the album cuts (only six altogether) come across sounding like the Electric Flag, minus their blues-loyal predication and Buddy Miles, doing straight rock.

An exception to the general tone of the album is Quicksilver's interpretation of folk-rock (remember?) singer Hamilton (Bob) Camp's "Pride of Man." This is an unusual number for them to have done, but it's really a better version than Camp's original. Another rock group, Clear Light, started off their album with a folk-oriented cut, Tom Paxton's "Mr. Blue," which they butchered unmercifully. Not so this version of "Pride," which the Quicksilver carry off admirably. The song itself has some surprisingly profound lyrics: "Oh God/Pride of man/Broken in the dust again."

The first inkling of the Flag influence is evident on "Light Your Windows," which is spaced by some obvious Bloomfieldian guitar breaks. John Cipollina is an excellent guitarist and his susceptibility to Bloomfield's techniques is understandable, and, since he plays so well, readily acceptable.

The guitar on "Dino's Song" wanders in and out of a Kaukonen, Garcia and Bloomfield-like garden of sounds, supporting a strong vocal of simple but intensely reflective lyrics endeavoring to explain that "All I ever wanted to do was know you/And maybe hope you could know me too."

"Gold And Silver" is (whether intended or not) a rock arrangement of Dave Brubeck's "Take Five." Cipollina's guitar excursions are singularly evocative of Paul Desmond's sax changes. They manage to get away from the "Take Five" theme a bit by going into some Vanilla Fudgish, sluggish tempo drags which develop into a takeoff reminiscent of the Flag's "Another Country," even adding some fluttery, tinkly sounds a la Country Joe & the Fish.

Gravenites' composition, "It's Been Too Long," is done in typical Flag style. The vocal is as close a duplication of Gravenites' singing as it could possibly be. It's a great piece, though, from its raw, Albert King intro, to a campy "whoa whoa whoa" Dion imitation and old 50's R&R fade out.

"The Fool" takes up most of Side Two but, unfortunately, not very justifiably. It starts out carefully, waiting for the guitar to move out, spaced by some beautiful bass runs which cut into some hard-rock movements only to be lost in a series of impotent semi-buildups. Some very handsome guitar phrasing sneaks through but whatever good it does winds up buried halfway through the track. It digresses into some disappointing, ineffable routines, including a guitar-growling sequence, followed by a Claptonesque wah-wah pedal ritual. But with the addition of the vocal it picks up somewhat—the words are intoned in a middle-eastern, Hebrew cantor-like quaver. It closes out with some Yardbird "Still I'm Sad" declensions, culminating in an organ-anchored Bach-Procol Harum denouement.

It's inevitable that a group will absorb a certain measure of influence from other bands —and the Quicksilver Messenger Service has emerged on record as a composite of influence, from their overbearing Flag-derived arrangements to a number of other easily identifiable characteristics. But, incredibly, their formula works. They have a good, even, remarkably honest sound. Theirs is a much finer record debut than the Grateful Dead's. The only problem seems to be a lack of original direction, something that will be impossible to locate anywhere but in their own individual musical sense.

—BARRY GIFFORD
7-6-68

SHADY GROVE
Quicksilver Messenger Service
(Capitol SKAO 391)

This is the first Quicksilver album in more than a year, and for those of you accustomed to *Happy Trails*, will come as something of a shock. The absorption of Nicky Hopkins and the departure of Gary Duncan have changed the sound and thrust of the Quicksilver-of-yore entirely. No more the Haight Street flashes, the extended Cipollina guitar solos, the rhythm and blues edges or the Bo Diddley echoes that seemed the essence of this "first generation" San Francisco band. "The Fool" from their first album and their "Who Do You Love" extensions on *Happy Trails* will remain as the hard-core Quicksilver cuts. This new album is something else.

The old Quicksilver was immediate, instrumentally flashing and frenzied. The Quicksilver on *Shady Grove* has had its collective head turned around by Nicky Hopkins. The result is a more precise, more lyrical, more textured Quicksilver.

But they pull it off quite well. Hopkins by no means totally dominates the music—he was the catalyst for the shift in outlook, no doubt, but the reaction is four-fold and sympathetic. You can tell that they all still enjoy what they are doing (and how many bands can you say that about after five years?) and, even though the rhythm section isn't recorded too well, this ambitious album should be well received.

Echoes of the old Quicksilver verve and abandon do crop up quite often. The title cut, "Shady Grove," after a classical-tempoed Hopkins introduction settles down into that old familiar Bo Diddley beat. "3 Or 4 Feet From Home" and "Joseph's Coat" also have that memorable brawlingness to them—the latter even having an extended guitar passage reminiscent of Duncan's "Calvary" on *Happy Trails*.

The rest of the cuts take some getting used to. They are muted, delicate and Hopkins-infiltrated. He switches from piano to celeste to harpsichord to organ on "Flute Song," "Too Far" and "Flashing Lonesome," all the time forcing the exploding essence of Quicksilver to focus on such matters as melody, tone and lyrics. It takes a few listenings to adjust to this switch and to absorb Hopkins' keyboard mastery, which except for the vocals, makes these cuts work. For me, the vocals tend to be too self-conscious and strained, even muddy at times. It seems as though each syllable has to match each chord with nary an inch given on either side—this only results in plasticity and a departure from the ethos of rock, which comes driving back at us in the final Hopkins-authored "Edward." It is stunning in its complexity of development and satisfies the need for a wide-open instrumental. Hopkins overwhelms on piano, but the supporting guitar/bass/drums should not be slighted. Hopkins fans should buy this album for this cut alone.

If it seems as though I'm hedging a bit in this review, well, maybe I am. I really liked the old Quicksilver and the frenzy they could work up to —they were the only consistently great instrumental-oriented band in the Psychedelic Shop-days and onward through *Happy Trails*. They had a certain mystique about their music matched only by the looming Warlocks and the Wild Wested Charlatans. Now, in a way, they have become the "straight men" for the facile Hopkins. Fine music is still the result—but that rock and roll, free-form jamming quality seems to have been sacrificed.

—GARY VON TERSCH
5-14-70

OAR
Alexander Spence
(Columbia CS 9831)

Poking around the shelves of bargain record shops, one will stumble across the wreckage of the rock and roll revolution— the hundreds of albums released in the last few years that no one ever listened to. Shoved against the wall, their hopefully outrageous psychedelic covers now limp and dull, one can almost judge the quality of the music by a glance at the jacket. And crammed in between the waste and the garbage are great records that got lost in the shuffle, LPs that had the misfortune to be released the same week as *Wheels of Fire* or *Cheap Thrills:* the already forgotten albums by the Good Rats, Bunky and Jake, and others. The hip FM stations never got around to programming them, Top 40 never heard of them, and the unlucky songwriters and musicians may soon be back toiling at the Sixties equivalent of the proverbial carwash.

Oar, the new album by Alexander (Skip) Spence of Moby Grape fame, will probably find its way onto the dingy shelves of the bargain shops—even a brand new copy may go for a dollar or less. "This album is an oasis of undersell," read the liner notes (if that's true, it shouldn't be said, right?). Not many new LPs will sell less, I'm afraid.

Much of *Oar* sounds like the sort of haphazard folk music that might have been made around campfires after the California gold rush burned itself out—sad, clumsy tunes that seem to laugh at themselves as Spence takes the listener on a tour through his six or seven voices: a coughing, halting bass on "Diana," a withered, half-dead moan on "Lawrence of Euphoria," or a dazzling, lyrical wail for "War in Peace" and "Grey/Afro."

In one way, this album is a joke. It's so unpolished and rude (as in "rude hut") that it sometimes seems merely incompetent—one might sit by and crack up over every cut. "Uh, uh, Di-an*na*," lurches Alexander Spence, and if it's not intended as a good laugh on Neil Sedaka then it's just plain bad. Nothing on *Oar* is irritating, though—the music is quiet and insinuating, so if it's not great rock like "Omaha" or cute like "Funky Tunk," this is still real music, not someone's half-baked idea of where it's at.

Spence recorded in Nashville, but lo, he didn't use Charlie McCoy, Kenny Buttrey, and Bob Johnston. He plays, sort of, all the instruments himself—bass, drums, electric and acoustic guitar—and produced his record. Sometimes his playing is about as good as Wildman Fischer, and sometimes

he's perfectly brilliant. The end result is music that has the same tone to it as the tapes Bob Dylan records for fun and doesn't release.

Oar's greatest blessings are "War in Peace" and "Grey/Afro." They're quintessential Spence cuts—anarchic in conception but somehow holding on to form and rhythm in execution. I've never been able to figure out how Spence's most astounding compositions—"Seeing" from *Moby Grape '69* and "Indifference" from *Moby Grape*—were ever performed, they sound like wild street fights, vocalists shouting back and forth, guitarists challenging one another for the lead, harmonies splitting the beat without a thought for the perfect order that's the triumph of Spence's revolutionary music. Spence triumphs again in *Oar*, though "War in Peace" and "Grey/Afro" are less immediate in their impact. "Weighted Down" precedes "War in Peace," and by the time it's over the listener may find himself half-asleep, only to be lifted out of the doldrums by the ghostly approach of Spence's electric guitar. Spence states a theme and then sets a mood, following it as far as it will go. His voice is another instrument—I've heard the record many times and not understood more than a score of the words, and though this may be an affront to Spence's lyrics more likely it's a tribute to the seduction of his music. "War in Peace" is pure San Francisco in its sound, but San Francisco long after the scene and Spence himself have passed from it, and the song has a slow, aging glimpse of what the music was all about.

Oar presents some of the most comfortable music I've ever heard—it's not good old rock and roll, the way Moby Grape plays it anyway, but that line from a thousand old rock ditties, "I just can't explain, I'm goin' insane" might be the musical father to Spence's new music. This unique LP is bound to be forgotten—some day it'll be as rare as "Memories of El Monte," the tune Frank Zappa wrote for the Penguins. Get ahead of the game and buy *Oar* before you no longer have the chance.

—GREIL MARCUS
9-20-69

THE SUBURBS

CREEDENCE CLEARWATER REVIVAL
Creedence Clearwater Revival
(Fantasy 8382)

On the liner notes to their album, Ralph Gleason states: "Creedence Clearwater Revival is an excellent example of the Third Generation of San Francisco bands." Really more like Third Level—behind the Airplane, Dead, Quicksilver, Grape and all the others. The only bright spot in the group is John Fogerty, who plays lead guitar and does the vocals. He's a better-than-average singer (really believable in Wilson Pickett's "Ninety-Nine and a Half"), and an interesting guitarist. But there's nothing else here. The drummer is monotonous, the bass lines are all repetitious and the rhythm guitar is barely audible.

Fogerty can't carry the load by himself, and when he does get going, as in two or three spots on "Suzie Q," their "big" number (over eight minutes long), he has no complementation from the other members of the group. He's no Albert King, but he plays a fine guitar at times. His singing on "Ninety-Nine and a Half" is beautiful. But even on that track, whenever it's suspended between riffs, the unimaginative drumming kills it. The whole record is unimaginative, poorly produced and a great waste of John Fogerty's talents.

"I Put A Spell On You" bears only a cursory resemblance to Alan Price's version, but maybe it's unfair to compare them with someone so polished and well-established.

Even Eric Burdon casts a heavier "Spell."

"I'd rather hear an old man coughing than listen to their (CCR's) rhythm section," says San Francisco jazzman Paul deBarros.

But Fogerty's versatility keeps sneaking through. He even comes on with a little Jeff Beck-ish feedback on "Porterville." He's really the only redeeming quality on the record, and even he gets buried beneath the mediocre non-arrangements and uninventiveness of the other members of the group.

I've heard them in person (they played free one day on campus in Berkeley), and they sounded much better than they do on their album. They should release "Ninety-Nine and a Half" as a single: I think it would tear up the Top-40 crowd and sell a million. Fogerty's a gas but Creedence Clearwater's Revival may not be worth it.

—BARRY GIFFORD
7-20-68

BAYOU COUNTRY
Creedence Clearwater Revival
(Fantasy 8387)

Creedence Clearwater Revival's new LP suffers from one major fault—inconsistency. The good cuts are very good; but the bad one just don't make it.

The group's sound is very reminiscent of that of the early Stones—hard rock, based in blues. John Fogerty carries the group with his good lead guitar, in addition to his good vocal and harp work. He also wrote all of Creedence's original songs, and arranged and produced the album. He probably swept out the studio when the recording was finished, too.

Despite John's dominance, the group has a solid overall sound. Stu Cook on bass, brother Tom Fogerty on rhythm guitar, and Doug Clifford on drums are all good musicians; they lay down a heavy backing for Fogerty, and the result is a very tight sound.

The main failing of the bad cuts is a lack of originality. "Graveyard Train" is a repeat of "Gloomy" on the first album. "Gloomy" wasn't worth much in the first place, and "Train," dragged out to eight minutes and thirty-two seconds, is simply boring. "Penthouse Pauper" is similar to "The Working Man," also on the first LP. The music and lyrics are good, but they've been heard before.

"Good Golly Miss Molly" is not nearly as exciting as Little Richard's original, though the group gets a good workout on this one. "Bootleg" is a good, short number which explains how something often becomes more attractive when it is illegal. Again, the lyrics are good.

But even here, Fogerty uses the same riff as on "Keep On Chooglin'." A few more fresh ideas would be helpful.

The good cuts do come off well. "Born On The Bayou" is a very bluesy thing which inspired the LP title. This contains some of John's best vocal work. "Proud Mary" is a good, easy-rolling song concerning a Mississippi river-boat. The Fogertys' guitars help to create a gentle, flowing mood. I take it that "Proud Mary" is the name of the boat.

"Keep On Chooglin'" is Creedence Clearwater Revival's "rave-up," a good, long, toe-tappin' type song. As is usually the case with such numbers, it sounds better in person than on record. Nonetheless, CCR has managed to capture some of the excitement of a live performance on this album. Exactly what chooglin' is, or how you do it, is not explained. However, Creedence Clearwater Revival would like us all to keep on doing it (apparently we've been doing it all along without knowing it) and it seems like a good idea in these troubled times.

Overall, the material in *Bayou Country* is not always strong, but Creedence Clearwater Revival plays with enough gusto to overcome this problem. With the stronger material, they are excellent. It seems to me though, that CCR has just about exhausted its supply of blues-rock numbers. They have produced two fine albums; so far, so good. But I think (and hope) that we will see new directions on their forthcoming albums.

—RAY REZOR
3-1-69

GREEN RIVER
Creedence Clearwater Revival
(Fantasy 8393)

Because Creedence Clearwater Revival first rose to prominence with hits like "Suzy Q" and achieved such immense popularity with a teenybopper audience, many people (myself among them) have until now refused to take them very seriously. But "Proud Mary" should have clued us in. It was more than simply a fine song by Top-40 standards; it was a superb song by any standards. Creedence's new album, *Green River*, demonstrates convincingly that "Proud Mary" was no fluke. Make no mistake about it; Creedence Clearwater Revival, despite some rather clear limitations, is one of the most exciting and satisfying bands around.

When I first heard "Green River," the initial cut on the album, I thought, "Oh, shit, another Creedence bayou song!" But John Fogerty's raw guitar quickly drew me in. The throbbing riff which introduces the song signals that Creedence's return to the bayou will be a complete delight. And it is. Fogerty's tough, gritty voice infuses the lyrics ("walkin' along the river road at night/barefoot girls dancin' in the moonlight") with a marvelously evocative feeling.

"Wrote a Song for Everyone," the only cut on the album in a slow tempo, creates a haunting mood somewhat akin to that of "The Weight." It features a graceful, tantalizing brief country guitar solo by Fogerty. The lyrics are really weird; as far as I can tell, their central message is the failure of message songs.

"Bad Moon Rising" was the follow-up single to "Proud Mary"; unlike most follow-ups, this song generates as much excitement as its predecessor. Like the Beatles' "Daytripper," it is marked by a curious ambivalence. The music is joyously kinetic; it is hard to listen to it without feeling like getting up and dancing. The words are something else again. Here is paranoia, 1969 style—"hope you got your things together/ hope you are quite prepared to die." "Bad Moon Rising" accurately measures the distance we've travelled since the Sunset Strip riots of "For What It's Worth."

But the true highlight of the album is "Lodi." This mournful tale of a musician stuck in a nowhere town has everything it takes to become a real classic. John Fogerty's masterful vocal makes "Lodi" one of the most convincing hard-luck stories I've heard in a long time. He never makes the mistake of straining to be "poetic"; he selects ordinary words and images which always manage to be incisive. With a fine sense of economy, he depicts an American landscape that is somehow both older and newer than Chuck Berry's classic rock description of America—older in its nostalgic visions, and newer in its nightmarish perils and traps. From "Proud Mary" and "Green River" to "Bad Moon Rising" and "Lodi," this heartbreaking American circle of beauty and ugliness is drawn. I wish John Fogerty could have written the score for *Easy Rider*.

Creedence's deficiencies are readily apparent. Their music tends to lack variety (sometimes giving the feeling that you can predict the next guitar lick) and occasionally to lack finesse. But their distinctive driving sound, when fused with Fogerty's vocals, results in something so fine that it makes such criticisms seem irrelevant. *Green River*, whatever its flaws, is a great album. Creedence Clearwater Revival have come a long way since "Suzy Q"; they are now creating the most *vivid* American rock since *Music from Big Pink*.

—BRUCE MIROFF
10-18-69

WILLY AND THE POOR BOYS
Creedence Clearwater Revival
(Fantasy 8397)

It was a benefit at the Fillmore West for KPFA, the Conscience and Culture radio station of Berkeley, and the place was filled much beyond the legal capacity. The bill was mixed; several eminent bores and some bands as talented as Commander Cody and His Lost Planet Airmen, a rising group that has succeeded in capturing the essence of country music.

But the crowd had come, virtually to a man, to see Creedence Clearwater. It was an overwhelmingly suburban audience, and from the remarks hovering in the air that was rank with sweat and deodorant-derivatives, most people had never heard of KPFA and would be scarcely impressed with it even if it was explained. "But, it's a vital part of the liberal-academic community, I tell you." So the clean-cuts and bouffants waited through several hours of barbiturate-rock. Only the light show and the passage of joints differentiated this show from 1960-Friday-Night-At-The-Boys'-Club.

When Creedence did come on, there was no stopping the audience. If you didn't manage to force your way to a point where you could barely see, you would have had no way of knowing whether Creedence was there or if their records were being played.

In all probability, there is no other rock group that can play its material so letter-perfect, exactly-like-the-record as Creedence. Even John Fogerty's harp solo on "Keep On Chooglin'" was note for note.

The crowd lived it, although spontaneity was as lacking in the crowd as in the band. Except for the dedication of "Bad Moon Rising" to R. Milhous Nixon, it was entirely predictable. As far as Fillmore groups go, it was more a demonstration than a performance. But, the crowd nearly became dangerous when Creedence refused to do an encore, and left in a bad mood.

Still, it was beautiful.

Song after song was clear, distinct and memorable. Lack of spontaneity can also be translated as lack of waste, and in the case of Creedence, it's the latter that's appropriate. They play songs. Period.

Creedence is simply not an improvising group (neither were the Beatles) and their approach is as successful as it is unusual. At this writing, they are the biggest draw in American rock. Their style and talents have also afforded them complete mastery of the AM radio. They think and play in terms of singles.

"A single means you've got

to get it across in a very few minutes. You don't have twenty minutes on each side of an LP. All it really means is you've got to think a little harder about what you're doing. We learned from the singles market not to put a bunch of padding on your album. Each song's got to go someplace." So says John Fogerty, the heart and brains behind Creedence Clearwater.

There are those who feel that to write for the AM radio is a sign of either decadence or lack of talent. Fogerty:

"Most of this is a built-in uptightness . . . 'Singles is what I dug when I was little, therefore I have to change now. I've grown up, I don't like top-40' . . . which is dumb. Why not change top-40?"

This attitude and goal characterizes the Creedence-Fogerty position. They have chosen to play to the popular audience at as high a level as possible. They are open and aboveground. No group that comes to mind has relied less on funk, esoterica, cultism, charisma or extravaganza and made it work so well, so successfully and so artfully. And this seems due to the talent and vision of John Fogerty and to the fact that Creedence has been together, playing rock, for ten years.

John Fogerty, as singer, lead guitar and songwriter, melds the band; Creedence's style

must, therefore, be largely his style, just as the Byrds' style is that of Roger McGuinn. Fogerty's singing is utterly distinctive, his guitar playing is expressive and unadorned, and his songwriting is rarely matched.

Fogerty's voice has ferocious power and an edge on it that can cut through the worst static on the cheapest car radio. He growls and shouts and scats. His range is not great, but neither is Mick Jagger's.

"When I first started singing, I really couldn't imitate anyone, because I didn't sound like anybody. The first song I really sang a lot with the band was 'Hully-Gully.' It happened to be in the right range for me and it sounded all right. . . . It was physically impossible for me to sound like a lot of the people I dug." He especially liked Little Richard and Howling Wolf, and slight ghosts of both can be detected in his style.

His guitar work isn't innovative; rather it's very solid and frequently beautiful. It complements and accompanies his singing and seems to spring from the same source and sound. "My favorite guitar player . . . and I only based it on two records I had . . . was Carl Perkins. Also Scotty Moore. Low boogie line stuff." Those elements are all present in John's guitar playing, but it's difficult to hear any particular source. After ten years, it's Creedence Clearwater.

As Creedence must have come a long way in their first eight years, they have come an equal distance since their first record. All too frequently, a group surfaces with an excellent album that proves to be the consummation of their talents and thereafter goes downhill. Partial proof that Creedence is no flash in the pan, as too many rock sophisticates tend to think, is that their albums have improved with each subsequent release. *Willy And The Poor Boys* is the best one yet.

Folk saying to the contrary, you can tell it's a good record just from the cover. The picture of the group standing around in front of Duck Kee's market in grungy West Oakland replete with gut-bucket bass, washboard, ol' git'ar an' mouf harp. Couple teeny little black kids standing around.

The picture was, in fact, shot about a block from the Fantasy studios. While the shooting was going on, they were fooling around on the jug-band instruments. They played something they liked, went back to Fantasy, cut it, and put it on the album. It appears as "Poorboy Shuffle" and while it won't eclipse Gus Cannon and the Jug Stompers, it is pleasant and might even turn on some kid enough to pursue some real jug band music.

The rest of the album is in the basic Clearwater mode, but with considerably more variation and imagination than Creedence has previously produced. There are probably six hit singles on the album; when Fogerty says, "We try to fill our albums with as many hits as possible," he means it.

"Down On The Corner" and "Fortunate Son"; you know those. Two of the other cuts are fully as powerful, and with regard to content, probably the most interesting things Creedence has done. Fogerty regards rock as being 80 per cent sound and beat; the other 20 per cent is worth playing around with. At this point, he feels no need to confine himself to love and its many distorted forms as subject matter.

The first two albums had no songs that could be construed as even slightly political. *Green River* had a couple of quasi-social songs. *Willy* has three songs of political impact, the most obvious being "Fortunate Son." Yet Fogerty denied that he was a more political person than he had been. "They put too much weight on political reference in songs. They think a song will save the world. That's absurd." Yet, at the same time he passionately believed that a song could have a message. This curious paradox can be resolved by listening to "It Came Out Of The Sky,"* which is message and comment without moralizing. It is also a very funny song, as funny as Dylan at his best. That's aside from being just a great rock song.

Fogerty's lyrics are usually difficult to distinguish—"A lot of the fun of rock is trying to figure out what he said"—but these are worth it.

The song is worth repeating in its entirety:

> Well, it came out of the sky, landed just a little south of Moline.
> Jody got out of the tractor, couldn't believe what he seen;
> Laid on the ground and shook for fearin' for his life;
> Then he ran all the way to town screamin' It Came Out Of The Sky.
>
> Well, the crowd gathered round and the scientists said it was marsh gas;
> Spiro came and made a speech about raisin' the Mars tax;
> Vatican said, "Well, the Lord has come";
> Hollywood rushed out an epic film;
> Ronnie the Popular said it was a Communist plot.

---

* Copyright © 1969 by Jondora Music.

> The newspapers came and made Jody a national hero;
> Walter and David said put him on a network TV show;
> White House said put the thing in the Pool Room;
> Vatican said, "No, it belongs to Rome."
> Jody said it's mine but you can have it for 17 million.

Comment would be superfluous. Yet, it shows at what Fogerty is superb—compression. He's managed to get three worlds of paranoia into one short, entertaining, musical song. If he fails to take the subject very seriously, well, to steal a quote, "it's too serious not to be taken humorously."

"Don't Look Now, It Ain't You Or Me," despite what was said before, is a song that both questions and moralizes. "Who takes the coal from the mines?/Who takes the salt from the earth?/Who makes the promise you don't have to keep?/Don't look now, it ain't you or me."

Why does that matter?

"Why does that matter? That's exactly why I wrote the song. We're all so ethnic now, with our long hair and shit. But, when it comes to doing the real crap that civilization needs to keep it going . . . who's going to be the garbage collector? None of *us* will. Most of us will say, 'That's beneath me, I ain't gonna do that job.' "

OK, it's a pretty straight point of view and one that can be used (and is used) against us all. But, it's one that is important, and it's to Fogerty's credit that he attempts to deal with it. His vision is broader than that of most rock lyricists. The song is simple and probably the most beautiful on the record.

Creedence dug up a couple of Kingston Trio era songs, "Cottonfields" and "Midnight Special," and added life to them. They don't sound bastardized nor do they sound as if they were crammed into the Creedence sound, nor do they sound folk-rock. They simply sound good. Either or both will, in all likelihood, make the top of the charts.

"Side of the Road" is an instrumental that just shows Fogerty to be one of prettiest-playing rock guitarists. Maybe the future will show more invention and longer sustained pieces.

The remainder of the tracks aren't much to talk about but make fine listening. You can dance to them, too.

Despite the variety present in *Willy And The Poor Boys,* there are those who still insist that it all sounds the same. Rather than point out that all banjo music or all classical music or all rock music sounds

the same unless you listen to it, I just take bets on who'll be around in five years . . . and it won't be Ten Years After.

—ALEC DUBRO
1-21-70

COSMO'S FACTORY
Creedence Clearwater Revival
(Fantasy 8402)

It should be obvious by now that Creedence Clearwater Revival is one great rock and roll band. *Cosmo's Factory,* the group's fifth album, is another good reason why.

Four of the eleven cuts have been on previous hit singles; John Fogerty wrote three of the remaining seven, only one of which, "Ramble Tamble," is unsatisfying. Apart from prolific writing, Fogerty's ability to consistently churn out good stuff is largely due to his penchant for rehearsing the band five days a week in a converted warehouse in Berkeley's industrial section. It's doubtless because of this that drummer Doug "Cosmo" Clifford refers to the group's studio as the factory.

The emphasis is not on modern derivatives but on authentic reproductions of, for example, Roy Orbison's vintage "Ooby Dooby." On "My Baby Left Me" the early-Elvis echo-chamber effect and the old Scotty Moore riffs on lead guitar reveal a considerable amount of careful study of the original. Both .cuts hold up very well as straight rockabilly.

"Travelin' Band" qualifies for historical authenticity, even though Fogerty grafts new lyrics onto a modified "Reddy Teddy" melody. He lays down a very credible Little Richard vocal and arrangement, substituting a good tenor shriek for a trademark upper register vibrato. In the absence of machinegun triads on keyboard, he dubs in saxophone—which he now plays.

Besides saxophone, Fogerty is now learning all the other instruments he's always wanted to play. In addition to lead guitar and vocal on Bo Diddley's "Before You Accuse Me" he drops in some fine blues piano riffs but apparently out of modesty keeps them pretty well buried in an easy-going, traditional arrangement. Elsewhere he picks dobro on "Lookin' Out My Back Door." Though not geared for a gut-level Creedence treatment, the song is good car music, great for summer and will probably be commercially successful.

"Who'll Stop the Rain" has the same commercial feel, and amounts to Fogerty's version of a sizable production number with a somber message delivered at a ballad's pace. Fogerty shows equal facility on "Long As I Can See the Light," a fine composition with more saxophone work and a strong Otis Redding flavor. Released as a single, it could easily end up on soul station play lists, as did "Run Through the Jungle" before it.

It's another damn good album by a group which is going to be around for a long time.

—JOHN GRISSIM
9-3-70

I FEEL LIKE I'M FIXIN' TO DIE
Country Joe and the Fish
(Vanguard VSD 79266)

Country Joe and the Fish, hereinafter referred to as CJ&TF, is another group which, between first and second records, has gone through a number of changes. The first thing that strikes you is the record cover, far more professional and, thank God, tasteful in execution than the first one. Similarly the production of the music and the songs is also done with more experience and taste.

Their first record was done far too early in their development and reflected a great deal of amateurishness on all sides. For example, the organ on the first LP, which many people found so appealing as a sound because it was so familiar and so easy to understand, has by comparison matured tremendously in approach and content.

Similarly the guitar work is much more sophisticated.

On top of this, CJ&TF have worked in a better studio and added sounds and effects to their record that are not a part of the group. However, there are certain problems that still remain; the CJ&TF cheer that opens the record is very funny and from it one can very well intuit the whole funky Berkeley bag that CJ&TF come from. On the other hand, the LSD commercial—listen to it twice—is an essentially tasteless bit.

"Janis," the song written for Janis Joplin of Big Brother and the Holding Company, hereinafter referred to as BB&THC, was not at all the track to pick for single release. The "Bomb Song" would have been more commercial. They are better at being political than at trying to be hip.

The music is fairly simple in concept. "Eastern Jam" is not as involved in Eastern-influenced electronics and patterns as Butterfield's "East-West." However it has an elementary hypnotic effect, and if that effect—as in "Colors for Susan" as well—is what they're after and that is the way they want to go about it, then CJ&TF are into their thing.

—JANN WENNER
12-14-68

TWO TRIPS WITH JESSE COLIN YOUNG
The Youngbloods
(Mercury SR 61273)

In early 1965, Jesse Colin Young recorded an excellent solo album on Mercury (now out-of-print) called *Young Blood*. Truckin' along in relative obscurity in the folk field, Jesse nevertheless was the subject of a three-page article in the November 1965 Hit Parade: "The Rockfolk Revolution: Jesse Colin Young and Fred Neil." (!) Shortly thereafter in Boston, Jesse met bluegrass musician Banana, jazz drummer Joe Bauer, and folkie Jerry Corbitt of Tifton, Georgia and ragtime fame. They all got together, amazingly, and said, "Hey man, why don't we all play together and be the best American rock group there'll ever be?" And so they were, hassles and all.

This new Mercury album is *not* pirated garbage; it is *not* a recording of the Youngbloods tuning up at their first rehearsal; it is *not* a rechanneled version of the early Youngbloods' practice tapes being run backwards. What it is, is a very good album—historically invaluable and in some ways equal to any of the Youngbloods' albums.

Side one has five performances by the Youngbloods: one Jerry Corbitt song and four

Jesse Colin Young originals. Three of the songs are gently rocking ballads, all beautiful and excellent in the classic Youngbloods vein, featuring their fantastic group singing. The fourth, "Another Strange Town," is a marginal hard rock song with solo vocal by Jesse; "Rider," the last, is a blues with Jesse singing alone again.

The second side consists of six cuts taken from the old *Young Blood* album: "Nobody's Dirty Business," "Doc Geiger," "Brother Can You Spare a Dime," and three of Jesse's eight originals on the album. Every one of the six songs is good. For that matter, the five which have been left off are also excellent. The striking thing is that Jesse Colin Young's singing here is as good as he has ever done, if not perhaps even better: clear and unaffected. The music (Jesse and his guitar, backed by John Sebastian on harp and Pete Childs on dobro) is really varied: some blues-type songs, some straight folk material, and other songs tending to bluegrass. In a nutshell, it is amazingly good; and this side, good as it is, only hints at the depth and larger mood of *Young Blood*. But good it is.

And so, what we have here is not a junky re-issue, but a beautiful and valid album that chronologically comes right before the Youngbloods' first RCA album. And, brothers and sisters, if you *still* haven't listened to the Youngbloods, if you *still* don't have some of the Youngbloods' albums—is there something *wrong* with you? Have a heart, give the Youngbloods a chance. The Youngbloods' music has enough heart to go around for everyone.

—MIKE SAUNDERS
6-25-70

A LONG TIME COMIN'
The Electric Flag, An American Music Band
(Columbia CS 9597)

Nobody who's been listening to Mike Bloomfield—either talking or playing—in the last few years could have expected this. This is the New Soul Music, the synthesis of White Blues and Heavy Metal Rock. "Groovin' is easy" with the Flag and their anti-Motown Background Shoeshine Quartet, their "American Music."

The album is not spectacular. It's good, truthful. The Flag are honest imitators as well as innovators. Nothing they do can be attributed to any one singular source. Nick Gravenites sings to himself but it's OK. The band isn't as tight as expected. I get the feeling Bloomfield's not quite sure if the group is kosher like this: he senses there can be no dualism in music or anything else.

A Long Time Comin' is suspended in a blues-soul limbo,

working feverishly to figure it- self out.

After a lead-in by LBJ ("I speak tonight for the dignity of man") is drowned out in laughter, the Flag mobilize into "Killing Floor," a blues number distinguished mainly by Bloom- field's singing guitar; Gravenite's vocal is partially lost under the horn riffs and since it's the first cut on the album I was impatient to hear Bloomfield get into something. This isn't one of the more remarkable tracks on the record. "Groovin' Is Easy" starts out sounding like the Left Banke backed by Little Anthony and the Impe- rials. But then Bloomfield does some Beatles-to-bagpipes phras- ing that splits up the piece ad- mirably. It ends with with a repeating soul chorus shuffling off to Berry Gordyland.

"Over Lovin' You" is a beau- tiful, driving screamer high- lighted by a vocal incarnation of James Brown and Stevie Wonder. It was written by Bloomfield and Barry Goldberg, who is heard here on organ but has since left the group. "She Should Have Just" is a mellow-down-easy blues with a break to some harsh rock chording reminiscent of Hen- drix on "Foxy Lady." "Wine" is an old "Rock-Around-the- Clock" type Bill Haley-ish num- ber sung well by Gravenites and annotated briefly but superb- ly at the finish by Bloomfield. Towards the end Gravenites

refers to Janis Joplin (of Big Brother) and her knowing all about "socking that wine."

But the entire complex of the record changes on side two. It leads off with "Texas," a slow, distinct blues of the sort that Bloomfield is so comfortable in. There aren't any gimmicks in this piece. Bloomfield knows what he's doing here—his lead is so well thought out you realize he's played it fifty mil- lion times before and was anx- ious to get it across on this record.

The highlights of the album are the next two cuts. "Sittin' In Circles," another Barry Goldberg composition, is sup- ported by strings and strong brass accompaniment. It's an outstanding piece—the tightest on the record—and the lyrics, unlike those of most of the other selections, are honest. But on "You Don't Realize," which is "dedicated with great respect to Steve Cropper and Otis Redding," the Flag reach their highest level. The song deals with woman's respon- sibility and what her actions really mean to her man. It comes across as a testament befitting the homage to Otis Redding. The song seems writ- ten for Redding—a pleading, heart-wrenching version of "Dock of the Bay."

"Another Country" gives dra- matic evidence of the balance the Flag have. Gravenites' vo- cal warrants a more than cursory comparison with Bugsy Maugh of Butterfield's band. (Listen to "Drivin' Wheel" on the *Resurrection of Pigboy Crabshaw* album.) The number is interrupted by a cacophony of distorted noises, mostly indecipherable—the whole thing is really unnecessary. The piece once again breaks into the main theme after a magnificent Bloomfield solo—the first time on the record he appears to get into something and out of the balanced mold of the group. Even the horns sound better here because they're being used to a fuller capacity and not constrained to rattling off disciplined rhythm accompaniment.

The last fifty seconds are devoted to a sweet, willowy, unaccompanied Bloomfield rendering of "Easy Rider" that is absolutely beautiful. I would have loved to hear him go on with it.

All in all, the debut of The Electric Flag is strangely stultifying. You realize how much the band has to offer, how much golden potential is trying to find a way to manifest itself properly into the open.

When they are finally able to channel the diverse forms of "American Music": (heard) in the air, on the air, in the streets; the blues, soul, country, rock, religious music, traffic, crowds, street sounds and field sounds, the sounds of people and silence as Mike Bloomfield

intends to do, it will be a magnificent testament to their composite musical genius. To borrow from Ouspensky, The Flag are "in search of the miraculous." The first evidence of this, *A Long Time Comin'* is only slightly overwhelming.

—BARRY GIFFORD
5-11-68

It should be pointed out that songs credited to "R. Polte" are actually compositions of Nick Gravenites.

AN AMERICAN MUSIC BAND
The Electric Flag
(Columbia CS 9714)

By now everyone involved knows of Mike Bloomfield's split with his briefly celebrated Electric Flag and too, of the demise of the same soon after his departure. Buddy Miles has gone on to form his Express, taken a couple members of the Flag with him; Nick Gravenites is due to record a solo album for Columbia; Harvey Brooks led the ill-fated Cass Elliot band in Vegas; and the rest are off on their own somewhere. But the Bloomfield-less Flag have left something behind: a strange record dominated in part by Buddy Miles, in part by Harvey Brooks and in the final analysis, dominated most of all by the lack of Bloomfield himself.

On their first album, *A Long*

Time Comin', Bloomfield's spirit was indefatigable, the Flag was exciting; and although they weren't half as good on wax as they were in person (and who is, these days?) they communicated a vibrancy that had been sorely missing in blues-oriented rock bands. In an enthusiastic review of that first album I used the words "the New Soul Music, the synthesis of White Blues and Heavy Metal Rock." I really believed it. I hoped they had stumbled upon the direction we'd all been looking for. The dissolution of the Flag was regrettable. And their new album is a sad testament to their inability to stick it out, to hang on and build on that "slightly overwhelming" foundation.

The first part of the new album is just fine—old Flag arrangements done with more precision and balance than was present in their debut. "Soul Searchin' " is a soulful answer to Butterfield's "Screamin' " (*The Paul Butterfield Blues Band*), a high and mighty organ-drum bash designed to get everybody off their ass, that drifts, or really, crashes, into the intro for "Sonny" which was always in the Flag's repertoire, and on which Buddy Miles distinguishes himself as the sweet vocalist he can be on occasion. Herbie Rich's solo is magnificent and well-controlled, something that had been lacking in earlier performances.

Stemsy Hunter, the first replacement for Peter Strazza, does the singing on "With Time There Is Change" but somehow misses the point. His voice just isn't up to carrying off Harvey Brooks' jazzy arrangement. "Nothing To Do" is a soft and mellow track featuring Gravenites' vocal—if you dig his style you'll really like this. His asides and sustained pauses work as well as they were intended to. And Hoshal Wright, Bloomfield's replacement, works some equally mellow magic on the guitar. He isn't really given much of a chance here, though. "See To Your Neighbor," another jumping exercise by Gravenites, closes the side admirably. Gravenites-penned numbers are instantly recognizable. He's really his own man.

Unfortunately, the second side just doesn't work the same. "Qualified," with an indecipherable vocal by Herbie Rich, just isn't fresh enough. It's too over-balanced, too LA, too many horns for this particular song, over-arranged, and, as a result, over-worked.

"Hey, Little Girl," by Gravenites, is the saving grace of the side. Rich does a neat little solo spin on organ—his versatility should be pointed out: he does a tenor solo on "Qualified" as well as the vocal. The band is extremely well-organized—everything is a little too overdone.

The other two cuts, "Mystery," with vocal by Miles, and "My Woman That Hangs Around the House," with vocal by Harvey Brooks—HARVEY BROOKS?!!?!—really strain to make it. And with the help of top-heavy production—mostly the work of John Simon—they nearly do; or rather, are almost successfully disguised. "My Woman" is the least offensive—it doesn't hit the ear as hard. I thought it was Tony Bennett singing.

This album has a few noble moments, a few overdeveloped moments, and just enough Flag-nostalgia to make it worthwhile. Gravenites is still a gas.

—BARRY GIFFORD
2-15-69

IT'S NOT KILLING ME
Michael Bloomfield
(Columbia CS 9883)

MY LABORS
Nick Gravenites
(Columbia CS 9899)

LIVE AT BILL GRAHAM'S FILLMORE WEST
Michael Bloomfield & Friends
(Columbia CS 9893)

It don't sound like blues. It sounds like some white kid trying to sing blues. It drags me, they're not funky. They don't have a good beat. I can't explain it. It's not the real shit, and it's not even a good imitation.

—Michael Bloomfield
in an interview
in *Rolling Stone,*
April 27, 1968

Bloomfield, in the above quote, was talking about the Grateful Dead, but he might have been describing these three albums. The same group recorded all these albums; they gig as "Bloomfield and Friends." *It's Not Killing Me* is Bloomfield singing his own songs. *My Labors* is Gravenites singing *his* own songs. *Live at B. G.'s* is an assortment of Bloomfield and Gravenites. Bloomfield and Gravenites grew up together musically, so it's no surprise that all three albums sound alike. The sound seems to come mostly from Bloomfield's head: languid guitar in front of an automotive herd of horns, playing very simple charts.

Bloomfield is a strange dude. When he's in the right scene with the right people, he can be great. As he is, for example, on the current *Fathers & Sons.* When it's someone else's trip—Muddy Waters, Butterfield, Buddy Miles—Bloomfield is at his best. That's what makes these albums embarrassing. They are *so* bad. The music is flat, unimaginative and badly played. The singing—with the exception of several cuts on Gravenite's album—is uniformly terrible.

It's Not Killing Me can only

be described as a specimen of boring exhibitionism. Bloomfield's singing should never have been released—he has a terrible voice. His playing is a caricature of itself; it sounds stale, full of instrumental mannerisms and little else. The band sounds ill-rehearsed and sloppy.

Bloomfield's material is clever and facile, but largely empty of the emotion it pretends. The songs that work best are not the blues, but the little excursions into different styles, like "For Anyone You Meet," a country and western lament for the Fallen Woman; "Why Must My Baby (be the onliest one for me?)," a cute old-timey piece, and "Don't Think About It Baby," a tuff-enuff bugaloo with tight lyrics. The rest of the songs are built from musical cliches—and sound it.

Gravenites' *My Labors* is slightly better because Gravenites' songs are real *songs,* not exercises in style. The melodies are standard-Chicago blues for the most part, but the lyrics have a fine intensity. He lived them. "Moon Tune" and "Throw Your Dog a Bone" are Gravenites at his best. He also

sings "As Good As You've Been To This World," but not nearly as well as Joplin does on her new album. In general, though, Gravenites' singing is not his best. The subtleties of his phrasing often get smothered in the horns and clatter of Bloomfield's arrangements. Ironically, Gravenites sounds best on the three cuts that were recorded with anonymous and modest studio musicians.

Live At B. G.'s is more of the same. The band is ragged, the singing is bad, Bloomfield's guitar is frequently out of tune. The audience was incredibly indulgent, applauding any and everything. The extremely poor recording and production doesn't help much. Even played on a good stereo, the album still sounds like a neglected jukebox. The one relatively bright spot on this dim album is a Gravenites tune: "Blue On a Westside." The rest, well . . . On the corner of the jacket of *It's Not Killing Me* is written "Bloomfield Shucks." Maybe that's it. Maybe.

—DAVID GANCHER
11-15-69

Down Home

Out West

and

Other Texans

~~~~~~

The big difference between Liverpool and San Francisco, often spoken of as the "new Liverpool," was that Liverpool, once you made it, was a place to leave.

People tend to settle in San Francisco. Not only the new bands out of the hippie scenes, but also thousands of musicians and dozens of groups from around the country. The biggest single contingent of them were from Texas: Steve Miller, Boz Scaggs, Doug Sahm, Tracy Nelson, many lesser known musicians, and, of course, Janis Joplin.

Janis actually arrived in San Francisco well before its "new Liverpool" days after the Family Dog threw their "Tribute to Doctor Strange." She was a part of the small coffee house scene of upper Grant Avenue, where she chanced to run across transplanted Illini like Nick Gravenites.

Chet Helms, the successor to the Family Dog mantle when the first group decided it was too much hassle, was himself from Texas and brought Janis back to sing with Big Brother and the Holding Company after she had disappeared with the folk scene itself.

Our reviewers never regarded Big Brother's records as artistically satisfying, though they surely secretly thrilled to them as did the hundreds of thousands who bought them. They *were* thrilling albums: their first on Mainstream Records, their live concert album, *Cheap Thrills* (Columbia KCS 9700), followed by albums Janis did after she left Big Brother. Included in this collection is her first solo effort (though all others really were, too) only. But all the others are recommended highly.

Johnny Winter, though he really had nothing to do with San Francisco, is worth putting in at this point. Winter was an obscure figure in Texas until his now manager, then club-owner, Steve Paul, picked up on a strong mention and photograph of him in a Texas special in *Rolling Stone,* and brought him to New York for fierce inter-company bidding and other hysterics associated with those salad days.

The rest of the albums in this collection are by Texas groups who did move to and settle in the Bay Area: The Steve Miller Band (who brought along with them friends from Chicago and Madison, Wisconsin), Mother Earth, including various Madisonites—lead singer Tracy Nelson among them—and the Sir Douglas Quintet.

They all traded off musicians, session men, ideas and licks. They developed some kind of recognizable common consciousness of earthy and "real" music. Boz Scaggs, after two albums with Steve Miller and session work with Mother Earth, broke out as a solo act (see section entitled Some Singing Voices). Steve Miller evolved into more of a pop act, Sir Douglas got involved with dozens of Latino musicians and Mother Earth moved to Nashville.

What joyful noise!

~~~~~~~~~~~~~~~~~~~~~~

CHILDREN OF THE FUTURE
Steve Miller Band
(Capitol SKAO 2920)

"We are Children of the Future/Wonder what in this world we are going to do . . . When I get high/I can see myself for miles . . . Takes a little bit of loving/A little bit of hugging . . . And if you don't think that you can find/And if

you don't think that it's a piece of mind."

The question begins with a lightly moving musical statement based primarily on the guitar and resolves into the rocking "takes a little bit of loving" answer. It's an instrumental version of a classic call/response pattern. The toms provide the transition, as well as the transition to "Pushed

Me To It," and the transition, moving from the toms to the bass while simultaneously moving from channel to channel, to "You've Got the Power." These latter two are beautifully moving under-a-minute passages, each based on a single repeating pattern. Simple, elegant, and accessible.

Steve Miller Band at its best is, among other things, a super tight and super rhythmic musical unit, creating a fine energy from those two strong points. Without instrumental frills and superfluous solos (which do often occur in live performance), all of the musical parts become essential, and by definition, important.

Steve Miller Band (*nee* The Steve Miller Blues Band) has, for a number of different reasons, done a superb job on their first album. It ranks with Moby Grape's first album in terms of economy and with *Sgt. Pepper* in terms of taste. They begin, in most of the songs, in fact on the first side, with a simple acoustic guitar line and build the whole rock and roll complement around it.

Jim Peterman establishes himself on the album as a musical force equally as dominant as the guitarists. He is excellent both as a soloist and as a rhythm player. His efforts with the instrument are diverse, ranging from straight blues patterns to a little shuffle (with the bass) to very churchy stuff

(without becoming at all tedious as so much of this quasi-religious stuff does indeed become). The organ is one of the most enjoyable parts of the entire album. It's precise and heavy, used all over the place without any excess.

"Children of the Future" (the entirety of side one) is constructed like *Sgt. Pepper,* a coherent whole of individual pieces, with a dominant theme (philosophical without pretentiousness) and, unlike the Beatles, recurring musical themes. Side two as well moves from song to song without break, held together solely by unity of concept.

There is a lot of material in the record which lends itself to Top-40 radio play. These include the first three cuts (considered as one) from side one, "Steppin' Stone," "Roll With It," and "Junior Saw It Happen." Even without this kind of radio play, the album should be quite successful, because like all of the best rock and roll it is good music and understandable by children of all ages.

Steve Miller Band demonstrates its ability in all of the current specialties of rock and roll. The crisp engineering and tasty production (done by the band itself with Stones' engineer Glyn Johns) and the eclectic influences make it very Beatle-ish in nature (especially in the vocal work, with the constant use of several voices for harmony and rhythm). If the album can be easily categorized, call it the marriage of the Beatles and the blues.

Like all the best rock and roll, the parts of the album are songs. Unlike most of the amateur efforts predominant today, the tracks here include such things as good vocals (Steve's voice is probably the most commercial and "pretty" blues voice around today), sound and intelligent instrumentation, interior structure and melody, and each one is recognizable by itself. They range from the folksy, to the driving, to the moody to straight blues. One would not characterize the record as being "far out" or revolutionary, but rather as being excellent.

—JANN WENNER
6-22-68

SAILOR
Steve Miller Band
(Capitol ST 2984)

The Steve Miller Band made an impressive debut with *Children of the Future. Sailor,* their new LP, is a most worthy successor. While their first album had a very strong blues flavor (especially on side two), *Sailor* has more of a rock and roll feeling.

"Song For Our Ancestors," which opens the album, tastefully blends ocean sound effects with an instrumental back-ground. This cut is much more successful than the Miller Band's previous attempt at a sound montage ("Psychedelic B. B.") which got a bit boring. "Dear Mary" is a very soft and slow ballad which makes me think about dancing close in the eighth grade when the lights were turned off. Miller sings the sentimental lyrics in an inoffensive falsetto.

The next tune is "My Friend" and it really rocks. The production is incredibly clean throughout the album, but this cut is the most outstanding. The arrangement is solid, with a good use of a sound effect simulating brass; in fact, the song has a strong feeling of Sly and the Family Stone.

"Living In The USA" starts off appropriately enough with drag strip sound effects. The song is a commentary on the US scene, but unfortunately some of the lyrics are rather weak. A good editor could have really perfected the words. The song is a real rocker though, and one cool moment occurs at the beginning of the fade out when Miller yells desperately, "Somebody get me a cheeseburger!" That line captures everything.

Side two begins with "Quicksilver Girl." This is a very commercial type of candy-rock song, and although it's pretty it is also quite ignorable. I like the line "She spreads her wings and she's free," but maybe I'm reading too much B. B. King into it.

"Lucky Man" features a very tasty acoustical guitar intro. It fades into the next cut, Johnny Guitar Watson's revived "Gangster of Love," which is a talking song in which the vocalist expounds his prowess as a lover ("Hey, Mr. Sheriff, that's your wife on the back of my horse"). This cut is pretty funny for a few times, but it tends to get old and "cute" pretty quickly. It is only a minute and a half long.

Following "Gangster" is a Jimmy Reed tune, "You're So Fine," which is the only straight blues cut on the album. It features some very good harp work. The song comes in heavy, but goes out weakly, and is thus not as successful as their earlier blues work. "Overdrive" is a strong Bo Diddley-type number, featuring a bottle-necked electric guitar. The lyrics are a bit "Oh wow, heavy!" but they don't get in the way. The guitar break is a bit disappointing however.

"Dime-A-Dance Romance" is really solid rock and roll. The bass line is nearly right out of "Jumpin' Jack Flash" and the whole song is really alive and exciting. The lyrics are excellent and blend well with the mood of the song. Both in its various parts and also as a whole, the song is perfectly constructed. This cut is the highpoint of the album.

The Miller Band is really together. If you like good solid rock-blues, they can really lay it down. They also can handle ballads with remarkable success. The production is superb, the performances are always high level. Though a few of the songs have rather mediocre lyrics, they are never obnoxious or pretentious. The only other fault in the album is that the guitar work as a whole is disappointing. None of the solos are up to par with either their first album or their better live performances. But this is not to say that they aren't good. Because they are quite good. Taste is evident throughout this LP.

In a sense this album is also disappointing. Harmonies (as on "Quicksilver Girl") are oftentimes sloppy and corny; cuts such as "Lucky Man" and "She's Fine" being straight blues in a rock and roll setting are ultimately weak. Despite these kinds of faults, faults of imperfection and unevenness, so much of this album is so well done that it is a fine record. "Dime-A-Dance Romance" is all one could ever expect or want in the way of a rock and roll song.

Buy this album if you liked the first one. If you haven't heard either, buy them both. The Steve Miller Band can be justly proud of *Sailor*. They are one of the two or three San Francisco bands which really deserve the praise which S.F.

bands seem to receive in such bulk. No shit!

It's a pity that *Sailor* is being promoted as a psychedelic item, because in contrast to the excess of that genre, this is in every sense a musical album. It is also a pity that the group is breaking up—and the tensions are evident in the construction of the album, so many fragments—because the best was still yet to come.

—MIKE DORN
11-23-68

BRAVE NEW WORLD
Steve Miller Band
(Capitol SKAO 184)

If you were hoping for some new music from the new Steve Miller Band—organist Jim Peterman and guitarist Boz Scaggs have left, and Miller, bassist Lonnie Turner and drummer Tim Davis are carrying on as a trio—you'll probably be a little bit disappointed with this album. Which is not to say that the music isn't good, but only that, in spite of the personnel changes, it is basically more of the same.

The only noticeable difference is that Miller has forsaken almost entirely the soft melodic material that turned up in several places on the first two albums in favor of the big beat. Virtually the whole album is uptempo and very loud. The

addition of two sidemen (co-producer Glyn Johns and Ben Sidran) gives the band the same instrumentation it has had in the past.

On stage, the Miller band is developing into a power trio a la Jimi Hendrix and the late Cream. The big beat of *Brave New World* reflects this, but the instrumentation tends to reject it. This is most noticeable on cuts like "Celebration Song," on which everyone seems to get in the way of everyone else. I'm tempted to describe this as a transition album, but it clearly isn't as the band hasn't decided whether it wants to be the power trio or the quintet of *Children of the Future* and *Sailor*.

The best cuts on the album are "Kow Kow," the title cut, and "Space Cowboy."

"Kow Kow" is near flawless. It opens with just a guitar, then the rest of the band comes in one by one and the song builds for about two minutes to a crescendo. That is suddenly cut off by a piano soliloquy with the organ whining in the background as the song fades out. Over the music, Miller sings a story about a smooth operator who had a pet alligator which he kept in a chrome elevator. Beautiful!

In their own bizarre way, "Space Cowboy" and "Brave New World" complement each other nicely. Both speak of a rebirth. Both provide a vehicle for the Miller band to show off its mastery of electronics (and they use them as well as anyone in rock, the Beatles and Hendrix not excepted), and both play Miller's guitar off against a steady rhythm section. "Space Cowboy" is especially nice: Davis pounding out a strong beat, Turner laying down a rugged fuzz bass line, and Miller bending off notes like he was born with a guitar in his hands. One of the high points of the album is the drumming of Davis, especially on his own "Can't You Hear Your Daddy's Heartbeat," a hard-driving ode to lust.

The main problem here comes in trying to reconcile the big beat of the trio with the quintet of yesteryear, which this album seeks to maintain through the use of sidemen. When this problem is solved, look for great things from the Steve Miller Band. In the meantime, though, *Brave New World* will do just fine.

—JOHN MORTHLAND
7-26-69

JOHNNY WINTER
Johnny Winter
(Columbia 9826)

Having listened to the new Johnny Winter LP for a couple of weeks, I have to say that I found it disappointing, despite the fact that in several respects

it's a more than respectable, even a fine album. But it hasn't the looseness, excitement, intensity, the real power and urgency of the best stuff on the earlier Sonobeat session. Most of the music on the Columbia set sounds tired, fussy, too worked-over and worried out of any real vitality. Undoubtedly there were strong pressures on Winter to come up with a truly "heavy" album that would justify all the hype that followed on his six-figure signing, so perhaps he can be excused for being a bit cautious. I'm damn sure I'd be. But it's too bad he wound up the victim of all the BS that went down.

This could have been a monster of an album. As it is, there are a couple of spots where it almost happens. Much of the difficulty with the tracks that might have made it is that they suffer from excess, as though Winter couldn't trust his instincts to leave well enough alone. He piles everything on.

"I'm Yours and I'm Hers" is an example of this overindulgence. The accompaniment consists of two electric guitar parts, one slide (channel A) the other plectrum lead (channel B), plus bass and drums (with the vocal in the center). Now, it's an interesting idea to have parallel guitar parts playing contrapuntally, but the end result here is just so much busyness. The two parts tend to cancel each other out because instead of being complementary, interlocking parts that work together as contrapuntal voices they pretty much attempt the same thing, with only the minor variations resulting from their not being played perfectly together. If we assume that the slide part was the basic accompaniment, then the other just muddies up the texture because it doesn't add anything significant (not even parallel voicing) but merely duplicates, with an excess of decoration, what the slide has laid down. Though the tune is credited to Winter, an almost identical piece, "She's Mine, She's Yours," was recorded by Jimmy Rushing for King Records seventeen years ago.

The same over-busyness mars the version of Robert Johnson's "When You Got a Good Friend" and again the problem is a two-guitar accompaniment for which no real part has been worked out. An imaginative but unobtrusive bass-guitar part would have been far more successful than the two lead parts —neither of which is properly a lead. It's too frantic. "Dallas," on the other hand, works out well. The accompaniment is a single slide guitar line, played on the National. The piece suggests several of Johnson's song accompaniments but perhaps the major source is his "Terra-Plane Blues," though Winter's playing is not as tightly focused

as it was on the Sonobeat "Broke Down Engine," which also used a Johnson-styled accompaniment. This one is a bit sloppy rhythmically and the texture somewhat thick. But, all in all, the best performance in this style on the album. If this is the 13th take, as the spoken introduction suggests, it might go a long way to explaining the rhythmicless stiffness.

The same rhythm difficulties plague the trio version of "Leland Mississippi Blues" (Winter's birthplace), with an accompaniment based on Muddy Waters' "All Night Long." Winter gets into Waters' guitar style nicely playing strongly and with feeling, but a rhythmic sluggishness creeps into the last half of the cut and the piece never quite recovers. "Mean Mistreater," with Walter Norton on harmonica and Willie Dixon on acoustic bass, is a fairly successful evocation of early Fifties Muddy. The guitar playing is authentic, true to the Waters rubric, fairly inventive, and the amplifier sound properly funky. A good, gutty performance marred only by an inaudible, badly distorted vocal. This is such a distinguishing feature of most of Winter's blues sides that I wonder if it represents a conscious artistic choice. If he feels vocals lack muscle, the answer is not to mix them in at a barely audible level but to use a number of recording techniques to help beef them up.

"Be Careful with a Fool" is in fairly conventional modern guitar style—fast, supercharged playing accompanied by bass, drums and an occasional over-dubbed guitar line. A good bit of excitement is generated—particularly in the second and third guitar choruses—but much of this is superficial, the result of speed in execution rather than substantial, musically logical improvised lines. The first chorus burns itself out; starting with a blistering barrage of notes, fast as hell. Winter stops dead when he runs out of steam and realizes he's at a dead-end. He recovers and takes a little more care with the two cho-ruses that follow. Vocal is okay, but again under-recorded.

"Good Morning Little School Girl," the old Sonny Boy Wil-liamson song but here credited to "D. Level-B. Love," whoever they may be, gets a solid performance from Winter, in-strumentally and vocally. Un-fortunately, we are treated to a horn accompaniment that is un-necessary on several counts: the arrangement is woefully un-imaginative and played sloppily in the bargain; moreover, it just gets in the way of the guitar part, which is a very inventive, exciting accompaniment when the horns don't obscure it, which is most of the time.

That brings us to "I'll Drown in My (Own) Tears," on which the horns are also present. Doing this was a mistake, pure and simple, and a classic ex-ample of sending a boy to do a man's job. Winter should have known better. A flyweight, no matter how agile, is no match for a heavyweight cham-pion, and if you think this simile excessive, just listen to the two recordings. The horns here are fine but, then, they offer a literal recreation of the horn arrangement on the Ray Charles original. The fact that they are well recorded and mixed at a decent level sug-gests—to me at least—that someone was justifiably self-conscious about their participa-tion on "School Girl" and mixed them in at a very low level. No guitar on this track, but effective gospel piano from Edgar Winter and, at the end, barely adequate vocal support from a chick vocal trio, which just escapes being amateurish.

And that's it. Now that the first album's out of the way and, hopefully, much of the pressure off, perhaps Winter can relax a bit and serve up some of the strong stuff of which he's proven himself capable. Take it easy, Johnny, and learn to trust your instincts. They were right at least half of the time on the Sonobeat LP.

—PETE WELDING
8-9-68

SECOND WINTER
Johnny Winter
(Columbia KCS 9947)

THE JOHNNY WINTER STORY
Johnny Winter
(GRT 10010)

Johnny Winter has been maturing for a long time, as the Imperial Sonobeat and GRT releases show; the latter is an unmitigated abortion, an offal-heap of very early tries for the Top 40 that sound like nothing so much as some nasal kind laboriously aping Jimmy Reed. That it was released at all is a travesty, and a triumph of the recording industry's undying tradition of greedy entrepreneurship.

The new Columbia release is a universe apart—a solid advance over his first set for the label—an unrelenting floodtide of throbbing, burning sound, a work of folk art which captures the tradition of blues and rock from the prehistoric Delta bottleneck sundown moans to the white-hot metal pyrotechnics of today and tomorrow. Winter has recognized that the blues is fluid and ever-present, from Robert Johnson to Little Richard to Dylan to the rampant feedback exorcisms of the Velvet Underground. He doesn't need to plow the same old pastures. *Second Winter* features few of the blues standards which glut releases from the Canned Aynsley Mac slaveyard. Beginning with Percy Mayfield's "Memory Pain," he wails through new, soon-to-be-classic versions of "Slippin' and Slidin'," "Johnny B. Goode," and "Highway 61 Revisited." Winter is stunning, with imaginative arrangements of very familiar material, ginmill earthy musicianship, and definitive rock and roll by anybody's standards.

Take "Highway 61 Revisited." Few but the Byrds seem able to transform a Dylan song into anything but a demonstration of self-consciousness. Folks strain their imaginations to smithereens trying to conceive an alternative approach that might measure up to that of the composer. But Winter doesn't need to sight it from such a self-defeating angle: he just takes the song and bends it to his own cry as he would any other, forgetting about Dylan entirely, for the moment. The performance is a masterful processing of the blues tradition that bodes new idioms by simultaneously sounding like everything that the blues emotionally *is* while sounding like no blues we've ever heard before. The cut sounds nothing like Dylan's version while it rumbles unmistakably with Dylan's deepest ethos. Winter is an alchemist mating paradoxes.

Winter's own compositions also show a distinct advance over the first Columbia release, when his songs sometimes came across as little more than un-credited cops from his black mentors. Here he quashes categories with a stunning succession of musical constructions that are often trailblazing, sometimes standardized, but always overwhelming. "I Hate Everybody" is a woolly ramble that builds one of the most banal fifties riffs—resounding waves of basic sock-hop bop—into a roaring musical juggernaut—Bill Haley preaching Armageddon and pressing on toward electronic renaissance. The album's most fully realized experiment, "Past Life Rider," is built from Bo Diddley drums and changing modern blues guitar into a ripping, searching improvisational foray aeons removed from the amphetamine strain of most "heavy" music. It's a triumph.

It's a joy that Johnny Winter has been brought among us, however irritating the hypes that accompany him. All the bullshit beomes meaningless now, precisely because the forced enthusiasm of flacks and ad copy is so totally antithetical to the vibrantly instinctive eruption of his talent.

—LESTER BANGS
12-27-69

ENTRANCE
Edgar Winter
(Epic BN 26503)

This album is not what you expect. Edgar is Johnny Winter's brother and organ/piano player—yet this album is definitely not blues or rock 'n roll. The closest classification that fits is free-form jazz—but even that, while explaining the musical framework, doesn't take into account Edgar's distinctive vocal style. He sounds like Mose Allison on some cuts ("Back in the Blues") but on most of the album Edgar's frenetic, high-pitched vocal style is all his own and very effective with the bebop-type lyrics (authored by the Winters) that most of the cuts contain.

The album is divided into two sections. The first side, entitled "Winter's Dream," features seven cuts that slide into and out of each other nicely and work effectively as a musical statement. Highlights are Edgar's vocal work-out on "Where Have You Gone," his sax solo on the extended "Fire and Ice" segment and brother Johnny's harp-playing on "Back in the Blues." While tight and together, this side does suffer from an occasional excess of strings and horns, that in many cases don't add a thing to what is, or could be, happening without them. But, in most cases, Edgar prevails.

The second side opens with the most exciting version of that old war-horse "Tobacco Road" I've heard in a long while. Johnny plays guitar on this one and Edgar sings with more fervor than I believed possible, besides playing sax and organ. Two tour-de-force jazz-shaded cuts on this side really pull things around. "Peace Pipe" opens with an "Eleanor Rigby" type organ riff on top of a scat vocal and then drives along with theme changes that eventually come back to a scat vocal/Rigby-ish close. The other jazz cut, entitled "Jimmy's Gospel," features a demonstration of just how well Edgar can play alto sax. This instrumental is a mellow yet forthright explosion that is the essence of this album, even though it comes last.

Had his brother not been such an overnight music phenomenon, Edgar would probably never have had the opportunity to assemble an album. And, even though this one is a little overdone in spots, one hopes that another is forthcoming soon.

—GARY VON TERSCH
9-3-70

JOHNNY WINTER AND
Johnny Winter
(Columbia C30221)

A bad title for a terrific album. The title implies: Superstar and . . . the boys. But this album is much more than Johnny Winter being Mister Ultimate Speedfingers while an anonymous rhythm section tries to keep up. Johnny plays *with* his new band, not on top of them. The new band consists of three ex-McCoys, a dyed-in-the-wool Rock Band. They still are. And good musicians—especially Rick Derringer, the guitarist-singer who shares the limelight with Johnny Winter.

This album contains—surprise!—no blues. It is Rock and Roll at its very best. Good, solid songs—a few of them instant classics. The singing is funky, full of raspy screams, pushing pushing the music towards some sort of ultimate . . . edge.

The soul of the album is the interplay between Johnny Winter and Rick Derringer. On stage, it's easy to see how it works. Derringer plays guitar straight from the groin: solid-snaky rock lines. The root. Winter seems to play guitar in a state of transported ecstasy, like the bare electric skeleton of rock dancing in the mind-juice river. The branch. Winter's guitar-imagination has greater scope than Derringer's. Winter's guitar builds on Derringer's, elaborating, decorating, getting slinky and sliding right out of your brain. All without ever losing the beat, the sexual thread of the music.

Together, they sound like Hendrix playing behind Clapton. In fact, the album will remind you of the best moments of early Hendrix and early Cream. "Am I Really Here" sounds much like Cream's

"White Room." The vocal to "Rock and Roll Hoochiekoo" has the same slide-punch inflections as Hendrix's singing. There are more examples of Influences At Work Here, but Winter and Derringer are much too good to be mere imitations. They have learned; they have transcended their influences and come up with something all their own.

Playing in a rock context has improved Winter's playing (if you can believe that possible). He seems more down-to-earth, more believable. You can dance to it. In fact, you'd better.

The material is surprisingly good—especially Derringer's compositions. "Rock and Roll Hoochiekoo" and "Funky Music" are both sturdy good-time rockers, and would make fine singles. Winter's compositions, though intense and moving, tend to lack form. They sometimes, as on "Nothing Left," fall apart in your ear. But what the hell. This is fine stuff, by far the best thing Johnny Winter has done. And that's saying something.

—DAVID GANCHER
10-29-70

HONKEY BLUES
Sir Douglas Quintet Plus Two
(Smash 67108)

Honkey Blues is not the latest, greatest rock and roll record to come out in the last week; it is, however, one of the most welcome records. First of all, it's rhythm and blues, in the vein of Bobby Blue Bland or even Horace Silver, because this record is also into the real jazz. The horn riffs are lyrical, the melodies beautiful with understated lyrics. None of it is totally unique, but all of it just right, spontaneous and fitted precisely into its place.

These qualities are largely a matter of the taste and ability to satisfy an audience on the part of Sir Douglas Sahm, the man himself. Sir Doug began playing steel guitar professionally at the age of nine, performing in country music, blues and R&B clubs around Texas into his early teens. At nineteen, Sir Doug has two national hits: "She's About A Mover" and "Rain, Rain, Rain."

After "Rain, Rain, Rain" Sir Douglas went virtually unheard of. About two years ago, Bob Dylan was asked in a press conference if he had heard anything lately, and he mentioned Sir Doug. Dylan had Sir Doug up to Woodstock for a while, and later he recommended that Grossman take Sir Doug on. But Grossman didn't see it, and Sir Doug moved on to Big Sur and then to Mercury Records, where for the past year he has been producing other groups (Junior Parker and Roy Head among them) and getting together this new record.

What we have on this record are tracks running from up-tempo Stax kind of things, through Latin tempo minor blues and very funky, jazzy instrumental things, as well as ballads and some straight pre-sixties stuff. All of the material except one song are originals. The *modes* are not new; the performance and interior ideas are.

The feeling of the performance is relaxed, free and mellow; the spirit is bright and enthusiastic, and the musicians have come up with some very tasty arrangements and hip solo work. Martin Ferrio should be credited for his fine solos and very bright horn section work and Wayne Talbert, the same, on piano. Both Talbert and Ferrio (the "plus two" in the title) will be in for some high recognition soon, especially Talbert whose soulful keyboard is remarkable. The texture and coloring of the whole record are greatly affected by Talbert's close-in attack and wandering right hand. George Raines is one of the most solid, versatile and imaginative drummers to appear lately.

The lyrics, generally speaking, seem to come out of the feeling of the music, and talk around that feeling. Sahm's language is direct and his images arise from the broad sense of the theme of the song. Sir Doug is just "talkin' to ya."

Anyway, as one conscientious critic, record-buyer, music-digger to another, this one's really got it. It's got them groovy blues and that pretty gospel and that down home, country righteous good tone to it. The record makes me dance around and sing along. I've copped some good licks from it and most generally enjoy myself all around when I hear it.

—BOZ SCAGGS
11-23-68

MENDOCINO
Sir Douglas Quintet
(Smash SRS 67115)

The Sir Douglas Quintet is back, thanking all their beautiful friends everywhere for all the beautiful vibrations, the voice at the beginning of the album says while the band comps in the background. Then they launch into their recent hit, "Mendocino." The lyrics are printed there on the back of the record jacket. Please don't look at them. They're not very good. But if you hear the song twice, you'll be humming it and it'll make you feel good.

That's the thing about this album. Despite its many faults, it makes you listen to it. It's poorly recorded, sloppily produced (dig the fade on "If You Really Want Me To I'll Go"), and could hardly be called innovative, but it's the kind of album you keep coming back to. It has something that very few albums I've heard recently have got—atmosphere.

Although I have never heard the Quintet live, I would imagine that this is the kind of set that they would play at the Fillmore or out in a park somewhere. Very natural, relaxed, eminently danceable and hummable. Unpretentious—the musicians banter back and forth ("Hey, boy, where'd you learn that freaky git-tar playin'?"), they dared to call a song "Lawd I'm Just a Country Boy in This Great Big Freaky City" (it works), and included an updated "She's About a Mover." Look at Doug Sahm smiling there on the back of the album. He knows something that a lot of lesser folk should learn, and I'll be happy to keep picking up on what he puts out as long as he promises to do a little better by it in the studio.

—ED WARD
5-17-69

TOGETHER AFTER FIVE
Sir Douglas Quintet
(Smash 67130)

The cover photo on this album is a straightforward, uncontrived shot of five uncontrived, down-home dudes. Among the self-conscious posturings we've gotten used to on album covers, it stands out like a cheeseburger in a medicine cabinet.

Inside, Sir Douglas continues working in his solid groove of Texas rock and roll, distinguished by its fully assimilated Cajun and Mexican influences. "Nuevo Laredo," the track that has been getting airplay so far, is a pure example of the easy, natural way his group makes music out of the material at hand: Doug Sahm's drawling vocal alternates with a high, close-harmony *norteno* chorus just the same way his loose-limbed country guitar alternates with Mexican fiesta trumpet figures. The simultaneous individuality and harmony of these elements is nothing but breathtaking. Listen to the way that full-hearted Mexican melody automatically translates into mellow country phrasing.

Though the up-tempo numbers stand out on this album, Sir Douglas has invested a generous imagination on ballads as well. He has the balls to follow up "Nuevo Laredo" with a song written to a tune which is essentially the same as "Honey," the suburban sob number of yore. It's worked over into his groove so you'd hardly know it and fitted with a folksong-like lyric about a Texan girl whose father couldn't approve her boyfriend's "long hair and far-out groove,/ But he knew he couldn't stop her./He only had about four or five million,/475 acres outside of Kingsville." It's a great song in its own right, as well as performing the valuable service of wiping up after "Honey." But—how it got there!

Probably the outstanding track here is "Backwood's Girl," which has almost the melodic variety of a medley. (There are two medleys on the album—a driving "Son of Bill Baety" which is the Leadbelly song plus Leadbelly's "When I Was a Cowboy," and another consisting of Dylan's "One Too Many Mornings" and Sahm's own "Got To Sing a Happy Song.") "Backwood's Girl" is one of the nicest-constructed songs in a long time, with a melodic strength and solid rhythmic buildup that is just plain *satisfying*.

The entire LP is like that: satisfaction.

—CHARLES PERRY
3-7-70

1 PLUS 1 PLUS 1 IS 4
Sir Douglas Quintet
(Phillips PHS 600-344)

AND

RISE
Love and the Lovers
(Epic E 30026)

There comes a time in every critic's life when he becomes tired of the virtuosi, the noise, the hype, the clutter of civilization. Things being what they are today, the way people solve these problems is usually to move to the country with their old ladies, raise a couple of kids, and only visit the city a couple of times a month. As for me, I can't drive, so I can't get any farther away than the last bus stop. I don't have an old lady, let alone any kids, and I have a job in the city that requires my presence five days a week. But don't think for a minute that *all* of the benefits of living an organic country life are missing from my day-to-day existence, no indeedy. Because when the sunshine's just right and it's just warm enough I can sit back and let the country come to me. That's right. Listen:

Doug Sahm is a product of West Texas, the same area that produced such giants as Buddy Holly and the Bobby Fuller Four. He scraped and scuffled and pulled together a fine band called the Sir Douglas Quintet which had a big hit with "She's About A Mover" a while back. From the way his record sales look, that's about the last time that a lot of you out there heard of him, unless it was when you heard "Mendocino" on the radio.

Well, let me tell you: *1 Plus 1 Plus 1 Is 4* is a masterpiece. Sir Doug has gathered some of the finest musicians in the country around him and has whipped them into action to produce some truly exciting music. It doesn't matter that you've never heard of any of these musicians before—maybe Pete Drake and Doug Sahm, but probably not Wayne Talbert or Jance Garfat —they just haven't been out there trying to make you notice them, but I guarantee that you'll be out looking for *them* after one listen.

Probably the most exciting aspect of the album is the revival of Doug's big band, the Honky Blues, which features all kinds of brass and Wayne Talbert's exciting piano work. Check out "Don't Bug Me!" which starts to fade out at what would be a reasonable place, but the excitement engendered by the first half of the song is so great that Talbert and Martin Pierre, playing tenor, just can't stop playing and keep on going for another couple of minutes, adding a whole 'nother dimension to the song. Among the other cuts with this band are "In the Dark," with its "jungle drums" right out of be-bop, and "Pretty Flower," which features the biggest band on the album—ten musicians just blowing their brains out, and yours, too, I'll bet. The Honky Blues have loosened up considerably since their last appearance with Doug back in 1968 on the album of the same name, which is not intended to run down that album in any way, and they manage to make the rest

of those big-band groups sound pretty watery at best.

Then there's the classic Quintet sound, in evidence here on three cuts, "Yesterday Get In the Way," "What About Tomorrow?" and "A Nice Song," which is just that. The Quintet is in fine form, bouncing out Spanish-tinged melodies and harmonies that always manage to sound fresh and new.

There's even a potential hit single here: "Be Real." If I were asked to summarize Doug Sahm's music in one phrase, that would be it. And, true to the title, that's just what it is. Fiddles, steel guitar and rocking Jerry Kennedy Nashville production back up one of the best Sahm vocals in a long while. The lyrics are simple: "Be real, baby, be real/That's all I ask you/Baby, be real." That's all Doug requires from his musicians, and, although these days it seems like quite a lot to ask, that's what he gets.

In fact, he gets it sometimes when he doesn't expect it. One day, about a year ago, someone in his home town of Salinas, California, asked him to listen to a rock and roll band some kids in town had and he did. They were Louie and the Lovers, and they knocked him out. They were playing music similar to the kind he was making, but with a freshness and purity that his salty old musicians had outgrown or lost years ago. "It just flows out, naturally and *really,* like Echo Valley," he says on the album cover, and he's right. In fact, Louie and the Lovers have a few lessons to teach the Sir Douglas Quintet, even though their drummer just celebrated his 17th birthday and Louie Ortega, the guiding genius behind the group and writer of all the songs on the album but one, is only 20.

Their debut album, *Rise*, is just plain incredible. It sounds a little like Creedence, but without that four-square dullness that makes Fogerty and company unlistenable for me. There's some Ritchie Valens in there, a whole lot of traditional Mexican music and plenty of just Louie and the Lovers. Until they went to San Francisco to record, they had stayed pretty much in their home town of Prunedale (that's right, Prune-dale), and that goes a long way towards explaining their unique-ness.

Unlike many first albums these days, there's not a bum cut or well-intentioned-but-failed experiment on the whole disc. These guys are stone pro-fessional, and they know what they want. Each song flows with a self-assurance and unity that is sadly missing in these days of frantic get-to-the-top-and-stay-there musicianship. And the songs are so genuine: after meeting his girlfriend for the first time, Louis went and wrote "I Just Met You." If you heard the song before you read

that, you probably know it al-ready. "Royal Oakie" is about a park near their home where they go on weekends and drink wine and fool around. Again, I didn't really need to tell you that.

Every cut on the album is exciting, and it is difficult to single out particularly praise-worthy numbers. Right at the moment, my favorites are "Rise," which could be a big hit if released as a single, "I Know You Know," "Royal Oakie," and "I Just Met You." One can only hope that the success that will follow the release of this album won't change Louie and the boys, and that they'll be treating us to their music for years to come.

Oh, yes, I was going to tell you how I manage to get all the benefits of living in the country even though I have to stick pretty close to the city. Well, I guess you'll just have to buy these albums and find out. . . .

—ED WARD
10-1-70

LIVING WITH THE ANIMALS
Mother Earth
(Mercury SR 61194)

The first thing you notice about this album, even before you extract the record from the jacket to hear what it's all about, is the collection of Mother Earth family picture-book photos on the cover and inside, handsomely wrought and printed in brown ink, like tintypes.

Mother Earth is a musical family of friends, a Texas family, mainly, with many of the good things and some of the bad, that implies. The family tree is diverse—Gospel, country blues, city blues, rock-a-billy, Tex-Mex, jazz, country and western, soul, folk, and straight-ahead rock and roll—but the two most prominent factions within Mother Earth can be described as Texas soul (groovy) and Texas Psychedelic Hokum (boring).

Tracy Nelson represents Texas Soul (though, curiously, she's one of the few non-Texans in the band), R. Powell St. John represents Texas Psychedelic Hokum, and since they get equal time, you'd have to say *Living With The Animals* comes as a mixed blessing.

St. John's quavery, thin, uncertain vocal delivery mars every track on which he sings. It would matter more if he were messing up good material, but since he's singing his own inconsequential ditties (they sound rather like radio commercials) in all but one case, it's difficult to get especially worked up about it. The exception is Willie Dixon's "My Love Will Never Die," which features a churning overlay of horns, blues piano and John Andrews' strong lead guitar. On this track,

St. John's ineptitude is really disconcerting; a real singer could have gotten *into something.* But St. John's own compositions sound just as corny as these lyrics read: "Through the incense and the candles/and the colors on the wall/your image stands reflected/as a princess come to call . . ."

Tracy's something else again. You get all the way through the first side of the album to the last tune, before—bam—it comes alive with her Gospel piano chording on "Down So Low," and the entry of her deep, intense voice really "down." "The pain you left behind/has become a part of me/'n' it's burned out a hole/where yer love used to be . . ."

It's her song and for just the few minutes it's on, with the Earthettes crooning and moaning behind her, you begin to get an inkling of the power of Mother Earth in person. Too much!

"Cry On" finds Tracy in a similar groove, down and longing, gritty, the horn section spreading funky tapestries behind her, Martin Fierro stepping up for a handsome tenor saxophone solo—his jazz playing is tasty if brief, everywhere on the album, though it gives little idea of what he is capable of, in person.

"Goodnight Nelda Grebe, The Telephone Company Has Cut Us Off," is a Tracy Nelson song that has nothing to do with

either Nelda Grebe or Ma Bell
—unless she's using some sort
of code—but it does get the
band into a strutting, uniquely
Texan 6/8 groove, has a strong
Tracy vocal and some more
nice blowing by Fierro. It's one
of three—out of ten—strong
tracks on the album, not a very
good batting average.

Two oddities are worthy of
note. Somebody named Makal
Blumfeld (say, you don't suppose that's a pseudonym
for . . .) plays blues guitar fills
and an undistinguished solo on
the Memphis Slim tune "Mother
Earth"—which Tracy gives a
strangely dispirited performance.
And the title tune, a clomp-
along St. John original, is in no
way as nutty as the liner photo
it inspired: 23 of Mother Earth
and friends posed with nearly a
dozen critters.

All in all, a disappointing
record, though it is a comfortable sort of thing to slap on
your stereo and just let it un-
reel. Family things—when it's
a happy family—are always
comfortable, and there's abun-
dant evidence here that there's
joy in Mother Earth's house-
hold. It's just that some members of the family are one hell
of a lot longer on talent than
others, and if you possess this
album, you are forced—in the
words of Mothers everywhere—
to take the good with the bad.

—JOHN BURKS
12-21-68

MAKE A JOYFUL NOISE
Mother Earth
(Mercury SR 61226)

What's remarkable to me is
that Mother Earth is so righ-
teously defiant in the face of
the first canon of success in this
business—which is, simply,
Don't Complicate Matters—and
so successful despite the com-
plications.

To begin with, you might ask
which Mother Earth. This is album 2-1/2 (counting their contribution to the soundtrack of
Revolution), and the change in
playing personnel from the last
album is no more remarkable
than the changes within the
albums themselves. The focus,
naturally, is on Tracy Nelson,
but there are new vocalists altogether, principally the Rev.
Ronald Stallings, who dominates
the "City Side" of the record,
which is stacked with horns and
Earthettes.

The "Country Side" interests
me more—it is a clean break
not only with the "City Side"
but with a good number of the
rockabilly tricks that a good
rock band uses when it plays
country, such as anchoring the
drums up front as do the Byrds
or the Band (something of an
anathema in pure country); or
slipping in feedback guitars as
do the Byrds again, or Sir
Douglas; or juicing up the lead
work with all those funky licks
that are sure to date guitar pick-

ing in our time, like the lead work on *Nashville Skyline*. These are examples of stuff that I admire for the most part, but which I hate to see choked to death with repetition.

Mother Earth, on some cuts, sounds a lot closer to the bands Hank Williams used than to any of the bands I have mentioned. Their sound is down home in a way that lets fiddles come across like fiddles, rather than like what some engineer always thought fiddles should sound like; down home in a way that has a venerable old sideman like Peter Drake (one of Dylan's studio men) playing steel guitar like Hawaiian guitar rather than Wurlitzer guitar. This means that the band allow themselves to do a very fine number by Doug Sahm ("I Wanna Be Your Mama Again") on an on-beat and let the song carry itself instead of letting it ride on some slick wheelchair rhythm track. R.P. St. John achieves the same effect with lyrics; his "I'll Be Moving On," is a fine song about a long-haired musician trying to talk a southern sheriff out of a bust. "Yes, sir, I'll take it easy, that's my code . . ."

There are exceptions to anything you can say about this album; for example, Bob Arthur, the bass guitarist, lays down a sound on the "Country Side" which is uniquely Bay Area. His vocal debut, on "Come On and See," reminds me of the famous stumbling drunk session Screamin' Jay Hawkins did on "I Put A Spell On You."

It's easy enough to accuse Mother Earth of being eclectic, to call them the greatest variety show on vinyl. But that's only an accusation when you can't pull it off. They can.

—PATRICK THOMAS
—11-15-69

KOZMIC BLUES
Janis Joplin
(Columbia KCS 9913)

Janis herself has never sounded better on record, but it took me four full listenings to the LP before I could hear her. That's how bad her band is. When (and if) you get hold of this record, my suggestion is that you listen really hard to how awful the backup is— everything from the arrangements to the level of musicianship. Those sons of bitches can't do anything really right. The only answer is to get superfamiliar with what they're doing so you can ignore it. And *then* dig Janis.

They can't be *that* bad, you say?

On "Try," they stutter along like Stax rejects, thudding out a 16-to-the-bar quick-step so metronomic it defies you to pat your foot, let alone get up and dance. Janis sounds great, but—

"One Good Man" contains perhaps the only instrumental

blessing on the whole record, wherein Sam Andrew plays a tolerable bottleneck introduction and obbligato to Janis' vocal. At least the rest of the band is relaxed on this track, even if they add nothing. (Disconcerting reminders of Canned Heat intrude late in the arrangement, however.)

"As Good As You've Been To This World" finds the band back in their accustomed groove: incredibly stiff ensemble passages which sound for all the world like a college marching band at half-time doing their big *Swing* routine. Snooky Flowers plays the worst baritone saxophone solo I have ever heard, discounting only a handful of amateur performers at jam sessions in people's garages. The tenor sax solo, while empty, is somewhat less embarrassing. The trumpet solo consists mainly of excruciating pauses where he was hung for ideas that never, alas, came. Then comes a big chug-CHUG-CHUG buildup to Janis' vocal, reminiscent of those fine, socking arrangements behind Otis Redding—except that Janis' band falls completely on its face. The big buildup is a huge, fumbling let-down, and only a massive effort of will on Janis' part manages to make the track in any way listenable. (The way it's recorded, her voice is buried in among the horns, so that, at times, it sounds like a grotesque duel between her and Flowers' ugly, snorting horn.)

On "To Love Somebody," Janis is positively impassioned, imparting a terrifying urgency to the repeated line "You don't know . . ." The band is *almost* mellow behind her, and the stomping arrangement is the only one on the record with any true character. It is marred, though, by uncertain intonation in the horns. Somebody's out of tune—and why producer Gabriel Mekler, Janis' organist, allowed this to happen is hard to imagine. *Anybody* can see to it that a band tunes up.

"Little Girl Blue" is a fine old Rodgers & Hart tune, and Janis is in fine form, unleashing her Texas furies (coupled with intimations of both Bessie Smith and Dinah Washington) upon the song's fragile melody. But the intro—Sam Andrew's guitar playing a fugal line—is almost identical to Big Brother's arrangement to "Summertime." Why should this be? Will every ballad Janis does get the same sweet/funky back-up? The string arrangement (!) is limber enough, and properly elegant— until at the very end, the final cello note (meant to cap off the whole thing) slides down at least a half-step flat. It destroys the whole beautiful mood Janis has created, really, because you are left with the feeling that the whole thing is essentially slipshod. Amazing that Columbia would release this!

"Work Me Lord" is excellent Joplin, despite an ensemble that steals the well-worn "Hey Jude" figure, and despite the ragged horns, which blow sour ones right and left. Janis gives this track (indeed, the whole record) whatever vitality it's got. Listen when she's not singing, here and elsewhere, where the band's on their own. Without Janis to lean on they sound lumpier than a beer hall accordion band.

One of the principal faults is the wooden, mechanical drumming. But it's not just the drummers, and not just the rhythm section. On the basis of this record, there's not a funky cat in the band—and that's the pure hell of it: nothing is more disgusting than listening to un-funky cats work at funk. It's fortunate for Janis that she's funky enough—all by herself—to overcome.

She sounds great. Just great. It's simply a matter of reaching the point where you are able to shut out the band—entirely—and listen to this woman sing. An odd strategy, admittedly, but guaranteed worth it.

—JOHN BURKS
11-1-69

Los Angeles,

Southern California

and

Other Extremities

~~~~~~

Surfers can be seen historically as the pre-drug wave of the great hippie explosion: middle class, back to nature, wandering from beach to beach in search of the next wave, and eminently, happily all-American.

The Beach Boys were the major and most popular voice of the surfers, and through their own genius for song, for arrangement and for production, they brought surfin' music, and the beginning elements of a "California sound" throughout the world.

If there is longevity in the American group scene, the Beach Boys certainly are the strength of it; their first great hits ("Surfin' U.S.A.") pre-date the Beatles, and in 1970, as this collection is assembled, we still see them together as basically the same group, putting out records of continuing high quality. That's a long time in the music business.

(Brian Wilson, the tanned eminence of the group, had a brief but influential association at that time with a young Los Angeleno named Van Dyke Parks, whose solo album is also included in this selection.)

If the Beach Boys spanned over and beyond the Beatle years (1963-1967)—and first identified that sunshine and outdoors ambience that was California music, it was the Byrds who began the new wave American rock after the appearance of the Beatles. They hit appropriately enough in 1965 with a version of Bob Dylan's "Mister Tambourine Man." In this collection, again we skip their early work (the excellent classical albums when the Byrds included David Crosby, Chris Hillman, Gene and Mike Clark) to the period when leader/founder Jim (later changing his name to Roger) McGuinn, took a series of

evolving and changing sidemen, through several different
albums and several different styles, all included here.

Out of the Byrds came the Flying Burrito Brothers
keeping the country-rock sound that McGuinn had discarded.

From another direction (in Los Angeles, the expression is ". . . and from another canyon . . .") came the
Buffalo Springfield. This was at a time parallel to the
development of the San Francisco band/club scene, that
Los Angeles was at the Trip and the Whisky A GoGo on
the Strip, the Hullaballoo on Sunset Boulevard, once the
home of "Queen For A Day" and across the street from
the Hollywood Palladium (Lawrence Welk's ballroom)
Bido Lito's, and a number of others. The bands were Taj
Mahal's Rising Sons, Arthur Lee's Love, Sons of Adam,
The Seeds, Canned Heat, and later the Doors. (The first
three Canned Heat records are reviewed in this collection.
See the section entitled Some Singing Voices for Taj
Mahal. The others, and other bands not even mentioned,
are regrettably not included.)

But the most bursting with talent (that ultimately could
not be contained in one group) was Buffalo Springfield.
Only their last album is reviewed here. (Their first three
records are superb.) From the group came Poco with
Ritchie Furay (also not included here) and Jim Mes-
sina; Neil Young struck out on his own for fine solo
efforts and later joined up again with ex-Springfield
Stephen Stills in one of the most popular groups of 1970:
Crosby (of the Byrds), Stills, Nash (from the Hollies of
England) and Young.

From out of the greasy suburbs came Frank Zappa and
the Mothers. Zappa, a prolific and perverse man, zipped
through a dozen or so records and musicians and styles
—some included here—and later began his own record
company, Bizarre, the efforts of which label are also
included here. Only in Los Angeles . . .

Meanwhile, the studio men were not lacking for work. A huge and talented bunch were playing anonymously on many of the great pop records of the time. James Burton, the guitarist with Ricky Nelson and in 1970 with Elvis Presley; Larry Knetchel on keyboards; Hal Blaine the drummer; Jimmi Haskell, string arranger extraordinaire. Some, like Sonny Bono, had begun with Phil Spector. Even Herb Alpert was a Spector session man. You can hear many of them on Mamas and Papas records, the *first* supergroup, who made a brilliant debut with those musicians under the direction of Lou Adler, *If You Can Believe Your Eyes and Ears* (Dunhill DS 50006).

One of those session men emigrated from Tulsa, Oklahoma, pianist/arranger Leon Russell. His first solo, post-dope, effort was *The Asylum Choir,* followed in a year by a quick succession of studio and production work with Bonnie and Delaney, Dave Mason (see section entitled The British Invasions), Eric Clapton, and supremely, the grand, magnificent Joe Cocker. In a Los Angeles-to-London leap focused around the many stylistic abilities of Russell, they all came together in a huge wave of Gospel Rock. And it was gorgeous. The *Mad Dogs and Englishmen* double set is not reviewed here, but is an absolute must. The early Delaney and Bonnie albums are not reviewed here but are also absolutely listenable.

As is all of it. From Los Angeles, with love . . .

~~~~~~~~~~~~~~~~~~~~~~~~

WILD HONEY
The Beach Boys
(Capitol T2859)

The fact that the Beach Boys are apparently formally back on the Capitol label, rather than on their own label ("Brothers Records" which was distributed by Capitol), is a good clue to the direction of their latest album. They have retrenched musical forces for a more solid approach after the disaster of their *Smiley Smile* (Brothers Records 9001), an abortive attempt to match the talents of Lennon and McCartney.

This new record is the convalescence after the illness, a necessary pause and—since standing still is moving into the past—a step backward. Through most of the album the approach is a simple one: add the Beach Boy harmony and vocal style to pre-existing ideas and idioms. Of course, the approach is still unsatisfactory compared to the time when the Beach Boys were making their own idiom.

The title track is one of the nicest: theremin, heavily chorded piano and a repititious melody line. The sexual associations are a touch too obvious, and the sock-it-to me line really out of place.

"Aren't You Glad" is a Lovin' Spoonful type song with the Beach Boy touch ("I've got a heart that just won't stop beating for you . . ."). The group puts the same sort of Southern California make on Stevie Wonder's fantastic "I Was Made to Love Her." It is a competent version; whether you like it depends on whether Stevie Wonder means anything to you.

"Country Air" is the most relaxed and naturally achieved synthesis of innocence and sophistication that the Beach Boys are aiming for. Whether or not they recognize the success of this inconspicuously placed song, hugely successful in terms of what they have so obviously been aiming for, is doubtful. The song is about the Rousseauian-styled life of simplicity in the woods. The opening orchestral riffs set a thoroughly pastoral mood, and the single, well positioned cry of a rooster signals the entrance of the voices. The lyrics are unconsciously simple-minded, the simplicity which is the beauty of the whole Beach Boy stance since "Surfin' USA." They say "Get a breath of that country air, Breathe the beauty of the everywhere."

"Darlin" is the song in which the Beach Boys really take R&B styling (which is what they did obviously with "I Was Made to Love Her," and less obviously, but not less subtly, on "Wild Honey") and make it work in an original way. "How She Boogalooed It" recalls, in another R&B effort, the surfin' guitar rhythms of the Beach Boys of yore.

It's kind of amusing that the Beach Boys are suddenly rediscovering rhythm and blues five years after the Beatles and Stones had brought it all back home, but it is probably indicative of the transmogrification of the blues that is making R&B currently so popular with the public at large.

In any case it's good to see that the Beach Boys are getting their heads straight once again.

—JANN WENNER

2-24-68

FRIENDS
The Beach Boys
(Capitol ST 2895)

The Beach Boys have tried faithfully to render who and what they are. That what they are is in some ways a simply (existential but) foolish denial of reality, that Hawthorne is not the world that Watts is, is nothing other than the fact that art, like human action, when it impersonally duplicates reality, is more schizophrenia.

The group takes risks, however. After *Pet Sounds,* the only flaw of which was its indulgence in a sometimes over-lush sound, they cleaned up and came out with *Smiley Smile,* so controlled, precise and tight that it risked (and at times lost to) sterility. "Wild Honey" bet on keeping tight and somehow simultaneously releasing everything they had in a sustained emotional burst. The bet paid off. *Friends* is a transition (note the jacket, the front of which is, like *Smiley Smile,* Rousseau-like, and the back a photograph of a sunset at the beach). Occasionally lapsing into the style of *Pet Sounds* (as on "Diamond Head," which is not as good as anything on that earlier LP), they more often mix the dry, silly-but-witty (like a fatigue high) style of *Smiley Smile* with the harder-driving, less still, more emotional feel of *Wild Honey.*

The best cuts are "Meant For You," the dedication; "Friends," a more mature (in that it lacks their usual immediacy) evocation of the surfer "pack" or "club" vision—why go out with a girl when you can go cruising with the guys on Saturday nights? It's really warm, simple, touching, saying in not so many words that friendship isn't about words. Other groups say what is happening, they talk about what has happened and what should have, and, by implication, why what has and why what should have hasn't.

Everything on the first side is great. These cuts, "Wake the World," "Be Here in the Morning," and "When a Man Needs a Woman," all evoke the elation of "Wild Honey." (The lyrics on the last are a weird synthesis of R&B raunchiness and the group's own wholesome naivete.) "Passing By," reminiscent of "Flying," is the best instrumental they've done, a smooth linear construction.

On the second side, "Anna Lee" is a trite melody, and "Diamond Head," except for a break in the middle, is uninteresting. But two cuts by Dennis Wilson and Steve Kalinich, "Little Bird" and "Be Still," are tight, emotional and beautifully done, with fine lyrics that do not exploit the California-nature-youth idiom that is, as vision, as artistic as the music itself. "Transcendental Meditation" is unfortunate, because

India Imports Gibranism is unfortunate, and because it experiments questionably with jazz. But for pop mysticism, it's not as pretentious as it might be.

"Busy Doing Nothing" words and music by Brian, is a great lyric, a matter-of-fact, vernacular exposition that well evokes a quiet mood with its small beauties. A good melody tapers off into embarrassingly sloppy jazz at its very end.

Like any entity that creates its own idiom, musically as well as culturally, the Beach Boys take getting into. Listen once and you might think this album is nowhere. But it's really just at a very special place, and after a half-dozen listenings, you can be there.

—ARTHUR SCHMIDT
—8-24-68

20/20
The Beach Boys
(Capitol SKAO 133)

The Beach Boys are one of the stranger phenomena of rock. In 1963, they were responsible for some of the best rock by whites before the Beatles. They created a style, now dated, more sociologically than musically. The style has altered (improved, even), though not as much as the music itself.

The current album is a collage of several different phases of the group's career. "Do It Again" is the best California rock song they've done since "Help Me, Rhonda," an authentic lyric, fine hand-clap drum, lush in a more disciplined way than on *Pet Sounds*. "I Can Hear Music" has an interesting alto chorus, a balance of strong vocals rather than, as on most of the other cuts, a solo with backing. Almost, but not quite, tight enough. "Bluebirds Over the Mountain" is distinguished by subtle, even humorous, but nonetheless driving piano (here, as throughout their later stuff, Brian's piano is the central instrument, rather than guitar). The chorus here is nasal, and is a disadvantage. The "psychedelic" guitar is seemingly out of place, but undeniably good.

"Be With Me," by Dennis Wilson, uses woodwinds effectively, with heavy emphasis on brass that is, but for a couple of notes, quite tasteful. Again, this is reminiscent of *Pet Sounds*, where the major influence on Brian seemed to be Motown—a creative influence that, however, also fit right in with the temptation to oversentimentalize the music. The fadeout on this piece is the highlight, a Space Odyssey-like distortion of strings and vocals. "All I want to Do," with fine piano and a simple but perfect bass line, uses guitar better than anywhere else on the album. The vocal is, ultimately, convincing. "The Nearest Faraway Place" is an alternately interesting and grotesquely overdone instrumental.

The second side has the record's two best pieces, one being the first band, "Cotton Fields" (*that* "Cotton Fields"), on which piano gives depth to harpsichord, the vocal is superb, the arrangement tight, and echo used better and more tastefully than by anyone since Phil Spector.

"I Went to Sleep" is not rock at all, but pop well-arranged. "Time to Get Alone" resolves the contradictions between pop and rock, with a real balancing of vocals tied together by simple but effective drums; violin, the most abused of all rock instruments, is employed with restraint. "Never Learn Not to Love" is a fine vocal, though the material itself is an uncertain mixture of pop and soul influences. "Our Prayer" is a nice prayer, but undemanding.

"Cabinessence," the last cut on the second side, is one of the finest things Brian has ever done, a product of the *Smiley Smile* collaboration with Parks, whose extraordinary gift it is to make a cliche grow into a world: "Lost and found you still remain there/I'll find a meadow filled with reindeer—/I'll build you a home on the range." The totally orchestrated cacophony was an innovation in rock when they used it in

Smiley Smile, and is still done here better than anywhere else. Piano imitates ukulele, and the solo vocal is gentle, but brilliant.

A good album, flawed mainly by a lack of direction (a sense of direction being last evident in *Wild Honey*), more a collection than a whole.

ARTHUR SCHMIDT
4-19-69

SUNFLOWER
The Beach Boys
(Brother/Reprise RS 6382)

After a long period of recovery, mediocrity, and general disaster, the Beach Boys have finally produced an album that can stand with *Pet Sounds*: the old vocal and instrumental complexity has returned and the result largely justifies the absurd faith some of us have had that the Beach Boys were actually still capable of producing a superb rock album—or, more precisely, a superb rock muzak album. "Add Some Music to Your Day"; hip supermarkets might program this album for contented browsing among the frozen vegetables and canned fruit.

As a reassuring note, most of the lyric impotence of the group remains, though not so prominently displayed as on colorful recent outings as *Friends*. In what is mainly a simple collection of love songs, Dennis Wilson has explored some aspects of rhythm and blues while Brian continues to work within his own distinctive framework. Thus on the one hand we have "It's About Time" and "Slip on Through," hints of the soft hard rock that marked "I Get Around," "Help Me Rhonda," etc., transferred to the domain of contemporary Motown. Dennis even pulls off a rib-tickling imitation of Barry Melton imitating James Brown on "Got to Know the Woman." All of these tracks are executed with a certain aplomb that often was lacking in post-"Good Vibrations" Beach Boy music, as if the self-consciousness of such homogenizing enterprise as making a new Beach Boy record has been again overcome. As a result, the naivete of the group is more astounding than ever—I mean, good Christ, it's 1970 and here we have a new, excellent Beach Boy's epic, and isn't that irrelevant?

In any case, Brian's new stuff is great, especially "This Whole World" and "All I Wanna Do." Which brings up the engineering and production work on this album: it's flawless, especially in view of the number of overdubs. There is a warmth, a floating quality to the stereo that far surpasses the mixing on, say, *Abbey Road*. The effects are subtle, except for the outrageous echo on "All I Wanna Do" that makes the song such

a mind-wrenching experience. And then there is "Cool, Cool Water," Brian's exquisite ode to water in all its manifestations, which, like "Add Some Music," is encyclopedic in its trivial catalogue of the subject at hand. "Cool, Cool Water" pulls off a *Smiley Smile* far better than most of the material on that disappointing venture.

The inevitable saccharine ballads are present in abundance. "Deirdre" and particularly Brian's "Our Sweet Love" rejoin the ongoing tradition of "Surfer Girl," although "Our Sweet Love" is almost reminiscent of the mood of *Pet Sounds*. Of course there is some lesser stuff here, like "At My Window." No matter: as a whole, *Sunflower* is without doubt the best Beach Boys album in recent memory, a stylistically coherent tour de force. It makes one wonder though whether anyone still listens to their music, or could give a shit about it. This album will probably have the fate of being taken as a decadent piece of fluff at a time when we could use more Liberation Music Orchestras. It *is* decadent fluff—but *brilliant* fluff. The Beach Boys are plastic madmen, rock geniuses. The plastic should not hide from use the geniuses who molded it.

—JIM MILLER
10-1-70

SONG CYCLE
Van Dyke Parks
(Warner Brothers 1727)

Rock music is finally becoming composed music, growing from Phil Spector and Burt Bacharach. Bacharach contributed a purely popular legacy while Spector with Jack Nitzsche remained in the rock mainstream; out of them grew the Beach Boys, with *Pet Sounds* remaining the greatest romantic statement in rock writing. The Beatles have never essentially participated in this field, theirs being ad hoc construction of sound, a field the Mothers have invaded, as well as remaining to rock what Kurt Weill was to the musical theater. Meanwhile Motown has always canned arrangements in metrically divided temporal space even more sophisticated than Spector; yet until now only the Mothers have broken away from song structure, the now being Van Dyke Parks, co-author of the last Beach Boy record of merit ("Heroes and Villains"), and now in charge of *Song Cycle*.

Van Dyke Parks may come to be considered the Gertrude Stein of the new pop music, for unlike the Beatles and the Rolling Stones, his is not mass circulation music, in fact it approaches being an inaccessible latice work of structured sound, which in itself is a major contribution to formalism in rock. In "The All-Golden" the possibility of sound as music within in the framework of form (and *not à la* Milton Babbit) comes through very clearly in several seconds of a train whistle that only slowly manifests itself as the train of such musical about-faces (such as the variations on "Donovan's Colours"), from tack piano to balalaika to bomb (the possibility explored with the suggestive silence between "The All Golden" and "Van Dyke Parks"). Parks is a romantic in many ways, but his structure is strangely open, progressing across space much as George Shearing's conceptions for guitar, vibes and piano.

Parks can't really sing (not like Brian), so his voice is transfigured into taped mutations, becoming an integral part of his lush/noise compositional structure. Compared to an earlier, quite pretentious try at composed rock (Chad and Jeremy's "Progress Suite"), *Song Cycle* presents us with the work of a creative genius. The album is hardly perfect, but familiarity breeds awe at what, for a first album, has been accomplished. If the Beatles pull themselves together, this may be their next stop in the breakaway from song form variations on a theme—significantly though, Van Dyke Parks is there first. Listening to *Song Cycle* may not bring love but it most certainly will bring music liberation.

—JIM MILLER
2-24-68

DR. BYRDS AND MRS. HYDE
The Byrds
(Columbia CS 9785)

The Byrds roll on.

With the exception of the Beach Boys they must hold the American pop group record for longevity, even though Roger McGuinn is the only surviving member of the group that started out in L.A., in 1964. Despite the endless personnel changes, the Byrds have remained the Byrds from beginning to end, which is to say that Roger McGuinn, despite the fact that he changed his name, remains Roger McGuinn.

While there is an underlying consistency to all their work, they have the capacity to grow in a way uncommon on the pop scene. They are always pushing themselves on to the next plateau, even with one eye glancing at their past.

The contrasts in the group's history were highlighted at a unique engagement at the Boston Tea Party, February 20-23. On that weekend, the Byrds were featured on the same program with the Flying Burrito Brothers, a newly-formed group comprised entirely of people who have either gigged with or were at one time members of the Byrds.

The engagement was concurrent with the release of the Byrds' eighth (and excellent) new album, *Dr. Byrds and Mrs. Hyde*. Throughout the weekend they received frequent ovations from a warm and affectionate audience.

Roger McGuinn was delighted with the gig, saying that the weekend had been beautiful for him and the other members of the group. "For the first time," he believes, "the Byrds are better live than on record." This new found success at performing is related to changes in McGuinn's own attitude; he seems more at peace than in the past. He is now 100% owner of the group (when Hillman was still there he owned 50%) and hires, at a fixed salary, the other Byrds. They are Gene Parsons on drums, John York on bass, and Clarence White on lead guitar.

With his new found control he is able to avoid some of the hassling and constant wars which have always exerted such a destructive influence on the Byrds—particularly as it affected them on stage.

Similarly, McGuinn has recently taken over the management of the group explaining, "When you reach the stage the Byrds have, the only thing a manager does is answer the phone. So now, $20 a month, I have an answering service and no manager. You save a lot of money that way."

Contributing to the overwhelming success of the weekend was the atmosphere engendered by the Boston Tea Party. That club goes to extraordinary lengths to provide conditions conducive to good performing. For example, despite the club's capacity of around 1000 (pitifully small for a rock club) and the fact that at least double that number of people showed up on Friday and Saturday nights, the club's management refused to turn people out after one show. The club's policy is "people pay to stay all night."

Club manager Don Law explains:

> There is no question that in the short run we could be making more money by going to a two show policy, but we would lose the spirit of the place. A good act needs to have the same audience all night to stretch out, to do things it doesn't normally do. We try to encourage that.

It is by this approach of encouraging spontaneity that the Tea Party avoids formalizing the presentation of rock. The featured group doesn't feel bound to do its "one show set," the one set that most

groups have ready when they are doing two or three shows in the evening. By the end of the weekend of such shows, most groups look like they are about to fall asleep on stage—if not that, then their efforts at looking involved with their material often appear contrived. The one-audience-a-night policy keeps the group from falling into a rut and encourages them to put out.

Which is why on the closing night of this gig, instead of the Byrds sounding tired, worn out, and bored, they were filled with enthusiasm and Roger McGuinn stood on the stage for an hour and a half with most of the Burritos and all the Byrds and they did every song they could think of, and when they were done, and the audience overwhelmed them with applause, McGuinn came back with the Byrds and did another half hour.

Among the outstanding country numbers is "Old Blue," done in the arrangement Bob Gibson lined out five or six years ago. Seeing it listed on the album gave me a start but there is nothing sentimenal or corny about the lilting vocal harmony or the marvelous lead guitar of Clarence White.

White is a long time flat picker who used to work in a bluegrass group called the Kentucky Colonels. He plays a Telecaster filtered through an attachment that makes it sound like a steel guitar. On the album he does a marvelous Doc Watson styled number—"Nashville West."

"Drug Store Truck Driving Man" is about a truck driver who is also a member of "Ku Klux Klan/and why he don't like me I don't understand." McGuinn spends a large amount of his spare time listening to the country stations as well as jazz, and spends virtually no time keeping up with the rock scene in general.

Among the rock tunes, "King Apathy III" and "Bad Night at the Whiskey" are both exceptional. But whereas Johnston's production on the country cuts is perfect, the sound of the rock cuts is inadequate. The instrumental tracks are too fragmented: the bass sticks out too much, the drums don't cut across the way they do live, and the rhythm is not consistent enough. The amazing power of the Byrds vocals are reduced to the status of vocal ornaments. Also, on record, Clarence White is a somewhat hit or miss lead. He is always first rate on the country cuts but lacks consistency on rock tunes. In particular the album track of "Wheels On Fire" suffers as a result.

Before seeing the group live I played this album several times and loved it without qualification. The various flaws became evident only after seeing

the group perform and hearing how much better they do everything live. After digging six sets of them in one weekend, the album becomes a mere "souvenir of a concert," as McGuinn himself puts it.

The Byrds are that good live.

On Thursday night—opening night—they started off with a medley which grabbed me at once: it included in entirety "Turn, Turn, Turn," "Mr. Tambourine Man," and "8 Miles High." McGuinn refers to the medley as the "nostalgia trip," and enjoys doing it when people respond, "even though it sometimes seems like writing the same sentence 1000 times in a row."

What struck me is how much the Byrds, despite White's country guitar, sound like the original records. That similarity is but another confirmation of the importance McGuinn has always had in shaping the identity of the group. For it seems that he can take any three musicians who want to do it, and teach them to play "byrds."

The evidence for this dates all the way back to the recording of "Mr. Tambourine Man." McGuinn says he was the only member of the original Byrds to play on that cut. Everything but his 12 string was done by L.A. studio musicians, mostly Lou Adler's regular crew, including Hal Blaine on drums. At that session the studio crew also cut the track for the flip side of "Tambourine," "I Knew I'd Want You." However, when it came to recording the album, everyone decided they would rather do it themselves, hence the other tracks on the album were all done by the real Byrds.

If one now goes back and compares the apparent "studio musician cuts" against the "Byrds cuts," there are practically no discernible differences in style, which indicates how much direction McGuinn was giving to both studio musicians and Byrds. It also explains why the new Byrds are able to play the old Byrds music with such sensitivity. The Byrds are style —primarily McGuinn's style— and each successive group of Byrds has mastered it.

Of course after the first album David Crosby was to exert an ever greater influence on the group, as did all the other Byrds. But the part of the old Byrds that McGuinn still does on stage is the part he created.

At the end of one set someone called out for him to do "Mind Gardens"; he looked at the person with an "are you kidding" sneer on his face.

"How about 'Chewy, Chewy'?" he inquired. "Mind Gardens" was a Crosby creation and is known by many Byrd *aficionados* as the permanent Byrds' bummer. In talking about old Byrds' albums McGuinn asked me what I thought of it. I told him it had come close to ruining the second side

of *Younger Than Yesterday* for me.

He looked at me blankly for a moment and said, "We tried to convince him of that at the time but he was sure it was right for the album. Now, I think even he thinks it was a mistake."

After the opening medley, the Byrds went through 11 additional songs. They don't believe in the current vogue of doing four ten minute songs as a set. "Too much chaff," says McGuinn. He prefers to do his tight little three minute songs and give people as many of them as possible. His performing repertoire includes over thirty songs.

Among the highlights of their live performance was "Wheels On Fire." McGuinn sings lead and gestures out some of the lines of the lyrics, while singing them. Clarence White stands perfectly still, looking, as always, petrified. At the chorus he and York join McGuinn and the vocal seems to cascade off the stage drowning out the instruments (do you believe that?) and engulfing everyone with its power.

They aren't fighting with you. There is no "wall of sound" between you and them. They play loud, but a beautiful loud —the kind of loud that draws you towards them. It all seems like an invitation to come along, like they are the original Tambourine Men.

The effect of the Byrds throughout the weekend was, as it should have been, cumulative and by Saturday even McGuinn seeemed surprised at how responsive the audience was. Towards the end of the second set on Saturday night he asked Gram Parsons to sing "Hickory Wind" with them.

Eyes closed, Gram seemed to be entranced and in touch with his music in a way that he is not with the Burritos. That group is a competent, straightforward country band which lacks imagination. Each individual is an excellent musician but the collective sound is seldom satisfying. They generally lack McGuinn's ability to transcend the parochial in country without cheapening the style. But Gram Parsons with the Byrds was beautiful on *Sweetheart of the Rodeo* and was beautiful that night.

Like everyone else on the stage, he was playing for himself.

On Sunday night the weekend culminated in an evening of perfect style. The Byrds' first set was as perfect as I have ever heard a rock band perform. They began with their lovely version of "You Ain't Goin' Nowhere." At the end McGuinn asked the audience to "sing along." Again, that amazing ability to do something you couldn't accept from anyone else and make you respond; he

seemed like the Pete Seeger of 1969 for a moment. From there they went through the material that was by now familiar to me but done with precision and complete effortlessness.

The Burritos followed but their set never really ended. After forty minutes, Gene Parsons took over for Michael Clark on drums and everyone else from both groups stayed on board. Everyone took turns singing the things they knew best. McGuinn did "Pretty Boy Floyd" and "I Like the Christian Life." Gram sang "Hickory Wind" and several others. Hillman offered "Time Between" from *Younger Than Yesterday*. Clarence White and Gene Parsons sang a haunting gospel tune together. John York did a beautifully soulful "Long Black Veil." You get the picture, I'm sure.

The best of it was "You Don't Miss Your Water." On the album, for some reason, McGuinn wound up singing the song even though it was Gram Parsons who had taught it to the group. Now Gram sang lead and the harmony between him and Roger was gorgeous in its flowing tranquility.

As is often the case in this kind of situation, things start out a peak of spontaneity and tend to decline as the group gets farther away from its best material. Gradually the Burritos drifted off stage, leaving things to the Byrds. And the

Byrds quickly shifted the energy level back to where it had been at the start with "Chimes of Freedom" and "So You Want to Be a Rock and Roll Star." When they thought they had finally exhausted the audience they did their best new piece of material, "Jesus Is Just All Right."

"Jesus" is a song McGuinn learned from Gram Parsons. It will probably be their next single and has the electrifying effect on an audience that Dylan's "Mr. Tambourine Man" used to have. The song is a spiritual which is sung as a quartet. Parsons leads off the singing which is *acappella*, except for drum accompaniment. He is gradually joined by each of the other Byrds. The instruments come in and the riff continues over a rock background. The arrangement goes back and forth between the two elements and on Sunday night it seeemed like they did it forever and it still wasn't long enough.

"Jesus Is Just All Right" defines the brilliance of the Byrds. They take a song with lyrics which might ordinarily seem campy to the average rock fan and infuse them with a spirit that touches everyone. They extract, from what might otherwise be a dated Southern hymn, the joyfulness and optimism which is a part of all religion and they allow you to participate in it.

Again they are pulling you into something. They transcend the quaintness of the song's background and give it that Byrds touch which simultaneously reduces and elevates everything it encompasses.

After that they made a fast exit, but obviously people weren't going to let them get away. Back they came. This time McGuinn just strummed a few chords and, "I think I'm going back . . ." The other parts slowly fell into place and the song gently but continuously built up to its "la-la-la" chorus. And then through a seemingly endless procession of largely obscure Byrds material ending with "Mr. Spaceman" and then good-bye.

The Byrds left most of the people there with a memory of the kind of thing an audience sees all too rarely. For during that weekend the Byrds were renewing their energy, spirit, and music. In a sense they were being reborn.

What made it so meaningful was that it was not just the Byrds whose spirit was being renewed but also that of the audience. There were no spectators at this spectacle. Everyone was a mid-wife. It's so much nicer that way.

—JON LANDAU
4-5-69

THE NOTORIOUS
BYRD BROTHERS
The Byrds
(Columbia CS 9575)

Lots of people are down on the Byrds. They haven't been able to perform decently in years. They are essentially a recording act unable to reproduce their music effectively on a stage. Like the Beatles, I suppose.

What is forgotten in this kind of attitude is that there is a distinction between performing and making a record, and the two ought to be judged separately. No one has ever seen the Beatles perform *Sgt. Pepper;* but who exactly is complaining? A lot of the West Coast groups and even the Cream have trouble doing things in the studio, and that doesn't keep people from loving them when they are on stage.

When the Byrds get it together on record they are consistently brilliant. And it is interesting to speculate about how many of the currently popular groups on the Coast or in England will still be as fresh and inventive as the Byrds are when they get around to recording their fifth album.

At their best—on records—the Byrds are graceful. No rough edges, no jarring protrusions. Their music is possessed by a never-ending circularity and a rich, child-like quality. It

has a timelessness to it, not in the sense that it is capable of forcing you to suspend consciousness of time altogether.

While *Younger Than Yesterday* seemed to upset the formal basis of this timelessness and circularity, it really had the effect of deepening it, and preparing us for their new album, *The Notorious Byrd Brothers.* The use of solo voices, the moving away from a strict, 12-string dominated sound and the greater rhythmic freedom on the earlier album expanded the wholeness of the Byrds' musical circle. Tension was created by counterposing the roundness of feeling inherent in the "Turn, Turn, Turn" mode with a classically linear style as in "Everybody's Been Burned," an exquisite song. The result was an album of deeply satisfying music which communicated a gentleness and warmth seldom attained through the electric syndrome of Rickenbacker 12-strings. It is from this foundation that the Byrds have continued their musical growth on their newest album.

The Notorious Byrd Brothers is the same old trip but, at the same time, a brand new one. The lyrics have greater force (the presence of the war is deeply felt) and there is a seriousness to even the lighter pieces. Stylistically, the eclecticism is so marked that one suspects McGuinn of having read an article about the Byrds' eclecticism. Yet the pervasive mood, as always, remains a continuous warmth and openness, perhaps for no other reason than McGuinn's inability to sound angry.

The Byrd's eclecticism is awesome: C&W, science fiction, light jazz touches, finger-picking rhythms, pop rock (two fine Goffin-King songs), and touches of strings all play their part on this album. Yet if one doesn't listen closely he may not notice even a fraction of the incongruities which are present. And therein lies a key to the Byrds' ability to assimilate everything that they touch.

Instrumentally, the group is stylized to accomplish this inconspicuous assimilation perfectly. Michael Clark, now replaced by Kevin Kelley, deserves much of the credit for this. He is a marvelous drummer who holds it all together with his hard, uncomplicated style. In a sense he serves the same practical function that Charlie Watts does with the Stones: he gives the group a floor, a bottom, which unifies whatever developments are happening at the top of the sound. He is especially effective here on straight Byrd material like "Goin' Back" and on slightly jazzier material such as "Natural Harmony."

Bassist Chris Hillman, who really came into his own on *Younger Than Yesterday,* holds off a little on this one. Like Clark, he seems to be more concerned with holding the sound together than with flying over the key board. While the brilliance of his performances on "Everybody's Been Burned" and "Renaissance Fair" is missed, his more solid and repetitious stylings on the new album are extremely effective (as in "Draft Morning" and his brilliantly syncopated style on "Change Is Now"). Meanwhile, McGuinn's mastery of his instrument continues to grow and while I miss Crosby on some of the cuts (and the fullness of the earlier Byrds on most of the album) there is ample compensation in the greater fluidity and melodiousness, and even freedom, in the overall impact of this album.

The only real technical problem is that McGuinn has trouble holding his own vocally. Producer Gary Usher has submerged his voice even more than usual owing to McGuinn's wavering pitch. This is more than unwise for whatever McGuinn's shortcomings in this area, they are more than compensated for by his charm and vocal expressiveness.

The songs on the album cover a vast range, highlighted by a couple of minor masterpieces. The second side contains two pieces that are culminations of the Byrds' history. "Space Odyssey" is a brilliant example of the Byrds' eclecticism—a synthesis of their ballad style with electronics and outer space. To listen to this cut is to become immediately aware of the sources of the Byrds' music: everything from Almeda Riddle and Pete Seeger to Paul McCartney and Stockhausen. But beyond that is the impressive coherence of the composition which always remains a perfectly accessible piece of music. At the other end of the scale is "Old John Robinson" which contains the pinnacle of the Byrds' work with geniune folk and C&W influences, dating back to "John Riley" on *5D* and "The Girl With No Name" on *Younger Than Yesterday*. The instrumental arrangement has its roots in such earlier 2/4 finger-picking pieces as "Mr. Spaceman" and "CTA 102," and the addition of strings on this cut helps it to transcend any of their previous efforts in this area. The vocal is also perfect.

Similarly, the quasi-jazz style of "Everybody's Been Burned" is further delineated on the new album on the Crosby-Hillman composition "Tribal Gathering" which is an unqualified success. The Byrds are one of the two or three rock groups that can sound jazzy without being incoherent, as both this cut and "Get To You" illustrate. The latter is a 5/4 composition that moves to 3/4 on its choruses. Yet there is nothing awkward or jarring about the transitions; they just happen. The idea of

superimposing a rich, major chord based progression over such a subtle and fluid rhythmic pattern is typical of the Byrds' type of creativity and the result is perhaps the best cut on the album. McGuinn's lyrics and vocal are among the best he has ever recorded.

The presence of two Goffin-King songs on the album probably surprised many—especially at this point in the Byrds' history. Yet, whatever their reason for being included, they fully justify themselves aesthetically. The words to "Goin' Back" have been considerably altered from the original—obviously for the better—and the song contains much of the feel of the early Byrds, except with a C&W flavor injected into the old style via the use of piano and dobro, allegedly by Clarence White. Michael Clark's brief drum break at the end of the cut is brilliant. "Wasn't Born to Follow," the other Goffin-King composition, again continues the Byrds' finger-picking style. It is an infectious piece in which both guitar and words seem to cascade off the record in a manner almost reminiscent of some of Hendrix's more verbal cuts on *Axis*.

Yet ultimately this album can't be dissected cut by cut because it is all part of a single attitude which dominates the entire record.

That attitude is an optimism

born out of a genuine awareness about what is going on over there and what it is doing to us right here. While acknowledging and even responding to the war, the Byrds refuse to give in to it, and for that reason the music on this album is deeply appropriate to 1968—appropriate in a way that songs like "Magical Mystery Tour" are not.

For example, a song like "Draft Morning" may seem pessimistic but ultimately it is not. The Byrds don't give themselves over to anger or despair. They precede the song with the exquisite "Natural Harmony" and follow it with "Wasn't Born to Follow" and "Get To You," two serious but optimistic songs. And the fact that "Draft Morning" is severely marred by its melodramatic touches further indicates that the Byrds can't be satisfied or comfortable with a pessimistic stance.

They sense the horror and paranoia that is all around us but they do not give up their search for innocence and natural harmony. They still sing about catching them if you can and they can still write "But I really only want to get to you." And it's good that they do. Somebody has to sing love songs like that.

What it gets down to is that the Byrds are still turning, or at least revolving. Their circle of feeling is large enough so that they can feel and sense

what really is happening. But sensing that, they continue the cycle. *The Notorious Byrd Brothers* is simply the latest rendition of "Turn, Turn, Turn." It's just that this time the turning isn't so self-assured or so automatic. In fact, it sounds like they had to think about it.

—JON LANDAU
4-27-68

SWEETHEART OF THE RODEO
The Byrds
(Columbia CS 9670)

The Byrds, during the not-so-great Folk-Rock controversy, attempted to qualify their own individual transition by saying: "If only one line of 'Mr. Tambourine Man' (which they had just recorded) gets through to the kids it'll have been worth it." The Byrds had all been Folkies and their subscription to Dylan's new method of "getting the message across" (something Dylan himself denied trying to do) was of no little significance. What Barry McGuire, Jody Miller and the Byrds were doing was sacrilegious to the hard-core Folkies. Not only were they put down severely at first by *Sing Out!* and *Broadside,* the Bibles of the Guthrie generation, but to some, like Randy Sparks, former leader of the New Christy Minstrels and Back Porch Majority, what they were singing (as ascribed to McGuire's "Eve of Destruction") was "fodder for the communists." Folk-Rock, such as it was, made the "Folks" uptight.

In light of the former *faux-pas*, it is suggested that no purist C&W fans listen to *Sweetheart of the Rodeo*, the Byrds' latest transition. The Yin-Yang cycle of the musical flow continues to hold true. From straight, unamplified Folk, to Folk-Rock, to Rock, to Acid-Rock, to semi-C&W— the next step appears all too obvious. But what we're confronted with at the moment is the current product.

The new Byrds do not sound like Buck Owens and his Buckaroos. They aren't that good. The material they've chosen to record, or rather, the way they perform the material, is simple, relaxed and folky. It's not pretentious, it's pretty. The musicianship is excellent. (They had to practice before playing the Grand Old Opry.) The songs are, with the exception of the Dylan tracks "You Ain't Goin' Nowhere" and "Nothing Was Delivered," all standard ballads. "Blue Canadian Rockies" is an old Gene Autry tune, "Pretty Boy Floyd" was written by Woody Guthrie, "Life In Prison" is a Merle Haggard number and their arrangements of "The Christian Life" and "I Am a Pilgrim" (not the Merle Travis version)

are in the traditional storytelling vein.

"You Ain't Goin' Nowhere" is the finest cut they've done since "Old John Robertson" on the *Notorious* album. But it's really more standard Bob Dylan than standard C&W. Buck Owens or Charlie Pride would never refer to Genghis Khan in a song. (Even Johnny Cash will sound a little silly singing it.)

Dylan has found his corner of C&W to relax in. With "I'll Be Your Baby Tonight" he proved he could master any Folk or Rock idiom, and with "Nowhere"—he's identified himself as a valid songwriter in a medium that he's apparently spurned long ago. The Byrds are gallant interpreters of his lyrics—"My Back Pages" was probably their most genuine effort. The other Dylan-penned track, "Nothing Was Delivered," starts out innocently enough with steel guitar backing, but following the first "are-you-true-to-me" verse it breaks into a rock chorus worthy of Sonny and Cher. It's plain enough otherwise, and does the job.

The dedication to simplicity is reflected best on "I Am a Pilgrim," a really sweet song rearranged by Roger (Jim) McGuinn and Chris Hillman. It includes only one minor repeated guitar run and the rest is reminiscent of Dylan's uninspired folk-strumming of "The

Times They Are A-Changing'" days.

"Blue Canadian Rockies" is a particularly nostalgic track for all old Gene Autry fans. To hear that "the golden poppies are bloomin'/'round the banks of Lake Louise" brings back visions of Ol' Gene and his horse Champion loping along the prairie.

"Rockies" sounds much more honest than their rendering of Merle Haggard's "Life In Prison," a much more citified contemporary song. The Haggard tune sounds too professional, too well laid out and unsympathetic with the plight of the unfortunate guy who murdered his girl friend. It would be better to listen to Haggard himself do this—it's not that much better but at least it's honest.

The Byrds have made an interesting album. It's really very uninvolved and not a difficult record to listen to. It ought to make the "Easy Listening" charts. "Bringing it all back home" has never been an easy thing to do.

—BARRY GIFFORD
9-14-68

THE GILDED PALACE OF SIN
The Flying Burrito Brothers
(A & M SP 4175)

Gram Parsons, the head Burrito, stares out of the cover photograph of this album wearing a suit made by Nudie of Hollywood, who specializes in the outfits with spangled cactuses and embroidered musical notes worn by such traditional country-western performers as Porter Wagoner and Buck Owens. But Parsons' suit is decorated with green marijuana branches, and there are naked ladies on the lapels.

Wonderful (in the Churchillian sense) as this is, it seems even more of a wonder when you know that Parsons comes from Waycross, Georgia, especially if you happen to know what Waycross, Georgia, is like.

Jerry Wexler of Atlantic Records, sitting around his Long Island house one night with Bert Berns, trying to come up with a real down-home song for Wilson Pickett, suggested that they write one about Waycross. "I figured there couldn't be any more down-home place than that," Wexler explained later. "Waycross, Georgia, would have to be the asshole of the world." Waycross, pop. approx. 20,000, is located 60 miles from the Atlantic Ocean, 36 miles from the Florida state line, about 15 minutes via alligator from the Okefenokee Swamp, close to the heart of Wiregrass, Georgia, a territory which may well be the deepest part of the Deep South. Memphis, Birmingham, Atlanta are southern; but they are nothing like Waycross. People around Waycross think of Atlanta the way you and I think of the moon—a place which, though remote, might possibly be visited someday by us or our children.

Wiregrass, the territory which includes Waycross, encompasses nearly 10,000 square miles of pine-and-palmetto forest, grading almost imperceptibly into the Okefenokee, in Seminole the Land of the Trembling Earth. The forest floor, carpeted with sweet-smelling dry brown pine needles, laced with creeks and rivers, becomes more unsteady under your feet, until another step, onto land that looks the same as the place where you are standing, will take you too far, the ground gives way, and you are sucked down into the rich peaty swamp, which, though it supports great pines, will not support you. Many men have walked into the Okefenokee, where even the pretty little plants eat meat, never to be heard from again. Finally there is more water than land, and the huge cypresses towering overhead, wild grey tresses of Spanish moss in their branches stirring in the wind, form the walls of corridors through the brown water, which is clear in the hand and good to drink.

The people of Wiregrass, dealers in, among other things, pine trees, tobacco, peanuts, sugar cane, moonshine whisky, trucks, tractors, new and used cars, Bibles, groceries, dry goods and hardware; in isolated farms on swamp islands; in turpentine camps deep in the woods, like Dickerson's Crossing, Mexico, the Eight-mile Still; in unincorporated settlements like Sandy Bottom, Headlight, Thelma; in towns like Blackshear, Folkston, Waycross; from banker to bootlegger, all share two curses: hard work and Jesus. Wiregrass must be one of the last places in the world where the Puritan ethic still obtains, making an almost unrelievedly strenuous way of life even more grim. Before smoking tobacco was known to be a health hazard, it was frowned upon by many people there, simply because it gives pleasure. Although Waycross has the Okefenokee Regional Library and once had a world movie premiere (a swamp picture called *Lure of the Wilderness,* starring Walter Brennan), Culture exists there only in the anthropological sense. The social life of the community has two centers, with, in general mutually exclusive clientele: churches and roadhouses. There is violence, illicit sex, drunkenness—in a word, sin—in south Georgia, but they have not become behavioral standards. The ideal still is to be a hardworking, God-fearing, man or woman, boy or girl.

So here we have Gram Parsons, from Waycross, Georgia, with shoulder-length hair, and dope and pussy on his jacket. Parsons' first record, as far as I know, was *Safe at Home* by his earlier group, the International Submarine Band. The album, "a Lee Hazlewood Production, produced by Suzi Jane Hokom," included songs associated with Johnny Cash, Merle Haggard, Big Boy Crudup, Elvis Presley, as well as a couple of country classics ("Miller's Cave" and "Satisfied Mind") and four Parsons originals. The music was fairly straight country-western, with piano, base, drums, rhythm, lead, and steel guitars. It was an honest, pleasant, but not a strongly exciting album.

Next Parsons joined the Byrds, staying with them long enough to make *Sweetheart of the Rodeo,* the country album recorded in Nashville, which, though not a complete success, was one of the best records of the last year. Parsons left the Byrds, refusing to appear before segregated audiences in South Africa, and with Chris Hillman, another ex-Byrd, formed the Flying Burrito Bros.

The Burritos' first album, with roughly the same instrumentation as Parsons' two previous ones, has perhaps less surface charm than *Sweetheart,* but is the best, most personal Parsons has yet done. *The Gilded Palace of Sin,* unlike *Safe at Home* and *Sweetheart of the Rodeo,* is about life in the big city, where even a pretty girl, as Parsons warns on the first track, can be a "devil in disguise." "Sin City," the second track, predicts destruction for the city, "filled with sin," where the slickers in their "green mohair suits" advise you to "take it home right away, you've got three years to pay." But, the song cautions, "Satan is waiting his turn":

> It seems like this whole town's insane
> On the 31st floor
> A gold-painted door
> Won't keep out the Lord's burning rain

The two following songs, "Do-Right Woman" and "Dark End of the Street" by Dan Penn of Memphis, the only ones on the album which Parsons had no hand in writing, are given new depth of meaning by their juxtaposition against what has preceded them. "Do-Right Woman" is especially outstanding; though obviously quite different it is in no way inferior to the original Aretha Franklin recording. "My Uncle," the last track on side one, does honor to the great tradition, equal to the tradition of Southern war heroism, of hillbilly draft-dodging. It is a delightfully good-humored "protest" in the best, healthiest, most direct and personal sense:

> I'm headin' for the nearest
> foreign border
> Ventura may be just my
> kind of town
> 'Cause I don't need the
> kind of law and order
> That tends to keep a good
> man underground

The second side opens with a return to a mood like that of "Sin City," except that the emphasis is on how out of place "this boy" feels, very much as in the old gospel song, "This World Is Not My Home." "Wheels" ends with a plea to "take this boy away." In "Juanita," the next song, "an angel . . . just seventeen, with a dirty old gown and a conscience so clean" finds him abandoned and alone "in a cold dirty room . . . with a bottle of wine and some pills off the shelf" and brings back "the life that I once threw away."

"Hot Burrito No. 1," which follows, is perhaps the best song Parsons has yet written, and he has written some very good ones. A rather old-fashioned rock-and-roll song, it might have been recorded in 1956 by the Platters, except for one line, the most effective on the album, "I'm you top—I'm your old boy," which no one but Parsons could sing so movingly. "Hot Burrito No. 2," an up-tempo secular love song, breaks the gospel-honkytonk taboo, which is just as strong as the black blues-in-church taboo, when Parsons sings, "You better love me—Jesus Christ."

The next-to-last song is the only repeat from an earlier Parsons album. "Do You Know How It Feels To Be Lonesome" from, ironically, *Safe at Home,* is the statement of a young man who must feel at home nowhere, not in the big city or in Waycross, Georgia. "Did you ever try to smile at some people," he says, "and all they ever seem to do is stare?"

"Hippie Boy," the final song, an updated version of Red Foley's "Peace in the Valley," is recited by Chris Hillman, possibly because his accent is less countrified than Parsons'. It tells a story with a moral: "It's the same for any hillbilly, bum, or hippie on the street. . . . Never carry more than you can eat." The album's ending somehow summons up a vision of hillbillies and hippies, like lions and lambs, together in peace and love instead of sin and violence, getting stoned together, singing oldtime favorite songs. The album closes with a fine, fractured chorus of "Peace in the Valley," with whistles, shouts, and rattling tambourines.

Perhaps Parsons, coming from the country, feels more deeply than most the strangeness and hostility of the modern world, but he speaks to and for all of us. Gram Parsons is a good old boy.

—STANLEY BOOTH
5-17-69

LAST TIME AROUND
Buffalo Springfield
(Atco SD 33-256)

As a final testament to their multi-talent, the Buffalo Springfield have released *Last Time Around,* the most beautiful record they've ever made.

This is the second record album by an originally Canadian group (the first was *Music From Big Pink* by the Band) of major importance to be released this month. They both have their country roots showing. The great difference lies in their separate "heaviness distinction." The Band are overwhelming seriousness and pointed profundity, and the Buffalo Springfield are happier sounding, more sweet-country flavored. They sound, as Jim Messina croons, like a "carefree country day."

"Four Days Gone" is one of the best tracks the Springfield has ever done. Stills' vocal is, as usual, uniquely trembly. It's a sad, C&W flavored song about a guy on the road running from the government, trying to get to his chick ("I'm four days gone into runnin' "), who can't tell his name because he's "got reason to live." The piano

tinkles Cramer-rily in the background as Stills tells the story. "Government madness," he complains.

Stills has written five of the cuts on the album. "Special Care" and "Uno Mundo" show his amazing versatility as a songwriter. Both are entirely different from the C&W-ish "Four Days Gone." "Special Case" is a rock number in the finest sense. After a keyboard intro in the style of Dylan's "Black Crow Blues," it's led by a furious, screaming guitar and a crashing, closely following organ. Stills trembles the paranoid lyrics: "Hey there you on the corner/staring at me/ Would you like to shoot me down?" The guitar's buzzing vibrato lays down the melody as he raves on in the background, yelling at the people. It sounds as if he's being dragged away.

"Uno Mundo" is a Latin-based maracas-congas-trumpet Jamaican ska-beat politi-calypso blast at the world: "Uno Mundo/Asia is screaming/Africa seething/America bleating/just the same."

On "I Am a Child" Neil Young sounds more like Tim Hardin than Tim Hardin. It's not very often that this happens, that two performers sound almost identical. Oscar Peterson sounds so similar to Nat "King" Cole that for years, during Cole's career, Peterson did not sing. Then, when Nat died, Oscar put out a memorial album dedicated to him—he sang all of Nat's best-loved songs—an almost perfect duplication of the King's original recordings. And the similarity was unintentional, as the likeness between Young and Hardin. Moreover, "Child" is done exactly in Hardin's electrified country-folk vein. It's a nice tune, very pretty, with some strikingly poignant lines: "You can't conceive of the pleasure in my smile." It's very simple and light. Even the harmonica bit reminds one of Herb Shriner playing "Back Home in Indiana."

Richie is a beautiful singer, and his best efforts here are the ballads "It's So Hard to Wait" and "Kind Woman." "Hard to Wait" is a plaintive love song: "I'll never forget you/I hope you care"—it moves slowly, backed by clarinet, acoustic guitar, drums and bass—all of which are played down appropriately, in order to highlight Richie's lingering falsetto. "Kind Woman" is similar and is performed just as nicely.

But the best track on the album is "Carefree Country Day." Jimmy's crackly-voiced lead vocal ("I get up in the morning with a cock-a-doodle doo/I get myself together if and when I choose") has the most relaxed country flavor this side of Jack Elliott. Some great backup harmony by Richie and Steve and a funky "wha-wha-wha" horn interlude complement Jimmy's vocal superbly. It even has a "dot-in-doo-wah-wap-en-doo-wat-en-dah" fadeout which is the finest bit of country doodling since Elliott's "Guabi Guabi."

Too bad this isn't the *first* time around.

—BARRY GIFFORD
8-24-68

NEIL YOUNG
Neil Young
(Reprise RS 6317)

This album by Neil Young (formerly of the Buffalo Springfield) and various friends is a flowing tributary from the overall Springfield river of twangs, breathless vocals and slim yet stout instrumentation. Especially vivid is Young's sense of melancholy and the ingenious clusters of images he employs in his lyrics (printed in full). In particular, one could very easily view this disc as an extension of Young's work on the *Buffalo Springfield Again* album, especially his compositions "Expecting to Fly" and the gaping "Broken Arrow," which closes the album.

This solo disc opens with "The Emperor of Wyoming," an instrumental which sets the tone musically for the side in a high-flying yet whining sort of way. It has that definite Springfieldian touch to it like wind between rocks or the people you see in dreams.

"The Loner" is a contemporary lament that features a nice blending of Neil's guitar with strings in non-obtrusive fashion, allowing Young's balanced ice-pick vocal to chip effectively at the listener. The stance and imagery are much the same as in the earlier "Expecting to Fly."

The next two selections are pieces of the same puzzle. "If I Could Have Her Tonight" is a slow, crystal-like effort. It features a heavy drum line, Byrds-like guitar and mellow lyrics that all together add up to that unique sense of melancholy yet joy in melancholy which the Springfield captured so well and which Young just continues doing. Like standing in all four corners of the night. "I've Been Waiting for You" is an extension of the theme, with a tinkly piano and organ.

The side ends with a longish song entitled "The Old Laughing Lady" that is so close to, yet so far apart from, Young's earlier song "Broken Arrow." A quivering piano and a halting string move around and around the melody line, here peeking between his words, there showing sky between his phrasings. The two pieces also have a series of mood/tone changes between verses—the strings, for instance, get increasingly lusher and fuller in "Laughing Lady." The fade-out piano chord here

is similar to the heartbeat fade-out on the earlier piece. The main difference between the two can be tersely put: the latter piece is tighter, more mature and has more of the quiet explosion to it that Young obviously intends.

The second side opens with a diminutive Jack Nitzsche piece entitled "String Quartet From Whiskey Boot Hill." It is a slow, deliberate ethereal introduction to Neil's vocal on "Here We Are in the Years." Musically the piece is string-dominated and very lush and full with Neil's voice incising between—the scraping fade-out says it all.

"The Last Trip to Tulsa" closes the album. It is nine minutes long and is the most stylistic, anti-Springfield piece on the album. Here we have only Young's chameleon voice and guitar—no strings, drums or piano. It proceeds to build from verse to verse—the vocal gets wider, the guitar more abandoned, more wanton. An innovative close to, in many ways, a delightful reprise of that Springfield sound done a new way.

—GARY VON TERSCH
4-5-69

EVERYBODY KNOWS THIS IS NOWHERE
Neil Young with Crazy Horse
(Reprise RS 6349)

Neil Young does not have

the kind of "good" voice that would bring praise from a high school music teacher. But you only have to listen to Judy Collins mangle "Just Like Tom Thumb's Blues" to realize that rock and roll does not flourish because of "good" voices. The best rock vocals (for example, those of Mick Jagger or Richard Manuel) are usually gritty or even harsh. Negating a formula prettiness, they push forward the unique temperament of the singer ("It's the singer, not the song"—Mick Jagger). Such vocals can never function as background music; they demand that you listen to them and feel them. Their essence is their intensity—and in light of that intensity the products of "good" voices usually sound pallid and dead.

While Neil Young is a fine songwriter and an excellent guitarist, his greatest strength is in his voice. Its arid tone is perpetually mournful, without being maudlin or pathetic. It hints at a world in which sorrow underlies everything; even a line like "you can't conceive of the pleasure in my smile" (from "I am a Child") ultimately becomes painful to hear. And because that world is recognizable to most of us, Young's singing is often strangely moving. In a natural and moving way, Neil Young is the Johnny Ray of rock and roll.

Everybody Knows This Is Nowhere is Young's second album since the demise of the Buffalo Springfield. In several respects it falls short of his previous effort. Young's new material is a little disappointing; nothing on this album touches the aching beauty of "If I Could Have Her Tonight" and "I've Loved Her So Long" or the quiet terror of "The Old Laughing Lady." His guitar work also suffers by comparison; the lyricism of the first album can only be found in faint traces here. But despite its shortcomings, *Everybody Knows This Is Nowhere* offers ample rewards. Young's music partially makes up for its lack of grace by its energy and its assurance. And his singing is still superb. Listen, for example, to the conviction which he gives to the title cut, a song about the need for and the impossibility of escape from Los Angeles.

The most interesting tracks on the album are "Running Dry" and "Cowgirl in the Sand." Building on a traditional folk melody, "Running Dry" interweaves electric guitar and violin into a disquieting blend. Its aura of strangeness is somewhat reminiscent of Young's magnificent "Out of My Mind." The lyrics are a bit over-dramatic, but the music and vocal manage to transcend them, creating the feeling of a dimly understood tragedy.

On "Cowgirl in the Sand" everything works. The lyrics are quietly accusative, while the lead guitar, alternately soaring, piercing, and driving, keeps the song surging forward. But it is Young's singing which is the real key to the success of this track. "Cowgirl in the Sand" demonstrates quite clearly the peculiar depths of Young's voice. It indicates how rock manages, again and again, to triumph over high school music teachers and their legions.

—BRUCE MIROFF
8-9-69

CROSBY, STILLS, & NASH
Crosby, Stills and Nash
(Atlantic SD 8229)

> *If you smile at me I will*
> *understand*
> *'Cause that is something*
> *everybody*
> *Everywhere does in the*
> *same language.*

This is an eminently playable record. The combination of talents creates a great sound—and it is a new sound, not merely music derived from the styles of previous groups. The vocals are warm and full, with a kind of built-in kineticism produced by three good voices emerging asynchronously on the same phrase, with rich, complementary harmonies reminiscent of Moby Grape's "8.05." Tasteful backing accompanies the superb compositions, some of them full-blown rock tracks, other cuts with simple acoustic guitar.

It's a happy sound—one feels the album was a labor of love to record. Confidence seems to pervade the trio and their music. They do what they please— singing a short blues phrase between cuts, performing their multi-melodies with a grand sense of their own uniqueness, throwing in clever bits, engaging in a musical conversation, combining songs. This new freeform is not to be found within the scope of their former associations, and it works well. They are in complete control of all they do, and the result is an especially satisfying work.

One may remember the voice of Graham Nash as harmony on the Hollies' "Bus Stop" and lead on "On a Carousel." His high tenor thresholds squeakiness at times, but most of his harmony parts are subdued and right. He wrote and solos on several songs: a couple of rockers, including the Top-30 bound "Marrakesh Express," and a soft ballad, "Lady of the Island," reminiscent of Pete Townshend's "Sunrise." On this cut, Nash's voice reaches its lower ranges and resembles that of Paul Simon. Besides his brand of harmony, Nash brings from the Hollies the catalyst for one of the best doo-doo-do-doot choruses yet—the final segment of Still's "Suite: Judy Blue Eyes" —which is quite similar to the introduction to the definitive Hollies song, "I'm Alive."

"Guinnevere," by David Crosby, completes a haunting mood-trilogy which was two-thirded by the Byrd's "Everybody's Been Burned" and Grace Slick's "Triad." On "Long Time Gone," Crosby reveals a great, thick bluesy voice which seems to round out the group and the album. In a fantastic arrangement, his voice is juxtaposed against neatly woven high harmonies in a framework of churning organ and crisp guitar. The lyrics are timely without being ostentatiously meaningful —and the whole performance turns out to be truly moving.

Steve Stills, who once told no tales about hot dusty roads, now appears in hiking boots. He evokes a soulful, country feeling in all he does. He pulls a Steve Winwood by tripling on organ, bass, and lead guitar—a crackling guitar, but muted, bouncing lyrically back and forth throughout the album. His singing is so lovely that the word "language," which is impossible to pronounce prettily, becomes a beautiful thing. His songs are life from where he stands—probably traipsing down a road or leaning on a fence somewhere.

What is important here is the music. For once, the sheet music deserves inclusion, along with the lyrics.

With no write-up detailing the illustrious careers of Crosby, Stills, and Nash, the album jacket pictures them relaxed and content, saying all that really matters: "We've done our part. Now listen."

—BARRY FRANKLIN
7-26-69

DEJA VU
Crosby, Stills, Nash, Young, Taylor, and Reeves
(Atlantic SD 7200)

Along with many other people, I had hoped that the addition of Neil Young to Crosby, Stills, and Nash would give their music the guts and substance which the first album lacked. Live performances of the group suggested that this had happened. Young's voice, guitar, compositions and stage presence added elements of darkness and mystery to songs which had previously dripped a kind of saccharine sweetness. Unfortunately, little of this influence carried over into the recording sessions for *Deja Vu*. Despite Young's formidable job on many of the cuts, the basic sound hasn't changed a whit. It's still too sweet, too soothing, too perfect, and too good to be true.

Take for example all of side two. Here we have a splendid showcase of all the Crosby, Stills, Nash, and Young strong points—precision playing, glittering harmonies, a relaxed but forceful rhythm, and impeccable twelve-string guitars. But are there any truly first rate songs here? If there are, I don't hear them. David Crosby's "Deja Vu" has little or no tune and fails totally to capture the eerie feeling that accompanies a real deja vu experience. "Our House" by Graham Nash is a flyweight ditty with nothing to say and makes this clear through its simpering melody. Steve Stills' "4+20" conjures up some quiet enigmas, but with such tepid questions at stake, who really cares? Neil Young's "Country Girl" continues his tradition of massive production numbers which includes the masterful "Broken Arrow" and "Down By The River." But compared to his earlier work, the piece is sadly undistinguished. In both this song and the next one, "Everybody I Love You," Young's voice is absorbed in the major key barbershop harmonizing of the other singers. C, S, N and Y could probably do the best version of "Sweet Adeline" in recorded history.

One's disappointment with the album is heightened by the absurdity of its pretensions. The heralded leather cover turns out to be nothing more than crimpled cardboard. What a milestone—fake leatherette! The grainy portrait of the "Old West" characters on the cover looks less like Billy the Kid, the James Gang and Buffalo Bill than the waiting room for unemployed extras for Frontier Atmosphere Inc. "Now then, which of you desperados is next?" And, of course, the

pretty gold leaf lettering turns out to be yellow Reynolds Wrap. *Deja Vu* would like to convince you that it has roots deep in the American soil. But a closer inspection reveals that its tap root is firmly implanted in the urban commercial asphalt.

There is much on this album of real merit. "Helpless," "Carry On" and "Teach Your Children" are excellent songs, well performed. But for me Crosby, Stills and Nash—plus or minus Neil Young—will probably remain the band that asks the question, "What can we do that would be really heavy?" And then answers, "How about something by Joni Mitchell?"

—LANGDON WINNER
4-30-70

WE'RE ONLY IN IT FOR THE MONEY
The Mothers of Invention
(Verve V6-5045)

Frank Zappa is a supreme genius of American music today. A direct function of this fact, perhaps, is the incredible obstacle course that each of his albums has had to follow between recording and release. One, *Lumpy Gravy,* hasn't made it at all. And it has been a good four months since this album was first advertised in the press.

Those four months have brought many delights, but now

once again it is Zappa's turn to claim our full attention. To lay it on the line, the Mothers' new album is the most advanced work to be heard in rock today. Whether it is the *best* is a moot point—how would you compare it with, for instance, Otis Redding? But Zappa's ingenuity in conception of form, in innovation of recording techniques, and in the integration of vastly differing types of music, beggars all competitors. His rhythms and harmonies are truly sublime, and his lyrics contain the most brilliant satire in the whole pop world.

He is the only man in the whole business who could get away with coming on the way he does. I'm referring mainly to the *Only Money* cover which is, of course, a spoof on *Sgt. Pepper*. But it's more than a spoof. You must look at it side by side with the *Sgt. Pepper* cover to see what heavy things the Mothers are saying. While paying the Beatles the supreme tribute of parody, the Mothers are also putting the gods of Liverpool in a slightly less exalted light than we've been used to seeing them in. Suddenly the Beatles look much too pretty, and not a little bit plastic in all those satin uniforms. And from the lyrics inside we read:

> I'm gonna tell you the way it is
> And I'm not gonna be kind or easy.

——"Harry, You're a Beast"

Zappa, the freewheeling experimentalist of *Freak Out* and the hilarious wit of *Absolutely Free,* has in this terrifying year of 1968 given us a message album. His humor is sharper and drier than ever, but now it's as grim as the headlines. A repeated theme is that of the World War II Japanese relocation centers, allegedly being prepared for the incarceration of socially and/or politically undesirable American citizens.

> Concentration moon
> Over the camp in the valley . . .

Most of the lyrics are slightly less grim than this, and Zappa provides plenty of belly laughs as he takes deadly aim on American Womanhood, "Bow Tie Daddy," "Flower Punk," the San Francisco scene, and many other people and places. Though the Establishment gets well roasted, Zappa saves his sharpest jabs for "hippies," brutally exposing the irrelevance of much of their world. "Flower power sucks," a voice says, and many other voices on this disc say the same thing more subtly. Zappa never lets your mind get too far away from ugly reality, as war, murder, police, Nazis crop up frequently in many contexts. One song, "Mom & Dad," is so grim that it leaves the realm of humor altogether for a moment, and it seems quite evident that Zappa has suffered a momentary lapse in taste. Perhaps he got carried away with this morbid story of a girl slain by policemen; perhaps he only wanted us to think so.

The timeliness of Zappa's message, the accuracy of his barbs, the consummate wit of all his writing tend to make the Beatles' lyrics look vacuous by comparison. But we must be aware that this tendency represents only one point of view. (A point of view pretty close to the Communist doctrine of art in service of the revolution.) The Beatles represent beauty for its own sake. And what purpose does a revolution serve other than making our lives, or someone's lives, more comfortable and more beautiful? If the Beatles were denied us, we'd have a lot less to live for, even in the most utopian of new societies.

With that cover, the Mothers are challenging Lennon, McCartney & Co. musically as well as ideologically. If the music on *Only Money* were anything less than titanic, the whole idea would appear rather ridiculous.

Among the great creators of pop music today, Zappa is one of a select few who developed a vastly sufficient musical language for himself without the aid of the Beatles. His original environment was the rhythm &

blues vocal group sound of the 1950s—especially the El Monte Legion Stadium variety that produced the Penguins, the Medallions, Marvin & Johnny and such stalwarts of the Oldies. Zappa came to know the scene intimately both as spectator and participant. Later, he became deeply involved in contemporary classical music. He has written many pieces of instrumental music, ranging from piano sonatas to that large orchestral work, *Lumpy Gravy*, recorded (for Capitol) but never released. His major influence in this field was probably Edgar Varese, a good selection of whose compositions for instruments and tape machines is available on Columbia (MS 6146).

Only Money contains by far the largest dose of composed electronic music ever heard on a rock record. Note that Zappa's electronic music is not at all the same thing as what Jimi Hendrix makes by skillfully manipulating the natural malfunctions of guitar amplifiers. Zappa's sounds are put together as painstakingly as a symphony. A few seconds of sound on this album will often represent hours of work on the part of Zappa and his recording engineers, using roomsful of sophisticated equipment, and the results of years of experimentation, to create the most powerful and appropriate possible sound.

Six minutes at the end of side 2, and substantial shorter segments on both sides, are filled with such sounds, alone and in combination with "live" instrumental sounds. Perhaps the most striking are the tones that begin and end the six-minute segment (which incidentally is supposed to represent an experience at "Camp Reagan," a penal colony for nonconformists). The manipulation of levels on the two stereo channels produces a really alarming effect, especially through speakers with heavy bass response.

There are many other effects in the engineering and editing which border on electronic music. Much of the editing also is analogous with the editing of modern cinema. There are many brief interludes where speaking voices are heard, often electronically altered. Speech, music, and sounds are all collaged together in bits of all sizes and shapes. At the end of the first side two conversations (one on each channel) are carried on simultaneously, along with the music. The editing throughout the disc is so rapid-fire as to allow the listener no peace.

The closest we get to respite from this is when the Mothers go into a song. Actually the songs themselves are the least revolutionary part of the album. Musically they fairly well resemble the songs on *Absolutely Free*. "Let's Make the Water Turn Black," "The Idiot Bastard Son" and several others are well into the *Absolutely Free* groove, which could well be called the only tenable contemporary approach to the musical comedy idiom. Beside these, and the electronic things, we have one sterling example of Zappa's writing in the oldtime rock idiom—"What's The Ugliest Part of Your Body." The juxtaposition of 1968 ideas to 1954 music is absolutely perfect.

The purely instrumental (meaning guitars, bass, drums) aspect of the Mothers' music is less in evidence on this album than on its two predecessors, both of which had a fair bit of jamming and soloing. Save for an amazing flash of Clapton at the beginning, guitar is mostly used for rhythm only. But Roy Estrada's bass and the double drums (Billy Mundi and Jimmy Carl Black) are with us fairly constantly, and are fairly constantly fantastic. "Flower Punk" (a burlesque of "Hey Joe") has them cutting some really hairy rhythms just like 1 2 3.

The voices also go through some changes. Mostly speed changes. About half the time, they are sped up in various degrees, as part of the whole electronic circus. In fact, there is for my taste just a taste too much of speeded-up vocal sound. The Donald Duck voices certainly make a point, but they satirize more eloquently when the little nuances can be heard at regular speed.

In the right circumstances, the first hearing of this album could well be the most profound record-listening experience a person has ever had. In a day when the term is tossed around very lightly, this album will assuredly and genuinely "blow your mind." The long-range effects, however, may not be quite as strong, for the Mothers depend an awful lot on shock value, and after twenty listenings there isn't so much shock value any more. The Beatles, and a lot of groups who couldn't hold a candle to Zappa for pure genius, do settle down in your mind much better with repeated hearings. There is much in rock music that is essential, that the Mothers do not, cannot, do not attempt to offer. But at the forefront of total creativity they stand alone.

—BARRET HANSEN
4-6-68

UNCLE MEAT
The Mothers of Invention
(Bizarre 2MS-2024)

While it's subtitled "most of the music from the Mothers' movie of the same name which we haven't got enough money to finish yet," it almost doesn't matter whether the movie gets finished or not, for this sound-track-without-a-movie is a consummate piece of work. In fact, from the sketchy description of the movie provided in the liner notes, the Mothers would probably do better to let the thing just rot.

While *Uncle Meat* is subject to the same sort of criticisms that any sound-track score is (from *Blue Hawaii* to *Dr. Zhivago*) it seems better to just evaluate the music as itself and let Frank Zappa hassle with the film.

The four sides are broken up into short musical vignettes, longer musical pieces, and some of the most revealing, incisive monologues in existence. While it is disjointed in the extreme, there is a unity which becomes more apparent when you take into account the music, the packaging, and the Mothers as they have come to be regarded.

That unity is a picture, a very unflattering and absolutely unretouched photograph of that hostile and incomprehensible environment known as Los Angeles. Not Los Angeles as a geographic entity, but Los Angeles as a state of mind. And with the impending Los Angelization of the world, this theme becomes universal.

Perhaps not even a photograph. *Uncle Meat* is an X-ray. It probes the soft underbelly of the Miracle Mile. It sees the freeways not so much as streams of cars or swaths of concrete, but as frantic tedium and open hostility. It examines, even revels in, those very real parts of plastic America that the plastic can't hide: "Nine Types of Industrial Pollution"; "The Dog Breath Variations"; "Our Bizarre Relationship," a monologue by Miss Christine which in 1:05 accurately describes show business glamor as a case of the crabs.

The longer pieces are overdubbings done with such incredible care and painstaking artistry, so exact as to be much closer in structure and in spirit to modern classical music. And yet they, too, are impressions, sometimes melodic, sometimes dissonant, but always honest of the Southern California syndrome. As Frank Zappa says, "basically, this is an instrumental album." And as instrumentation, it is artistry.

The shorter songs are much in the same vein as those on *Ruben and the Jets*, that is a parody of Fifties R&R, except that these have much more outrageous lyrics. "Cruising for Burgers," and "Electric Aunt Jemima" are like that. The only way the Mothers (or anyone else with any sensitivity, for that matter) can face the Plastic Life is to sneer and burlesque.

"We are the ugly remainder," Zappa once said. And here, in part, is presented that remainder. It's pretty apparent from their expertly crafted cynicism, that the thing the Mothers dread most is being taken too serious-

ly. But *Uncle Meat,* more than any of their previous albums, is a serious piece of music. You can't just put it on the set and grab it with half an ear. You've got to listen to it, hard. Much of it isn't easy to follow, although some of it, like their version of "God Bless America," is sheer delight.

The longer instrumental pieces, particularly the whole fourth side, the King Kong suite, takes a good deal of concentration. But it's worth the effort in every way.

—ALEC DUBRO
5-31-68

CRUISING WITH RUBEN AND THE JETS
The Mothers of Invention
(Verve V6 5055-X)

"The present-day composer refuses to die!"
Edgar Varese, July 1921

"Ruben Sano was only 19 when he quit the group to work on his car . . . His girlfriend said she would leave him forever if he didn't quit playing in the band and fix up his car so they could go to the drive-in and make out."
Verve Records Vault Research

"Darling hear my plea . . ."
The Pleas

A few miles outside of Detroit, just about ten years ago,

was a little town consisting of twenty-five hard working souls, a gas station, a church, and six cops—who were there to hassle Jack Scott's Dance Ranch and the eight hundred teenagers who showed up every weekend. Most guys went there to dance with and to pick up the chicks that weren't picked up by the pachukes with the tattoos and the little scar-crosses on the backs of their hands. Kids who weren't that tough came to dance close and watch the pachukes play pool and also to cheer them from a distance when they'd stare down the cops or fight the locals.

It might as well have been Ruben and the Jets that used to play there almost every weekend. Though no one thought they were any good, no one cared, because Ruben and Natcho and Louie and Pana and Chuy knew enough to keep playing no matter if people were cutting each other with broken booze bottles, or actually fighting. One night, when everybody was juiced out of their skulls, the fat cop and his five buddies snuck into the Dance Ranch and pulled out the plug to Ruben's amplifier. The six cops had almost made it out the door when they disappeared under scores of pool cues, boots, bottles, and fists. The kids, totally blasted, dragged the unconscious cops out to their car, handcuffed them, and drove the squad car to the

police station and left it there. It was one of the greatest nights in rock and roll history. The next day the State Police showed up, nailed the Dance Ranch closed, and left it to rot, as it does to this day. Things had gone too far—or at least, Ruben and the Jets no longer had a place to play.

But their music lives on. Years later, Ruben and the Jets have somehow gotten transmogrified into the Mothers, who've finally waxed all those great unforgettable and unrememberable songs that are always just on the tip of everyone's tongue. We tried for years, but we could never quite remember all of "Cheap Thrills, all over the seat/Cheap thrills, your kind of lovin' can't be beat . . ."

Or Ruben's great tribute to Chuck Higgins' classic "Pachuco Hop," his own "Jelly Roll Gum Drop," a tune that contains one of the shittiest chord changes in the history of the recording industry: "You know I wish I might/Get a tiny bite/Of your . . . Jelly Roll Gum Drop." All thirteen cuts are great, right down to the last boppa dooaydoo (except that the drums and bass are played with a little too much imagination, something that can be corrected by playing the record in mono or on a Macy's phonograph).

You can see where Dion and the Belmonts got it from—just listen to "Deseri," especially the dramatic spoken monologue with its echoes of crippled Don Julian and the Meadowlarks: "Deseri, the first day we met/ I'll never forget/I saw you walking down the street/And my heart skipped a beat . . ." (As a favor to people who like to analyze lyrics but don't like to listen to music, all the words are printed on the cover!) Not to mention the lyric roots of all the Mark Denning—"Teen Angel" songs of the late Fifties, obviously a cop from Ruben's classic "Stuff up the Cracks": "Stuff up the cracks/—Turn on the gas/I'm gonna take my life . . ." Cool.

If you were there, you'll love it. "The present-day Pachuco refuses to die!"

—GREIL MARCUS
12-21-68

HOT RATS
Frank Zappa
(Bizarre RS 6356)

This recording brings together a set of mostly little-known talents that whale the tar out of every other informal "jam" album released in rock and roll for the past two years. If *Hot Rats* is any indication of where Zappa is headed on his own, we are in for some fiendish rides indeed.

In the past both Zappa's high-flown "serious music" and his greasy Fifties routines grew heavy-handed, but this album suggests he may be off on a new and much more individual direction, inspired by Captain Beefheart, who is featured prominently on *Hot Rats* and whose *Trout Mask Replica* set him several frontiers beyond anything we've heard from Zappa. Beefheart is one of the true originals of our day, and his raffish dadaism is an excellent tonic for a Zappa too often preoccupied with polemics—his influence shows clearly in much of this record, whether he's actually performing or not.

The new Zappa has dumped both his Frankensteinian classicism and his pachuko-rock. He's into the new jazz heavily, same as Beefheart, and applying all his technical savvy until the music sounds a far and purposely ragged cry from the self-indulgence of the current crop of young white John Coltranes. Ian Underwood's reed work in particular is far more advanced than anything he did with the Mothers.

The album's instrumental highlight comes on "The Gumbo Variations," spotlighting the wildest, most advanced piece of free-form electric violin playing I've ever heard (*who* is "Sugar Cane Harris"?), a slithery performance that sings with the rusty purity that only the most corrosive music can muster.

Zappa himself has an extremely long guitar solo on "Willie the Pimp," but as past numbers like "Invocation of the

Young Pumpkin" have shown, he's really not a jazz improvisor, and his repetitious and surprisingly simple patterns get boring before he's half-way through. But those words! The wily Beefheart spirit strikes again: "I'm a little pimp with my hair gassed back . . . Man in a suit with a bow-tie neck/Wanna buy a grunt with a third-party check/Standin' on the porch of the Lido hotel/Floozies in the lobby love the way I sell . . ."

If you're eager for a first taste of Beefheart or interested in the new approaches to instrumental style and improvisational technique being developed these days, this is as good a place to start as any; a good stepping stone to folks like Ayler, Don Cherry and Cecil Taylor—the real titans these cats learned it from.

—LESTER BANGS
3-7-69

WEASELS RIPPED MY FLESH
The Mothers of Invention
(Bizarre/Reprise 2028)

"Yes, well, Zappa is always delightful, isn't he?" And for once, here is a jacket that *is* worth the price of the record alone. (How can you possibly describe a record cover that lives up to the title *Weasels Ripped My Flesh?*)

Here it is! Another nifty collection of music inspired by Frank Zappa's pre-occupation with Edgar Varese, death, bopping and jacking off.

Once I thought that Zappa and his group might be the saviors of pop music. Now after all the music that they've produced since their Suzie Creemcheese period I'm not sure that I don't still feel much the same. This random collection of editing room snippets recorded at Mothers' concerts over the last few years finds the group peerless in the field of amalgamating satire, musical adventuresomeness, and flash. This could be because they're the only ones attempting it, but no matter.

It's all here: more assaults on the calibrated sexuality of early rock, and jousts at the pomposity which musical avant-guardism has traditionally engendered. Held together with Zappa's Spike Jones-ish bag of tricks and the Mothers' usual impressive control over electronic technology.

Everytime a live audience demands that the group re-hash its circa '67 Supremes imitations the Mothers seem to advance one step further into the realm of musical extremism. "Weasels" is a grand example of the latter. But it's not all Alban Berg revisited by any means; for this latest Zappa comes closer than any other record I can think of to meeting the needs of both rock and jazz listeners. A consummate example of this is the group's version of Little Richard's

"Directly From My Heart To You." The song is rendered against a hard-edged blues back-up that manages to integrate into its midst a swinging Forties-style jazz violin. It coalesces into something at least as "nouveau nouveau" as anything you'll find in recent release on ESP Records.

At the very least this must be one of the most impressive collection of out-takes ever.

—BILL REED
11-1-70

PRETTIES FOR YOU
Alice Cooper
(Straight Records STS 1061)

Alice Cooper is a West Coast Zappa-sponsored group: two guitars, bass, drums and a vocalist who doubles on harmonica. Echoes of 1967 psychedelia in the oscillators and distorted guitars. Showing here the influence of the Mothers, here the first-wave San Francisco sound, there and almost everywhere the Beatles. But their overall texture and the flow of randomly-selected runs interspersed by electronic gimmicks place them closer to a certain rivulet in that deluge of pre-packaged groups which can be defined as marginal acidrock (references: recent debut albums by Aorta and Touch). Droning fuzz leads overlaid by droning (or is it whining?) Bee Gees vocal harmonies, and ponderous quasi-"baroque" organ wallowings a la Vanilla Fudge. Stereotyped guitar solos, a great many of which seem to derive directly (and not surprisingly) from Ray Davies' great fuzztone explosions on early Kinks hits like "You Really Got Me" and "All Day and All of the Night." Apocalyptic raveups patented by the Yardbirds. Spoken "poetry" or "trippy" declamations muttered half-comprehensibly over "atonal" guitar gimmicks (dragging the pick across the strings below the bridge, etc.).

I'm not trying to denigrate Alice Cooper's abilities: within the context of their self-imposed limitations, the album is listenable. But there is a way to do these things. I think simplicity and the imaginative use of the cliche are at the essence of rock; but the cliches have to hit you a certain way, with a certain conviction and energy and timing, to get it on, to spark that certain internal combustion of good feeling and galvanized energies that lifts you out of your seat irresistibly and starts you dancing, balling, just whooping, or whatever—Black Pearl is the most stunning recent realization of this. And it is this that is lacking in Alice Cooper's music. Everything falls where it should, there are none of the gross, ugly, idiotic juxtapositions of the totally incongruous found in much other studio-assembled art-rock. But neither is there any hint of life, spontaneity, joy, rage, or any kind of authentic passion or conviction. As such, Alice Cooper's music is, for this reviewer at any rate, totally dispensable.

—LESTER BANGS
7-12-69

TROUT MASK REPLICA
Captain Beefheart and His
Magic Band
(Straight STS 1053)

Captain Beefheart, the only true dadaist in rock, has been victimized repeatedly by public incomprehension and critical authoritarianism. The tendency has been to chide C. B. and his Band as a potentially acceptable blues band who were misled onto the paths of greedy trendy commercialism. What the critics failed to see was that this was a band with a *vision,* that their music, difficult, raucous and rough as it is, proceeded from a unique and original consciousness.

This became dramatically apparent with their last album. Since their music derived as much from the new free jazz and African chant rhythms as from Delta blues, the songs tended to be rattly and wayward, clattering along on weirdly jabbering high-pitched guitars and sprung rhythms. But the total conception and its execu-tion were more in the nature of a tribal Pharoah Sanders-Archie Shepp fire-exorcism than the ranting noise of the Blue Cheer strain of groups.

Thus it's very gratifying to say that Captain Beefheart's new album is a total success, a brilliant, stunning enlargement and clarification of his art. Which is not to say that it's in any sense slick, "artistic," or easy. This is one of the few bands whose sound has actually gotten *rawer* as they've matured —a brilliant and refreshing strategy. Again the rhythms and melodic textures jump all over the place (in the same way that Cecil Taylor's do); Beefheart singing like a lonesome were-wolf screaming and growling in the night. The songs clatter about—given a superficial lis-tening, they seem boring and repetitious. It's perhaps the ad-dition of saxophones (all played by the five men in the band) that first suggests what's really happening here and always has been happening in this group's music.

On "Hair Pie: Bake One," for instance, the whole group gets into a raucous wrangling horn dialog that reveals a strong Al-bert Ayler influence. The music truly meshes, flows, and excites in a way that almost none of the self-conscious, carefully crafted jazz-rock bullshit of the past year has done. And the reason for this is that while many other groups have picked up on the trappings of the new jazz, Cap and the Magic Band are into its essence, the white-hot stream of un-"cultured" energy, getting there with a minimum of strain to boot. This is the key to their whole instrumental approach, from the drummer's whirling poly- and even a-rhythmic patterns (compare them to Sonny Murray's on Ayler's *Spiritual Unity* or Ed Blackwell's on Don Cherry's *Symphony for Improvisers*), to the explosive, diffuse guitar lines, which (like Lou Reed's for the Velvet Underground or Gary Peacock's bass playing on *Spiritual Unity*) stretch, tear, and distend the electric guitar's usual vocabulary past its present strictly patterned limitations—limitations that are as tyrannically stultifying for the rock musician today as Charlie Parker's influence was for the jazzmen of the late Fifties.

I mustn't forget the lyrics. You certainly won't; the album on a purely verbal level is an explosion of maniacal free-association incantations, eschewing (with the authentic taste that assassinates standards of Taste) solemn "poetic" pretensions and mundane, obvious monosyllabic mindlessness. Where, for instance, have you heard lyrics like these: "Tits tits the blimp the blimp/The mother ship the mother ship/ The brothers hid under the hood/From the blimp the

blimp . . . all the people stir/ 'n' the girls' knees tremble/ 'n' run 'n' wave their hands/'n' run their hands over the blimp the blimp . . ."

The double record set costs as much as two regular albums, but unlike most of these super-long superexpensive items it's really sustained, and worth the money, which is perhaps not so much to pay for 27 songs and what may well be the most unusual and challenging musical experience you'll have this year.

—LESTER BANGS
7-26-69

PERMANENT DAMAGE
The GTO's
(Reprise STS 1059)

When the first sign of spring burst upon Fullerton in late November, the local kids decided, according to the sunny circumstances, to bypass winter altogether that year.

"It's all fucked up," Paulie told his mother as he dropped his books on the table one warm Monday afternoon. Paulie's silent friend, Mark, stood next to him, regarding the mother as Paulie poured them each a glass of lemonade. "We don't *need* winter."

"But you can't just do away with it," his mother frowned as she handed the sixth-graders some cookies. "I mean, you . . ."

Paulie turned and gave her a severe look.

"What do you mean, Mother?"

She lowered her eyes as all good ladies did when Paulie or any of his friends gave them the look.

"Well, I mean, Paulie, that . . . that winter is too important to too many people. It means many different things to many different people, important things, Christmas, New Year's, sledding, fireplaces . . ." She felt the situation slipping away from her. Her eyes shifted about unsteadily. "You know, Paulie, I have many good memories of winter, like growing up in Philadelphia, a teenager on . . ."

Paulie cut her off like a razor through hot lather.

"A teenager on *Bandstand?* A big TV favorite? Steve Rossi, Franny Giordano, *Sixteen,* and all that other crap? Yes, Mother, I know. I've heard it all before, and frankly I'm getting a bit sick of it!"

"Oh, Paulie, I don't understand you sometimes anymore." She sighed and sat down exhausted. "What's happened to you? You were such a nice little boy when you were taking acid. But now . . ."

"Shut up, Mother!" And he suddenly snapped out a smart left jab that caught her squarely in the forehead, splitting the smooth white skin to the bone. "You ain't messin' with my head no more."

Her dark eyes registered nothing but fear for a moment as a trickle of blood crept from the small wound. Her shoulders rose momentarily and then fell with great violence as she buried her face in her hands, sobbing out of control.

"Let's go, Mark," Paulie growled, and he ran off through the stainless steel utility room.

Mark, however, lingered a moment. He had more on his mind as he stood looking down on his best friend's mother. He watched her long body quiver, and then in one insane motion stolen from the late movies he grabbed the woman by her Philadelphia ponytail, wrenched her tearstained face up to his, and pressed his small mouth on her trembling lips. It was over in a second.

"Great lemonade, Mrs. Giammatteo," Mark said, and taking the last cookie, he bounded from the room.

Mrs. Giammatteo sat for many minutes afterward, struck deaf and dumb, her face still inclined toward the ceiling, her eyes half closed. *Speed,* she thought, *it must be speed,* but she didn't really know for sure. She only knew what she read in the papers and she didn't know *anything* for sure. That much she knew. And at that, she knew she was even more afraid of knowing. It was terrifying.

An hour later, however, after a long hot bath, Mrs. Giammatteo sat semi-relaxed on the couch with a Coke, in the den, watching the afternoon soaps and drying her thick hair under the Professional Beauty Jet Hair Dryer. It was a huge bulbous machine that jammed down over her entire head and shoulders, leaving only her face and naked shoulders exposed. She wore only a bathrobe. The great unwieldly machine also made her hearing next to impossible under the roar of the jets. When out of nowhere Paulie's face loomed large in front of her, her heart lept up her throat. She suddenly saw herself in some sort of do-it-yourself electric chair.

Paulie, however, was smiling down at her, his lips moving with a deliberate and certain ease. She couldn't hear him, but she saw his eyes were calm and reassuring, narrowing at times in a manner of genuine sincerity that she hadn't seen in two years. He seemed to be apologizing, agonized and grimacing at times as if angry at himself, overwhelmed perhaps by his own heinous acts, but then she couldn't be too sure. He brought his face down very close to hers, his eyes fluid, a humble crooked smile spreading on his lips as he kissed her bandaged wound softly. *Sweet*, she thought.

Paulie stood up tall again, and from behind him he brought a thin package, obviously a record, and he placed it on her lap. He smiled, pleased with his present. He nodded and gestured at her to open it.

Mrs. Giammatteo slid the album from the bag, and looked it over carefully. *He knows I like music,* she thought ("And they call it puhpee lah-ah-ahve . . . just because we're, we're seventeen"), but the cover didn't ring any recognizable bells in her musical index.

"THE GTO's?" she said in a much too loud voice that she assumed was normal under the incessant rush of air. "Very nice. A pretty cover," although what the strange debauchery on the jacket actually meant was difficult for her to ascertain.

Paulie nodded wildly, a strange maskface taking possession of his features, his wet eyes darting as he backed toward the door.

"Very nice, Paulie. I like it!" she shouted again. "Are there any Paul Anka songs on it? You know I like him." But when she looked up again, her Paulie was gone.

"Paulie?" She glanced around, but the room was empty, empty until her eyes stopped at the window . . . and there she saw two strange and familiar eyes, silent eyes, peering in at her over the window sill.

"Paulie," she called out, but no one answered.

"Paulie?"

—J. R. YOUNG
4-16-69

CANNED HEAT
Canned Heat
(Liberty LST 7526)

BOOGIE WITH CANNED HEAT
Canned Heat
(Liberty LST 7541)

LIVING THE BLUES
Canned Heat
(Liberty LST 27200)

The best of Canned Heat is exactly what Canned Heat wants it to be: good-rockin blues music suitable for balling, dancing, doping, boozing, whatever your thing happens to be, all of them at once maybe. It's a tight band with a tough bass player and a heavy lead guitar, and, if only these were the good old days out of which Canned Heat draws its style and its best material, we might have one really good album from them instead of three so-so ones. In the 1940s, a blues band would put out 78s for years, and finally, if their output warranted it, the parent record company would assemble the best into an album. Today the accent has shifted from quality to quantity; and one result is far too much Canned Heat.

A *Best of Canned Heat* album, culled from all this bulk, would be a gas. It would have "Rollin' and Tumblin'" and "Catfish Blues" and "Dust My Broom" from the first LP; "Evil Woman," "Amphetamine An-nie," "An Owl Song" and "Fried Hockey Boogie" from *Boogie;* and from *Living the Blues* it would take "Walking By My-self," parts of "Parthenogenesis" and lead guitarist Henry Ves-tine's solo on "Refried Boogie." That might be a bit much for one LP, but you could drop even a couple of those without heartbreak.

Until such a record exists, the best bet is probably the *Boogie* album, side two, where Canned Heat gets it together pretty well. They take "Amphetamine Annie" at a nice, chomping, Muddy Waters-like clip, belting these dope lyrics about this chick who's "always shovelin snow":

> *Your mind might think
> you're flyin', babe,
> On those little pills,
> But you ought to know
> it's dyin', 'cause
> (Chorus) Speed kills . . .*

And somehow it's a happy thing, even to the weeping over Annie's death at the end. Along the way, Vestine rips off a preaching, cooking solo. He's nearly always strong, with his big buzzy sound and saxophone-like phrasing.

"An Owl Song" is perhaps Al Wilson's strongest vocal outing to date—his peculiarly high crooning mumble grooving along over a kicking, chugging rhythm section. Vestine is really *down* on the blues "Marie

Laveau." And then comes "Fried Hockey Boogie," which is, at once, the best and the worst of Canned Heat.

It starts with a lot of words from Bob Hite, the lead singer, about the beneficial attributes of boogie-ing, and then a lot more chatter out of Hite all through the whole thing, while you're trying to hear what the musicians are laying down. He talks far too much, and the way he talks—a hype black plantation accent that doesn't make it, sounding instead like the interlocutor at a minstrel show— is perfectly offensive. "Doncha feel gud naow thatcha lissen tuh all 'at boo-geh," he intones over Vestine's storming solo, and reminds us at the end: "An' don't fo-git tuh boo-geh!"

Hite, like all the rest of Canned Heat, is white, and as a means of getting the blues sound he wants, he tock lak lotta dem cats done on dem Libraree uh Con-gress records. And on "Catfish," the first album, when Hite bellows "Ah been knocked out all night . . . Ah's drunk, don't know whut ah'm doin . . . But ah do feel lak boogie-in . . ." it's Tomming in white-face, no other way to slice it; one big drag.

Such is the ethnic cul-de-sac in which an "authentic" white blues band like Canned Heat places itself. If they simply copied the old stuff, it would be easy enough to write them off entirely, but the fact is they

approach nearly every tune afresh. Canned Heat's got its own flavor, its own identity, and not many rock bands can cut them on the energy and musicianship. It's pointless to complain that they do a lot of things old bluesmen have done before, since they make it no secret that this is their point of departure. Indeed, Vestine and Hite have two of the largest blues record collections extant, Wilson is an authoritative researcher into early blues, and the band was begun as a sort of tribute to the music they love.

Either you dig the idea of playing old blues in more or less the old style, or you don't. (Canned Heat does muddy the water even more, however, with a lot of sad packaging. What other band would distribute bumper stickers saying BOO-GIE? And what other band would choose nicknames for its players like "Mole" and "Bear" and "Blind Owl" and "Sunflower"? Can you dig "Blacksnake" Hendrix? "Groundhog" Dylan?)

A quick look at the rest of Canned Heat's output. You'll enjoy the first album if downhome country blues blowing is your thing. They lift a few licks from here and there, but the finished product is their own and it wails. On *Boogie*, we find the rhythm section beginning to loosen just a bit, to get more things going, still blues basically, but in the direction of rock. There's still no indication on *Boogie,* though, of the more personal direction Canned Heat has taken in performance lately. They have begun to use "Refried Boogie" as a vehicle for free playing—for improvisations that often depart completely from tempo, key and the basic chord structure, while retaining the blues feeling. They get into this on "Refried" on *Living the Blues,* though they have done it better. Only places this comes across well are on Larry Taylor's bass solo (not too far out, but nice), and Vestine's volcanic ten-minute excursion. Trouble with "Refried" is that it's 41 minutes long, two whole sides, and only Vestine and Taylor are up to that kind of extended soloing. Al Wilson can play screwy little things, but over the long haul he gets plenty tiresome. And while all long drum solos are boring, Fito De La Parra's are excruciatingly so; it would be hard to think of a less imaginative ten minutes than his "Refried" stint.

Oddly enough, Canned Heat seems listless almost everywhere on the new two-record release. A lot of it sounds so much alike it's hard to distinguish among tracks. The exception is "Parthenogenesis," a 19-minute, 54-second, psychedelic adventure which Canned Heat almost brings off. Had it been edited with more care (and De La Parra's heavy-handed drum solo excised), "Parthenogenesis" (the title means development of an unfertilized egg, appropriately) might have worked. As it is, it sandwiches some heavy Vestine, some crazy blues piano (the album notes don't say who's playing), and a pretty little neo-raga by Wilson on mouth harp, in amongst some dull singing and second-rate electronics.

A problematic band, Canned Heat. There's plenty wrong with them, they're still discovering who and where they are, the best is probably yet to come, etc., etc., etc. But still, and despite each and every objection, it's hard not to dig Canned Heat.

—JOHN BURKS
12-7-68

LOOK INSIDE THE ASYLUM CHOIR
Asylum Choir
(Smash SRS 67107)

As you might guess from their name, Asylum Choir is a Los Angeles group. Like L.A., it is sometimes tasteless and crass, but it is vital, freaky and exciting. Leon Russell and Marc Benno wrote and produced the album, apparently in a frenzy. Reportedly they play all the instruments heard on it, with the help of an electronic synthesizer.

The music is good-times rock;

it has the same funky joy that the Spoonful used to do, before Fame and Changes cut their strings. The influence of Dylan is evident in the many country harmonies, and you can hear the ghost of Jerry Lee Lewis stalking the keyboard. The instrumental is slithery and funky, punctuated by outrageous sound effects. It is freaky stuff, but it hangs together well; the sound effects are well-done and funny, and almost never become tiresome game-playing. The vocals are rough and even rude, but rock could use a bit more rudeness. Some few times the lyrics and the production are not daring, but merely stupid, but still, their stupidity is unpretentious and interesting.

The album begins by putting its feet solidly in L.A. "Welcome to Hollywood" is brassy and satirical, complete with Movietone Fanfare of Imperishable Brass, and some strange sound-things that sound like King Kong attended the session. "Icicle Star Tree" is spaced fantasy, which lurches along at a funny, uneven tempo. "Soul Food" has the sort of upfront outrageous humor that makes singles into hits. "Indian Style," which has been getting a fair amount of play on the San Francisco rock stations, is not a George Harrison tedium-raga, but is a whooping satire on the fad for Indian Philosophy and style: "New Yawwkk City's going Indian style/With an Indian Flower Child." The album has no bad tracks at all —each song makes its point, insanely but amusingly.

As rock becomes more and more a producer's medium, there has been a tendency for excitement and musical daring to fade away, filtered out by days and days spent in the studio. So many of the best groups—the Airplane, the Dead, Moby Grape—sound stifled and stuffed on records. The Asylum Choir's is a well produced album, but it has not lost *presence;* you can feel the music as well as hear it.

The Choir's impact is partly due, undoubtedly, to its insanity. It isn't psychotic in the same way that Hendrix, say, is—the Choir's insanity is enjoyable in much the same way the movie *King of Hearts* was enjoyably insane.

The Choir hasn't been receiving a lot of attention, but they are already well developed and together. If they survive the second-album temptation to go through changes, they may prove to be a major voice in rock.

—DAVID GANCHER
11-23-68

LEON RUSSELL
Leon Russell
(Shelter SHE 1001)

Fine and funky—that's Leon Russell's first album out on his

own, away from his producer/ arranger/back-up role with De- laney and Bonnie, Joe Cocker, even the Stones ("Live with Me"). But that word "away" is misleading, since all those folks —and then some—are present, if not accounted for, on his al- bum too; gentlemen with such Christian surnames as Harrison and Starr, Wyman and Watts, Clapton and Voorman. An au- gust assembly, you might say.

Yet no sense of heavy-handed helping out, or high-minded seriousness, or superstar-gazing accrues. That's the Russell funk- iness at work—every cut, for all the polish evidenced, still retains a feeling of late-night, good-time get-together. Like Clapton and Harrison joining up with the Bramletts just to enjoy themselves, you sense that Russell's friends are there be- cause working with him is fun. The earthiness is there too, what Gram Parsons—who ought to know—means when he desig- nates somebody as "funky": "people who don't know nothin' 'cept the bottom of a beer can when they see it through the hole." In Russell's case, that be- comes his gospel get-it-on en- thusiasm, his mushmouthed and straining vocals, his omnipres- ent down-home piano, and his Southern subject matter.

So every cut has something going for it. A few of the 12 collapse en route, but most make it. Oddly enough, the very first cut is one of those

that falters, a resonating love ballad called "A Song for You" with too much in the way of agony-vibrato and Gershwin piano from Russell. But that number and an amusing novel- ty, Russell singing "Masters of War" while playing the national anthem, are his only solo out- ings.

On to the good, good stuff, like two ragged and happy gos- pel shouts, Russell originals with, for some reason, "bor- rowed" titles: "I Put a Spell on You" and "Give Peace a Chance." Both feature laughter and false starts, the soulful Bramletts and, on the former at least, the Stones' own rhythm section; and there's a home- grown, mess-around air to each that knocks me out, especial- ly the distinctly *un*peaceful tambourine-piano crescendo in "Peace." Eric Clapton adds his own indelible mark to another semi-gospel number, "Prince of Peace": "Never treat a brother like a passing stranger . . . It might be the Prince of Peace returning." Russell's piano lies low, as does the bass (by Voor- man?), and Clapton picks im- pressively in his "new," relaxed, flowing manner.

It's the Beatles' turn on the album's nicest ballad, a slow rocker called "Hummingbird." George Harrison alone starts the tune moving in a Missis- sippi-Delta, "Can't Be Satisfied" vein, then Russell's piano stut- ters in, clashing just enough to keep things lively—and can that really be Ringo doing the fingers-and-palm drumming? Too much. And it gets even better as Russell sings movingly and convincingly, "She gets me where I live,/I give her all I have to give,/talking 'bout that hummingbird," while someone's heavily comping organ builds behind and, finally, the Bramlett gang joins in for the spirited finish.

Ringo's supposedly around too on the album's most interesting cut of all, the bizarre "Shoot Out on the Plantation." If any of Russell's tunes is truly low-down and funky, this is the one. First off, it's his retelling of an actual incident that occurred among L.A.'s crowd of transplanted Tulsa musicians (which mean the "Plantation" of the song is probably that building once occupied by Taj Mahal and Indian Ed Davis and the others). An infamously funky cat named Junior Markham got into some "woman poisonin'" trouble with another musician, a Galveston boy who took out after the knife-wielding Markham with a gun. From this barren incident, Russell has constructed an incredible song: "Junior's been livin' in the blackboard jungle with his Elvis Presley hair . . . And stabbin' your friend is such a drag to boot." Ringo's drumwork is typically straightforward, Russell himself drives things with his flailing piano, and Chris Stainton mixes in as well. Slowly, gradually, the disparate elements behind Russell's slurred yet tense vocal build to an overwhelming cacophony, a creative chaos of jarring, *warring* sounds that somehow still remain . . . musical. It's a regular tour de funk.

Funky people, deceptively amateurish production, thoroughly professional musicianship, and a Bull Durham barn full of fun—that's Leon Russell's Shelter album.

—ED LEIMBACHER
4-16-70

DELANEY & BONNIE & FRIENDS ON TOUR WITH ERIC CLAPTON
Delaney & Bonnie & Friends with Eric Clapton
(Atco 33-326)

"FREE THE PEOPLE"
Delaney & Bonnie & Friends
(Atco 45-6756)

Six Archbishops of Canterbury are buried in Croydon, England, and if you're a connoisseur of orange marmalade, the variety that comes in those handmade earthenware crocks comes from Croydon, too. It's also a "swinging place for big shows," because Croydon was the scene of a concert that was to become Delaney & Bonnie & Friends' first album for Atco, *On Tour With Eric Clapton.*

The Croydon audience, which

more than likely went to see their local-boy-made-good Eric Clapton, rather than Delaney & Bonnie, ended in giving D & B a most enthusiastic reception. Rightly so, for even though they occasionally laid things on a bit thick, Delaney & Bonnie & Friends with Eric Clapton put on a show that was a beautiful hybrid of southern funk and British rock.

The Friends were fantastic at Croydon, especially Carl Radle on bass and Jim Gordon on drums, probably the tightest rhythm section going these days. The horns don't get it on quite so well, and sometimes get carried away with second-hand Beatles licks more than they should. "Only You Know And I Know," is really overdone by the horns, and they overwhelm everyone except themselves.

Eric Clapton is a whiz on guitar, though he keeps to himself a lot, for fear of taking the spotlight from Delaney or Bonnie. On "Things Get Better," for example, Clapton takes an extended solo exploring the possibilities of one note. Eric seems to have found a new humility during his association with Delaney Bramlett, and it is reflected in his playing. Diehard Clapton fans might be disappointed, but it's nice to see someone of obvious talents decide to quit being a Pop Star and start being a good musician.

Delaney is developing into an amazing singer, as shown on his tribute to Robert Johnson, "Poor Elijah," and his work with Bonnie is getting into the realm of the finest boy-girl soul duets that anyone's done. Bonnie sings one solo, "That's What My Man Is For," and she's not bad, but she's been in better voice on the Bramletts' previous albums for Elektra and Stax. Ah, well, perhaps the girl can't help it.

If there was ever any doubt as to the future of Delaney & Bonnie & Friends after Clapton's departure, it's all been forgotten. Their first, post-Clapton single, "Free the People," is a sheer delight. Opening with Salvation Army horns playing "Rock of Ages," Bonnie sings in her best Sunday schoolgirl voice, "Free the people from the fire/Pull the boat out of the raging sea./Tell the devil he's a LIEyuh,/Come and save the likes of me." Delaney picks it up with his verse, punctuated by some hilarious horn riffs, and then they take off—just like "Hey, Jude" with a tuba. Some Top 40 stations have picked up on it, and with luck, it'll be a hit.

And next time you spread orange marmalade on your English muffins (or whatever you spread it on), think of Croydon. A lot of people there love Delaney & Bonnie.

—CHAS. BURTON
7-9-70

ERIC CLAPTON
Eric Clapton
(Atco SD 33-329)

"Bet you didn't think I knew how to rock and roll . . ."

Well, to tell you the truth, Eric, we had begun to wonder. What with all the running around you've been doing of late, we'd begun to worry that you'd become just another studio musician, hobnobbing with the rich and famous. After all, overexposure to Leon Russell has been known to turn some people into wind-up tambourine-beating rocknroll dolls.

But no. Even though it's a "supersession," even though the personnel is liberally salted with old Delaney and Bonnie Friends, it comes off as a warm, friendly record of the kind that I haven't heard since the first Delaney and Bonnie album. Of the tunes, we have some good old tambourine beaters, one beautiful all-acoustic piece authored entirely by Clapton (most of the rest are by him and Delaney Bramlett, who produced), and a bunch of simply delightful D&B-styled gospel-type numbers, which, unlike a lot of the recent attempts in this genre, succeed because they build sensibly to a climax rather than indulging in the type of excess that spoiled Leon Russell's album, at least for me.

Clapton's voice is a revelation. He'd been scared to use it before because he thought it was terrible, but Delaney told him that his voice was a gift from God, and if he didn't use it, maybe God would take it away from him. Which, I thought, is maybe a nice way of saying "Well, maybe it ain't too hot, but you should sing along anyway." But Clapton's voice is just fine; rough and unfinished, maybe, but it adds to the rustic quality of the music.

"Bet you didn't think I knew how to rock and roll . . ."

Sure I did, Eric. And you play a mean guitar, too.

—ED WARD
9-3-70

WITH A LITTLE HELP FROM MY FRIENDS
Joe Cocker
(A&M SP 4182)

Joe Cocker and the Grease Band were ending a performance they gave recently at the Whiskey in Los Angeles. As they went into their explosive version of "With A Little Help From My Friends," a nubile young admirer, apparently driven wild by Cocker's amazing voice and insane spastic contortions, stationed herself on her back between Cocker's legs and, reaching up, began to work the Cocker cock with considerable fervor. Moments later Joe delivered the scream of his career.

Which is not to say that everyone will react with such frenzy to this latest and perhaps greatest British bearer of the Ray Charles tradition, but that Cocker's first album, a gem, should cause an awful lot of excitement. Despite the fact that he's a twenty-four-year-old product of Sheffield, England, Cocker's voice is that of a middle-aged Southern black man—and the quality of his voice enables him to transcend (as does Ray Charles on his coke commercials) the lyrics and the traditional happy associations of such originally sprightly tunes as "Bye Bye Blackbird," turning them into astonishing, compelling expressions of pain and desperation.

That Cocker is a Charles imitator is beyond argument—at various places on his album he even receives vocal backing from former Raelettes. But Cocker has assimilated the Charles influence to the point where his feeling for what he is singing cannot really be questioned. And, in answer to the question of why someone should listen to Cocker when there is Charles to listen to—how many times in recent years has the latter applied himself to such exceptional modern material as Dave Mason's "Feelin' Alright?" or such contemporary Dylan as "I Shall Be Released" (of which Cocker does the most evocative, moving version I've yet heard)?

Denny Cordell, late of Procol Harum fame, deserves a feverish round of applause for producing this album, in spite of such momentary lapses as stealing almost intact Havens' arrangement of "Just Like A Woman" and letting Jimmy Page nearly capsize "Bye Bye Blackbird" with a completely inappropriate solo. Cordell was so determined to come up with a perfect album (and the album *is* nearly perfect) that he spent over a year and a small fortune getting everything just so. For instance, he's reportedly got ten excellent takes of "Released" in a can somewhere, having decided that none of the takes—done by Al Kooper and Aynsley Dunbar among others—were quite good enough. Cordell's success in fusing a consistently marvelous backing unit out of America's premier studio soul singers and England's most famous rock musicians and delicate egos cannot be exaggerated.

Besides such material as the Dylan, Mason and Beatle stuff there are three originals written by Cocker and Grease Band keyboard man Chris Stainton: "Marjorine" (a Stainton puppet show score to which Joe added words), "A Change in Louise," and "Sandpaper Cadillac," all of which are brilliant rock tunes. It's a triumph all around. And the thought of Cocker's next album, which will include new Harrison and McCartney songs and a lot more Grease Band originals, is an exceptionally pleasant one.

—JOHN MENDELSOHN
8-23-69

JOE COCKER!
Joe Cocker
(A&M SP 4224)

Joe Cocker's delightful second album is ample proof that the imagination that transformed a song so fixed in our minds as "With A Little Help From My Friends" has not run out of things to do, nor fallen into the trap of "stylization."

Joe, his Grease Band, and their friends—who together form one of the toughest rhythm and blues bands outside of the Motown studios—start from the bottom up in re-arranging material as familiar as "Dear Landlord" or "She Came In Through the Bathroom Window." It's not a matter of "improving" the songs, but of removing them from their original sound and conception to such a degree that they remain great music and still don't really remind the listener of the original versions. The feeling one gets when listening to, say, Aretha's version of "The Weight"—"Wow, they must have really been *reaching* on that one"—doesn't happen when Joe and his band make music.

Not just anyone can carry off lines like those, from Leonard Cohen's "Bird on the Wire": "Like a bird on the wire . . . I will try, in my way, to be free." When Joe sings it those words seem as timeless as the wisdom of the blues.

If Cocker himself is beginning to sound like a master, his band has surprised as well. Their introduction to "She Came In Through the Bathroom Window" sounds like a fat man splitting his pants—and then Cocker falls in like he slipped on a bar of soap. The song itself has that hilarious circus sound of Dylan's "Can You Please Crawl Out Your Window." And maybe that's not a coincidence.

It would be fun to hear Cocker experiment with different sorts of back-up groups. While there are certainly limits to what he can do, they are broad enough to keep him going for a long, long time. Limits or no, what's special about Joe Cocker is that he is so much fun to listen to, because the fun he's having—on stage, picking his phantom guitar with mad frenzy, or on record, letting his own excesses communicate his real emotion—is completely infectious.

—GREIL MARCUS
2-21-70

Music

That

Will

Endure

~~~~~~

Even the most successful records in rock and roll have only a fleeting popularity. The average life of a hit single on the Top 40 is approximately five weeks. Some of the music, however, has lasting significance which makes it listenable year after year. *Rolling Stone* reviewers have always been quick to call these rare masterpieces to our attention.

~~~~~~~~~~~~~~~~~~~~~~~~~~~~~~~~~~

LORD SUTCH AND HIS HEAVY FRIENDS
Lord Sutch
(Cotillion Records 9015)

Lord Sutch is one of those names that's been popping up in the English scene for years, appearing with the Animals here, Manfred Mann there, Gerry and the Pacemakers back then, and so on, and as the liner notes point out (significantly?), "he originated the long hair trend back in 1960." Apparently he's been resting on such laurels ever since, because he's terrible, absolutely terrible. The album is even more regrettable because his "heavy friends" (Jimmy Page, Jeff Beck, Noel Redding, Nicky Hopkins, Jon Bonham and others . . . not exactly a dearth of talent, by any means) try to get it together with their own particular brand of heavy sounds, but with the absolute restriction of Lord Sutch's not-so-singular lack of talent (singing, writing, and arranging are not his strong points . . . but since it is his album . . .), the big boys end up straining on each track, and thus in the final analysis sound like a fouled parody of themselves.

It's hard to imagine that Page or Beck or Hopkins could be pleased with what went down, especially when Lord Sutch relied so heavily upon them (the album is full of tracks with the Lord screaming inane lyrics such as "gotta be played on Jeff's guitar," or "with Jimmy Page you can't go wrong." Bet again, man). Either Lord

Sutch is a very dear and old friend of them all, or they owe him some incredible debt of gratitude, because there's no other reason for any of them to be there. If it's a debt, let's hope this pays it. If they're old friends, let's hope they don't burden us again with such an unnecessary public demonstration. It hurts too much.

—J. R. YOUNG
4-2-70

SALVATION
Original Cast
(Capitol SO 337)

I took this record home and put it on my hi-fi. The changer mechanism clicked and paused. The record dropped. And then the tone arm went limp.

I mean, to say they don't get it on is an understatement.

Since the ordinary record buyer never sees any examples of that extraordinary intra-industry phenomenon called a "promo packet," I'd like to share with you the artifacts that are coming to music biz people with this record. In a WW II surplus K-Rations pack, we find: (1) gloves, surgeons', pure natural latex, one pair (2) first-aid dressing, carlisle model, one small (3) lip Ivo, one stick (4) Heatabs, emergency heating, 8 units (5) pork slices, with juices, 5-½ oz. tin (6) corn flake bar, survival type, type 1 (7) rubber prophylactic in foil

(8) emergency drinking water, one tin (9) Song and Service Book for Ship and Field. Also a pair of goggles and a can opener (10, 11).

The message in all this is perhaps not obvious, unless it's too obvious. The Army-Navy field hymnal makes one meaning plain, though: something for everyone. There is a Protestant Section, then a Catholic Section, then a Jewish Section. Then Christmas carols, assorted hymns, patriotic songs. Then spirituals and Stephen Foster songs ("Old Black Joe").

See, what *Salvation* depends on is B'd-way ballads, fake rock, and fake soul that will send wrinkles up and down your spine. Just once, for the experience, see whether you can listen to the unforgettable spiritual, "There Ain't No Flies on Jesus!"

—CHARLES PERRY
12-13-69

STORMY WEEKEND
Mystic Moods Orchestra
(Philips PHS 600-342)

I have a friend who has a psychedelic pad. He approached me the other day at work and said: "You oughta see my pad now, man. I've got it fixed up all psychedelic—fishnet hanging from the ceiling with beercans and starfish in it, purple lights, posters on the walls, and a whole wall covered with stacked beercans. Only trouble is I need some psychedelic music to go with it."

"Don't you have any records?"

"Oh yeah, I've got some by the Mystic Moods Orchestra—that's real *love* music. Just before I start to maneuver the broad into the bedroom I put on those Mystic Moods albums. It's got lotsa violins, but the part that really gets 'em is the sound effects of crickets and falling rain. It's got a whole storm on it. By the time those train whistles blow they're just like butter in my hands!"

"Then what do you need with psychedelic music?" I wondered.

"The preliminaries, man, the preliminaries! You know, used to be when you try to make a chick you had to have a good car. You got a Vette like me, they'd say 'Let's go fuck.' But now they all want you to have all kindsa psychedelic stuff. You get a lotta records in the mail —why don't you bring me some real, you know, *weird* ones; some of that acid-rock!"

I did just that. I went home and got albums by the Chocolate Watchband, Hapshash and the Colored Coat, Alice Cooper, the Electric Lucifer and several other outstanding acts, and sold them to him for a dollar apiece. Two weeks later I asked him how he liked them, and he said: "I haven't finished listening to them yet."

I didn't tell him, but personally I find that those hippie broads come across quicker for the Mystic Moods Orchestra. If the music doesn't get 'em, the psychedelic poem on the jacket will: "Stormy Weekend forecasting—Music showers from the Milky Way—Thunder dust from a blue black puff—Electric stars seep into the sultry night. . . . Or is it an illusion?"

So, men, if you want those hot little pussies to tumble rapturously into the old sack, just comb your hair down and pick up on the romantic sounds of the Mystic Moods Orchestra. It works!

—LESTER BANGS
6-25-70

THE AMERICAN REVOLUTION
David Peel and the Lower East Side
(Elektra EKS 74069)

Picture this: the group down the street is rehearsing in a garage. They have a guitar, a beginner drum, and a tambourine. They do not have a sound system for voice, so the "singer" screams as loud as he can to get over the blasting guitar, which is turned up all the way on its huge amp (which mom bought for Christmas). Now, put it in stereo, have Peter Siegal produce it, and put it on Elektra. You have *The American Revolution* by David Peel and the East Side. The gist of the album is as follows: side one/ doing what you like is good pot is very very good it should be legalized the pigs are bad and stupid and everyone should get high because it is good; side two/violence is bad girls are made to love and draft board is bad and nasty God is good and as this thing says "Why is there war, God?" If you ever have the chance, instead of folding the album cover out, try folding it *in*. Then fold it over again and again until it is about one inch square and a foot high. Leave the record in the jacket while you are folding.

—MARK LEVITON

4-30-70

The

Motor City

Madness

~~~~~~

Detroit will forever go down in history as the home of the Motown (Motor Town) Sound. If and when that history is written, and a little marginal space is left over for a footnote, you'll find the names of the MC-5 (Motor City Five) and the Stooges, nee The Psychedelic Stooges, two bands that came from suburban, collegiate Ann Arbor, Michigan.

The search for new talent and new commodities led Elektra Records to an urban commune where poet/revolutionary/White Panther John Sinclair was supporting some several dozen of his hippie radicals and a *rock as revolution* theory off the energies and gate receipts of the MC-5. Friendly with the Five's musicians were another group, the Stooges, and they made Elektra Records, too.

That's not all . . .

KICK OUT THE JAMS
MC-5
(Elektra 74042)

Whoever thought when that dirty little quickie *Wild in the Streets* came out that it would leave such an imprint on the culture? First the Doors (who were always headed in that direction anyway) grinding out that famous "They-got-the-guns-but-we-got-the-numbers" march for the troops out there in Teenland, and now this sweaty aggregation. Clearly this notion of violent, total youth revolution and takeover is an idea whose time has come—which speaks not well for the idea but ill for the time.

About a month ago the MC-5 received a cover article in *Rolling Stone* proclaiming them the New Sensation, a group to break all barriers, kick out all jams, "total energy thing," etc. etc. etc. Never mind that they came on like a bunch of 16-year-old punks on a meth power trip—these boys, so the line ran, could play their guitars like John Coltrane and Pharoah Sanders played sax!

Well, the album is out now and we can all judge for ourselves. For my money they come on more like Blue Cheer than Trane and Sanders, but then my money has already gone for a copy of this ridiculous, overbearing, pretentious album; and maybe that's the idea, isn't it?

The set, recorded live, starts out with an introduction by John Sinclair, "Minister of Information" for the "White Panthers," if you can dig that. The speech itself stands midway between *Wild in the Streets* and Arthur Brown. The song that follows it is anticlimactic. Musically the group is intentionally crude and aggressively raw. Which can make for powerful music except when it is used to conceal a paucity of ideas, as it is here. Most of the songs are barely distinguishable from each other in their primitive two-chord structures. You've heard all this before from such notables as the Seeds, Blue Cheer, Question Mark and the Mysterians, and the Kingsmen. The difference here, the difference which will sell several hundred thousand copies of this album, is in the hype, the thick overlay of teenage-revolution and total-energy-thing which conceals these scrapyard vistas of cliches and ugly noise.

"Kick Out the Jams" sounds like Barret Strong's "Money" as recorded by the Kingsmen. The lead on "Come Together" is stolen note-for-note from the Who's "I Can See for Miles." "I Want You Right Now" sounds *exactly* (down to the lyrics) like a song called "I Want You" by the Troggs, a British group who came on with a similar sex-and-raw-sound image a couple of years ago (remember "Wild Thing"?) and promptly disappeared into oblivion, where I imagine they are laughing at the MC-5.

—LESTER BANGS
4-5-69

SIRS:

Your coverage of the MC-5 thus far has been characterized, I believe, by a not unusual inability to understand the climate or culture of Detroit, which remains the most explosive city in the nation.

"Revolution is Poetry" exclaimed the surrealist Breton, and for over four years the MC-5 have been living by that maxim. I lived near the Five in the Detroit ghetto, and heard the midnight bombs blasting their commune apart.

The MC-5 are serious revolutionaries, and John Sinclair—for all his hulking, almost crude, simplicity—has a profound grasp of the theory of revolution, art, and media. In their efforts to radicalize white youth, the White Panthers —the political arm of the Five's philosophy— —have been publishing broadsheets as well as books, organizing underground papers as well as visiting high schools. The emphasis is on obtaining access to, and building, media in order to liberate kids from the false consciousness perpetrated upon them by their parents and the authorities.

We grew up with hard rock and roll, and before Carl Perkins and Little Richard became vogue again, Sinclair and I were taking old records and dope into the college classroom to explain how rock has been integrally related to the rebellion of our generation.

Well how far does it go, man? How far can rock and roll be pushed? The MC-5 say to the wall—to revolution in our lives, leading to revolution in our institutions.

The MC-5's first album should be judged in perspective, as the first album of a knowledgeable group breaking into—and trying to lead the public into—a new thing. (Some of the tapes of the Five recorded in Detroit bars with black jazz groups like Lyman Woodard is incredible.)

Kick Out the Jams is hardly a flawless album, but the extraordinary cuts, including "Come Together," suggest a power that has not been heard in rock for a decade. If the Five's second album lives up to its potential, it may predicate a new direction in rock, and a reversal of the present counterfeit trend toward pseudo-serious, pseudo-hip, commercialized "super" rock.

The power structure— including the rock establishment—is vitally interested in suppressing the MC-5, the only group in America that is dedicated first to our revolutionary culture, and then to our music as an extension of that culture. What other group would have the balls to run a full-page ad reading "Kick out the Jams Motherfucker, and if the store won't sell you the MC-5, kick the doors down!"

I hope *Rolling Stone* doesn't come to identify with and be an apologist for the genteel hip-capitalist establishment.

—ART JOHNSON,
WHITE PANTHER
SAN FRANCISCO

THE STOOGES
The Stooges
(Elektra EKS 74051)

As we all remember, in 1957, it was conclusively proven that there exists a causal relationship between rock and roll and juvenile delinquency. This record is just another document in support of this thesis.

The Stooges, formerly the Psychedelic Stooges, hail from Ann Arbor, Michigan, where, in case you've never been told, they do things high-powered—high-powered music, high-powered doping, high-powered fucking, high-powered hyping. The Stooges used to share a house with another local band whom they greatly resemble—the MC-5. The picture on the cover of the album shows the Stooges to be four nice middle-class-kids-gone-wrong wearing brand-new synthetic leather jackets and pouting at the camera in a kind of snot-nosed defiance. They don't look at all that bright, although they may be college dropouts, and I'm sure that all the high school kids in the area dig the hell out of them. Three of them play guitar, bass, and drums, while picturesque Iggy sings in a blatantly poor imitation early Jagger style. The instrumentalists sound like they've been playing their axes for two months and playing together for one month at most, and they just *love* wah-

wah and fuzz just like most rank amateur groups. The lyrics are sub-literate, as might be inferred by the titles: "No Fun," "Not Right," "Little Doll," and "Real Cool Time." This last is the monument of the Stooges' artistry: "Can-uh Ah come ovuh/Tognat-uh?/We will have a real cool tam-uh/We will have a real cool tam-uh . . ." Their music is loud, boring, tasteless, unimaginative and childish.

I kind of like it.

Granted that the Stooges are all I have said them to be, how can I explain this away? Well, it is certainly an understatement to say that they have a marked lack of pretension. They are a *reductio ad absurdum* of rock and roll that might have been thought up by a mad D.A.R. general in a wet dream. They suck, and they know it, so they throw the fact back in your face and say "So what? We're just havin' fun." They emit a raw energy reminiscent of the very earliest British recordings—ever listen to the first two Kinks records?—and while there is ample reason to put them down, the fun is infectious, and that's more than you can say about most of the stuff coming out nowadays.

The album itself is, I am told, far better than the Stooges are in person, where they rely heavily on visual effects and loud freak-out scrapings of guitar strings and bashing of amps. Producer John Cale, a former member of the Velvet Underground, has squeezed everything he could out of them, and he has done a fine job. The only place where the album falls down, it falls with a resounding thud. "We Will Fall" is a ten-minute exercise in boredom that ruins the first side of the record. The rest of it—well, when something is as simple as the Stooges' music, it would take an artist to ruin it.

So, cats and kitties, if you want to have a real cool time, just bop on down to your local platter vendor and pick up the Stooges' record, keeping in mind, of course, that it's loud, boring, tasteless, unimaginative, childish, obnoxious. . . .

—ED WARD
10-18-69

FUNHOUSE
The Stooges
(Elektra EKS 74071)

Ah, good evening my good friend. Good evening and welcome to the Stooges' Funhouse. We are so glad you could come. Oh, do not be alarmed, dear one, if things should seem a trifle unusual . . . or, as the natives say, "oh-mind" . . . at first. You'll doubtless get used to it. Perhaps, you may even begin to . . . *like* the things you see.

Why do you look so pale, my friend? Why, that's only tenor saxophonist Steve Mac-

kay vigorously fucking drummer Scott Asheton, dog-style. Steve is a new member of the band, you know, but like Iggy and the rest of the boys are saying, he really fits in, *n'est-ce pas?* How smart he looks in his new black leather jacket. And that swastika on Scott's lapel. How *killer* . . . how terribly, terribly *killer.*

And that man over there? The one being slowly whipped with the long, curly tendrils of that young lass' hair? Why, that's none other than Don Galucci, who produced the Stooges' latest album. He was the producer of the song "Louie, Louie" by the Kingsmen, you know. Here. I have the original words to it written on this piece of paper. Perhaps you would like to read them.

Oh, thank you, Mr. Galucci. Please *do* put on the new Stooges record. It would be *so* nice for our guest to hear.

Mercy! "Down On the Street," what a super killer jam! That is why I love the Stooges so, you know, and why I have stayed here at the Funhouse with the boys for so very long. They are so exquisitely horrible and down and out that they are the ultimate psychedelic rock band in 1970. Don't you agree?

Don't laugh. You mustn't laugh. The new record is much more sophisticated than their first. And you cannot deny that they are the best Detroit area rock band. Why, Iggy was just telling me that when he plays with other Detroit and Michigan area bands, that he feels, not like King of the Mountain, but King of the Slag Heap! Can you imagine that? King of the Slag Heap! How super oh-mind, no?

Do you think you might like to . . . see Iggy? Well, all right. But you must take care not to disturb him. When Pop is really "Jonesed," there's really no telling what could happen. His scars *do* take so long to heal, you know, and he is so slight, sometimes I can't help worry about him, but can you blame me?

He should be behind that door, in that room. Perhaps, if we're lucky, he might be spreading peanut butter upon his phallus. Why, sometimes, he'll lock himself in there for days screaming, "I feel all right!" at the top of his lungs until he passes out. And then, it is said, before he can arise again, a 14-year-old girl must perform oral intercourse upon his comatose body. Oh! He has heard us! Do be quick, my friend, before he can get it together to react! Heavens! What a close shave, eh, *mon ami?*

Ah, no, you mustn't be leaving so soon. There is yet so much you have not yet seen, so many things strange, killer, and oh-mind. Well, if you must, then I suppose you must. Sometime soon you will pay us a return visit, all right, dear one? Thank you for stopping by ever so much.

You. Out there. What are you doing? Do you long to have your mind blown open so wide that it will take weeks for you to pick up the little, bitty pieces? Do you yearn for the oh-mind? Do you ache to feel all right?

Then by all means, you simply must come visit us at the Stooges' Funhouse. I know the boys would look forward to seeing you. In fact . . . they'd be . . . simply *delighted.*

—CHARLIE BURTON
8-29-70

The

Masked Marauders

and

Other Curiosities

The fads come and go. Among these was the "super-session," basically a one-time grouping of star musicians to make a record. Al Kooper, the organist from New York City, is credited with the idea, although it is just a slightly more commercialized all-star jazz jam thing brought up to date.

Kooper's first record at it was pretty good. (It introduced Stephen Stills as a *lead* guitarist.) For the record, that review is in this chapter.

Back to the perishability of popular art: the super-session led to one imitation after the next, each one becoming increasingly worthless (though there are exceptions to every rule).

Out of this confusion came the Masked Marauders, an innocent hoax dreamed up by Greil Marcus and Bruce Miroff. Under the pseudonym of T. M. Christian (The Magic Christian) they reviewed a non-existent album titled the Masked Marauders, claiming it was a super-session done in Hudson Bay Canada featuring . . .

You read it. And if you believe it, well, what is going on these days?

(The Masked Marauders hoax occurred, by the way, simultaneously with the rise of Spiro Agnew and the Paul McCartney death rumor. Somehow they seem intimately connected.)

The response to the review was enormous. Thousands believed it. A few readers letters are included here from a subsquent issue's letter section. And Warner Brothers, two months later, issued an album of that name, following the track by track analysis of the review, and sold over 100,000 copies of it. At $4.98.

For the historical record, "I Can't Get No Nookie," the single released from the album, was attacked by Federal Communications Commission Chairman Dean Burch as "obscene." Would you believe what our parents listen to?

~~~~~~~~~~~~~~~~~~~~~~

SUPER SESSION
Mike Bloomfield, Al Kooper,
    Steve Stills
(Columbia CS 9701)

Taking into consideration the various parts that Kooper has played in the production of this album, the fact that he does play more than the others (including the parts on which he backs up a given soloist and the generous periods of group interaction) this must be considered his latest LP. Latest, since the Blood Sweat and Tears album, and an excellent follow-up to that most extraordinary of past LPs.

The personnel shifts slightly (from side to side) in the form of the lead guitarist. Side One features Bloomfield, Side Two is Stills. The music on Side One seems to be fitted closer together, generally contemplating that specific area of the Blues which Bloomfield and Kooper combined carve out for themselves. Side Two deals more generally with music, exploring various territories. Each tune

standing out and up as an individual treatment and track.

The backup group which so faithfully supports and inserts its powerfully defined talents to aid the "headliners" are from left to right: Harvey Brooks (Bass); Eddie Hoh (Drums); and added on the first two tracks on Side One. Barry Goldberg (Electric Piano). The Bloomfield side is particularly excellent. Michael is heard playing better than one can hear him on records ever since these early Butterfield recordings. There is a firmness, a real steady handedness, a determinedly sure feeling to what he puts out here. He must have been hearing what he was about to play, licks ahead. Except for that piano solo on the Moby Grape's *"Grape Jam"* LP and the tiny beatific tune, "Easy Rider" on his Flag flop LP, his playing has gotten increasingly more predictable and flabby. He hasn't lent such coherence to his playing in quite some time.

"Stop" features this new Bloomfield, fullblown phrases

pouring out miles of tough intricate patterns. Mike handles this track-length solo with a rare tone of surefire authority and soma-human cool magnetism, slightly akin to that of Hendrix, except with some things that Jimi would never try. The horns pouring in over the top of the guitar and organ purring in the backdrop, which with the addition of Goldberg's piano, sounds as if it's a few miles to the other side of the studio. "Man's Temptation" features a fine throaty Kooper vocal. The opening passage of the song switching smoothly between speakers. The horn arrangement on this track reminds one of those beautifully portrayed slower tunes on both the BS&T & EF LPs. Widening depths behind and shouting voice in front. Bloomfield roaming around the vocal.

"His Holy Model Majesty" plots the course of a nicely jazz-inspired trip. Kooper's interesting Coltraneish Ondioline solo opening up to the organ, over to Bloomfield's solo slightly reminiscent of those of his East-West performances and back to that shrill solo on the one-finger-at-a-time instrument. Kooper should listen to some of Coltrane's "later" pieces and absorb them into his music (Suggestion: "Up 'Gainst The Wall"). Harvey Brooks countering with his heavily-throbbing bass underneath, pushing things along. Michael coming back to

take it all down to a chilling silence between tracks. "Really" features Bloomfield in perhaps his favorite guitar role, a very deep and darkly King Brothersish vocal guitar, a most graphic style, crying out in sputtering passages and continually building up his song. Kooper trails in on his mild-mannered slashing organ solo. Licks from Jimmy Smith, all those old changes brought out and dusted off and battered out for us to thrill to. So good to hear it all from out of the lips of two of America's favorite musical sons. Incidentally, Bloomfield's relaxed 'second solo' is breathtaking. It's no wonder that B. B. King recently said that Michael is his favorite young guitarist.

Side Two. Enter Steve Stills. The Springfield defunct, one of the very few bands today that was able to bridge a few gaps and effectively utilize plasticity. Steve Stills, who every time one hears him, you've got to think that the best of his obviously considerable talents is, like the iceberg, still more than halfway below the surface. The introduction to the first number, Dylan's "It Takes A Lot To Laugh, It Takes A Train To Cry" combines the raw buzzing guitar-tones that Kooper let fire on a Tom Rush LP he once played on and helped produce and Stills' great string-loose and fancy mellow guitar solo tune. The mixed-in backup Who-Do-

You-Love changes, high hillbilly "no smoking" drawn-out vocals, Eddie Noh's crisp cymbal work locking everything up. A wonderfully playful rendition.

Next track, Steve locks horns with wah-wah box and delivers a most delicious version of Donovan's "Season Of The Witch." Kooper's vocal takes advantage of the full range of phrasing-possibilities this song has to offer. At times, especially during Kooper's highly charged organ solo, the horn arrangements get to be a bit too much. Slightly overstated heavy musical passages, but it all drops back to Stills who proves, as Michael Thomas' backcover notes point out, that "the wah-wah pedal's not just a war toy." I don't particularly care for this rendition, but it is certainly bombastic. And Stills is so good!

"You Don't Love Me" can be remembered best in the version by John Mayall. This song seems to be having a revival as there are quite a few groups to be heard on Los Angeles FM radio playing it, frequently "to death." The song as it's presented here is surprisingly fresh and likewise pulsating, with that gimmick soaring jet roaring throughout (the technical name of this effect is "phasing"). It's the best tune on this side, holds together and seems to stand completely apart from all the other tracks, as does the next and final band of this LP, "Harvey's Tune." Brooks' "Tune"

carries a heavy scent of Woody Herman, 1945 memories of ball rooms and 52nd St. supper club moods. Sounds like there was a lot of smoke in the studio when they were making a take. Brian Wilson will just love it.

When Manfred Mann comes to collect my empties, I'll play this all for him, he wouldn't say "No."

—JIM BRODEY
10-12-68

THE MASKED MARAUDERS
The Masked Marauders
(Deity DKS 9001/2)

They began months ago, the rumours of an event that at first seemed hardly believable but which in the end was accepted as all but inevitable. After all, with *Grape Jam, Super Session, The Live Adventures of . . .,* Blind Faith, Joe Cocker's LP, Crosby Stills Nash & Young, *Jammed Together* and *Fathers & Sons,* it had to happen. Set for release late this month, the "Masked Marauders'" two-record set may evoke an agonizing, tip-of-the-tongue, lobe-of-the-ear recognition in some, or cries of "No, no, it can't be true" in others. But yes, yes it is —a treasured, oft-xeroxed sheet of credits (which, for obvious contractual reasons, will not be reproduced on the album), and the unmistakable vocals make it clear that this is indeed what it appears to be: John Lennon,

Mick Jagger, Paul McCartney and Bob Dylan, backed by George Harrison and a drummer as yet unnamed—the "Masked Marauders."

Produced by Al Kooper, the album was recorded with impeccable secrecy in a small town near the site of the original Hudson Bay Colony in Canada. Cut in late April, only three days were required to complete the sessions, though mixing and editing involved months of serious consultations on both sides of the Atlantic. Word has it that the cover art was intended as a "send-up" of Blind Faith, but none of the principals were willing to comment on the situation.

The LP opens with an eighteen-minute version of "Season of the Witch" (lead vocal by Dylan, on which he does a superb imitation of early Donovan). The cut is highlighted by an amazing jam between bass and piano, both played by Paul McCartney. Then, the tone of the album is set by the next track, "With a Little Help from My Friends" (all), followed by a very brief "In the Midnight Hour," which collapses in giggles and is the "joke" of the set.

Side Two begins with a extremely moving acappella version of "Masters of War," sung by Mick and Paul. You'll truly wish, after hearing this cut, that you "could stand over their graves until you're sure that they're dead." This is followed by an indescribable twelve-minute John Lennon extravaganza, James Brown's "Prisoner of Love," complete with a full ten-minute false ending. "Don't let me be a prisoner . . . ooo, ah, eee, uh . . . please don't let me be a prisoner . . . ak, ow, arrrggghhh, ooo."

The oldies craze is not slighted; Dylan shines on Side Three, displaying his new deep bass voice, with "Duke of Earl," Jagger with "The Book of Love," and John, of course, with "I'm the Japanese Sandman." Paul showcases his favorite song, "Mammy," and while his performance is virtually indistinguishable from Eddie Fisher's version, it is still very powerful, evocative, and indeed, stunning. And they say a white boy can't sing the blues!

After the listener has recovered from this string of masterpieces, Side Four opens with a special treat, two songs written especially for this session: Dylan's "Cow Pie," which is very reminiscent of Billy Ed Wheeler's "The Interstate is Coming Through My Outhouse," and Mick Jagger's new instant classic, "I Can't Get No Nookie."

In line with the present trend toward "simplicity," the album nears an end with a very simple duet on acoustic guitars—George and Bob—a marvelously sensitive, yearning, melancholy exploration of "Kick Out the Jams." The final cut, a group vocal, is, what else, "Oh Happy Day." This track will probably be released as a single.

All the hassles of creating a special label, of re-arranging schedules, chartering planes, and minimizing the inevitable "ego-conflicts" were worth it. It can truly be said that this album is more than a way of life; it *is* life.

—T. M. CHRISTIAN
10-18-69

CORRESPONDENCE

SIRS:

Very clever, my boys! An interesting survey might be to find out how many of your so-hip readers actually asked their record stores to order *The Masked Marauders.*

DAVID PORTER
LOS ANGELES

SIRS:

Only one thing bothers me. Why was all mention deleted from the *Masked Marauders* review of perhaps the most charming cut of all—Mick Jagger and Paul McCartney's splendid duet of "You've Lost That Lovin' Feeling?" Under Al Kooper's tastefully spare production, the two mop-tops have etched an accurate and moving portrait of America in 1969.

JACK NOOGER
SAN FRANCISCO

SIRS:

It all began the day before Issue No. 44 of *Rolling Stone* hit the streets here in Philadelphia, hard on the heels of *The Great White Wonder*. People were calling us every five minutes or so, to ask when we expected to receive *The Masked Marauders*. We started calling various record distributors around the country, and wasted most of the afternoon in this fashion. While we were unable to locate a source for the album, we did locate two distributors who claimed to represent Deity Records, but neither of them had any information about *The Masked Marauders*. Then T. M. Christian's review of the album was noted by us the next day. . . .

Incidentally, we have learned of a forthcoming four-LP set, titled *Crime Does Not Pay,* which includes private tapes by Donovan, Jimi Hendrix, Arlo Guthrie, Laura Nyro, Louis Armstrong, Janis Joplin, Pete Seeger, and Paul Butterfield. The set contains the legendary "94-Minute Raga" with the famous spoken introduction by David Peel. The record album is packaged in an ivory-and-ebony-inlaid teakwood box with platinum feet. The front depicts a detailed rendering of Janis' left nipple. Inside, the four records are pressed on clear vinyl. The discs have no labels, but imbedded in each is a cutout, 3-D plastic (a la *Satanic Majesties*) picture of each artist appearing on that LP. These cutouts are so arranged that when the records are placed in a stack they will form a stereo, full-color photomontage of the entire battery of musicians.

WARREN LANGILL
PENN RECORDS
PHILADELPHIA

*If it is not obvious by now, the Masked Marauder review (*ROLLING STONE, *October 18th) was just a laugh. In other words, a fabrication, a hoax, a jest, an indulgence, or—in the word of the trade—a shuck. If you should happen to see an album by that name in your local record store, do not be misled. The persons who made such a record—musicians and manufacturers alike— are merely masquerading as the Marauders, a double-negative if you like, reduced to nada, nothing, not there, non-existent.—* Editor.

The Review

as Fiction

~~~~~~

~~~~~~

Sometimes a record contains one of those ineffable qualities that drives even the most skillful and technically proficient reviewer into a state which is only communicable by parable. The record doesn't have to be good, of course, but it does have to be, in one way or another, outstanding.

The problem of communicating one's thoughts about an album by writing a story rather than directly dealing with bass lines, influences, production flaws, and the like, is nearly insurmountable. Perhaps the only reviewer to come to terms with this exacting form has been J. R. Young, a mild-mannered young man who lives on a lush 15-acre farm in a tiny town in Oregon "where we have a nice garden, but we also have these funny little bugs in the cold water." Don't let his Master of Fine Arts from the University of Oregon or his two years' teaching experience at the State University of New York fool you— the man's a good writer.

The following chapter documents J. R.'s development of the fictional review. It leads off with what is perhaps his most famous work, a review of *Live Dead.* Next we are treated to a two-part story of The Wise Kid and Ten Years After, followed by radiophonic ruminations on B. B. King and "The Thrill Is Gone." The last two are perhaps his masterpieces. The *Deja Vu* story almost found itself onto the Big Screen, and is known to have frightened "hip" record store owners from Secaucus to Sacramento. And *Woodstock* is a moving, poignant portrait of a member of the members of Woodstock Nation's silent majority. Each of these stories transcends its subject. Read 'em and grin.

~~~~~~~~~~~~~~~~~~~~~~~

LIVE DEAD
The Grateful Dead
(Warner Brothers 1830)

Marsha Steinburger and her best friend, Starglow Peterson, had hitchhiked into Mill Valley from Sacramento in the early afternoon and were now sitting in Sheila Titterwell's front room on the hillside of Mount Tam. Sheila lived with some guy neither Marcia nor Starglow knew, but about whom they had heard nice things. He was at work now and would be home shortly. In the meantime, the three young lovelies were smoking some very potent dope, and were sitting on Sheila's floor watching the orange sun go down. By dusk, they were all four joints to the cosmos, and everything was a barrel of laughs.

"And that crazy fart is going to be home any minute," Sheila laughed as she took the toilet paper roll from Starglow. "You know what he does now? He comes screaming up that hill each night with Hugh Jardon, hollering as loud as he can like an asshole, 'GET OUT THE PIPE, PUT ON THE DEAD, AND SPREAD!' And like the cat is stark raving naked by the time he hits the front door."

Sheila laughed again and shook her head, and then inhaled deeply on the roll.

"Put on the dead, and spread?" Marcia looked puzzled. Sheila raised one slim finger, held her breath a few seconds longer, and then exhaled slowly.

"Right. As in the Grateful Dead and legs. Real George thinks that it's the greatest to . . ."

She was interrupted as the quiet of the early evening disintegrated around them in a confusion of sound and squalor as the high whine of a VW wound down to a quick halt, and a huge voice called up to them.

"PUT ON THE DEAD AND SPREAD, 'CAUSE I'M LOADED AND READY TO GO!"

"It's Real George now," Sheila said jumping to her feet. "Excuse me." She pulled her sweater up over her head and off her arms, and then slipped out of her jeans. She was naked in a jiffy. "It's been like this for a week now, almost two."

She quickly crossed the room to the tape deck, threaded a reel, and turned the machine on.

The two visiting girls peered at her for a long moment, and

then turned their attention to the strange shadowy figure charging up the front steps and leaving a trail of clothes strewn wildly behind him. He was going like sixty.

"Ever since he got that album," Sheila said as she opened the bedroom door, "Real George likes nothing better than to fuck to the Grateful Dead. It makes him on fire." She winked. "It's groovy." Sheila then disappeared in the darkness of the bedroom.

And just as the Dead began "Dark Star," Real George hit the front door with his naked pink and hairy body and crashed through into the living room.

"Da da!"

Marcia's and Starglow's mouths fell open as the fleeting vision swept through the room for a brief moment before disappearing along with Sheila in the darkness.

"Ahhh," someone said in there as Marcia and Starglow exchanged quizzical glances. "Ahh." The music grew louder.

"That's far out," Starglow said.

"Very far out," Marcia nodded.

The two girls turned around and looked back out into the hills. Already lights were beginning to come on as the land grew blacker.

"Gee, I wish I had a date tonight," Marcia finally said.

—J. R. YOUNG
2-7-70

SSSH
Ten Years After
(Deram DES 18029)

Perhaps a week or two ago, a very wise kid shuffling about in an old pawn shop was approached by an aging but slick pawnshop keeper. The old man watched with amusement as the young longhair looked through all the shiny and not so shiny instruments hanging in the yellowed window and stuffed into the backroom.

"What can I do for you, young man," the keeper said, rolling back on his heels, his hands in his pockets, the standard toothpick hanging out of the corner of his tight dry lips.

"Looking for something to play," the kid answered with nary a glance up to the sly old man. The kid's fingers were busy threading their way into the darkest recesses of all the back corners of the room, in quest of some forgotten treasure.

"Ah," the shopkeeper smiled, rolling his eyes toward the ceiling. "A tuba; perhaps, so you can join the high school band." He paused chuckling for a second, and then leaned forward, his sallow eyes quickly ablaze, his voice close and whispering loudly. "Or a guitar, an electric guitar, a Gibson Les Paul so you can make loud noises and maybe next week be a big star? Eh?"

The kid pushed the hair out of his eyes and grimaced at the pawnshop keeper. "No," he said.

"No? That's not it?" The old man drew back askance. "You don't want to learn to play the guitar?"

"Naw," the kid answered without any apparent interest, adding what seemed mere token explanation. "A lot of guys can play the guitar, and play it real well." He was silent for a moment as his hand settled gently on an old red Les Paul Junior. The kid turned, looked up at the aging keeper, and said in a very strange and remorseful voice, "What's the use anyway? And ten years after what could I do that a million guys can't do now?" The kid smiled, obviously struck by something he had said. "Ten Years After. Ha. Isn't that funny. I'd almost forgotten." And he laughed once more. "Ha. Do you know what I said? Do you know that last week I was really tired of listening to the guitar, no matter who was trying to get it on?" The hair settled back over his eyes, and the old man drew his hands from his pockets and cocked a thick finger under his chin. "Clapton, B.B., Page, all of them. The same old stuff. They weren't moving, ya know? Refinements, not extensions. I really thought the days of the guitar were numbered." The kid picked up the smooth red axe and plucked the metal strings

lightly. "Then I heard the new album."

"New album?" the old man quizzed, puzzled by the whole thing. "What new album?"

"Sssh," the kid said with a smile, "Ten Years After."

"What?" The man looked around suspiciously. "When? Who?"

"Ten Years After," the kid said again.

"Ten Years After?" the old man asked, furrowing his eyebrows. "And whom pray tell is that?"

"Ten Years After is . . ."

There was a singularly long pause, with not so much as the blinking of an eye. The boy lowered the guitar to its resting place, and then added his last words.

"And Alvin Lee . . . I think perhaps he is God."

The boy smiled at the old man for the final time and turned toward the front entrance. Just before closing the door, he paused and looked back in, still smiling, and said, "What's left for me to do but pass the Word? Why do I have to play? Why does anyone? It's already been done."

He closed the door and slipped out, humming an Alvin Lee run. A passing freak and businessman both nodded.

"Mellow," they said in unison.

"Yeh," the kid answered. "Mellow."

And as they moved by one

another, the kid hoped that they understood, and were not just talking as so many are prone to do.

—J. R. YOUNG
11-1-69

CRICKLEWOOD GREEN
Ten Years After
(Deram 18038)

It wasn't more than six months ago that I happened by chance to come across a certain record review in a rock and roll magazine (and a magazine of no little repute, I might add), and that review concerned a very old and dear friend of mine, a very wise young lad who had been a classmate of mine in Junior High three years ago. Where he went to school now, if he even did, or what he was up to in general, I had no idea. From what I had read, however, I gleaned that, yes, he was still the same wise kid I had known, and that he was at the time of the review a great, great admirer of Ten Years After and Alvin Lee.

It also seemed that people had taken a paternal interest in him and in his musical tastes, and that they were willing to listen to what he had to say, and so I thought to myself, I thought, "Why not, yes, why not me." Why shouldn't I get first crack at him this time for a brief interview about what he thought about Ten Years After's

new album. If I didn't do it, someone else surely would, and so, strapping my trusty tape recorder to my side, I went in search of him. After perhaps five phone calls to old girl friends and such, I finally located him in a small California deli having a pork sandwich. He recognized me immediately, and after cordialities, a few more Cokes and French fries, I finally brought the conversation around to Alvin Lee, Ten Years After, and *Cricklewood Green*. This is what went down:

Did you really mean what you said about Alvin Lee in the November 1st ROLLING STONE *review of 'Sssh,' and I believe I'm quoting you correctly, 'I think perhaps he is God'?*

Sure, sure. I said it, didn't I? And not only that, but I said that Alvin was "the pure water and pure fire of a black mountain stream." [*Laughs.*] But they didn't print that. I never did know what that writing cat had on his mind. But back to the question, yes, I said what I felt. Sure.

How did you handle the usual criticism that followed 'Sssh' in which most critics felt that Lee played with speed just to be playing with speed? (The kid smiled.) *What I mean to say is that his solos are fast for no apparent reason other than to show how clever he is.*

Oh, that. Well, man, I mean even God shows off, too. Sometimes. Have you ever been to the Grand Canyon, or Crater Lake? Talk about a show, man. Shit, what do you want to do, hold somebody back who can really go, really get it on? That's a heavy notion.

Is that what you think now?

Oh, *now.* You want to know what I think now. Oh, no.

No?

No, man.

No, what?

No, I don't think that now. No, I mean, yes, that I don't think that now. Right. Forget all that shit I just said. (*A long pause ensued.*) Yes, I don't. Believe that anymore. (*He smiled.*)

Well, what do you think now?

A lot of things, but specifically about what?

Specifically about Ten Years After.

Oh, them. *Cricklewood Green?* That?

Yes.

Well, first of all, the cover and inside spread is a crock of Hallmark Postcard shit. That's first.

And the album itself?

The album itself. Humm. It's crazy.

How?

It's just crazy, man. Crazy. It's Alvin Lee on the trip of "On the Trail of the Big Hit Single." Roy Rogers and Dale Evans. For what reasons, God only knows, meaning, of course, Him up there.

Alvin may even have a bundle of them in *Cricklewood Green.* I'm happy for him. But even Johnny Rivers had some big ones, man, Big Hits. Even Walter Brennan. I mean, have you heard "Working On the Road"? Alvin even sounds like Johnny Rivers.

Like I said it's crazy. I mean, I know a lot of shit goes down after each album, but this is just weird. It's like you can enjoy it but it still fucks you up. I mean, I hate to say this, with all the strange connotations and everything, but it's like Chinese food, you know? It fills you up, but like ten minutes later you're hungry again. For a hamburger, this time, though. Can you dig how many waitresses have gone through that "ten minutes later you're hungry" routine. But back to the record, yeh, it's a real Chun King trip. But then, most albums today are like that. I mean why the fuck should Alvin Lee do an imitation "Sympathy for the Devil." It's been done, for Christ's sake. It's like some kind of old Guess Who trip, riding around on somebody else's coat tail.

Then you're disappointed with 'Cricklewood Green'?

Yeh, you can say that. I really expected more from it, more of Alvin's head than his fingers, but I guess it's like Clapton said, "You don't have to be intelligent to play music." And you know what the cat down the street said.

What?

Never trust a Rock and Roll Star. Now, I can really dig that.

—J. R. YOUNG
6-11-70

"THE THRILL IS GONE"
B. B. King
(Dunhill 1449)

"The Thrill Is Gone," reflections on the B. B. King single of that name.

When Bud had been an undergraduate at Oregon, he and Phil Hill, an older fraternity brother of his, had ridden back and forth to his folks' place in Sacramento innumerable times. That was back in '62 and '63, and the two guys in those years had learned every white-tile wayside diner from Wolf Creek to Live Oak. They had become good friends.

Phil was smart, deep into phenomenology and African Lit (even then) and other such things, and Bud liked to think he was hot on Phil's intellectual trail. One night, as Phil pushed his old '55 Pontiac through the dark mountain passes outside of Dunsmuir, he glanced over and asked if his younger friend knew anything about sound. Bud, an American Lit major, of course didn't know much, except that it moved in waves.

"Right," Phil nodded. "Now dig this. If those waves begin, like now when I'm talking, what's to stop them as long as they have an elastic medium to

ride upon? Doesn't it stand to reason that each sound ever created is still moving somewhere, but is merely beyond the realm of the human ear, like the proverbial tree in the forest? Like it's deflected off the earth in a matter of seconds, and is gone into outer space, kind of like lost in space?"

Bud frowned at this because he really had no idea as to the feasibility of Phil's hypothesis. He also had difficulty in determining when Phil was putting him on.

"I don't know, Phil. I guess so."

"Then listen to this," Phil continued. "When I drove across the country last year, something really weird happened." He paused as he passed an old pickup. "It was late, about two in the morning, perfectly clear out on the Nebraska flatlands. I turned on the radio and heard, now dig this, a program that was from the *late Forties*. Not a recording of great moments or anything like that, but the real thing." Bud frowned again, but Phil nodded and went on. "I mean I think that somehow that radio wave or beam in its outward movement collided with something that reflected it back and somehow the car receiver picked it up and broadcast it."

"Are you shittin' me?"

"No," Phil laughed. "It happened. It was like walking backwards. Harry Truman was the

President on that highway. Gordon Jenkins. Doc Blanchard. John Garfield. Stalin. All this weird stuff piped into the car." There was a pause.

"Ever happen again?" Bud asked.

"No, never happened to anyone I know. But I'm always waiting. Like on nights like this. It's something to think about."

Bud thought about it, but didn't know what to think. He didn't know to this day about Phil's story. Phil once told Bud that someone had pictures, almost a film, of Christ on Calvary. The pictures had been discovered buried, wrapped in a parchment tube. What it was, so Phil's story went, was a series of rabbit retinas. Someone had lined up a row of rabbits facing the cross and then chopped their heads off in quick succession. The final retinal imprint was somehow made permanent in each eye, and thus, when all the retinas were lined up, there was a pictorial study of Calvary. The story had bothered Bud for a long time.

That, however, was years ago, and Bud hadn't seen Phil since '64. Bud now was a book salesman, and for the first time in many years he found himself in late February driving over the same mountain road he and Phil had taken those many times before. It was night again and the road had changed little.

Bud pushed the button of his radio and waited for some music, but he got only static. He remembered how hard it was to pick up anything in the mountains. He slowly turned the tuning knob. Nothing but static . . . until slowly the dial seemed to ease into and lock on a strangely haunting tune, a lonely guitar rising somewhere from the past, and then a full and plaintive voice.

The thrill is gone
The thrill is gone away

There was something about it, an unknown quality conjured up from the past that told Bud something, a song for long driving nights in the dark mountains, calm and clear as the lush strings rolled gently under the full white moon above and the silver road ahead. It moved on endlessly, soothing his mind, and Bud thought that, yes, here it was again, a single beam from out of the sky, vibrational energy, a wave again trapped before beginning its second stellar flight, and he found himself taking deep breaths, trying to inhale it all, the sinuous and sharp strings, the fragile tones, and that voice . . . that voice.

It slowly began to fade, and Bud reached for the volume and tried to keep pace with the dying sound, but he couldn't hold it. It still fell away as Bud reached full volume. And then the sound was lost altogether.

Bud thought he had lost the beam.

"Crap," he muttered.

"AWRIGHT, BABY . . . B. B. KING AND 'THE THRILL IS GONE.' " The radio suddenly boomed at an incredible volume that almost knocked Bud's head off, "AND WE GOWAN TO DA NEWS BABY AT TWELVE THUTY TWOO." Wolfman Jack from San Diego, and the news was today's news, and the beam was just as powerful, not interstellar, and Bud then snapped the radio off in a half second and sat quite still for a few moments, still slightly shaken, his ears ringing.

Then he smiled and rapped the steering wheel with his knuckles. "That Phil," he laughed. "What a card."

—J. R. YOUNG
4-2-70

DEJA VU
Crosby, Stills, Nash, Young, Taylor, and Reeves
(Atlantic SD 7200)

The record business hadn't been good lately. Some said it was a recession, others said suppression, while others said mere direction, but whatever the reason, the plasticware wasn't moving through the stores. Records hadn't been turning anybody on in recent weeks and many thought that was bad. The capitalists with the hip facades throughout the supposed counter-culture all shook their furry little heads like crazy over the weeklies, because not only wasn't there anything strong on the racks, there wasn't anything on the way except perhaps the long awaited *Deja Vu*. They'd been hearing about it for months.

Dave worked at the counter of one such establishment and he made change all day. His boss was one of the hip capitalists, a stone business man, and thus it was with more than mere interest that Dave watched him look the rack up and down at the end of the day, grimace, and finally bolt from the store, snorting over the lack of integrity, the failing hypes, the excessive delays, but more than anything, the real lack of good new releases and guaranteed sales. In short, moola.

Dave watched the scene enacted daily, and each day muttered something about "assholishness" as the boss jumped in his GTO and shot out of view. Dave liked his job, however, because here it seemed correct to come to work stoned, hipper than thou, together, or as they said on the radio every eight minutes, "From Eugene, getting it *right on* . . ."

Dave was a very serious lad, into a much heavier stint than that of a mere desk clerk, for he fancied himself a bombmaker in the coming revolution, bombs now only in the blueprint stage . . . but what blueprints. They were so large and meticulously drawn and so thorough that they covered three walls of the bedroom. He stood and admired the blue papered walls each night before taking his old lady to bed.

His old lady was something else, too, because her scene, as she so candidly admitted, was a "mixed bag," anything from "politico-revolutionary theatre" to blue ribbon winner at the Lane County Fair for her apricot conserve. She said "Sorry 'bout that" more than three time a day, and talked on endlessly about good karma.

Clipper, the cat who lived next door to them, thought "her act was nowhere" privately, although he still would have loved to ball her. He was an older cat, and presumed he was terrifically sexual, and was into all kinds of "villes," such as "I'm in Turned-onsville," or "He's from Hostilesville." He had a freaky girl friend who always wore a peasant blouse and jiggled her tits on purpose.

"Nipplesville," Clipper often laughed as he made a grab for the big ones.

They were all heavy record freaks and well into dope, always dropping "pure Owsley" and tripping at the beach, stashing joints, and things like that, and always to the big beat of the sounds that Dave brought home from the record store. Music and the dope went hand in hand in their households—

whether fucking in the shower, eating dinner, talking revolution, reading Mao, answering the door, whatever, they were wacked. Even during his most serious moments, such as when working out a complicated detonator on paper, Dave still had half a joint, "just to keep my thing together." Yes, the new life was a good alternative.

One day, a very strange dude moved into the complex. He had red bushy hair and never smiled, didn't talk much, kept to himself, and read thick books and apparently wrote a lot, too. About what was a mystery. He brought only one suitcase, a pillow, a blanket and an ancient army cot. He ate little, too.

"Music, man, he doesn't listen to The Music. Isn't that far out," Dave's old lady exclaimed. "I mean, aaahhh," and she rolled her crazy red eyes back in her head as the other three passed the joint.

"Yeh," Dave said, inhaling quickly. "Weird."

"And probably No Dope, man. You know, probably No Dope. I mean AAAHHHH."

"Weird, man. You know what I mean?"

They all knew.

As time passed, however, the strange dude, one Jordan Rover, began making inroads upon their heads with his consistent demeanor of general togetherness, a clean brand of intense calm, his eyes flickering just slightly at the mention of People's Park or the slamming of a car door.

Thus it was that following a macrobiotic meal in Dave's place one night they all sat around the living room as Dave filled the bamboo pipe. Jordan sat alone in the corner. It had been his first meal with the four, and he seemed a bit ill at ease at the dope development. When the pipe was handed to him, he merely kept it moving without taking the customary hit. The four friends all exchanged secret and knowing glances.

"Not tonight, huh, Jordan?" Dave asked as the pipe went around for a second time.

"Not tonight. Fucks my head around a little too much. Can't smoke it anymore. I used to really dig it, too. Same with music, man. Dangerous stuff." He nodded at them.

Dave's old lady, her lids heavy, leaned forward.

"No music? No dope? Man, where is that?"

Jordan Rover didn't react, but only met her thick eyes with his clear eyes until she had to look away. They all looked away. Then he did speak, glancing around the apartment:

"I'll tell you where it's at, because it's not where those blueprints are that you showed me earlier, if you know what I mean. The question is, 'where are you people?'"

Dave stiffened.

"What about the blueprints?" he asked.

"They're posters, man, just like Jane Fonda and Elvis Presley and the Marx Brothers. Can you dig that?"

"No, man. What the fuck are you talking about?"

"They're plans, then," Jordan shrugged, "for you, but nothing more. Always planning, always waiting."

"Wait a minute, man. So they are plans. Right on. Right?"

"But it's a game. It's all a game. The dope's a game, the music's a game. Your fuckin' revolution is a game. You're really into all this other shit, man, and it has you locked in this room. It's all too comfortable for you to leave."

"You're crazy, man," Dave said shaking his head. "He's crazy, right?" and Dave turned looking for help, but the other heads were fogged.

"You think I'm crazy, when what it really comes down to is your ultimate concern this month is 'where the fuck is *Deja Vu?*' I've been hearing that rap ever since I moved in, and you can still say I'm crazy? What a waste, man. *Deja Vu.*"

"Now wait a minute." Dave held up his hands, blinking his eyes. "Wait a minute." A long pause ensued, broken only by the rustle of Clipper's hand up his chick's blouse.

"You know what I think, man," Jordan Rover finally said

as he looked around at them, "I think that if you're ever going to get it together about the Change, man, Real Change, then you'll be hoping the *Deja Vu* will be shit, no good, 'cause like it's close this time."

"What are you talking about. What's close? You're crazy."

"Crazy? Then try this. There's a lot of energy in the air, and people are getting uptight. The market is slow, bad records, and there is no release, nothing to buy, right?"

"Right?"

"So dig it. It's energy, man, and it's building and it's going to have to move somewhere somehow, and if your *Deja Vu* suddenly appears and is a trip, *well*, man, then it's just another energy drain. *Abbey Road* and *Let It Bleed* all over again, another reprieve for Them. They've locked you up in here. Atlantic and all those people have you in jail and you don't even know it. You're the old people in *Wild In The Streets*. You put on the record, smoke a little dope, draw up a few bombs, and go to bed so you can get up and begin again tomorrow, and it's dumb, man, dumb. Nothing ever changes." Jordan was on his feet standing over them waving his arms as he talked on. "You folks call yourselves revolutionaries, but that's really crazy. You ought to lay off the music, lay off the shit, burn them rock and roll mags, and really get it on, put

your energy in the street. That's where it's at!" He nodded slowly at them, signifying his message. "That's where it's at. Deja Vu *isn't the question. It's the problem!*" And with one final wave, Jordan Rover bowed, thanked his host for the dinner and split.

The remaining four were quiet for a long while. Dave was the first to speak, leaning forward and snubbing out the roach.

"A righteous cat, man, a righteous cat. He's right on." He grinned at them all. "Right on!"

That night some changes were made at Dave's place.

Two nights later the record shop blew up taking half the block with it.

"Can you dig it?" Clipper said, still fluffing his chick's tits as the flames shot up 60 feet across the street from where the four sat watching.

"A righteous explosion, man," Dave laughed, but exuding a new determined grimness all the time. "Right out of the Mantovani section. A righteous explosion." They all stood proudly and watched as the three-alarm fire became a four and stretched on into the early morning. Clipper and his chick left early. Dave and his old lady were almost the last to leave.

"Oh, man, when I heard it, when I heard it my heart almost burst. So far out. BOOM!" He threw his head back and roared. His old lady unlocked the door of the apartment and they went in. The place was now nothing more than bare walls and floors, save for the bed. Only essentials remained.

"So far out," Dave laughed again, and he fell on the bed, his eyes closed, his face aglow in the candlelight. His old lady sat at his side, looking down reverently at her longhaired radical.

"Did you dig it?" he asked as he slipped a hand up inside her blouse to her warm breasts.

"I dug it," she said, smiling softly at him. They fell together almost immediately and balled.

Perhaps forty minutes later, they lay silent in bed, breathing easily and thinking private thoughts, private until both were aware of low throbbing sounds coming from down the hall.

"Do you hear something," she finally asked, "like music?"

"Sure do," he answered, and they listened some more.

"Know who is it?" she asked.

"Well, if I'm not mistaken, it's Crosby, Stills, Nash, and Young. I know *Deja Vu* came out today."

"No, silly. I couldn't care less about what the record is. I want to know who's playing it around here."

"Who else but Clipper. I mean, the cat's crazy. No will. He's at it again." Dave reached for a cigarette.

"Now, I can't believe that," she said sitting up.

"You know him."

"I'm gonna see," and wrapping a blanket around her, she crept to the door.

"It *is* coming from there, and I smell dope, too."

Dave jumped out of bed.

"I think I better go rap with him about this," he said "after all the shit he was laying on us the other night how he was gonna make it."

"Me, too," his old lady chipped in.

They marched to Clipper's door, and just as Dave was about to knock, he stopped. The sound strangely enough wasn't coming from Clipper's place at all, but from the next room. Dave and his old lady exchanged quizzical glances and edged that way, unsure of their discovery. But sure enough, it was Crosby, Stills, Nash, and Young on the stereo. *Deja Vu.*

Dave slowly cracked open the door, and there on the floor on his mattress in front of a KLH portable sat Jordan Rover, naked, a fresh lid of grass at his side, and a huge joint hanging from his lips. When he saw Dave and his old lady at the door, he beamed at them, chuckling easily.

"Hey, man, com'on in." He lifted his eyebrows and nodded at them. "Com'on in and smoke a little shit, open yer ears. Sit down," and he patted the mattress at his side.

"But . . . you said . . ." Dave stammered, pointing at him.

"Oh, man, sit down," Jordan grimaced jocularly, and then smiled. "You've got to hear this. It's sooo far out."

"But, what I said, man. I know what I said. Right on." He thrust a fist feebly into the air.

"But you were right. It's an energy . . ."

"Yeh, man, it's a drain, a real energy drain . . . but it feels so good . . . *It feels so fuckin' good, man*," and his head fell back as he turned up the volume and let the music pour into their heads. And he was right.

"Gee, it does sound good, doesn't it?" Dave's old lady said as she blithely dropped the blanket at her feet and sat her pink little body down on the mattress. She went for a joint immediately. It wasn't more than a second later after a final shrug that Dave, too, sat down and took the joint in his turn.

And it wasn't more than twenty minutes later that Dave in sweet serenity was heard to remark to no one in particular: "Neil Young is a heavy man, Neil Young is a real heavy."

—J. R. YOUNG
4-30-70

SIRS:

First, what possible justification can there be for printing something like J. R. Young's jejune bullshit next to Langdon Winner's legitimate review of *Deja Vu*, or anyplace else?

Printing stuff like that is irresponsible, and reading it is a pain in the ass.

PETER DAVIS
NEW YORK CITY

SIRS:

Well, to be perfectly honest with you, I actually *prefer* J. R. Young's jejune, bullshit reviews to legitimate reviews. More!

DAN DONALDS
CLEVELAND, OHIO

WOODSTOCK
Various Artists
(Cotillion SD 3-500)

Bill hadn't been to Woodstock that August weekend the summer before, although Plattsburgh, his home, was less than 300 miles due north on the Northway. He'd gone drinking at Filion's Friday night, and when he awakened terribly hungover the next afternoon, as did most of his 18-year-old buddies, it was too late to make the trip down to Bethel. You couldn't have convinced anyone in the months that ensued, however, that not only was Bill not *at* the Music and Art Show in the alfalfa fields, but that he hadn't also played some integral part in the whole proceeding—a dope runner for the Airplane, perhaps ("Hey, Bill, you got a bomber?" Grace, resplendent in white, tits high and firm, asked him standing behind the giant platform as the Who finished up their set with the sun edging orange up the mountain from its resting place), or a candy bar for Jerry Garcia. Bill believed, too, and if pressed he had a whole Abbie Hoffman Rap about the "actuality" of being there not actually being the important thing, but only a minor side trip.

"I *live* in Woodstock nation," Bill told people when the topic came up, "If you can dig it. I mean how many were actually there. You don't know. We'll never know. But it doesn't make any difference. The Woodstock actuality has become a media trip. That's where it's at. More cameras, writers, and that kind of shit than at Kennedy's funeral. Like the people on the outside probably know more than those who were actually there. What it's come down to is Woodstock Nation, and Woodstock Nation, man, is in your head if you want it to be."

Probably. But Bill still knew a whole lot about the Music Show itself, and took great pains to seek out said information. He had clippings, articles, ads, the illustrious *Life* Magazine Special Edition, *Rolling Stone's Woodstock*, the *Village Voice* issue, and now in late spring had seen the movie three

times at four bucks a throw, and also had the album committed to memory. His head, in fact, was a living monument to the whole Woodstock thing, even down to the little things. Somehow Bill had found someone who had some of the infamous "brown acid." He paid ten bucks for the tab so that he could find out "what was going down." True to form, he took it the second time he saw *Woodstock*.

"Man, that brown acid at Woodstock was a real bummer," he told assorted freaks at assorted gatherings. "A real bummer. Knocked me out for hours. Paranoia personified."

As time passed, Bill became more assertive in such situations. No one now bothered to question him directly as to whether he had been there, but merely what was it like. Bill went along with them because he felt he really knew what it was like.

"Cocker was crazy, man, beautiful. And Alvin Lee, wow."

"Were there really a lot of naked people," a far out chick asked handing him a joint, "like cunt and cock and everything?"

"Well," Bill would smile, "you saw the movie didn't you?"

"Yeh."

"What else do you want to know?"

"Far out."

Woodstock was now the new American Dream, a pipe dream, how it had been those three glorious days of sun and rain, mud and music, and the 500,000 patriots whose ranks were growing day by day, patriots of Woodstock "flying their freak flags high," Groupies, the Dope, and good ol' Rock & Roll, and the national anthem, understood for the first time by Hendrix and his buzz saw guitar. It was all coming home to rest now, and Bill, like many, was proud to stand up and be counted for his own People, for Life, Liberty, and the Pursuit of Happiness, for his Country. Woodstock Nation was a reality.

So it was, until one night at a party in West Chazy when the conversation once more found its way to Woodstock as it always did whenever Bill happened to show. Bill dropped facts and recollections amidst the circle of listeners who sat rapt about him like Leary dropped acid. They all shook their heads at the good dope being passed and at the general incredulity of the whole Woodstock affair. But they believed. That is, all but one believed, and this one hairy ragamuffin of hipdom lay back against a sofa, hitting on his own kief, and cooly taking in Bill's polished exposition. He listened for a long time. At some point, undiscernible to the rest of the gathering, he apparently had heard enough.

"Hey, man," he said, leaning his well-coiffed head into the circle. "Did you ever understand what happened down front just before the Band went on?"

Bill looked up and smiled.

"No, I wasn't there when that happened. I must have been somewhere else. What happened?"

"I don't know. I was sitting about 50 yards out." The kid leaned back out again.

Bill eyed him for a moment, and then continued on from the point where he had disengaged. He had his stuff down.

Seconds later however, the kid again poked his head inside the circle.

"What happened, man, when that weird rumor. . . ."

"About Dylan showing up?" Bill cut him off in stride.

"No, man, that was a media hype. No, the rumor just before Creedence Clearwater went on about the latrines?"

Bill looked at the kid again, and didn't answer for the longest time. And then it was only a reticent shrug.

"Well, where, man, did you take a dump after that? Where'd you spend most of your time?"

Everyone turned and looked at Bill, but Bill had nothing to say, no one to look at, nowhere to go.

"I mean," the kid went on, driving his point home, "when

I arrived, the can situation, and that strange tale, well, it was weird. Right? You do remember that, don't you?"

"Sure, but. . . ."

"Did you fork out any bread to get in?"

"No," Bill answered, looking down at the flickering candle, "but. . . ."

"Did you get back to Leon's down the. . . ."

"Groovy Way?"

"Wrong direction, man, wrong direction."

There was a silence, a certain moment of embarrassment because now everyone knew. Bill didn't look up.

"You're right, though," the kid finally said, "the movie was pretty far out. But it wasn't like being there. Nothing was like being there." A second silence followed, and then the kid turned to the far out chick. "Hey, you got anything to drink or eat, man? This is your place, isn't it?"

"Yeh," someone echoed, and in seconds the crowd was on its feet, eager to be up and away. Everyone but Bill. He was still on the floor staring into the flame. The rest of the gang trooped to the kitchen.

* * *

"Look, man, it was clear he hadn't been there if you'd been there."

"And you'd been there," the girl said.

"Yeh. Anybody who had would have known immediately he was shucking us. It was obvious, if you knew."

"Sure, maybe, but dig where it's at. Two wrongs don't necessarily make a right, as my grandmother used to tell me, if there were even two wrongs. You know what I mean?"

"But, look. He'd been sold a bill of goods, man, a product that had little to do with anything but money, and that's what he was selling. What, I'm supposed to feel bad for coming down on him for fucking around with us? He's an asshole, it's that simple. I mean, like he really believes it, and that's weird."

"Apparently you believe it too. Perhaps more so than Bill. But then you *were* there. You are Woodstock Nation, and if it's come down to this, then that's sad. That's why there will never really be a Woodstock Nation. You won't let anybody live on your land. You were there. Bill wasn't. Bang, bang. Sad. It's too bad you didn't remember what Dylan said."

"What?"

" 'Those dreams are only in your head.' " She turned and walked away. At the door she paused and looked back at the kid, and smiled. " 'I'll let you be in my dreams, if I can be in yours.' "

—J. R. YOUNG
7-9-70

Some

Pop Music

In the general preoccupation with what was happening in the "new music" (a hard term to define exactly, but the perimeters are roughly that which *looked* underground, that which was primarily album music, that which generally was not exposed on the Top-40, those artists who generally speaking came to popularity after 1967, and those artists who generally stayed within the guitar/drum/piano arrangement), much of what was happening in the deliberately commercial areas has often been ignored.

On the other hand, much of it was reviewed. It was, after all, music as good as the best in any other subdivision of popular music. Some of it was substantially better. The following selection is anything but comprehensive or complete. All it really represents are a few particular interests and loves of some of our record reviewers.

The first album in this selection, *Dusty in Memphis* is simply a great album. In the first paragraph, reviewer Marcus explains the problem. "A few months ago, I walked into the *Rolling Stone* offices and palely inquired if the journal might possibly be interested in a review of the then-new Dusty Springfield album. Blank stares and a few snickers."

No longer.

DUSTY IN MEMPHIS
Dusty Springfield
(Atlantic SD 8214)

A few months ago I walked into the *Rolling Stone* office and palely inquired if the journal might possibly be interested in a review of the then-new Dusty Springfield album. Blank stares and a few snickers. Today, Jackie De Shannon's "Put a Little Love in Your Heart" is one of the day's events on AM radio and I still dig *Dusty in Memphis*.

Dusty started out with a nice little rocker called "I Only Want to Dance With You," her first hit, riding in on the heels of Beatle boots in 1964, and then scored, with some of us anyway, a monster, "Wishin' and Hopin.'" As opposed to Leslie Gore's great single, "You Don't Own Me," Dusty's song was the ultimate anti-Women's Liberation ballad: "Wear your hair, just for him . . ." We used to turn it up loud on double-dates. Dusty had this way with words, a soft, sensual box (voice) that allowed her to combine syllables until they turned into pure cream. "AnIvrything'inboutH'greeeaaate true love *is* ..." And then a couple of years later she hit the top with "The Look of Love" and seemed destined to join that crowd of big-bosomed, low-necked lady singers that play what Lenny Bruce called "the

class rooms" and always encore with "Born Free."

It didn't happen, and *Dusty in Memphis* is the reason why. This album was constructed with the help of some of the best musicians in Memphis and with the use of superb material written by, among others, Jerry Goffin & Carol King, Randy Newman, and Barry Mann & Cynthia Weil. Now Dusty is not a soul singer, and she makes no effort to "sound black"—rather she is singing songs that ordinarily would have been offered by their writers to black vocalists. Most of the songs, then, have a great deal of depth while presenting extremely direct and simple statements about love. Unlike Aretha, who takes possession of whatever she does, Dusty sings around her material, creating music that's evocative rather than overwhelming. Listening to this album will not change your life, but it'll add to it.

There are three hits on this LP, and they are representative of the rest of it. "Son of a Preacher Man" is as downhome as Dusty gets; it has an intro that's funky, a vocal that's *almost* dirty. The bass gives the song presence and Dusty doesn't have to strain to carry it off. No one has topped her version of this yet and no one's likely to. "Don't Forget About Me" is to my ears the best cut here—it opens with a counterpoint between bass and vibrating guitar that's tremendously exciting, and then Dusty enters, her voice almost like another instrument. The song picks up Gene Chrisman's woodblock and the Sweet Inspirations and it's a fast race home. Piano cues Reggie Young's sizzling guitar (and it's a crime that Atlantic mixed Young down from the version used on the single) toward the end, and it's his show from then on. Better musicianship is not to be found, and I include Dusty as one of those musicians.

Finally, there's "The Windmills of Your Mind," a slick song that served as the soundtrack for the slickest movie of recent years, *The Thomas Crown Affair*. The rest of the album falls somewhere in between this cut and the other hits, but not to be missed are superb versions of "No Easy Way Down," "So Much Love," and "Just a Little Lovin.'"

Most white female singers in today's music are still searching for music they can call their own. Dusty is not searching—she just shows up, and she, and we, are better for it.

—GREIL MARCUS
11-1-69

CHILD IS FATHER TO THE MAN
Blood, Sweat and Tears
(Columbia CS 9619)

This album is unique. More precisely, it is the first of its kind—a music that takes elements of rock, jazz, straight blues, R&B, classical music and almost anything else you could mention and combines them into a sound of its own that is "popular" without being the least bit watered down.

That Blood, Sweat and Tears is a band and not merely a melange whose diverse constituents (a trumpet player from Maynard Ferguson's college-dance-and-concert big band, a drummer who has gigged with Eric Anderson and whose elder brother is Thelonious Monk's personal manager, several young white New York jazz horn men who were technologically unemployed by the New Thing revolution and physically unemployed by the shrinkage of available nightclub and record jobs, an L.A. bass player out of the Mothers of Invention and a pair of old Blues Project-ers) are at war with each other is greatly to the credit of Al Kooper, its organist, pianist, vocalist, arranger and general head honcho, *Child* is even more complex than that, what with the addition of a string section, a "soul chorus" and assorted sound effects on several of the cuts. But Kooper and the other musicians involved knew the sound they were after, and having achieved it, they kept the effects strictly secondary.

Two of the songs, "I Love You More Than You'll Ever

Know" and "Somethin' Goin' On" are very nearly perfect, self-contained masterpieces. Both written by the leader, they are extremely bluesy, but without the credibility gap that afflicts almost all white blues performances. This is because these are Al Kooper's blues, Blood, Sweat and Tears' blues and not anyone else's, not Robert Johnson's or B. B. King's or Wilson Pickett's blues or, on the other side, Hank Miller's blues—just as "She Belongs to Me" is Bob Dylan's blues and Gerry Mulligan playing "Blueport" is the blues, and those are two *pale* cats. They are big city blues, New York blues, too much happening blues, they are the blues used as a frame for deeply felt experiences and that's what the form, any form, is all about anyway. If you use it your way.

Musically these cuts are tight where they should be tight, loose, etc. What they do is swing, a term of honorable antecedents (see Duke Ellington) that is too little heard these days. For a working definition Fred Lipsius's alto solos are more than just adequate; they are, quite frankly, better saxophone playing or just plain better anything playing than one would expect to hear on a rock and roll record. Lipsius blows right up to the limits of the form and even makes them bulge a little, but he neither pierces nor transcends them. He doesn't need to and it is doubtful that he wants to. What he sets out to do is play the blues, and a booting, exciting pair of blues solos they are.

It would have been a minor miracle if the entire album had maintained that level. Most of it is merely very good. The only weakness lies in Steve Katz's vocals, and his choice of material does nothing to minimize the dull graininess of his voice: Tim Buckley's "Morning Glory" and Katz's own "Meagan's Gypsy Eyes" are the two folkiest songs on the record. They make pretty limp vehicles for the horn section—and why did Kooper and Lipsius choose to frame "Morning Glory" with the corniest kind of Ferguson over-arranged opening and closing riffs? Probably this, like the animal sound effects, will be forgotten by the time they record again.

Compared to The Mothers, say, not to mention Sun Ra or Roswell Rudd, Blood, Sweat and Tears is not very far out musically. But they come across, baby, they do come across.

—JERROLD GREENBERG
4-27-68

BLOOD, SWEAT AND TEARS
Blood, Sweat and Tears
(Columbia CS 9720)

The new Blood, Sweat & Tears album is a perfect example of the rock record that "tries harder." While at some points on the record the basic style of the group resembles rock and roll, more often the listener is being bombarded with non-rock arranging devices, non-rock solos, and non-rock material, all of which tells him that "something else" is going. The obvious response is that we are hearing something new: rock being mixed with jazz, rock being mixed with soul, etc. Ultimately, someone at Columbia will come up with a name for it: "jazz-folk-soul-baroque-C&W-latin-show-tune-rock." And for once the hyphenated labeling would be appropriate because B, S & T play hyphenated music: first they play folk, then they play jazz, then they play latin, etc. Styles exist in tangent on their record, but never merge into one.

There is an understandable reason why B, S & T have adopted this approach. Most efforts by musicians to merge varying styles have been more than dismal. Perhaps they thought it would be better to maintain the integrity of each style and to combine them without mixing them. Unfortunately, the only result of such an approach can be a pastiche of styles that are fitted together in an artificial way. The elements often have little musical relationship with each other. The listener responds to the illusion that he is hearing some-

thing new when in fact he is hearing mediocre rock, OK jazz, etc., thrown together in a contrived and purposeless way. In their first album, B, S & T managed their material (which was—in the form of Kooper's songs—considerably better than the new material) in a beautiful way. Here they are too intent on proving that they can out-do the first album and wind up letting the material manage them.

I realize that these are harsh criticisms but I think a careful listening to several songs in particular bear them out. "Smiling Phases" is well known as one of Traffic's finest recordings. They did the song as a largely straight R & B piece, with Jim Capaldi playing a primitive and simple four beat on drums. B, S & T have taken the edge off of Traffic's version. The song begins with an over-elaborate horn intro. The verses are done at rushed pace and the rhythm is syncopated so as to fragment the lines of the verse instead of holding them together. Bobby Colomby's drumming is particularly at fault: he overplays everything. After two verses they find their way into a piano solo which involves several changes, several breaks, and which gets farther and farther into a jazz thing. Once having done that, they have to find a way to get back into the rock style of the song in order to end it. Hence, coming out of the piano solo we get what sounds like a horn transition, but this only leads to a longer, lush, horn segue, which in turn leads into the real horn transition, which is the already overly elaborate horn intro used at the beginning of the cut. Now back into the song, the final verse seems —oddly enough—to be lacking in any sense of climax or tension. The over-elaboration of musical ideas makes it all sound limp.

In a similar vein, Laura Nyro's "And When I Die" is over-arranged right into the ground. The verses are done in an imitation-Cowboy musical style (a la "Oklahoma"). These cute little items lead into choruses which are done in a smooth shuffle, except that the last line of the chorus is broken up. Following the first chorus we are given a piano solo in the spirit and style of the verses. After the second, we get a horn riff played over a Lawrence Welk styled effect of hoof-beats. The rest of the cut continues like this, all of it involving innumerable rhythm changes, various instrumental patterns, all of which accomplish nothing except to bury the song beneath layers of musical irrelevance and nonsense. It wasn't a very good tune to begin with, and Peter, Paul and Mary did it better three years ago.

Even on a song as poignant and eloquent as "God Bless the Child" they are unable to contain themselves or to allow something beautiful to speak for itself. In the middle of a perfectly fine reading of the song we are given an intrusion of a latin styled horn solo which is so vile and obnoxious, and so lacking in taste, that it's hard to believe the same minds are responsible for both parts of the cut. B, S & T are constitutionally incapable of leaving well enough alone. A computer could have arranged this song with more sensitivity.

There are two musicians on this record who come through in excellent form and who ought to be exempted from some of these comments. David Clayton Thomas is an extremely able vocalist who has more depth than most and happily avoids vocal "blackface." Jim Fielder has been, since his superb performance on the first B, S & T album, one of the finest bassmen on the scene. On this album he shows he can play anything. But beyond that, he exhibits an excellent sense of what goes where, i.e., how to use his knowledge in a musically effective way. *Blood, Sweat and Tears* would have been a much better record if some of his colleagues possessed that same knowledge.

—JON LANDAU
3-1-69

DIMENSIONS
The Box Tops
(Bell 6032)

NONSTOP
The Box Tops
(Bell 6023)

SUPER HITS
The Box Tops
(Bell 6025)

The Box Tops have been plowing some cautious fields and raking in bushels of money for a couple of years now. First appearing in the season of Question Mark and the Mysterians and Count Five, they have endured in the survey market by seldom repeating a Sound from single to single and maintaining a high level of disciplined musicianship, seasoned with just enough real soul to catch a few unlikely listeners— like me. I liked "The Letter" and "Cry Like a Baby" and "Choo Choo Train" until endless AM repetitions made me hate them. "Cry Like a Baby," for instance, had a certain yearning bluesy quality that sounded quite refreshing in that gross Blue Cheer spring of '68, with its funky electric sitar, girl backup vocal group, and the sad restrained wistfulness of Alex Chilton's singing. "Choo Choo Train" came out later that year, and it was a good radio song too, which meant you didn't lunge for the dial

the instant it began. Nice chugging homestead-nostalgia song for hicks. But *buy* a Box Tops album? Shit, one glance at the cover of their current one, *Nonstop,* was enough: five shiteating Gary Lewis grins framed in immaculate early-Beatle manicures, posing stupidly on an old locomotive. Christ.

And this year a set called *Dimensions:* the photo on the back (deBryllcreamed, sloppy unmatched duds, grim weltschmertz scowls) suggested that they had entered their solemn don't-give-a-shit stage, Artists now with extended jams and experimental gestures and sermon lyrics. Nine-minute version of "Rock Me Baby." Nope.

Of the two regular albums, *Dimensions* is the more ambitious, eclectic, "adult"—and the weaker. "Rock Me Baby" is of course a dragged-out bore, and "I Must Be the Devil," a passable Ray Charles-ish piano roll blues, is ruined (although it gets a laugh) when a tinkling piano suddenly surfaces from the slow-boiling funk for a keyboard-spanning Liberace-an arpeggio (you know, that stairway to the cocktail stars)—and you suddenly realize anew how very much these guys have to learn.

But maybe that very limitation is the source of their strength. A song like "Soul Deep" is obvious enough, a patented commercial sound, yet within those strictures it communicates with a depth and sincerity of feeling that holds the attention and brings you back often. A number of their songs have this same half-definable quality, an approach just this side of Neil Diamond's pretensions, combined with a clear, airy funk. Blue-eyed soul plus helium, overt melodrama repressed for a clear undemanding flow. A good example is "Together," one of the Box Tops' several-teenage love songs. Again the maudlin side of the cliche is boiled away until the slight taste of it remaining acts as a fine seasoning, even enhancing the song.

Nonstop, however, is a much better album. "Choo Choo Train" sounds as good as ever. In '68 the record might have gathered dust, but times have changed, we've O.D.'d on Art, and the artlessness of these packaged crackers suddenly sounds quite authentic, as rock and roll, as self-expression, as a valid manifestation by its very commerciality of the rock tradition, which after all is rooted in the sheerest decadence of our glittering cornucopial American culture.

Next is the Box Tops' surprising version of Hank Snow's "I'm Movin' On," one of the very best versions of that song ever, complete with a great rolling bass solo that expresses beautifully a sense of traveler's wonder as the great golden Rocky Mountain crags of echoing brass loom up. Enter lead guitar, dancing rockabilly pirouettes around this wash of sound, followed a chorus later by rocking cowboogie piano, all jamming joyfully as the brass oozes past mountain shadows into the fadeout.

"She Shot a Hole in My Soul" and "People Gonna Talk" are also fine songs, throbbing soul progressions transfused via the Box Tops' own unique approach into beautiful buoyant stretches of pure rolling pleasure, somewhat like the Rascals' sweet-soul songs but more airy. At times, yes, the Box Tops *do* get a mite raw and low-down—the three-minute version of "Rock Me Baby" on this album finds them about as "heavy" as they'll get, Chilton's gravelly voice out front of shrill Brian Jones-ish harp, terse edgy organ, grunting trombones and blues guitar riffs trilling with a subtle tinge of shitkicker sentimentality. A fine track at 3.49.

The *Super Hits* album is typical of groups like the Box Tops: note-for-note renditions of other people's hits like "Whiter Shade of Pale" alternating with all those tunes we started to like and grew to hate over the radio these last two years. This is where the Box Tops are at right now, and it's a greedy mindless approach to a superhits album.

—LESTER BANGS
12-13-69

JUDY IN DISGUISE WITH GLASSES
John Fred and His Playboy Band
(Paula LPS 2197)

John Fred, for those who manage never to listen to AM radio, is a kid from Louisiana who sold two-and-a-half million copies of a single called "Judy in Disguise (With Glasses)." The radio is the center of your life when you're driving a lot—in the old days, many producers used to play their produce through a car radio speaker to make sure they had it right—and "Judy in Disguise" soon distinguished itself as a great car song.

It had the simple melody and the heavy beat, but it was good music over and above that—the instrumental work was very tight, the arrangement original with several good gimmicks (a heavy breath for punctuation and a short filter-distort at the close), and the lyrics, well, strange, not what is called rock poetry but not "yummyyummyyummy igotloveinmytummy" either. Furthermore, it sounded like John Fred and His Playboy Band had a fine time making the record.

One does not expect a good album from a John Fred. Even the Box Tops, a Top-40 group that has never released a second-rate single, make terrible albums, and the Tommy Jameses are much worse.

On the cover of this album in its original release was a corny picture of the band. On the back were pictures of John's two previous LPs—John has been a star in Louisiana for a long time—and some acknowledgements ("Sitar Furnished By —Kenny Gill Music, Baton Rouge, La."). But it is a great record.

The album is now entitled *Judy in Disguise* and has a not-bad cartoon on the cover. Paula, which hadn't wanted to release "Judy" as a single because it was a little, well, er, far out, decided to play the freak for what it was worth. But the album didn't sell much. All those singles sales were to the 12-year-old market. And in a couple of years, chances are that John Fred will be back in the South playing dances, or maybe in the administrative end of the music business.

Like many white singers from the South (Alex Chilton of the Box Tops, for instance), John Fred's bag is pop R&B. He is tuned to Memphis and to white singers like Eric Burdon and Stevie Winwood, the Eric and Stevie of "When I Was Young" and "Gimme Some Lovin'." And just like them, he has ambitions. Obviously, he and his collaborator, sax player Andrew Bernard, listened carefully to the Beatles and decided to do some studio stuff of their own.

Similar decisions have produced a lot of bad music in the past year.

But stuck down there in Shreveport, Fred and Bernard were principally entertainers who wanted to fool around a little. So when they use crowd noises in "Achenall Riot" they integrate them cleanly into the music. They write obscure lyrics but link them to things known and seen, so that "Agnes English," a Top Ten record in places like Dallas that reached 70 or so nationally, is obviously about a whorehouse. They employ a sitar and a girl chorus and part of the Dallas Symphony Orchestra but (out of pure caution, probably) never overdo it. Those three songs are the "experimental" ones. All were written by Fred and Bernard, who also contributed two more conventional songs (including an exceedingly catchy bopper-trap called "Up and Down," which should have been the follow-up and wasn't) and an arresting talk thing called "Sad Story." There is one song by Bernard and other group members (I suspect Bernard is the musical talent of the organization) and five by outsiders. The only one that doesn't work is "Out of Left Field," mostly because it's hard to redo Percy Sledge. Fred and Bernard produced the whole record.

Judy in Disguise is energetic, intelligent and refreshing. It is reminiscent in spirit of the Hollies, who in albums like *Evolution* combine first-rate musicianship with an utter disdain for the lugubrious. The Airplane and Stones have succumbed to excesses, but Fred and Bernard do not. Of course, they had much less to work with—the lyrics are high-pop in quality, and while the music is precise and well-realized, it is not brilliant. (The band is exceptionally tight live, but Fred is not a good performer, and his choice of material is unfortunate—he does other people's songs because he believes his young audiences won't recognize his own.)

But for anyone who caught himself liking "Judy" or has a prejudice for happy music, the album is a worthwhile gamble. Just tell your friendly neighborhood record dealer to write Paula Records, 728 Texas Street, Shreveport, Louisiana. He'll get it eventually.

—ROBERT CHRISTGAU

7-6-68

WRITER: CAROLE KING
Carole King
(Ode SP 7700)

Carole King started her career as a singer. In 1963 she had a hit with "He's a Bad Boy." But she's been much more famous as half of the fabulous Goffin-King songwriting team, which has been responsible for innumerable great songs over the past decade: "One Fine Day," "The Locomotion," "Baby, It's You," "Will You Still Love Me Tomorrow," "Don't Bring Me Down," "A Natural Woman." The list could go on for a long time. Thus, although the title of her album emphasizes Carole's writing (all the songs are by Goffin-King anyway), a major part of its interest is in her return as a singer. Alas, her singing is the weakest element of what is in all other respects a very good album.

At its best, her voice is quite adequate, reminiscent of Cass Elliot's cold-in-the-nose low register, complete with a slightly irritating accent of some kind (New York? Philadelphia?). The best singing is on songs where she does not try to exceed her own capabilities, as on "To Love," which is done in a very nice semi-country voice, free from mannerisms or strain.

The album is very relaxed, almost mellow in mood; by no means hard rock. Carole did the arrangements, which are excellent, and is backed by a band which includes herself on piano, James Taylor on acoustic guitar, a sensitively used Moog, strings where needed, and a fine group of electric musicians. The sound is sophisticated studio, and in a few places the band *sounds* like a studio band: not completely welded to the singer. For the most part the musicians are excellent.

The songs themselves range from the ordinary to the very good. The former category includes some songs, such as "Eventually," which lack the characteristic melodic quality of Goffin-King's best efforts. Goffin-King songs are eminently hummable, not to mention singable. Standouts in the latter category include two of the team's oldies, "Goin' Back" and "Up on the Roof," which, possibly by virtue of sheer familiarity, emerge as among the best on the album. "Sweet Sweetheart," an Aretha-type soul number which could as easily be done in country style, and "No Easy Way Down," a slow song with a Procol Harum/Band rhythm, are also good.

Though flawed, this is still a listenable, indeed nice, record. You might like it. Any album with a real live piano *has* to be good.

—MELISSA MILLS
10-29-70

ELI AND THE THIRTEENTH CONFESSION
Laura Nyro
(Columbia CS 9626)

I wasn't at Monterey. Consequently, I don't really know what Laura Nyro did there that turned so many people off. She must have done something, because the word was so thick that it convinced me that there wasn't any point bothering with her first album. It took a lunatic friend of mine, barging into my apartment a couple of weeks ago, frothing at the mouth about the record, to get me to listen to it seriously. All I can say is I'm glad he did.

Laura Nyro's music is a mixed marriage of diverse styles. Her melodies and lead vocal betray a Bacharach-David type of sophistication. Her harmony and some of her rhythms show she's been influenced either directly or indirectly by Curtis Mayfield's Impressions. To that nucleus she adds a rock, almost soul, beat with lyrics that occasionally sound like sophisticated Bobbi Gentry ("Let's go down by the grapevine/drink your daddy's wine"). In both lyrics and melodies there is a generally attractive combination of the ornate and elementary.

Laura is at her best when she leans more towards the simple side. Perhaps "Lu" shows that side best. The chorus, which contains the Impressions' lyric phrase "keep on pushin'" is exquisitely simple and driving. The beat hits very hard and it can sweep you off your feet. The whole chorus sounds like it was drawn from the same bag as Steve Miller's "Pushed Me To It," it has that same type of harmony only done with infinitely more grace.

She's at her worst when she breaks her rhythms too much and misuses her falsetto. I say misuses because she employs both beat changes and falsetto on practically every cut, sometimes, as on "Lu," to great effect. However, when she overdoes it, she clutters the track up with superfluous emoting. In such cases, both techniques begin to sound like artificial gimmicks. The introduction to "Timer" is subject to both of these faults and severely damages what is in other ways a fine cut. Similarly, "Poverty Train," which has a powerful chorus, might have been more effective if the arrangement had been tighter. Yet, even with defects, that cut comes out very powerfully.

The cumulative impact of Laura's excesses make this a difficult album to listen to all the way through. Yet the strong cuts (which far outnumber the weak ones) when listened to individually, reveal the mark of an original and brilliant young talent. When she gets into a steady, solid groove, whether fast or slow, she can make you feel it deep down inside. Dig her especially on "Luckie," "Eli's Comin'," "Stone Soul Picnic" (which the Fifth Dimension took note for note), and "Emmie."

Laura Nyro has a long way to go. But she also has a lot going for her: a fine voice, a great melodic and lyrical sense, and plenty of style. What she mainly needs now is a little more self-restraint and control. It will come.

—JON LANDAU
9-28-68

COLLAGE
The Raiders
(Columbia CS 9964)

One of the things about long-lived Top-40 groups is that they certainly learn how not to mess around on record; no forty minute guitar freak-outs, no highly-convoluted masterpieces, no feedback for the sake of feedback. They simply take care of business, accomplishing things with a minimum of waste and self-indulgence, putting in each piece as if it were a logical part of a puzzle. The main object is to pulse out a beat and message just as fast and hard as possible, and then let the mixture fly wherever it may.

The Raiders are no exception. Under the direction of Paul Revere, they've produced a string of classic singles over the past few years: "Steppin' Out," "Just Like Me," "Hungry," "Good Thing." At times, you may not have cared much for what they were saying ("kicks just keep gettin' harder to find"), but you could never deny the power in the way they managed to put it over. Now, guided by Mark Lindsay in an attempt to bring them up-to-date, they've continued doing the same sort of thing with *Collage*.

This is a great album from the very moment it takes off. For openers, the Raiders light into a version of Laura Nyro's "Save The Country" which is remarkable for the original treatment it gives to a song quite undeservedly on its way to being this year's Muzak superhit. They begin with a riff reminiscent of Otis Redding's version of "Satisfaction" and then move into one of those eternal rock and roll arrangements that will probably never lose its effectiveness, no matter how many times it's overused. Adding some tasteful horns, some rather obvious military drumming and a fine Lindsay vocal, it sits there waiting for you, all set to be played a half dozen or a million times.

Similarly, when the Raiders get into their own material (mostly penned by Lindsay and co-Raider Keith Allison), they continue in much the same direction. There's nothing overwhelmingly original here—you know that you've heard it all *somewhere* before—but the blend never fails to be carefully constructed and well-done. "Think Twice" is the old reliable so-you-want-to-be-a-rock-and-roll-star song, "Dr. Fine" seems like a synthesis of any number of Top 40 FM radio hits, and "Just Seventeen" never even tries to hide its Led Zeppelin roots. You could probably go through most of the other cuts on the album in a similar fashion, picking out the "sound" each song was built upon and moving from there.

Yet derivative though it is, Lindsay's music and lyrics manage to do that one extra thing to make the song rise above any average level. "Gone Movin' On" is probably the best example on the album of the Raiders' approach: simple lyrics, even to the point of reciting that time-worn phrase of "It was easy come/But now it's easy go," a great rocking beat reminiscent of many of their earlier hits, and a fine arrangement that makes the song move and consequently work. Lindsay's power as a vocalist also adds another dimension to the album. Forget all the silly "Arizona" type things he's been doing on his own of late; just listen to him gleefully say "just 17 and that's a *crime*" on "Just Seventeen." Beautiful.

With all the good, however, there are times when the Top 40 satisfy-everybody format of the album becomes a bit much. There is a mandatory social commentary song ("We Gotta All Get Together"—of course), and a couple of things which border on pretension—though it must be noted that one carries the strangely significant title of "Interlude (to be forgotten)." Through it all, though, Mark Lindsay never fails to give the

impression that he knows what he is doing. Almost single-handedly, he's brought the Raiders to a stronger position than they've occupied for the past couple of years, and if future albums build on the strengths of *Collage,* we should be in for some fine music indeed. More power to him.

—LENNY KAYE
6-11-70

TIME PEACE
The Rascals
(Atlantic SD 8190)

The Rascals should probably be considered one of the best white hard rock bands recording in the rhythm and blues idiom; after all, vocalist Felix Cavaliere not only has an honest full voice, but with Eddie Brigati he has also penned some rhythm and blues classics, "Groovin'" in particular. In spite of this fact critical attention recently has tended to ignore the Rascals, and not entirely without justification. *Time Peace,* a collection of the Rascals' "greatest hits," offers an opportunity to review in retrospect just exactly what the Rascals have contributed to rock music.

From the outset the Rascals, like most rhythm and blues performers, have built their art within the confines of the commercial single. Their early work arises out of a definite white hard rock tradition, and these initial recordings, especially when considered in the context of the Righteous Brothers, the Kingsmen, and the early Paul Revere and the Raiders, still sound significantly better than most white rhythm and blues efforts of the era.

The instrumentation on the early tracks is the standard white hard rock one: guitar, bass, organ and drums. Since none of the Rascals is an outstanding instrumentalist, most of their charts stay pretty close to the bare essentials of rhythm and blues conventions: there is no trace of the virtuosity of Booker T. and the M.G.'s here. In "I Ain't Gonna Eat My Heart," the first "Young" Rascals single, Eddie Brigati adopts a rather fey tough-guy stance in his vocal and somehow almost makes it work; although the instrumental break is elementary, and the whole song plods through its changes, the result sounded quite tolerable on the AM airwaves of late 1965.

The group's second single, "Good Lovin'," introduced Cavaliere as lead singer; his voice has more range and depth than Brigati's, and on "Good Lovin'" he uses it to fine effect. Cavaliere is no Stevie Winwood, but in many ways he is closer to the spirit of rhythm and blues than Winwood; like Winwood, his phrasing and vocal quality distinguish him, among white rhythm and blues singers.

The several efforts by the Rascals immediately succeeding "Good Lovin'" were all more or less stylistically akin: the early Rascal originals were credible genre pieces, but little more. The listener feels keenly the unimaginative rhythm work that is the curse of so many white rhythm and blues bands; the Rascals employ few of the little syncopations and rhythmic off-accents that are generally one of the main factors in gracefully forcing the heavy rhythm and blues rhythm to swing.

These faults are most glaring in the two Rascals' interpretations of the rhythm and blues classics "Mustang Sally" and "Midnight Hour." Neither is in any way comparable to the Wilson Pickett versions, and both serve as case studies in the weaknesses of white rhythm and blues: both tracks, but particularly "Mustang Sally," suffer from the absence of horns; on both tracks guitarist Gene Cornish suffers in comparison with either Steve Cropper or Jimmy Johnson; on both tracks Dino Danelli's drumming suffers from monotony, hardly a problem with either Al Jackson or Roger Hawkins. Nevertheless a song like "Love Is a Beautiful Thing" shows that the Rascals were in the process of evolving an original rhythm and blues style, not in inconsiderable achievement.

"Groovin'" opened up a new

phase for the Rascals. The instrumentation, which before that time had been crying out for expansion, was augmented; the Rascals began to settle into a relaxed, unselfconscious rhythm and blues groove that was unique in a white hard rock group; and, most importantly, the group recorded some beautiful rock tracks. "Groovin'," to begin with, is a classic Cavaliere-Brigati composition, a simple, unassuming yet appealing bit of rock magic. The production work attains a new high for the Rascals—even the sound effects of birds that open the track are tastefully mixed. There are effective (if unobtrusive) overdubs of piano and organ (and piano and piano), as well as some appropriate fills on a vibraharp. The rhythm section of bongos and tambourine enhances the easygoing aura of the record, an aura and mood so perfectly sustained that the original Rascals' version is quite capable of standing on its own merits next to Aretha Franklin's more complex reading and arrangement of the song.

"A Girl Like You" is also representative of the Rascals at their best. The original composition is set off by a nice loping figure for horns that imparts a jazz flavor to the track, while Cavaliere sings beautifully throughout, especially in the opening section of the song. By this record Cavaliere had developed an appealing unforced quality to his singing, and even the back-up vocal work had acquired a distinctive rhythm and blues character.

Of course, the later Rascals are not without their faults, since they are capable of both the pretentious (a disaster in their case) as well as the cloyingly sentimental. For instance, Brigati's rather strained vocal effort on "How Can I Be Sure" is splendidly set off by violins, accordion and horn, but the song hangs suspended over a syrupy abyss. If this song doesn't fall into its self-set trap, "It's Wonderful" does, with devastating results—apparently "It's Wonderful" represents the Rascals' fling with psychedelia. Unfortunately, the echoed interjections refuse to let the song alone, standing as a signal instance of tasteless tape work.

The last song on *Time Peace*, "It's a Beautiful Morning," represents the recent Rascals performing one of their own songs in a typical vein. The group is together, the production work is tasteful, and the arrangement achieves a pleasing textural fullness; the vocal group work is superior, and Cavaliere's singing, as usual, leaves little to be desired. If some of the old faults persist, the Rascals here, as elsewhere in their recorded output, prove that they have evolved a distinctive and not unappealing approach to the rhythm and blues idiom. They may not be consistent, but the Rascals' undeniable mastery of their chosen craft not only makes their best work excellent, but also makes *Time Peace* a collection of tracks well worth listening to.

—JIM MILLER
5-17-69

DON'T IT MAKE YOU WANT TO GO HOME
Joe South
(Capitol ST 392)

Top forty radio is better than ever these days. Singles by such artists as Brainbox, the Hollies, Fleetwood Mac and Shocking Blue are all getting air-play and are all eminently fine market creations. Most all singles are "market creations" because they are all basically chosen or recorded with a sales factor in mind. Usually instantaneous and fleeting in concept, the above groups and others are now creating singles of true durability.

All of which brings us to Joe South's current hit, "Walk A Mile In My Shoes," a song that contains all the textures and abandonment that characterize his new album. The single, in itself, is a fine four-minute review of this album. The first fifteen seconds feature South's bobbing rhythm guitar and hand-thumped drums that introduce the extensions of the main song-riff. Then there is a pause which somehow slides right into South's drawling lyrics of "point-of-view" in the Seventies. Each chorus is screamed out, revival-style, by South's back-up group of girls and acts as a shot of auditory adrenalin that moves the record along. The unique factor here is that, though basically identical, each chorus riff is subtly different as South slips in and out at his leisure. Strings also slide gradually into the song, about halfway through, augmenting and emphasizing South's infective vocal and straining out the sound of the chorus into a marvelous fade-out that, very effectively, slides away with the same off-the-beat guitar progression that it slid in with. I never thought I'd hear the word "ego" in a top forty effort, but South proves me wrong and does it magnificently with variety, spontaneity, inflection and honest lyrics.

The album is an extension of the single—both are a refreshing change of pace as far as sound is concerned—South starts with country and western, yet before most of the cuts are over he winds up blending in gospel and soul along with the above-mentioned vocal back-up group that features Barbara South, who, I assume, is his wife. The arranging avoids gimmickry, and, while stacked with horns and those tempestuous Spector-ian back-up climaxes, *sounds* as though it was recorded in Atlanta, Georgia.

In addition to these factors on the album there is one cut, "A Million Miles Away," which is possibly as relevant as Chicago's "The Whole World Is Watching" number, during which South attempts to speak to Nixon with train-kept-a-rollin' drumming and funky Ventures/Johnny & the Hurricanes guitar-work boggling in the background.

All in all, it's as tight an album as recent efforts by other rejuvenated country artists such as Jerry Lee Lewis, Carl Perkins, the Everlys and Lonnie Mack. But South isn't rejuvenated—he has borrowed from the idiom (like the Spoonful, Beatles, Dylan and the Band before him) yet managed to add his own diverse elements. On tracks like "Shelter" (which is the flip of "Walk A Mile") and "Before It's Too Late" South sounds as though he could have done the arranging for the Edwin Hawkins Singers "Oh Happy Day" album—the gospel fervor is that real (down to handclapping percussion on the latter cut), and, ultimately, convincing. What we get a glimpse of on the single is magnified ten-fold on the album. Perhaps the most "country" element on the album is South's voice, which, particularly on the up-tempo ballads, is almost a duplicate of vintage Roy Orbison, who actually was a predecessor to the things that South accomplishes here.

If you dig "Walk a Mile," try this album. Half of the cuts make it totally and the others, though over-arranged, are a sign of things to come from this man South. At times he allows his sly production techniques to get in the way of his voice, but it is still a remarkable album by a former session-guitarist for Dylan, among others. I just hope Capitol doesn't saddle him with a producer and arranger next time (he does it all himself here) or, worse yet, bring him to Hollywood to record. Atlanta's nice.

—GARY VON TERSCH
3-7-70

B. J. THOMAS GREATEST HITS, VOL. 1
B. J. Thomas
(Scepter SPS 578)

B. J. Thomas is a respectable journeyman who has sustained himself for several years by regularly filling our season's quota of AM survey annoyance with singles, and removed from the torturous redundance of the radio, his hits have a certain catchy charm, exuding high school sentimentality and teenage melodrama in Sta-Prest Levis modern dress. If the trite, maudlin anguish of many of the songs of this record seems absolutely unbelievable in this post-hip era, remember that no one could ever count the tears shed to them when they were singles of yore—Because They Spoke To Youth In Their Own Language.

Take "Billy And Sue," the plight of two young lovers sundered by the military-industrial complex because "when Billy was old enough to take a wife/He was old enough to fight for his country/And his way of life." Sue sends him a Dear John letter in Vietnam, but he's saved from a lifetime of mundane pining because "He'd rather die from a bullet than to die/From a broken heart."

"Hooked On A Feeling" must have been the ultimate Dating Game euphemization of the 1967 drug-song syndrome: slick Box Tops organ, electric sitar, and: "I'm hooked on a feeling/High on believing/That you're in love with me." Solid. It was a good record, too.

The album reaches its emo-tional climax with "Plain Jane," a True Confessions tearjerker about that poor homely chick we all knew in high school, the one shut out from the madcap social whirl of maindrag cruising and technical virginity, sustaining her lonely soul with romantic novels and candy bars. A figure drawn from real life, yes, as true as the new abstract Lady Madonnas and Ruby Tuesdays. But dig the denouement: the kids pull a fake phone call from a football hero, "inviting" her to the prom, and when he fails to materialize on the big night she commits suicide! Take a lesson from that, kids. Your brothers and sisters certainly did, at least until the next day at school, where class lines were the lesson that mattered, where pariahs were pariahs, and the sentimental compassion mushed up from pop songs was just that: sentiment.

—LESTER BANGS
4-3-70

Some

Singing Voices

A number of solo artists working in the rock idiom emerged despite the overwhelming popularity of the group as a format. Some of them, like John Phillips, were once members and even leaders of groups that preceded them.

By no means a comprehensive selection, in fact, a catch-all category, this chapter is one in which the emergence of the solo artists can be traced, both from the folk and rock fields. It is an unusually fine aggregation of singers.

VINTAGE VIOLENCE
John Cale
(Columbia CS 1037)

It was about 3:30 in the afternoon. Down 7th Street, a parade of parochial school girls wended its way towards the projects on Avenue D, the sidewalks coming alive with the plaid skirts swishing not quite in unison as they walked in twos and threes. People sat on the stoops reading papers, and a game of stickball was in progress in the vacant lot.

Suddenly, an argument flared up—in staccato Spanish—Dee Christian, a Robin-Hood-like figure among the 7th Streets amphetamine junkies (A-heads, we called them), had once again run into Spanish Eddie.

Guns were drawn, and the argument moved out into the street. Interested heads peeped from tenement windows and watched as Dee Christian went down, four bullets in his stomach. Eventually, I think, an ambulance came.

"Gideon lied/And Gideon died/The force of Cain felt."

New York is, of course, not such a nice place. And the New York scenemakers are a breed apart from their brethren elsewhere. To make *joie de vivre* coexist with the cockroaches takes some doing, or, perhaps, some help. Can Andy Warhol get behind cockroaches? See, the question answers itself. New York, New York, says the old show tune. It's a hell of a town.

"So hold on tightly/The show's on nightly/They speak so very slow/It gets so hard to follow . . ."

John Cale has been around. First with the Velvet Underground, where he played electric viola and wrote some stuff for them. Then he disappeared for a while, re-emerging as an employee of Elektra Records, where he helped Nico and her album *The Marble Index,* a work formidable in its unapproachability, and (paradox upon paradox) he then produced the Stooges' first album, which is so staggeringly simple that most people can't take it.

Now he has showed up on Columbia, with an album of amazing complexity. Most of the songs sound like a Byrds album produced by a Phil Spector who has marinated for six years in burgundy, anise, and chili peppers. Does that help? I didn't think it would.

Well, then, suffice it to say that this is an important album, even though it takes a while to take hold. It stands up well next to such masterpieces as *Astral Weeks,* Jesse Winchester's album, and—yes, I dare say it—*Highway 61.* It is a deeply moving personal statement by an artist who just doesn't compromise in any direction and I believe that it is destined to become one of the most important albums of the past few years.

Obviously, there is a story here. There is a list of characters on the back, and times and places crop up as they would in a diary. The story goes untold in a literal sense, though, and the inferences don't make a whole. No matter, because it's just as interesting to listen and let the total gestalt form slowly. About all you can tell after the 60th listening is that there is more to be gotten, and it may take years. Like Van Morrison's lyrics, Cale's pop out at you at odd times and sock you right in the stomach: "Gideon sighed/As Gideon died/The thought of China helped," a fleeting reference to "my proud amphibian bride."

The songs themselves are delightful, melodic things which almost (but not quite) belie the spirit of the lyrics. In fact, "Big White Cloud" could easily be a Top-40 hit, with its sing-along chorus. Other standouts are "Gideon's Bible," "Ghost Story," "Charlemagne" and "Please," which seems to me to be the most thoroughly realized composition on the album, with the instruments unfolding layers of sound reminiscent of a forest of sea anemones on the ocean floor.

Mention should also be made of another of the album's enigmas—the musicians. I have never heard a backup band—overdubbed as they may be—with such an incredibly organic flow. At times, there seem to be two pedal steel guitars and a regular electric guitar, bass, piano, organ, acoustic guitar, and drums, and the interplay they achieve (try on "Gideon's Bible" or "Please," or the eerie ending of the aptly-titled "Ghost Stories") is masterful and chilling. Special notice must go to the pedal steel player, who has invented a whole new approach to the instrument that can only be termed rhythm/lead pedal steel. And, of course, there is Cale's electric viola, providing everything from white noise to the seductive sussurance the instrument was created for. In keeping with the album's enigma, there is little indication who they are, although it would be a safe bet to say that they include members of a band called Grinder's Switch, who put out a perfectly awful album a few months back. But if that's so, why are they so good here? If we're lucky, we'll never find out.

Dee Christian, incidentally, recovered and detoxified. A few days after the incident, somebody sold Spanish Eddie a bag of Drano, which he promptly did up. He lived, too.

—ED WARD
9-17-70

THE SONGS OF
LEONARD COHEN
Leonard Cohen
(Columbia CS 9533)

There are, in *The Favorite Game,* Leonard Cohen's first novel, several scenes in which people ask the hero (presumably Cohen, since everything else fits) to sing. A friend of mine read the book and finished with one question: if the guy was Leonard Cohen, why did they keep asking him to sing? I think that is untrue—the more I listen to this LP the more I like his voice. It is a strange voice—he hits every note, but between each note he recedes to an atonal place—his songs are thus given a sorely needed additional rhythm.

The record as a whole is another matter—I don't think I could ever tolerate all of it. There are three brilliant songs, one good one, three qualified bummers, and three are the flaming shits.

The problem is that, whether the man is a poet or not (and he is a brilliant poet), as those ridiculous ads announce in hushed tones of reverence, he is not necessarily a songwriter; his three successes ("Suzanne," "The Master Song," and "The Stranger Song") are stories, ballads whose progression of meaning becomes more important to Cohen than his poetic bag of tricks. Elsewhere, this kind of delicacy, put to the rigid demands of music, sinks into doggerel: "I lit a thin green candle /To make you jealous of me/ But the room just filled up with mosquitoes/They heard that my body was free."

Worse, in the same song, "One of Us Cannot Be Wrong" (only forgivable if a parody of Dylan, and then questionable) Cohen does what has become reputable for the songwriter aspiring to poetry; he has confused the marijuana or fatigue silly high with the insight of poetry (one can blow one's mind promiscuously): "Then I took the dust of a long sleepless night/And I put it in your little shoe,/Then I confess that I tortured the dress/That you wore for the world to look through." Then there is the standard Dylan trick of reversed images ("smoked my eyelids and punched my cigarette"): "I showed my heart to the doctor/He said I'd just have to quit/Then he wrote himself a prescription/And your name was mentioned in it." The poet-become-songwriter runs the risk of imprisonment in his new discipline, because he does not come to it naturally.

The arrangements are beyond even sympathy; a fact I take Cohen to recognize in his notes to the album: ". . . they were forbidden to marry. Nevertheless, the arrangements wished to throw a party. The songs preferred to retreat behind a veil of satire." Would that it were that easy. In "Marianne," the lyrics of which are reasonably unpretentious, there is a chorus, the musical ancestors of which are the Hi-Los. In "Teachers" there is a hard guitar sound, ridiculously inappropriate, copped, if I remember correctly, from Marty Robbins' "El Paso," a better song. On the last song ("One of Us Cannot Be Wrong") the arrangement fades into a hilarious cacophony—but the Beach Boys did this kind of thing better in *Smiley Smile* (and they aren't even poets). If this is satire, it is satire after the fact. In back of most of the songs is an indistinguishable Muzak hum.

But three songs make the LP worthy of purchase (unless one is interested in culture heroes, like Janis Ian, in which case the other songs are infinitely more valuable).

"Suzanne" is a song of distance; doggerel exists when there is no place to go: this song goes into a center and out again, resting, finally, closer to the center than it began. Cohen, with the second person, is telling you how you (he) feels. Further distance.

"The Master Song" is ambiguous—but the art of its ambiguity does not interfere with its ability to move. There is, in Cohen's novel, and in places on this LP, a kind of faith in the regenerative power of degeneration, of sadness, perhaps even of evil. The song works also—I don't know whether this is the intention as a song for two of the characters of *Beautiful Losers*, Cohen's second novel.

"The Stranger Song" is perhaps the best. Cohen the aphorist here realizes that aphorism is more insight than surprise. The simplicity of the imagery does not interfere with the feelings of the characters nor the situation, nor do the images crowd the loneliness. Here is perhaps the most moving statement Cohen can make: "And he wants to trade the game he plays for shelter/And he wants to trade the game he knows for shelter."

—ARTHUR SCHMIDT
3-9-68

BABYLON
Dr. John, the Night Tripper
(Atco SD 33-270)

Try to imagine Mose Allison stoned and trapped in a swamp with a chorus of mistaken Baptist harmonies. Do you remember Dr. John's first album? It was really underground stuff: smoky and aquatic, a sort of voodoo-funk. His second album, *Babylon,* has some of the mystery and charm of the first, but on the whole it's disappointing. It's not at all together; it seems to fall apart inside your ear.

What's wrong is the relationship between the lyrics and the music. The music itself is still Generally Weird—lots of electronic effects and distant, unthinkable rhythms. But the music is also vague and centerless. None of the musicians are credited on the jacket, and with reason. None of them are there. Except for some mediocre guitar on "Lonesome Guitar Strangler," none of the musicians can be heard. The music just floats in the background; it's really a sound-environment, a sustained mood. The songs are definitely songs—with beginnings, middles and ends, but they still don't stand up as individual pieces. For one thing, Dr. John's singing is not melodic—instead, it's a sort of meandering chant. The sound is sinister and fascinating at first, but eventually it becomes tiresome. A few of the songs have interesting parts—"Lonesome Guitar Strangler" has funny lyrics and funky imitations of Jimi Hendrix and Wes Montgomery. "Twilight Zone," the longest piece on the album, is a spaced science-fiction ballad with visionary lyrics: "Martians kidnap the First Family, they gonna demand New York City for ransom money. We gonna outsmart 'em, leave a note for 'em to read—the best they can get is Milwaukee. . . ."

The album really stumbles on the words. There are too many of them and the music (what there is of it) gets smothered by their weight. The lyrics are long, involved raps; they demand attention, while the music doesn't. The effect is that of literature chanted to jazz and a chorus of demented angels. The literature is somewhat lacking.

Dr. John was much the better when his songs didn't even try to make sense. After all, what the hell *is* Gris-Gris on the first album? Who cares? The lyrics on *Babylon* come on heavy, but they're actually ordinary, too thin to sustain the mood that the music seems to imply. It would be interesting to hear Dr. John try this sort of thing with better lyrics—maybe a middle-period Dylan song, or a chunk of William Burroughs' more scabrous fantasies, or even some Henry Miller. Could it be that Dr. John is actually a Ph.D.?

—DAVID GANCHER
5-31-68

REMEDIES
Dr. John, the Night Tripper
(Atco SD 33-316)

Break out the hash pipe and heat up the gumbo—Dr. John is back again with music from that steamy, swampy place in your mind that only Dr. John can reach. *Remedies* is not get-it-on rock music; it's too loose and languid for that. The rhythms—by far the best part of Dr. John's music—are lyrical and liquid; they flow and throb, like blood, like fucking. Dr. John's music is not mind-music, not body-music—at its best, it is emotional—beyond words, almost beyond form. It is ecstasy without pleasure, misery without pain.

Remedies is Dr. John's third album, and his music has gone through some changes. Dr. John himself, née Mac Rebbenack, seems to have taken over the musical direction. He wrote and arranged all the songs. The choir of heavy ladies that haunted the first two albums has been replaced by a horn section. The sound is more solid, more predictable, almost rock-and-roll. Dr. John sings better than ever; his voice is rougher, raspier, meaner. In Dr. John's mouth, a seemingly innocent song takes on a sinister and almost nasty edge; the melodies never seem quite solid. The singing sounds like a blood ritual made crude by a dark kind of dope. Satanic, the Kenneth Anger or Charlie Manson image.

The songs on Side One—the commercial side—are loose and rappy, full of funny rhymes, street slang, and double meanings. The opener, "Loop Garoo" is most like the songs on the first Dr. John album. The lyrics are magic incantations, incomprehensible, evocative. The rhythms are slinky and wet, and the horns sound like Wilson Pickett's horn section lost in a swamp and stoned on belladonna. "Wash, Mama, Wash" is great—about a funky washerwoman who drinks too much and blows the family food money playing the numbers.

The lyrics are just as funky as the subject; the chorus goes "Rub-adubba-dubba-mama, bustlin' suds/Scrub, mama, scrub." After that, it just gets better. And the piano, the *piano!* "Chippy, chippy" is about: chippying. "Everybody in the neighborhood loves to chippy, and they chippy goooood." And chippying is . . . well, if you don't know, don't mess with it. These songs are the most successful pieces on the album—they are so clever, so right-on.

Side Two consists of a 17-minute voodoo aria called "Angola Anthem." It is a long, meandering lyric on top of some good but aimless Afro drumming. The instrumental parts are sparse, weak, and easily lost. The lyrics, where they can be heard, do little to redeem the piece. They try to invoke the terror of living under a fascist regime in Angola, but the piece fails. And in a 17-minute piece, if you do not succeed, you really fail. Despite an occasional interesting part, the piece lacks drama, lacks words, lacks music. You can't listen to it, and you can't even dance to it.

Remedies is good Dr. John, but Dr. John is not for everyone. His audience is an esoteric bunch. If you dig *jive,* pure jive; if you dig dreaming, if you dig Wolfman Jack, if you ever order barbecue at 4 AM; if you get stoned to watch TV commercials while eating Colonel Sanders fried chicken and drinking warm Ripple—then you are weird enough for Dr. John. And he is, sure as sin and rain, weird enough for you.

—DAVID GANCHER
6-11-70

SPIRIT IN THE SKY
Norman Greenbaum
(Reprise 6365)

Some years back, a dim star sputtered in the sky of Pop Music. Dr. West's Medicine Show and Junk Band, hailing from Chicago, put out a single entitled "The Eggplant That Ate Chicago," which made it fairly high on the charts and brought the band fleeting fame. But, in spite of a pretty good album, the Junk Band took the short step from Chicago to nowhere and Chicago, alas, remained uneaten.

This woeful story is recounted because the guiding genius of the Junk Band is alive and living in Petaluma, California, and has just put out a truly inspiring first-class album. Norman Greenbaum has emerged as a man of real talent. He writes and sings all the material on *Spirit in the Sky,* and although it doesn't say who did the arranging, if he did that, too, he is doubly good.

Spirit in the Sky represents a most enjoyable approach to a white soul sound. Greenbaum doesn't bother trying to sound black and lets himself sound like Greenbaum—a kind of flat whiny voice with power—if you can imagine that. But, instead of sounding like a Mouseketeer trying out with the Stax-Volt band, he totally dominates the music. Whoever worked out the band and the backup chorus had a great deal of imagination and total familiarity with his material. No musician, and there appear to be a great many used, is permitted an indulgence or any extraneous music. Nothing drags. There isn't a boring note on this album.

But the record would only be pretty good but for Greenbaum's songs themselves. "Catchy" may not be the heaviest adjective to tack on a rock singer, but it suits him and his songs. Many of the cuts on this album are the sort that keep running through the mind at odd hours. And they all lift things up. They're not heart rending, but neither are they trivial.

The title cut, "Spirit in the Sky," is representative of the album; it's making it on Top-40, and with good reason. It starts off with the dirtiest heavy-industrial fuzz-tone heard outside a machine shop and moves into a handclapping/snare drum rhythm. Norman, backed by a super chick chorus, generates a great deal of enthusiasm. Infectious is the word.

There is humor and melody, a lot of music and a lot of joy on this record. It demands virtually nothing from the listener, nor does it patronize him, and in return it gives pleasure.

A good deal. Norman Greenbaum.

—ALEC DUBRO
3-19-69

ORIGINAL RECORDINGS
Dan Hicks and His Hot Licks
(Epic BN 26464)

The Charlatans never became a really name band, but if they had, Dan Hicks surely would have been the star. A talented songwriter, Hicks wrote some of their best, and his pleasant voice added a welcome element of softness to their sound.

But even while a Charlatan, Hicks was working on his own, first gigging as a single act and then with His Hot Licks—two chick singers, violinist Sid Page, lead guitarist Jon Weber and Jaime Leopold on standup bass. Finally, Hicks decided to leave the Charlatans.

Epic offered him a good contract (about $50,000 in front money) and he started working up some "original recordings" for his first LP. It was produced by Bob Johnston (*John Wesley Harding, Nashville Skyline*) but Johnston did such a poor job that Hicks had to re-mix the entire album himself. It was the first time he'd worked that side of the studio so, naturally, it reflects his inexperience. (One wonders in what shape *Johnston* left the tapes.)

Yet, by and large, it's a good album; not very exciting, but pleasant, with imaginative arrangements for simple (though not banal) lyrics.

One problem is that the overall effect is so low-key that unless you listen to it several times, parts tend to be forgettable—even though most of the tunes *are* enjoyable. Not that every cut sounds the same. There is considerable variety—from straight country humor on "How Can I Miss You When You Won't Go Away?" to the haunting "I Scare Myself" that blends background vocals and some fine violin work by Page. Yet the supporting vocals by Sherry Snow and Christina Gancher have little variety: they are always pleasant, but are literally, too much. (Hicks is auditioning for two new girls.)

"Waitin' for the '103'" exemplifies the best spirit of the album. It's light, tight, a really fine song that shows Hicks' writing talent. "Slow Movin'" recalls remnants of Ricky Nelson's "Travelin' Man." "Jukie's Ball" probably had its genesis with a radio spot Hicks did some months ago for Leonard Schaeffer's *A Boy and His Dog*, surely the worst album ever to come out of San Francisco. The spot was never aired, but in it Hicks introduces a character called Jimmy the Talking Harmonica; "Jukie's Ball" opens with dialogue about Jimmy the Talking Dummy "in his record debut"—a bouncy ditty featuring Page's violin. "Bad Grammar," too, is excellent.

In all, the album is interesting, in its potential if not always exciting in the execution. Criticism about the production rightfully belongs to Bob Johnston; much of the other liabilities can be chalked up to the fact that this is a first effort. Hicks will certainly distinguish himself on future LPs.

—GEOFFREY LINK
12-13-69

THE NATCH'L BLUES
Taj Mahal
(Columbia CS 9698)

Taj Mahal may not be the most authentic, the most technically proficient, or the most emotionally cathartic practitioner of the blues today, but he certainly is one of the most enjoyable and entertaining performers around. He's a quiet, soft-spoken man who enjoys fishing and building model airplanes and being a vegetarian. And his records are a solid joy to listen to.

The songs he plays are mostly blues standards—"Statesboro Blues," "E Z Rider," "Dust My Broom"—and it is a measure of his amazing musicianship that he is able to make them come off absolutely fresh and vital. His band is superb. Jesse Edwin Davis, the lead guitar player, is easily one of the best blues guitarists around. (Incidentally, he's an American Indian; you blues purists out there toy with *that* for a while!) His sound is pure and fluid and the lines he plays are wonderfully natural and unlabored. Gary Gillmore and Chuck Blackwell, bass and drums, are both ex-country musicians and are also excellent.

It's no surprise that Taj's second album is called *The Natch'l Blues*, because the music seems to be an extension of the band's life-style. I have seen Gary Gillmore peel an orange with the same infinite care that the band puts into their music. When someone asked him a question he seemed to put an imaginary bookmark in the orange, answer the question slowly and carefully, and then go back into the orange.

The key to the music is given in the liner notes to the first album: "You gotta get it right there in the first few bars." The first few bars really do have a way of hooking you, and before you realize it, you're involved with the song, jumping around and grooving with the music. What makes it all so easy is that Taj Mahal is an extremely engaging vocalist whose appeal is direct and immediate; he's one of the few people you can actually hear smiling.

Of the two albums he's put out, the first one is probably the better by a nose. The band personnel changes a bit from cut to cut, with Davis the only consistent member of each group, but it hardly shows. The second album is slightly marred by an attempt at "You Don't Miss Your Water," a song that isn't too well suited to Taj's voice. The use of brass on this cut and the next is tastefully handled, but for no other reasons than personal taste I prefer the cuts with the band, all of which are excellent. Do yourself a favor and pick up on Taj Mahal, if you haven't already.

—ED WARD
5-17-69

GIANT STEP/DE OLD FOLKS AT HOME
Taj Mahal
(Columbia GP 18)

One of the things I've always admired Taj Mahal and his band for is their incredible rhythmic flair and loose but tight way of flinging it at the listener. Taj has always been able to do just the right things with his voice and harp, and Jessie Davis has always played riffs that spiral up and around the backing, but which ultimately land at just the right time, and the rhythm section is as tight as can be.

On *Giant Step*, though, the

band takes a back seat, and their parts are mostly reduced to chunka-chunka mechanical backings for Taj, who sounds like he is straining and over-extending himself. There are some good cuts; "Give Your Woman What She Wants (When She Wants It)" and "Six Days on the Road" deliver the old Taj, albeit in a kind of frenetic way, bursting with exuberance and pepper. The former song is very poorly recorded, as is most of the first side, and Taj's voice sounds as if it had just been sandpapered.

"Giant Step" is a Goffin-King number, one of those songs that you may not care so much for at first, but which gradually insinuates its way into your head, possibly because of the authors' Top-40 slant on song-writing. Anyway, it's nice and sunny, but the rest of the disc is really nothing special. In fact, it's downright dull. "Ain't Gwine Whistle Dixie" is a throwaway instrumental that makes a nice lead-in to "Giant Step." "Good Morning Little Schoolgirl" has been bowdler-ized in tone—you really do get the impression that all he wants to do is walk her home. "Bacon Fat," which is credited to Robbie Robertson, is mainly a rhythm track with some dull rap about how groovy it is to be playin' to all dem people out dere in dat land listenin' to de phonograph. It sounds like he's reading the dialect out of

some Civil War-vintage book, and it's embarrassing to hear him going through all that just to prove to us how down-home he is. Hmmm . . . Maybe that's why you never see him with his hat off.

The other record, "De Ole Folks at Home," is the telling one, though. The idea of Taj solo singing old folk songs is appealing, but here, at least, there's more ham than grits. The instrumentals are passable, even if they do meander a bit, but the songs range from OK to terrible. It becomes apparent that Taj is really straining in his vocal work, relying on poorly disguised cliches and a breathiness that sounds forced. When we get to "A Little Soulful Tune" and hear Taj going "unh-unh-*unh*-unh" for a few minutes, it becomes apparent that he is trying just *so* hard to be cute and lovable and only succeeding in being cloying.

Taj Mahal is having trouble confronting the realities of his material, which may be a weird thing to say about a black blues performer, but it's beginning to sound as if he's become a black counterpart to John Hammond—all the technical problems have been solved, and all that remains is to put them together right. I sure hope he's able to do it (I hold out *some* hope that he has more soul than John Hammond, that is), because I find this to be a very depressing album, and that's something I really don't expect from Taj Mahal. After all, Taj is fantastic.

—ED WARD
2-7-70

THINKING OF WOODY GUTHRIE
Country Joe McDonald
(Vanguard VSD 6546)

"This record is a collection of songs I just naturally learned and loved in my early years of playing and singing," Country Joe drawls at the close of this record of Guthrie tunes. Gathered here are some of Nashville's finest instrumentalists (Martin, Bradley, Putnam, Robbins) playing sympathetically behind Country Joe's surprisingly adept vocals. Together they make it seem so easy that even if you buy this album only because of Country Joe's presence, you won't be disappointed. Whatever McDonald gets into, be it STP-oriented lyrics or acid-chorale instrumentals, he gets into it all the way. Here he doesn't play guitar at all—he just interprets the lyrics, phrases and feelings of this man Guthrie. Admittedly, this is a low-key, non-fiery record, but it has a certain honesty.

And it also lets you hear what a truly fine vocalist Joe is—he handles such diverse songs as "Tom Joad," "Talkin' Dust Bowl" and "Roll On Columbia" with ease and just

the proper amount of fervor. It is so easy to over-sing Guthrie, to strain and force the rhymes or to fall into a monotone. But Country Joe never stumbles. In fact, at times, you get the feeling he's rushing a little. Eight of the ten songs are under three minutes long, yet you'd swear they're longer. And that is not to mention Joe's marvelous epilogue to Woody that could have been so corny and maudlin, but as it stands, seems to be an intrinsic piece of conversation that sums up Woody and what he means to this one man in these late Sixties.

An album of nostalgia and an album of affirmation; if you have never heard of Woody Guthrie, or were never sure what he was all about, let Country Joe be your introduction. He knows the way.

—GARY VON TERSCH
2-21-70

TAPE FROM CALIFORNIA
Phil Ochs
(A&M SP 4148)

DAVID ACKLES
David Ackles
(Elektra EKS 74022)

THESE TWENTY-THREE DAYS IN SEPTEMBER
David Blue
(Reprise 6296)

These three albums have interesting and even entertaining

places. With the possible exception of David Blue's, they are not really very good.

Phil Ochs, in a beautifully produced record, is no less Phil Ochs. Van Dyke Parks and Jack Elliot helped with the music, which is splendid. But Phil's political vision and/or insight is still pubescing, it has not matured. "Joe Hill," a seven-minute ordeal in which Ochs employs a droning melody, is a song about enemies, and Ochs, like most old-style protesters, can simply find nothing vaguely amusing in enmity itself, revealing his (and their) basic lack of wit. Two other directly political songs, "White Boots Marching in a Yellow Land" and "The War Is Over" (the latter with the two great lines "freedom will not make you free" and "even treason might be worth a try") are poorly arranged, not one but both using bugles and military drums to make their over-obvious point (points?). The latter song shifts to Ochs' new "thing," in which Ochs enters a nightmare world of fleeting, unrelated images, some quite striking. But the impetus of the writing plainly comes not from any point being made, but from the rhyming word of the previous line. He rhymes "Mother Goose" and "Lenny Bruce" not for the relationship between the two (though there is one), but because "goose" and "bruce"

rhyme. It is as if the nightmare is bordered by—even induced by—the surrounding rhythm. This makes for isolated good lines, but the songs don't hold together, even the best, the title cut, which is especially well-arranged and has one of Ochs' better melodies.

David Ackles' arrangements and accompaniment are, once again, excellent, and especially Michael Fontara's very fresh, very clean organ. (This might be the stage of rock music, however, like the stage in the evolution of B movies where technical excellence can and should be expected as a matter of course.) Ackles is one of the best singers I've ever heard. He gets into a song the way Richie Havens does, without indulging himself in stylistic excesses the way Havens does. (Havens is to rock what Streisand is to her brand of pop.) But his melodies, lines of which are occasionally interesting, are at best frail, almost no melodies at all, on the order of Mel Brooks' "Thirty-One German Soldiers Hurt Their Knees." Their frailty simply forces the listener's attention off the words, which are themselves breathtakingly ordinary. ("Hey people, can you hear the children singing?" Sure, why not?) His influences seem to be pure blues and pure folk.

David Blue's first LP strikes something like a warning with

the cover, a vintage *Highway 61* shot with a sullen Blue in a leather jacket. His delivery is quite like Dylan's on *Blonde on Blonde*. But behold, the lyrics are among the best I've recently heard. Though the stance is like Dylan's, the words themselves indicate he really knows some things Dylan knows, and some things the master doesn't. So fine is his ear for speech that the words tend to overshadow the otherwise quite adequate music. Blue does not try for Dylan's explosions, his examinations are more like microscopic (if not more subtle). The Dylan influences overreach themselves on only two songs, "Grand Hotel" (nice autoharp) and "The Fifth One" (good Buttrey-like drumming). But it is hard explaining that something which so easily lends itself to comparison with another specific thing is really quite unique, and in Blue's case, a promising first offering as well. The music is quite good, particularly the piano, and even provides an instance of humor when a sitar run backs up the word "philosophy." Unlike Ackles' LP whose accompaniment is superior, and even most of Ochs' LP, it's actually fun to listen to.

—ARTHUR SCHMIDT
9-28-68

JOHN PHILLIPS
John Phillips
(Dunhill 50077)

Once upon a time, in a magic city called Los Angeles, there lived a Supergroup known as the Mamas and the Papas. Of course, nobody called them a Supergroup, because in those days, before there was Alvin Lee or even Jimi Page, that word hadn't been invented yet.

Although the Mamas and the Papas were rich and famous and lived in big houses near the magic city called Los Angeles, they were not happy. They fought among themselves, and threw things, and screamed, and yelled, and hurt each other's feelings, until finally they all went away, locked the doors to their big houses, and sulked.

And they never made any more beautiful record albums.

Oh, sure, every now and then one or two of them would come out of their houses and go down to the beach and sing, all by themselves, but it was never the same, and it didn't sound as good, and it never would, ever again.

This is what you're expecting, right?

Wrong. . . .

The John Phillips album is a masterpiece. And we can all put away our Golden Era albums, and stop reciting Kaddish for the Mamas and the

Papas, because the old familiar feeling is back with us. No, not the sound, but what was behind the sound, the incredible songwriting of John Phillips. In this album, backed by the same old gang of L.A. studio musicians, and assisted on vocals by an amazing chick trio (featuring, for all Phil Spector fans, none other than Darlene Love), Phillips has come to terms with himself, his own talents, his own mythology, and the result—well, I think it compares favorably with *Nashville Skyline*.

Go ahead, raise your eyebrows. The facts remain—there isn't a boring or repetitious cut on this album—nothing is forced, exaggerated or indifferent, and it is original, unselfconsciously and helplessly original without gimmickry, gadgetry, or goofery.

The songs are (like *Nashville Skyline*) mostly about love and other related problems; but where the Dylan album presented us with an archetypical set of situations, from which we could pick and choose, and substantiate with our own meanings as they applied, John Phillips' songs have their own prefabricated reality. "April Anne," for example, is rather like Peggy Day, except that this time she sounds like someone you know. In "Topanga," and throughout the first side, for that matter, the entire idea of introspective and personal songwriting, which certainly has

been all kinds of popular lately, is taken one step further. Phillips is not breaking his head trying to write universal songs —fortunately, he doesn't have that kind of image to live up to—yet what we're getting, diffused through his word patterns and syruped over by Buddy Emmons' pedal steel, is a set of personal experiences and reactions that we (with little cries of joy and amazement, natch) just happen to recognize.

The same thing, it seems, is going on in the music. Opening off side two, in "Captain," he comes up with a third cousin to the 12-bar blues form, throws in some fine shouting in the middle, and finally adds a country fiddle, bumbling and scratching around the edges of the song. In "Mississippi," which has been released as a single (and I might add, this is the first time in years that I've sat huddled by the radio, enduring hours of bubble-gunk, in the hopes, in the hopes . . .) he comes out with an informal, exuberant, intense performance that, along with the happily insane lyrics, emerges as my favorite Little Groovemaker.

Without the big voices and the fancy arrangements, without the elaborate chord changes, without all the musical trappings that characterized his former days (but with Lou Adler) Phillips comes across fresh and sweet, like that one delicious Delicious in a barrel full of otherwise disappointing apples. Sure, he still sings in three-syllable "yeahhhhs"—why not?—he invented them. And the twist and feint of the lyrics couldn't be unfamiliar. But that's all in a different perspective now. This album, *John Phillips,* has zilch to do with that departed Supergroup from the magic city called you-know-what. This is John Phillips' album, and you get the impression that that's how he wants it.

In that case one can only admire his judgment. It's a brilliant album.

—SYLVIA A. WEISER
7-23-70

BOZ SCAGGS
Boz Scaggs
(Atlantic SD 8239)

In this era of hick *Hee-Haws* and Hollywood cowboys, Nashville cronies and Nudies creations, seems like everybody and his musical brother (and also his chaste sister) has to make it to Tennessee or Alabama, or he jes' cain't make it a-tall. Most of the transient residents at 3614 Jackson Highway, for example, site of the much-favored Muscle Shoals Sound Recorders, have no business recording there. Things really aren't all *that* magical in Muscle Shoals—what counts is what a musician brings into town with him.

Fortunately, Boz Scaggs travels with talent to spare. You knew that listening to the early Steve Miller albums. But then Boz split. He resurfaced briefly a while ago, providing some back-up on Mother Earth's second release, and now Boz has emerged from his own session in Muscle Shoals—and it must have been something! Boz moves effortlessly all the way from gospel to rock and back again, ringing all the changes and making all the whistle-stops between. You want a Fifties-style rock-ballad arrangement? Saunter along with "Another Day." A slice of everlovin' country pie? Join the honky-tonkin' in "Now You're Gone": tipsy slide guitar, skittish fiddle, and break-your-heart, saloon-gal vocal-backing from Tracy Nelson and others.

For gospel-soul, listen to "I'll Be Long Gone": the gentle opening interplay of Barry Beckett's organ and Boz's understated vocal (with just a hint of horns); then hear him hit those high notes—no strain, no explosion, just *whoo-o-ops* and you're there. "I'm gonna get up and make my life shine," he sings. Mine too, Boss Boz.

Or how about a bit of railroads blues, courtesy of the Original Blues Yodeler himself? Dig "Waiting for a Train"—but understand that's *Boz* doing the weaving with the fiddle and the ricky-tick pieanner. Jimmie

Rodgers is looking down from on high with a proud smile.

The album's other beauties and sweet C&W moments multiply. (Only "Finding Her," with its precious lyrics and *Moonlight Sonata* piano, falters; and it's rescued by Duane Allman's slide guitar magic at the end.) But the peak of the disc is the 13-minute "Loan Me a Dime." Most extended cuts—face it, folks—are a drag. Can't be sustained. Your ear tends to blot them out on most every record, picking out the briefer, tighter numbers instead.

But not this time. "Loan Me" makes it all the way. Boz's vocalizing seems relaxed and mournful at the same time; and then, midway, the singing stops and the cooking begins—horns soaring (the same figure over and over), organ romping along, drums pushing, and some spinetingling guitar work by Duane Allman. That guitar fools around with the horns part of the time; and they seem to prod it into new inventiveness the rest of the way.

That's Boz. Style. *Panache.* One of the few. He sounds right at home in Muscle Shoals. Like his namesake, the illustrator "Boz" who brought Dickensian London to vivid life, this Boz belongs to, yet shapes and transcends, his milieu. No wonder he's smiling.

—ED LEIMBACHER
11-15-69

JOHN B. SEBASTIAN
John Sebastian
(Reprise 6379)

John Sebastian's new album opens with "The Red-Eye Express," a great burst of enthusiasm that immediately brings back all those wonderful bits of style and wisdom that brought so much joy a few years ago. "Hurry up Lorey,/Hurry up Sue/We can't hardly wait for you/Starving for your love, it's true." Sebastian's marvelously rich voice slides all over the lines of the song, and his warm harp edges in a bit later on as an extra delight. The man who wrote one of the best songs about rock and roll *ever* is making music again.

He has famous friends along to help—Dallas Taylor, David Crosby, Steve Stills, Bruce Langhorne, to name a few—they never sound like guest stars, but merge into a solid framework, supporting whatever Sebastian brings to each cut. It's his show, good or bad.

The album is by no means completely successful. Most of the songs, even some of the best ones, lack tension and flair, as if they'd been worked out with such care that the final takes were absolutely *perfect* in terms of their execution but somewhat stiff in spirit. "Rainbows All Over Your Blue" and "Baby, Don't Ya Get Crazy," two good songs, suffer from this sort of vaguely forced enthusiasm. There are other numbers, notably "Magical Connection," a Sergio Mendes bore with vibes, that simply doesn't make it at all. Two cuts, "The Room Nobody Lives In" and "I Had A Dream," are plain old schmaltz—bad movie music with, on the latter, a harp (not harmonica). "Room" even has more or less the same melody as Frank Sinatra's "All the Way." Here, as in most soundtrack music, sentiment does not evoke lasting emotion, and prettiness falls far short of beauty.

Sebastian sang "How Have You Been" ("My darling children/While I have been away in the west") at Woodstock, and it seems just as insufferable now as it did then. The idea is lovely, the result extremely pretentious, and the performance almost maudlin. It's a Paul Simon trip that Paul Simon has had the good sense to avoid.

All of this granted, the album has proof that Sebastian's talents are still with him; "What She Thinks About," a crashing, explosive rock and roll song, stands out from this record the way Boz Scaggs' "Dime a Dance Romance" did on Steve Miller's *Sailor*. This is what you can't tell a stranger about! It has all the expertise of the hard rock we get from the Band, with a special lift from Sebastian's own sense of the

music: "Well, you say you been around and you got it all together and you're diggin' where it's at and you really feel groovy/Well, that's not quite true but nice to meet you . . ." You can say it all if you get the sound right.

It's a good album, mostly, and in places really exciting. But it could have been a lot better, and hopefully, the enormous popularity this one will have won't see Sebastian resting on his laurels next time he enters the studio.

—GREIL MARCUS
4-16-69

JAMES TAYLOR
James Taylor
(Apple SKAO 3352)

James Taylor is the kind of person I always thought the word folksinger referred to. He writes and sings songs that are reflections of his own life, and performs in them in his own style. All of his performances are marked by an eloquent simplicity. Mr. Taylor is not kicking out any jams. He seems to be more interested in soothing his troubled mind. In the process he will undoubtedly soothe a good many heads besides his own.

Taylor's music is a mix between country, blues, and some antique folk styles. Whichever idiom he is leaning on in any particular song, both his lyrics and his voice flow with a lyricism that connotes a deeply personal style. Taylor is aware of his mastery of his material and therefore tends to understate things. His reserve is a sign of his maturity. He sings with resonance and plays with grace; he refuses to let himself get lost in anything that obscures his identity as an artist.

Of the songs on the album, each seems to reflect a different shade of Taylor's style—although on first hearing the album may sound a bit repetitious. "Taking It In" has the simple beat and instrumentation common to most of the tracks, but watch the rhythm changes fly right past you on the third line of each verse: "Morning sing me a song/Afternoon bring it along/Nighttime—show me a friend/say it again/send a good dream my way." Taylor is subtle enough to put this funky bit of syncopation across without making the listener raise his eyebrows.

In a similar way, Taylor is capable of making unusual chord changes while never jolting the ear. All such changes, whether rhythmic or melodic, are absorbed by Taylor's coherent and naturalistic lyrics and singing "Sunshine Sunshine," a lovely song about Taylor's sister Kate, is a marvelous example of his musical coherence.

"Knocking Around the Zoo" combines a subdued sense of humor with more naturalism.

The song is about life in a mental hospital where "there's bars on all the windows and they're counting up spoons." "Something In the Way She Moves" is concerned with transcendence of a sort and is done without accompaniment. Again Taylor's restrained delivery contributes to the power of his presentation. He lets the melody, lyric, guitar, and voice speak for themselves. He doesn't hit you up with anything that isn't absolutely necessary to get the song across.

The two most deeply affecting cuts are "Carolina On My Mind" and "Rainy Day Man." The latter is noteworthy for its melody, the excellent vocal background, and the perfection with which the simple but important transitions are made. "Carolina" is also a beautiful song and has, in addition, an absolutely perfect arrangement. The bass playing is extraordinary, as are the background vocals (done by James and producer Peter Asher), drums—just everything.

There is only one problem with this album: some of the production is superfluous. There are a few string arrangements that serve no real function. The horn arrangements sound a bit too British. And on some cuts, James' voice is not as "up front" as it should have been. These reservations notwithstanding, this album is the coolest breath of fresh air I've inhaled in a good long while. It knocks me out.

—JON LANDAU
4-19-69

SWEET BABY JAMES
James Taylor
(Warner Brothers 1843)

Last August James Taylor was quoted in *Rolling Stone* thusly: "I hope my next album will be simpler. It has to be, because the music is simple and a big production job just buries all my intentions." Well, this first post-Apple album dovetails nicely with that anticipation, even down to the inclusion of Stephen Foster's "Oh, Susannah," buck-wheat cakes in her mouth and all.

Peter Asher (formerly at Apple with Taylor) produced this album, as well as Taylor's first, and, one can hear, let Taylor have free rein this time. Echoes of the Band, the Byrds, country Dylan and folksified Dion abound, yet somehow Taylor pulls through it all with a very listenable record that is all his own. The gentle, intelligent manipulation of piano, steel guitar, fiddle and a few brass arrangements alone deserve a close listening to by any erstwhile producers.

And it is hard to fault Taylor's lyrics. "Sweet Baby James," with its "cowboys waiting for summer/his pastures to change" and "Fire and Rain" with its "Sweet dreams and fire machines in pieces on the ground" are just a few of the images that Taylor develops. Throughout, his vocal stance is low-key and perfectly matched to the country-styled guitar work. No acute solos or overstressed melodies appear as musicians and vocalist together manage to mandala their way through Taylor's persistent lonely prairie/lovely Heaven visions that, at times, work their way up to the intensity of a haiku or the complexity of a parable.

Taylor only shifts from this stance a couple of times. "Oh Baby, Don't You Loose Your Lip On Me" is less than two minutes long; bluesy yet random, it sounds like studio hijinks used to fill out an album. But the other exception, "Steam Roller," is a different story. Here Taylor is earthy and lowdown with definitely crude electric guitar behind him as he moans "I'm gonna inject your soul with some sweet rock and roll and shoot you full of rhythm and blues." Then a miasmic, brass riff to make sure things stay tough, followed by a particularly timely and potent couple of verses: "I'm a napalm bomb for you baby/stone guaranteed to blow your mind/and if I can't have your love for my own sweet child/there won't be nothing left behind." A double-entendre tour-de-force pulled off effortlessly.

This is a hard album to

argue with; it does a good job of proving that his first effort was no fluke. This one gets off the ground just as nicely, as Taylor seems to have found the ideal musical vehicle to say what he has to say.

—GARY VON TERSCH
4-30-69

BLACK AND WHITE
Tony Joe White
(Monument SLP 18114)

Tony Joe White is a young singer-songwriter who originally hails from somewhere in the deep South and now works out of Houston. He is one of those grass-roots personalities that come upon the scene full-blown and overflowing with talent and a flair for overcoming even the most seemingly impossible odds placed in his path by the public, the record business, and/or the label. His songs reflect a gutsiness and warmth that is missing in many of today's song-writer-performers, and he is possessed of a natural delivery ("soulful," the liner notes call it—I'll leave it to you to quibble over that one) that must make grunters like John Hammond bilious with envy. His guitar playing is superb, with a sensible, one might say even sensitive, approach to the wah-wah pedal that almost makes me stop wishing it hadn't been invented. His songs are wonderfully in-

fectious and he's already had one of them in the top ten.

Strangely enough, though, his debut album is a lump mixture of country, soul, pop, blues, and, oh yes, his own songs. Fortunately, the shit is all on side two: "Who's Making Love," "Scratch My Back," "Wichita Lineman," and "Look of Love." I guess it's to White's credit that someone with such a superb naturalness should sublimate it so successfully in order to turn out these dull, mechanical tracks, but anyway, side two's not what the record's all about. Side one gives us six slices of Tony Joe White, served up quite nicely. True, the band behind him is nothing special, but that only serves to emphasize his talents better. Two of his songs have already achieved national attention: his hit "Polk Salad Annie" and "Willie and Laura Mae Jones," which was recently recorded by Dusty Springfield. This last-named could only have been written by a southerner; it deals with the black family that used to have the farm down the road and how they've been acting a bit more distant recently. No preaching, no judging, just a gentle commentary on the way things are—a superb song. "Whomp Out on You" and "Don't Steal My Love" are opportunities for some vocal and instrumental expertise, as is "Soul Francisco," a humorous ditty that was a big hit in

France, of all places. "Aspen, Colorado" is an easy-listening type ballad that I rather enjoy for its nice melody, although I can see how some people might object to it.

Now, if you're the affluent type that can go out and buy albums that have only one listenable side, you'll be pleased with this record. If you're not, wait around till the next one, and we'll see if it's any better.

—ED WARD
10-18-69

BEACOUPS OF BLUES
Ringo Starr
(Apple SMAS 3368)

Correct me if I'm wrong, but I would venture the guess that not too many people reading these words could say that they look to Ringo Starr for New Horizons in Pop Music.

Still with me? Then, I am prepared to say that you won't be disappointed with Ringo's all-country and western album, *Beaucoups of Blues*. Shucks, you'll probably even *like* it.

Anyone who can recall Ringo's rollicking renditions of Carl Perkins' "Matchbox" or Buck Owens' "Act Naturally," or even Ringo's own "Don't Pass Me By" from the eldest white album, will know of the Beatle's affection for country and western, and I don't think I'm alone in knowing that I'll never be able to hear Lorne

Greene sing his oldie-but-goodie, "Ringo," without picturing Richard Starkey, cute and majestic atop his pony, the high noon sun bathing down on his neck, sending rays glinting off his sheriff's badge and his rings.

So Ringo has always had a vaguely country and western image anyway, so why not put out his first solo record (let's be generous and forget *Sentimental Journey*) in the country and western genre? That sounds like a good idea. So Ringo went all the way to Nashville to record what sounds like Marion Lorne attempting to sing the Tammy Wynette songbook.

Beaucoups of Blues is an unusually apt title for this collection of 12 songs, each one sounding more ridiculously degenerate than the one before. And the very thought of Ringo Starr being backed by the cream of Nashville's studio musicians from Jerry Reed right on down to the Jordanaires, produced by Pete Drake, the man who made the steel guitar fucking *talk*, and engineered by Elvis' old guitar player, Scotty Moore, is, well . . . Ringo doesn't even play drums on the record, and I thought he played drums.

Make no mistake about it, though, this record is a real winner. After the opening, title song, there's a tune that is so utterly *heavy* in its lyrics that I'm willing to bet that even

Bobby Goldsboro would think twice before recording a song like "Love Don't Last Too Long." Try this story on for size, pardner:

> A young man was unlucky and got
> Busted in Kentucky
> Asked his dad to go his bail.
> But his dad had big ambitions with
> The local politicians
> Told his son to go to hell.
> He hung his self that morning and
> The note that they found on him
> Said "dad, please take me home."

Um. Love don't last long. And as though that wasn't enough, in "Fastest Growing Heartache in the West," Ringo's own true love seems to have abandoned him to look for those well-hung studs that put ads in the "Personals" column of the L.A. *Free Press,* he has to live his life "Without Her," gives his love to one of those "Women of the Night," and ends up singing, "If I had talked about the good times/ There wouldn't be much to say."

Whew! And that's only the end of the first side! Pretty maudlin, eh? It's a good thing Ringo isn't a better singer than he is, or this record could have ended up being as depressing as Hank Williams' *Luke the*

Drifter album, and that one is so depressing that Commander Cody himself broke the record over his knee the very first time he heard it. Fortunately, the only reason Ringo can carry a tune is that the composers of the tunes were singing along with him on most of the songs, just out of mike range. No matter how morose the material gets, Ringo's easy-going baritone assures us that he has little idea of what's going on, anyway.

If *Beaucoups of Blues* reminds one of any record, it's *Nashville Skyline,* only instead of being lovable, spaced-out Bobby Dylan in front of those luxurious Nashville backups, it's lovable Richard Starkey who is crooning his heart out.

Like *Nashville Skyline, Beaucoups of Blues* opens side two with what will doubtless be one of Ringo's greatest hits, "$15 Draw," about a Nashville Cat who neglects his home life to sit and pick his guitar:

> I'm sure daddy always knew that Tom
> Would be the one to take his place
> And when he tried to lecture me I'd
> Sit and pick and sing and let him nag
> But way down deep inside I think he
> Knew that hardware ain't my bag.

It's a terrific rocker, and who

really cares if it's Jerry Reed and not Ringo Starr who plays the fantastic guitar riffs on "$15 Draw"? There's a nice photo of Ringo fingering a "C" chord on the inside cover.

Side two also features some pure honky-tonky songs, like "Loser's Lounge" and "Wine, Women, and Loud, Happy Songs," the latter containing some of my favorite lines on the album: "It's strange how the wine/Works on a fool/It seeps through his mind/Leaves him blued to the stool."

Credit for the amazing songs on the album are shared by some of the backup musicians, Sorrels Pickard, Chuck Howard, Larry Kingston, and Bobby Pierce, all of whom have a good ear for making bizarre twists to country and western cliches. Coming from the lips of Ringo Starr, the songs sound terrific, but it's hard to imagine any more traditional country singers who would take them seriously enough to record elsewhere.

Take the last song on the album, an anti-war song called "Silent Homecoming." Now, normally there's nothing terribly funny about a girl waiting for her beau to come home from the war, wondering if the killing he has done will have changed him, and all those other thoughts that would run through one's mind while standing at an airfield. Anyway the guy has come home from the war, all right, but he's in "That hearse filled up with flowers." Not too funny, right? So right after that, Ringo asks us the question, "Did he really have to die?" Quite a ponderous question for anyone, let alone Ringo Starr (who, if we are to believe rumors from early Beatlemania, has an I.Q. of, well, less than, say, John Lennon). Ah, but Ringo proceeds to answer the ponderous question, singing, "No, no, no . . ." as the song fades out. It's all so unbelievable that it's not even in poor taste. After all, can you really imagine Ringo Starr trying to hurt anyone's feelings?

No, right? So why don't you go ahead and buy *Beaucoups of Blues*. Ringo plays the part, and it sounds as though he hardly did any rehearsing. All he had to do was act naturally. Natural Ringo Starr may not exactly be New Horizons in Pop Music, but, hell. He's really pretty good after all.

—CHARLES BURTON
10-29-70

The Voices

of Upstate

New York

Two of the most remarkable and totally individual new record artists emerged from the Saugerties Mountains and the woods of upstate New York near Woodstock, Bob Dylan's now legendary country retreat.

One of them is Dylan's own rehearsal and backing band—known variously as the Crackers, and the Hawks when working behind first Ronnie Hawkins and later Dylan himself. On their own, they called themselves The Band and issued one of the more extraordinary albums of 1968, reviewed here by Al Kooper, also an old Dylan friend. Their second, superb album was reviewed by Ralph J. Gleason.

The other artist is the Irish singer Van Morrison who sang with Them (out of Belfast) during the first British Invasion. After a stormy career outlined in the essay here, Van Morrison emerged from a Woodstock retreat first with *Astral Weeks* and then the stunning *Moondance*. The albums of this chapter were all worthy of association with Woodstock's most famous adopted son.

MUSIC FROM BIG PINK
The Band
(Capitol SKATO 2955)

Every year since 1963 we have all singled out one album to sum up what happened that year. It was usually the Beatles with their double barrels of rubber souls, revolvers and peppers. Dylan has sometimes contended with his frontrunning electric albums. Six months are left in this proselytizing year of music; we can expect a new Beatles, Stones, Hendrix, perhaps even a mate for JW Harding; but I have chosen *my* album for 1968. *Music from Big Pink* is an event and should be treated as one.

Very quietly, for six years, a

band has been brewing. They'd pop up once in a while behind Ronnie Hawkins, or on their own as the Hawks, or affectionately called "the Crackers," but it was sort of hip to know who they were outside of Toronto. They left Toronto three years ago to tour with Dylan. But when the concerts were over, and the boos had turned to standing ovations, what was to become of these nameless faces?

They came home to Woodstock with Dylan and put down firm roots for two years. It was Dylan's "out of touch" year and they began to spawn this music, this hybrid that took its seeds in the strange pink house. Whereas the Dylan "sound" on recording was filled with Bloomfielding guitar, Kooper hunt and peck organ and tinkly country-gospelish piano, a fortunate blending of the right people in the right place etc., the Big Pink sound has matured throughout six years, picking up favorites along the way, and is only basically influenced by the former.

I hear the Beach Boys, the Coasters, Hank Williams, the Association, the Swan Silvertones as well as obviously Dylan and the Beatles. What a varied bunch of influences. I love all the music created by the above people and a montage of these forms (bigpink) boggles the mind. But it's also something else. It's that good

old, intangible, can't-put-your-finger-on-it "White Soul." Not so much a white cat imitating a spade, but something else that reaches you on a non-Negro level like church music or country music or Jewish music or Dylan. The singing is so honest and unaffected, I can't see how anyone could find it offensive (as in "white people can't pull this kind of thing off").

This album was made along the lines of the motto: "Honesty is the best policy." The best part of pop music today is honesty. The "She's Leaving Home," the "Without Her's," the "Dear Landlord's" etc. When you hear a dishonest record you feel you've been insulted or turned off in comparison. It's like the difference between "Dock of the Bay" and "This Guy's In Love With You." Both are excellent compositions and both were number one. But you believe Otis while you sort of question Herb Alpert. You can believe every line in this album and if you choose to, it can only elevate your listening pleasure immeasurably.

Robbie Robertson makes an auspicious debut here as a composer and lyricist represented by four tunes. Two are stone knockouts: "The Weight"— probably the most commercial item in the set with a most contagious chorus that addicts you into singing along . . . "take a load off Fanny, take a load for free, take a load off Fanny and . . . you put the load right on me . . ." "To Kingdom Come"—starts out smashing you in the face with weird syncopations and cascading melody lines and then goes into that same groovy bring-it-on-home chorus that earmarks "Weight."

Individually what makes up this album is Robbie Robertson whose past discography includes "Obviously Five Believers" on *Blonde on Blonde,* the "live" version of "Just Like Tom Thumb's Blues" and the much ignored Dylan single, "Crawl Out Your Window." Rick Danko, on bass and vocals, is one of the more outgoing people in the band, he can be depended upon to give you a lot of good matured shit whenever you see him; he of the new breed in bass players, the facile freaks like Harvey Brooks, Jim Fielder and Tim Bogert. He is only different from these three in his tasteful understanding.

Richard Manuel is affectionately called "Beak" or was at one time; a deft pianist with a strong feeling for country-gospel big-pink music. A strong contributing composer: "Tears of Rage," "In A Station," "We Can Talk," and "Lonesome Suzie."

Garth Hudson is one of the strangest people I ever met. If Harvey Brooks is the gentle grizzly bear of rock and roll then Garth is the gentle brown bear. He is the only person I know who can take a Hammond B3 organ apart and put it back together again or play like that if it's called for. While backing Dylan on tour he received wide acclaim for his fourth dimensional work on "Ballad Of A Thin Man."

Levon Helm is a solid rock for the band. He is an exciting drummer with many ideas to toss around. I worked with him in Dylan's first band and he kept us together like an enormous iron metronome. Levon was the leader of the Hawks.

John Simon, a brilliant producer-composer-musician, finally has this album as a testimonial to his talent. The reason the album *sounds* so good is Simon. He is a perfectionist and has had to suffer the critical rap in the past for what has not been his error, but now he's vindicated.

These are fiery ingredients and results can be expected to be explosive. The chord changes are refreshing, the stories are told in a subtle yet taut way; country tales of real people you can relate to (the daughter in "Tears of Rage") the singing sometimes loose as field-help but just right. The packaging, including Dylan's non-Rembrandt cover art, is apropos and honest (there's that word again). This album was recorded in approximately two weeks. There are people who will work their lives away in vain and not touch it.

—AL KOOPER
8-10-68

THE BAND
The Band
(Capitol STAO 132)

It's homemade, Robbie Robertson says, done in the house they rented in Hollywood last winter in which they fixed up a room with baffles and a projector for flicks and the recording equipment. Robbie was engineer for about 90% of the work and they really produced the album themselves. John Simon, aside from being odd man in for the horn section, became "that outside ear and outside opinion you could trust."

So it really is just the Band.

There are twelve tracks, Robbie wrote eight of the songs himself and collaborated on one with Levon Helm and on three with Richard Manuel. Richard Manuel sings lead on five of them, Levon sings lead on four, Rick Danko on three and there are numerous occasions when the lead voice is joined by another and sometimes two others. Robbie and Garth Hudson do not sing at all on the album, unless they are way in the background on some of the ensemble vocal bits.

The band doubles all over the place on various instru-

ments. Richard Manuel, for instance, not only sings but plays piano, drums, baritone sax and mouth harp; Garth plays organ, clavinette (which he keeps on top of the organ), accordion, soprano, tenor and baritone sax and slide trumpet. Levon plays drums, mandolin and guitar; Rick Danko plays bass, violin and trombone and John Simon plays tuba (a fine effort, too, it is), baritone and pack horn, and Robbie plays guitar.

About the only way I can go about discussing the content of the album is to use as an illustration a view of Mt. Tamalpais on the Pacific Coast shore line above San Francisco. The western part of that mountain runs right down to the sea and the more you look at it, the more you see. Week in, week out, month by month, hour by hour even, nature conducts a change which rings through the twelve months and the four seasons, and there is the change in daylight when the sun shifts and the shadows bring out silhouettes and crevices in the rocks and accentuates the gullies and the draws and at night when there's moonlight, it is a different mountain altogether.

The album is like that. It is full of sleepers, diamonds that begin to glow at different times. As with the Beatles and Dylan and the Stones and Crosby, Stills and Nash, the album seems to change shape as you continue to play it. The emphasis shifts from song to song and songs prominent in the early listening will retreat and be replaced in your consciousness by others, only in later hearings to move to the fore again. Little things pop up unexpectedly after numerous listenings and the whole things serves as a definition of what Gide meant by the necessity of art having density.

Take "The Night They Drove Old Dixie Down," a Civil War song sung by Levon ("I aimed it right at him, I wrote it for him, he gets to say it all," Robbie says). It is the story of a Rebel soldier who served on the Danville and Richmond railroad which supplied Richmond during the war and which was cut several times by Gen. George Stoneman's Union Cavalry. Virgil Kane is the soldier's name and the song builds a story of the winter after Appomattox, lean and sparse like a Hemingway short story.

Nothing that I have read, from Bruce Catton to Douglas Southall Freeman, from Fletcher Pratt to Lloyd Lewis, has brought home to me the overwhelming human sense of history that this song does. The only thing I can relate it to at all is the *Red Badge of Courage.* It is a remarkable song, the rhythmic structure, the voice of Levon and the bass line with the drum accents and then the heavy close harmony of Levon, Rick and Richard Manuel in

the theme, make it seem impossible that this isn't some oral tradition material handed down from father to son straight from that winter of '65 to today. It has the ring of truth and the whole aura of authenticity. Yet after playing the album a dozen times, I began to feel that "Dixie" was an obvious song, the superficial standout number on the album and I acquired other favorites. But I kept coming back and coming back until now I am prepared to say that, depending on one's mood, these songs stand, each on its own, as equal sides of a twelvefaceted gem, the whole of which is geometrically greater than the sum of the parts.

Just as "Dixie" evokes history, "Up On Cripple Creek" throws images of trucks and trailers rolling down the great inland highways, putting the Danville and Richmond Railroad, as well as many others, out of business. "Up On Cripple Creek" is a modern song, its rhetoric is the rhetoric of today and even the line "When I get off of this mountain, y' know where I'm gonna go, straight down the Mississippi River to the Gulf of Mexico" (on Highway 61 from Minneapolis to New Orleans, paralleling Ole Miss?), which is, as a friend remarked, surely the oldest line in American folk history, does not date it. "Cripple Creek" is the story of a trucker and the gal he has stashed away in Lake Charles, "a drunkard's dream if I ever did see one." It is a salty, sexy, earthy (rather than funky) ballad and it is Levon who sings it with a little help from his friends Rick and Richard. (Levon's chuckle towards the end is surely the nastiest, dirtiest, evilest sexual snort in the history of the phonograph record.) And again the rhythmic tension created between the interplay of the bass and drums and the line of the voice sets up a tremendously moving pulse. It vies with "Dixie" as the song that hooks you first and like the former it fades and then returns to fade and return again.

I hear these songs as a sound track to James Agee's *Let Us Now Praise Famous Men,* to the real documentary of the American truth. They are sparse songs with never a superfluous note or an unnecessary syllable. And yet the sparseness, like a Picasso line, is so right that it implies everything needed. Lean and dusty, perhaps, like Henry Fonda walking down the road at the beginning of *Grapes of Wrath,* it says volumes in a phrase ("me and my mate, we were at the shack, we had Spike Jones on the box. I can't take the way he sings, but I love to hear him talk") and though the device is folkish the images are contemporary ("I'll bring over my Fender and I'll play all night for you" in "Jemima Surrender," a racy love song).

There is, paradoxically, no paradox at all in the electrical band giving forth the simple philosophy of country living backed by the sounds of Fender bass and electric guitar (there hasn't been, really, since TVA). Robbie's wah-wah pedal makes a human sound and the snarl of his guitar string twisting through the amplifier is the triumph of the man over the machine. That they could produce this contemporary marvel in the basement, home cookin', so to speak, is in itself a triumph of man over the increasing complexities of the electronic studio and its 60 hours of recording, twelve track machines and God knows how much overdubbing. The simple way, with only as much overdubbing as is needed to allow Garth to play organ and then dub on a horn track, turns out in the end to be more effective (and greater art) than the electronic marvels.

With their flashing images of the American continental landscape, Canadians though they are, they speak for the continent in "King Harvest Has Surely Come." They could have called the album *America,* Robbie says, and after you play it a few times you know what he means. We live in these cities and we forget that there is more than 3000 miles between New York and the smog of Los Angeles and those 3000 miles are deeply rooted to another world in another time and with another set of values. "King Harvest" takes us there.

The hymn-like quality of the voicings, the use of counterpoint and contrapuntal rhythms by the singers, the weaving of the voices in and out into a pattern that grows each time you hear it, are the things that make the sound of this music so compelling. In "King Harvest," as in other songs, individual sections with contrasting timbres, moods, rhythms and sounds are juxtaposed to make a totality that is so open it can cover whatever you feel. The sense of doom, almost Biblical in its prophetic warning, of "Look Out, Cleveland" is unique in contemporary popular song, so far removed from the obvious morbidity of some of the songs of past years as to be an adult to their child. (This music, of course, *is* mature, made by men who know who they are and what they want to do. Its appeal to the teenybopper Top-40 audience seems, on the evidence, to be limited.)

In a way, it seems to me that the use of the drums in this band typifies how their music in constructed. The drums are not used solely to keep time nor solely to underscore a line or emphasize a rhythm. Rather the drums are used as sound, as punctuation, as the spine for the whole skeleton of the song. Levon uses wooden drums and

tunes the bass so that it gets a crunchy, not a zappy sound, as Robbie explains it, which is like a punch in the stomach. You hear the drums if you listen for them, but, like the bass, you feel them all the time. That is how the music is made, out of the flesh and blood of human beings and part of their flesh and blood and its humanity sings to you, music that you feel you know. It has the sound of familiarity in every new line because it is ringing changes on the basic truths of life, you *have* been there before, and like the truths of life itself, it nourishes you. As the old pitchman used to say, "it's good for what ails you and it gives you what you haven't got."

—RALPH J. GLEASON
10-18-69

**HERE COMES THE NIGHT.
     (or GLORIA)**
Them
(Parrot PA 61005)

THEM AGAIN
Them
(Parrot PA 61008)

BLOWIN' YOUR MIND!
Van Morrison
(Bang BLB 218)

ASTRAL WEEKS
Van Morrison
(Warner Brothers-Seven Arts
     WS 1768)

Van Morrison is a unique

and often forgotten figure in the history of rock and roll. From the time of his first recordings with Them in 1964, the image and the reality was that of a fiery Irish temper, a violent refusal to adhere to the discipline and the directives of unlucky A&R men, in a demand for freedom that was both personal and artistic.

Van formed Them in Ireland as a trio in 1963, and added another member in 1964; they played tough, hard R&B. On "The Story of Them," an English single recorded in 1964 and released in 1967, Van described their origins: scrambling in bars, hassled by straights over long hair, what every group went through in those days. Such were "the good times, the sad times."

Van's angry need for freedom was evident in the first years. The group began to break up almost immediately, and continued to drop and add members with eerie regularity. Them's first album, entitled *The Angry Young Them* in England, showed the musical side of Van's attempt, in the midst of driving, powerful group efforts like "Baby Please Don't Go" and the blazingly sexual "Gloria," to walk his own road.

He wrote most of the songs on the first record, and in two instances began to show his discomfort with the limits of traditional R&B. One, "Philos-ophy," was a Jaggerish rap sung over a monotonous blues theme, just Van letting it out for no particular reason, a piece that forced the listener to focus on the words, which were singularly uninteresting.

"Mystic Eyes," though, was a triumph for both Van as an artist responsible to no one but himself, and for the band. The vocal consisted in essence of Van chanting virtually demonic incantations over a mad tempo and the harsh chords of a biting guitar.

Them and Van had made it, with hits on both sides of the Atlantic; but by the time of their second album, only one member apart from Van remained from the original crew. On *Them Again* (released in early '66), aided by the excellent lead guitar of Jimmy Page, Van truly *participated,* musically, in one of the finest of all rock and roll recordings.

The band had added piano and organ, vibes, flute, and sax. The performance, within the limits of a normal song format, was expert, imaginative, and dramatic; this album might be described as what Traffic would have done had they been together at that time. It was a serious band, less exciting than the Stones and without their humor, but far more original than the Spencer Davis Group and flashier and tougher than the Yardbirds.

The cuts on *Them Again* are

the equal of those by all but the very best of today's groups. There is "How Long Baby," a searing vocal punctuated by a shimmering guitar solo, the definition, in good taste, of all that "psychedelic" music ever aspired to; "Don't You Know," a mixture of jazz flute and piano and R&B, extremely simple and elementary, yet very satisfying; and "Call My Name," playing on a basic theme in rock and roll that reaches out to all of us, Van's yearning softened by a soothing run by Page, a climactic and memorable cut.

Van's singing on this album seems to represent an attempt to communicate all he knows and all he feels, never letting down, never throwing away a line, not coming on like The Grand Preacher of Love and Sorrow, just excitement and emotion in a brash yet committed manner. It was a signpost in Van's growing maturity as a singer, but not proof of the freedom for which he was searching; without such a superb band backing him up, this album would not be extraordinary.

Only on Dylan's "It's All Over Now, Baby Blue" does Van truly shatter all the limits on his special powers. The band composes itself out of a very hard, dominant bass, working over crucial notes instead of patterns; an acoustic guitar; organ; drums; and electric vibes, as a high-pitched, painful lead instrument.

Each note stands out as a special creation—"the centuries of emotion that go into a musician's choice from one note to the next" is a phrase that describes the startling depth of this recording. Played very fast, Van's voice virtually fighting for control over the band, "Baby Blue" emerges as music that is both dramatic and terrifying. The only song I know that is comparable in both conception and performance is the Buffalo Springfield's "Out of My Mind," another cut made for the loneliness of a dark night.

Them's best music signaled the end of their commercial success. One last tour of America, and they split for good in 1966. Van shifted to New York, under the wing of the late Bert Berns (who wrote Them's "Here Comes the Night" and co-authored Irma Franklin's "Piece of My Heart"). Van's new home was to be Bang Records, once the source of the Strangeloves' "I Want Candy," Terry Southern's contribution to rock and roll. Berns and Van put together a soulful and bouncy Top-40 hit, "Brown Eyed Girl," and if the song didn't quite match Van's previous recordings, it was proof that he was still with us.

It was the follow-up album, *Blowin' Your Mind!*, complete with a monstrously offensive super psychedelic far-out out-of-sight exploding cover, that made one wonder if Them had been one big happy accident. Painfully boring—the music, the vocals, the lyrics—*Blowin' Your Mind!* seemed to be made up of three sweet minutes of "Brown Eyed Girl" and thirty two minutes of the sprawling, sensation-dulling "T.B. Sheets," a track that stood out from the rest if only in its embrace of the grotesque. The other cuts simply merged into one endless, uninspired blues run, be it "She Who Drove the Red Sports Car" or "He Ain't Give You None" or any of the other faceless chunks of time.

This was Van Morrison free from all restrictions, of song, of melody, of verse and chorus, free from all limits, but far too early. It went back to the blues-raps of "Philosophy" and "The Story of Them," neither of which had ever had much merit as music to begin with. Imagine a half-hour of Elvin Bishop's "Drunk Again," only much much worse, and one has something akin to *Blowin' Your Mind!* A year and a half went by with no further sign from Van Morrison, and that appeared to be that.

And yet Van Morrison, who seemed to have been captured by Donovan's "freedom in a lie," has now released a unique and timeless album, called *Astral Weeks.* The limits and restrictions are no more in evidence than on the previous record, but the limits of the blues, as they exist for Van Morrison, have been abandoned as well. Van sings in and around what might be called a modern chamber orchestra, a group of half a dozen musicians on bass, drums, guitar, sax and flute, with the participation of a cello or a violin at times, not smoothing out the music, but entering into the spirit of the album, a spirit of risk and experiment.

The music is not rock and roll in any ordinary or hyphenated sense; rather it is music that is intelligible to us because of rock and roll, intelligible, given the complexities which hide behind the simplicity of intent, because of *John Wesley Harding.* What might seem arty at first proves to be a new place to go, a new kind of music to hear, as conductor Larry Fallon often abandons the structured comforts of conventional melody, rhythm, and time in an attempt to create and sustain mood, a basis for Van's own creations.

Once Van establishes control of that mood the music flows toward him, rather than forcing him into a conception to which he must adhere. The musicians give Van space in which to walk without abandoning him.

Astral Weeks is strong, serious stuff. It's not really for fun, the way a good song on the car radio is for fun. Some songs, "Brown Eyed Girl" for one, are car songs no matter how one hears them—speed up, pound on the upholstery, "dance dance dance right here in the car"—that can happen anywhere, with the right music. Other songs might be different; once I heard Bob Dylan singing "Mr. Tambourine Man" on an AM car radio, and I almost ran off the road into a ditch, because that song isn't driving music, and I went with it to another place where it belonged.

Astral Weeks is serious, and it is also a profoundly intellectual album. Not in the sense that it requires some grand intelligence to "understand" it or to dig it, or in the sense that Van's music is now something to be "figured out"—rather, it is "intellectual" in the same way that Nathaniel Hawthorne's room, filled with moonlight, was a place and a time for the intellect and the emotions to live together. *Astral Weeks* has the same powers as such a room.

It is pointless to discuss this album in terms of each particular track; with the exception of "Young Lovers Do," a poor jazz-flavored cut that is uncomfortably out of place on this record, it's all one song, very much "A Day in the Life." *Astral Weeks* represents for Van Morrison the same kind of maturity that "Abraham, Martin and John" did for Dion, except that Van has so very much more to offer, as he takes his themes not from the newspaper but from strange mansions in which very few of us have ever truly lived.

That mansion, for Van, is on "Cyprus Avenue," the last cut of "In the Beginning," the first section of the music, a place to which Van returns, "Afterwards," with "Madame George." Wherever "Cyprus Avenue" might be for the artist as a man, it seems very close to Desolation Row, not as Van's conception, but in terms of the myths and metaphors that exist within the world of rock and roll, those things that give us our understanding. "Caught one more time/Up on Cyprus Avenue/Yes, I may go crazy/Before that mansion on the hill."

Not everything works; there are poor lines, like "the viaducts of your dreams," awkward moments, shouts of "breathe in, breathe out, breathe in, breathe out," but such moments fade very quickly, and do not intrude on the fine sections of this album, which seem very heavily influenced by Bob Dylan, influenced in a way that is as strong a tribute as was Them's "Baby Blue." If this record reflects *John Wesley Harding*, it is by capturing the spirit of that music, not by dully incorporating steel guitars and Hank Williams riffs in a frantic sense of where it's at. Morrison has captured a sad manner of gentleness, almost a gesture of forgiveness toward life.

And yet there is an air of tension on this record. The opening notes of "Madame George," very calm, spare, and restrained, just bass and Van's acoustic strumming, like the beginning of "The Weight," signal, in a dramatic way, the major section of the album, the most fully commit themselves, place where Van and the band as Van goes back to Cyprus Avenue to go beyond it, vague riffs on a cello intertwined with striking lines:

> She jumps up and says
> Lord have mercy, I think
>   that it's the cops
> And immediately
> Drops everything she gots
> Down into the street
> Below

moving into quiet announcements of situations with no solutions, "playing dominoes in drag," until, "round that train from Dublin/Up the sandy road . . . say goodbye/To Madame George," never understood, only left behind.

I went to the Avalon Ballroom in San Francisco to hear Van Morrison perform with a stand-up bass player and a hornman. After a brilliant set in which he sang all of *Astral Weeks* as well as three songs from his previous record, we talked about the failure of *Blowin' Your Mind!*

"I've got a tape in Belfast with all my songs on that record done the way they're supposed to be done," he said. "It's good and simple, doesn't come on heavy. 'TB Sheets' isn't heavy. It's just quiet." The soft, seductive rhythms of *Astral Weeks* had surrounded "Red Sports Car" and "She Ain't Give You None" that night, and it had made them seem, at least this listener, as if they were new songs.

"It was the producer who did it, and that record company. They had to cover it all with the big electric guitar and the drums and the rest. It all came out wrong and they released it without my consent." He said that with a gentleness that almost nullified the fact that the album had ever existed at all. *Blowin' Your Mind!* had seemed like the pointless chaos of Morrison on his own —too much freedom—but it had been, once again, the bars of someone else's prison. The bars are down now; the freedom Van has achieved has less to do with chaos than with grace.

—GREIL MARCUS
3-1-69

MOONDANCE
Van Morrison
(Warner Brothers 1835)

Long ago, Van Morrison reached that point where the

influences on his music no longer mattered. It is as pointless to attempt to detect those influences as it would be for any musician to try to imitate him.

Van Morrison's music cannot really be imitated, because, as with Dylan's music, what one hears is not style, but personality. With each record—*Them Again, Astral Weeks,* or *Moondance*—one gets a sense that Van has achieved some ancient familiarity with his band and with his songs; no matter how the music changes, the long inventions of Van's singing, his full command of the musicians that play with him, and the striking imagination of a consciousness that is visionary in the strongest sense of the word, create an atmosphere that instantly sets its own terms. Morrison's powers are clear: his strong gift for melody, his ability to move freely within virtually and sort of contemporary instrumentation, his verbal magic as inventive and literate as Dylan's, and most of all, the authenticity of his spirit.

Moondance is his first album in over a year. Unlike Van's masterful *Astral Weeks,* this one will be immensely popular; Van's picture already fills the windows of record stores and his new music is getting more airplay on FM stations than anything in recent memory.

Van's new album might send one back to the bright enthusiasm of "Brown-Eyed Girl" and the magic blues of *Them Again;* Van now sings with a magnetically full electric band, complete with piano, organ, vibes, and intricately controlled saxophones and flute. The band's performance has a stately brilliance; and if it recaptures some of the feeling of the earlier music, the past is serving as a rite of passage toward the celebrations of *Moondance.*

Van opens with "And It Stoned Me," a tale of boys out for a day's freedom, standing in the rain with eyes and mouths open, heads bent back: "Oh, the water, let it run all over me . . ." The sensuality of this song is overpowering, communicated with a classical sort of grace. "And it stoned me/To my soul/Stoned me just like jelly roll . . ." There is no strain for meaning in Van's words or in his voice. "Let it run all over me . . ."—you feel the exhilaration almost with a sense of astonishment. The band, playing subtle, gentle rock and roll, surrounds the singer; here, as everywhere on *Moondance,* the horn arrangements are absolutely exquisite, as eloquent as a sermon in a backwoods chapel.

With "Caravan" one might begin to remember the early Impressions: that instantaneous aura of fantasy and desire that Curtis Mayfield created for "Gypsy Woman" tumbles down again as a fanfare on piano and the roll of drums and guitar open a composition of seductive grandeur. "Caravan" is a strange song; the images are easily real and the music is profoundly comforting, yet there's the edge of a story here that fades without ever revealing all it has to tell. "Now the caravan has all friends/Yes, they'll stay with me until the end . . . Gypsies . . . tell me all I need to know . . ." Woven between the fragments and framed by the textures of the horn section is a love tale, drawn with blazing imagination: "Turn up your radio/And let me/ Hear the song/Turn on your electric light/So we can get down/To what is really wrong." The singer moves from the gypsy campfire to his lover and back again, with a lovely sort of affection. Van's singing is pure expression, pure sound; the band moves off and then forward again. A graceful soprano saxophone holds notes behind Van's words: "Now, the caravan is painted red and white/That means everyone is staying overnight . . ."

"It's a good thing he doesn't have much stage presence," said a friend after watching Van perform this song. "Otherwise it'd be too much to take."

"Into the Mystic" is the heart of *Moondance;* the music unfolds with a classic sense of timing, guitar strums fading into watery notes on a piano, the bass counting off the pace. The lines of the song and Morrison's

delivery of them are gorgeous: "I want to rock your gypsy soul/Just like in the days of old/And magnificently we will fold/Into the mystic." The transcendent purity of the imagery seems to turn endlessly, giving back one's own reflection. Van's more abstract songs are mosaics of brilliantly chosen metaphors—ambiguous and instantly recognizable. Morrison communicates directly even when he is most obscure; his visions have power, and the ambiguity of those visions is always unified by the sympathy of the music—there is no "back-up band" on *Moondance* anymore than there is on "Lay Lady Lay." Something's been made; it stands, it won't be broken down.

Perhaps "Glad Tidings," which ends *Moondance,* is the song that most makes one want to come back to this album without even thinking about it. "Glad Tidings" is a vital, leaping promenade through the streets of the town; fast, clean rock and roll moves it along as striking horns guide the song, until they cue the chorus into an explosion of real joy: "Yeah, we'll send you glad tidings/From New York/DO DO DO DOOT DO DO/ Open up your eyes that you may see/DO DO DO DOOT DO DO/Ask you not to read between the lines/Hoping that you come right in on time."

Moondance is an album of musical invention and lyrical

confidence; the strong moods of "Into the Mystic" and the fine, epic brilliance of "Caravan" will carry it past many good records we'll forget in the next few years. Van Morrison plays on.

—GREIL MARCUS AND
LESTER BANGS
3-19-70

Bob Dylan

If there is a single figure who dominated rock of the Sixties like Elvis Presley dominated rock and roll of the Fifties, it was, of course, Bob Dylan ("from that little Minnesota town").

To roughly divide up Dylan's career to date, one first has the folk period of his first records when Bob came to New York full of Woody Guthrie and the folk boom of the early Sixties. With *Another Side* he began the transition to rock that encompassed the albums *Bringing It All Back Home* through *Blonde on Blonde.*

Following a year-long recuperation from a motorcycle accident in which he nearly died, and the release of a *Greatest Hits* collection, Dylan entered a stage in which the country influence predominated. It began with *John Wesley Harding,* considered his most perfect album.

(Dylan was so enamoured of the review of *JWH* in this chapter that he selected it for reprinting in the book of lyrics from that album.)

Though he had used the Nashville session men as early as *Blonde on Blonde,* and used them exclusively for *John Wesley Harding, Nashville Skyline* was really Dylan's first totally country album. It even had a duet with Johnny Cash with whom Dylan enjoys a long-standing mutual respect and friendship dating from the Newport Folk Festival days when Cash presented Dylan with his own guitar onstage.

Paul Nelson, who reviewed *Nashville Skyline,* was also an old acquaintance of Dylan's from the days in Minneapolis, where Dylan played the folk clubs in college before he headed for New York.

Shortly after the release of *JWH,* tape copies of a demo session Dylan did with The Band during his recuperation in Woodstock began to be widely circulated. There were various versions of this collection of songs, literally a thousand generations of dubbed copies—passed on from performers, publishers, managers and agents for whom the songs were originally intended, to friends, other performers, more friends, friends of friends—until a lead story in a Summer, 1968 issue of *Rolling Stone* described all the songs, dubbed it "The Basement Tape," and called for its release.

Shortly thereafter it was. As a bootleg. The album was called *The Great White Wonder,* and was the first in a long series of white cover, white label bootlegs circulated throughout the new music underground. It was a double set including other numbers, both tapes of live performances and copies of outtakes from various Dylan recording sessions.

Greil Marcus, in the same issue with Dylan's only interview since his motorcycle accident, wrote a fairly complete discography of The Basement Tape, the various other bootlegs and tapes, performances and outtakes that have been circulating among Dylan fans for years.

The point of *Self Portrait,* coming at the time it did and during the clamor for all the unreleased, second-rate Dylan songs and performances, is that both reviews included here were right in their way. *Self Portrait* wasn't his best, or even among them, but on the other hand, Dylan was still a great singer, writer and the consummate artist.

And then, as the year 1970 ended and the Seventies were about to begin, Dylan released *New Morning.*

"LIKE A ROLLING STONE" AND OTHER UNRELEASED DYLAN

Bobby Darin had three hit records under his belt when he announced his goal in life: "I want to be a legend by the time I'm twenty-five." He didn't make it, but Bob Dylan did.

Searching out the sources of every sort of American music —from the rock and roll childhood he shares with his fans to the depression ballads our parents might have known, from the apocalypse of Robert Johnson to the city flash of Muddy Waters, from the old testament of the Carter Family to the ageless earth of Johnny Cash— Dylan found what he was looking for, and his impact on the Sixties has been devastating and magnificent.

That impact is perhaps as much a result of Dylan's personal stance as it is a result of his music. Hard to find, hard to find out about, Dylan held back from the usual nonsense and the honest curiosity that surrounds the star and created, perhaps to protect himself, perhaps for fun, a style of resistance, allegory, irony and humor that pervaded both his songs and his appearances in public. And more than ever, the fans could not bear to be without him and musicians could not afford to ignore him. The shifts in Dylan's own musical approach brought havoc to

the "styles" of more groups and performers than would like to admit it. "If I didn't dig his stuff so much I'd have to hate him," said one; "In fact, maybe I do hate him anyway." Or as Dylan put it: "I got a friend who spends his life/Stabbing my picture with a bowie knife . . . I got a million friends."

And yet in eight years he has released only nine albums. The sparing manner in which Bob Dylan has presented both his own charismatic self and his special music to the public has brought about an amazing interest in and collection of rare and unreleased songs and performances. Some search these out because they want to listen, some because they want to hold them in their hands, some because they provide The Key.

Whatever the reason, it soon becomes obvious that far more material remains unreleased than has ever appeared on Columbia LPs. The *Great White Wonder* records are only a taste of it—forgotten albums from the early Sixties, demos made for publishing companies, basement tapes, session rejects, live performances and songs deleted from LPs or withdrawn from the market—all this and more indicates that the recorded history of Dylan's career has been presented in a form that has been, perhaps, tailored for its impact on us. Ironically, it has been the impression made on us by the music we *have* been given that makes us want to hear the rest of it.

The "discography" that follows makes no claim to be complete; no doubt a great deal more remains to be heard. This is merely a chronicle of what is available, formally and informally: what we have missed.

[HARMONICA RECORDS]

In last year's interview with *Sing Out*, Dylan mentioned that his first recordings were made with Big Joe Williams (in an older and more obscure interview Dylan talked about his early rock and roll days—touring with Bobby Vee and, if you choose to believe all the stories, with Buddy Holly and Bo Diddley as well—and records he cut previous to his arrival in New York). The Williams recordings came about as a result of Bob's meeting with Victoria Spivey, a blues singer who was performing at Gerde's in the Village. Miss Spivey was recording Williams and allowed the young folksinger to perform with his idol. Two cuts remain in the vaults, but two have been released on *Three Kings and the Queen*, Spivey LP 1004 (Williams, Roosevelt Sykes, Lonnie Johnson, V. Spivey). Recorded in 1961, issued in 1964, Dylan accompanies Williams on harp for "Wichita" and provides a deep blues back-up vocal for "Sitting On Top of the World."

"When Bobby first hit the Village he wasn't singing Woody Guthrie songs. That came later. That first time, he was into Harry Belafonte." So said an old New York folkie. Thus: *Midnight Special*, Harry Belafonte, RCA LSP 2449, issued May 1962, produced by Hugo Montenegro, with Bob Dylan, harmonica, on one cut, "Midnight Special."

Just before the release of his own first album, Dylan accompanied Carolyn Hester on her first and only Columbia LP. Gorgeous, but hopelessly without talent, Carolyn now heads up the Carolyn Hester Coalition, a "rock group." *Carolyn Hester*, Columbia CL 1796, Bob Dylan, harmonica.

Sometime in 1963 Dick Farina and Eric Von Schmidt (from "the green pastures of Harvard University . . .") found themselves in Europe and proceeded to cut an album, "singing, shouting and playing American ballads, work songs, and blues, with Ethan Singer and occasionally Blind Boy Grunt . . . Blind Boy Grunt showed up from Rome and nobody got much sleep . . ." The album is rather wretched, but for the record, Dylan plays harp on "Glory, Glory," "You Can't Always Tell," "Christmas Island," and "Cocaine." *Dick Farina and Eric Von Schmidt*, Folklore Records (English), F-LEUT/7.

Finally, the old Elektra *Blues*

Project set (not the group), EKS 7264, apparently includes Bob ("Bob Landy") on piano for "Downtown Blues." Now, with this out of the way, we can skip to 1969 for—

[JOHNNY CASH AND THE NASHVILLE SKYLINE RAG]

In 1969 The National Educational Television network aired a long documentary on Johnny Cash made by Granada Films. A fine show, it also included a duet between Dylan and Cash on "One Too Many Mornings." The song was widely taped, and is in wide circulation (it was part of the same session that produced "Girl From the North Country"—released on *Nashville Skyline*—as well as "I Walk the Line," "Wanted Man," "Big River," "Careless Love," and "Understand Your Man," among others). "One Too Many Mornings" seems to be one of the songs that has aged best for Bob—he was performing it with the Hawks in 1966 (see below) and of course recorded it on *The Times They Are A-Changin'*. The Dylan-Cash version is a bit of a burlesque, especially the final choruses, which go on and on and on. The film showed Dylan cracking up as he listened to the playback.

Dylan returned to Nashville in June of this year to tape his appearance on Cash's first TV show, and included the new "Living the Blues" in his set.

As just about everyone who heard it has said, the tune catches the feel of the Guy Mitchell's "Singing the Blues." This too was taped by many, and was included on the *Great White Wonder* discs. At the same time, Dylan cut a number of other songs, including "Take A Message To Mary," the old Everly Brothers number, and "Blue Moon," backed by Doug Kershaw on fiddle. One would hope, but doubt, that Bob's version would be patterned after the Marcels' hit —but Elvis' would be alright too. And now on to what this article is really about.

[THE MINNESOTA TAPES— OFF HIGHWAY 61]

Back in December, 1961, Bob Dylan recorded twenty-six songs in a hotel in Minneapolis. In this voluminous session, he put down a good bit of his repertoire—a young artist searching out his own material, perhaps for an audition tape to be used to gain jobs or as preparation for a recording date. Having returned to Minnesota from New York, the tapes reflect things Dylan most likely learned from Dave Van Ronk and others, as well as songs that might have been picked up in any part of the country. There's a much greater range in this session than in the material that eventually surfaced as Dylan's first album. There is little sense of "packaging" or image; from the old Lord Buckley rap about Hezekiah Jones to the pounding gospel-rock of "Wade in the Water," from the clumsy, happy "Sally Gal" to the difficult "Man of Constant Sorrow," this is a young man attempting to understand American music, and beginning to succeed.

A brief run-down, with highlights: (1) "Candy Man." (2) "Baby Please Don't Go"—one of Dylan's best blues performances—a stinging, harsh vocal and rough, rhythmic guitar, with a bass drum pushing it on. Very similar to the brilliant hit version by Them. This number would have shaken up a lot of people had it been included on Dylan's first LP. (3) "Hard Times In New York"—Dylan finds the big city unpleasant and polluted, yearns for wide open spaces, etc. (4) "Stealin'"—Bob's version of the old blues theme of infidelity; rough, clumsy, and a lot of fun.

(5) "Poor Lazarus"—the depth of talent that made Dylan a young sensation emerges on this number. It is simply not that easy for a twenty-year-old to sing a song about death and treachery and carry it off, but Dylan does it. He could *play* the roles of fathers and sons as he sang about them; and if he could not yet sing with the presence of Robert Johnson, he was beginning to understand what it might mean to do so. (6) "Ain't Got No Home"—a crude version of the Guthrie

song. (7) "It's Hard To Be Blind"—a reworking of the old "It's Hard To Be Poor." "I wrote my own words to it," says Bob. (8) "Dink's Song"—"I learned it from a lady named Dink. I don't know who wrote it." The number has an infectious rhythm; it would make a great rock and roll performance. The drama of Dylan's soft guitar almost makes the listener feel strings have been added—there is that much projection in the take. It's a simple farethee-well, but unspeakably lovely, and a hint of what was to come with "Corinna, Corinna" and "Boots of Spanish Leather." (9) "Man of Constant Sorrow"—another brilliant version of the song included on Dylan's first LP. (10) "East Orange, NJ"—a long shaggy dog story about the perils of being a musician in a hick town. Dylan would never have made it as a stand-up comedian, though. (11) "Only Wise"—a lovely, ancient song of lost love and death. (12) "Wade in the Water"—an up-tempo charger. Today they'd call it "heavy." Dylan's bottle-necking gives the take its guts.

(13) "I Was Young When I Left Home"—"I sorta made it up on a train," Bob says. This is the most brilliant song of the session; an aching, desperate marriage of several traditional songs, and modern themes: "Five Hundred Miles," Bobby Bare's "Detroit City," and others. "It's so *blue,*" said a

friend when he heard it. One has the image of a single, solitary young man floating in his mind from station to station, riding whatever train might pass through with the old hope of someday finding someone there to meet him when he gets off at the end of the line. "I was young when I left home . . . an' I been a-ramblin' round . . . and I never wrote a letter to my home." It has a maturity youth deserves to be spared. (14) "Get Lonesome Sleeping By Yourself"—a mean blues, with dirty, beautifully restrained harp and percussion. (15) "Baby Let Me Follow You Down"—a long, wildly exuberant take of the number that illuminated the first album. (16) "Sally Gal"—"I'm gonna get you, Sally Gal!" Why not? (17) "Gospel Plow"—again, on the first LP. (18) "Long John"— one of those superethnic Dave Ray train hollers, and pretty dismal. (19) "Cocaine Blues"— not exactly up to the job Dave Van Ronk has done on this, but a lovely, relaxed version of the song every East Coast folksinger had to master. "Yonder comes my baby, all dressed in purple/Hey, baby, I wanna see your nipples."

(20, 21, 22 & 23) The Infamous Medley: "VD Blues," "VD Waltz," "Gunner's Blues," and "VD City." "VD City" is the best of them—it might remind one of "Heartbreak Hotel" —"The cold horrible dungeons, where the victims of syphilis lie . . . there's a street named for every disease here, Syph Alley and Clap Avenue . . . must you pay your way to this city with an hour of passion and vice . . ." (24) "See That My Grave Is Kept Clean"—repeated on the first album. (25) "Ramblin' Round." (26) "Black Cross"—the Lord Buckley story of a black non-believer from a Southern town, lynched for his honesty. Dylan's vocal mannerisms are a clear debt to or cop from Buckley, but it's a better effort than, say, "The Death of Emmett Till," which Dylan had recorded three months earlier on a radio show for WBAI-FM.

That show was never aired, for some reason; included were Izzy Young, Pete Seeger, Sis Cunningham, and Gil Turner. Dylan performed a song called "The Ballad of Donald White" as well, an interesting tale of a man demanding to be returned to prison because he cannot function in normal society. White kills a man, and is hanged instead of being allowed to find a home in prison. This number prompts Young to announce, in a beautifully patronizing tone, that "this is the first psychological song," which was nonsense, but part of the game that was being played in those days. The interview includes a few other priceless bits, including one where Pete Seeger asks Bob how he writes songs. "Do you just spread out the newspaper in the morning until you find a story that gets you upset?" Bob Dylan, re-write man. The show closes with a moanin' and groanin' of "Blowin' in the Wind." "I really do just take 'em out of the air," Bob had been saying.

[THE BROADSIDE RECORDINGS AND THE RISE OF BLIND BOY GRUNT]

In the Fall of 1963 (according to best information) Dylan made a number of recordings for Broadside Records—really, for the *Broadside* scene. Sitting in on this session were Gil Turner, Phil Ochs, Gordon Friesen, and Sis Cunningham. Three of the cuts recorded have been released on an LP, still available, called *Broadside Ballads No. 1,* Broadside Records BR-301, issued November 1963. The songs include "John Brown" (discussed below in the "live" section), "Only A Hobo," a rather poor song about the death of a tramp (of which a couple of other versions exist), and "Talking Devil," which is a gas. The song predates a verse from the Stones' "Jigsaw Puzzle": "The gangster looks so frightening/With his luger in his hand/But when he gets home to his children/He's a family man." Dylan's "Talking Devil" is the brief tale of a nightrider, "the devil," and Bob asks, "Wonder if his kids know who he is?" It's the only bit

of humor on the whole Broadside LP.

None of the other Broadside recordings have been released, perhaps because of contract problems or perhaps because Bob chose to keep them in the past. The most surprising of these is "The Cough Song"—none other than "Nashville Skyline Rag" for guitar and harmonica! The harp sketches out the part the band plays on the 1969 recording, and keeps right on until Dylan laughs. "That was the end. Right there before I coughed. It fades out." And then everyone cracks up.

The other recordings don't stand up so well, save for "Walking Down the Line," a fine road song with a bit of displaced humor: "I saw the morning light/I saw the morning light/It's not because I'm an early riser, but I didn't go to sleep last night." Another version was also cut for a publishing demo. "Hey, Hey, I'd Hate to Be You on That Dreadful Day" is a rough blues that might have surfaced as a tough rocker had Dylan held on to it and worked it out; as it is, the cut has a few flashes: "You're gonna walk naked, can't ride in no car/Everyone's gonna see just what you are." "Playboys and Playgirls" reveals Dylan claiming he won't be sold down the river by the Hugh Hefner crew; "Train-a-Trailin' " is just that; and "Cuban Blockade" is a stiff number about that day "when everyone thought the world would end." As one of *Broadside*'s editors said when *Highway 61 Revisited* hit the stores, "I wouldn't mind what he's doing now, if only he'd just write one good song against the war. . ."

References to the bustling metropolis of East Orange, New Jersey pop up occasionally in Dylan's career: on "Talkin' New York" from the first album, in the little folk tale about a coffeehouse recorded for the "Minnesota Tapes." Sometime in early 1962, it seems, Dylan recorded a number of Woody Guthrie songs at the home of Sid and Bob Gleason, in, as the gig would have it, East Orange, N.J. Bob never released a Guthrie song commercially, though many of his songs have rung changes on Guthrie themes— most recently, "John Wesley Harding." Strangely, it was Dylan's love for Guthrie, not Bob's own music, that brought him his first national attention. Years ago, *Time* ran a short story about an itinerant folksinger who'd journeyed across country to visit the dying man, a kid hyped as a perfect choice to play Guthrie in a film biography. And *that* is a project still talked about.

Thinking back, it seems odd that given the nature of industry packaging Bob never recorded an album of Guthrie songs. It would have been a natural product for Columbia to suggest, along with the raft of other folksingers with their Guthrie albums and country singers with their Jimmie Rodgers and Hank Williams records. Simply, Dylan was pushing ahead of the game, making up his own songs, looking for his own music even as he reached for a surer hold on his roots.

Most of the numbers are pretty much straightforward runthroughs, lacking in projection or feeling, adding little to the music, though the takes would no doubt delight Dylan fans simply because of the nature of the material. "San Francisco Bay Blues," "Jesus Met the Woman at the Well," "Gypsy Davy," "Jesse James," and "Remember Me" receive this sort of performance—careful, studied, and a bit stiff. And then, in contrast to the rest of the session, Dylan begins to draw on that incredible reserve of spirit and tension that has made him a performing curator of the museum of American music. Slowly picking out the notes to "Pastures of Plenty," on his harp for the first time on the takes, he captures a sense of age the song perhaps never knew before —a sense of passing. The pastures of plenty are a memory, a desire, a hope—never a reality. The "journey through valleys till the day that I die," the broken witness "on the edge of your cities," is more a search than an affirmation, an attempt to find what has been lost, what perhaps never existed at all.

It happens again with "On the Trail of the Buffalo." Guthrie set the song in the 1880s, but its power came from the fact that Guthrie *himself* was on that trail, looking for those endless herds that formed their own horizons. The harsh strumming of Dylan's guitar gives the song a deathly, scary tone; you know there was *never* a chance for the animals to last. The beasts were doomed even before they had captured our imagination, and the threat of death hovers over the cowboys of the song, riding the trail the buffalo had cut into the earth. "Outlaws watching to pick us off/From the hills of the buffalo." It's this sense of forgotten history, alive in the soul of a man in the present, that is the source of the power of the best American music, music that reaches for America, wherever and whatever it was, always with the sense that if we can uncover what it felt like to live when the country was young we can learn how to live when the country is old.

Dylan's "As I Went Out One Morning" and "The Wicked Messenger" and "Tears of Rage," the Band's "Rockin' Chair," "Across the Great Divide," and "King Harvest" are all songs of age, songs of a spiritual, not a factual adoles-

cence. Unlike the "rock and roll revival," these songs and those that Guthrie wrote do not have to be "revived." They endure, and they last, and it is the burden of age that they carry that fixes their agelessness.

[THE GASLIGHT TAPES]

These tapes, recorded in the Gaslight Cafe in Greenwich Village in 1962, are interesting mainly because they comprise what seem to be the only available recorded versions of three fine songs. The tape seems to have been made with an on-stage recorder—a semi-formal session, so to speak.

"There Was An Old Man" is a radically different version of that staple of Dylan collectors, "Only A Hobo." It's a dramatic, sensitive portrait of the tramp dead on the curb, the cop poking him into the gutter; not a shouting eulogy, but a story that is part of the city.

"He Was a Friend of Mine" is a beautiful soft song to a friend who "died on the road." It seems to have a sense of the dues one has to pay simply to live: "He never had enough money/To pay his fine . . . and he was a friend of mine." The Byrds kept the title and the tune for their song about the Kennedy assassination.

Then comes "Talking Bear Mountain Picnic Massacre Disaster Blues," all about an excursion boat that's oversold and sinks from the crush of bodies, baskets, kids, and fried chicken. Dylan used to crack up his audiences with this one back in 1963 and 1964, but the humor's not nearly as sharp as "Talking World War III" or "Talking John Birch."

The tape ends with Dylan and Dave Van Ronk combining for "Car Car," the gay little automobile song Woody Guthrie wrote to sing to his kids, and a short "Pretty Polly" by Bob. All in all, the tape is a nice memory of the days when Fourth Street wasn't "such a drag."

["... UNLIKE MOST OF THE SONGS NOWADAYS BEING WRITTEN UP IN TIN PAN ALLEY ..."— THE WITMARK DEMOS]

Dylan's first songs were published by Duchess Music (BMI), but by the time of the *Freewheelin'* album Bob had affiliated with M. Witmark & Sons, one of the first music publishers in American history—a founder of Tin Pan Alley and a house of the most eminent prestige. It was virtually unprecedented for a "folksinger" to publish through such an agency, and this stroke of financial and PR genius set Dylan apart from the rest of the Village crowd as much as his songs did. Dylan wrote a large number of songs from 1962 and 1964 that he did not release on his albums, and these were cut as demos for Witmark. Many of these were

eventually recorded by other artists, while some eventually reached the general public only through songbooks (*Bob Dylan, The Original,* Warner Bros.-7 Arts purchased M. Witmark some time ago). Some of the tapes discussed below may not in fact be Witmark demos—it's hard to tell—but they fall more readily into *that* category than any other.

Piano songs. In 1963 or 1964 Dylan recorded a number of songs, accompanying himself on piano, featuring what Al Kooper has called Bob's "beautifully untutored" keyboard work. Others, perhaps with more accuracy, have referred to the "ultimate flowering of the whorehouse piano." Whatever one calls it, the music brings to mind a strange amalgam of Jerry Lee Lewis, Skip James, Mose Allison, Memphis Slim and Nicky Hopkins—a wilder, freer style than on, say, "Dear Landlord" or "Ballad of a Thin Man." The vocals and the composition of a couple of these numbers represent a maturity and a grasp of the finest subtleties of American popular music that is simply not to be found in any of the recordings Dylan had released up to the time. A spare sense of restraint and an effortless timing characterize the singing—a feel, again, of age beyond years.

"I'll Keep It With Mine" is a song written for, of all people, Nico, who was a European groupie when Dylan and Grossman met her on a visit to the Continent. Nico eventually did come to the US, as they had urged, and recorded the song on her first album for Verve, *Chelsea Girl*. A. E. Mac. Denny of the Fairport Convention has also recorded the song, magnificently, for the Fairport Convention's album on A&M. None of these versions, though, give a hint of Dylan's performance. His piano accompaniment is a succession of quarter-note triplets, with the first heavily accented and reinforced by his tapping foot. The lyrics—reminiscent of *Another Side*—tell a train story, the singer softly pleading for a girl to remain. The melody is one of his best up to that point, with a fine understated verse and a gradual build-up in the chorus: "Everybody will help you/Discover what you set out to find/But if I/Can save you any time/Come on, give it to me/I'll keep it with mine." The performance is a tour-de-force that really should have been released.

"California" is a little ditty in the vein of "Outlaw Blues," with a line that later found its way into that song: "I got my dark sunglasses/I got for good luck my black tooth . . ." It's title comes from the verse, "San Francisco is fine/It sure gets lotsa sun/But I'm used to four seasons/California's got but one." The piano here is much

like that on "Black Crow Blues."

"Hmmmm," says Bob, and hits his rinky-tink piano for Arthur Crudup's "That's Alright Mama," also Elvis' first record. The piano work is extraordinary; Dylan performs some finger-breaking pyrotechnics that must be heard to be believed. Near the end, he abruptly changes tempo, riffs, changes tempo again—and then the tape is out. The listener is invariably left breathless.

"Denise, Denise" is a pounding rocker with an infectious rhythm, the singer casting a cold eye at a girl who just won't cop out to being real. Maracas, piano and harp drive the best version of this number until Bob is ready for a line that would have entered our common language had the song ever been released: "I'm looking deep in your eyes, babe/But all I see is myself."

There are three versions of "Bob Dylan's New Orleans Rag"—an incomplete take, a live cut from an unreleased LP (see "Live Performances") and a full, rocking performance with harp and piano. We find Bob sitting on a stump in New Orleans: "Along came a stranger and he didn't even ask/He said I know 'bouta woman who can fix you up fast." He leads the singer to a door marked "103" and then the fun starts. All sorts of laid-out wiped-out, freaked-out fellows stumble out the door, moaning, crawling, unable to speak; Bob sees one that "looked like he'd been through a monkey wrench." The kid splits fast: "I musta run a mile in a minute or less." The piano pushes this remarkably fluid number to crazy heights of rhythm, until Bob wheezes: "Man, you're better off/In your misery/Than to tackle that woman/At one-oh ... *three!*"

Dylan also recorded demos of "Paths of Victory," a song of better-times-in-the-future later cut by by Hamilton Camp; "Walking Down the Line" (see "Broadside Recordings"); "Percy's Song" (there are three demos of this—see "Live Performances"); "The Ballad of Emmett Till"; "The Walls of Redwing," a song about the Minnesota boys' reform school, recorded by Joan Baez; and "Seven Curses" (see "Live Performances"). One of his best performances for a demo comes on "Tomorrow Is a Long Time," the song recorded by Elvis for the sound-track of *Spinout* (RCA LSP 3702). The lyrics ride the same Elizabethan melody Dylan used for "Seven Curses," [See "Live Performances"] moving toward Dylan's finest statement of loneliness: "If tomorrow wasn't such a long time/I'd lie in my bed again." The loveliness of the performance impresses one with the depth of feeling Dylan had invested in this song.

Even this take pales next to Dylan's vocal on the traditional Southern ballad "I've Been a Moonshiner," which Dylan called "The Bottle Song." The singing is among the best Bob has ever recorded, as he ornaments and phrases beautifully, demonstrating a control, especially when he soars to the highest notes, that is chilling in its power. It would have been good to have had this song around a few years ago when people complained that Dylan couldn't sing. The guitar and harmonica virtually lead the vocal—the drama of this performance which seems so aged that it might be from the edge of the grave, is like nothing Dylan has released to the public. "I'll go to some barroom/And drink to my fill/Where the women can't follow/And see what I spend."

"Hero Blues" is a funny number in the vein of "It Ain't Me Babe," though closer in tone to Country Joe's "Not So Sweet Martha Lorraine" than to Dylan's own very serious song. "She reads too many books/She got nails inside her head [!]/She will not be satisfied until I wind up dead." And: "You need a different kinda man, babe/You need, you need a Napoleon Bona-part." All he wants to do is love her, not kill for her. Too tough to be a hero, at least this time.

"Whatcha Gonna Do" is a gospel-styled member of the

"where will *you* be on Judgment Day?" sort; "Ain't Gonna Grieve" affirms that the singer will not, in fact, grieve. These two numbers and "Farewell" seem to be from 1962; "Farewell" is an honest goodbye that moves quite nicely: "So it's fare three well, my own true love/We'll meet another day, another time/It's not the leavin', that's a grievin' me/But my true love who's bound to stay behind." Bob and Joan Baez used to sing this together, some years ago.

"Sometimes I'm In the Mood" may not be a demo; it's a weak song that may have been recorded around the same time as "Born To Win, Born To Lose" and "Quit Your Lowdown Ways." These three are not fully worked out, and play on very limited sorts of themes, with lyrics that do not go much beyond the song titles themselves.

Finally there's "The Eternal Circle," a sad, funny number about someone waiting for a song to be over—that someone being the singer, who wants to get at a good-looking girl who is watching him perform. The problem, as the lyrics say, is that "the song it was long" and the first thing is to finish it. Of course, when he finishes, she's gone, so what does he do? "I picked up my git-tar and began the next song."

[ON COLUMBIA—MIXED-UP CONFUSION]

Dylan's career on Columbia has been marked by a number of mistaken releases, changes in album art (the liner photos on *Blonde on Blonde* were re-arranged shortly after the LP's release), mixing and album programming (for a time, the most familiar version of "From a Buick 6" was replaced by an alternate take with different lyrics, and then removed and replaced by the original take). This sort of confusion has only added to the vinyl charisma of Dylan's recordings.

The Freewheelin' Bob Dylan. Sharp-eyed fans will have noticed that the liner notes to *Freewheelin'* announce the presence of a band (Bruce Langhorne, guitar; George Barnes, bass; Dick Wellstood, piano; Gene Ramey, string bass; and Herb Lovelle, drums) on "Don't Think Twice" and "Corrina, Corrina." While the group is vaguely audible on the latter cut it's obvious that "Don't Think Twice" was recorded as a solo performance. Columbia, however, released a single prior to *Freewheelin'* that *did* include the band—a different, stronger take of "Corrina" (a fully realized accompaniment, brilliant harmonica, and a vocal close to Chuck Wills') and the dazzling rocker, "Mixed-Up Confusion." "Confusion," an original, is a full-bopping tune with bouncy piano triplets and snappy drumming—"And I'm lookin' for a woman/who's head's mixed up like mine!/ And I'm lookin' for some answers/But I don't know who to ask!" Had this little gem been in circulation from 1963 through 1965 the fans at Newport might have been kinder to Bob when he returned to rock and roll. However, the single didn't exactly bust the charts, and was withdrawn soon after release. It was later issued in Holland in 1966 (CBS 2476) and was available in the Benelux countries and in Germany as late as 1968.

Following the release of "Confusion," someone at Columbia mixed up the programming for *Freewheelin'* itself. A small number of the LP's included four cuts omitted from the standard version: "Ramblin', Gamblin' Willie" (a delightful tale of a card shark who finally drew that dead man's hand—"He had twenty-seven children/And never had a wife!"); "Rocks and Gravel" (a railroad gang blues, very southern in tone, backed by the band mentioned above); "Let Me Die in My Footsteps" (an anti-fallout shelter song); and the famous banned-by-Ed Sullivan "Talking John Birch Society Blues" (a very funny routine about paranoia and bed-looking-under: "Looked deep down inside my toilet bowl—they got away!" and the priceless line, "I discovered there was *red stripes* on the American flag! Oh, Betsy Ross?").

Most of these albums were recalled immediately but a number remained on sale in California for at least three months after release. The songs deleted pretty much match up to those actually released: "Masters of War" replaced "Let Me Die in My Footsteps" (on an out-take of "Footsteps" Bob stops the song in the middle and asks, "Do you want this one? It's so long . . . it's not that it's long, but it's such a drag . . . I've sung it so many times"); "Girl From the North Country" replaced "Rocks and Gravel"; "Bob Dylan's Dream" replaced "Ramblin' Gamblin' Willie"; and "Talking World War III Blues" replaced "Talking John Birch Society Blues."

Another Side of Bob Dylan. There are a number of out-takes from this session, and "East Laredo" seems to be one of them. Produced by Tom Wilson, it's a piano solo with echoes of Ben E. King's "Spanish Harlem," a pretty number that would have made a good B-side for a single. Also from this session is "Lay Down Your Weary Tune," a song that seems to be a call to the quest for the perfect, unobtainable music. Stately, restrained and majestic, it is as much a break with the past as "My Back Pages," though the metaphors are musical, not political: "Lay down your weary tune/Lay down the songs you strum/And rest yourself 'neath the strength of strings/No voice can hope to hum."

It's also possible that the versions of "Bob Dylan's New Orleans Rag" and "Denise, Denise" that are recorded with piano, maracas, and harp are from this session.

Bringing It All Back Home. Dylan broke loose as a rock and roll singer on this album, with "On the Road Again," "Outlaw Blues," and "115th Dream," but it was "If You Gotta Go, Go Now," a natural, sexy rock and roll song, that had hinted at what was going to happen on *Bringing It All Back Home.* Dylan had been performing this number acoustically for some time, and it never failed to stop the show, as laughter and cheers broke over the singer's grin as he smiled back to the crowd: "It's not that I'm questioning you/To take part in any kinda quiz/It's just that I ain't got no watch/And you keep asking me what time it is." A "Let's Spend the Night Together" with jokes. Supposedly set for American release in 1967, it seems clear that the cut was recorded as part of the sessions for *Bringing It All Back Home:* the piano-styled guitar of Bruce Langhorne is a delight, as are the back-up vocals, which seem quite girlish. It was released as a single in Europe in 1967 (b/w "To Ramona") and is still available in the Benelux markets (CBS 2921). Manfred Mann's excellent ver-

sion prompted Dylan to announce that they did his material more justice than anyone else. "It's not that I'm asking/For anything you never gave before/It's just that I'll be sleeping soon/And it'll be too dark for you to find the *door.*"

Highway 61 Revisited. Aside from producing one of the two or three finest rock and roll albums ever made, the sessions for *Highway 61 Revisited* also produced their share of rarities. "Killing Me Alive (Barbed Wire Fence)" is the most outstanding—a tough, solid, tremendously exciting blues, with Kooper on organ and Bloomfield in his brash, I-Can-Play-Anything - Better - Than - You groove (and he just about could, too). Kooper chords for the rhythm and Bloomfield solos for fun, Bob shouting out the lyrics that ultimately give it all away: "You're gonna think this song is just a riff/I *know* you're thinking this song is just a riff/Unless you've been inside a tunnel and fell down 69,000 feet over a *barbed* wire fence." The lyrics also bear out what Dylan has said time and time again to disbelieving audiences: he makes up his songs as he goes along, building around lines and images that he really digs. The alternate version of "From a Buick 6" demonstrates this in-the-studio process, as do these words from "Killing Me Alive"; "The Arabian doctor comes in, gives me a shot but he wouldn't tell me what it was that I got"—lines that later appeared, in different form, in "Just Like Tom Thumb's Blues." The pattern is repeated in many other unreleased songs.

Also a product of this session was the first version of "Won't You Please Crawl Out Your Window," which featured what sounds like a xylophone and magnificent guitar from Bloomfield. Columbia accidentally released it under the title "Positively Fourth Street" (some gremlin must have mixed the labels), recalled it a week later, and then some months after released a different version of the song that included Robbie Robertson and probably the rest of the Hawks as a backing band. Very little is known about the sessions that produced this take. The standard release take of "Crawl Out Your Window" has a weird, circus sound, with odd jangling rhythms something like the Band's "To Kingdom Come." The lyrics seem to echo a follow-up to "Like a Rolling Stone"—come on, honey, get out of there, you can go back if you want to, but look at this cat you're with: "If he needs a third eye he just grows it." The standard version is still available (Columbia 4-43477, CBS EP 6288), while the mellow, seductive "mistake" gets rarer by the day.

[THE BASEMENT TAPE]

"The Basement Tape," recorded before *John Wesley Harding* in Woodstock on a home machine, is the best-known, most accessible and perhaps the most striking of all of Dylan's unreleased material (whether or not this ought to be called "unreleased" is up to the reader—all of it is now available on the *Great White Wonder* and *Troubled Troubador,* bootleg LPs). *Rolling Stone* ran a review of the session (June 22, 1968, Vol. II, No. 2), and since then most of the songs have been covered by various performers. One of the compositions, "I Shall Be Released," has been covered by almost everyone, from Joan Baez to the Box Tops. Dylan's magnificent performance has not been touched; his vocal may well be the best he has ever recorded.

The sessions, which included the Band as a backing group, musically and on vocals, set down basic performances of songs Dylan was not intending to release himself but which were to be included in the Dwarf Music catalogue. Copies of the tape in the form of acetate discs were sent to Manfred Mann, the Byrds, and the Rolling Stones, among others. Unlike the songs on *John Wesley Harding,* almost none of which have formal choruses, the songs from this session use the device of a chorus with a great deal of imagination; with so much imagination, in fact, that the choruses often do not have a logical relationship to the verses. The relationship is often one of mood, or, simply, of dramatic impact. Richard Manuel is extremely effective on some of the choruses, especially on "I Shall Be Released."

The Basement Tape is anything but unique; it's rather a semi-public version of what might go on at Dylan's house and at Big Pink any day of the week. "There're lots more," said one member of the Band. "They're just for fun." For after all, making music, writing songs, changing the old music and inventing the new music is simply what Dylan and the Band *do;* it's their life, their vocation.

A rather rare version of The Basement Tape gives one some idea of what this invention is like. Aside from the well-known fourteen songs, this copy also includes two partially worked-out versions of "Tears of Rage," two of "Open the Door Richard," one other of "Quinn the Eskimo," and a hilarious version of "Nothing Was Delivered." As Dylan and the Band move from setting up to fooling around to the finished product, the songs are changed. "No," someone says after giving up on "Tears of Rage," "it's got to be in rock tempo." And the lyrics are altered to fit the beat, the phrasing changes, Robbie Robertson chooses a new riff, Manuel and Danko try out the high notes they muffed the first time around. Sometimes, as on the rejected "Nothing Was Delivered," something special happens. On this take, the tempo is speeded up, making the song less like the dirge of the final take and more like the theme song of a fun-loving gang leaning hard on a burn artist. Dylan steps out with an extravagant Elvis Presley riff: "You must provide some kind of answer—*you must —you must do that!*—you must provide those answers!" Dylan's Fats Domino piano work makes the cut a hilarious delight. The lyrics are not the same as on the better-known version; they change from take to take, as they do on the alternate versions of "Quinn the Eskimo," "Tears of Rage," and "Open the Door Richard."

The fact that The Basement Tape was not released by Dylan is indicative of a couple of things. First of all, this was music worked out—and in some cases written—with the Band; it was music, most likely, that would have been commercially recorded with them and not with the Nashville musicians of *Blonde on Blonde* or *John Wesley Harding.* Why Bob chose not to record with the Band is pretty obvious; it was time for them to try and make it on their own, to see if they could cut it without help. Secondly, this material was clearly not what Bob wanted to present to his audience when he returned to public life—something "older," something with more restraint and with superficially more clarity was what he had in mind. Like any artist, Dylan chooses what to reveal and what to keep for his own. That such a choice has, in this case, been taken out of his hands is something about which most must feel ambivalent. Garth Hudson's magnificent organ pushing Dylan's unmatched vocal on "This Wheel's On Fire," the kicks of "Tiny Montgomery" (a Southern dragster champ, word has it), or the still water of "I Shall Be Released" are moments that few would trade for anything. The Basement Tape is the album that almost never was.

[LIVE PERFORMANCES—"I EXPOSE MYSELF EVERY TIME I GO OUT ON STAGE"]

Dylan's first live recordings appeared in 1963, on Vanguard and Broadside Records—and while Columbia and Leacock-Pennebaker have recorded reels and reels of live material, only one cut of it has ever been released. There are, of course, the movie "soundtracks," which some have taped: *Don't Look Back,* with it's brilliant, shining hotel-room "It's All Over Now, Baby Blue"; *Festival,* showcasing Dylan's first electric performance with pieces of Paul Butterfield's band ("Maggie's Farm" was included in the film —"Tombstone Blues" and "Like a Rolling Stone" remain in the can); the film shot and the sound recorded for the movie to be made of the Guthrie Memorial Program, at which Dylan and the Band recorded "Mrs. Roosevelt," "Grand Coulee," and "Ain't Got No Home"; and the completed and unreleased film of Dylan's 1966 tour of Europe with the Hawks.

Dylan's earliest live recordings are of mostly academic interest. They include two LPs made from the Newport Folk Festival, 1963: *Evening Concerts at Newport,* Vol. I, 1963, Vanguard VSD 79143 (Dylan sings "Blowin' In the Wind") and *Newport Broadside* (Topical Songs), Vanguard VSD 79144 (Dylan sings "Playboys and Playgirls" with Pete Seeger, "Blowin' in the Wind" again with the whole gang). Dylan also appeared at the 1963 March On Washington, singing "A Pawn in Their Game," which was preserved on the Broadside LP that commemorated the event: *We Shall Overcome,* BR-592.

Then in 1964 Columbia recorded Bob's first solo concert at Carnegie Hall. They wanted a live album, and apparently so did Bob, but disagreements over what songs were to be included doomed the project. The LP did reach the acetate stage, however (Job No. 77110), and the list of cuts seems to indicate that Columbia was trying to capitalize on Dylan's new fame as "the conscience of the nation's youth," while Dylan may, by this time, have become disillusioned with singing songs "written for other people." The album itself is not all that impressive, mostly due to the poor programing, for much of Dylan's weaker material was included: "When the Ship Comes In," "John Brown" (a bitter war story about a kid with a patriotic mother who doesn't recognize her boy when he returns home from the battlefield, mutilated and shattered; a theme taken from many resentful Irish songs about English conscription), and the anti-boxing pure-protest grind-it-out guilt-cruncher, "Who Killed Davey Moore?".

The LP opens with what Columbia calls "Poem To Woody." "Woodie Guthrie is really something more than a folk-singer," Dylan says, introducing his poem. "And this is called 'Last Thoughts On Woody Guthrie.'" That chilling title leads into a long, stream of consciousness reading, very simply the story of a boy looking for himself, down the road, on the street, in the fields. Somehow, Bob is saying, Guthrie was a companion on that road, in the "trash can alleys."

Then Dylan moves into a compelling "Lay Down Your Weary Tune," and then lets loose with a rare song, "Dusty Old Fairgrounds," a charming number about carnivals and arcades, perhaps a memory of the annual Minnesota State Fair, always an important event for a town like Hibbing. After the three cuts mentioned in the paragraph above comes "Percy's Song." A friend has been involved in a fatal accident, sentenced to 99 years in Joliet Prison, and the singer meets with the judge to plead for a lesser sentence. The judge, inevitably, orders the young man from his chambers, and there is nothing to be done. "I played my guitar through the night and the day/But all it could play was the cold, the cruel, rain and the wind." It is a musician's song of stolen friendship. The Fairport Convention performs the composition on their A&M LP, *Unhalfbricking*.

Then comes "Bob Dylan's New Orleans Rag," and the LP closes with "Seven Curses," a brilliant song in the old English manner, with an appropriately dramatic melody. In mood, the number is not all that different from Joan Baez' magnificent "Matty Groves" from her *In Concert* LP. Dylan sings of a horse thief who can escape death if he allows the judge a night with his daughter. He refuses, but the girl insists. The deal is made and the deed is done—and the hanging takes place. The daughter hurls seven curses on the judge: ". . . that five walls cannot hide him; that six diggers cannot bury him; and that seven deaths will never kill him." Dylan's timing in the delivery of these verses is extraordinary, and the song provides a chilling, desperate close to the album.

Later that same year Columbia recorded Dylan's Hallowe'en concert in New York City—17 songs, four with Joan Baez. The performances are not all that different from the studio recordings of the same tunes, with the exception of the show-stopping "If You Gotta Go, Go Now" and the performance of the unrecorded "Mama/Daddy You Been On My Mind," with Joan. The concert is refreshing; it reminds one that Dylan was able to take his songs far less seriously than much of his audience. "This is a sacrilegious lullaby in G-minor," he says, introducing "The Gates of Eden." And later, that classic line: "Well, hope you're all having a good time . . . it's Hallowe'en, and uh, I've got my Bob Dylan mask on."

Fade to 1966. "Like A Rolling Stone" has hit the top of the charts, and Columbia is pressing for another hit. "Positively Fourth Street" is successful, "Crawl Out" flops, "One of Us Must Know," though one of Dylan's best records, flops, and finally they

score with "Rainy Day Women No. 12 & 35." And then, just before the release on *Blonde on Blonde,* comes the pretty bouncy "I Want You." Those who bought it got a surprise; on the flip of Columbia 4-43683 was "Just Like Tom Thumb's Blues," live in Liverpool, 1966: five minutes and thirty-six seconds of tearing, devastating hard rock. Where was the rest of the concert, the rest of that long tour of Europe? Tapes of a performance in Dublin have leaked out, the acoustic part of the show only—"Desolation Row," "Visions of Johanna," "Just Like A Woman," and others, with blazing harp work; but of Bob Dylan and the Hawks on stage, only three numbers have escaped from Columbia's vaults, Pennebaker's files, and Dylan's own collection.

[WHEN THE CIRCUS WAS IN TOWN]

Bob Dylan and the Hawks. They were, without exception or qualifications, the finest rock and roll band I have ever seen or heard. If you weren't there it will be difficult to convey the visual power of their performances. There were Bob and Robbie Robertson, like twins on the stage, charging each other for the solos, their fingers only inches apart; Rick Danko, puffing out his cheeks and bending his body deep, dancing through the cables and wires; Garth Hudson and Richard Manuel, each off to one side of the stage sitting back and making sounds one might have thought came from the guitarists, simply because one could not take his eyes off them; and Mickey Johns or Bobby Greg, sitting high above it all, holding it together, never missing.

The sound they produced was stately, extravagant, and visionary—there is nothing with which to compare it in all of Dylan's recordings. At the bottom of that sound was a rough, jerking marriage of blues and honky tonk, but over that were grafted the sorts of echoes that come from the music box of a circus merry-go-round: the fire and ice of Garth Hudson's organ and the young, brash clinches of Robbie Robertson's guitar. And it was loud, louder than anyone played in those days, but so musical and so melodic that the band could dance free and their audiences easily went with them.

There was an urgency to those performances, an urgency that is captured in the three recordings that have filtered out of New York City. It's certainly there on "Just Like Tom Thumb's Blues," the single that is at least available in Europe (CBS 2258b). Dylan's voice is tired, raspy, but even at the end of an endless tour he wouldn't quit. The music and the phrasing are nothing like the version on *Highway 61 Revisited*, and the real stars are Hudson and Robertson, Garth soloing weirdly in between the lines, Robbie punching notes in and out of Bob's shouts and screams until there is no separation between the singer and the musicians: "And picking up ayyn-gel/Who just arrrrryyyved here/BAM/From the cohhhhhhst/Who looked so fiiiine at firstbutleft-looking/Just . . . like a ghohhhhhhst! Yeah!" And then Robertson and Hudson are into their own music, so fast they literally have to slow down the tempo in order to catch the last verse. It's a stunning performance.

Probably recorded the same night was "One Too Many Mornings," which has surfaced on a tape of professional quality. It is almost pure honky-tonk in its structure, with Dylan rushing the verses, stretching out his vowels more than he ever did on record. Danko and Manuel join him on the choruses, lending a high, moaning dimension to the song that it hasn't known before or since. "Just one too many mornings/And a thousand/*myyles*/BA-DA - DA - DUMP - DA - DUMP/BE-*HIND*." There is virtually no resemblance between this performance and the soft, sorrowful ballad of years before. Dylan sings it almost as if it was a memory that belonged to someone else.

And then, finally and ultimately, there is "Like a Rolling Stone"—Dylan's greatest song, and on this tape, in my opinion, his greatest recording. The performance lasts a full nine minutes.

The Hawks—and especially Robbie Robertson—brought out something in Dylan that allowed him to project, and to reach his audiences, in a way that he had never done before. "If I told you what our music was really about we'd probably all get arrested," he said to an interviewer in 1965. More than just sound, the Hawks gave Dylan the dramatic back-drop he needed to step out all the way and sing. He did it, then, night after night, all over the world. It was glorious—Dylan was a triumphant rock and roll star in a manner that will not be repeated. The parallel, visually, and in its musical excitement, was Elvis Presley. The Hawks made it possible—because Dylan could be sure it was all there without looking over his shoulder.

"Like A Rolling Stone" would be the last encore. The three guitarists would turn their backs on the audience and face the drummer, he'd raise his stick above his head and bring it down with the crash of a cannon shot. Bob would leap into the air and the three of them would hit the first note just as he hit the ground; instantly, they'd have it all. On the live tape the song is slowed down greatly from the recorded version, giving Bob more space in which to sing, more room for those long, stretched-out phrases and the shouts that end each line. It opens with that gunshot and rises immediately with a riot of sounds and colors, with Garth Hudson playing as if he's standing on one key of his organ, shooting out a scream that seems constant throughout the nine minutes. The key to the performance is Robbie Robertson—he hits the toughest, hardest note imaginable at the beginning of every other phrase, signaling the changes and setting up Dylan for every image that's shouted into the microphone. The song moves up and down with Robertson's rhythm, fading and returning: "They used to be/Briiiinnnng!/Sohhh amused/Baaaaah/With Napoleon in rags/Briiiinnnng!" Robertson cuts each line in half and doubles its impact, like the "mathematical guitar genius" Dylan said he was.

But in the end the performance belongs to Bob. Burning his lines with a power he had only suggested on record, he pulls his way to the climax: "You better take your diamond ring down and/*PAWN IT/ BABE!!!*" Dylan crashes it down and then fades while Robbie solos for a verse, letting it out until the band is ready to end it. Printed below is the end of that; of the song, the concert, and the high point of Bob Dylan's career, the way he sang it that night in Liverpool:

How does it *feel?*
Ahhhhhhh, How does it *feel?*
To be on your *own?*
With No Direction HOME?
LIKE A COMPLETE UNKNOWN?
LIKE A ROLLING STONE!

—GREIL MARCUS
11-29-69

JOHN WESLEY HARDING
Bob Dylan
(Columbia CS 9604)

So, there is this semi-recognizable cat on the front of the album out there in the woods, looking like some friend of Baudelaire, way back in 1844 in "Le Vieux Quartier" of Paris —with a few friends from inside the walls. You might well ask, "What's it all about?"

The music is again a brilliant electronic adaptation of rural blues and country and western sounds. A swaying harp picks out the title track, "John Wesley Harding." A statement is made about the concept of everyday Good and Evil. Harding is Johnny Cash's outlaw figure, "he was never known to hurt an honest man" —folk-hero of a different kind, John Wesley Harding— "a friend to the poor." Call him Robin Hood if it means more to you. He was offering you "a helping" hand, and was this a man really to be hunted and punished?

With all the spiced crispness of the Elizabethan verse of some Samuel Daniel, Dylan expresses in this early morning incident, "As I Went Out One Morning," all the beauty of a different concept of Love: in his knowing, he can only refuse the hand of this "fairest damsel," as he must. This Sad-eyed Lady, reaching out for another answer, finds only a rejection. In her asking she condemns herself: "I will secretly accept you, and together we'll fly South." Dylan lets her go her own way, also so "sorry for what she's done."

In "Dreaming of St. Augustine," some parallels are found with the bent track of all our lives. St. Augustine, who also sought an answer in a life of deprivation, of spiritual and physical agony ("with a blanket underneath his arm" as he went "searching for the very souls that already have been sold"), found in the end a similar humility to that expressed by Dylan here. The two concepts of Saint and Devil blended here—"There is no martyr amongst you now"; compared to Mozart, so "Come out you gifted Kings and Queens" and do your thing. And "know you're not alone." The immense compassion Dylan feels is shown only too clearly: he tells us that "He put his finger to the glass and bowed his head and cried."

There is hope for those still on the other side. With a delicate rippling harp-ending, Dylan tells us with all his gentleness how easy it is to break once and for all the clouded glass.

The opening lines of "All Along the Watchtower" resemble a wandering entrance through Dark Portals ("There must be someway out of here"). Dylan speaks in an almost apocalyptic vein of the Fall to come. He has told us frequently in his poetry of his acceptance of Chaos: "businessmen may drink my wine, ploughmen dig my earth; none of them along the line know what any of it is worth."

Yet there is some hope in the minds of those who watch eagerly from the turrets: "There are many here amongst us who feel life is just a joke." There could be a New Day for the Princes and their Ladies—of realized, once thought impossible, differences, and a dancing tapestry of endless sounds and colors. For those who wait, "the hour is getting late."

Perhaps the most important track on the album is "Frankie Lee and Judas Priest." This too real, even surrealistic, dialogue between two opposed parties attains a steam-hammer urgency. (It recalls the "Lonesome Death of Hattie Carroll"

in its intensity.) The enormous gulf between the turned-on honesty of Judas Priest and his charity ("My loss will be your gain") as he pulled out a roll of tens, and the baffled, suspicious questioning of Frankie Lee is a stage-piece. Judas, the knowing, says the money will all disappear and "Pointed down the road and said 'Eternity'."

This vision of a Golden Age—though "you might call it Paradise"—is not so far off. Judas the Priest, the one who has really seen, does not put Frankie down, but rather as a friend is just willing to wait until he can also find the laughing way out of it all. The limits of conventional Paradise are well known to the young, as they are to the "neighborhood child who walked along with his guilt so well concealed." And as Dylan whoops his way through a jubilant exit, one cannot help thinking of what might be changed soon, if one does "not go mistaking Paradise for that home across the road."

"Drifter's Escape" is a weird Kafkaesque judgment. Dylan, as ever, catches the exact pulse of these days—just as with "The Times They Are A'Changing" and *Highway 61*. Here is the nation, as its own jury and judge, and the Trial has commenced. The Vietnam war, symbolized in the court and its process, has a personal and national level: "help me in my weakness" for "my time it isn't long." The choice is there. The consequences of no rational answer to the whole problem were made only too clear in Peter Watkins' *The War Game*. The choice is Black and White ("you fail to understand, why must you even try"). Good and Evil exist only on Man's terms. The tapping chords of a bass guitar ("outside the crowd was stirring") as an asking minstrel voice tells us of the lightning that could strike and who will be the victor then—the Drifter?

Side Two begins in the simple terms typical of the whole album. The elegant restraint of his plea for sanity ("my burden is heavy, my dreams are beyond control") amid the grasping hand of capitalistic machinery is overawing. Gone is the harsh attack of Dylan's previous compositions; "Dear Landlord" is a statement of what goes on around here sometimes. Dylan knows that they too "have suffered much although in that you are not unique" and questions the emptiness, bitterness and unhappiness of the *supposedly rich* and the vacuous non-reality of "things that you can feel, but just cannot touch." The song is a plea to those out there. Dylan "is not about to argue or move to some other place." With final resignation he says "If you don't underestimate me, I won't underestimate you."

"I Am A Lonesome Hobo" recalls (as does the picture of Bob, on the sleeve) a 15-year-old Arthur Rimbaud on the cobbled streets of Belgium, and his miniature masterpiece *My Bohemian Existence*. The serving of "time," that first questioning of established values of many career and personal desires, that unique nature of personal choice, brought us all down here with Dylan.

Brilliantly Dylan reverses the role of the Hobo and tells us what road one may end up on if one does not "stay free from petty jealousies, live by no man's code," hold your judgment for yourself and keep cool.

In "I Pity the Poor Immigrant," almost to the tune of "Irene Goodnight," Dylan suggests the immense sympathy he has for those who have dared to cut the rope and be free from the life of being one, "who lies with every breath, who passionately hates himself, and likewise fears his death." He realizes the trials of anybody who pushes through to this side of the Looking Glass. The immigrant, having seen through the enormous paradox of wealth and poverty on this earth, seeks another way. The song ends with open tenderness for those who have made the journey.

Just who the "Wicked Messenger" is, is unimportant, except to say that one knows his faces only too well. With "his mind that multiplied the smallest matter," and all the old hang-ups of flattery and dealing, Messenger is but total Self-deception. With epic descending interludes Dylan tells us to reject it all: the bid was made behind the Assembly Hall and it did not come to pass. Seek the truth as it is, not as it is laid upon you. Many now seek a way, but, "if you cannot bring good luck, then don't bring any."

"I'll Be Your Baby Tonight" is such a simple answer. The minor chords jangle the shattered staircases of all our fears: "You don't have to worry anymore," "You don't have to be afraid." Woman's age-old fear of unwanted and unloved children has no more relevance. The song ranks alongside "Ramona" and "It Takes a Lot to Laugh, It Takes a Train to Cry," as an epic, lyrical love song. So tonight "kick your shoes off, do not fear." As the hang-ups recede you will forget the moon when somebody lies in your arms tonight. Love really isn't anything to regret on equal terms.

Without a doubt this is another major musical step for Bob Dylan. The predominance of country blues—white and black—from Hank Williams to Leadbelly is unprecedented in the new electric music. The steel guitar conjures shades of the Black Ace on many a front porch down South. As to the usual message and meaning, anybody can feel the return to a cooler, more hip, almost shrugged-shoulder awareness of the whole scene revolving around here. The commitment is, as always, frighteningly sincere. And Bob would no doubt agree that J. S. Bach did try also, so really so hard, to tell us that the seagulls had wings to fly.

—GORDON MILLS
2-24-68

NASHVILLE SKYLINE
Bob Dylan
(Columbia KCS 9825)

Bob Dylan's ninth album poses fewer mysteries and yet, paradoxically, offers greater rewards than any of his previous work. Its only difficulties aren't metaphysical or interpretative— indeed, the beauty and openness within is kept almost rigorously simple in genre—but rather those of taking the artist's newfound happiness and maturity for exactly what they appear to be. That smiling face on the cover tells all—and isn't it wonderful?

Most obviously, *Nashville Skyline* continues Dylan's rediscovered romance with rural music (here complete with a more suitable, subtle "country" voice). The new LP represents a natural progression, both historically and emotionally, from the folk-music landscapes of

John Wesley Harding into the more modern country-and-western worlds of Hank Williams, Elvis Presley, Johnny Cash, Buddy Holly, the Everly Brothers, and Jerry Lee Lewis.

In *Harding,* Dylan superimposed a vision of intellectual complexity onto the warm, inherent mysticism of Southern Mountain music, rather like certain French directors (especially Jean-Luc Godard) who have taken American gangster movies and added to them layers of 20th-century philosophy. The effect is not unlike Jean-Paul Sartre playing the five-string banjo. The folk element gains a Kafka-esque chimericality, and the philosophy a bedrock simplicity that leaves it all but invisible and thus easy to assimilate. "Down Along the Cove" and "I'll Be Your Baby Tonight," exceptions to the above and the record's last two songs, are almost a microcosm of the geography to come.

Nashville Skyline is a jewel of construction with three distinct beginnings. The much-anticipated guitar-and-vocal duet with Johnny Cash, a stately and beautiful rendition of "Girl from the North Country," is a thoughtful bonus to the listener, a musical postcard to an old Minnesota love, and a reminder that Dylan has always been capable of tenderness. The song's most painful verse— "Many times I've often prayed/

In the darkness of my night"— has been deleted here.

The second beginning—or, if you prefer, an intermission in which each performer gets a chance to solo—"Nashville Skyline Rag," serves as an instrumental introduction to the album's excellent personnel: Kenny Buttrey, Charlie McCoy, Pete Drake, Norman Blake, Charlie Daniels, and Bob Wilson. It's country music at its joyful, shit-kicking best.

Dylan finally announces the LP's "real" beginning, "To Be Alone With You," when he asks producer Bob Johnston, "Is it rolling, Bob?" Unlike the Beatles, he may not want to take us home with him, but he makes it quite clear that what follows should be viewed as a personal confrontation: "Everything is always all right/When I'm alone with you."

"I Threw It All Away," the first of the record's three classic love songs, couples a haunting melody and magnificent singing to the hard-won realization that "Love is all we need/It makes the world go round." In contradiction to the earlier "It Ain't Me, Babe," Dylan, cast as someone who has formerly tried to do without deep affection, now wants very much to be "A lover for your life and nothing more." This is clearly going to be an album of staying, not leaving.

A good-natured exercise in country wordplay ("Love to

spend the night with Peggy Day . . . Love to spend the day with Peggy Night"), complete with a Presley rave-up finale, "Peggy Day" presents two delightful sides of one ideal woman; or maybe two delightful women, each with one ideal side. "By golly, what more can I say!"

Side two begins with another classic. "Lay Lady Lay" has the organ sound of *Highway 61* Dylan, and the lyrics are not as stringently genre-bound. "Whatever colors you have in mind/I'll show them to you and you'll see them shine" is more a metaphysical leap than a naturalistic hop, while "His clothes are dirty/But his hands are clean" seems a self-conscious attempt to needlessly bring it all back home.

"One More Night" and "Tell Me That It Isn't True" are My-baby-left-me songs, but, as is befitting the structures of country music, there is little or no bitterness, and Dylan even calls one of the girls his "best pal." The former, with its "Tonight, no light will shine on me" line, echoes the "dark side of the road" imagery of "Don't Think Twice," but its protagonist, unlike the hero of "It Ain't Me, Babe," can only mournfully state, "I just could not be/ What she wanted me to be." The latter bears a superficial resemblance to "Positively 4th Street" in that the singer has been put down strongly by

someone dear to him. Rather than rage, the reaction here is a gentle "Darling, I'm counting on you/Tell me that it isn't true."

In some ways, the final song of the LP should logically be "Country Pie," an unabashed tribute to country music ("Love that country pie!") and a clear statement of Dylan's present credo: "Ain't running any race/ Get me my country pie/I won't throw it up in anybody's face."

As with *Sgt. Pepper's Lonely Hearts Club Band, Nashville Skyline* saves the best until last. "Tonight I'll Be Staying Here With You" fuses personal commitment with professional preference, and functions as a sort of very content "A Day in the Life." Musically, it's brilliant, with a powerful Jerry Lee Lewis stride piano leading the way. Although the symbolism is hobo-traditional, the *mise-en-scene* of melody, lyrics, and performance overpowers and explodes any genre limitations in a glorious flow of every sort of imaginable triumph.

Perhaps, after all, it is more difficult to convey meaningfully a total fulfillment of marriage and family life than it is to create a nightmare world of complex hallucination, even though the latter seems more painfully our own. In many ways, *Nashville Skyline* achieves the artistically impossible: a deep, humane, and interesting statement about being happy.

It could well be what Dylan thinks it is, his best album.

—PAUL NELSON
5-31-69

SELF PORTRAIT
Bob Dylan
(Columbia C2Y 30050)

SELF PORTRAIT NO. 25
Written and Arranged
by Greil Marcus

Chorus: Charles Perry, Jenny Marcus, Jann Wenner, Erik Bernstein, Ed Ward, John Burks, Ralph Gleason, Langdon Winner, Bruce Miroff, Richard Vaughn and Mike Goodwin

(1)

What is this shit?

(1) "All the Tired Horses" is a gorgeous piece of music, perhaps the most memorable song on this album. In an older form it was "All the Pretty Ponies in the Yard"; now it could serve as the theme song to any classic western. Can you hear the organ standing in between the beautiful strings and voices? 'Shane' comes into view, and 'The Magnificent Seven': gunmen over the hill and out of time still got to ride. It sounds like Barbara Stanwyck in 'Forty Guns' singing, as a matter of fact.

The beauty of this painted signpost promises what its words

belie, and the song's question becomes the listener's: he can't ride when the horse is asleep in the meadow.

(2)

"I don't know if I should keep playing this," said the disc jockey, as the album made its debut on the radio. "Nobody's calling in and saying they want to hear it or anything . . . usually when something like this happens people say 'Hey, the new Dylan album,' but not tonight."

Later someone called and asked for a reprise of "Blue Moon." In the end it all came down to a telephone poll to determine whether radioland really cared. The DJ kept apologizing: "If there is anyone who needs . . . or deserves to have his whole album played through it's Bob Dylan."

(2) After a false beginning comes "Alberta #1," an old song now claimed by Dylan. One line stands out: "I'll give you more gold than your apron can hold." We're still at the frontier. The harmonica lets you into the album by its nostalgia, and it's the song's promise that matters, not the song itself, which fades.

(3)

"What was it?" said a friend, after we'd heard thirty minutes of *Self Portrait* for the first time. "Were we really that impressionable back in '65, '66? Was it that the stuff really wasn't that good, that this is just as good? Was it some sort of accident in time that made those other records so powerful, or what?

"My life was really turned around, it affected me—I don't know if it was the records or the words or the sound or the noise—maybe the interview: 'What is there to believe in?' I doubt if he'd say that now, though."

We put on "Like a Rolling Stone" from *Highway 61 Revisited* and sat through it. "I was listening to that song five, ten times a day for the last few months, hustling my ass, getting my act together to get into school . . . but it's such a drag to hear what he's done with it . . ."

*(3) Something like a mood collapses with the first Nashville offering, "I Forgot More Than You'll Ever Know," a slick exercise in vocal control that fills a bit of time. After getting closer and closer to the Country Music Capitol of the World—and still keeping his distance with 'Nashville Skyline,' one of the loveliest rock and roll albums ever made—the visitor returns to pay his compliments by recording some of their songs. How does it sound? It sounds alright. He's sung him-*self into a corner. It sounds alright. Sign up the band.*

(4)

GM: "It's such an unambitious album."

JW: "Maybe what we need most of all right now is an unambitious album from Dylan."

GM: "What we need most of all is for Dylan to get ambitious."

JW: "It's such a . . ."

GM: ". . . though it is a really . . ."

GM & JW: " . . . *friendly* album . . ."

(4) "Days of '49" is a fine old ballad. Dylan's beginning is utterly convincing, as he slips past the years of the song (listen to the vaguely bitter way he sings "But what cares I for praise?"). He fumbles as the song moves on, and the cut collapses, despite the deep burr of the horns and the drama generated by the piano. It's a tentative performance, a warm-up, hardly more than a work tape. The depths of history the song creates—out of the kind of pathos Johnny Cash gave "Hardin Wouldn't Run" (sounding like it was recorded in the shadows of an Arizona canyon) or "Sweet Betsy from Pike"—has been missed. The song is worth more effort than it was given.

(5)

"It's hard," he said. "It's hard for Dylan to do anything real, shut off the way he is, not interested in the world, maybe no reason why he should be. Maybe the weight of the days is too strong, maybe withdrawal is a choice we'd make if we could . . ." One's reminded that art doesn't come —perhaps that it can't be heard—in times of crisis and destruction; art comes in the period of decadence that precedes a revolution, or after the deluge. It's prelude to revolution; it's not contemporary with it save in terms of memory.

But in the midst of it all artists sometimes move in to recreate history. That takes ambition.

(5) When you consider how imaginative the backing on other Dylan records has been, the extremely routine quality of most of the music on 'Self Portrait' can become irritating. It is so uninteresting. "Early Mornin' Rain" is one of the most lifeless performances of the entire album; a rather mawkish song, a stiff well-formed-vowel vocal and a vapid instrumental track that has all the flair of canned laughter.

(6)

THE FOUR QUESTIONS: The four sons gazed at the painting on the museum wall. "It's a painting," said the first son. "It's art," said the second son. "It's a frame," said the third son, and he said it rather coyly. The fourth son was usually considered somewhat stupid, but he at least figured out why they'd come all the way from home to look at the thing in the first place. "It's a signature," he said.

(6) "In Search of Little Sadie" is an old number called "Badman's Blunder" (or sometimes "Badman's Ballad" and sometimes "Little Sadie") that Dylan now claims as his own composition. As with "Days of '49," the song is superb—it's these kinds of songs that seem like the vague source of the music the Band makes—and what Dylan is doing with the tune, leading it on a switchback trail, has all sorts of possibilities. But again, the vocal hasn't been given time to develop and the song loses whatever power it might have had to offer, until the final chorus, when Bob takes off and does some real singing.

This bit about getting it all down in one or two takes only works if you get it all down. Otherwise it's at best "charming" and at worst boring, alluding to a song without really making music.

(7)

Imagine a kid in his teens

responding to *Self Portrait*. His older brothers and sisters have been living by Dylan for years. They come home with the album and he simply cannot figure out what it's all about. To him, *Self Portrait* sounds more like the stuff his parents listen to than what he wants to hear; in fact, his parents have just gone out and bought *Self Portrait* and given it to him for his birthday. He considers giving it back for Father's Day.

To this kid Dylan is a figure of myth; nothing less, but nothing more. Dylan is not real and the album carries no reality. He's never seen Bob Dylan; he doesn't expect to; he can't figure out why he wants to.

(7) The Everly Brothers version of "Let It Be Me" is enough to make you cry, and Bob Dylan's version is just about enough to make you listen. For all of the emotion usually found in his singing, there is virtually none here. It is a very formal performance.

(8)

"Bob should go whole-hog and revive the Bing Crosby Look, with its emphasis on five-button, soft shoulder, wide-collar, plaid country-club lounge jackets (Pendleton probably still makes them). And, like Der Bingle, it might do well for Dylan to work a long-stemmed briar pipe into his act, stopping every so often to light up, puff at it, raise some smoke and gaze, momentarily, toward the horizon, before launching into [this is John Burks in *Rags*, June 1970] the next phrase of 'Peggy Day.' Then, for his finale—the big 'Blue Moon' production number with the girls and the spotlights on the fountains—he does a quick costume change into one of those high-collar 1920s formal shirts with the diamond-shaped bow tie, plus, of course, full length tails and the trousers with the satin stripe down the side, carnation in the buttonhole, like Dick Powell in *Golddiggers of 1933*. Here comes Dylan in his tails, his briar in one hand, his megaphone in the other, strolling down the runway, smiling that toothpaste smile. "Like a *roll*-ing stone . . ."

(8) "Little Sadie" is an alternate take of "In Search of . . ." I bet we're going to hear a lot of alternate takes in the coming year, especially from bands short on material who want to maintain their commercial presence without working too hard. Ordinarily, when there are no striking musical questions at stake in the clash of various attempts—alternate takes have been used as a graveyard rip-off to squeeze more bread out of the art of dead men or simply to fill up a side. "Little Sadie" fills up the side nicely.

(9)

"It's a high school yearbook. Color pictures this year, because there was a surplus left over from last year, more pages than usual too, a sentimental journey, 'what we did,' it's not all that interesting, it's a memento of something, there's a place for autographs, lots of white space, nobody's name was left out. . . . It is June, after all."

(9) "Woogie Boogie" is fun. The band sounds like it's falling all over itself (or maybe slipping on its overdubs) but they hold on to the beat. There is as much of Dylan's feel for music here as on anything else on 'Self Portrait.' If you were a producer combing through a bunch of 'Self Portrait' tapes for something to release, you might choose "Woogie Boogie" as a single—backing "All the Tired Horses," of course.

(10)

Self Portrait most closely resembles the Dylan album that preceeded it: *Great White Wonder*. The album is a two-record set masterfully assembled from an odd collection of mostly indifferent recordings made over the course of the last year, complete with alternate takes, chopped endings, loose beginnings, side comments, and all

sorts of mistakes. Straight from the can to you, as it were. A bit from Nashville, a taste of the Isle of Wight since you missed it, some sessions from New York that mostly don't make it, but dig, it's Dylan, and if you wanted *Great White Wonder* and *Stealin'* and *John Birch* and *Isle of Wight* and *A Thousand Miles Behind, Self Portrait* will surely fill the need.

I don't think it will. It's true that all of the bootlegs (and the *Masked Marauders,* which was a fantasy bootleg) came out in the absence of new music from Dylan, but I think their release was related not to the absence of his recordings but to the absence of the man himself. We are dealing with myth, after all, and the more Dylan stays away the greater the weight attached to anything he's done. When King Midas reached out his hand everything he touched not only turned to gold, it became valuable to everyone else, and Dylan still has the Midas touch even though he'd rather not reach out. It is only in the last two years that the collecting of old tapes by Dylan has really become a general phenomena, and there are many times more tapes in circulation than are represented on the bootlegs. There is a session with the Band from December of 1965, live albums, ancient recordings, tapes of Dylan at the Guthrie

Memorial, with the Band last summer in Missouri, radio shows from the early Sixties, the live "Like a Rolling Stone." It sometimes seems as if every public act Dylan ever made was recorded, and it is all coming together. Eventually, the bootleggers will get their hands on it. Legally, there is virtually nothing he can do to stop it.

He can head off the theft and sale of his first drafts, his secrets, and his memories only with his music. And it is the vitality of the music that is being bootlegged that is the basis of its appeal. The noise of it. *Self Portrait*, though it's a good imitation bootleg, isn't nearly the music that *Great White Wonder* is. "Copper Kettle" is a masterpiece but "Killing Me Alive" will blow it down. *Nashville Skyline* and *John Wesley Harding* are classic albums; but no matter how good they are they lack the power of the music Dylan made in the middle Sixties. Unless he returns to the marketplace, with a sense of vocation and the ambition to keep up with his own gifts, the music of those years will continue to dominate his records, whether he releases them or not. If the music Dylan makes doesn't have the power to enter into the lives of his audience—and *Self Portrait* does not have that power—his audience will take over his past.

(10) Did Dylan write "Belle Isle"? Maybe he did. This is the first time I've ever felt cynical listening to a new Dylan record.

(11)

In the record industry music is referred to as "product." "We got Beatle product." When the whirlwind courtship of Johnny Winter and Columbia was finally consummated everyone wanted to know when they would get product. They got product fast but it took them a while longer to get music. Such is show biz, viz. *Self Portrait*, which is already a triple gold record, the way "O Captain! My Captain!" is more famous than "When Lilacs Last in the Dooryard Bloom'd," is the closest thing to pure product in Dylan's career, even more so than *Greatest Hits*, because that had no pretensions. The purpose of *Self Portrait* is mainly product and the need it fills is for product—for "a Dylan album"—and make no mistake about it, the need for product is felt as deeply by those who buy it, myself included, of course, as by those who sell it, and perhaps more so.

As a throw-together album it resembles *Flowers;* but it's totally unlike *Flowers* in that the album promises to be more than it is, rather than less. By its title alone *Self Portrait* makes claims for itself as the definitive Dylan album—which it may be, in a sad way—but it is still something like an attempt to delude the public into thinking they are getting more than they are, or that *Self Portrait* is more than it is.

(11) "Living the Blues" is a marvelous recording. All sorts of flashes of all sorts of enthusiasms spin around it: The Dovells cheering for the Bristol Stomp, Dylan shadow-boxing with Cassius Clay, Elvis smiling and sneering in 'Jailhouse Rock' ("Baby you're so square, I don't care!"). The singing is great—listen to the way Bob fades off "deep down insyyy-hide," stepping back and slipping in that last syllable. For the first time on this album Dylan sounds excited about the music he's making. The rhythm section, led by the guitar and the piano that's rolling over the most delightful, rock and roll changes, is wonderful. The girls go through their routine and they sound— cute. Dylan shines. Give it 100.

(12)

". . . various times he thought of completing his baccalaureate so that he could teach in the college and oddly enough [this is from "A Rimbaud Chronology," New Directions Press] of learning to play the piano. At last he went to Holland, where, in order to reach the Orient, he enlisted in the Dutch Army and sailed for Java in June of 1876. Three weeks after his arrival in Batavia [Charles Perry: "We know Dylan was the Rimbaud of his generation; it seems he's found his Abyssinia"] he deserted, wandered among the natives of the jungle and soon signed on a British ship for Liverpool. After a winter at home he went to Hamburg, joined in a circus as interpreter-manager to tour the northern countries, but the cold was too much for him and he was repatriated from Sweden, only to leave home again, this time for Alexandria. Again, illness interrupted his travels and he was put off the ship in Italy and spent a year recovering on the farm at Roche. In 1878 he was in Hamburg again, trying to reach Genoa to take a ship for the East. Once more he tried to cross the Alps on foot [Charles Perry: "We know that Dylan was the Rimbaud of his generation; it seems he's found his Abyssinia"] but in a snowstorm he almost perished. Saved by monks in a Hospice, he managed to reach Genoa and sail to Alexandria where he worked as a farm laborer for a while. In Suez, where he was stopped on his way to Cyprus, he was employed as a ship-breaker to plunder a ship wrecked on the dangerous coast at Guardafui. Most of the first half of 1879 he worked as foreman in a desert quarry on Cyprus, and went home in June to recuperate from typhoid fever."

(12) "Like A Rolling Stone" —Dylan's greatest song. He knows it, and so do we. Not only that, but the greatest song of our era, on that single, on 'Highway 61 Revisited; on the tape of a British performance with the Hawks in 1966. If one version is better than the other it's like Robin Hood splitting his father's arrow.

1965: "Alright. We've done it. Dig it. If you can. If you can take it. Like a complete unknown, can you feel that?"

We could, and Bob Dylan took over. All that's come since goes back to the bid for power that was "Like a Rolling Stone."

"Can you keep up with this train?" The train no longer runs; I suppose it depends on where your feet are planted.

Dylan from the Isle of Wight is in your living room and Dylan is blowing his lines, singing country flat, up and down, getting through the song somehow, almost losing the whole mess at the end of the second verse. You don't know whether he dropped the third verse because he didn't want to sing it or because he forgot it. It's enough to make your speakers wilt.

'Self Portrait' enforces or suggests a quiet sound. "Like a Rolling Stone" isn't "Blue Moon" but since most of 'Self Portrait' is more like "Blue Moon" than "Like a Rolling Stone," and since it is a playable album that blends together, you set the volume low. But if you play this song loud—really loud, until it distorts and rumbles, you'll find the Band is still playing as hard as they can, for real. The strength was cut in half by the man who recorded it, but volume will bring it back up.

Some of "Like a Rolling Stone" is still there. A splendid beginning, announcing a conquest; Levon Helm beating his drums over the Band's Motown March (ba-bump barrummmp, ba-bump barrrummmp), smashing his cymbals like the glass-breaking finale of a car crash; and best of all, Garth Hudson finding the spirit of the song and holding it firm on every chorus. Near the end when the pallid vocalizing is done with Dylan moves back to the song and he and the Band begin to stir up a frenzy that ends with a crash of metal and Bob's shout: JUST LIKE A ROLLING STONE!" There is something left.

1965: "BAM! Once upon a time . . ." The song assaults you with a deluge of experience and the song opens up the abyss. "And just how far would you like to go in?" "Not too far but just far enough so's we can say we've been there." That wasn't good enough. "When you gaze into the abyss, the abyss looks back at you." It peered out through "Wheel's On Fire" and "All Along the Watchtower," but it seems Dylan has stepped back from its edge.

The abyss is hidden away now, like the lost mine of a dead prospector. "Like a Rolling Stone," as we hear it now, is like a fragment of a faded map leading back to that lost mine.

(13)

I once said I'd buy an album of Dylan breathing heavily. I still would. But not an album of Dylan breathing softly.

(13) Why does "Copper Kettle" shine (it even sounds like a hit record) when so many other cuts hide in their own dullness? Why does this performance evoke all kinds of experience when most of 'Self Portrait' is so one-dimensional and restrictive? Why does "Copper Kettle" grow on you while the other songs disappear?

Like "All the Tired Horses," it's gorgeous. There are those tiny high notes punctuating the song in the mood of an old Buddy Holly ballad or "The Three Bells" by the Browns, and that slipstream organ, so faint you can barely hear it— you don't hear it, really, but you are aware of it in the subtlest way. There is the power and the real depth of the song itself, that erases our Tennessee truck-stop postcard image of moonshining and moves in with a vision of nature, an ideal of repose, and a sense of rebellion that goes back to the founding of the country. "We ain't paid no whiskey tax since 1792," Bob sings, and that goes all the way back—they passed the whiskey tax in 1791. It's a song about revolt as a vocation, not revolution, merely refusal. Old men hiding out in mountain valleys, keeping their own peace.

[The old moonshiners are sitting around a stove in 'Thunder Road,' trying to come up with an answer to the mobsters that are muscling in on the valley they've held since the Revolution. "Blad sprat muglmmph ruurrrp fffft," says one. The audience stirs, realizing they can't understand his Appalachian dialect. "If you'd take that tobacco plug out of your mouth, Jed," says another whiskey man, "maybe we could understand what you said."]

What matters most is Bob's singing. He's been the most amazing singer of the last ten years, creating his language of stress, fitting five words into a line of ten and ten into a line of five, shoving the words around and opening up spaces for noise and silence that through assault or seduction of the gift of good timing made room for expression and emotion. Every vocal was a surprise. You couldn't predict what it would sound like. The song itself, the structure of the song, was barely a clue. The limits were there to be evaded. On "Copper Kettle" that all happens, and it is noticeable because this is the only time on 'Self Portrait' that it happens.

"Not all great poets—like Wallace Stevens—are great singers," Dylan said two years ago. "But a great singer—like Billie Holiday—is always a great poet." That sort of poetry—and it's that sort of poetry that made Dylan seem like a "poet" —is all there on "Copper Kettle," in the way Bob changes into the lines ". . . or ROTTEN wood . . ." fading into "(they'll get you) by the smo-oke . . ." The fact that the rest of the album lacks the grace of "Copper Kettle" isn't a matter of the album being "different" or "new." It is a matter of the music having power, or not having it.

(14, 15, 16)

". . . very highly successful in terms of money. Dylan's concerts in the past have been booked by his own firm, Ashes and Sand, rather than by [this is from *Rolling Stone*, December 7th, 1968] private promoters. Promoters are now talking about a ten city tour with the possibility of adding more dates, according to *Variety*.

"Greta Garbo may also come out of retirement to do a series of personal appearances. The Swedish film star who wanted only 'to be alone' after continued press invasions of her life is rumoured to be considering a series of lavish stage shows, possibly with Dylan . . ."

And we'd just sit there and stare.

(14) "Gotta Travel On." Dylan sings "Gotta Travel On."

(15) We take "Blue Moon" as a joke, a stylized apotheosis of corn, or as further musical evidence of Dylan's retreat from the pop scene. But back on Elvis' first album, there is another version of "Blue Moon," a deep and moving performance that opens up the possibilities of the song and reveals the failure of Dylan's recording.

Hoofbeats, vaguely aided by a string bass and guitar, form the background to a vocal that blows a cemetery wind across the lines of the song. Elvis moves back and forth with a high phantom wail, singing that part that Doug Kershaw plays on Dylan's version, finally answering himself with a dark murmur that fades into silence. "It's a revelation," said a friend. "I can't believe it."

There is nothing banal about "Blue Moon." In formal musical terms, Dylan's performance is virtually a cover of Elvis' recording, but while one man sings toward the song, the other sings from behind it, from the other side.

(16) "The Boxer": remember "How I Was Robert Mac-Namared Into Submission," or whatever it was called, with that friendly line, "I forgot my harmonica, Albert?" Or Eric Anderson's "The Hustler"? Maybe this number means "no hard feelings." Jesus, is it awful.

(17)

Before going into the studio to set up the Weathermen, he wrote the Yippies' first position paper, although it took Abbie Hoffman a few years to find it and Jerry Rubin had trouble reading it. A quote:

"I'm gonna grow my hair down to my feet so strange till I look like a walking mountain range then I'm gonna ride into Omaha on a horse out to the country club and the golf course carrying a New York Times shoot a few holes blow their minds."

"Dylan's coming," said Lang.

"Ah you're full of shit," [said Abbie Hoffman in *Woodstock Nation*], "he's gonna be in England tonight, don't pull that shit on me."

"Nah I ain't kiddin, Abby-baby, he called up and said he might come . . ."

"You think he'd dig running for president?"

"Nah, that ain't his trip he's into something else."

"You met him, Mike? What's he into?"

"I don't know for sure but it ain't exactly politics. You ever met him?"

"Yeah, once about seven years ago in Gertie's Folk City down in the West Village. I was trying to get him to do a benefit for civil rights or something . . . hey Mike will you introduce us? I sure would like to meet Dylan . . . I only know about meetin' him through Happy Traum . . ."

"There's an easier way . . . Abbs . . . I'll introduce you. In fact he wants to meet you . . ."

Would *Self Portrait* make you want to meet Dylan? No? Perhaps it's there to keep you away?

(17) "The Mighty Quinn" sounds as if it was a gas to watch. It's pretty much of a mess on record, and the sound isn't all that much better than the bootleg. The Isle of Wight concert was originally planned as an album, and it's obvious why it wasn't released as such— on tape, it sounded bad. The performances were mostly clumsy or languid and all together would have made a lousy record. Two of the songs had something special about them, on the evidence of the bootleg, though neither of them made it to 'Self Portrait.' One was "Highway 61 Revisited," where Bob and the Band screamed like Mexican tour guides hustling customers for a run down the road: "OUT ON HIGH-

WAY SIXTY-ONE!" The other was "It Ain't Me Babe." Dylan sang solo, playing guitar like a lyric poet, transforming the song with a new identity, sweeping in and out of the phrases and the traces of memory. He sounded something like Billie Holiday.

(18)

It's certainly a rather odd "self-portrait": other people's songs and the songs of a few years ago. If the title is serious, Dylan no longer cares much about making music and would just as soon define himself on someone else's terms. There is a curious move toward self-effacement; Dylan removing himself from a position from which he is asked to exercise power in the arena. It's rather like the Duke of Windsor abdicating the throne. After it's over he merely goes away, and occasionally there'll be a picture of him getting on a plane somewhere.

(18) "Take Me As I Am Or Let Me Go." The Nashville recordings of 'Self Portrait,' taken together, may not be all that staggering but they are pleasant —a sentimental little country melodrama. If the album had been cut to "Tired Horses" at the start and "Wigwam" at the end, with the Nashville tracks sleeping in between, we'd have a good record about which no

one would have gotten very excited one way or the other, a kind of musical disappearing act. But the Artist must make a Statement, be he Bob Dylan, the Beach Boys, or Tommy James and the Shondells. He must enter the studio and come out with that masterpiece. If he doesn't, or hasn't bothered, there'll be at least an attempt to make it look as if he had. If Dylan was releasing more music than he's been—a single three times a year, an album every six months or so—then the weight that fixes itself on whatever he does release would be lessened. But the pattern is set now, for the biggest stars—one a year, if that. It's rather degrading for an artist to put out more than one album a year, as if he has to keep trying, you know? Well, three cheers for John Fogerty.

(19)

Because of what happened in the middle Sixties, our fate is bound up with Dylan's whether he or we like it or not. Because *Highway 61 Revisited* changed the world, the albums that follow it must—but not in the same way, of course.

(19) "Take a Message To Mary": the backing band didn't seem to care much about the song, but Dylan did. My ten-year-old nephew thought "It Hurts Me Too" sounded fake

but he was sure this was for real.

(20)

Ralph Gleason: "There was this cat Max Kaminsky talks about in his autobiography who stole records. He stole one from Max. He *had* to have them, you know? Just had to have them. Once he got busted because he heard this record on a juke box and shoved his first through the glass of the box trying to get the record out.

"We all have records we'd steal for, that we need that bad. But would you steal this record? You wouldn't steal this record."

You wouldn't steal *Self Portrait*? It wouldn't steal you either. Perhaps that's the real tragedy, because Dylan's last two albums were art breaking and entering into the house of the mind.

(20) Songwriting can hardly be much older than song-stealing. It's part of the tradition. It may even be more honorable than outright imitation; at least it's not as dull.

Early in his career, Bob Dylan, like every other musician on the street with a chance to get off it, copped one or two old blues or folk songs, changed a word or two, and copyrighted them (weirdest of all was claiming "That's Alright Mama,"

which was Elvis' first record and written—or at least written down—by Arthur Crudup). As he developed his own genius, Dylan also used older ballads for the skeletons of his own songs: "Bob Dylan's Dream" is a recasting of "Lord Franklin's Dream"; "I Dreamed I Saw St. Augustine" finds its way back to "I Dreamed I Saw Joe Hill." "Pledging My Time" has the structure, the spirit, and a line from Robert Johnson's "Come On In My Kitchen"; "Subterranean Homesick Blues" comes off of Chuck Berry's "Too Much Monkey Business." This is a lovely way to write, and to invent, history, and it is part of the beauty and the inevitability of American music. But while Dylan may have added a few words to "It Hurts Me Too," from where he sits, it's simply wrong to claim this old blues, recorded by Elmore James among others, as his own. That 'Self Portrait' is characterized by borrowing, lifting, and plagiarism simply means Bob will get a little more bread and thousands of kids will get a phony view of their own history.

(21, 22)

That splendid frenzy, the strength of new values in the midst of some sort of musical behemoth of destruction, the noise, the power—the *totality* of it! So you said well, alright, there it is . . .

The mythical immediacy of everything Dylan does and the relevance of that force to the way we live our lives is rooted in the three albums and the two incredible singles he released in 1965 and 1966: *Bringing It All Back Home, Highway 61 Revisited, Blonde on Blonde,* "Like a Rolling Stone" and "Subterranean Homesick Blues." Those records defined and structured a crucial year—no one has ever caught up with them and most likely no one ever will. What happened then is what we always look for. The power of those recordings and of the music Dylan was making on stage, together with his retreat at the height of his career, made Dylan into a legend and virtually changed his name into a noun. Out of that Dylan gained the freedom to step back and get away with anything he chose to do, commercially and artistically. The fact that more than a year now separates one album from another heightens their impact, regardless of how much less they have to offer than the albums which established this matrix of power in the first place. In a real way, Dylan is trading on the treasure of myth, fame, and awe he gathered in '65 and '66. In mythical terms, he doesn't have to do good, because he has done good. One wonders, in mythical terms of course, how long he can get away with it.

(21) *"Minstrel Boy" is the best of the Isle of Wight cuts; it rides easy.*

(22) *The Band plays pretty on "She Belongs To Me" and Dylan runs through the vocal the way he used to hurry through the first half of a concert, getting the crowd-pleasers out of the way so he could play the music that mattered. Garth Hudson has the best moment of the song.*

(23)

VOCATION AS A VOCATION: Dylan is, if he wants to be, an American with a vocation. It might almost be a calling—the old Puritan idea of a gift one should live up to—but it's not, and vocation is strong enough.

There is no theme richer for the American artist than the spirit and the themes of the country and the country's history. We have never figured out what this place is about or what it is for, and the only way to even begin to answer those questions is to watch our movies, read our poets, our novelists, and listen to our music. Robert Johnson and Melville, Hank Williams and Hawthorne, Bob Dylan and Mark Twain, Jimmie Rodgers and John Wayne. America is the life's work of the American artist because he is doomed to be an American. Dylan has a feel for it; his impulses seem to take him back into the forgotten parts of our history, and even on *Self Portrait*, there is a sense of this vocation; Bob is almost on the verge of writing a western. But it's an ambitious vocation and there is not enough of that, only an impulse without the determination to follow it up.

Dylan has a vocation if he wants it; his audience may refuse to accept *his* refusal unless he simply goes away. In the midst of that vocation there might be something like a Hamlet asking questions, old questions, with a bit of magic to them; but hardly a prophet, merely a man with good vision.

(23) "Wigwam" slowly leads the album to its end. Campfire music, or "3 AM, After the Bullfight." It's a great job of arranging, and the B-side of the album's second natural single, backing "Living the Blues." "Wigwam" puts you to bed, and by that I don't mean it puts you to sleep.

(24)

SELF PORTRAIT, THE AUTEUR, AND HOME MOVIES: "*Auteur*" means, literally, "author," and in America the word has come to signify a formula about films: movies (like books) are made by "authors," i.e., directors. This has led to a dictum which tends to affirm the following: movies are about the personality of the director. We should judge a movie in terms of how well the "*auteur*" has "developed his personality" in relation to previous films. His best film is that which most fully presents the flowering of his personality. Needless to say such an approach requires a devotion to mannerism, quirk, and self-indulgence. It also turns out that the greatest *auteurs* are those with the most consistent, obvious, and recognizable mannerisms, quirks, and self-indulgences. By this approach *Stolen Kisses* is a better film than *Jules and Jim* because in *Stolen Kisses* we had nothing to look for but Truffaut while in *Jules and Jim* there was this story and those actors who kept getting in the way. The spirit of the *auteur* approach can be transferred to other arts; and by its dictum, *Self Portrait* is a better album than *Highway 61 Revisited*, because *Self Portrait* is *about* the *auteur*, that is Dylan, and *Highway 61 Revisited* takes on the world, which tends to get in the way. (*Highway 61 Revisited* might well be about Dylan too, but it's more *obvious* on *Self Portrait*, and therefore more relevant to Art, and . . . please don't ask about the music, really . . .)

Now Dylan has been approached this way for years, whether or not the word was used, and while in the end it may be the least interesting way to listen to his music it's occasionally a lot of fun and a game that many of us have played (for example, on "Days of '49" Dylan sings the line "just like a roving sign" and I just can't help almost hearing him say "just like a rolling stone" and wondering if he avoided that on purpose). One writer, named Alan Weberman, has devoted his life to unraveling Dylan's songs in order to examine the man himself; just as every artist once had his patron now every *auteur* has his critic, it seems.

[CONTINUED]

(24) 'Self Portrait' is a concept album from the cutting room floor. It has been constructed so artfully, but as a coverup, not a revelation. Thus "Alberta #2" is the end, after a false ending, just as "Alberta #1" was the beginning, after a false beginning. The song moves quickly, and ends abruptly. These alternate takes don't just fill up a side, they set up the whole album, and it works, in a way, because I think it's mainly the four songs fitted in at the edges that make the album a playable record. With a circle you tend to see the line that defines it, rather than the hole in the middle.

SELF PORTRAIT, THE AUTEUR, AND HOME MOVIES, CONT.: We all play the *auteur* game: We went out and bought *Self Portrait* not because we knew it was great music—it might have been but that's not the first question we'd ask—but because it was a Dylan album. What we *want*, though, is a different matter—and that's what separates most people from auteurists—we *want* great music, and because of those three albums back in '65 and '66, we expect it, or hope for it.

I wouldn't be dwelling on this but for my suspicion that it is exactly a perception of this approach that is the justification for the release of *Self Portrait*, to the degree that it is justified artistically (the commercial justification is something else—self-justification). The *auteur* approach allows the great artist to limit his ambition, perhaps even to abandon it, and turn inward. To be crude, it begins to seem as if it is his habits that matter, rather than his vision. If *we* approach art in this fashion, we degrade it. Take that second song on *John Wesley Harding*, "As I Went Out One Morning," and two ways of hearing it.

Weberman has determined a fixed meaning for the song: It relates to a dinner given years ago by the Emergency Civil Liberties Committee at which they awarded Bob Dylan their Thomas Paine prize. Dylan showed up, said a few words about how it was possible to understand how Lee Harvey Oswald felt, and got booed. "As

I Went Out One Morning," according to Weberman, is Dylan's way of saying he didn't dig getting booed.

I sometimes hear the song as a brief journey into American history; the singer out for a walk in the park, finding himself next to a statue of Tom Paine, and stumbling across an allegory: Tom Paine, symbol of freedom and revolt, co-opted into the role of Patriot by textbooks and statue committees, and now playing, as befits his role as Patriot, enforcer to a girl who runs for freedom—in chains, to the *South*, the source of vitality in America, in America's music—*away* from Tom Paine. We have turned our history on its head; we have perverted our own myths.

Now it would be astonishing if what I've just described was on Dylan's mind when he wrote the song. That's not the point. The point is that Dylan's songs can serve as metaphors, enriching our lives, giving us random insight into the myths we carry and the present we live, intensifying what we've known and leading us toward what we never looked for, while at the same time enforcing an emotional strength upon those perceptions by the power of the music that mowes with his words. Weberman's way of hearing, or rather seeing, is more logical, more linear, and perhaps even "correct," but it's sterile. Mine is not an answer but a possibility, and I think Dylan's music, is about possibilities, rather than facts, like a statue that is not an expenditure of city funds but a gateway to a vision.

If we are to be satisfied with *Self Portrait* we may have to see it in the sterile terms of the *auteur*, which in our language would be translated as "Hey, far out, Dylan singing Simon and Garfunkel, Rodgers and Hart, and Gordon Lightfoot . . ." Well, it is far out, in a sad sort of way, but it is also vapid, and if our own untaught perception of the *auteur* allows us to be satisfied with it, we degrade our own sensibilities and Dylan's capabilities as an American artist as well. Dylan did not become a figure whose every movement carries the force of myth by presenting desultory images of his own career as if that was the only story that mattered—he did it by taking on the world, by assault, and by seduction.

In an attack on the *auteur* approach, as it relates to film, Kevin Brownlow quotes an old dictionary, and the words he cities reveal the problem: "The novel [the film] [the song] is a subjective epic composition in which the author begs leave to treat the world according to his own point of view. It is only a question, therefore, whether he has a point of view. The rest will take care of itself."

A Second Look at SELF PORTRAIT

Several years ago John Cohen in a *Sing Out!* interview asked Dylan if he thought he'd ever get a job playing for Muzak, "airplane style" music. It was all a joke, but Bob curiously answered, "Well I'd give it a try if they ask."

But what if he did try playing Muzak? This would be hard to accept, even from Dylan. Few could listen seriously. Mass media might turn away, and there would be little excitement from radioland over the new Dylan LP. He'd be called "commercial," taking the easy way out. Could Bob Dylan ever get booed on a Forest Hills stage again?

There certainly is an "easy listening" sound to much of *Self Portrait*. The voice is mostly soft and smooth, the harmonica has mellowed; there are strings, repeat and climactic endings, girl choruses, yes, even "Dylanettes." Some pop hits from the Fifties are reworked, and the old Dylan masterpieces are done in quicker, lighter tempos.

But Dylan still hasn't joined the ranks of Muzak, just as he never really was a folk or a rock musician. Even in his "Hollis Brown" heyday, there were always muffled complaints from the faithful that Dylan's folk music was not "genuine"

enough. Sometime in 1966 Susan Sontag said, "The great thing about Bob Dylan is that now kids can frug and think about the war at the same time." I did not think then that we were doing *either* with Dylan. He never wrote real dance music, the true rock and roll.

Dylan is a pretty strong fellow. Rather than work in the service of a style of music, he will twist the medium for his own purposes. Dylan assimilates, he rarely accommodates. Just as once he used folk, rock, and then country, now he has also adapted a kind of easy listening sound. The music escapes these categories as easily as water leaking through cupped hands.

The critics have creamed Dylan on this one, and it's important to know why. Though he has taken plenty of chances in the past, never before has he left himself so vulnerable. For one thing, *Self Portrait* is the most daring title Dylan has ever chosen, and he has used it for an album with little of his own writing. But the heart of the matter is this new sound. It simply does not have the glorious tradition of folk-country-rock, particularly for those of us who never were Tin Pan Alley fans. Easy listening means for us the landscape of supermarkets, and we would rather recall that trip down Highway 61.

What counts, though, is that

Self Portrait is alive musically. It is beautiful to listen to, an evolution in attitude and sound that works as well as anything Dylan has ever done.

Look at the way Dylan handles the classics, "Like a Rolling Stone" and "She Belongs to Me." The choice of these two for *Self Portrait* was an inspiration. They have always been, and now more than ever, as opposite sides of the same coin. Both written, at one level, to a woman, the first is a bitter put-down, the latter an act of worship. But the point of view remains identical: you get the sense that the contempt for Miss Lonely and her pretty people comes from the same source of values as does the reverence for she the artist.

We do not forget the days when Dylan once wailed, *"Aw, you've gone to the finest schools, all right . . .,"* or gently sang, "She never stumbles . . ." That's forever. But from the Isle of Wight we have something more. Dylan now flips the words out over his shoulder, a waterfall of familiar syllables without stress or pause. You couldn't keep up with them, except that you already *know* what they say. That spectacular history of pain, of anger, of love—we've been there before with these songs; we're still there. But the new presentations have enlarged the spectrum.

It is not that Dylan is now above caring, just that he doesn't seem to take it all so personally. There is a sense of acceptance and a sense of humor: a new forgiveness in his "Rolling Stone" that is paralleled by a trace of laughter in the latest "She Belongs to Me." The original power is not lost or faded, but Dylan's new distance has expanded the meanings. There is a broader feeling here, or more simply a broader smile—perhaps a shrug of the shoulders and a wink to boot. How fantastic that now we can be reminded *three times* to give her a trumpet, buy her a drum. He is that much more in control.

This is why I love the way Dylan picks up the second takes of "Alberta" and "Little Sadie." There is no one way to sing or feel about a story, and the second time around Dylan unbinds us from the moods of the first. When "In Search of Little Sadie" turns into "Little Sadie," Dylan surely has found the song. The first version is a fine, emotional rendition, with cymbals, melodramatic guitar rolls, and Dylan's high-tension voice sliding around restlessly in between keys. He really *shouts* "Oh no!" at the end, and I know this is how *I* would feel if hit with a 41-year jail sentence.

Then comes "Little Sadie" herself. The guitars and banjo take over, and we are suddenly into a square dance tune rather than the anguish of a captured killer. Neither the events nor the word meanings have changed. All that remains from the first version is the joy of making music, purer now that the song's mood has become more casual.

Same with Alberta, only the changes are more subtle. After an introductory "All the Tired Horses," the actual *Self Portrait* begins with the melancholy "Alberta #2" at the end of the album, Dylan sounds less sad, more on top of it. He adds a piano to lighten things up, picks up some speed and then shakes out the melody a little to suit his new mood ("worri*ed* and both*ered* all *of* the time"). This one makes you want to laugh instead of cry, though the words don't change.

Dylan plays with his songs like a little kid trying out new toys. The child creates as many possibilities as he can think of: he will make a pencil into a hammer, or into a hat. The more resourceful the child, the more uses he can find. Whether or not the toy is "supposed to" serve a special function does not matter much to the child.

The new sound even transforms Dylan's latest statement of independence. When he croons, "Take Me As I Am or Let Me Go," the feeling is quite different from that of a "Maggie's Farm." The silky tone of "Take Me . . ." puts people off in 1970, just as the

electric band in "Maggie" was disturbing in 1965. And the warnings are similar: There's no use in making him "the image of someone you used to know," even if that someone happens to be the old Dylan. But "Take Me As I Am or Let Me Go" is still, and first, a love song. The feel is gentle, and friendly. It comes across a lot easier than does "Maggie's Farm."

It's been said over and over that Dylan destroyed folk music by his explosion into rock. Damage certainly was done. We simply were not as interested in hootenannies once "Subterranean Homesick Blues" had conquered the airways.

Self Portrait has a way of opening up the past rather than rendering it obsolete. It might be the most inclusive work of music ever assembled; all kinds of old songs shine again in its light. Bessie Smith blues, Simon and Garfunkel, the earliest Dylan records, even Elvis sounds better after *Self Portrait*. Dylan has done more than dig for his roots, he has kept them alive.

In the East, painters often did not sign their paintings. The idea was that art should be a group expression of universals from the lives of all men. Indian art saw mankind as a whole, and so was less concerned than is Western art with the emotions of individuals. It was faceless, but expansive.

Now this is only part of the

story; but what is revolutionary about *Self Portrait* is Dylan's movement in this direction. He is after universals now, the basic bonds between men. He selects from the music of other writers—songs of the sorrow, the violence, the warmth and the laughter. Lines of communication are opened: the human scope of the stories is broad enough to include Tom Moore's saucy crew and the maiden of Belle Isle, the hip Quinn as well as that lonely minstrel boy. And while performing these songs Dylan attains such astonishing unity with the music that in the end it makes little difference who wrote them.

There is that hollow "rotten" of "Copper Kettle," in which Dylan becomes the wood, or the kettle, whichever you like. There is the final take-off in "Early Morning Rain," the climactic "way-ay-*ay*" of the last stanza. Dylan prepares us for this three-note variation by the rising "ho-*ome*" of the previous verse, and then lands us smoothly after it with a gently falling "early *morning* rain." You are right there on the runway.

In "The Boxer" the harmonies linger apart for so long, then come together at last for the sharp ". . . every blow that's laid him low and *cut* him . . ." Dylan approaches this song with a high-intensity understatement, so that each small change reflects a new

mood. My favorite moment follows the man's confession that he has been with the whores on Seventh Avenue. Dylan drifts into a solemn "*ooh* lie lie" that becomes both a self-reproach and a consolation. Dylan sings "The Boxer" with his own harmony part done in his "old" voice. Substitute the word "singer" for "boxer" and it's really a song about himself.

Listen to the story line of "Belle Isle," a model of nonlinear narrative. Not since "Boots of Spanish Leather" has a ballad so captured the delicate interplay of dialogue between lovers. Or hear Dylan bring "Take a Message to Mary" back to the Code of the West. The frontier lad is a defeated outlaw, and it is only his predicament that we recall from the Everly Brothers. But Dylan turns it around so that we focus on the young man's strength and honor. You can feel his pride in his principles as he announces, "You can *say* she'd better not *wait* for me, but don't tell her I'm in jail."

Dylan has worked magic with hidden blues before— "Tom Thumb," for example— but never anything like "It Hurts Me Too." This is a conventional number, but if you float with the melody and with the exquisite pauses the old pattern disappears. It is a love song beyond form or structure. And again, those powerful small changes: Dylan begins with ". . . baby, put your little hands in mine" and ends by saying, "put your little *hand* in mine." Try acting it out.

The musical unity is everywhere. Slips and recoveries become exciting within the process of music-making. In "Days of '49," Dylan stumbles halfway through Poker Bill's verse and is in genuine trouble until he pulls it all back together with his mock "Oh, my goodness!" Is it part of the song or part of the moment? No matter, they're both the same now. The band snaps back for an ending so solid it takes your breath away.

With all of its unity and inclusiveness, *Self Portrait* is too complete to have a point of view. It is Eastern in its egolessness; and I imagine that this is true of Dylan himself when he comes to terms with his art. How else could he make such music? For this reason I could not accept the idea that Dylan is an *auteur* when I first read it (*Rolling Stone*, July 23).

But he is an *auteur*, among all the other things. He has brought to *Self Portrait* his myth, his images and his past. These add force and interest to his work, we can't deny it. And further, Dylan does remind us on this album, more than he has done before, of all the ways we have known him. We even hear whispers of the old voice from time to time, pronouncing the familiar language.

But Dylan's image serves only his music. It is an elusive, chameleon-type image anyway. It changes for the song, intruding when it can provide needed charisma, disappearing again into the music. Which Dylan is it? Only the song will tell. For he can be cynical, silly, mystical, can even play the fool if that's what's called for. He is not a Truffaut or a Hemingway, whose later works have a purpose in establishing their *auteur*'s personal myth. When Dylan uses his myth it is to give freedom and power to his work. The paradox of *Self Portrait* is that while Dylan seems more here than ever, he dominates the music far less.

After all, isn't it true that we learn nothing about Dylan the man from *Self Portrait,* and as much as we want to know about his twenty-four songs?

Since *Blonde on Blonde,* Dylan and the world have suffered the mutual misfortunes of growing in opposite directions. Dylan's final expression of outrage came with the visions and nightmares of that album. Perhaps his turning point was the apocalyptic period that produced the basement tape—I don't know, I wasn't there. But by *John Wesley Harding* the frustration that had electrified Dylan's earlier work was breaking down.

Now he was singing "Dear

Landlord" and saying that he was "not about to argue, not about to move to no other place." This was no longer the Dylan of "Baby Blue." The worldly mysticism of *John Wesley Harding* had bred a music of acceptance rather than of alienation. Dylan moved cautiously over the new ground. He presented a possibility, not quite yet an affirmation: if there was human conflict, it could be met with understanding rather than rejection. In *Nashville Skyline*, down to the basics, Dylan would become bolder: "Love is all there is, it makes the world go round . . ."

Self Portrait is another musical explosion for Dylan, a breaking out from the constraints of his past work. He has extended his reach in all directions from the archetypal patterns of the *Nashville Skyline* songs. Dylan has adapted a new sound, and with it has explored relationships and emotions that are no longer elemental, but which approach the complexity of life. Communication can mean laughter, forgiveness, or the lover's sympathy of "It Hurts Me Too." And the *humor*, one of art's truest tests, is everywhere, beginning with Dylan's joke on himself in "All The Tired Horses" (the way they sing it almost sounds like "How'm I supposed to get any writin' done?"). *Self Portrait* brings this all together; but the world,

from where I stand, isn't listening easily.

—BILL DAMON
9-3-70

NEW MORNING
Bob Dylan
(Columbia KC 30290)

Well, friends, Bob Dylan is back with us again. I don't know how long he intends to stay, but I didn't ask him. Didn't figure it was any of my business.

Put simply, *New Morning* is a superb album. It is everything that every Dylan fan prayed for after *Self Portrait*. The portrait on the cover peers out boldly, just *daring* you to find fault with it, and I must admit that if there is a major fault on the album, I haven't found it. Nor do I care to. This one comes easy, and that's what it's all about, isn't it? A newly rediscovered self-reliance is evident from the first measure to the last fadeout, the same kind of self-reliance that shocked the old-timers when this kid dared to say "Hey-hey Woody Guthrie, *I wrote you* a song." That may have been his own modest (as it turns out in retrospect, anyway) way of saying "Here I am, world." Calling his latest outing *New Morning* may very well be his way of saying, "I'm back."

But that's reading things into it already, and I'd like to get through this review without reading much into what's already there, because what's there is very impressive indeed, and needs no help from the likes of me. Instead, let's look at what is there, pausing now and again to comment on it.

To begin with, there's the cover. Dylan, looking like he's been through some rocky times, but confident. And the back cover, with Young Zimmerman and Victoria Spivey, self-appointed "Queen of the Blues," standing by her piano. He's holding a guitar that Big Joe Williams had just given him, and she is beaming up at him, immensely pleased. The look on his face seems to say, "I thought I could do it, and I could. Shit, man, I'm Bob Dylan, that's who I am." And indeed, that's who he was. And is.

"If Not For You" starts it all off. A kind of invocation to the muse, if you will, only this time, instead of crying "I *want* you *so bad,*" he's celebrating the fact that not only has he found her, but they know each other well, and get strength from each other, depend on each other. 'Twas always thus, it seems, and the Kooperishly bouncy organ and brisk tempo go back a long ways.

Everyone seems to think that "Day of the Locusts" is about Dylan picking up his degree at Princeton, but it could as easily be any kid in this day and age,

perplexed, uptight, and not a little unnerved by this juncture of his life, graduating from college. But putting all that aside, musically, this is where the whole thing gets off the ground. Dylan makes his first appearance here playing piano (piano cuts wisely ticked off on the cover, probably by Kooper who knows a great keyboard artist when he hears one, and who hears one in Dylan), and the entire production, from the locust organ discord to the subtly mixed-down vocal back-up, is just fine. This cut sounds like a lot of work was put into it, which is a break from Dylan's usual studio practice of doing a song about twice and leaving it at that.

After the hero of "Locusts" has run off to the Black Hills, he tells us that "Time Passes Slowly." More superb pianistics here, although the erratic ending makes me think that this was done on the spot in the studio. No matter, it's a nice piece of fluff, and it fits.

"Went to See the Gypsy" is what the side's been building up to, and there is no doubt in my mind that it is a masterpiece. The hardest rocker from Dylan in a 'coon's age, it builds beautifully, ending in some fantastic electric guitar work. Dylan's voice is back in its raspy, rowdy glory; after a list of unusual achievements credited to the gypsy by his dancing girl, we hear Bob growl, "He did it in Las Vegas and he can do it here." Really! I whooped the first time I heard that. For some unknown reason, the story line in this song reminds me of the scene in *Juliet of the Spirits* where Juliet and her friend go to see the androgynous Indian at the grand hotel. And the meaning, if indeed there is one, of the line about the "little Minnesota town" escapes me, but I don't really care.

Side one ends on two comic notes. "Winterlude" is lewd, and makes me wish I'd learned to ice skate when I was still back East. The line about going to get married and then coming back and cooking up a meal reminds me of Bing Crosby crooning, "In the meadow we can build a snowman" in "White Christmas." And "If Dogs Run Free" puts me in mind of a beatnik poetry reading at the Fat Black Pussy Cat Theatre in Greenwich Village. Everybody—and especially Maeretha Stewart—sounds like they're having a good time, and Al Kooper can play in my piano bar any time he wants.

On the surface, the second side would seem to be the "serious" side of the record, but that notion is belied immediately by the fact that somebody's guitar (Bob, is that *you?*) is horribly out of tune. But there is a lot of gusto to Dylan's singing and, for a change, the backup girls add just the right touch.

The unquestioned masterpiece of the album is "Sign on the Window." It ranks with the best work he's done, and the fact that he plays such moving piano and sings with just everything he's *got* makes it one of the most involved (and involving) pieces he's ever recorded. It's right up there with "Sad Eyed Lady of the Lowland," "Just Like Tom Thumb's Blues," "Like A Rolling Stone," and the unreleased "I'm Not There" in intensity. "She and her boyfriend went to California." And baby, that's a long, long way. It's gonna be wet tonight on Main Street, and with that pronouncement, Dylan communicates a despair mixed with resignment. And is the cabin in Utah the panacea that it would seem, the glue to mend this broken heart? I'm not convinced, and Dylan doesn't sound like he is either. If poetry can be a story that must be sent by telegraph, then this is certainly one of Dylan's foremost achievements as a poet. Words, music, singing, piano work, all of the highest order. Yes, Doubting Thomas, he can still do it. And how!

And if there is any doubt left try on "Leopard-Skin Pillbox Hat Volume Two," otherwise known as "One More Weekend." It's such a good rocker, and so full of energy that I still haven't bothered to listen to the words. No matter, they surely say what they must, which, in the grand old rock lyric tradition, is not much.

Speaking of lyrics, who among us would have thought that we'd see the day when Bob Dylan would start out a song with "La la la la la . . ."? I've never heard Dylan sounding so outrageously *happy* before. The tune to the verse is similar to "I Shall Be Released," but the sentiments here show that the release has already happened. I just love this number, and I hope that the likes of Joe Cocker will think twice before attempting a cover version of it.

The second side ends with two "religious" songs that will doubtless be plumbed for "meanings" they don't contain. "Three Angels" is an old-fashioned Dylan word-riff, the kind of thing that we've seen before in "Gates of Eden" and "Desolation Row." It is so corny that it is funny, and this is the one cut on the album that makes me wonder if it'll stand up under repeated playings. And regardless of what others say about "Father of Night," *I* think that Dylan

found a good gospel riff on the piano and used it. Anybody can make up words to it; they simply aren't that important. I guess it could also be seen as the leavetaking of the muse too, but I'll leave it to others far more erudite than myself to figure that out. Praising the maker of the night is an awfully good way to end a New Morning, anyway.

In the end, this is an album that, the less said about it, the better. I have my favorite moments (like the part in "Sign On the Window" where he modulates up and then, when he says "Looks like it's gonna rain", he hits a major chord—right out of the blue), but so will you. It seems almost superfluous to say that this is one of the best albums of the year, one of Dylan's best albums, perhaps his best. In good conscience, all I can really say is get it yourself and prepare to boogie.

After all, what better recommendation for an album—be it Dylan or a bunch of unknowns —is there?

—ED WARD
10-26-70

WE'VE GOT DYLAN BACK AGAIN!

It came on the radio in the late afternoon and from the first note it was right. Bob Dylan bringing it all back home again.

I couldn't believe it. There was no warning, only the knowledge that it had been, in fact, completed and was due out shortly. But there it was with that warm, rich, groovy sound and Bob singing out to all of us that everything is all right. "I'd be lost without you, and you know it's true," and I thought, what about us?

Then there was that great line about the locusts singing, "the man standing next to me, his head was exploding, while I was praying the pieces wouldn't fall on me." Ah, there we were. Back home again.

I was driving along a Berkeley street then, and I had the fantasy that all the other car radios were tuned to KSAN and the Dylan album was blowing their minds that very minute and I looked at the drivers as they went past me and they had smiles on their faces. I resisted the impulse to start blowing the horn like at the end of the war or something. Crazy? Sure! Only this dude thinks you're fine.

God, it's beautiful. I have played it an even dozen times in two days. I can't find a weak track, not that I'm lookin', but you know. Time passes slowly when you're searching for love and we've all been searching this past long time, searching blindly and searching almost mechanically, fatalistically, hoping against hope that something would happen.

This album is a sign. You believe that? I think I do.

It is surely the best thing new to come over the airwaves and out of the grooves in I don't know when and after these grim weeks of Agnew and Reagan and Nixon and Billy Graham and all that shit, it was like the cool, clear water from a mountain spring to hear his voice so true, so good.

The album makes me feel good. Every song on it. It is the most reassuring thing that has happened this year of the bombings. Ah, I can hear the crazies say, it is more pap for the people. It is avoidance. It is meaningless. Rejoice, rejoice, we have no choice. Those love songs are a celebration of life, that description of country living is everyman's dream come true. You'd have stayed there too, wouldn't you?

Then Elvis in the big hotel. He did it in Las Vegas and he can do it here! It all makes me feel so good. All the little turns of phrases, the humor, the flashing images, the sentimentality.

Even the waltz-time country & western love song and the simplistic "If Dogs Run Free" with its jazz piano copping Avery Parish's solo on "After Hours," the classic blues of the big band years. Kooper has turned into a hell of a piano player. He's got his chops up. He must have been working at that. And the scat vocal throw-back to Gloria Wood and Pete Condoli.

Then "New Morning" came on. Like an early mist. So clean, so sweet. "This must be the day that all my dreams come true." What a love song! What a message to all of us blinded as we are by paranoia, grimly trying to see through the murk and the smoke and the blood. "So happy just to be alive underneath the sky of blue. . . ."

You want folk music? Songs about people with stakes coming out of them and heads rolling off? Brighton girls are like the moon . . . and then the raunchy married-couple-with-kids-down-home song and then the parables of Dan. And the rest—.

It's all there. All that it ever was and all we'd hoped for and you don't need a weberman to know which way *this* wind blows. He's coming out again. Come on, Bob! We need you. That's the truth, man, we really do. Come out, Bob, come out!

And he will, just as sure as God made little apples. Didn't he bring it all back home again just to show us where it really was at? With Victoria Spivey on the cover and all? Jesus. What do you *want*, man, what do you want? I mean I wouldn't do a thing like that to *you*. Come on out, Bob, there's nothing you can do now after such a bright new morning except to come on out into the day.

Sure, the Gypsy fled in the night and the dancing girl, too, and the room was empty and dark but that was Vegas. We're still the real world, no matter what they say in Washington. Still there, still waiting and still digging it all. If not for you! Of course, what a great thing to say right now at this moment in history like he had been waiting for just the right second to answer the doubts.

His song poems are so open, just as they have always been so open, that you can find it all in there if you look. Sometimes you don't even have to look very hard, it comes right out to speak to you. But every time it's there. In every track of this album there's something for all of us to chew on.

Here we are. Tim Leary armed and dangerous in Algiers. Nixon armed and dangerous in the White House. Bombs bursting in Rochester and guns firing at random in Cairo. The Kent State massacre being blamed on the massacred, Jackson's dead accused of violence and the poison spreading all around, as no man can trust his brother and the country an armed camp. Five dead in Santa Cruz and the old folks arming against the longhairs even though the clues that turned up the killer came from longhairs. Voluntarily.

"Shoot them!" the sheriff said in Washington and Mitchell predicts we'll rush to the right and in Canada it's martial law.

As we go into this dark night we will need what light, what sustenance we can get and that is just what he has given us. The brightest light and the strongest sustenance of all—hope. This is a hopeful album and my God how we need it. America may be greening but you wouldn't know it from where we stand, any of us looking around numbly at the bumper stickers and the scum on the water.

There is nothing to fear but fear itself, our last real president said. I'm old enough to remember him saying it. Franklin Roosevelt's words coming out over the Atwater Kent that Lenny called the first cathedral we knew. FDR would have dug Dylan, had him in the study for talk and songs and Eleanor would have stood with him as she stood with Josh White. Back then, there was honor on Pennsylvania Avenue.

Yes, this is a message from home to all of us. A message of hope, of joy, of good will and above all of cheer. Good cheer, the kind they don't make so much of anymore. So he got older and caught rainbow trout and had a bunch of kids and all the rest—and what a lovely woman she must be to inspire love songs like these—that really and truly is what it all is about and now he's said it loud and clear.

There will be more. He will be back. He will sing for us again, one man with the stage fright, and he'll stand up there and give it all his might. Because when he gets to the end, he wants to start all over again.

Just remember, though, that when he says that he's afraid, take the poor boy at his word. And remember, we're all afraid, all of us, everywhere. Come back, Bob, we need you. And thank you for that letter from home.

—RALPH J. GLEASON
11-26-70

Index

547